Working Memory

Working Memory

State of the Science

Edited by

ROBERT H. LOGIE, VALÉRIE CAMOS, AND
NELSON COWAN

OXFORD
UNIVERSITY PRESS

OXFORD
UNIVERSITY PRESS

Great Clarendon Street, Oxford, OX2 6DP,
United Kingdom

Oxford University Press is a department of the University of Oxford.
It furthers the University's objective of excellence in research, scholarship,
and education by publishing worldwide. Oxford is a registered trade mark of
Oxford University Press in the UK and in certain other countries

Published in the United States of America by Oxford University Press
198 Madison Avenue, New York, NY 10016, United States of America

British Library Cataloguing in Publication Data
Data available

Library of Congress Control Number: 2020935781

ISBN 978–0–19–884228–6

Printed and bound by
CPI Group (UK) Ltd, Croydon, CR0 4YY

Foreword

It is hard to believe, but it has been almost a quarter century since we started to work on our edited volume (Miyake & Shah, 1999a), *Models of Working Memory: Mechanisms of Active Maintenance and Executive Control* (*MWM* hereafter). Around that time, working memory research had become quite popular, leading to the proliferation of distinct theoretical models. Our goal was to provide a forum for clarifying points of agreement and disagreement among these models and promote their theoretical synthesis by asking a common set of important theoretical questions.

We are truly honoured that the editors of this new volume, *Working Memory: State of the Science* (*WMSS* hereafter), adopted the same common-question approach in editing this major update of the theoretical scene, more than 20 years after the publication of the *MWM* volume. In fact, we find it amazing that working memory is most likely the only research topic in cognitive psychology (and even in the entire field of psychological science) that comes with three edited volumes implementing this common-question approach, with the third one being the *Variation in Working Memory* volume with a focus on individual differences (Conway, Jarrold, Kane, Miyake, & Towse, 2007).

When the planning for the 1999 *MWM* volume began, we were only a brand-new assistant professor (Miyake) and a postdoctoral research associate (Shah), but we felt that our aforementioned goal was timely and important enough to be worth our time and effort. So we organized and hosted a 4-day workshop in Colorado in 1997 (with a lot of help from our colleagues) and did our best to produce a highly integrative volume that met our initial goal and the field's need. Although we are really happy that we successfully implemented this common-question approach, what we were most proud of about our *MWM* volume was the fact that we were able to offer two substantial synthesis chapters that we think provided thoughtful reflections on the theoretical state of the field circa 1999, inspired by the contributors' answers to our common questions (Kintsch, Healy, Hegarty, Pennington, & Salthouse, 1999; Miyake & Shah, 1999b).

In writing this foreword, in addition to the chapters in this *WMSS* volume, we also reread the two aforementioned synthesis chapters from the *MWM* volume (along with the answers to our common questions provided by the contributors) to gain some insights into how working memory research and its theoretical landscape have changed since 1999. When we wrote our own synthesis chapter in *MWM* (Miyake & Shah, 1999b), we found it really useful and insightful to read Norman's (1970) edited volume on memory, entitled *Models of Human Memory*, and reflect on the field's progress since.

As we highlighted in the *MWM* book, we were impressed with the transformation of our conceptualization and understanding of working memory from 1970 to 1999. Most of the models described in that 1970 volume conceptualized short-term memory as a separate passive storage buffer for the sake of memorization, and, with the publication of Baddeley and Hitch's (1974) seminal working memory chapter, the conception of working memory reflected in the models represented in the 1999 *MWM* volume seemed radically different from those represented in the 1970 volume. Moreover, a surge of interest in examining individual differences in working memory capacity in North America in the 1980s and 1990s, inspired by the development of complex span tasks (e.g. Daneman & Carpenter, 1980; Turner & Engle, 1989), has led the field to fully embrace the critical relevance of working memory in complex cognitive activities, such as reading comprehension and reasoning. We are glad that this *WMSS* volume provides a great new opportunity for working memory researchers to reflect on not only the current state of the field but also the progress the field has made in the last 20 years or so (1999–2021).

Unfortunately, space limitations do not allow us to fully flesh out our own thoughts on the theoretical development in the field (e.g. what changed, what has not, where to go from here). However, we were really impressed with various new theoretical ideas and empirical findings outlined in the individual chapters. At the most global level, major theoretical progress (and even innovation) made since 1999 in the specification of key working memory processes and mechanisms was quite evident when we read the chapters in this volume (e.g. the process of updating, re-examining of ways in which items are refreshed and maintained, the nature of working memory limits, and individual differences in working memory capacity). And such theoretical advances are supported by impressive arrays of empirical evidence (e.g. experimental, individual differences, cognitive neuroscience, and computational modelling), derived from more sophisticated research and data-analytic methodology than was the case back in 1999.

At a more specific level, what struck us as the most exciting new trend in the field, clearly reflected in the current volume throughout, concerns some positive changes in the way we do science, something we had hoped to see when we edited the *MWM* volume. In our 1999 synthesis chapter (Miyake & Shah, 1999b), we suggested that one important future research direction was more competitive argumentation and further theoretical synthesis. Specifically, we argued that 'it is time to move forward and start rigorously testing competing, mutually incompatible claims through competitive argumentation as well as actively synthesizing mutually compatible ideas within a coherent framework' (pp. 472–473). The current volume (as well as recent publications cited in the chapters) suggests that the field of working memory research has been moving in that direction.

Indeed, competitive argumentation is at the forefront of the *WMSS* volume, with a new common question dedicated to asking authors to discuss evidence that is inconsistent with their theoretical framework (Question 7). Several of the chapters are admirably direct in their responses to this question. It is also reflected in the 'adversarial collaboration' approach taken by the editors of this volume and their colleagues and discussed in several of the chapters here (see also Cowan et al., 2020; Doherty et al., 2019).

Attempts for theoretical and empirical synthesis are also featured prominently in different parts of the *WMSS* volume. Most noticeably, the question requiring authors to define working memory (Question 1) was inspired by Cowan's (2017) attempts to crystallize different conceptions of working memory and his observations about the importance of clear shared definitions to support synthesis. Similarly, meta-analytic synthesis mentioned in some of the chapters (e.g. as applied to the working memory training literature) is another important recent development that has contributed to increased efforts for synthesis. Moreover, recent attempts across multiple laboratories to delineate a set of 'benchmark' working memory phenomena that must be explained by any model (see, for example, Oberauer et al., 2018) are also important in terms of not only forging consensus but also encouraging further competitive argumentation and model comparison.

Despite these (and various other) highly visible and impressive advances in working memory research in the last 22 years, however, we were also struck by the fact that many of the theoretical ideas and questions discussed in the *MWM* volume (especially in the last two synthesis chapters) are still quite relevant, even today. In light of what we considered radical changes in theoretical conceptualizations of temporary memory between 1970 and 1999, we were perhaps envisioning equally radical changes in theoretical developments between 1999 and 2021 (e.g. in the 1999 volume, we even briefly speculated about the possibility that an umbrella term like working memory might be no longer necessary!). Instead, after reading the chapters of the current *WMSS* volume, we thought that our 1999 volume was not entirely obsolete and still offers some insights relevant to the current working memory models, even though major updates to the volume (of the sort offered by the current *WMSS* volume) are clearly needed.

For example, in our synthesis chapter in the *MWM* volume, we identified and presented six common themes that we thought ran across all ten models covered in the *MWM* volume:

1. Working memory is not a structurally separate box or place in the mind or brain.
2. Working memory's maintenance function is in the service of complex cognition.
3. Executive control is integral to working memory functions.
4. Capacity limits reflect multiple factors and may even be an emergent property of the cognitive system.
5. Completely unitary, domain-general view of working memory does not hold.
6. Long-term knowledge plays an integral role in working memory performance.

Even though some of these themes from the 1999 volume may need some tweaks and updates (especially Theme 5), they are still generally applicable to the models included in the *WMSS* volume. In fact, it might be an interesting and even inspirational exercise for readers to try to identify such common themes that cut across all the models covered in the *WMSS* volume and examine how different those new themes are from those six themes listed that we identified back in 1999.

We believe that it is important to have an up-to-date, state-of-the-art knowledge of the current research and theoretical ideas and, for that purpose, this *WMSS* volume will serve as a terrific tool. So, any serious researchers and students interested in studying working memory should read this volume.

At the same time, we invite readers to also take a close look at our 1999 *MWM* volume (perhaps a second look for some readers) and engage in some historical reflections, asking questions such as: what changed in our theoretical thinking over the last 20 years or so? Are there any general changes in the way working memory is defined and conceptualized between 1999 and 2021 (i.e. compare the answers provided to Question 1 in the two volumes)? Which unresolved issues have been compellingly resolved since 1999, and what unresolved issues still remain unresolved despite their importance (the decay versus interference debate covered in detail in the *MWM* volume, for example, is still highly relevant in this *WMSS* volume, and we are not sure whether we are any closer to the resolution of this debate now)? What are the most important future directions of research and theoretical development?

Typically, readers of an edited book take a look at only some of the chapters and do not reflect much on the book as a whole, let alone on the historical progress of the field. Edited volumes such as *MWM* and *WMSS*, in contrast, require (and deserve) a much greater commitment from readers. We hope that readers will use this *WMSS* volume as a starting point to engage in such active reflections about the past, present, and future of working memory research and theories and thereby help continue to move the field forward.

Akira Miyake, University of Colorado Boulder, USA

Priti Shah, University of Michigan, USA

References

Baddeley, A. D., & Hitch, G. J. (1974). Working memory. In G. H. Bower (Ed.), *The psychology of learning and motivation: Advances in research and theory* (Vol. 8, pp. 47–89). New York, NY: Academic Press.

Conway, A. R. A., Jarrold, C., Kane, M. J., Miyake, A., & Towse, J. N. (Eds.). (2007). *Variation in working memory*. New York, NY: Oxford University Press.

Cowan, N. (2017). The many faces of working memory and short-term storage. *Psychonomic Bulletin & Review, 24*, 1158–1170.

Cowan, N., Belletier, C., Doherty, J. M., Jaroslawska, A. J., Rhodes, S., Forsberg, A., . . . & Logie, R. H. (2020). How do scientific views change? Notes from an extended adversarial collaboration. *Perspectives on Psychological Science, 15*, 1011–1025.

Daneman, M., & Carpenter, P. A. (1980). Individual differences in working memory and reading. *Journal of Verbal Learning and Verbal Memory, 19*, 450–466.

Doherty, J. M., Belletier, C., Rhodes, S., Jaroslawska, A., Barrouillet, P., Camos, V., . . . & Logie, R. H. (2019). Dual-task costs in working memory: An adversarial collaboration. *Journal of Experimental Psychology: Learning, Memory, and Cognition, 45*, 1529–1551.

Kintsch, W., Healy, A. F., Hegarty, M., Pennington, B. F., & Salthouse, T. A. (1999). Models of working memory: Eight questions and some general issues. In A. Miyake & P. Shah (Eds.), *Models of working memory: Mechanisms of active maintenance and executive control* (pp. 412–441). New York: Cambridge University Press.

Miyake, A., & Shah, P. (Eds.) (1999a). *Models of working memory: Mechanisms of active maintenance and executive control*. New York, NY: Cambridge University Press.

Miyake, A., & Shah, P. (1999b). Toward unified theories of working memory: Emerging general consensus, unresolved theoretical issues, and future research directions. In A. Miyake & P. Shah (Eds.), *Models of working memory: Mechanisms of active maintenance and executive control* (pp. 442–481). New York, NY: Cambridge University Press.

Norman, A. D. (Ed.). (1970). *Models of human memory*. New York, NY: Academic Press.

Oberauer, K., Lewandowsky, S., Awh, E., Brown, G. D. A., Conway, A., Cowan, . . . Ward, G. (2018). Benchmarks for models of short-term and working memory. *Psychological Bulletin, 144*, 885–958.

Smith, E. E., & Jonides, J. (1997). Working memory: A view from neuroimaging. *Cognitive Psychology, 33*, 5–42.

Turner, M. L., & Engle, R. W. (1989). Is working memory capacity task dependent? *Journal of Memory and Language, 28*, 127–154.

Acknowledgements

The editors acknowledge support for their work on this book from the UK Economic and Social Research Council (ESRC) within the project 'Working memory across the adult lifespan: An adversarial collaboration' (WoMAAC) ES/N010728/1 (for more details see https://womaac.psy.ed.ac.uk). Nelson Cowan acknowledges support for his research from National Institutes of Health (NIH) Grant R01 HD021338. The editors would like to thank Martin Baum at Oxford University Press for support, encouragement, and patience during the gestation of this volume.

Contents

Contributors

Richard Allen, PhD
Associate Professor
School of Psychology
University of Leeds
Leeds, UK

Duarte Araujo, PhD
Associate Professor of Sport and Health
Faculty of Human Kinetics
University of Lisbon
Cruz Quebrada, Lisbon, Portugal

Edward Awh, PhD
Professor
Department of Psychology
University of Chicago
Chicago, IL, USA

Alan Baddeley, CBE, FRS, FBA, FMedSci
Professor
Department of Psychology
University of York
York, UK

Pierre Barrouillet, PhD
Full Professor
Faculty of Psychology and Educational Sciences
Université de Genève
Geneva, Switzerland

Clément Belletier, PhD
Assistant Professor
Department of Psychology
Laboratoire de Psychologie Sociale et Cognitive,
Centre National de la Recherche Scientifique
(CNRS), Université Clermont Auvergne
Clermont-Ferrand, France

Alexander P. Burgoyne, PhD
Post-Doctoral Researcher
School of Psychology
Georgia Institute of Technology
Atlanta, Georgia, USA

Valérie Camos, PhD
Professor in Developmental Psychology
Department of Psychology
Université de Fribourg
Fribourg, Switzerland

Nelson Cowan, PhD
Curators' Distinguished Professor
Department of Psychological Sciences
University of Missouri
Columbia, Missouri, USA

Jason M. Doherty, MA, MScR, PhD
Postdoctoral Research Assistant
Department of Psychology
University of Edinburgh
Edinburgh, UK

Randall W. Engle, PhD
Professor
Department of Psychology
Georgia Institute of Technology
Atlanta, GA, USA

Nicole Hakim
PhD Student
Department of Psychology
University of Chicago
Chicago, IL, USA

David Z. Hambrick, PhD
Professor
Department of Psychology
Michigan State University
East Lansing, MI, USA

Graham Hitch, MA, MSc, PhD
Emeritus Professor
Department of Psychology
University of York
York, UK

Alexandru D. Iordan, PhD
Postdoctoral Research Fellow
Department of Psychology
University of Michigan
Ann Arbor, MI, USA

Robert H. Logie, PhD
Professor of Human Cognitive Neuroscience
Department of Psychology
University of Edinburgh
Edinburgh, Scotland, UK

Randi C. Martin, PhD
Elma Schneider Professor
Department of Psychological Sciences
Rice University
Houston, TX, USA

Cody A. Mashburn, BS
Graduate Student
School of Psychology
Georgia Institute of Technology
Atlanta, GA, USA

Candice C. Morey, PhD
Senior Lecturer
School of Psychology
Cardiff University
Cardiff, Wales, UK

Moshe Naveh-Benjamin, PhD
Professor of Psychology
Department of Psychological Sciences
University of Missouri
Columbia, Missouri, USA

Klaus Oberauer, Dr
Professor
Department of Psychology
University of Zurich
Zürich, Switzerland

Bradley R. Postle, PhD
Professor
Departments of Psychology and Psychiatry
University of Wisconsin–Madison
Madison, WI, USA

Jeremy Purcell, PhD
Research Scientist
Maryland Neuroimaging Center
University of Maryland
College Park, MD, USA

Brenda Rapp, PhD
Professor
Department of Cognitive Science
Johns Hopkins University
Baltimore, MD, USA

Patricia A. Reuter-Lorenz, PhD
Department Chair, Michael I. Posner Collegiate
Professor of Psychology and Neuroscience
Department of Psychology
University of Michigan
Ann Arbor, MI, USA

John Spencer, PhD
Professor
School of Psychology
University of East Anglia
Norwich, UK

Jason S. Tsukahara, MA
Graduate Student
School of Psychology
Georgia Institute of Technology
Atlanta, GA, USA

André Vandierendonck, PhD
Emeritus Professor
Department of Experimental Psychology
Ghent University
Ghent, Belgium

Edward K. Vogel, PhD
Professor
Department of Psychology
University of Chicago
Chicago, IL, USA

Sobanawartiny Wijeakumar, Dr
Assistant Professor
School of Psychology
University of Nottingham
Nottingham, UK

1

The State of the Science of Working Memory

An Introduction

Robert H. Logie, Valérie Camos, and Nelson Cowan

Why This Book and Why Now?

Working memory (WM) refers to our ability to keep a small amount of information readily available for our current activities, and to support decisions, guide actions, make statements, and keep track of conversations, to navigate and support creative thinking and problem-solving, to remember to do things, and to update what is going on around us throughout the day. In other words, it is an ability that we use every waking moment of our lives. It is also one of the most popular research topics in psychological sciences and cognitive neuroscience, and is now widely used in everyday conversation throughout society. A search for the term on Google Scholar resulted in over two million hits. The general concept was identified by the philosopher John Locke (1690) who referred to 'contemplation' in contrast with the 'storehouse of ideas', and a number of related concepts were proposed over the following three centuries (for historical reviews, see Logie, 1996; Logie & Cowan, 2015). The use of the term WM to refer to this human mental ability was first mentioned briefly by Miller, Galanter, and Pribram (1960), but major theoretical and empirical developments are widely considered to have been stimulated by Alan Baddeley and Graham Hitch (1974), and subsequent work by Baddeley and colleagues (e.g. Baddeley, 1986; see chapter by Baddeley, Hitch, & Allen, 2021).

Over the following nearly five decades since that 1974 chapter, a large volume of research has been generated, leading to the development of multiple theoretical frameworks regarding how WM works, what are its capacity limitations, how it is organized, how its functions are implemented in brain structure and function, and how it is affected by damage to the brain. Although there are large numbers of journal articles and books on aspects of WM, for the last 20 years the 'go to' definitive collection of theoretical and empirical reviews has been a book published in 1999 and edited by Akira Miyake and Priti Shah. That book was remarkable in bringing together the ideas of the most high-profile WM researchers at the time, reflecting a diversity of theoretical perspectives, and the book and the chapters within it are still very widely cited.

A lot has happened in research on this topic in the last 20 years, with major theoretical and empirical developments, and it is an increasingly popular topic both with researchers and policymakers, as well as with a range of other stakeholders and the general

Robert H. Logie, Valérie Camos, and Nelson Cowan, *The State of the Science of Working Memory* In: *Working Memory*. Edited by: Robert H. Logie, Valérie Camos, and Nelson Cowan, Oxford University Press (2021). © Oxford University Press. DOI: 10.1093/oso/9780198842286.003.0001 public. With these developments has come a scientific diaspora, with multiple different definitions (reviewed in Cowan, 2017), and competing theoretical frameworks fuelled by new behavioural, cognitive studies of healthy and brain-damaged individuals across the lifespan, and by dramatic developments in neuroimaging techniques that were nascent and used by very few research groups at the time of Miyake and Shah's book. So, it seems particularly timely for this new book *Working Memory: State of the Science* that brings together many of the most productive and well-known WM researchers in Europe and the United States to highlight current empirical and theoretical developments as well as pointing to what has changed since Miyake and Shah's (1999) book.

One reason for the major success of the Miyake and Shah volume was that the chapter authors were each asked to answer a common set of questions about their own theoretical perspective. This unique feature gave the book a much more integrated character than most edited texts at the time, and it remains extremely rare in edited texts today. Our new book follows this excellent idea by asking the authors of each chapter to address questions that remain unresolved as well as new questions that have arisen over the last two decades. However, unlike the previous book, each author also has been asked to state how they deal with research findings that are not consistent with their own theoretical assumptions. This highlights contemporary debates, but also encourages authors to step out of their own paradigms and findings and to consider new and contrasting theoretical arguments rather than focusing only on their own work and work of their like-minded colleagues.

The encouragement for chapter authors to consider contrary evidence has arisen from a long-term 'cooperative adversarial collaboration' within a common research programme between the three editors (Logie, Camos, and Cowan), four of their chapter co-authors (Barrouillet, Naveh-Benjamin, Belletier, and Doherty), and other colleagues (see Cowan et al., 2020) whose theoretical perspectives differ, as will be evident from their chapters. Details of that adversarial collaboration and of resulting publications and other outputs are available at http://www.womaac.psy.ed.ac.uk, and some of the results of the empirical work are summarized in the chapter by Logie, Belletier, and Doherty (2021). Our book also has been guided by the aim of recruiting, as authors of the other chapters, leading representatives of approaches to WM that differ widely in their theoretical approaches, research methods, and domains of application.

The Designated Questions for All Authors

The designated questions for authors addressed seven core issues, plus up to five optional issues depending on the relevance for their research. At the start of each chapter, authors were asked to provide a table with a summary of their responses to each question. The intention is that this general structure and the summary table for each chapter will facilitate comparisons of the differences in theoretical assumptions across authors. The summary table also provides a theoretical context for each chapter before reading the detailed text.

The instructions to authors and the designated questions are laid out in Table 1.1.

Table 1.1 The instructions and designated questions given to authors

---

When writing your chapter, please address the following seven questions plus any of the optional questions that are relevant for your research. Add a table at the start of your chapter that summarizes very briefly your answer to each question.

---

1. Definition of working memory (WM)

Cowan (2017) has delineated a range of different definitions of WM, although there may be other definitions assumed by researchers in the field. What is the definition of WM within your own theoretical framework?

2. Describe and explain the methods you use, and their strengths and limitations

What research methods do you use most frequently in your research, and are there any methods that most uniquely characterize your research? Briefly highlight what you see as the major advantages and limitations of these methods compared with alternatives. What new developments in methods might help enhance empirical and theoretical advances in WM research?

3. Unitary versus non-unitary nature of WM

Does your theoretical framework assume that WM is essentially activated long-term episodic and semantic memory, or do you view WM as a separate system that interacts with long-term memory (LTM)? Is WM a highly flexible domain-general system that supports both temporary maintenance and ongoing processing, or a collection of domain-specific systems that cooperate in supporting task performance? What evidence supports your views? Is there evidence that is inconsistent with your views, and how does your theoretical framework deal with contrary findings?

4. The role of attention and control

A common assumption across cognitive psychology is that there is centralized control of mental activity, and of which aspects of the environment are perceived and encoded. These aspects of cognition often are referred to as controlled attention, or 'top-down control' but this raises questions about the nature of the control system. How does your theoretical framework account for 'top-down control' of mental activity? What is doing the controlling, and how do you address the implicit assumption of a homunculus acting as an executive controller? What, if any, theoretical differences are there between selective attention through the senses to stimuli in the environment and selective attention to mental events?

5. Storage, maintenance, and loss of information in WM

How is information encoded in WM, and how is the information retained? Is there passive storage and/or active maintenance to prevent loss, and what are the mechanisms for loss? How are these processes affected by strategies?

6. The role of LTM in WM storage and processing

How do episodic, semantic (declarative and procedural) aspects of LTM contribute to WM capacity and function, and how does WM contribute to LTM? What evidence and theoretical considerations support your theoretical views about the relationship between WM and LTM? What is the role of WM in learning, and how does learning affect WM capacity and function? What is the role of domain-specific expertise in WM? How does training on WM tasks impact WM function, and how does your theoretical framework account for the presence or absence of an impact of WM training?

7. Is there evidence that is not consistent with your theoretical framework, and how does your framework address that inconsistency?

This can be addressed as a separate question, or incorporated in your answers to each of the other questions.

Additional optional questions—please also try to consider one or more of the following questions that are relevant for your research. They may be considered in the context of the previous core questions, or in addition.

A. Early life development

What are the sources and kinds of change that occur in WM during development from early life to early adulthood that are incorporated in your theoretical framework? How does your framework account for these changes, and what are the most important sources of evidence that are consistent with, and those that present a challenge to your framework?

(Continued)

Table 1.1 Continued

B. Adult ageing

What are the sources and kinds of change that occur in WM across the adult lifespan that are incorporated in your theoretical framework? How does your framework account for these changes, and what are the most important sources of evidence that are consistent with, and those that present a challenge to your framework?

C. Individual differences and limits in WM capacity

What limits WM capacity and what are the factors that underlie differences in that capacity between individuals? Are gender differences important for WM function and capacity?

D. Neural correlates

How does your theoretical framework relate to findings from brain imaging and brain stimulating studies of WM (e.g. functional magnetic resonance imaging, electroencephalography, magnetoencephalography, transcranial magnetic stimulation, transcranial direct current stimulation, and near-infrared spectroscopy)?

E. Neuropsychology

How does your theoretical framework relate to findings from cognitive/behavioural studies of individuals with focal brain lesions or with neurodegenerative diseases that impair some or all WM function?

F. WM applications

Does your theoretical framework for WM have any implications for everyday cognition, e.g. in accounting for learning, training, mental arithmetic, language learning, prospective remembering, autobiographical remembering, problem solving, decision-making, multitasking, holding conversations, or design of human–digital interaction?

A Summary of the Chapters

The chapters are intended to represent most, if not all of the current most prominent theoretical perspectives and empirical research on WM. The first group of five chapters reflects different theoretical frameworks and approaches. Chapter 2 is by the authors who, in their seminal publication in 1974 asked the question 'What is short-term memory for?'. This led Baddeley (1986) to the idea of multicomponent WM as a dynamic mental workspace with domain-specific temporary memory capacities respectively for verbal (the phonological loop) and for visuospatial (the visuospatial sketchpad) material together with a controlling central executive. Baddeley and Hitch are joined in this chapter by Allen, discussing how their view of the multicomponent model of WM has developed over the last 46 years. They point to key findings from studies of healthy adults and from individuals who show very specific deficits linked with brain damage that have resulted in gradual expansion and greater sophistication in the understanding of the phonological loop, and of executive function, with the addition of an amodal episodic temporary buffer. They emphasize the approach to theory development based on its utility to account for empirical findings and to be applied to a wide range of questions outside the cognitive laboratory. In Chapter 3, Cowan, Morey, and Naveh-Benjamin provide a detailed account of empirical work that has driven the development of the embedded processes framework, originally proposed by Cowan (1988). This views WM as the currently activated area of long-term memory (LTM) coupled with a limited capacity focus of attention, and the control of attention is key to WM capacity and function. In Chapter 4, Barrouillet and Camos describe evidence for, and the current instantiation of the time-based resource sharing framework, the core of which is the time for which attention is focused on a specific task. So, for example, if there is a requirement to remember some material while having to deal with some other cognitively demanding task, memory performance will be determined by how long attention is directed to refreshing and hence maintaining the to-be-remembered material before switching attention to deal with the contrasting cognitive demand. In the latter case, the contents of memory degrade until attention switches back to memory maintenance. In the fifth chapter, Oberauer argues that evaluation of a theory requires that it makes strong predictions that can be tested empirically and with the use of computational modelling. He acknowledges that the implementation of a computational model typically involves focusing on very specific empirical phenomena and research questions, and describes three such specific models. He suggests a roadmap for developing a more general model as predictions are supported or falsified by the data, and that any such general model should incorporate specific requirements for a WM to function effectively. In the sixth chapter of this set, Vandierendonck describes a general computational model of WM that is inspired by the Baddeley et al. multicomponent view comprising both domain-general and domain-specific components. Importantly, he demonstrates how executive control can be distributed across the multiple components without the need for a central executive controller, a theme that is also explored in Chapter 13 by Wijeakumar and Spencer, and in Chapter 14 by Logie, Belletier, and Doherty.

The next three chapters explore individual differences in WM capacity and how it is used. Individual differences can include age differences, variation within an age group in capabilities and experiences, and psychopathologies as well as neuropathologies. They are inherent in several of the common questions, so many of the chapters address them in one way or another. However, they are the main focus for Chapters 7–9. In Chapter 7, Mashburn, Tsukahara, and Engle discuss the use of both experimental and correlational studies focused on how individuals differ in their overall WM capacity, which is viewed as the control of executive attention to inhibit irrelevant information and focus on current task goals. They identify the latent factor of attention control using multiple different measures of WM capacity across large groups of individuals with diverse mental ability levels. Like Cowan et al. in Chapter 3, Reuter-Lorenz and Iordan in Chapter 10, and Postle in Chapter 12, Mashburn et al. view temporary memory as currently activated aspects of LTM. Chapter 8 by Hambrick, Burgoyne, and Araujo argues that much of WM research has been short-sighted in exploring WM primarily from the perspective of the individual or group and within controlled laboratory studies. This approach neglects how WM is used outside of the laboratory and how the environment contributes to WM function. For example, they show how the capacity of an individual's WM can be substantially supplemented by external cues in cognitively demanding environments such as a busy restaurant kitchen, or when landing an aeroplane. This is followed in Chapter 9 by Martin, Rapp, and Purcell who provide an extensive and detailed review of how studies of individuals and groups with brain damage have led to significant insights into the cognitive impairments from which these individuals suffer, and to insights into the relationship between brain function and WM function. In focusing on domain-specific orthographic, phonological, semantic, and visuospatial characteristics of verbal WM, as in the chapters by Baddeley et al., by Vandierendonck, and by Logie et al., they provide evidence for multiple WM functions that work together in the healthy brain and that can each be selectively impaired by specific brain damage.

Chapters 10, 11, 12, and 13 explore neural correlates of WM functions, starting in Chapter 10 with Reuter-Lorenz and Iordan, who demonstrate that semantically based false memories are observed both in LTM and WM experimental paradigms. They then review brain imaging studies that point to WM and LTM cognitive constructs being linked with different activation states of the same neural networks, consistent with Cowan et al.'s view that WM comprises activated LTM. The relationship between neural activation and the cognitive understanding specifically of visual WM is discussed in Chapter 11 by Hakim, Awh, and Vogel from the perspective of evidence from electroencephalography studies that track the time course of electrical signals during WM task performance. They concur with Cowan et al. and Reuter-Lorenz and Iordan, that WM is reflected in active neural firing of networks that store information long term, but diverge from those views by demonstrating that different mechanisms support representation of the visual characteristics of individual items separately from the prioritization of spatial locations. In Chapter 12, Postle also argues that visual WM function arises from activation states of networks in the brain. However, he goes further in suggesting that the functions attributed to WM are emergent properties of systems that support the processing of sensory inputs, the representations from those inputs, the control of attention, and the representation and control of action rather than a separate memory system. The argument is supported by studies using functional magnetic resonance imaging, electroencephalography, and computational modelling of recurrent neural networks. In Chapter 13, Wijeakumar and Spencer consider the neural correlates of visual WM across the lifespan within dynamic field theory. This explores the use of behavioural measures and computational modelling of WM representations comprising strong interactions between sustained self-excitation and lateral inhibition within a collection of active neural networks, each serving a specific function, and referred to as dynamic fields. Like Postle, there is a strong argument made for visual WM as a property of sensorimotor systems, but as in Vandierendonck's computational model and consistent with the Logie et al.'s arguments, there is no central control of attention, with executive control arising from the interaction between several dynamic fields.

In the final chapter, Chapter 14, Logie, Belletier, and Doherty argue that differences between the competing theoretical views of WM might be more apparent than real, and differences arise from the research questions being addressed and the level of explanation that is appropriate for those questions. They argue that in the healthy brain, there are multiple domain-specific functions that dynamically and seamlessly interact, giving the impression of a single general capacity. Moreover, these domain-specific systems can be used in different combinations for any given cognitive task, depending on the strategy that a participant adopts to support task performance. The domain-specific systems then only become apparent when one or more system is impaired following brain damage as also described in the chapters by Baddeley et al., Martin et al., and Logie et al. Moreover, the different cognitive functions could be distinguished at the neural level by the mechanisms for activation and inhibition, by synaptic growth, or by the way in which different brain networks interact. There is no need to assume that a domain-specific cognitive function would necessarily map on to a specific brain structure. By considering the level of explanation sought, there is considerable potential for more theory integration than for increasing theoretical diversity.

Associated Electronic Material

This book has been published electronically as well as in print. Many of the chapter authors have, and will, make associated electronic material available in the form of demonstrations, datasets, computational and statistical models, and links to online experiments and supplementary discussions. Links to most of the electronic material will be made available at http://womaac.psy.ed.ac.uk, and these links will continue to be updated after publication of the book. Some of the electronic material will be uploaded to the Open Science Framework (https://osf.io/).

Some authors will make electronic resources available via their own web pages. Updates and additions to these electronic resources will continue to be made available after the book has been published. We hope that all of these additional electronic features will allow readers to become engaged with WM research well beyond their reading of the book chapters. This broader perspective should make the book distinctive, and we hope this will attract WM researchers who are experienced or new to the area, postdoctoral researchers, and graduate students and also provide background activities for advanced undergraduates on cognitive psychology courses.

References

Baddeley, A. D. (1986). *Working memory*. Oxford, UK: Oxford University Press.
Baddeley, A. D., & Hitch, G. J. (1974). Working memory. In G. A. Bower (Ed.), *The psychology of learning and motivation* (Vol. 8, pp. 47–89). New York, NY: Academic Press.

Baddeley, A. D., Hitch, G. J., & Allen, R. (2021). A multicomponent model of working memory. In R. H. Logie, V. Camos, & N. Cowan (Eds.), *Working memory: State of the science* (pp. 10–43). Oxford, UK: Oxford University Press.

Barrouillet, P., & Camos, V. (2021). The time-based resource-sharing model of working memory. In R. H. Logie, V. Camos, & N. Cowan (Eds.), *Working memory: State of the science* (pp. 85–115). Oxford, UK: Oxford University Press.

Cowan, N. (1988). Evolving conceptions of memory storage, selective attention, and their mutual constraints within the human information processing system. *Psychological Bulletin, 104*, 163–191.

Cowan, N. (2017). The many faces of working memory and short-term storage. *Psychonomic Bulletin & Review, 24*, 1158–1170.

Cowan, N., Belletier, C., Doherty, J. M., Jaroslawska, A. J., Rhodes, S., Forsberg, A., . . . Logie, R. H. (2020). How do scientific views change? Notes from an extended adversarial collaboration. *Perspectives on Psychological Science, 15*, 1011–1025.

Cowan, N. Morey, C., & Naveh-Benjamin, M. (2021). An embedded-processes approach to working memory: How is it distinct from other approaches, and to what ends? In R. H. Logie, V. Camos, & N. Cowan (Eds.), *Working memory: State of the science* (pp. 44–84). Oxford, UK: Oxford University Press.

Hakim, N., Awh, E., & Vogel, E. K. (2021). Manifold visual working memory. In R. H. Logie, V. Camos, & N. Cowan (Eds.), *Working memory: State of the science* (pp. 311–332). Oxford, UK: Oxford University Press.

Hambrick, D. Z., Burgoyne, A. P., & Duarte Araujo, D. (2021). Working memory and expertise: An ecological perspective. In R. H. Logie, V. Camos, & N. Cowan (Eds.), *Working memory: State of the science* (pp. 212–234). Oxford, UK: Oxford University Press.

Locke, J. (1690). *An essay concerning human understanding.* Book II, Chapter X, 1–2. [First edition consulted in University of Aberdeen, UK, Archive Library.]

Logie, R. H. (1996). The seven ages of working memory. In J. T. E. Richardson, R. W. Engle, L. Hasher, R. H. Logie, E. R. Stoltzfus, & R. T. Zacks (Eds.), *Working memory and human cognition* (pp. 31–65). New York, NY: Oxford University Press.

Logie, R. H., Belletier, C., & Doherty, J. D. (2021). Integrating theories of working memory. In R. H. Logie, V. Camos, & N. Cowan (Eds.), *Working memory: State of the science* (pp. 389–429). Oxford, UK: Oxford University Press.

Logie, R. H., & Cowan, N. (2015). Perspectives on working memory: Introduction to the Special Issue. *Memory and Cognition, 43*, 315–324.

Martin, R. C., Rapp, B., & Purcell, J. (2021). Domain-specific working memory: Perspectives from cognitive neuropsychology. In R. H. Logie, V. Camos, & N. Cowan (Eds.), *Working memory: State of the science* (pp. 235–281). Oxford, UK: Oxford University Press.

Mashburn, C., Tsukahara, J., & Engle, R. W. (2021). Individual differences in attention control: Implications for the relationship between working memory capacity and fluid intelligence. In R. H. Logie, V. Camos, & N. Cowan (Eds.), *Working memory: State of the science* (pp. 175–211). Oxford, UK: Oxford University Press.

Miller, G. A., Galanter, E., & Pribram, K. H. (1960). *Plans and the structure of behavior.* New York, NY: Holt, Rinehart and Winston, Inc.

Miyake, A., & Shah, P. (Eds.) (1999). *Models of working memory.* New York, NY: Cambridge University Press.

Oberauer, K. (2021). Towards a theory of working memory: From metaphors to mechanisms. In R. H. Logie, V. Camos, & N. Cowan (Eds.), *Working memory: State of the science* (pp. 116–149). Oxford, UK: Oxford University Press.

Postle, B. R. (2021). Cognitive neuroscience of visual working memory. In R. H. Logie, V. Camos, & N. Cowan (Eds.), *Working memory: State of the science* (pp. 333–357). Oxford, UK: Oxford University Press.

Reuter-Lorenz, P. A., & Iordan, A. D. (2021). Remembering over the short and long term: Empirical continuities and theoretical implications. In R. H. Logie, V. Camos, & N. Cowan (Eds.), *Working memory: State of the science* (pp. 282–310). Oxford, UK: Oxford University Press.

Vandierendonck, A. (2021). Multicomponent working memory system with distributed executive control. In R. H. Logie, V. Camos, & N. Cowan (Eds.), *Working memory: State of the science* (pp. 150–174). Oxford, UK: Oxford University Press.

Wijeakumar, S., & Spencer, J. (2021). A dynamic field theory of visual working memory. In R. H. Logie, V. Camos, & N. Cowan (Eds.), *Working memory: State of the science* (pp. 358–388). Oxford, UK: Oxford University Press.

2

A Multicomponent Model of Working Memory

Alan Baddeley, Graham Hitch, and Richard Allen

1. Definition of Working Memory

A limited capacity system for the temporary maintenance and processing of information in the support of cognition and action.

2. Describe and Explain the Methods and Their Strengths and Limitations

The multicomponent model is assumed to form an important interface between a range of cognitive processing systems including perception and both episodic and semantic long-term memory (LTM). Attention is assumed to play an important role in working memory (WM) which is also essential for conscious awareness. WM thus covers many aspects of cognition, a fact reflected in the sheer number of publications with 'working memory' in their title. This has increased (within psychology-related fields) from 6 in 1980 through 306 in 2000, to 845 in the year 2016 (Baddeley, Hitch, & Allen, 2019).

Scientific theories tend to fall into two broad categories. The first is based on Newtonian physics where the aim is to postulate laws reflecting basic assumptions resulting in clear predictions that if not fulfilled should lead to the rejection of the theory, an approach typified by Newtonian physics and advocated, for example, by Braithwaite (1953) and Popper (1959) who stressed the crucial importance of potential falsification of the theory. The second approach is to treat theories as equivalent to maps that represent existing knowledge in a coherent way that encourages further investigation. This assumes that theories are validated in terms of their productivity in generating new findings, an approach typified by Darwin's theory of evolution. The first type emphasizes precision and mathematical elegance, while the second, typified by biology, acknowledges the complexity of the world to be explained, emphasizing the way in which evolution can result in several different ways of solving the same problem with none necessarily being the most elegant (Crick, 1990). Sanbonmatsu and Johnston (2019) suggest that 'In the study of complex phenomena there is an extreme trade-off between generality and precision' (p. 6720), illustrating this claim across a range of areas of social and behavioural research. Our own view is that given the complexity of WM, a precise and testable model of the whole system is currently unlikely to meet with success. Others, however, such as Klaus Oberauer are more optimistic (see chapter by Oberauer, 2021).

Alan Baddeley, Graham Hitch, and Richard Allen, *A Multicomponent Model of Working Memory* In: *Working Memory*. Edited by: Robert H. Logie, Valérie Camos, and Nelson Cowan, Oxford University Press (2021). © Oxford University Press. DOI: 10.1093/oso/9780198842286.003.0002

Table 2.1 Basic questions

Question	Response
1. Definition of working memory (WM)	A limited capacity system for the temporary storage and processing of information required for complex cognition.
2. Methods used	We use a range of methods including (a) experimental effects of concurrent tasks and materials, (b) neuropsychological evidence, (c) developmental evidence, (d) effects of strategies, and (e) computational modelling. We use these as converging operations because each has both strengths and weaknesses.
3. Unitary or non-unitary?	We regard WM as comprising an alliance of subsystems, each of which can be further fractionated. This aspect of our model is continually evolving. We began with a homunculus-like central executive serving as a marker for the attentional control processes that were important but not at that time directly investigated. Our approach has been to successively explore potential components to executive control, with a view to eventually 'retiring' the homunculus. This led first to the proposal of the fourth component, the episodic buffer, followed by more detailed exploration, with our most recent work focusing on the role of attention in visuospatial WM.
4. Role of attention and control	We make a broad distinction between selective attention to the external environment and internally driven attentional control. The central executive is principally concerned with internally oriented attentional control processes but also has a role in the attentional selection of perceptual information.
5. Storage, maintenance, and loss	We began by focusing on verbal WM and emphasizing the role of both temporary storage and articulatory rehearsal. We now accept that this is probably atypical, with non-verbal maintenance depending on 'refreshing', maintaining a representation by attentional focus. We have tended to accept a trace decay theory of forgetting, largely on grounds of simplicity while acknowledging the role of interference and of overloading limited capacity. We do not regard trace decay as an essential component of our model but rather as a simple and convenient current assumption.
6. The role of long-term memory (LTM)	WM is influenced by a range of types of LTM including semantic, episodic, and procedural. These operate at different stages and in different ways, with the crucial questions being what where and how. Hence, we do not regard the concept of 'activated LTM' as helpful.
7. Theoretical consistency	We regard our model as representing a map of a central area of cognition. As such it brings together existing knowledge in ways that allow further tractable questions to be asked regarding both the details of the model and its practical and theoretical scope. Progress has been crucially dependent on well-established negative results. These then suggest that the model needs to be modified but not abandoned unless a better model can be produced. In this context the value of the theory should be measured by its productivity rather than its capacity for falsification. On this criterion we regard our model as currently successful.

However, we fully accept that more precise and detailed models will prove necessary as *part* of a broader overall framework. A good example is the lack of a mechanism for storing the order in which items have occurred in a simple serial memory span task within our initial WM model (Baddeley & Hitch, 1974). This led to a very fruitful line of detailed modelling, with its application to a multicomponent framework, as discussed later.

This leaves open the question of how to develop such a broad framework. As described later, our own approach started with a simple question, namely, what function did the earlier concept of a short-term temporary memory serve, other than the frequently used example of remembering telephone numbers? We wanted a framework that was sufficiently general to be applied across a range of paradigms and that could be useable in tackling issues that extend beyond the laboratory. As will be discussed later, the framework developed gradually, being expanded only when empirical evidence demanded it. The role played by negative results here is crucial. Rather than regarding such results as a reason for abandoning the model, we have consistently used it as a stimulus to increase the complexity of the model from its initial unitary concept of a single short-term memory (STM), first to the assumption of three separate components, and eventually after many years including a fourth component. Our basic principle in using this method was to be parsimonious and not to simply add another assumption whenever an inconvenient result occurs, but rather to first ensure that the negative results are reliable and then to ask whether the proposed extension could prove fruitful in asking further tractable questions.

This means that the model is continuously developing, not a very convenient characteristic for others who might wish to use it, although happily the broad outline of the model has itself remained constant for over 40 years, with the single additional structure, the episodic buffer added 20 years ago (Baddeley, 2000). At a detailed level, however, things are constantly changing with the advent of investigators from other areas, for example, visual attention and the use of other tools such as neuroimaging adding to the richness of the field. Different people approaching WM from different orientations, however, tend to conceptualize WM in somewhat different ways. We ourselves like to think of this as analogous to the blind men attempting to identify an elephant by touch, one starting with its trunk and deciding that it is snake, another with its ears deciding it is a bird, and so forth. You will not be surprised to learn that we think we are describing the whole elephant! The present book, however, is a very good opportunity for the reader to sample the various approaches to decide for themselves.

We therefore welcome the opportunity to present a broad outline of our current views on the questions posed by the editors. In doing so, we are very aware that there is no 'authorized version' of the multicomponent model. This is partly because of the way in which it developed, not through a series of large grants supporting substantial teams of investigators as is often the case today, but rather through a series of often informal collaborations, initially involving a sequence of postdoctoral fellows who have gone on to develop their own viewpoints (e.g. Andrade, 2001; Jarrold, 2001; see chapter by Logie, Belletier, & Doherty, 2021) with the three authors of the present chapter collaborating rather more closely over the last decade or so. There remain, however, differences in emphasis between the three of us with AB being more influenced by neuropsychological collaborations and with attempts to link WM and LTM, an interest shared by

GH whose ongoing involvement with computational and mathematical modelling will be reflected in a later section. Much of our recent work has involved visual WM, with RA playing a particularly strong role. However, we like to work together, interact, and continue to influence each other with the result that answering the various questions did not prove difficult.

What would be much more difficult is to describe the precise nature of the model on which our answers are based, partly at least because, although a broad framework has emerged, predicting exactly how individual components will interact in specific experiments is likely to prove difficult. We admire the attempt to do so in the 'adversarial collaboration' in which the editors of the current book attempted to decide between the apparently diverse approaches represented by the embedded-processes model (see chapter by Cowan, Morey, & Naveh-Benjamin, 2021), the time-based resource-sharing model (see chapter by Barrouillet & Camos, 2021), and Logie's version of the multicomponent model (see chapter by Logie et al., 2021), but were not surprised that no clear 'winner' seems to have emerged. We interpret this as reflecting the broad equivalence of the three approaches despite their apparent differences.

What follows therefore is an attempt to use the questions raised by the editors as a means of communicating our own approach, with its emphasis on breadth and applicability, combined with an appreciation of the importance of gradually providing a more detailed account of the components of this complex system and of their interaction. In discussing detail, however, our focus will be on those areas that we ourselves have investigated. Hence, although the concept of a phonological loop is assumed to link into more detailed models of speech perception and production, we ourselves have not worked on these aspects and hence do not attempt to cover them. Similarly, while we are certainly interested in the mapping of our model onto underlying brain structures, as indicated by our use of neuropsychology, our emphasis has been on the psychological implications of such evidence rather than its anatomical basis. Thus, having little experience of using neuroimaging, we do not attempt to cover the extensive literature based on such techniques.

We began with the hypothesis that an integrated system combines STM and attention to facilitate a wide range of cognitive activities. We have proceeded through a method of progressive fractionation with the basic ground rules that the system should operate across a range of modalities and paradigms and that additional subsystems should be proposed only when necessary. This has resulted in a deliberately broad model that combines a fixed multicomponent structure with flexible, goal-driven control processes. The latter allow strategies for making optimal use of the limited resources of the system in different situations. Rather than attempting precise modelling of the entire system, we use converging operations, asking the same question using a range of different approaches to constrain and test the proposed hypothesis.

One advantage of this approach is that it allows us to combine evidence across a range of methods and populations to answer a carefully targeted set of questions. Another advantage is that it reduces the risk of artefacts and problems of generalization associated with relying too heavily on any one paradigm, methodology, or population. This has resulted in a relatively simple broad framework that is readily applied beyond the laboratory.

Limitations of this approach are the inherent complexity of the system and the need to leave large areas of the model currently unspecified, for example, how does the operation of the phonological loop link to theories of speech perception and production? This does, however, allow for continuous growth gradually linking into other areas of psychology and neuroscience.

The principal converging operations we use are as follows.

Dual-Task Methodology

Our methods have relied heavily on dual-task methodology whereby a task is analysed by requiring the simultaneous performance of tasks thought to load on a specific subsystem of WM. For example, articulatory suppression is used to prevent subvocal rehearsal. This has the advantage of isolating subcomponents of the model and focusing on the extent to which they are involved in specific activities such as reading or arithmetic. The method can be used with considerable flexibility across a wide range of paradigms and practical situations, as, for example, in the study of chess (Robbins et al., 1996) where, by selecting appropriate tasks we were able to show an important role for the visuospatial sketchpad and the central executive while ruling out the previous claim for a verbal contribution. In contrast, we found an unexpectedly substantial contribution of the loop to task switching with a much smaller role for executive processes (Baddeley, Chincotta, & Adlam, 2001).

However, it is important to accept that most tasks are not process-pure and are likely to place some load on the central executive, as shown by the selection of dual-task studies combining visual and verbal activities discussed by Morey (2018a) which all show some degree of impairment when simultaneous performance of visual and verbal tasks is required. Experiments using concurrent tasks also need to be designed skilfully in order to avoid confounding by ceiling and floor effects and/or interference at a perceptual rather than executive level. Given the complexity of the multicomponent model there can also be difficulty in interpreting potential interactions, particularly where different degrees of reliance on executive processing are involved. Hence, while broad dissociations may be relatively simple to demonstrate, more precise fractionation adds considerable complexity and depends on the method of converging operations rather than simple or double dissociation. A good example is the study by Klauer and Zhao (2004) who make a strong case for separating the visual and spatial components of the sketchpad where, despite building on a substantial existing literature, they require a further six experiments to pin down the evidence for the visual–spatial distinction by systematically ruling out alternative explanations.

More generally, however, dual-task methods have been used widely and productively in analysing a broad nature of a range of complex tasks. More recent application to answering more precise questions will be illustrated in the later section on visual WM.

Materials

We also make extensive use of item characteristics including similarity and spoken length. Such relatively simple paradigms produce substantial and reliable effects which make them readily applicable across a range of different tasks and populations. Indeed, our model evolved from a study contrasting effects of phonological and semantic similarity on verbal STM (Baddeley, 1966a), finding a large negative effect of phonological similarity (e.g. MAN, CAT, CAN) with a minimal effect of semantic similarity (e.g. HUGE, BIG, LARGE). When the task was changed to require LTM by requiring the learning of lists of ten such words, the pattern changed with semantic similarity proving much more important (Baddeley, 1966b). The phonological similarity effect, first noted by Conrad (1962) provides a clear marker of the use of the phonological loop, particularly valuable in analysing STM deficits in patients (see later). A marker of subvocal rehearsal is provided by the word length effect, the observation that immediate serial recall declines systematically with the increasing length of the words to be remembered (Baddeley, Thomson, & Buchanan, 1975). The role of rehearsal is also indicated by the effect of articulatory suppression, the requirement to repeatedly utter a single word such as 'the' while attempting to recall verbal material. Suppression abolishes the word length effect, and as first demonstrated by Murray (1968) also eliminates the phonological similarity effect for visually presented material, suggesting that articulation is necessary to convert the visual stimuli into a verbal code.

Limitations to these methods include the need to select material with care in order to rule out alternative explanations. An example is provided by the word length effect where we initially attempted to test the importance of trace decay, as marked by temporal delay, by comparing retention of sequences of five bisyllabic words with long vowels (e.g. HARPOON, FRIDAY) or short vowels (e.g. BISHOP, WICKED) finding span greater for the short-vowel words (Baddeley et al., 1975). However, others using a different set of words failed to replicate the advantage (Caplan & Waters, 1994; Lovatt, Avons, & Masterson, 2000). A later experiment by Mueller, Seymour, Kieras, and Meyer (2003) which attempted to separate the effects of spoken time from others such as phonological similarity, concluded that duration was the better predictor. Other studies have resulted in evidence against a trace decay interpretation of the word length effect (Guitard, Gabel, Saint-Aubin, Surprenant, & Neath, 2018), but accept that there are likely to be other dimensions that would need to be controlled before a clear conclusion can be reached. Our own view is that the problem of adequately balancing material makes this paradigm unsuitable to answering the decay versus interference question.

Neuropsychology

This has played a crucial role in developing the model and in particular in separating the influence of the visuospatial and phonological subsystems. Carefully selected patients who have a very precise cognitive deficit allow theoretically important questions to be addressed in a way that is typically much more difficult in healthy participants. In this respect, the well-established literature on patients with phonological loop deficits has been particularly valuable.

The importance of such patients was first demonstrated by Shallice and Warrington (1970) who reported a patient, KF, who had a greatly reduced STM as reflected both in a digit span of only two items and an absence of a recency effect in the free recall of verbal materials while having well-preserved LTM, the opposite pattern to classic amnesic patients such as HM who had preserved STM and grossly impaired LTM. There have now been many patients reported with a specific deficit in verbal STM (Shallice & Papagno, 2019; Vallar & Shallice, 1990). A deficit in STM is not uncommon among aphasic and other language disorder patients (Vallar, Corno, & Basso, 1992), although patients with more than one deficit tend to be harder to interpret theoretically with a problem of deciding which of the two or more deficits is responsible for performance on a given task.

Our own involvement with such patients came with the discovery in Milan of patient PV who following a stroke had a very clear and limited STM deficit which Vallar and Baddeley (1984) were able to show followed the pattern of phonological similarity, word length, and suppression effects that would be expected from a phonological loop impairment. We went on to explore the possible function of the loop by studying what PV could and could not do, beginning with language comprehension. Earlier approaches to psycholinguistics suggested that comprehension might involve holding sentences in STM while they were syntactically and semantically analysed (e.g. Savin & Perchonok, 1965), potentially suggesting that PV should have problems in sentence comprehension. She did not (Vallar & Baddeley, 1987) except for highly artificial sentences that were expressly devised so that comprehension required holding an initial subject across many intervening words. Hence PV could correctly reject a sentence such as *Sailors are lived on by ships* but not *Sailors, it is commonly believed with some justification frequently tend to be lived on by ships*, a task performed correctly by control participants.

A more promising hypothesis proved to be the proposal that the phonological loop was important for initial phonological learning. Supportive evidence came from our attempt to teach PV to associate words in Italian with their Russian equivalent, a task she completely failed, while showing a normal capacity for learning to associate pairs of words in her native Italian, a task known to depend principally on semantic coding (Baddeley, Papagno, & Vallar, 1988). We went on to show that a similar disruption of new phonological learning could be achieved in healthy young subjects by disrupting the phonological loop either by articulatory suppression (Papagno, Valentine, & Baddeley, 1991), word length, or similarity (Papagno & Vallar, 1992). A final stage was to extend this to new learning, first by demonstrating that children with a specific language disorder, coupled with normal non-verbal intelligence, showed the predicted phonological loop deficit. We went on to show that non-word repetition, the capacity to hear and echo back a non-word, was a powerful marker of vocabulary development in healthy young children (see Baddeley, Gathercole, & Papagno, 1998 for further discussion). Single-case studies in patients with visuospatial STM deficits have also been conducted (Farah, 1990; Hanley, Young, & Pearson, 1991) although our own involvement in this area has been much less.

This might be a good point to discuss some recent suggestions that the evidence from such studies is flawed. Morey (2018a), for example, discusses two papers by Hanley and colleagues (Hanley, Pearson, and Young, 1990; Hanley et al., 1991), concluding that their evidence is inconsistent with the assumption of a temporary visuospatial subsystem such as the sketchpad. However, as pointed out by Hanley and Young (2019), these conclusions are based on erroneous reporting of the original data, a point subsequently acknowledged by Morey (2018b), although not resulting in any change in her conclusions. A similar type of criticism based on the claimed inability of the phonological loop hypothesis to account for an apparent feature of the impairment of verbal STM was made by Morey, Rhodes, and Cowan (2019) resulting again in a detailed refutation, this time by Logie (2019). It is worth bearing in mind in this context that the theoretically important neuropsychological cases have typically been built across a range of different measures and different cases within a literature that was vigorously challenged and rigorously defended. A good example of this is provided by Shallice and Papagno (2019) who consider and answer the range of possible criticisms faced by the proposal of a separable verbal buffer store. It is also worth noting that the strength of the multicomponent hypothesis lies not in the detail, whether forgetting represents trace decay or interference, for example, but in its capacity to integrate a range of phenomena and to apply these successfully beyond the laboratory.

One limitation of the neuropsychological approach is that suitable patients are rare, making replication a problem although as shown in the case of patients with a phonological loop deficit, they can, over time be sufficiently frequent to allow an overall evaluation of the conclusions they support (Shallice & Papagno, 2019). Group studies using less pure cases can also be useful but may be harder to interpret unequivocally due to additional potentially confounding deficits. Another problem is that the approach depends on access to neuropsychologists who regularly see potentially interesting patients and who have the theoretical background knowledge to recognize such patients and the time to follow them up sufficiently carefully. This is by no means easy given the increasing pressure of work on clinicians in the United Kingdom at least. Finally, the fact that this approach is not available to most investigators can lead to scepticism from colleagues outside neuropsychology.

Neuroimaging

We ourselves have made relatively little use of neuroimaging. Early imaging studies were successful in showing an association between our three-component model and its broadly based links to anatomical location with phonological storage depending on a temporoparietal junction location, rehearsal reflected in Broca's area, the sketchpad depending on a series of principally right hemisphere locations, with a largely frontal basis for executive processing (Jonides et al., 1993, 1998; Paulesu, Frith, & Frackowiack,

1993; Smith & Jonides, 1997). However, later attempts to use location as a guide to more detailed function seem to have proved less successful (see reviews of the very extensive literature in this area by D'Esposito & Postle, 2015; Eriksson, Vogel, Lansner, Bergström, & Nyberg, 2015).

An example of the problems of mapping complex cognitive tasks onto their anatomical basis is provided by the N-back task which is frequently used as an indicator of executive function in neuroimaging studies, but proves to be anatomically highly complex, as shown by Owen, McMillan, Laird, and Bullmore (2005) whose meta-analysis finds activation in no fewer than eight different brain areas. In a similar vein, the attempt by Kane, Conway, Miura, and Colflesh (2007) to use meta-analysis to link a range of candidate executive processes to their anatomical basis led only to a broad visual-verbal distinction. We suspect that some techniques, while effective when applied to more basic perceptual processing, are not yet sufficiently developed to allow the more detailed complexities of WM to be analysed. However, new techniques, such as representational analysis seem more likely to allow the detailed complexities of WM to be explored, as Kalm and Norris (2014) have shown.

Human Development

Applications of the multicomponent model to children have proved fruitful in shedding new light on the nature of developmental changes. Early findings showed that the word length effect in verbal STM extends throughout childhood (Hitch & Halliday, 1983; Hulme, Thomson, Muir, & Lawrence, 1984; Nicolson, 1981), there being a striking linear relationship between amount recalled and speech rate. This suggested a simple interpretation according to which the speed of refreshing the phonological loop increases with age while the rate at which information is lost remains constant. This in turn stimulated a good deal of further investigation that led to a more nuanced account in which the crucial factor is the speed at which information can be read out from the phonological store during either rehearsal or recall (Gathercole & Hitch, 1993). Another finding was developmental fractionation, whereby experimental manipulations have qualitatively different effects according to children's age (Hitch, 1990). A good example is the sensitivity of STM for nameable objects to item similarity and retroactive interference. Thus, children younger than around 5–6 years were found to be more sensitive to visual than verbal interference whereas 10–11-year-olds showed the opposite pattern (Hitch, Halliday, Schaafstal, & Schraagen, 1988; Longoni & Scalisi, 1994). This suggested a developmental progression in the way nameable pictures are remembered, from initial reliance on the visuospatial sketchpad to later use of the phonological loop through verbal recoding. However, other evidence indicated that older children continue to use the visuospatial sketchpad but that its contribution to recall is usually masked by the more pervasive phonological component (Hitch, Woodin, & Baker, 1989). Subsequent investigation indicates that in memory for nameable pictures use of phonological coding emerges around 6–8 years of age (Henry, Messer,

Luger-Klein, & Crane, 2012; Palmer, 2000), which contrasts with its much earlier emergence in memory for spoken stimuli (see earlier, also Hitch, Halliday, Dodd, & Littler, 1989). Overall, evidence for the importance of presentation mode in children's use of the phonological loop converges neatly with data from adults and neuropsychological patients indicating that spoken and visual stimuli access the phonological loop via different pathways (Vallar & Papagno, 2002).

An early attempt to apply the multicomponent model to individual differences in children aged 6–15 years also proved encouraging, indicating three factors corresponding to executive processes, phonological storage, and visuospatial storage (Gathercole, Pickering, Ambridge, & Wearing, 2004). Subsequent studies (summarized in Gray, Green, Alt, Hogan, Kuo, Brinkley, & Cowan, 2017) have given broadly consistent results. However, Gray et al. reported that Cowan's (2001) three-factor model gave a slightly better account of their data and also failed to obtain evidence for the four-component version of the multicomponent model (Baddeley, 2000). In our view, Gray et al.'s observations illustrate some important methodological issues. One is that individual differences are a somewhat blunt tool, with limited capacity to distinguish between models when they make highly similar predictions and with limited power to identify multiple factors when measures are highly intercorrelated. The other limitation is the familiar problem that outcomes are constrained by the choice of measures used, which in the case of Gray et al.'s attempt to assess the episodic buffer were at best exploratory.

The question of how the executive component of WM develops has become a major area of research in its own right, much of it using alternative theoretical approaches and distinguishing a number of different aspects of executive function (Anderson, 2002). Much of this work is inspired by the view that executive processes can be subdivided into a number of different categories (Miyake et al., 2000). The general picture to emerge is one in which executive functions emerge gradually, beginning with the ability to deploy selective attention and progressing to full executive control. This is not an area where we have been particularly active ourselves, and we have tended for simplicity not to differentiate within the executive, while accepting the need to fractionate at a finer level of analysis (Baddeley, 2002). Our findings do, however, fit a general pattern of a developmental increase in executive control. One example comes from our work on visual STM showing that instructing adults to prioritize particular items leads to reliable costs and benefits in their recall. We have shown that these strategy effects depend on executive processes and are superimposed on an underlying recency effect (see later). When we used the same task with 7–10-year-old children, we saw the recency effect but no effect of instructions, suggesting the executive resources needed to implement them have yet to develop (Berry, Waterman, Baddeley, Hitch, & Allen, 2018). Later work showed that these children can prioritize when the task context is made more motivating, though the effect appears to be somewhat smaller than for adults (Atkinson, Waterman, & Allen, 2019).

Evidence on spontaneous strategies points to a similar broad developmental progression. Much of this comes from variants of the 'working memory span' task developed by Just and Carpenter (1992) to assess the capacity for resource sharing by measuring the amount of information that can be stored temporarily at the same time as engaging in cognitively demanding processing operations. In our own experiments using tasks of this sort we found that children are relatively passive, making little attempt to engage in resource sharing by reactivating items in memory during processing operations, a result that also seemed to extend to adults (Towse, Hitch, & Hutton, 1998). This led other investigators to explore what happens with less demanding schedules for processing operations allowing more opportunity for resource sharing. Under these conditions it is clear that children can actively refresh WM while processing (Barrouillet, Gavens, Vergauwe, Gaillard, & Camos, 2009), just like adults (Barrouillet, Bernardin, & Camos, 2004). However, even in these simpler tasks, the very youngest children appear to be passive during processing operations (Barrouillet et al., 2009; Camos & Barrouillet, 2011), consistent with the pattern found by Towse et al. (1998) in older children and adults under task conditions less favourable to resource sharing. Overall, there appears to be a pattern of increasing flexibility in executive control as development proceeds, with its appearance in behaviour varying markedly with factors such as task demands.

A major limitation in using developmental evidence is that age differences are accompanied by a raft of covariates, which can make it difficult to draw conclusions. Nevertheless, the multicomponent model is clearly applicable to children, enriching our description of developmental differences and providing valuable theoretical feedback. This in turn has stimulated numerous applications of the model to the analysis of developmental disorders and educational attainment in areas such as reading and mathematics (see section on Applications).

Strategies

Theoretical interpretation can be complicated by differences in strategy use, and this can vary across ability groups. While care should be taken not to simply appeal to strategy use when a preferred hypothesis is not supported, we assume that participants will often make use of different strategies to optimize performance and/or ease cognitive load. The availability and effectiveness of these strategies will depend on the nature of the task, and the cognitive and metacognitive abilities of the individual. Strategy use can be observed by obtaining participants' reports (e.g. Dunning & Holmes, 2014; Logie, Della Sala, Laiacona, Chalmers, & Wynn, 1996; Morrison, Rosenbaum, Fair, & Chen, 2016), though these will inevitably be subjective in nature. It can also be manipulated through the instruction for participants to adopt particular strategic approaches, in terms of prioritizing some items over others within a single task (e.g. Hu, Hitch, Baddeley, Zhang, & Allen, 2014), prioritizing one method of encoding over another (e.g. Atkinson, Baddeley, & Allen, 2018; Campoy & Baddeley, 2008), prioritizing one task over another (Hitch & Baddeley, 1976), or adopting particular methods of encoding and maintaining items, such as rehearsal, chunking, or visualization (e.g. Turley-Ames & Whitfield, 2003). This approach offers ways of harnessing the naturally occurring variability in how tasks are performed, with the aims of better understanding the cognitive mechanisms involved and the optimal ways in which limited capacity systems can be employed, though difficulties lie in assuming participant compliance. Finally, additional experimental manipulations can be applied with the aim of establishing whether certain strategic approaches are being implemented (e.g. Campoy, Castella, Provencio, Hitch, & Baddeley, 2015).

Computational Modelling

Our main use of computational modelling has concerned the phonological loop. Despite being the best specified part of the conceptual model, it gradually became clear that a range of effects required further explanation. These fell into two broad categories: effects associated with memory for the serial order of a series of items and interactions with LTM.

Our first efforts at modelling focused on serial order. We used a connectionist approach with separate representations for items and their serial positions, the latter represented by states of a context signal that evolves gradually during sequence presentation. Connections between the current item and the current state of the context signal were strengthened during encoding. Separately, items were linked to representations of their phonological content. Once strengthened, connections were subject to rapid decay and a certain amount of noise, resulting in errors when it came to recall. An initial version of the model showed this approach was promising (Burgess & Hitch, 1992) and a subsequent more ambitious revision successfully reproduced a range of effects associated with memory for serial order in combination with signature effects of the phonological loop such as those of phonemic similarity, word length, and articulatory suppression (Burgess & Hitch, 1999).

At about the same time, a number of alternative computational models were developed. These differed in many aspects, most notably in their solutions to the problem of serial order. Some were similar to ours in assuming some form of context signal (e.g. Brown, Preece, & Hulme, 2000; Lewandowsky & Farrell, 2008; Henson, 1998). Others sought to avoid this step by assuming information about order is carried by a gradient of activation levels over items, the first being the highest, as in the primacy model (Page and Norris, 1998), or by the formation of 'chaining' associations between successive items, as in the TODAM model (Lewandowsky & Murdock, 1989).

Chaining seemed to us unlikely given that memory for sequences of alternating phonemically similar and dissimilar items shows extra errors *on* rather than *after* the similar items (Baddeley, 1968; Henson, Norris, Page, & Baddeley, 1996). Botvinick and Plaut (2006) did succeed in showing that a chaining model could simulate this result, but the complexity of their model rendered it open to the objection that it achieved this by learning positional representations (Hurlstone, Hitch, & Baddeley, 2014).

Given a growing plethora of models, with numerous points of overlap and differences, we sought to simplify by identifying the underlying principles on which they differ and then weighing the experimental evidence for each assumption (Hurlstone, Hitch, & Baddeley, 2014). As part of this we extended a method first developed by Farrell and Lewandowsky (2004). This involves creating a family of models that incorporate different principles in various combinations and comparing their outputs with human data. The best-fitting model of serial ordering to emerge was one that combines both position–item associations and a primacy gradient. In terms of behavioural signatures, a primacy gradient is indicated by the high frequency of 'fill-in' errors where, having recalled the Nth item one position too soon, the following error is much more likely to be the $N − 1$th item than the $N + 1$th (Page & Norris, 1998, Surprenant, Kelley, Farley, & Neath, 2005). This bias would not be seen if recall was driven solely by positional cues (or indeed by chaining) but follows from a primacy gradient as item $N − 1$ is more highly activated than item $N + 1$. By contrast, the need to assume position–item associations is clearly indicated by the distinctive pattern of order errors in memory for temporally grouped sequences in which groups of items are separated by pauses. These show clear influences of the positions of items within groups and of groups within the sequence (Ryan, 1969a, 1969b), a two-dimensional pattern that would not be expected from a primacy gradient.

More recently we have shown how the context signal can be computed directly from a spoken input by a bank of filters that analyse its temporal structure. Some of these filters respond to the presentation rate of individual items, others to the durations of temporal groups, and others to the duration of the list. We have demonstrated that such a model successfully predicts how recall varies with differences in the way a sequence is grouped, going substantially beyond current models (Hartley, Hurlstone, & Hitch, 2016). Initial findings from neuroimaging using the technique of multivoxel pattern analysis provide independent confirmation of the use of positional coding in immediate verbal recall and, incidentally, no support for chaining (Kalm & Norris, 2014). Overall, we conclude that computational modelling has been fruitful in tackling the problem of serial order and in providing the initial outline for a more detailed, mechanistic account of the phonological loop. One spin-off from this work is preliminary evidence that serial order is handled in similar ways in the spatial and visual domains (Hurlstone & Hitch, 2015, 2018).

In contrast, progress in modelling interactions with LTM has been somewhat limited, most likely reflecting the greater extent of the challenge. An exception is the role of the phonological loop in long-term learning, as reflected in the Hebb effect (Hebb, 1961) where unbeknown to the participant, a sequence is presented for immediate recall on multiple occasions embedded within other non-repeated sequences. This results in gradual learning of the repeated sequence, regardless of whether the repetition is detected. We have succeeded in showing that an extended version of the context signal model can simulate the Hebb effect (Burgess & Hitch, 2006). It does this by assuming that context–item connections undergo slow as well as fast decay and uses a cumulative matching process to recognize a sequence as familiar. The model provides a good account of why long-term learning is slower when the temporal grouping structure of a repeated sequence changes but is unaffected by phonemic similarity of the items or articulatory suppression (Hitch, Flude, & Burgess, 2009). A similar model has been applied to the learning of new words, as in vocabulary acquisition (Gupta & MacWhinney, 1997). More generally, we note the existence of resemblances between models of this type and models of speech production (see, e.g. Acheson & MacDonald, 2009), suggesting an opportunity for greater integration and scope in future work.

Another way LTM is important is through effects of previously acquired skills and knowledge in immediate recall. Perhaps the best-known example is the use of past experience to recode groups of items into higher-order chunks, which George Miller (1956) showed can have a big effect on performance. Another is word frequency. Effects such as these can be readily incorporated in current computational models (e.g. Burgess & Hitch, 1999; Page & Norris, 2009). However, more complex phenomena such as the substantial improvement in memory for a sequence of words when they form a meaningful sentence (Allen, Hitch, & Baddeley, 2018; Baddeley, Allen, & Hitch, 2011) go beyond such models as they require extra assumptions about syntactic and semantic processes.

Problems of scale and complexity assume even more importance when it comes to computational modelling of the WM system as a whole. The challenges here include mechanisms for top-down executive control, processes for binding information within and between subsystems, and endowing the system with a sufficient range of usable long-term knowledge. A recent attempt to identify empirical benchmarks for WM illustrates the potentially large number of constraints to be satisfied (Oberauer et al., 2018). So far, attempts to model the WM system have tended to focus on specific tasks such as complex span (Oberauer, Lewandowsky, Farrell, Jarrold, & Greaves, 2012). However, there is a risk of too early a commitment to a particular experimental paradigm restricting subsequent generalization to the wide range of contexts in which WM is used. So far, we ourselves have limited our use of computational modelling to a specific aspect of WM, serial order in the phonological loop, where there is a clear general question (Lashley, 1951) and empirical constraints set by human data are relatively few and well established. Although highly focused, we have shown this approach can be used to simulate neuropsychological impairments (Burgess & Hitch, 1996), generate novel predictions (Burgess & Hitch, 2006), and allow generalization to non-verbal domains (Hurlstone & Hitch, 2015, 2018).

3. Unitary Versus Non-Unitary Nature of Working Memory

We regard WM as a unitary system comprising an alliance of interactive components. We regard it as unitary in the sense that the components interact in an integrated and coherent way making it useful to consider the system as a whole, as well as to study its various components. However, the verbal and visual subsystems themselves depend on input from a range of other potentially separable systems. In the case of the phonological loop, for example, we assume that it has evolved from separable language-based auditory input and articulatory output systems (e.g. Vallar & Papagno, 2002). These in turn will depend on more peripheral aspects of cognition such as hearing, and articulatory movement control. In a similar vein, we assume that the sketchpad involves the integration of information from visual, spatial, kinaesthetic, and tactile processing to form objects which themselves will reflect existing visual semantic knowledge. Finally, we assume that visual and acoustic/linguistic information can be combined within the multimodal buffer to create consciously accessible episodes. In short, we regard WM as a single overall system comprising many interacting components.

4. The Role of Attention and Control

We assume a centralized control system that can potentially be fractionated into a set of interacting executive processes which together comprise a limited capacity central executive that is yet to be fully specified. We initially used the concept of the central executive, as a homunculus capable of performing a wide range of attentionally related functions. It is important to note, however, that we did not assume that this provided an explanation, but rather a placeholding concept which would in due course be fractionated and eventually, we assumed, become itself a well-specified attentional control system.

While we initially avoided the complexity of the central executive, more recently we have separated out its memory storage function as a separate subsystem, the episodic buffer, which evidence suggests is principally a passive storage system maintaining integrated information that is available to conscious awareness. It does, however, depend on input from a range of other sources for its content. We assume that it has limited storage capacity and is closely linked to the central executive, providing a system that has much in common with the focus of attention in Cowan's approach to WM.

More recently, we have been applying methods developed for the study of verbal STM to its visuospatial equivalent using briefly presented coloured shapes. We used dual-task methodology and prioritization instructions to investigate the role of executive resources and we used the effect of a post-stimulus visual distractor to study the role of perceptual attention. The distractor, or 'suffix', was a further coloured shape that participants were instructed to ignore (Ueno, Allen, Baddeley, Hitch, & Saito, 2011). The different effects of these manipulations are especially clear when the coloured shapes are presented sequentially. Under these conditions, memory for the final item is especially good and there is a recency gradient over earlier items, with memory for colour-shape bindings declining more rapidly than individual features (Allen, Baddeley, & Hitch, 2006). We interpreted these recency effects as suggesting that the sketchpad is subject to rapid forgetting, possibly involving overwriting, with information about feature bindings particularly fragile. Turning to our experimental manipulations, we found that performing a concurrent task impaired memory for all except the final item (Allen, Baddeley, & Hitch, 2014), whereas a post-stimulus visual distractor had broadly the converse effect, principally disrupting memory for the final item (Hu et al., 2014). This dissociation suggests the need to separate two aspects of attention, internal control (used to refresh items in store) together with external attentional selection (used to select memory items and not distractors), a distinction routinely made in the field of research on attention (Chun, Golomb, & Turk-Browne, 2011). In line with these results, we extended the multicomponent model to include externally oriented, perceptually based visual attention as the gateway to the visuospatial sketchpad, and a source of overwriting, contrasting this with internally driven executive attention and its deployment in counteracting forgetting. The most recent version of the model is illustrated in Fig. 2.1.

Further evidence for our interpretation comes from the effects of manipulating strategies using instructions to prioritize memory for particular items in the sequence. We find that prioritizing an item boosts its retention at the cost of poorer memory for low-priority items (Hu et al., 2014), and that these effects disappear under dual-task conditions (Hu, Allen, Baddeley, & Fitch, 2016). These observations are what would be expected if prioritization instructions bias the way limited capacity executive resources are deployed in offsetting forgetting. Intriguingly, we discovered that the boost

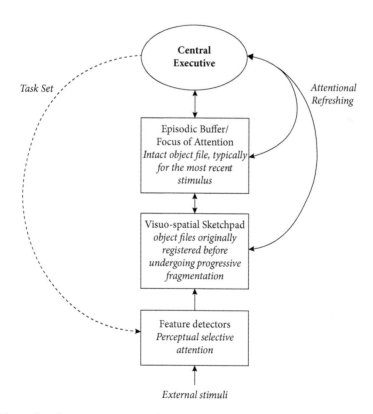

Fig. 2.1 The authors' current views on the processes involved in visuo-spatial working memory.

Reproduced from Graham J. Hitch, Richard J. Allen, and Alan D. Baddeley, 'Attention and binding in visual working memory: Two forms of attention and two kinds of buffer storage', *Attention, Perception, and Psychophysics*, 82 (1), pp. 280–293, Figure 9, https://doi.org/10.3758/s13414-019-01837-x Copyright © 2020 The Author(s)/CC BY-SA (https://creativecommons.org/licenses/by-sa/4.0).

in retaining a prioritized item tended to disappear when the series was followed by a visual distractor (suffix), even when the prioritized item was not the final item (Allen & Ueno, 2018; Hitch, Hu, Allen, & Baddeley, 2018; Hu et al., 2014). We interpreted this as suggesting that prioritizing an early item tends to give it equivalent status to the most recent item, a state in which information is highly available and immediately accessible, but at the same time highly fragile and vulnerable to perceptual interference. We identify this privileged state with the episodic buffer in the multicomponent model and with the focus of attention in Cowan's and Oberauer's models (Cowan, 1999; Oberauer and Hein, 2012). The amount of information that can occupy this privileged state at any moment is a topic of current debate (Cowan, 2011) and is, we suggest, likely to be influenced by organizational factors such as chunking. Thus, our own results suggest a lower capacity than we have assumed for the episodic buffer, but this may reflect a limited opportunity for chunking in our task of remembering a series of coloured shapes. Overall, we are pleased to note that our conclusions are broadly in line with those drawn by colleagues who have approached visual WM from the field of visual attention (for a recent review, see Hitch, Allen, & Baddeley, 2020).

5. Storage, Maintenance, and Loss of Information in Working Memory

We assume a range of encoding processes, some perceptual and others based on LTM. We assume that both are involved in most situations, for example, perceiving a scene will depend on both the perceptual input and the processing of that scene via LTM and prior experience. Furthermore, we regard the way in which information is encoded, as opposed to modality of presentation, as a defining characteristic of buffer storage in the case of both the phonological loop and the visuospatial sketchpad. We are relatively open on the method of retention and suspect that this will differ according to the individual component and the amount of material to be retained. Particularly important in this respect is the role of strategy where the nominal task as specified by the experimenter may be very different from the method of processing adopted by an individual participant. The traditional approach to this problem within experimental psychology and in single-case neuropsychology is to use a range of converging operations to constrain potential strategies, accepting evidence only if it is consistent across a range of methods. Unfortunately, this is impractical for most neuroimaging studies which can present major problems of interpretation. Methods of attacking this are starting to appear, including instruction to use a particular strategy (Campoy & Baddeley, 2008; Campoy et al., 2015). An important potential area for development would be to use neuroimaging to obtain an independent indicator as to whether a given system was or was not being used by an individual (Logie, Pernet, Buonocore, & Della Sala, 2011; Zeman et al., 2010).

More generally, it seems clear that interference effects play an important role in forgetting, as reflected in the effect of similarity and on the impact of exceeding the capacity of one or more components of WM. However, we would not wish to rule out the concept of trace decay which could indeed be perceived as non-specific disruption through neural noise within the system, as a further cause of forgetting. This does of course leave open the question of how to study the differential effects of these two forms of potential interference, one specific and the other general, and whether interference can occur as we suspect, at different points within the system. Due to its complexity we have tended to leave open the question of trace decay or interference within our overall conceptual model. While accepting that it is important for a full specification of any WM model, we do not regard it as currently crucial for the use of our broad framework.

A good deal of our work has involved the process of subvocal rehearsal within the phonological loop. This provides a convenient method of maintaining verbal material, provided that the material is familiar enough to articulate accurately. It provides a useful way of retaining the order of spoken material operating with a relatively light attentional demand. It is, however, limited in capacity and is, we suspect, atypical of rehearsal more generally. Here we accept the concept of 'attentional refreshing' (e.g. see chapter by Barrouillet & Camos, 2021) as the most likely form of rehearsal within other modalities such as vision. While we have not investigated this in any detail, we accept the proposal that it involves the focusing of attention on the representation of material which we assume occurs within the episodic buffer, a subsystem of limited in capacity that is open to strategic control.

An illustration of different storage mechanisms is represented by the recency effect. We regard this as the application of last-in-first-out strategy to primed internal representations for which the priming may be either intentional or incidental. The representations primed may be either within short-term or long-term systems. An example of different modes of recency is provided by patient PV who shows little evidence of a recency effect in immediate verbal free recall. However, she does show normal long-term recency in a task requiring delayed recall of anagram solutions (Vallar, Papagno, & Baddeley, 1991). In the case of long-term recency, retrieval appears to depend on the relative recency of the target versus that of the closest rival stimuli, approximately following a ratio rule as proposed by the SIMPLE model proposed by Brown, Neath, and Chater (2007). From the practical viewpoint we assume that long-term recency provides a quick and convenient means of orientation in time and place that allows the maintenance of an ongoing representation of our environment.

6. The Role of Long-Term Memory Knowledge in Working Memory Storage and Processing

We assume a complex pattern of interaction between WM and LTM via the episodic buffer. This operates at a range of levels; in the case of the simplest component of the multicomponent model, the phonological loop, we assume that long-term lexical and semantic knowledge will influence the representations within WM, as evidenced by effects of factors such as item lexicality, frequency, concreteness, and neighbourhood size (e.g. Allen & Hulme, 2006; Hulme, Maughan, & Brown, 1991; Roodenrys, Hulme, Alban, Ellis, & Brown, 1994; Roodenrys, Hulme, Lethbridge, Hinton, & Nimmo, 2002), Broader language habits will influence chunking thus allowing memory span for five unrelated words to be increased to a span of around 15 if the words comprise a meaningful sentence (Baddeley, Hitch, & Allen, 2009; Brener, 1940). Similarly, if verbal information is presented within a familiar visuospatial configuration, this additional representational support can serve to boost recall performance, as in the case of visuospatial bootstrapping (Darling, Allen, & Havelka, 2017). Rehearsal will depend on fluent subvocal articulation which in turn reflects long-term procedural language learning. Finally, the whole process will depend on the strategy adopted by the participant, whether this is specified by the experimenter (Campoy & Baddeley, 2008; Campoy et al., 2015, Logie et al., 2011; Zeman et al., 2010) or devised on the basis of experience (Salame & Baddeley, 1986). Bearing this in mind, the assertion that WM is simply activated LTM is not erroneous, but is unhelpful, other than as a placeholder for further research.

However, while we regard the role of LTM in WM as pervasive, its influence will vary depending on the particular aspect of WM concerned. We regard this as providing a series of empirical questions rather than reflecting basic assumptions within the model. We therefore use hypotheses as a way of exploring the limits of the model rather than directly testing its validity. For example, our assumption that chunking in prose recall might depend on executive processes proved unfounded. Disrupting executive processing using a demanding concurrent task reduced overall retention of both sentences and strings of unrelated words but did so to an equivalent extent (Baddeley et al., 2009), suggesting the advantage from language was coming via LTM rather than through the operation of the central executive.

WM, however, certainly does influence LTM through its general effect of reducing available attentional capacity in complex LTM tasks as reflected, for example, by the effect of expertise on remembering chess positions (Robbins et al., 1996) and importantly, through the differential impact of the separate subsystems on specific types of learning. Hence, their impaired phonological loop capacity interferes with the acquisition of new foreign language vocabulary in patients with a phonological loop deficit (Baddeley et al., 1988). Similarly, tasks that constrain the phonological loop disrupt the acquisition of foreign language words by healthy young adults, but do not disrupt paired associate learning in their native vocabulary (Papagno et al., 1991). This finding has been extended to individual differences in second-language learning where a meta-analysis of some 79 samples involving over 3000 participants finds clear evidence of the importance of both the central executive and phonological components of WM (Linck, Osthus, Koeth, & Bunting, 2014).

There has in recent years been considerable interest in attempts to train WM. While we have not ourselves been involved in this area, the evidence seems to suggest that given an appropriate programme, improvements can be made that will generalize to other broadly similar WM tasks, but that this gain does not generalize to improvement in more broadly based intelligence measures or in scholastic performance

(Melby-Lervag & Hulme, 2013). The most promising way of explaining this is offered by the recent research by Gathercole, Dunning, Holmes, and Norris (2019) who present evidence to suggest that individual subcomponents of tasks may be improved by practice and that this will enhance performance on other tasks that require broadly equivalent sub-skills. However, there seems to be little evidence that training leads to a more general improvement in WM capacity.

7. Is There Evidence That Is Not Consistent with Your Theoretical Framework and How Does Your Framework Address This Inconsistency?

This question goes to the heart of our theoretical approach to WM. We regard theories as broadly equivalent to maps that capture what is already known and that this helps to frame questions that will extend our knowledge. Theories can operate at a range of different levels. In our own case we wanted to keep the model as simple and general as possible. This meant only suggesting additional components when the evidence forced it while testing the theory wherever possible by attempting to generalize across domains. Where a less central assumption has been brought into question, as in the challenge to our initial view that the phonological loop is subject to trace decay, an assumption that is still controversial, it remains possible, if the evidence demands it, to accept an alternative interpretation of short-term forgetting while maintaining the broader concept. Hence, none of the evidence for a role of the loop in language acquisition would need to change. This approach differs from that of Popper (1959) who assumed a method based on falsification, proposing that to be useful, theories must make precise predictions, which if not supported should lead to the rejection of the theory, a view that was later rejected by his colleague Lakatos (1970) who evaluated theories on the basis on how *productive* they were in extending their scope and generating new and valid further information. He warned that theories faced with Popper's rather draconian criterion are likely to become defensive in nature based on the need to avoid falsification. We suspect that this may be a problem with complex computational models that may depend too heavily on free parameters and are therefore in danger of simply turning into a complex curve-fitting exercise. This issue is discussed further as part of an account of the development of the multicomponent model (Baddeley et al., 2019). However, we accept that our model leaves a wide range of unanswered questions which will eventually we assume be filled by more detailed theorization, though initially at least probably by focusing on specific limited questions. Others of our colleagues clearly disagree (see, e.g. Oberauer et al., 2018). Time will tell.

Given our approach to modelling as mapping therefore, evidence inconsistent with the model provides an essential stimulus to further development, provided that it is replicable and can be incorporated within the broad existing structure. If not, the structure will need to change.

Representing the Model

An important feature of the model is the way in which it has been presented graphically. As Logie (2016) pointed out, although Baddeley and Hitch (1974) referred to all three components, very little was said about the visuospatial sketchpad, and a visual representation of the three components seemed unnecessary. This was not because of lack of earlier research on visual (Phillips, 1974; Phillips & Baddeley, 1971) and spatial STM (Gilson & Baddeley, 1969; Warrington & Baddeley, 1974), but rather that these occurred earlier and were not influenced by the model, unlike the studies by Baddeley, Grant, Wight, and Thomson (1973) and Baddeley and Lieberman (1980) which were directly prompted by the need to expand the framework leading to the initial graphic version of the three-component proposal that appeared over a decade after our initial proposal (Baddeley, 1986). The specific format shown in Fig. 2.2a attempted to stress the conceptual nature of the model while avoiding a more standard 'box-and-arrows' representation. This continues to be an important point because we do not wish to suggest, for example, that the components are strictly modular in a Fodorian sense (Fodor, 1983), but rather that they reflect a common and integrative storage point for a range of incoming stimulus streams.

At some point the model seems to have been rotated through 90°, a transformation we accepted when modifying it to incorporate research on the role of the phonological loop in the acquisition of new vocabulary as shown in Fig. 2.2b. This requires the addition of LTM, with bidirectional arrows reflecting the relationship between the loop and phonological LTM. A similar process is hypothesized for the visuospatial sketchpad, although this does not seem to have yet been explored in any detail.

Bearing in mind the frequent criticism of box-and-arrow models that, when in doubt they simply add another box, we resisted adding further components until, forced by the evidence, we proposed a fourth box, the episodic buffer (Baddeley, 2000) arguing that one new box in 25 years was not excessively profligate! The later four-component model is shown in Fig. 2.2c which represents a separation of the executive into two components, attentional control and a separate temporary storage system, the episodic buffer, capable of binding information from a wide range of sources including visual, verbal, and LTM. This system was also assumed to make the resulting episodes available to conscious awareness.

Our initial hypothesis was that the buffer depended only on the central executive, regarded as the simplest assumption, represented by the single arrow. A series of subsequent experiments, however, convinced us that this was not the case, with a wide range of sources having potential access to this limited capacity storage system (Allen et al., 2006; Baddeley, et al., 2009). This is reflected in Fig. 2.2d, which also takes account of the extensive research suggesting that both the loop and the sketchpad can themselves be accessed from a range of lower-level encoding streams (Baddeley, Hitch, & Allen, 2011).

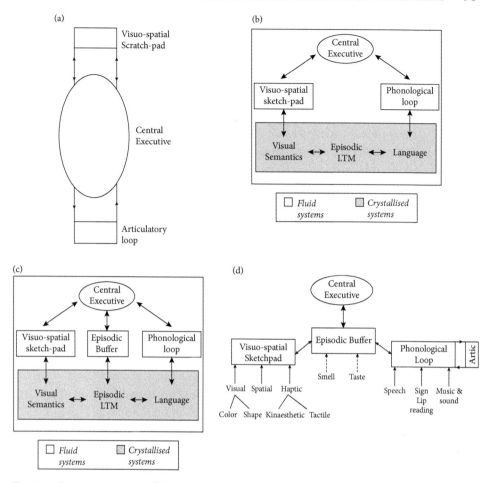

Fig. 2.2 Successive stages of the development of the multicomponent model are shown in panels (a) to (d) (for further details see text).

(a) Reproduced from Baddeley, A., *Working Memory* © 1986, Oxford University Press. (b) Reproduced from Alan Baddeley, 'The episodic buffer: a new component of working memory?', *Trends in Cognitive Sciences*, 4 (11), pp. 286–291, Box 1 Figure 1b, https://doi.org/10.1016/S1364-6613(00)01538-2 Copyright © 2000 Elsevier Science Ltd. All rights reserved. (c) Reproduced from Alan Baddeley, 'The episodic buffer: a new component of working memory?', *Trends in Cognitive Sciences*, 4 (11), pp. 286–291, Figure 1, https://doi.org/10.1016/S1364-6613(00)01538-2 Copyright © 2000 Elsevier Science Ltd. All rights reserved. (d) Reproduced from Alan D. Baddeley, Richard J. Allen, and Graham J. Hitch, 'Binding in visual working memory: The role of the episodic buffer', *Neuropsychologia*, 49 (6), p.1399, Figure 8. https://doi.org/10.1016/j.neuropsychologia.2010.12.042 Copyright © 2011 Elsevier Ltd. All rights reserved.

Figure 2.2d illustrates the current version of our multicomponent framework, comprising storage capacities for phonological and visuospatial information (the loop and the sketchpad respectively), a domain-general capacity capable of representing information drawn from different sources in the environment and LTM (the episodic buffer), and a set of central executive control resources. Each of these storage and resource components are limited in capacity, though there is variation in what determines these limits and the extent to which the components can be successfully employed in any given context.

We assume that information is fed in from a range of peripheral sources (e.g. vision, touch, hearing) and registered within the sketchpad and loop, leading to their temporary retention. Any of these sources can be maximized through selective attention, with information that is either prioritized in this way and/or encountered in the form of salient, abrupt-onset input being more likely to held at least briefly in a privileged, highly accessible state within the episodic buffer. As noted in Question 4, we would see this latter component as being broadly equivalent with the concept of a focus of attention as described by Cowan (1999; see chapter by Cowan et al., 2021). Information retained in this state is more likely to be successfully recalled and to influence ongoing processing, while other recently encountered information continues to be retained in the more specialized subsystems, though only temporarily and in an increasingly fragmented form.

The central executive then supports WM function in several ways. During encoding, it is likely to be important in guiding the direction of attention towards goal-relevant information, particularly during complex encoding events. Executive control is also likely to play a role in supporting the identification and implementation of strategic approaches that help optimize task goals. Post-encoding, these control resources are important in maintaining items within focused attention and supporting attentional refreshing in order to keep multiple items available within WM. There is also evidence to suggest a role in supporting consolidation (Wang, Theeuwes, & Olivers, 2019). Finally, active attentional processing will also play a strategic role in retrieving items into the focus of attention when required for recall.

This account would explain why at least some general cross-modality interference is typically observed when combining distinct tasks involving visual and auditory input. Firstly, these different forms of input are likely to compete for privileged storage within the focus of attention/episodic buffer, even when drawn from different modalities. Secondly, each task will draw on central executive control resources to some extent. However, it is also likely that visuospatial storage has a relatively greater dependence on these resources in the support of successful maintenance. The phonological loop is able to benefit from an atypical rehearsal mechanism that is privileged in drawing on speech output functions. The analogous form of rehearsal for visuospatial retention may draw on spatial and motor function, as in Logie's (1995) inner scribe mechanism, but this is not as effective and likely to be itself more dependent on executive control. Speculatively, this could help explain why relative dual-task cost asymmetries have been observed between verbal and visuospatial modalities (e.g. Morey & Miron, 2016; Morey, Morey, van der Reijden, & Holweg, 2013) why visual STM can be more closely associated with the focus of attention and central executive control (e.g. Gray et al., 2017), and also why visuospatial WM appears to show more precipitous decline with healthy ageing (e.g. Johnson, Brockmole, & Logie, 2010).

A current area of uncertainty is represented by the dotted lines in Fig. 2.2d reflecting a possible role of WM for taste and smell. We assume that these senses are accessible to conscious awareness via the episodic buffer, available for temporary storage, and presumably capable of temporary maintenance through attentional refreshing, although we are not familiar with any evidence in this field. We assume that such representations can also be combined within the episodic buffer, for example, to create the visual and olfactory representation of a banana. Other examples of the need for cross-modal binding occurs, for example, in sign language or Braille, both of which are likely to involve the combination verbal/phonological input from the loop and visuospatial input from the sketchpad. Our assumption of an episodic buffer available to conscious awareness resembles Cowan's emphasis on activated LTM. We accept that representations within LTM are likely to play an important role in most such episodic representations but do not regard the activation of LTM as providing an adequate representation of the processes underpinning conscious awareness.

By this stage, the model was becoming rather complex, and importantly did not include our assumptions about the links with LTM. These are reflected in Fig. 2.3 which is clearly not intended to reflect the relative importance of WM and LTM but simply to emphasize that we see WM as providing a link between cognition, broadly defined, and action.

Finally, it is important to bear in mind that all four systems can and should be fractionated into more explicit sub-processes. As outlined earlier, Fig. 2.1 represents our most recent attempt to capture the relatively complex pattern of results from our studies of the links between the perceptual and visuospatial components of WM (Hitch et al., 2020).

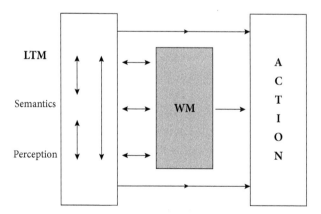

Fig. 2.3 Working memory (WM) as an interface between cognition and action. LTM, long-term memory.

Advantages and Drawbacks

We ourselves find that the attempt to represent our ideas visually provides a useful discipline, often pointing out areas of indecision. The fact that the core of the model has remained the same is also useful in explaining it to colleagues in other disciplines. A drawback is that it can lead the unwary to assume that our model is much more rigidly modular than is in fact the case, leading to a tendency to conclude that because individual modules cannot explain all the available data, that this reflects a failure of the model as a whole (e.g. Morey, 2018a; Nairne, 2002).

Additional Optional Questions from the Editors

Most of these have been covered already but we would like to focus on optional Question F.

Applications

Throughout its development, the multicomponent model has been strongly influenced by the philosophy of the Medical Research Council Applied Psychology Unit (Cambridge, UK) where both Baddeley and Hitch trained, of attempting to combine basic theory with its practical application. While this is not always practicable, it can provide both a means of testing the generality of the theory while presenting possible fruitful ways of extending the model. Keeping the basic model relatively simple and stable has had the advantage of encouraging others, either through collaboration or independently, to use it across a wide range of areas hence expanding relevant work on the model far beyond what would have been possible given our relatively limited resources. Applications have included the study of reading and vocabulary acquisition (Baddeley et al., 1998), dyslexia (Baddeley, Logie, & Ellis, 1988), aphasia (Baddeley & Wilson, 1985), language comprehension (Baddeley & Hitch, 1974), second-language learning (Baddeley et al., 1988), pronunciation (Mattys & Baddeley, 2019), puns (Baddeley & Lewis, 1981), counting (Logie & Baddeley, 1987), arithmetic (Hitch, 1978), following instructions (Yang, Gathercole, & Allen, 2014), complex problem-solving as, for example, in chess (Robbins et al., 1996), and neuropsychological disorders ranging from Down syndrome (Jarrold, Baddeley, & Hewes, 1999) to Alzheimer's disease (Baddeley, Bressi, Della Sala, Logie, & Spinnler, 1991). We regard our model's principal strength as providing a broad overarching and applicable theoretical framework, a framework that will of course require considerable further and more detailed elaboration. We see this as a strength, provided it continues to raise tractable questions that allow the model to gradually continue to grow in both breadth and depth. The multicomponent model does in short fulfil the Lakatos criterion of productivity and will we trust continue to do so while being enriched by the more detailed and analytic models generated by our colleagues.

Conclusion

The multicomponent model has much in common with the approach taken by many of our colleagues but differs in emphasis. We all agree with the concept of a limited capacity system based on some form of attentional control that plays an important role in a wide range of cognitive activities. We all agree on the importance of the attentional control component, which in our case we regard as a collaboration between the central executive and the episodic buffer. However, while many of the approaches begin with this important central issue, leaving the remainder of the system underspecified, we ourselves chose a bottom-up approach beginning by tackling the more tractable subsystems using the methods that were an extension of earlier work on STM. We acknowledged the importance of executive control but postponed its investigation on the grounds that it was likely to prove the most difficult part of the system to understand. We eventually went on to attempt to tackle this crucial issue, emerging with an attentional concept that we suggest is not unlike that of our colleagues who started using a top-down approach (see, e.g. the contributions to this discussion in the chapters by Barrouillet & Camos, 2021; Cowan et al., 2021; Mashburn, Tsukahara, & Engle, 2021). The result of our bottom-up approach, however, is that we have developed a more elaborated view of the systems feeding into executive control, the phonological loop and the visuospatial sketchpad, together with a series of well-tried methods of investigating their impact. These all form part of a relatively simple broadly based model that can readily be understood by colleagues investigating related areas. Furthermore, we regard such generalized application as an important way of testing the ecological validity of our model, and where appropriate, amending or enriching it.

References

Acheson, D., & MacDonald, M. (2009). Verbal working memory and language production: Common approaches to the serial ordering of verbal information. *Psychological Bulletin*, *135*, 50–68. doi:10.1037/a0014411

Allen, R. J., Baddeley, A. D., & Hitch, G. J. (2006). Is the binding of visual features in working memory resource-demanding? *Journal of Experimental Psychology: General*, *135*, 298–313.

Allen, R. J., Baddeley, A. D., & Hitch, G. J. (2014). Evidence for two attentional components in visual working memory. *Journal of Experimental Psychology. Learning, Memory, and Cognition*, *40*, 1499–1509. doi:0.1037/xlm0000002

Allen, R. J., Hitch, G. J., & Baddeley, A. D. (2018). Exploring the sentence advantage in working memory: Insights from serial recall and recognition. *Quarterly Journal of Experimental Psychology*, *71*, 2571–2585.

Allen, R., & Hulme, C. (2006). Speech and language processing mechanisms in verbal serial recall. *Journal of Memory & Language*, *55*, 64–88.

Allen, R. J., & Ueno, T. (2018). Multiple high-reward items can be prioritized in working memory but with greater vulnerability to interference. *Attention, Perception, & Psychophysics, 80*, 1731–1743.

Anderson, P. (2002). Assessment and development of executive function (EF) in childhood. *Child Neuropsychology, 8*, 71–82.

Andrade, J. (2001). A contribution of working memory to conscious experience. In J. Andrade (Ed.), *Working memory and perspective* (pp. 60–78). Hove, UK: Psychology Press.

Atkinson, A. L., Baddeley, A. D, & Allen, R. J. (2018). Remember some or remember all? Ageing and strategy effects in visual working memory. *Quarterly Journal of Experimental Psychology, 71*, 1561–1573.

Atkinson, A. L., Waterman, A. H., & Allen, R. J. (2019). Can children prioritize more valuable information in working memory? An exploration into the effects of motivation and memory load. *Developmental Psychology, 55*, 967–980.

Baddeley, A. D. (1966a). Short-term memory for word sequences as a function of acoustic, semantic and formal similarity. *Quarterly Journal of Experimental Psychology, 18*, 362–365.

Baddeley, A. D. (1966b). The influence of acoustic and semantic similarity on long-term memory for word sequences. *Quarterly Journal of Experimental Psychology, 18*, 302–309.

Baddeley, A. D. (1968). How does acoustic similarity influence short-term memory? *Quarterly Journal of Experimental Psychology, 20*, 249–264.

Baddeley, A. (1986). *Working memory*. Oxford, UK: Oxford University Press.

Baddeley, A. (2000). The episodic buffer: A new component of working memory? *Trends in Cognitive Sciences, 4*, 417–423.

Baddeley, A. (2002). Fractionating the central executive. In D. Stuss & R. T. Knight (Eds.), *Principles of frontal lobe function* (pp. 246–260). Oxford, UK: Oxford University Press.

Baddeley, A. (2012). Working memory: Theories, models, and controversies. *Annual Review of Psychology, 63*, 1–29.

Baddeley, A. D., Allen, R. J., & Hitch, G. J. (2011). Binding in visual working memory: The role of the episodic buffer. *Neuropsychologia, 49*, 1393–1400.

Baddeley, A. D., Bressi, S., Della Sala, S., Logie, R., & Spinnler, H. (1991). The decline of working memory in Alzheimer's Disease: A longitudinal study. *Brain, 114*, 2521–2542.

Baddeley, A. D., Chincotta, D., & Adlam, A. (2001). Working memory and the control of action: Evidence from task switching. *Journal of Experimental Psychology: General, 130*, 641–657.

Baddeley, A. D., Gathercole, S., & Papagno, C. (1998). The phonological loop as a language learning device. *Psychological Review, 105*, 158–173.

Baddeley, A. D., Grant, S., Wight, E., & Thomson, N. (1973). Imagery and visual working memory. In P. M. A. Rabbitt & S. Dornic (Eds.), *Attention and performance V* (pp. 205–217). London, UK: Academic Press.

Baddeley, A. D., & Hitch, G. J. (1974). Working memory. In G. A. Bower (Ed.), *Recent advances in learning and motivation* (Vol. 8, pp. 47–89). New York, NY: Academic Press.

Baddeley, A. D., Hitch, G. J., & Allen, R. J. (2009). Working memory and binding in sentence recall. *Journal of Memory and Language, 61*, 438–456.

Baddeley, A. D., Hitch, G. J., & Allen, R. J. (2019). From short-term store to multicomponent working memory: The role of the modal model. *Memory & Cognition, 47*, 575–588.

Baddeley, A. D., & Lewis, V. J. (1981). Inner active processes in reading: The inner voice, the inner ear and the inner eye. In A. M. Lesgold & C. A. Perfettie (Eds.), *Interactive processes in reading* (pp. 107–129). Hillsdale, NJ: Lawrence Erlbaum.

Baddeley, A. D., & Lieberman, K. (1980). Spatial working memory. In R. S. Nickerson (Ed.), *Attention and Performance VIII* (pp. 521–539). Hillsdale, NJ: Erlbaum.

Baddeley, A. D., Logie, R. H., & Ellis, N. C. (1988). Characteristics of developmental dyslexia. *Cognition, 29*, 197–228.

Baddeley, A. D., Papagno, C., & Vallar, G. (1988). When long-term learning depends on short-term storage. *Journal of Memory and Language, 27*, 586–595.

Baddeley, A. D., Thomson, N., & Buchanan, M. (1975). Word length and the structure of short-term memory. *Journal of Verbal Learning and Verbal Behavior, 14*, 575–589.

Baddeley, A. D., & Wilson, B. (1985). Phonological coding and short-term memory in patients without speech. *Journal of Memory and Language, 24,* 490–502.

Barrouillet, P., Bernardin, S., & Camos, V. (2004). Time constraints and resource sharing in adults' working memory spans. *Journal of Experimental Psychology: General, 133,* 83–100.

Barrouillet, P., & Camos, V. (2021). The time-based resource-sharing model of working memory. In R. H. Logie, V. Camos, & N. Cowan, (Eds.), *Working memory: State of the science* (pp. 85–115). Oxford, UK: Oxford University Press.

Barrouillet, P., Gavens, N., Vergauwe, E., Gaillard, V., & Camos, V. (2009). Working memory span development: A time-based resource-sharing model account. *Developmental Psychology, 45,* 477–490. doi:10.1037/a0014615

Berry, E. D. J., Waterman, A. H., Baddeley, A. D., Hitch, G. J., & Allen, R. J. (2018). The limits of visual working memory in children: Exploring prioritization and recency effects with sequential presentation. *Developmental Psychology, 54,* 240–253.

Botvinick, M., & Plaut, D. C. (2006). Short-term memory for serial order: A recurrent neural network model. *Psychological Review, 113,* 201–233.

Braithwaite, R. B. (1953). *Scientific explanation.* Cambridge, UK: Cambridge University Press.

Brener, R. (1940). An experimental investigation of memory span. *Journal of Experimental Psychology, 26,* 467–483.

Brown, G. D. A., Preece, T., & Hulme, C. (2000). Oscillator-based memory for serial order. *Psychological Review, 107,* 127–181.

Brown, G. D. A., Neath, I., & Chater, N. (2007). A temporal ratio model of memory. *Psychological Review, 114,* 539–576.

Burgess, N., & Hitch, G. J. (1992). Toward a network model of the articulatory loop. *Journal of Memory and Language, 31,* 429–460.

Burgess, N., & Hitch, G. J. (1996). A connectionist model of STM for serial order. In S. E. Gathercole (Ed.), *Models of short-term memory* (pp. 51–72). Hove, UK: Psychology Press.

Burgess, N., & Hitch, G. J. (1999). Memory for serial order: A network model of the phonological loop and its timing. *Psychological Review, 106,* 551–581.

Burgess, N., & Hitch, G. J. (2006). A revised model of short-term memory and long-term learning of verbal sequences. *Journal of Memory and Language, 55,* 627–652.

Camos, V., & Barrouillet, P. (2011). Developmental change in working memory strategies: From passive maintenance to active refreshing. *Developmental Psychology, 47,* 898–904. doi:10.1037/a0023193

Campoy, G., & Baddeley, A. D. (2008). Phonological and semantic strategies in immediate serial recall. *Memory, 16,* 329–340.

Campoy, G., Castella, J., Provencio, V., Hitch, G. J., & Baddeley, A. D. (2015). Automatic semantic encoding in verbal short-term memory: evidence from the concreteness effect. *Quarterly Journal of Experiment Psychology, 68,* 759–778. doi:10.1080/17470218.2014.966248

Caplan, D., & Waters, G. S. (1994). Articulatory length and phonological similarity in span tasks: A reply to Baddeley and Andrade. *Quarterly Journal of Experimental Psychology, 47A,* 1055–1062.

Chun, M. M., Golomb, J. D., & Turk-Browne, N. B. (2011). A taxonomy of external and internal attention. *Annual Review of Psychology, 62,* 73–101. doi:10.1146/annurev.psych.093008.100427

Conrad, R. (1962). An association between memory errors and errors due to acoustic masking of speech. *Nature, 193,* 1314–1315.

Cowan, N. (1999). An embedded process model of working memory. In Miyake, A., & Shah, P. (Eds.), *Models of working memory* (pp. 62–101). Cambridge, UK: Cambridge University Press.

Cowan, N. (2011). The focus of attention as observed in visual working memory tasks: Making sense of competing claims. *Neuropsychologia, 49,* 1401–1406.

Cowan, N. Morey, C., & Naveh-Benjamin, M. (2021). An embedded-processes approach to working memory: How is it distinct from other approaches, and to what ends? In R. H. Logie, V. Camos, & N. Cowan, (Eds.), *Working memory: State of the science* (pp. 44–84). Oxford, UK: Oxford University Press.

Crick, F. (1990). *What mad pursuit: A personal view of scientific discovery.* London, UK: Penguin Books.

Darling, S., Allen, R. J., & Havelka, J. (2017). Visuospatial bootstrapping: When visuospatial and verbal memory work together. *Current Directions in Psychological Science, 26*, 3–9. doi:10.1177/0963721416665342

D'Esposito, M., & Postle, B. (2015). The cognitive neuroscience of working memory. *Annual Review of Psychology, 66*, 115–142. doi:10.1146/annurev-psych-010814-015031

Dunning, D. L., & Holmes, J. (2014). Does working memory training promote the use of strategies on untrained working memory tasks? *Memory & Cognition, 42*, 854–862.

Eriksson, J., Vogel, E. K., Lansner, A., Bergström, F., & Nyberg, L. (2015). Neurocognitive architecture of working memory. *Neuron, 88*, 33–46. doi:10.1016/j.neuron.2015.09.020

Farah, M. J. (1990). *Visual agnosia.* Cambridge, MA: MIT Press.

Farrell, S., & Lewandowsky, S. (2004). Modelling transposition latencies: Constraints for theories of serial order memory. *Journal of Memory and Language, 51*, 115–135.

Fodor, J. A. (1983). *The modularity of mind.* Cambridge, MA: MIT Press.

Gathercole, S., Dunning, D., Holmes, J., & Norris, D. (2019). Working memory training involves learning new skills. *Journal of Memory & Language, 105*, 19–42. doi:10.1016/j.jml.2018.10.003

Gathercole, S. E., & Hitch, G. J. (1993). Developmental changes in short-term memory: A revised working memory perspective. In A. Collins, S. E. Gathercole, M. A. Conway, & P. E. Morris (Eds.), *Theories of memory* (pp. 189–209). Hove, UK: Lawrence Erlbaum Associates Limited.

Gathercole, S. E., Pickering, S. J., Ambridge, B., & Wearing, H. (2004). The structure of working memory from 4 to 15 years of age. *Developmental Psychology, 40*, 177–190.

Gilson, E. Q., & Baddeley, A. D. (1969). Tactile short-term memory. *Quarterly Journal of Experimental Psychology, 21*, 180–184.

Gray, S., Green, S., Alt, M., Hogan, T., Kuo, T., Brinkley, S., & Cowan, N. (2017). The structure of working memory in young children and its relation to intelligence. *Journal of Memory and Language, 92*, 183–201. doi:10.1016/j.jml.2016.06.004

Guitard, D., Gabel, A. J., Saint-Aubin, J., Surprenant, A. M., & Neath, I. (2018). Word length, set size, and lexical factors: Re-examining what causes the word length effect. *Journal of Experimental Psychology: Learning, Memory, and Cognition, 44*, 1824–1844. doi:10.1037/xlm0000551

Gupta, P., & MacWhinney, B. (1997). Vocabulary acquisition and verbal short-term memory: Computational and neural bases. *Brain and Language, 59*, 267–333.

Hanley, J. R., Pearson, N. A., & Young, A. W. (1990). Impaired memory for new visual forms. *Brain, 113*, 1131–1148.

Hanley, J. R., & Young, A. W. (2019). ELD revisited: A second look at a neuropsychological impairment of working memory affecting retention of visuo-spatial material. *Cortex, 112*, 172–179.

Hanley, J. R., Young, A. W., & Pearson, N. A. (1991). Impairment of the visuo-spatial sketch pad. *Quarterly Journal of Experimental Psychology Section A, 43*, 101–125. doi:10.1080/14640749108401001

Hartley, T., Hurlstone, M. J., & Hitch, G. J. (2016). Effects of rhythm on memory for spoken sequences: a model and tests of its stimulus-driven mechanism. *Cognitive Psychology, 87*, 135–178. doi:10.1016/j.cogpsych.2016.05.001

Hebb, D. O. (1961). Distinctive features of learning in the higher animal. In J. F. Delafresnaye (Ed.), *Brain mechanisms and learning* (pp. 37–46). Oxford, UK: Blackwell.

Henry, L. A., Messer, D., Luger-Klein, S., & Crane, L. (2012). Phonological, visual and semantic coding strategies and children's short-term picture memory span. *Quarterly Journal of Experimental Psychology, 65*, 2033–2053. doi:10.1080/17470208.2012.672977

Henson, R. N. A. (1998). Short-term memory for serial order. The Start-End Model. *Cognitive Psychology, 36*, 73–137.

Henson, R. N. A., Norris, D. G., Page, M. P. A., & Baddeley, A. D. (1996). Unchained memory: Error patterns rule out chaining models of immediate serial recall. *Quarterly Journal of Experimental Psychology, 49A*, 80–115.

Hitch, G. J. (1978). The role of short-term working memory in mental arithmetic. *Cognitive Psychology, 10*, 302–323.

Hitch, G. J. (1990). Developmental fractionation of working memory. In G. Vallar & T. Shallice (Eds.), *Neuropsychological impairments of short-term memory* (pp. 221–246). Cambridge, UK: Cambridge University Press.

Hitch, G. J., Allen, R. J., & Baddeley, A. D. (2020). Attention and binding in visual working memory: Two forms of attention and two kinds of storage. *Attention, Perception, & Psychophysics, 82*, 280–293.

Hitch, G. J., & Baddeley, A. D. (1976). Verbal reasoning and working memory. *Quarterly Journal of Experimental Psychology, 28*, 603–621.

Hitch, G. J., Flude, B., & Burgess, N. (2009). Slave to the rhythm: experimental tests of a model for verbal short-term memory and long term sequence learning. *Journal of Memory and Language, 61*, 97–111.

Hitch, G. J., & Halliday, M. S. (1983). Working memory in children *Philosophical Transactions of the Royal Society London, Series B, 302*, 325–340.

Hitch, G. J., Halliday, M. S., Dodd, A., & Littler, J. E. (1989). Development of rehearsal in short-term memory: Differences between pictorial and spoken stimuli. *British Journal of Developmental Psychology, 7*, 347–362.

Hitch, G. J., Halliday, M. S., Schaafstal, A. M., & Schraagen, J. M. C. (1988). Visual working memory in young children. *Memory & Cognition, 16*, 120–132.

Hitch, G. J., Hu, Y., Allen, R. J., & Baddeley, A. D. (2018). Competition for the focus of attention in visual working memory: perceptual recency versus executive control. *Annals of the New York Academy of Sciences, 1424*, 64–75.

Hitch, G. J., Woodin, M., & Baker, S. L. (1989). Visual and phonological components of working memory in children. *Memory & Cognition, 17*, 175–185.

Hu, Y., Hitch, G. J., Baddeley, A. D., Zhang, M., & Allen, R. J. (2014). Executive and perceptual attention play different roles in visual working memory: Evidence from suffix and strategy effects. *Journal of Experimental Psychology: Human Perception and Performance, 40*, 1665–1678.

Hu, Y., Allen, R. J., Baddeley, A. D., & Hitch, G. J. (2016). Executive control of stimulus-driven and goal-directed attention in visual working memory. *Attention, Perception & Psychophysics, 78*, 2164–2175. doi:10.3758/s13414-016-1106-7

Hulme, C., Maughan, S., & Brown, G. G. A. (1991). Memory for familiar and unfamiliar words: Evidence for a long-term memory contribution to short term memory span. *Journal of Memory and Language, 30*, 685–701.

Hulme, C., Thomson, N., Muir, C., & Lawrence, W. A. (1984). Speech rate and the development of short-term memory span. *Journal of Experimental Child Psychology, 38*, 241–253.

Hurlstone, M. J., & Hitch, G. J. (2015). How is the serial order of a spatial sequence represented? Insights from transposition latencies. *Journal of Experimental Psychology: Learning, Memory and Cognition, 42*, 295–324.

Hurlstone, M. J., & Hitch, G. J. (2018). How is the serial order of a visual sequence represented? Insights from transposition latencies. *Journal of Experimental Psychology: Learning, Memory and Cognition, 44*, 167–192.

Hurlstone, M. J., Hitch, G. J., & Baddeley, A. D. (2014). Memory for serial order across domains: An overview of the literature and directions for future research. *Psychological Bulletin, 14*, 339–373. doi:10.1037/a0034221

Jarrold, C. (2001). Applying the working memory model to the study of atypical development. In J. Andrade (Ed.), *Working memory and perspective* (pp. 126–150). Hove, UK: Psychology Press.

Jarrold, C., Baddeley, A. D., & Hewes, A. K. (1999). Dissociating working memory: Evidence from Down's and Williams syndrome. *Neuropsychologia, 37*, 637–651.

Johnson, W., Logie, R. H., & Brockmole, J. R. (2010). Working memory tasks differ in factor structure across age cohorts: Implications for dedifferentiation. *Intelligence, 38*, 513–528. doi.org/10.1016/j.intell.2010.06.005

Jonides, J., Schumacher, E. H., Smith, E. E., Koeppe, R. A., Awh, E., Reuter-Lorenz, P. A., … Willis, C. R. (1998). The role of parietal cortex in verbal working memory. *The Journal of Neuroscience, 18*, 5026–5034.

Jonides, J., Smith, E. E., Koeppe, R. A., Awh, E., Minoshima, S., & Mintun, M. (1993). Spatial working memory in humans as revealed by PET. *Nature, 363*, 623–625.

Just, M. A., & Carpenter, P. A. (1992). The capacity theory of comprehension: Individual differences in working memory. *Psychological Review, 99*, 122–149.

Kalm, K., & Norris, D. (2014). The representation of order information in auditory-verbal short-term memory. *Journal of Neuroscience, 34*, 6879–6886. doi:10.1523/JNEUROSCI.4104-13.2014

Kane, M. J., Conway, A. R. A., Miura, T. K., & Colflesh, G. J. (2007). Working memory, attention control and the N-back task: A question of construct validity. *Journal of Experimental Psychology: Learning, Memory and Cognition, 33*, 615–622.

Klauer, K. C., & Zhao, Z. (2004). Double dissociations in visual and spatial short-term memory. *Journal of Experimental Psychology: General, 133*, 355–381.

Lakatos, I. (1970). Falsification and the methodology of scientific research programmes In I. Lakatos & A. Musgrave (Eds.), *Criticism and the growth of knowledge* (pp. 91–195). Cambridge, UK: Cambridge University Press.

Lashley, K. S. (1951). The problem of serial order in behavior. In L. A. Jeffress (Ed.), *Cerebral mechanisms in behavior: The Hixon symposium* (pp. 112–146). New York, NY: John Wiley.

Lewandowsky, S., & Farrell, S. (2008). Short-term memory: New data and a model. *The Psychology of Learning and Motivation, 49*, 1–48.

Lewandowsky, S., & Murdock Jr., B. B. (1989). Memory for serial order. *Psychological Review, 96*, 25–57. doi:10.1037/0033-295X.96.1.25

Linck, J. A., Osthus, P., Koeth, J. T., & Bunting, M. F. (2014). Working memory and second language comprehension and production: A meta-analysis. *Psychonomic Bulletin & Review, 21*, 861–883. doi:10.3758/s13423-013-0565-2

Logie, R. H. (1995). *Visuo-spatial working memory*. Hove, UK: Erlbaum.

Logie, R. H. (2016). Retiring the central executive. *The Quarterly Journal of Experimental Psychology, 69*, 2093–2109.

Logie, R. H. (2019). Converging sources of evidence and theory integration in working memory: A commentary on Morey, Rhodes, and Cowan (2019). *Cortex, 112*, 162–171. doi:10.1016/j.cortex.2019.01.030

Logie, R. H., & Baddeley, A. D. (1987). Cognitive processes in counting. *Journal of Experimental Psychology: Learning, Memory, and Cognition, 13*, 310–326.

Logie, R. H., Belletier, C., & Doherty, J. D. (2021). Integrating theories of working memory. In R. H. Logie, V. Camos, & N. Cowan, (Eds.), *Working memory: State of the science* (pp. 389–429). Oxford, UK: Oxford University Press.

Logie, R. H., Della Sala, S., Laiacona, M., Chalmers, P., & Wynn, V. (1996). Group aggregates and individual reliability: The case of verbal short-term memory. *Memory & Cognition, 24*, 305–321.

Logie, R. H., Pernet, C. R., Buonocore, A., & Della Sala, S. (2011). Low and high imagers activate networks differentially in mental rotation *Neuropsychologia, 49*, 3071–3077.

Lovatt, P., Avons, S. E., & Masterson, J. (2000). The word length effect and disyllabic words. *Quarterly Journal of Experimental Psychology, 53A*, 1–22.

Mashburn, C., Tsukahara, J., & Engle, R. W. (2021). Individual differences in attention control: Implications for the relationship between working memory capacity and fluid intelligence. In R. H. Logie, V. Camos, & N. Cowan, (Eds.), *Working memory: State of the science* (pp. 175–211). Oxford, UK: Oxford University Press.

Mattys, S., & Baddeley, A. D. (2019). Working memory and second-language accent acquisition. *Applied Cognitive Psychology, 33*, 1113–1123. doi.org/10.1002/acp.3554

Melby-Lervåg, M., & Hulme, C. (2013). Is working memory training effective? A meta-analytic review. *Developmental Psychology, 49*, 270–291.

Miller, G. A. (1956). The magical number seven, plus or minus two: Some limits on our capacity for processing information. *Psychological Review, 63*, 81–97.

Miyake, A., Friedman, N. P., Emerson, M. J., Witzki, A. H., Howerter, A., Miyake, A., Friedman, N. P., . . . Wager, T. D. (2000). The unity and diversity of executive functions and their contribution to complex "frontal lobe" tasks: A latent variable analysis. *Cognitive Psychology, 41*, 49–100.

Morey, C. (2018a). The case against specialized visual-spatial short-term memory. *Psychological Bulletin, 144,* 849–883.

Morey, C. (2018b). Correction to Morey. *Psychological Bulletin, 144,* 1246.

Morey, C., & Miron, M. D. (2016). Spatial sequences, but not verbal sequences, are vulnerable to general interference during retention in working memory. *Journal of Experimental Psychology: Learning, Memory, and Cognition, 42,* 1907–1918. doi:10.1037/xlm0000280

Morey, C., Morey, R., van der Reijden, M., & Holweg, M. (2013). Asymmetric cross-domain interference between two working memory tasks: Implications for models of working memory. *Journal of Memory and Language, 69,* 324–348. doi:10.1016/j.jml.2013.04.004

Morey, C., Rhodes, S., & Cowan, N. (2019). Sensory-motor integration and brain lesions: Progress toward explaining domain-specific phenomena within domain-general working memory. *Cortex, 112,* 149–161.

Morrison, A. B., Rosenbaum, G. M., Fair, D., & Chen, J. M. (2016). Variation in strategy use across measures of verbal working memory. *Memory & Cognition, 44,* 922–936.

Mueller, S. T., Seymour, T. L., Kieras, D. E., & Meyer, D. E. (2003). Theoretical implications of articulatory duration, phonological similarity, and phonological complexity in verbal working memory. *Journal of Experimental Psychology: Learning, Memory, and Cognition, 29,* 1353–1380.

Murray, D. J. (1968). Articulation and acoustic confusability in short-term memory. *Journal of Experimental Psychology, 78,* 679–684.

Nairne, J. S. (2002). Remembering over the short-term: The case against the standard model. *Annual Review of Psychology, 53,* 53–81.

Nicolson, R. (1981). The relationship between memory span and processing speed. In M. Friedman, J. P. Das, & N. O'Connor (Eds.), *Intelligence and learning* (pp. 179–184). New York, NY: Plenum Press.

Oberauer, K. (2021). Towards a theory of working memory: From metaphors to mechanisms. In R. H. Logie, V. Camos, & N. Cowan, (Eds.), *Working memory: State of the science* (pp. 116–149). Oxford, UK: Oxford University Press.

Oberauer, K., & Hein, L. (2012). Attention to information in working memory. *Current Directions in Psychological Science, 21,* 164–169.

Oberauer, K., Lewandowsky, S., Awh, E., Brown, G. D. A., Conway, A., Cowan, N., & Ward, G. (2018). Benchmarks for models of short term and working memory. *Psychological Bulletin, 144,* 885–958.

Oberauer, K., Lewandowsky, S., Farrell, S., Jarrold, C., & Greaves, M. (2012). Modeling working memory: An interference model of complex span. *Psychonomic Bulletin & Review, 19,* 779–819.

Owen, A. M., McMillan, K. M., Laird, A. R., & Bullmore, E. (2005). N-Back working memory paradigm: A meta-analysis of normative functional neuroimaging studies. *Human Brain Mapping, 25,* 46–59.

Page, M. P. A., & Norris, D. (1998). The primacy model: A new model of immediate serial recall. *Psychological Review, 105,* 761–781.

Page, M. P. A., & Norris, D. (2009). A model linking immediate serial recall, the Hebb repetition effect and the learning of phonological word forms. *Philosophical Transactions of The Royal Society B, 364,* 3737–3753.

Palmer, S. (2000). Working memory: A developmental study of phonological encoding. *Memory, 8,* 179–193.

Papagno, C., Valentine, T., & Baddeley, A. D. (1991). Phonological short-term memory and foreign language vocabulary learning. *Journal of Memory and Language, 30,* 331–347.

Papagno, C., & Vallar, G. (1992). Phonological short-term memory and the learning of novel words: The effect of phonological similarity and item length. *Quarterly Journal of Experimental Psychology, 44A,* 47–67.

Paulesu, E., Frith, C. D., & Frackowiak, R. S. J. (1993). The neural correlates of the verbal component of working memory. *Nature, 362,* 342–345.

Phillips, W. A. (1974). On the distinction between sensory storage and visual short-term memory. *Perception and Psychophysics, 16,* 283–290.

Phillips, W. A., & Baddeley, A. D. (1971). Reaction time and short-term visual memory. *Psychonomic Science, 22,* 73–74.

Popper, K. (1959). *The logic of scientific discovery.* London, UK: Hutchison.

Robbins, T., Anderson, E. J., Barker, D. R., Bradley, A. C., Fearnyhough, C., Henson, R. N. A., ... Baddeley, A. D. (1996). Working memory in chess. *Memory & Cognition, 24,* 83–93. doi:10.3758/bf03197274

Roodenrys, S., Hulme, C., Alban, J., Ellis, A. W., & Brown, G. D. A. (1994). Effects of word-frequency and age of acquisition on short-term-memory span. *Journal of Experimental Psychology: Learning, Memory, and Cognition, 22,* 695–701.

Roodenrys, S., Hulme, C., Lethbridge, A., Hinton, M., & Nimmo, L. M. (2002). Word-frequency and phonological-neighborhood effects on verbal short-term memory, *Journal of Experimental Psychology: Learning, Memory, and Cognition, 28,* 1019–1034. doi:10.1037//0278-7393.28.6.1019

Ryan, J. (1969a). Grouping and short-term memory: Different means and pattern of grouping. *Quarterly Journal of Experimental Psychology, 21,* 137–147.

Ryan, J. (1969b). Temporal grouping, rehearsal and short-term memory. *Quarterly Journal of Experimental Psychology, 21,* 148–155.

Salamé, P., & Baddeley, A. D. (1986). Phonological factors in STM: Similarity and the unattended speech effect. *Bulletin of the Psychonomic Society, 24,* 263–265.

Sanbonmatsu, D. M., & Johnston, W. A. (2019). Redefining science: the impact of complexity on theory development in social and behavioral research. *Perspectives on Psychological Science, 14,* 672–690.

Savin, H. B., & Perchonok, E. (1965). Grammatical structure and the immediate recall of English sentences. *Journal of Verbal Learning and Verbal Behavior, 4,* 348–353.

Shallice, T., & Papagno, C. (2019). Impairments of auditory-verbal short-term memory: Do selective deficits of the input phonological buffer exist? *Cortex, 112,* 107–121. doi:10.1016/j.cortex.2018.10.004

Shallice, T., & Warrington, E. K. (1970). Independent functioning of verbal memory stores: A neuropsychological study. *Quarterly Journal of Experimental Psychology, 22,* 261–273.

Smith, E. E., & Jonides, J. (1997). Working memory: A view from neuroimaging. *Cognitive Psychology, 33,* 5–42.

Surprenant, A. M., Kelley, M. R., Farley, L. A., & Neath, I. (2005). Fill-in and infill errors in order memory. *Memory, 13,* 267–273. doi:10.1080/09658210344000396

Towse, J. N., Hitch, G. J., & Hutton, U. (1998). A reevaluation of working memory capacity in children. *Journal of Memory & Language, 39,* 195–217.

Turley-Ames, K., & Whitfield, M. (2003). Strategy training and working memory task performance. *Journal of Memory & Language, 49,* 446–468. doi:10.1016/S0749-596X(03)00095-0

Ueno, T., Allen, R. J., Baddeley, A. D., Hitch, G. J., & Saito, S. (2011). Disruption of visual feature binding in working memory. *Memory & Cognition, 39,* 12–23.

Vallar, G., & Baddeley, A. D. (1984). Fractionation of working memory. Neuropsychological evidence for a phonological short-term store. *Journal of Verbal Learning and Verbal Behaviour, 23,* 151–161.

Vallar, G., & Baddeley, A. D. (1987). Phonological short-term store and sentence processing. *Cognitive Neuropsychology, 4,* 417–438.

Vallar, G., Corno, M., & Basso, A. (1992). Auditory and visual verbal short-term memory in aphasia. *Cortex, 28,* 383–389.

Vallar, G., & Papagno, C. (2002). Neuropsychological impairments of verbal short-term memory. In A. D. Baddeley, M. D. Kopelman, & B. A. Wilson (Eds.), *Handbook of memory disorders* (2nd ed., pp. 249–270). Chichester, UK: Wiley.

Vallar, G., Papagno, C., & Baddeley, A. D. (1991). Long-term recency effects and phonological short-term memory: A neuropsychological case study. *Cortex, 27,* 323–326.

Vallar, G., & Shallice, T. (Eds.), (1990). *Neuropsychological impairments of short-term memory.* Cambridge, UK: Cambridge University Press.

Wang, B., Theeuwes, J., & Olivers, C. N. L. (2019). Momentary, offset-triggered dual-task interference in visual working memory. *Journal of Cognition, 2,* 38. doi.org/10.5334/joc.84

Warrington, E. K., & Baddeley, A. D. (1974). Amnesia and memory for visual location. *Neuropsychologia, 12,* 257–263.

Yang, T., Gathercole, S. E., & Allen, R. J. (2014). Benefit of enactment over oral repetition of verbal instruction does not require additional working memory during encoding. *Psychonomic Bulletin & Review, 21*, 186–192.

Zeman, A. Z., Della Sala, S., Torrens, L. A., Gountouna, V.-E., McGonigle, D. J., & Logie, R. H. (2010). Loss of imagery phenomenology with intact visuo-spatial task performance: A case of 'blind imagination'. *Neuropsychologia, 48*, 145–155. doi:10.1016/j.neuropsychologia.2009.08.024

3

An Embedded-Processes Approach to Working Memory

How Is It Distinct From Other Approaches, and to What Ends?

Nelson Cowan, Candice C. Morey, and Moshe Naveh-Benjamin

The *embedded-processes model* (Cowan, 1988, 1995, 1999, 2001, 2005/2016, 2019) is a simple, graphic, and conceptual model of how information is processed in the human mind. It is not designed to answer every question at this point, but rather to assemble what we know into a structure that is hopefully compatible with subsequent research findings and with brain research. Questions asked of all the chapter authors in this volume are summarized in Table 3.1 and addressed further in the following sections.

The model points to similarities between different modalities (visual, audition, touch, etc.) and codes (verbal, spatial, etc.) in how they are retained and processed. The components of the model can be summarized simply. (1) The first component is a brief sensory store that persists for a few hundred milliseconds after presentation of a stimulus as it is registered in the brain, and is experienced as continuing sensation even if the actual stimulus has abruptly ceased. (2) The brief sensory store activates elements of the long-term memory system. (3) A small part of the activated information at any one time can be in the focus of attention, where at most several meaningful items or ideas can be kept. (4) Features from both incoming and recently attended items can remain active for a while in long-term memory; elements of meaning are activated in memory primarily, or even solely, after items have been attended. Poorly consolidated items become inactive within seconds, whereas well-consolidated items can remain activated longer. (5) A neural model of the environment is formed from the activated elements of long-term memory. Any detected change in the neural model attracts attention, causing an orienting response (e.g. an abrupt change in lighting; a sudden sound; an interesting new topic in a podcast to which one is listening). (6) Other parts of the mind together termed central executive processes allow deliberate control of attention to achieve various goals, but there is sometimes a struggle between the deliberate processes and uncontrollable orienting responses. (7) In neural representation, the frontal lobes are primarily representative of central executive processes, areas in the parietal lobe are primarily representative of the focus of attention, and diverse posterior cortical regions represent long-term memory representations that can become temporarily active. (8) There may well be subdivisions of long-term memory, but the organization is not considered as simple as in some models (e.g. verbal and spatial

Nelson Cowan, Candice C. Morey, and Moshe Naveh-Benjamin, *An Embedded-Processes Approach to Working Memory* In: *Working Memory*. Edited by: Robert H. Logie, Valérie Camos, and Nelson Cowan, Oxford University Press (2021). © Oxford University Press. DOI: 10.1093/oso/9780198842286.003.0003

Table 3.1 Summary responses to designated questions

Question	Embedded-processes response
1. Definition of working memory	The ensemble of components of the mind that hold a limited amount of information temporarily in a heightened state of availability for use in ongoing information processing.
2. Methods of embedded-processes approach	All methods are relevant, e.g. accuracy, reaction time, error distributions, computational modelling, electrophysiology, neuropsychology, and functional magnetic resonance imaging, cautiously influenced by phenomenology as well.
3. Unitary versus non-unitary nature of working memory	Items in working memory interfere with one another based on overlap of many kinds of features, so no simple modular separation of stores; but focus of attention acts differently than just items in activated long-term memory.
4. The role of attention and control	Critical role of attention and control in shuttling items into and out of the focus of attention, allowing binding and conceptual formation to take place.
5. Storage, maintenance, and loss of information	Storage in activated long-term memory including rapidly formed new memories during trial. Maintenance by attention-based refreshing and verbal rehearsal. Decay of poorly encoded information.
6. The role of long-term memory knowledge in working memory storage, processing	Critical to allow a small-capacity focus of attention to deal with a large amount of complex information through chunking and concept formation.
7. Inconsistencies with the framework	The framework has continued to evolve, e.g. in the use of attention versus off-loading for storage and in severe limits on semantic processing of unattended information.
A. Early life development	Evidence for the development of ability to store information efficiently and work with it efficiently for maintenance.
B. Adult ageing	Older adults may become inefficient once more, like children; control of attention issues.
C. Individual differences	Processing method depends on adaptive choices in strategies; but adaptive choices may be influenced by individual differences in attention capabilities.
D. Neuropsychology	Good evidence for frontal-parietal attention system and posterior representations; regarding dissociations, many questions remain.
E. Working-memory applications of the embedded-processes view	Applications have to do with learning to allocate attention effectively and to process stimuli with patterns that will reduce the memory load.

stores). It is considered more likely to be feature based and complex (e.g. with separate representations of colours, orientations, pitches, shapes, phonemes, spatial layouts, touch sensations, smells, abstract ideas, etc., and various combinations of them) and, given unknowns, a detailed taxonomy is not explicitly shown in the model. Here is its history.

In 1988, Cowan published a *Psychological Bulletin* article that reviewed premises of common information processing models, not with an emphasis on working memory per se but with an emphasis on trying to arrive at a structure depicting human information processing that was consistent with available evidence and parsimonious, albeit not complete; one that could be filled in later with further details as the field advanced.

Although the model dealt with the relation between memory and attention generally, it was the concept of working memory that was most noted by subsequent mentions of that theoretical view. Within the model, working memory was defined as the collection of mechanisms capable of keeping a limited amount of information in a temporarily very accessible state. It was noted that two types of mechanism contribute to working memory: (1) the presently activated set of elements in long-term memory, which we mean to include not only previously learned information but also any information rapidly learned during the trial and still active, such as a new word or the order of items in a just-presented list; and (2) the contents of the focus of attention, limited to a few items or units about which the person is currently 'thinking'. These uses have precedence in different traditions within psychology: activated memory, in Hebb's (1949) cell assemblies; the focus of attention, in James' (1890) primary memory; both concepts, in prior work by Wundt summarized by Cowan and Rachev (2018). The terms working memory, short-term memory, primary memory, and immediate memory have been used with only subtly different meanings by different investigators (see Cowan, 2017a), but discussing differences between the terms is beyond the scope of this chapter.

The aim of this chapter is to explain why the embedded-processes model was formulated as it was, how this approach differs from other approaches, what purposes it can serve, and what unknowns it leaves for future work. The first part of the chapter adheres to our own organization, which is intended to provide insight into the fundamental properties of previous models of information processing and then to explain the most consequential aspects of the embedded-processes model in light of these earlier approaches. Most of the remaining part of the chapter is a question-and-answer session based on common questions that all the chapter authors were asked to consider (also summarized in Table 3.1). We answer both the compulsory questions and all the optional questions, to try to portray the embedded-processes model in as many ramifications as we can. Within these sections, we address controversies that have arisen in relation to specific questions. Last, we sum up the reasons why we think that the embedded-processes modelling framework has an exciting future.

Differences in the Structural Assumptions for Different Models

Our first point is that different basic cognitive models come with different ground rules for how the model can be structured (Fig. 3.1). Some such structural assumptions can be too confining to represent the breadth of evidence that one may want to consider.

Earlier Models

Stage models, which have the simplest ground rules, include Sternberg's (1969) model of memory search. They progress through a series of temporally defined phases: encoding, central processing (e.g. memory scanning), and decision and response.

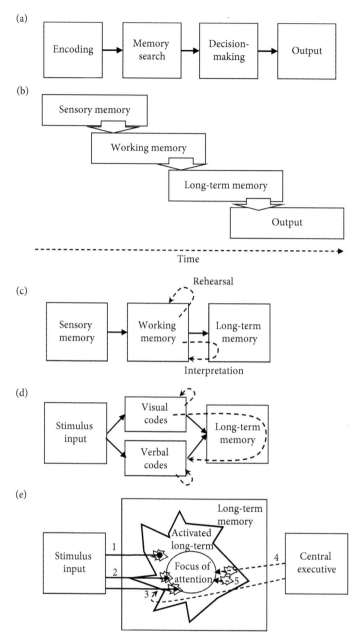

Fig. 3.1 Examples of different types of graphic model of processing. (a) Stage model. (b) Cascade model. (c) Model with recursion in time (dashes). (d) Parallel-processing model with concurrent visual and verbal maintenance. (e) Cowan's (1988) embedded-processes model. Within (e), (1) habituated stimulus, (2) physically changed stimulus recruiting attention and orienting, (3) deliberately attended stimulus, (4) information deliberately retrieved from long-term memory, and (5) automatic association that attracts attention.

Cascade models include transfer from one store to another while processing in the first store is still ongoing (e.g. McClelland, 1979). In short-term memory, Murdock (1967) advanced one example, with the notion that research at the time led to a 'modal model' with three phases. A temporary sensory memory was limited by decay. It fed into a primary memory limited by displacement, and therefore small in capacity. In turn, this fed into a secondary memory (today's long-term memory), limited by interference and therefore subject to the conditions of storage and retrieval. This model is cascade in that, for example, a primary memory representation of a stimulus can be constructed before sensory memory has decayed.

In *recursive models*, the notion of processes being reached earlier versus later in processing is not preserved. Instead, some models allowed information to feed back from a later step to an earlier step; an example is the Atkinson and Shiffrin (1968) model, in which we find the statement (p. 115) that, 'In general, information entering STS [short-term storage] comes directly from LTS [long-term storage] and only indirectly from the sensory register'. The notion is that the sensory information about, say, a dog, can be entered into a limited-capacity short-term storage only after it has been identified and categorized with the help of information from long-term memory. This kind of model no longer has parts strictly representing periods of time or serial phases between the stimulus and response; its parts are modules, each carrying out a specialized kind of operation as in a computer program. Information can be shuttled from one module to another as needed, using control processes (represented in Fig. 3.1c by dashed lines).

In *parallel-processing models* (e.g. McClelland & Rumelhart, 1985), multiple processes can be carried out at once. This term could apply to Baddeley and Hitch (1974), who found that there was more specialization in short-term storage than other modellers had supposed, with different domains of mental codes and more interference within a domain as opposed to between domains. Baddeley (1986) consequently designated the term working memory to reflect a more specialized multicomponent system. If, for example, one sees a neon sign, a visuospatial module could help in the assessment of its colours and shapes while, concurrently, a phonological module could help in the assessment of what words it forms. These separate streams could be brought together subsequently for a unified judgement of the object's implications.

The Embedded-Processes Model

The embedded-processes model (Fig. 3.1e), described by Cowan (1988) but named by Cowan (1999), addressed what appeared to be some infelicities in the order in which information was accessed, or apparent paradoxes. The modal model described by Murdock (1967), and varieties of it (notably Atkinson & Shiffrin, 1968; Broadbent, 1958), showed information flowing from sensory memory to short-term (or working) memory to long-term memory. Yet, as noted earlier, it was clear that the contents of working memory include not only sensory information, but also knowledge about the identifications and meanings of the information seen and heard, supplied by long-term memory. It seems reasonable to assume that information cannot be entered into working memory until it makes contact with long-term memory, yet also that the new information often must be held in working memory before it can form new long-term memory traces (inasmuch as working memory is needed to hold the information while the person carries out the most complete assessment of its meaning, value, etc.). To resolve the apparent paradox about the order in which stores are accessed within the modal model, one could represent this situation with two-way arrows between working memory and long-term memory. A more explicit and perhaps organic way to represent the situation, however, is with embedded processes, so that instead of different modules with multiple transactions between them in both directions, the representation more simply shows modules within modules. It is easy to grasp that, after incoming sensory information activates elements of long-term memory (cf. Logie, 1995), some of these elements give rise to a more integrated representation in the focus of attention, which does not deal with all the activated elements, but only a subset of them.

The embedded-processes representation was also useful to reconceptualize the deployment of attention, where again there were apparent paradoxes. Broadbent (1958) conceived of attention as a filter going between the many streams of information entering the brain from the senses, versus the very limited sub-portion of these streams that passed through the attention filter to gain entry into working memory. That conception, however, left some puzzles unresolved. Cherry (1953) observed that people were able to notice when information in an unattended channel changed its physical properties. A real-life analogy would be when you are listening to one person in a crowded room and cannot notice what was said by other people in the room, until someone with a very distinctive voice speaks (as when, for example, a young child starts speaking in a room full of adults). When something like that happens, you may involuntarily shift attention to the change in the acoustic properties of the previously unattended sound of people speaking in the background. Similarly, a suddenly flickering light or burning smell can cause distraction.

Any of these abrupt changes in the environment recruit attention away from what you were thinking about. But how does changed physical information get registered to attract attention, when it was supposedly being filtered out? There was a proposal of the filter being leaky so that it only attenuated information that was not being attended (Treisman, 1964), and strong information could still get through the filter to engage attention. A possibly more comprehensive way to accommodate such findings, however, existed in an embedded-processes representation. All information coming into the brain presumably activates features; it appears to be primarily sensory features of unattended stimuli but also semantic features of attended stimuli. All the features that can be analysed, to the extent that they are analysed, contribute to a neural model of the environment, and when a discrepancy from the neural model is detected, attention is recruited to the change. This process is supported by evidence about the attentional orienting response, which is assumed to continue until the neural model can be altered to accommodate the changes, at which point the orienting response habituates (Sokolov, 1963).

In principle, there is nothing about an embedded-processes model that states that all modules must have strictly embedded relations to one another. It would be possible, for example, to have a model in which the activated portion of long-term memory was divided into separate visuospatial and phonological modules, with the focus of attention subsuming parts of both of them. The reason why that kind of model was not proposed is that Cowan (1988) was aiming for a more general formulation. There were (and are) too many unanswered questions to formulate specific modules on a system-wide basis. Can all kinds of stimuli somehow be assigned to verbal and visuospatial stores or would more stores have to be added? If not, are these the correct names of the modules? How about the spatial locations of tones or speech? Is orthographic information stored in the same visuospatial buffer as non-verbal information? What about touch, smell, and so on? What about activated semantic information? To what extent is the organization of specialized stores innate versus learning dependent? How are associations between different kinds of information retained, like a bird and its song? Absent answers to these kinds of questions, Cowan simply suggested a functional property, that items interfere with other items in activated long-term memory to the extent that the activated features of the items are similar. (This could include similarities in sensory and motor activations, as well (see Morey, Rhodes, & Cowan, 2019).) The episodic buffer of Baddeley (2000) can be viewed as an attempt to grapple with these kinds of unanswered questions, and especially the questions about the storage of binding and semantic information; but this approach seems to impose an assumption that one mechanism can address all the unanswered questions, which is not assumed in the presentation of the activated portion of long-term memory without being explicit in the structure and subspecies of that activation.

A key point about the activated portion of long-term memory is that it can underlie an adequate understanding of working memory only if it includes rapid new learning of information during a trial, which most models do allow. Norris (2017) was apparently unaware that the embedded-processes model relied on this rapid new learning, and consequently emphasized that activated long-term memory is inadequate to understand working memory. For example, if one is trying to remember the digit series 8–5–8, it is not enough to activate the digits 5 and 8. One must activate three serial positions and assign a digit to each one, information that may not already exist long-term memory. Cowan (2019) responded by emphasizing that rapid learning of new information has always been part of the model (e.g. Cowan, 1988, 1999) and, indeed, is implicit in most models. Whatever mechanism holds the newly created information may be considered a specific short-term store, but it also may be considered the front end of new long-term learning, albeit often not learning strong enough to be retrieved after the context has changed unless there is a strong reminder (e.g. in a forced choice with the question, *which of these two lists have you seen before?*). Of course, there is the danger that any result could be explained as coming from the focus of attention when there is a capacity limit versus activated long-term memory when there is no capacity limit, so validation of the theory depends on the discovery of boundary conditions for each mechanism in the model, for example, severe capacity limits for sets of repeated items from trial to trial, allowing proactive interference, as in Cowan (2001); no such limits for sets of familiar objects without this repetition, as in Endress and Potter (2014) or Wolfe (2012).

The point about short-term storage being the front end of new long-term learning came up in a response by Cowan (2019) to Norris (2017). It is not clear that Norris disagrees with this conjecture that working memory is the front end of long-term learning, but a first reading of his article shows an emphasis (Norris, p. 993) on patients with 'grossly impaired verbal STM [short-term memory] capacity of perhaps 2–4 items, combined with relatively intact LTM [long-term memory]'. That condition would seem at first glance to rule out working memory or short-term memory as a portal for long-term learning. Reading further in Norris' article or Cowan's (2019) response, short-term memory impairment does not rule out short-term memory as a portal for long-term memory because impaired short-term memory in a certain domain is typically accompanied by selective, closely related deficits in long-term memory.

In his response to Cowan, Norris (2019) suggested that Cowan's formulation of processing still should be considered as including a 'separate' short-term memory, in particular the mechanism that first encodes serial order and other new associations among the elements of the stimuli (whether or not that same mechanism also underpins long-term memory learning). This does not seem like a critical difference between the views of Cowan and Norris. Our favoured interpretation (since Cowan, 1988) is that the mechanism that begins the process of the association between elements in activated long-term memory is the focus of attention.

The issue of whether working memory mechanisms serve as the front end of long-term learning is, we believe, not just a semantic argument, but an open and interesting issue. The answer to the question can fall along a spectrum. In one extreme, new information that is retained for immediate recall or recognition would result in a long-term trace that is easily recalled. There is evidence that this is not the case. For example, in procedures in which a whole array of six coloured shapes is presented and then the array is presented a second time, intact or with two colours swapped or two shapes swapped, repeating the same array every trial or every third trial did not result in learning of the repeated array sufficient for improved recognition of whether there was a swap (Logie, Brockmole, & Vandenbroucke, 2009; but for conflicting results see Fukuda & Vogel, 2019, discussed in the concluding section of the chapter). In the other extreme, it could be that short-term bindings do not contribute at all to long-term learning. We know that this is not the case, given results like Experiment 3 of Logie et al., in which a recall task with the array repeated every trial did result in rapid learning (cf. Shimi & Logie, 2019). Logie et al. argued that learning occurs from the act of recall. In the traditional Hebb effect (Hebb, 1961), in a list-recall procedure, there are repetitions of the same list every third trial and performance on that list increases with repetitions.

An intermediate case is that short-term information, such as the serial order of items in a list or coloured shapes in an array, forms a long-term representation, but one that is often difficult to retrieve and use in delayed recall. This would be an expectation of any theory that emphasizes temporal distinctiveness in recall (e.g. Bjork & Whitten, 1974;

Crowder, 1976; Glenberg & Swanson, 1986). There is supposedly a lot of temporal distinctiveness of the last few items compared to previous items. When one is supposed to retrieve the just-presented list, it is typically easy to retrieve the correct list representation. Suppose, though, that one was presented with many, similar lists for immediate recall, as in the typical list-recall experiment. Then, after a delay, there may be insufficient cues to recall the correct list as compared to other lists in which some of the same items appeared (or a mixture from different lists). It is also possible that the learning of a list may be fragmented into several different parts of the necessary information. For example, suppose one receives the list *brick, desk, fish, hand, fire, sheet*. One might memorize *brick–desk, fish–hand–fire*, and *sheet*. One may also form a higher-level representation of joint membership of these three units in the same list, and a representation of the order of these three units (e.g. perhaps in this case, *start with the two-word unit, progress to the three-word unit, and then recall the single-word unit*). However, in delayed recall, it is possible that only some of the needed associations are retrieved; resulting, perhaps, in recalls such as *fish, hand, fire, brick, desk, shirt*. Each multi-word unit in this example was correctly retrieved, but the order of units was switched, and the single-word unit was replaced by a similar-sounding word. If this intermediate view is correct, it should be relatively easy to remember new ordering information when there are very few trials in total using such stimuli and the items are not reused; and this, in fact, is what has been found. In particular, Nairne and Neath (2001) presented lists of two to nine words and required pleasantness ratings of the words. There was next a 5-minute geometric filler task. Then, in a surprise memory test, the words in each list were presented in alphabetical order, and the participant was supposed to reproduce the order of items in the list. Performance decreased as a function of list length and, overall, about half of the words were recalled correctly in five-word lists, for a capacity of about 2.5 items in position. The key to this excellent recall of items within lists originally presented for a different task was perhaps that only 22 words were used in all, distributed among lists of different lengths, with only a single trial per length and with 205 participants. The most likely account of the literature, we believe, is that the mechanisms that produce short-term remembering also produce long-term learning, except that what is retrieved long-term depends a lot more on the amount of specific interference that must be overcome and the retrieval cues that allow the correct information that was encoded to be reinstated at the time of recall (e.g. Morris, Bransford, & Franks, 1977). It may be that the conditions that produce the best short-term recall, therefore, are not identical to the conditions that produce the best long-term learning as tested after long delays. (Long-term learning might still contribute considerably to immediate recall because the retrieval context has not changed much (e.g. see Loaiza & McCabe, 2012).)

The relation between short-term and long-term memory may depend on the match-up between the two. If you have learned some Episode 1 and now you are experiencing Episode 2, the tendency to interpret Episode 2 as following the same rules as Episode 1 may depend on the participant's belief about the relation between the two. In the array repetition experiments of Logie et al. (2009), it would be reasonable for a participant to expect different arrays on every trial, and therefore to resist using information from long-term memory that seems similar but may be irrelevant (e.g. an array with a similar, but not identical makeup). Oberauer, Awh, and Sutterer (2017) have findings reinforcing the idea that long-term memory can be used instrumentally to advantage in working memory tasks. They found that participants were able to benefit from facilitation in array memory based on long-term learning of some coloured shapes, when those objects were repeated in a working memory recall task, but without suffering interference when a mismatching but similar object was presented in the working memory task.

One argument against the proposal that short-term serial memory is the front end of long-term learning is that the serial order is difficult to retrieve in delayed recall. However, additional factors of proactive interference between trials could have an effect on long-term retrieval that is not a problem in the short term. To examine such effects, Tzeng (1973) studied immediate and delayed memory for ten-item lists, with the list items separated by a distracting task to increase their distinctiveness from one another. He found not only a recency effect in short-term recall but, after four lists, a robust recency effect in final free recall as well. These findings suggest that when items remain sufficiently distinct, short-term recall does promote long-term recall. (For convergent results with a very different, visual array detection procedure, see Fukuda & Vogel, 2019.) A further argument along these lines is the incidental learning of serial order called long-term memory span (Nairne & Neath, 2001) mentioned earlier, and a similar finding for inter-item associations by Cowan, Donnell, and Saults (2013).

The embedded-processes model has adapted executive control processes from other sources to suit the model (e.g. Cowan, 1988). Executive functions directed largely by frontal lobe areas enter information into the focus of attention by highlighting certain incoming stimulus information or certain activated long-term memory (see the chapters by Postle, 2021, and by Wijeakumar and Spencer, 2021, as well as Cowan, 2011; Cowan et al., 2011; Li, Christ, & Cowan, 2014; Majerus et al., 2016; Majerus, Péters, Bouffier, Cowan, & Phillips, 2018). Information can be re-entered recursively using attention, a process now called refreshing (e.g. see chapter by Barrouillet & Camos, 2021; Barrouillet, Portrat, & Camos, 2011; Cowan, 1992; Raye, Johnson, Mitchell, Greene, & Johnson, 2007), or verbal items can be recited to reactivate information with minimal involvement of attention (e.g. Naveh-Benjamin & Jonides, 1984). Attention apparently inhibits, suppresses, or removes unwanted or no-longer-needed information to allow room for desired information (e.g. Oberauer, 2013).

In sum, the embedded-processes model acknowledges many of the dissociations and key effects proposed by the prior models of working memory but holds that (1) these effects are best explained without a special reference to structurally separate verbal and visuospatial storage bins, inasmuch as the overlap of many kinds of activated features of memory seems important to explain interference between stimuli in working memory; and (2) what is of special importance is the allocation of attention in working memory and the rapid formation of new memories that can relieve the load on attention during working memory tasks.

Answers to Questions About the Embedded-Processes Model

Next, we address questions asked of all the chapter authors in this volume. The answers are summarized in Table 3.1 and expressed in greater detail in the following sections.

1. Definition of Working Memory

We adhere to Cowan's (2017a, p. 1159, Table 1, Item 6) 'generic definition' of working memory: that it is 'The ensemble of components of the mind that hold a limited amount of information temporarily in a heightened state of availability for use in ongoing information processing'. This definition is important for the embedded-processes view because it allows joint consideration of the effects of the activated portion of long-term memory generally, and the focus of attention more narrowly. Yet, if various investigators who all say they are examining working memory had to agree on a common definition of working memory that subsumed their work, we suspect that it would be something like this generic definition.

The issue of definition is important because many different definitions have been used or implied (Cowan, 2017a), and we have observed that investigators typically assert they are examining working memory under the assumption that an unstated definition will be clear enough for readers. Unfortunately, though, investigators often seem to overestimate the extent to which others would naturally understand their definition. For example, some investigators consider working memory to be a multicomponent system, in distinction from earlier models in which a single component represented short-term memory. Baddeley and Hitch (1974, p. 80) commented that 'Our work so far has concentrated exclusively on verbal tasks, and the question obviously arises as to how general are our conclusions. It seems probable that a comparable system exists for visual memory which is different at least in part from the system we have been discussing'. After reviewing a few visual studies they noted (p. 80), 'From these and many other studies, it is clear that visual and auditory short-term storage do employ different subsystems. What is less clear is whether we need to assume completely separate parallel systems for different modalities, or whether the different modalities may share a common central processor'. Baddeley (1986) asserted the multicomponent nature of working memory more confidently. Some distinguish between short-term memory versus working memory based on only the latter involving processing as well as storage, consistent with Baddeley (1986), but inspired largely by the complex span procedures of Case, Kurland, and Goldberg (1982), Daneman and Carpenter (1980), and Conway et al. (2005); and others use the term working memory for temporary storage while not directly appealing to either of these distinctions (e.g. Cowan, Saults, & Blume, 2014; Luck & Vogel, 1997). In our view, a definition of working memory should be broad enough to encompass the phenomena that specific tasks are meant to tap, and should be consistent with multiple plausible theoretical constructions.

2. Methods of the Embedded-Processes Approach

The embedded-processes approach originated in a literature review (Cowan, 1988) in the spirit of attempting to accommodate all existing evidence. It is therefore under-standable that, subsequently, almost every major method in use in cognitive psych-ology and cognitive neuroscience has proven relevant to the model and is considered by it. Some key examples are discussed here.

Recall and recognition accuracy

In the embedded-processes view, the level of accuracy is considered the most important evidence because it is a rough indication of how much of the original information has been preserved. According to the embedded-processes view (Cowan, 1988, 1999, 2001), accuracy should decrease by time (because of decay when the participant is pas-sive), though at a rate dependent on the completeness of consolidation into working memory (Ricker & Cowan, 2014), and by the amount of intervening interference from similar items (Nairne, 1990; Oberauer & Lin, 2017). Both sources of forgetting presum-ably affect the activated portion of long-term memory. Accuracy also should decrease as a function of the number of items to be retained in working memory concurrently, for several reasons: because it is impossible to encode too many items at once, because some items from a list can be lost while others are being encoded, and because only a limited number of items can be preserved at once in the focus of attention.

Error analyses

Although Cowan and colleagues have rarely relied directly on error analyses, they play an important role in the field, which is relevant for the interpretation of results from an embedded-processes view. According to the embedded-processes approach, infor-mation should linger in the activated portion of long-term memory, often after that information has become no longer relevant to the current trial. Among the lingering information, there could be newly formed associations between items and their serial positions in the list, which could be accidentally retrieved because of close associations with the correct answer (e.g. when they both occupy the same serial position of their respective lists). Errors in favour of this notion include intrusion errors in which the item that is incorrectly recalled comes from the same serial position of a previous list (Henson, Norris, Page, & Baddeley, 1996; Osth & Dennis, 2015).

Meta-knowledge judgements

Another kind of behavioural evidence that is relevant is one in which participants judge their own state of mind. This information can be used to refine models of working memory. For example, Cowan et al. (2016) carried out an experiment in which an array of coloured items was presented on each trial, followed by another array; participants were to estimate how many colours had changed between the two arrays (from zero to all of them). Additionally, on some trials, there was an interruption after the first array, during which participants were to estimate how many of the array items they had in mind, a meta-knowledge judgement about the state of their working memory knowledge. What was of most interest was the relation between meta-knowledge and working memory knowledge (in particular, a kind of error analysis, namely, how many more or fewer items were said to have changed versus the actual number that changed). Because participants generally thought they had more items in working memory than they really did, they were likely to presume incorrectly that they could not have missed many changes in the items, and therefore they generally underestimated the number of changes.

Reaction time

Reaction time is an important measure for the embedded-processes model because of the assumption that items in the focus of attention can be recalled more quickly than items that have to be retrieved from the activated portion of long-term memory into the focus of attention before they are used in responses. Several lines of research are relevant to this notion.

Cowan, Johnson, and Saults (2005) suggested that items held within the focus of attention are not susceptible to proactive interference from previous trials, whereas items held within the activated portion of long-term memory would be susceptible to it. On every trial, they presented a list of three, four, six, or eight printed words, followed by a probe word to be judged present in the list or absent from it. In high-proactive-interference trials, words of the same semantic category as the list items had been used in four to seven immediately preceding trials whereas, in low-proactive-interference trials, the semantic category of the list items had not been used in other trials. The results showed that set sizes of three or four items, within the capacity of the focus of attention, showed little effect of proactive interference on reaction time, whereas larger set sizes showed a substantial effect. Although there could be some effect of proactive interference even in the focus of attention (e.g. Carroll et al., 2010), the results still suggest that the focus of attention helps to protect items from proactive interference (cf. Oberauer et al., 2017).

Our embedded-processes theory has been slightly modified by Oberauer (2002) and Oberauer and Bialkova (2009) so that the multiple-item, capacity-limited focus of attention is called a region of direct access and, within it, a single-item focus of attention is postulated. Gilchrist and Cowan (2011) showed that at least two items could be in focus at once. On every trial, the participant studied a link between two shapes and two letters (e.g. square and L, circle and R), as well as a link between two colours and two numbers (e.g. green and 3, blue and 5). Then, when a *colour + shape* probe was presented, the participant was to select the square on a grid in which the correct *letter + number* combination appeared. A key variable in the experiment was the switch from trial to trial in the colour or shape. If either the colour or shape changed from the previous trial, the reaction time was slowed, as if an item had to be replaced or updated in working memory, and if both changed, the reaction time was slowed more, as if both items had to be replaced in working memory. If, however, a pre-learned colour-shape combination was presented (i.e. a learned chunk), then a subsequent change in either colour or shape caused as much slowing as if both had been changed, indicating that one cannot update part of a learned chunk without replacing the entire chunk and starting over. Oberauer (2013) modelled this task and suggested (p. 14), essentially in keeping with our own view, that 'any limitation of the focus of attention to a single context and/or a single item arises from the function of the focus as a selection device'. It implies that the focus of attention can zoom in and out as necessary, though zooming out only to the capacity limit of several items at once (Cowan et al., 2005).

Metaphorical and graphic modelling

A core feature of earlier models of cognition is that graphic models are used based on an analysis of the parts of the cognitive process, each part representing a phase, component, or subprocess (Fig. 3.1). This core feature is now controversial because it involves a kind of reasoning by metaphor. Practically nobody literally believes that there are boxes inside the head doing the work, let alone boxes within boxes as in the embedded-processes model. However, the purpose of the metaphorical, graphic model is to gain a grasp over processes that are rather abstract and relate them to domains that are easier to think about, such as plumbing (sharing of water resources), electricity (sharing of wattage, activation), and computer science (with separable hardware components). A good metaphor can contribute to hypothesis formation because something that you know a lot about and can easily think about (the area of metaphor; physical boxes and items within them) can be used to suggest potential properties of the system under consideration (the area of investigation). Beyond an abstract metaphor, the embedded-processes model portrays cognition in a manner that we think is rather compatible with the organization of the brain, and this compatibility will be discussed further in the electrophysiological and neuroimaging sections.

Measurement-directed theoretical modelling

In another kind of modelling heavily used in the embedded-processes approach, a very simple mathematical model is formed, not because it is presumed to be the most sophisticated model available, but because it is a simple model that approximates reality and can be used to examine other variables in a principled way. In a similar manner, linear regression models are used even if one does not believe that the driving causes of behaviour have entirely linear effects, so long as the linearity picks up a large amount of variance that can be used to express meaningful relationships between variables.

Cowan and colleagues (Cowan, 2001; Cowan et al., 2005) proposed a measurement model, inspired by Pashler (1988), used to estimate the number of items in working memory, k, in recognition tasks. They are based on a simple logic in which one assumes that out of N items in the set to be remembered, k of them are remembered. If one is questioned about whether a particular item has changed or not, the probability that it is in working memory is k/N, leading to a correct response, and if it is not in working memory (in $1 - k/N$ of the trials), the remaining probability of a correct guess is g. This logic leads to a formula in which $k = N(hits\ minus\ false\ alarms)$, where *hits* are the proportion of changes that were detected and *false alarms* are the proportion of non-changing items incorrectly judged to have changed. Slight alterations in the paradigm lead to changes in the calculation of the number of items in working memory (Cowan, Donnell, & Saults, 2013; Pashler, 1988; Rouder, Morey, Morey, & Cowan, 2011). This type of approach has been applied mostly to visual working memory but has also been adapted to working memory for tone series (Clark et al., 2018) and verbal lists (Cowan, Rouder, Blume, & Saults, 2012). Complete success of this set of measurement models would include an estimate of the number of items in working memory that increases as the presented set size increases, until an asymptotic level is reached, the participant's capacity, after which no further increase should be found. Sometimes this pattern is observed (e.g. Cowan et al., 2005), whereas other times larger arrays are poorly encoded by lower-span participants (Cusack, Lehmann, Veldsman, & Mitchell, 2009).

Rouder et al. (2008) showed that the simple model presented previously, if made more sophisticated in some basic ways (allowing for attention lapses even when $N < k$), correctly predict a pattern of receiver operating characteristics curves that are linear as a function of the proportion of trials in which the probe has changed from the studied array, and as a function of the set size (cf. Donkin, Tran, & Nosofsky, 2014) and correctly predict response time distributions (Donkin, Nosofsky, Gold, & Shiffrin, 2013). The models are improved further when guessing is informed by the set size along with k (Rhodes, Cowan, Hardman, & Logie, 2018). Zhang and Luck (2008) introduced a more sophisticated approach in which one could distinguish between two sources of error for simple stimuli that could apply to recognition: the item could be absent from working memory, or it could be present but without enough precision to answer correctly in a recognition procedure.

Computational modelling

As mentioned previously, there are many researchers who invest in computational models of aspects of working memory (e.g. see chapter by Oberauer, 2021). Although we have not done so often, Cowan et al. (2012) used this approach to help understand the capacity limits of working memory. Participants saw lists of single words, familiar multi-item word series (e.g. *leather brief case*; *summer squash*), or combinations of unit lengths. Each list was followed by a test in which the participant was to indicate which of two words came from the list (e.g. *brief* or *door*). Various models were tested, based on whether there was a constant capacity in terms of units (words or series) or some other description of performance. The winning model involved a constant capacity that came to about three units, with the added qualifications that (1) not every multi-word series was perfectly learned, and (2) for long lists of singletons, there was an extra contribution of rapid long-term learning. Chen and Cowan (2009) trained participants to 100% learning of two-word series and found a constant capacity of about three items, remarkably constant across many word and list lengths, provided that the serial order of responding was ignored and articulatory suppression was used to prevent rehearsal, which can supplement the core capacity.

The approach of these studies stands in stark contrast with most of the computational modelling literature, which focuses on serial order memory. Norris (2017) promoted the thesis that short-term memory was more than the activated portion of long-term memory based on the need for a short-term representation in which the same activated element could appear more than once, for example, in the series 8–5–8. Cowan (2019) responded that this type of example does not rule out the embedded-processes approach because whatever mechanism forms and holds the serial representation in the short term also may serve as the front end of a long-term learning system that can learn rapidly enough to be of use even in the current trial of a serial recall task. In terms of the mechanism of serial learning, Cowan did not offer a new mechanism but did not reject mechanisms proposed by others.

Electrophysiology: event-related potentials

Electrophysiological approaches can be of great use in addressing the nature of working memory (e.g. see chapter by Hakim, Awh, & Vogel, 2021). Cowan, Winkler, Teder, and Näätänen (1993) used event-related potentials to help investigate the nature of the activated portion of working memory. According to the embedded-processes model, that activated portion includes sensory features. In event-related potentials, a series of identical standard tones followed by a deviant tone gives rise to an electrical response at the scalp, the mismatch negativity, which occurs even when the tones are unattended during their presentation (with attention directed to reading a book). The mismatch negativity can be clearly seen when trials are averaged across numerous comparable presentations. It takes several standard tones for the standard representation to be built up so that a mismatch negativity will occur. Moreover, if there is a 10-second break between the standard tones and the deviant tone, the standard tone's representation is no longer active and no mismatch negativity emerges. Cowan et al. (1993) considered that if the standard tone representation is newly learned information within activated long-term memory, and if it becomes inactive, a single reminder of the standard tone should reactivate the standard tone representation. The findings confirmed this expectation. After a 10-second delay, if and only if a single standard tone was presented that matched the prior series, then a mismatch negativity response to the deviant occurred immediately afterward. Winkler, Schröger, and Cowan (2001), by separating tones in a series, showed that the loss of information over a long delay occurred not because of simple decay, but because the standard tones were no longer perceived as forming a current context for the deviant.

Functional magnetic resonance imaging

The technique of magnetic resonance imaging (MRI) allows an examination of blood oxygenation thought to reveal the related pattern of neural activity across the brain. In functional MRI (fMRI), the pattern of brain activity from a control condition (e.g. reading text) is subtracted from that of a critical condition (e.g. reading and memorizing text) to indicate aspects of neural function arising specifically from the critical aspect of the task (e.g. memorizing). Criticisms have been levelled at fMRI in that (1) the response is too slow to pick up the sub-second-speed changes in neural activity that are known to play a role in cognition, and (2) identifying the location of neural activity would not tell us what processes are occurring, and therefore could be irrelevant to cognitive theory (e.g. for a review, see Norris, 2017). Working memory, however, is an area in which fMRI has proved relevant to theory despite these concerns. Methodologically, one can be concerned about neural activity during a maintenance period lasting several seconds, well within the temporal purview of fMRI. A number of fMRI techniques and results are useful for understanding working memory (see chapter by Postle, 2021) and have contributed to clarification of the embedded-processes approach.

Chein and Fiez (2010) used fMRI to compare four models of working memory (a multicomponent model, and object-oriented episodic record model, a feature-overwriting model, and the embedded-processes model). What was examined is neural responses to articulatory suppression, irrelevant speech sounds, and irrelevant non-speech sounds during a visual list memory task. The different models were assumed to attribute behavioural effects of the different manipulations to different processes. The results favoured the embedded-processes model over the others on the assumption that this model attributed articulatory suppression effects to a disruption of rehearsal and the other two effects to a disruption of attention. Specifically, brain areas known to be related to rehearsal and attention were differentially affected by the manipulations in the manner the theory predicted.

Todd and Marois (2004) carried out fMRI during maintenance of an array of coloured spots in working memory for recognition of a probe colour. The intraparietal sulcus on both sides of the brain yielded larger fMRI signals during the maintenance period when more items were included in the array. This increase in the fMRI signal reached an asymptote at about three items in the array, and strongly resembled the function of the estimated number of items in working memory, or k (Cowan, 2001), based on the behavioural responses.

Although Todd and Marois (2004) considered their finding to reflect a visual working memory area, Cowan (1995) previously had summarized brain damage and anatomical evidence suggesting that the region instead could be a general area for the focus of attention. Cowan et al. (2011) tested this hypothesis in an fMRI study by requiring maintenance of various numbers of coloured spots, spoken letters, or both together. Examining the whole brain, the only area that robustly responded to increases in memory load from either modality was the left intraparietal sulcus. The only discrepancy of this result from what was theoretically expected was the absence of a multimodal (or amodal) response from the right intraparietal sulcus, but this finding may be consistent with the observation of responding by the left intraparietal sulcus to item information in working memory, versus order information in the right intraparietal sulcus (Majerus et al., 2016). Li et al. (2014) further showed that the left intraparietal sulcus was functionally connected to the posterior regions for whichever type of material was being held (occipital for colours, temporal for spoken letters). The notion was that the intraparietal sulcus contains not a copy of the information, but rather pointers to the information in the posterior regions.

The recent advent of multivoxel pattern analysis (MVPA) in fMRI research has offered a level of specificity in identifying what is being held in the focus of attention (versus activated long-term memory) that makes the results theoretically more relevant than previously. MVPA allows the computer to learn to classify a pattern of fMRI results indicating that the participant is thinking about a particular kind of stimulus (e.g. line orientations, faces, or words).

Lewis-Peacock, Drysdale, Oberauer, and Postle (2012) used MVPA to identify which of three categories was held in working memory. Their procedure involved presentation on each trial of items from two categories out of the three used in the experiment (words for semantic memory, pseudo-words for phonological memory, and lines of particular orientations). The presentation was followed by a cue indicating that the item from a particular category would be tested first, followed by the test, followed in turn by a cue indicating the category from which the second test would occur. Sometimes the same category was tested twice, and other times there was a category switch. Both categories that were presented on the trial at first showed an MVPA signal well above the baseline indicated by the third category, the one not used on the trial. After the first cue was presented, the MVPA signal for the category to be tested first remained high, whereas the signal for the other category used on the trial returned to baseline. When the second cue was presented, if the same category was to be tested again, its MVPA signal remained high but, if there was a switch in the category to be tested, the MVPA signal for the category to be tested returned from baseline to a high level, whereas the first-tested category dropped back to baseline. It was suggested that the MVPA signal only occurred for items in the focus of attention, and its activity was centred on the appropriate posterior regions.

The information still potentially needed in the trial but not currently cued, and presumably not in the focus of attention, yielded no discernible MVPA signal. It may reflect a representation that is in the activated portion of long-term memory, but outside of attention. It may be retained not by the present firing of neurons, but by information stored chemically or anatomically, for example in the synapses where neurons are connected, which would allow the relevant neurons to begin firing again to represent that particular information (in the focus of attention) if it proves to be needed later in the current trial or episode. That theory will be reinforced in the section on transcranial magnetic stimulation by research (Rose et al., 2016) showing that, while the information is still task relevant, inducing electric flow at the right neural locations revives the dormant memory representations.

Majerus et al. (2016) provided further support for the notion that the attention system contains pointers to items in the focus of attention but does not itself contain a separate copy of the information. They presented either verbal letter or visual colour information for recall during fMRI and found that the intraparietal sulcus was the centre of a pattern that represented not the particular items in working memory, but rather their number (the memory load). Moreover, when the MVPA classifier was trained on verbal information, it then also succeeded at classifying the number of spatial items in working memory, and vice versa; that is, memory load was identifiable in the same way across verbal and spatial stimulus codes.

Neuropsychology

Cowan (1995, 1999) related human brain lesions to the embedded-processes approach. Whereas frontal lesions typically produce deficits in the control of attention, parietal lesions typically produce deficits in the experience of attention, including unilateral neglect and anosognosia (unawareness of an accompanying physical disability). Within the parietal lobe, the intraparietal sulcus is a most likely region for representation of the focus of attention given its involvement not only in working memory, but also attention in other domains, including perception (see Cowan, 2011; Cowan et al., 2011), mathematics (Price, Mazzocco, & Ansari, 2013), and reaching and grasping (Frey, Vinton, Norlund, & Grafton, 2005). The various posterior regions of the cortex that are involved in the perceptual analysis of stimuli feed fibres into the parietal areas and are good candidates themselves for material in activated long-term memory (e.g. Rose et al., 2016). Damage to the frontal areas, tied strongly to the parietal areas, result in deficits in the planning and executive control of behaviour, and appear to be the substrates of executive function that control the attentional focus. When new information is to be attended and recorded into long-term memory, the hippocampus is recruited for that process. Questions about the potential incompatibility between the embedded-processes model and apparent multiple, separate components of working memory according to the multicomponent model will be addressed later.

Transcranial magnetic stimulation and other brain research

This method of magnetically stimulating a spot in the brain has been used to produce a temporary lesion. Postle et al. (2006) used it to show that storage and processing of working memory items are separable brain functions. Transcranial magnetic stimulation in parietal regions impaired memory in two tasks: one in which a random series of letters was to be recalled, and one in which the series was to be alphabetized and then recalled. Transcranial magnetic stimulation in the frontal regions impaired only the task that required alphabetization.

Rose et al. (2016) provide information that clarifies what may be involved physiologically in the activated portion of long-term memory. In the fMRI procedure in which one category at a time was thought to be in the focus of attention and another was outside of that focus (Lewis-Peacock et al., 2012), transcranial magnetic stimulation at the posterior region appropriate for a given type of stimulus was capable of reactivating the MVPA signal for that type of stimulus, provided that there was still a chance that this type of stimulus might be needed later in the trial. When it could no longer be relevant, no reactivation was observed, consistent with the notion that there could be a synaptic mechanism holding information outside of attention. Single-cell recordings have also reinforced this notion of retention of working memories through synaptic means (Stokes, 2015). Although the terminology of activated long-term memory was originally most aligned to the idea of neural activity (Cowan, 1988), activation can be reconceived to include retention through synaptic means, without a problem for the cognitive model of embedded processes.

Phenomenologically influenced data collection and theorizing

An important but rarely discussed aspect of psychological model-building is that some researchers try to make their models and theories consistent with their experience as humans, whereas other researchers find this kind of influence misleading, and avoid it (see Logie & Cowan, 2015). We fall into the former camp (though we maintain caution in how we use phenomenology). One of the motivations for a model with a unified focus of attention supplemented by activated long-term memory of many types is that it seems consistent with the common human experience of a unified stream of consciousness (cf. Baars & Franklin, 2003) and activated long-term memory impinging on the focus of attention seems consistent with the spontaneous activation of thoughts, dreams, and daydreams, and the creative recombination of known elements from past experience to form new imagery.

This inclusion of phenomenology is in common with the leader of the first experimental psychology laboratory, Wilhelm Wundt, who aimed to clarify consciousness. Cowan and Rachev (2018) explored Wundt's history, including some newly available information (e.g. Araujo, 2016). Cowan and Rachev found remarkable commonalities between Wundt's view and the embedded-processes view. Wundt based his view on data from experiments in which participants yielded accuracy and reaction-time data, holding that the quality of the data depended on the faithful collaboration of the participant in adopting the desired frame of mind. Few modern psychologists cite this early work, perhaps because much of it has not been accessible in English (but see Sperling, 1960). There has been little attempt in modern cognitive psychology to read or replicate Wundt's research. As an example of its uniqueness, Cowan and Rachev (2018, p. 235) note about Wundt that 'in his work with his assistant Ludwig Lange, participants were asked to pay special attention either to the sensations to which they were to respond or to the muscular movements that they were about to make, the latter shortening the reaction times (presumably by allowing earlier formulation of the response while evaluation of the stimulus was ongoing)'. This early era of research led to a model of memory that appears very similar to Oberauer's (2002) version of the embedded-processes model. More could be done to bring back Wundt's type of method as convergent evidence now that phenomenology has made something of a comeback (e.g. in a study of the neural counterpart to the seen display during binocular rivalry by Zaretskaya, Thielscher, Logothetis, & Bartels, 2010).

3. The Unitary versus Non-unitary Nature of Working Memory

The embedded-processes model would be considered unitary in that it does not reify a distinction between visual and verbal domains the way that the multicomponent models do. However, this is not to say that the model assumes a unified field of equipotential responding across large swaths of the brain, as in the theory of Lashley (1950). It is assumed that every stimulus can give rise to many different kinds of representations, and often multiple types at once: phonological, morphological, syntactic, visual, tactile, olfactory, semantic, motor, and so on. It is further assumed that these codes rely on neural circuits that differ, though the circuits may overlap or rely on some of the same neurons. The scenario is complex enough, though, and unknown enough, that we think it best for now to represent all of these kinds of codes as different types of activated long-term memory rather than concrete modules.

The multicomponent focus on phonological and visual codes is seen as reflecting the kinds of studies run by authors coming from that tradition (e.g. Baddeley, 1986). We assume that concurrent codes in working memory can interfere with one another more when they contain more similar features, an assumption that produces the main kinds of dissociation that have been taken as evidence for multiple visuospatial and phonological components. Isolating measurement of short-term storage is an empirical difficulty: arguably, no task succeeds in measuring short-term storage (whether phonological or visual) without also implicating sensory and long-term memory, as well as the perceptual systems needed to capture the information or the motor system used to generate an appropriate response.

Could we agree on separate phonological and visual components regardless of how many other components there are, or whether these components refer exclusively to short-term stores and their immediate maintenance processes? Not necessarily. There may be phenomena that fractionate or combine these codes. For example, what are taken as phonological codes might be partly acoustic, partly phonetic (having to do with speech sounds as they are pronounced), partly phonological or phonemic (having to do with speech categories that make a meaningful difference in one's language), partly morphological (having to do with the rules of word formation), and partly motor (having to do with mouth movements to make the speech).

4. The Role of Attention and Control

The human mind is characterized by opposites: the very small amount that can be perceived or held in mind at once when there are few established patterns (Broadbent, 1975; Cowan, 2001; Glanzer & Razel, 1974; Graesser & Mandler, 1978; Luck & Vogel, 1997; Simon, 1974) versus the vast amount that can be perceived or memorized rapidly on the basis of patterns and known objects (e.g. Chong & Treisman, 2003; Endress & Potter, 2014; Ericsson, Chase, & Faloon, 1980; Wolfe, 2012). We take this contradiction to be the result of a focus of attention that is quite limited, but is facilitated by humans' ability to learn new structures quickly and make use of what they know, perceiving known patterns in new stimuli.

The severe limit in attention describes the limit in how much can be perceived or held in the focus of attention at once. Because of this severe limit, there are conflicts between two sets of items to be held in working memory even when one is visual and the other is verbal (Cowan et al., 2011, 2014), and when storage has to occur at the same time as processing (Doherty et al., 2019; Rhodes et al., 2019). The conflict is not severe (cf. Baddeley & Hitch, 1974), which we believe is the case because information can be off-loaded from the focus of attention to activated long-term memory to reduce interference between two tasks. Other control processes include moving items into the focus of attention, updating the contents of the focus of attention and of long-term memory in the process, and presumably protecting information from being affected by distraction, by suppressing the distraction.

5. Storage, Maintenance, and Loss of Information in Working Memory

Passive storage in the activated portion of long-term memory is complemented by active storage in the focus of attention. The passive storage can be interrupted either by time-based decay in the absence of mnemonic activities, or by overwriting from subsequent stimuli with similar features. The idea of time-based decay was dealt a blow by research suggesting that there is no decay even when rehearsal and refreshing are prevented (Oberauer & Lewandowsky, 2008). Recent findings, however, have suggested that there is memory loss over time when the information cannot be well encoded into memory, presumably either because the items are unfamiliar or because the time for encoding is short given items such as letters presented in a brief, multiple-item array (for a review see Ricker, Sandry, Vergauwe, & Cowan, 2020). The indication so far is that this loss over time is not merely a loss in temporal distinctiveness of the information in the most recent trial as a function of time, but an actual decay in absolute time regardless of the time between trials (Ricker, Spiegel, & Cowan, 2014).

Attention-based refreshing of representations can occur (Barrouillet et al., 2011; see chapter by Barrouillet & Camos, 2021). A limit in the capacity of the focus of attention could occur because of the limit in the speed with which items can be refreshed compared to the decay rate, as Barrouillet et al. have proposed on the basis of a negative linear relation between cognitive load and span. Of course, elsewhere we suggest that there may not be much decay in the situations that Barrouillet et al. have studied (cf. Oberauer & Lewandowsky, 2008), but there is still interference from ongoing stimuli and responses that could reduce memory representations over time. Alternative to the approach of Barrouillet et al., the observed speed limit could occur partly because multiple items are refreshed in parallel and the number of items that can be concurrently refreshed is limited by the capacity of the focus of attention to just a few at once (Lemaire, Pageot, Plancher, & Portrat, 2018). This issue is an important one for future research, to understand capacity and processing limits.

6. The Role of Long-Term Memory Knowledge in Working Memory Storage and Processing

It should be clear from what we have said that knowledge is quite important in overcoming the limits of the capacity of the focus of attention and in making representations long-lasting in the activated portion of long-term memory. At the same time, it appears that working memory training cannot make a person's basic capacity increase (e.g. Redick et al., 2013). Instead, the impact of working memory training is to improve strategies and efficiency for the trained task (e.g. Ericsson et al., 1980) and other tasks using very similar skills (Diamond & Lee, 2011). So, in understanding what people can and cannot do, one must consider the constrained nature of basic capacity along with the remarkable ability to form new chunks and learn structures, which allows a small capacity to accomplish big things.

7. Inconsistencies with the Framework

The framework has continued to evolve to account for inconsistencies. One apparent inconsistency is evidence for some part of working memory dedicated to specific modalities or codes. In our earlier examination of this issue, these specific components were not observed. Saults and Cowan (2007) presented, on each trial, a simultaneously presented set of four spoken digits remembered along with an array of multiple coloured squares, and concluded that the items were held together in the focus of attention. However, subsequent work (Cowan et al., 2014) has suggested that this result of Saults and Cowan was not the final word, inasmuch as the capacity for the spoken digits was only about two items and did not allow an unambiguous analysis. Using a more sophisticated analysis and series of verbal items with articulatory suppression rather than using an acoustic array, Cowan et al. found that only a limited component of memory was shared between the modalities (about one item); a substantial part of memory was not shared between them. The parts of memory not shared between the modalities are consistent with separate verbal and spatial modules as in the multicomponent view. Alternatively, though, within the embedded-processes framework, they could instead be accounted for by the idea that information from each modality can be off-loaded to the activated portion of long-term memory through new learning, relieving much of the burden of attention (for a similar proposed process, see Unsworth & Engle, 2007). There perhaps would still be a need for some shared attention after off-loading of both sets of items, to refresh the sets in memory or improve their organization. This rapid new learning of the materials (the off-loading process) need not lead to good delayed recall of the sets, because of the difficulty of identifying a particular trial in memory given later interference from other trials in the retrieval process. When interference is small enough, there is long-term learning (Nairne & Neath, 2001).

One inconsistency may be evidence that the model is too undifferentiated regarding different kinds of materials in working memory (e.g. visuospatial versus verbal materials). Our ongoing work addresses this issue by potentially pointing to more, not less, differentiation than in the multicomponent approach. Ongoing work with retention of two working memory sets (presented one at a time) suggests that there is some organization of information in activated long-term memory, but that the idea of micromodules for different features fits better than several simple modules. For example, we have examined memory for an array of colours of spots concurrent with memory for an array of bars at different orientations, and we have examined memory for a series of tones at different frequencies concurrent with memory for a series of white-noise bursts at different intensities. These mixed-feature trials produce memory that is superior to trials in which both sets include the same feature (e.g. colour in both cases), but is nevertheless inferior to trials in which sets occur in different modalities (one acoustic and one visual).

The nature of the working memory capacity limit is a work in progress. The embedded-processes approach to this issue (e.g. Cowan, 2001; Cowan et al., 2012), in which the focus of attention has a fixed capacity limit of a few items, should be viewed as a first approximation to understanding a more detailed mechanism. On one hand, there is good evidence consistent with the notion that capacity is not unlimited and can include at most a few items (e.g. Adam, Vogel, & Awh, 2017). If participants had some information about every item in an array to be held in working memory, they would never have to guess about an item, but there is good evidence that they sometimes do guess (e.g. Nosofsky & Donkin, 2016; Nosofsky & Gold, 2018; Pratte, 2019; Rhodes, Cowan, Hardman, & Logie, 2018; Rouder, Thiele, & Cowan, 2014).

On the other hand, when it comes to objects with multiple features that have to be retained separately, there is more than one kind of capacity limit, which the embedded-processes model needs to accommodate somehow. A revised model that has worked well in several reports (Cowan, Donnell, & Saults, 2013; Hardman & Cowan, 2015; Oberauer & Eichenberger, 2013) is one in which there is a capacity limited to about three objects, but sometimes with incomplete feature representation of some of those objects (e.g. some objects for which the colour is known but the shape is unknown). Perhaps this pattern of results can be explained with a single capacity limit that has to be applied reiteratively during consolidation of the objects into working memory. For example, in the spirit of a proposal by Wheeler and Treisman (2002), activated long-term memory could include a map for each feature, and a capacity limit therefore might apply at slightly different times at which, say, first the colours and then the shapes are consolidated into working memory.

Another aspect of capacity not formally in the model is that, when materials are open to higher-level average information or organization of the stimulus set, these higher-level regularities clearly do influence the observed capacity (e.g. Brady & Alvarez, 2015; Brady & Tenenbaum, 2013; Chekaf, Cowan, & Mathy, 2016; Chong & Treisman, 2003; Jiang, Olson, & Chun, 2000). It is possible to account for this kind of finding in the model with the idea that structures are rapidly built up in long-term memory, with the focus of attention used to index key notes in the structure. More research is needed to explore such possibilities.

One situation that would seem counter to the spirit of the embedded-processes model would be a situation in which information from perception is copied into a separate location that is used for short-term memory responses but is not saved to become part of long-term memory. Yue, Martin, Hamilton, and Rose (2019) provide evidence of activation of a region they term the *left supramarginal gyrus*, not during input of the verbal items to be remembered, but during the retention interval. However, the nature of that region remains to be seen. For one thing, it is possible that this region actually is a long-term memory storage area, here in an activated state. Long-term retrieval data would be helpful to examine that possibility. Also, rather than being a separate storage area that is not involved in processing, it is possible that some sort of maintenance process takes place in this area. Buchsbaum and D'Esposito (2019) pointed out an area they termed *Spt* to link aural and vocal information about speech (see the later neuropsychology section). A close examination of the brain areas highlighted and given different labels by these authors actually have a high degree of neural overlap with one another, as shown in Fig. 3.2. It is not clear that what they have termed the left supramarginal gyrus and Spt are really two different areas, one for storage and one for processing. It could be that the embedded-processes model will be proven wrong by further evidence, but we do not believe that the evidence is strong enough at this point.

Of the optional questions, we address the ones not covered previously in this chapter.

(a)   (b)

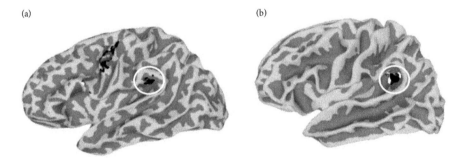

Fig. 3.2 A comparison of the brain areas demarcated in different works as, respectively, (a) the left supramarginal gyrus, specialized for phonological retention based on fMRI evidence (Yue et al., 2018, Figure 4, left side); and (b) area Spt for the integration of sensory and vocal tract information based on the overlap of lesion and fMRI evidence (Buchsbaum et al., 2011, Figure 4, right side). These two areas, shown within white circles in their respective brain diagrams, appear to have a high degree of overlap.

A. Early Life Development

Cowan has researched the childhood development of working memory during the elementary school years and beyond, throughout his career. Most of the findings and relevance for the embedded-processes approach have been summarized in two articles in *Advances in Child Development and Behaviour* (Cowan, Elliott, & Saults, 2002; Cowan, 2017b; see also Cowan, 2016). The 2002 summary shows systematic changes during childhood in the speed of recitation and the speed of memory search during recall of digit lists. These speed changes were unrelated to each other and accounted for much of the age-related change in digit span (Cowan et al., 1998). If there had been a single speed-of-processing change, it might have been considered a fundamental cause of change (cf. Kail & Salthouse, 1994). Given that there were two unrelated changes in speed, though, a more likely account is that the improvement in other aspects of processing (verbal rehearsal and search quality) accounted for changes in the respective speeds. The embedded-processes model has always allowed that verbal rehearsal is a special process that proceeds with little investment of attention after the necessary representation is established (Guttentag, 1984; Naveh-Benjamin & Jonides, 1984), whereas memory search is used in retrieval to search for the next item to be recalled, and therefore occurs at a pace that depends on the list length and on capacity (Cowan, 1992). The latter is likely to require attention, consistent with the refreshment process of Barrouillet et al. (2011). Cowan et al. (2002) also showed an age-related change in the decay rate of auditory sensory memory for the last digit in a series unattended at the time of presentation, though that finding seems unique and therefore should be explored further.

There is an increase in the capacity of the focus of attention in working memory during the elementary school years (for reviews see Cowan, 2016, 2017b). A difficulty for this research is that many kinds of qualities improve with development, including knowledge, the ability to filter out irrelevant items, encoding speed, and rehearsal. The various studies reviewed suggest that, even with these various factors held constant or controlled one by one, capacity still increases markedly during childhood.

Cowan (2016, 2017b) addressed the issue that some research suggests adult-like capacities of about three items in infancy. How is this possible, when the research on older children suggests a developmental progression? One resolution of the paradox (Cowan, 2017b) is that development occurs not in the number of items in working memory per se, but in the completeness of the representations in working memory. Showing incompleteness of representations, for example, Zosh and Feigenson (2012) examined the ability of 18-month-old children to retrieve toys from a box after having viewed the toys' placement in the box. In a critical condition, the toys were covertly removed and replaced with other toys. With one or two toys placed in the box, infants kept searching for the original toys, as if they remembered their identities. With three toys placed in the box, infants stopped searching after retrieving three new toys and were apparently no longer concerned with the disappearance of the original toys; they may have representations of three objects, but without the specific identities or details of those objects.

Cowan, Li, Glass, and Saults (2018) carried out a study modelled after an adult study by Cowan et al. (2014), to determine age differences in the ability to share working memory between an array of four coloured squares and series of either spoken digits or tones. Working memory was divided into the number of sounds and colours that were remembered no matter whether one or both modalities had to be retained in memory, called peripheral portions of working memory, and the number of slots that could be divided between colours and sounds, called the central portion. Whereas the central portion stayed fixed across ages at about one item, the peripheral portions markedly increased during the elementary school years. The suggested account was that, with age, participants learn to off-load information into the activated portion of long-term memory, allowing more information to be retained without much interference between the two sets. In keeping with this notion, Morey, Mareva, Lelonkiewicz, and Chevalier (2018) found that children under 8 years old showed different looking patterns to-ward incoming spatial memoranda than the patterns characteristic of older children and adults (Lange & Engbert, 2013). Older children and adults fixated spatial items presented serially for progressively shorter times, whereas children under 8 years old looked at each incoming item for longer periods. Decreases in fixation towards items during encoding may also reflect an increasingly efficient use of peripheral resources with maturation (e.g. proactively rehearsing the to-be-remembered information or preparing their response progressively; either of these assumed processes may boost measured span, resulting in increased memory spans across development).

B. Adult Ageing

There has not been a long-standing set of predictions about adult ageing from the embedded-processes standpoint. However, the model needs to explain the ubiquitous age-related decline from young adulthood to old age (65+ years) in working memory, as measured by different span measures, including, reading span, listening span, and operation span, with a meta-analysis by Bopp and Verhaeghen (2005) on verbal working memory showing that working memory capacity in older adults reached only 74% that of younger adults. This decline could be related to several basic mechanisms, including speed of processing (Salthouse, 1996), inhibitory control (Hasher & Zacks, 1988), and inter-item binding deficits (Peterson, Decker, & Naveh-Benjamin, 2019), although the exact manner in which these mechanisms affect the machinery suggested by the embedded-processing model needs to be investigated and specified. For ex-ample, slowing of speed of processing in older adults may explain the decline in the rate and efficiency in which information enters into the focus of attention or being off loaded from it to the activated portion of long-term memory.

Some studies that have started looking at the role of components of the embedded-processes approach in age-related declines in the capacity of working memory, have indicated that this decline for spoken language is related to a smaller number of chunks created by older adults (Gilchrist, Cowan, & Naveh-Benjamin, 2009). Other studies used the N-back task to assess age-related declines in working memory that may be due to a decline in focus switching; that is, the ability to shift items from the focus of attention into working memory (probably the activated portion of long-term memory), and back. Verhaeghen et al. (2004, 2019), used an N-back task, in which participants are presented with a sequential list of digits or letters, and are being asked whether the item currently presented matches the item presented N positions in the stream back. It is conceivable that to perform this task, participants pay attention to the current item and store the previously presented items in the activated long-term memory part (what Verhaeghen calls the outer store), and access these items one at a time as needed for comparison with the currently presented item. Age-related differences in such a process of swapping items in and out of the focus of attention (focus switching) was investigated in several studies, with results indicating much larger age-related differences when $N > 1$ than when $N = 1$ (e.g. Basak & Verhaeghen, 2011). These results were confirmed in meta-analysis (Bopp & Verhaeghen, 2018), which showed that across all published studies in the field, the average adult age-related difference for 1-back accuracy was significant (Cohen's $d = 0.50$), but about half the size of that for 2-back accuracy (Cohen's $d = 0.97$). Interestingly, this age-related decline in focus switching was not related to proactive interference or to dual tasking, but once encoding resolution was equated for younger and older adults, no age-related differences were shown in N-back >1, leading Verhaeghen et al. (2019) to claim that one possibility is that there is no age-related decline in focus switching but instead, older adults' deficits may be related to deficits in sensory processing (perceptual and attentional resolution).

Some suggestion raised in the context of age-related changes in long-term memory may have implications to the assessment of age-related changes in working memory. For example, studies on long-term memory suggested the notion of environmental–schematic support as a way to reduce older adults' decline in long-term memory by providing cues and information from semantic memory, a memory system known to be mostly preserved in older adults (Craik, 1983). Such cues may help older adults who are deficient on self-initiated processes. This notion of environmental and schematic support may highlight a potential important role of the activated portion of long-term memory in older adults' working memory performance, possibly as a compensatory mechanism, and it a potential topic for future research.

It stands to reason that the results regarding age-related changes in working memory should mirror what is found in childhood development, and we are currently testing the procedure of Cowan et al. (2018) with older adults. One reasonable prediction is that older adults have a more difficult time controlling attention, but that hypothesis has been only partly confirmed in a procedure involving storage of a list of letters during arithmetic processing (Rhodes et al., 2019). The priority of the storage versus the processing task was manipulated, and it was found that older adults were more impaired by a dual task compared to storage or processing alone, but that they prioritized the two tasks as efficiently as young adults. Other research suggests that they may have a restricted focus of attention compared to younger adults (Naveh-Benjamin et al., 2014), which can also result in binding deficits—both intra-item (Cowan, Naveh-Benjamin, Kilb, & Saults, 2006) and inter-item (Chen & Naveh-Benjamin, 2012). Further studies show that storage of verbal and arithmetic information is relatively preserved compared to spatial information (see chapter by Logie et al., 2021; Park & Festini, 2017); we suspect that the verbal and arithmetic information is better practised.

C. Individual Differences and Limits in Working Memory Capacity

There clearly are both individual and developmental differences in capacity. Given that there are multiple reasons for these differences, Cowan et al. (2005) concentrated on tasks that do not allow rehearsal and seem to index the focus of attention. In such tasks, capacity differences are linked to aptitudes on scholastic and intelligence tests. One especially interesting finding was that ordinary span was closely related to aptitudes in children too young to use rehearsal, but not closely related in older children or adults. In digit span tasks, older children and adults may have the adaptive choice to use rehearsal instead of a more attention-intensive means of remembering (cf. Camos, Mora & Oberauer, 2011; Oftinger & Camos, 2018) and it is the use of attention that relates to aptitudes. This relation could occur for many reasons, one being that learning new information depends on the ability to create new bindings between elements to form and retain new memory traces in a way that depends on the capacity of attention. For example, a young child's understanding of what a tiger is, and is not, depends on noticing and binding the features of being a cat (so, not a zebra), being large (so, not a house cat), and being striped (so, not a lion). This concept formation may depend on the capacity of the focus of attention of working memory.

D. Neuropsychology

The multicomponent model of working memory depends to a large degree on neuropsychological cases in which there is selective deficit in visuospatial working memory maintenance but not verbal-phonological working memory maintenance or vice versa, and no deficit in accompanying acts of perception, motor processing, or long-term recall (e.g. Baddeley, Hitch, & Allen, 2019; Logie, 2016; Shallice & Papagno, 2019). This is a particularly difficult set of conditions to meet. There have been recent reviews from an embedded-processes point of view suggesting that the conditions are not met (Morey, 2018; Morey et al., 2019; but see Hanley & Young, 2019; Logie, 2019; and replies by Morey, 2019; Morey, Rhodes, & Cowan, 2020). Researchers have suggested that it may not be storage in a domain that are deficient, but a particular mnemonic process that is applicable to that one domain, such as verbal rehearsal (Cowan, 1988). Others have suggested that it is the mapping between sensory input and motor response that is affected instead of domain-specific storage (Buchsbaum & D'Esposito, 2019; Morey et al., 2019), that there are processing deficits not specific to short-term or working memory (Surprenant & Neath, 2009), or that the specific short-term memory deficits are aberrant cases of a more general syndrome in which processing is affected, and not just storage (Majerus, 2009).

The Buchsbaum and D'Esposito (2019) position could be viewed as supporting a type of phonological store, but its quality involves processing integrated with storage more than might be suggested in the conventional multicomponent approach. For example, they state, 'We propose that in pure short-term memory cases, where there is relatively preserved spontaneous speech and impaired repetition, that the lexical speech pathway is largely intact, but that the non-lexical (direct phonological input-output mapping) pathway is severely damaged. We further propose that Spt is the critical linking node in this direct input-output pathway' (Buchsbaum and D'Esposito, 2019, p. 141). We believe that the intended implication is that speech perception and production per se are spared in pure short-term memory cases not because they are ordinarily separate from verbal short-term memory, but because they can proceed in these particular cases using the preserved lexical pathway.

Although there many publications on the neuropsychological data (see, e.g. chapters in this volume by Baddeley, Hitch, & Allen, 2021; Martin, Rapp, & Purcell, 2021; Logie, Belletier, & Doherty, 2021) we believe that the field could benefit from a process in which researchers with differing views about working memory do neuropsychological research together in an adversarial collaboration, a method of operation that has proven useful in recent cognitive behavioural research on working memory (e.g. Cowan et al., in press; Doherty et al., 2019; Rhodes et al., 2019). This could help shape future research with an approach in which opposing views might be reconciled, and contradictions resolved.

E. Working Memory Applications of the Embedded-Processes View

We were asked to reply to the following question: *Does your theoretical framework for working memory have any implications for everyday cognition, for example, in accounting for learning, training, mental arithmetic, language learning, prospective remembering, autobiographical remembering, problem solving, decision-making, multitasking, holding conversations, or design of human–digital interaction?* As a heavily attention-dependent view of working memory, the embedded-processes view can be useful in putting forward the notion that people can learn to allocate attention strategically, and therefore can learn to improve their performance on specific tasks of importance to them. The same can be said for any theoretical model with both long-term memory and central executive function. More specific links between the theory and everyday cognition can be found in terms of the control of attention, the capacity of attention in working memory tasks, and the use of activated long-term memory.

Control of attention

One area in which the embedded-processes approach in particular stands out is in understanding the coordination of deliberate and non-deliberate processes in the control of the focus of attention (Cowan, 1988, 1995, 1999). It was suggested that a person continually updates a neural model of the environment. That neural model includes physical features of the entire environment, plus semantic features of the environment for attended items. If a sudden change occurs in an environmental feature that is processed (e.g. a change in the room lighting or sudden noise; a change in topic by an attended speaker) then that change attracts attention. The focus of attention is a struggle between this orienting to changes and the deliberate, voluntary control by central executive processes, which can be directed to some degree through task instructions and payoffs. This approach led to the finding that pre-exposure to a type of stimulus that will later be presented as a distractor can be helpful, as it can be added to the neural model (Elliott & Cowan, 2001).

The approach provides the grounds to understand why it is that low-span young individuals often notice their names presented in an unattended channel in selective listening (Conway, Cowan, & Bunting, 2001) whereas older adults who have equally low spans but are high-functioning for their age rarely notice their names in the unattended channel (Naveh-Benjamin et al., 2014). Apparently, young adults with low spans have a particular problem with attention control and display wandering attention (cf. Kane et al., 2007), which allows attention to wander to the spoken message to be ignored, whereas the older adults examined by Naveh-Benjamin et al. had good attention control but a restricted focus of attention, allowing only mediocre span but with little attention-wandering. The role of the attention-dependent view of working memory in real-life situations can be exemplified by studies that indicate that older adults show working memory deficits in remembering the visual scene context in which a person has been seen (Chen & Naveh-Benjamin, 2012), an inter-item binding deficit that was shown to be mediated by reduced attentional resources (e.g. Peterson et al., 2019).

Capacity of attention

The conception of the embedded-processes model in which the limited capacity of the focus of attention is a core cognitive limit has played an important role in accounting for individual and age differences in cognitive ability. The key reason why studies of working memory capacity have relied on complex span that incorporate both storage and processing (e.g. Engle, Tuholski, Laughlin, & Conway, 1999; see chapter by Mashburn, Tsukahara, & Engle, 2021) is that they engage all aspects of working memory, allowing a better correlation between working memory and cognitive aptitudes (e.g. intelligence test scores, and scholastic achievement and ability scores). From the standpoint of the embedded-processes view, however, these complex span tasks are assumed to show these high correlations primarily because the processing component makes it impossible to complete the task with verbal mnemonic strategies like rehearsal, reducing the need for the focus of attention in the task. Thus, in children too young to rehearse, even simple span tasks correlate well with aptitudes (Cowan et al., 2005); the same is likely to be true in adults with long list lengths that demand attention (cf. Unsworth & Engle, 2007). In running span, in which the endpoint of a long list is unpredictable and recall of as much as possible from the end of the list is required, mnemonic strategies cannot be carried out and attention is critically required at the time of recall (Bunting, Cowan, & Colflesh, 2008). From our point of view it is therefore not surprising that running span correlates highly with aptitudes (Broadway & Engle, 2010; Cowan et al., 2005), assuming aptitudes are attention-dependent. In a latent variable analysis based on many span tasks in 9-year-old children (Gray et al., 2017), it was found that the embedded-processes model outperformed the multicomponent model, largely because acoustically presented running digit span loaded with visual span tasks, thought to require attention (Morey & Bieler, 2013), instead of loading with verbal tasks that presumably allowed mnemonic strategies.

Use of activated long-term memory

The embedded-processes model highlights the difference between a very limited capacity for information in the focus of attention versus a large capacity for information that can be maintained in the activated portion of long-term memory. Thus, the ability to remember items that cannot be rehearsed or memorized easily is typically limited to three to four items in adults and can be attributed to a heavy involvement of the focus of attention (Cowan, 2001), whereas people can retain a much larger number of items that are known objects that do not repeat from trial to trial (Endress & Potter, 2014) or search for large numbers of different known objects at once (Wolfe, 2012), presumably because of persistent activation in long-term memory. Thus, the embedded-processes model has a specific way to bridge the gap between the small limit of working memory in laboratory tasks and the remarkable feats of memory that people often demonstrate in daily life.

Concluding Observations

The embedded-processes model was never intended as a complete model but rather as a framework to be filled in by further findings. As a framework, the embedded-processes model is particularly suited to understanding rich interactions between working memory, attention, and long-term memory. Initially, the supposition was that the activation of unrehearsed items in long-term memory would decay within a number of seconds (Cowan, 1988). Recent findings, however, have suggested that activation decays for poorly consolidated information but lasts considerably longer for well-consolidated information. Poor consolidation can occur either because the materials are rapidly presented and unfamiliar (Ricker & Cowan, 2014) or because the materials are familiar items presented in brief, simultaneous arrays (Ricker et al., 2021; Zhang & Luck, 2009). Activation of clear categories in long-term memory apparently does not decay quickly, but is subject to interference.

The utility of the embedded-processes approach is clear in understanding a recent article on the role of working memory and its limited capacity in determining long-term memory for repeated arrays of items (Fukuda & Vogel, 2019). They first classified individuals as low or high span based on performance on a colour array change-detection task. Then they presented arrays of familiar objects in a change-detection task, followed by long-term memory recognition of these objects, the foils being objects never presented in the arrays. For familiar objects learned in sets of two, long-term recognition did not depend on individual capacity. For objects learned in larger sets of four or six, there was an increasing advantage of high-span individuals over low spans, no matter whether the long-term learning was intentional or incidental. Additional experiments showed that arrays of items repeated in a single-probe change-detection procedure were learned and that, again, the amount of learning of items within supraspan arrays depended on an individual's working memory capacity, and that the amount of time for consolidation of array items had a large effect on the amount of learning. These findings suggest that the focus of attention, with its limited capacity, is the seat of new long-term learning of stimuli and their configurations, as Cowan (1988, 2019) suggested. The embedded-processes model so conceived, with longer-lasting activation for known objects, is useful in understanding how transcranial magnetic stimulation can restore a category of objects back into the focus of attention, but only if this object category is still relevant to the current task (Rose et al., 2016). Activation may be represented not only by ongoing neural activity (e.g. for all input for a short time), but also by longer-lasting changes in synaptic weights (for familiar objects).

People resonate to the embedded-processes view because it provides a basis for understanding that our unified sense of conscious awareness makes sense (originating from the focus of attention) and that our experience of purpose makes sense (originating from central executive processes). It also predicts intrusions of unwanted thoughts that people often experience (originating from changes or significant stimuli in the environment, or unintentionally activated associations from long-term memory). Brain researchers find this view compatible with an organic theory of the brain in which attention does not entail separate re-processing of information, but rather making use of the ongoing processing in other systems (such as sensory input and retrieval from long-term memory) and in some way indexing and enhancing that ongoing processing. The view is ambitious and therefore goes well beyond the kinds of evidence that we have been able to collect in our own laboratories, and may prove most useful because of this attempt to be inclusive of everything known, though at this point there are, at best, many holes left to be filled in.

References

Adam, K. C. S., Vogel, E. K., & Awh, E. (2017). Clear evidence for item limits in visual working memory. *Cognitive Psychology, 97*, 79–97.

Araujo, S. D. F. (2016). *Wundt and the philosophical foundations of psychology: A reappraisal.* Cham, Switzerland: Springer.

Atkinson, R. C., & Shiffrin, R. M. (1968). Human memory: A proposed system and its control processes. In K. W. Spence & J. T. Spence (Eds.), *The psychology of learning and motivation: Advances in research and theory* (Vol. 2, pp. 89–195). New York, NY: Academic Press.

Baars, B. J., & Franklin, S. (2003). How conscious experience and working memory interact. *Trends in Cognitive Sciences, 7,* 166–172.

Baddeley, A. D. (1986). *Working memory.* Oxford, UK: Clarendon Press.

Baddeley, A. (2000). The episodic buffer: a new component of working memory? *Trends in Cognitive Sciences, 4,* 417–423.

Baddeley, A. D., & Hitch, G. (1974). Working memory. In G. H. Bower (Ed.), *The psychology of learning and motivation* (Vol. 8., pp. 47–89). New York, NY: Academic Press.

Baddeley, A. D., Hitch, G. J., & Allen, R. J. (2019). From short-term store to multicomponent working memory: The role of the modal model. *Memory and Cognition, 47,* 575–588.

Baddeley, A. D., Hitch, G. J., & Allen, R. (2021). A Multicomponent Model of Working Memory. In R. H. Logie, V. Camos, & N. Cowan (Eds.), *Working memory: State of the science* (pp. 10–43). Oxford, UK: Oxford University Press.

Barrouillet, P., Portrat, S., & Camos, V. (2011). On the law relating processing to storage in working memory. *Psychological Review, 118,* 175–192.

Basak, C., & Verhaeghen, P. (2011). Aging and switching the focus of attention in working memory: Age differences in item availability, but not item accessibility. *Journals of Gerontology: Psychological Sciences, 66,* 519–526.

Bjork, R. A., & Whitten, W. B. (1974). Recency-sensitive retrieval processes in long term free recall. *Cognitive Psychology, 6,* 173–189.

Bopp, K. L., & Verhaeghen, P. (2005). Aging and verbal memory span: A meta-analysis. *The Journals of Gerontology. Series B, Psychological Sciences and Social Sciences, 60,* 223–233.

Bopp, K. L., & Verhaeghen, P. (2018). Aging and N-back performance: A meta-analysis. *Journals of Gerontology. Series B, Psychological Sciences and Social Sciences, 75,* 229–240.

Brady, T. F., & Alvarez, G. A. (2015). No evidence for a fixed object limit in working memory: Spatial ensemble representations inflate estimates of working memory capacity for complex objects. *Journal of Experimental Psychology: Learning, Memory, and Cognition, 41,* 921–929.

Brady, T. F., & Tenenbaum, J. B. (2013). A probabilistic model of visual working memory: Incorporating higher order regularities into working memory capacity estimates. *Psychological Review, 120,* 85–109.

Broadbent, D. E. (1958). *Perception and communication.* New York, NY: Pergamon Press.

Broadway, J. M., & Engle, R. W. (2010). Validating running memory span: Measurement of working memory capacity and links with fluid intelligence. *Behavior Research Methods, 42,* 563–570.

Broadbent, D. E. (1975). The magic number seven after fifteen years. In A. Kennedy & A. Wilkes (Eds.), *Studies in long term memory* (pp. 3–18). Oxford, UK: John Wiley & Sons.

Buchsbaum, B. R., & D'Esposito, M. (2019). A sensorimotor view of verbal working memory. *Cortex, 112,* 134–148.

Bunting, M. F., Cowan, N., & Colflesh, G. H. (2008). The deployment of attention in short-term memory tasks: Tradeoffs between immediate and delayed deployment. *Memory & Cognition, 36,* 799–812.

Camos, V., Mora, G., & Oberauer, K. (2011). Adaptive choice between articulatory rehearsal and attentional refreshing in verbal working memory. *Memory & Cognition, 39,* 231–244.

Carroll, L. M., Jalbert, A., Penney, A. M., Neath, I., Surprenant, A. M., & Tehan, G. (2010). Evidence for proactive interference in the focus of attention of working memory, *Canadian Journal of Experimental Psychology, 64,* 208–214.

Case, R., Kurland, D. M., & Goldberg, J. (1982). Operational efficiency and the growth of short term memory span. *Journal of Experimental Child Psychology, 33,* 386–404.

Chein, J. M., & Fiez, J. A. (2010). Evaluating models of working memory through the effects of concurrent irrelevant information. *Journal of Experimental Psychology: General, 139,* 117–137.

Chekaf, M., Cowan, N., & Mathy, F. (2016). Chunk formation in immediate memory and how it relates to data compression. *Cognition, 155*, 96–107.

Chen, T., & Naveh-Benjamin, M. (2012). Assessing the associative deficit of older adults in long-term and short-term/working memory. *Psychology and Aging, 27*, 666–682.

Chen, Z., & Cowan, N. (2009). Core verbal working memory capacity: The limit in words retained without covert articulation. *Quarterly Journal of Experimental Psychology, 62*, 1420–1429.

Cherry, E. C. (1953). Some experiments on the recognition of speech, with one and with two ears. *The Journal of the Acoustical Society of America, 25*, 975–979.

Chong, S. C., & Treisman, A. (2003). Representation of statistical properties. *Vision Research, 43*, 393–404.

Clark, K. M., Hardman, K., Schachtman, T. R., Saults, J. S., Glass, B. A., & Cowan, N. (2018). Tone series and the nature of working memory capacity development. *Developmental Psychology, 54*, 663–676.

Conway, A. R. A., Cowan, N., & Bunting, M. F. (2001). The cocktail party phenomenon revisited: The importance of working memory capacity. *Psychonomic Bulletin & Review, 8*, 331–335.

Conway, A. R. A., Kane, M. J., Bunting, M. F., Hambrick, D. Z., Wilhelm, O., & Engle, R. W. (2005). Working memory span tasks: A methodological review & user's guide. *Psychonomic Bulletin & Review, 12*, 769–786.

Cowan, N. (1988). Evolving conceptions of memory storage, selective attention, and their mutual constraints within the human information processing system. *Psychological Bulletin, 104*, 163–191.

Cowan, N. (1992). Verbal memory span and the timing of spoken recall. *Journal of Memory and Language, 31*, 668–684.

Cowan, N. (1995). *Attention and memory: An integrated framework.* Oxford Psychology Series, No. 26. New York, NY: Oxford University Press.

Cowan, N. (1999). An embedded-processes model of working memory. In A. Miyake & P. Shah (Eds.), *Models of working memory: Mechanisms of active maintenance and executive control* (pp. 62–101). Cambridge, UK: Cambridge University Press.

Cowan, N. (2001). The magical number 4 in short-term memory: A reconsideration of mental storage capacity. *Behavioral and Brain Sciences, 24*, 87–185.

Cowan, N. (2005/2016). *Working memory capacity.* Psychology Press and Routledge Classic Edition. New York, NY: Routledge. [Original edition 2005. New Foreword to the Classic Edition.]

Cowan, N. (2011). The focus of attention as observed in visual working memory tasks: Making sense of competing claims. *Neuropsychologia, 49*, 1401–1406.

Cowan, N. (2016). Working memory maturation: Can we get at the essence of cognitive growth? *Perspectives on Psychological Science, 11*, 239–264.

Cowan, N. (2017a). The many faces of working memory and short-term storage. *Psychonomic Bulletin & Review, 24*, 1158–1170.

Cowan, N. (2017b). Mental objects in working memory: Development of basic capacity or of cognitive completion? *Advances in Child Development and Behavior, 52*, 81–104.

Cowan, N. (2019). Short-term memory based on activated long-term memory: A review in response to Norris (2017). *Psychological Bulletin, 145*, 822–847.

Cowan, N., Belletier, C., Doherty, J. M., Jaroslawska, A. J., Rhodes, S., Forsberg, A., . . . Logie, R. H. (in press). How do scientific views change? Notes from an extended adversarial collaboration. *Perspectives on Psychological Science.*

Cowan, N., Blume, C. L., & Saults, J. S. (2013). Attention to attributes and objects in working memory. *Journal of Experimental Psychology: Learning, Memory, and Cognition, 39*, 731–747.

Cowan, N., Donnell, K., & Saults, J. S. (2013). A list-length constraint on incidental item-to-item associations. *Psychonomic Bulletin & Review, 20*, 1253–1258.

Cowan, N., Elliott, E. M., & Saults, J. S. (2002). The search for what is fundamental in the development of working memory. *Advances in Child Development and Behavior, 29*, 1–49.

Cowan, N., Elliott, E. M., Saults, J. S., Morey, C. C., Mattox, S., Hismjatullina, A., & Conway, A. R. A. (2005). On the capacity of attention: Its estimation and its role in working memory and cognitive aptitudes. *Cognitive Psychology, 51*, 42–100.

Cowan, N., Hardman, K., Saults, J. S., Blume, C. L., Clark, K. M., & Sunday, M. A. (2016). Detection of the number of changes in a display in working memory. *Journal of Experimental Psychology: Learning, Memory, and Cognition, 42,* 169–185.

Cowan, N., Johnson, T. D., & Saults, J. S. (2005). Capacity limits in list item recognition: Evidence from proactive interference. *Memory, 13,* 293–299.

Cowan, N., Li, D., Moffitt, A., Becker, T. M., Martin, E. A., Saults, J. S., & Christ, S. E. (2011). A neural region of abstract working memory. *Journal of Cognitive Neuroscience, 23,* 2852–2863.

Cowan, N., Li, Y., Glass, B., & Saults, J. S. (2018). Development of the ability to combine visual and acoustic information in working memory. *Developmental Science, 21,* e12635, 1–14.

Cowan, N., Naveh-Benjamin, M., Kilb, A., & Saults, J. S. (2006). Life-Span development of visual working memory: When is feature binding difficult? *Developmental Psychology, 42,* 1089–1102.

Cowan, N., & Rachev, N. R. (2018), Merging with the path not taken: Wilhelm Wundt's work as a precursor to the embedded-processes approach to memory, attention, and consciousness. *Consciousness and Cognition, 63,* 228–238.

Cowan, N., Rouder, J. N., Blume, C. L., & Saults, J. S. (2012). Models of verbal working memory capacity: What does it take to make them work? *Psychological Review, 119,* 480–499.

Cowan, N., Saults, J. S., & Blume, C. L. (2014). Central and peripheral components of working memory storage. *Journal of Experimental Psychology: General, 143,* 1806–1836.

Cowan, N., Winkler, I., Teder, W., & Näätänen, R. (1993). Memory prerequisites of the mismatch negativity in the auditory event-related potential (ERP). *Journal of Experimental Psychology: Learning, Memory, & Cognition, 19,* 909–921.

Cowan, N., Wood, N. L., Wood, P. K., Keller, T. A., Nugent, L. D., & Keller, C. V. (1998). Two separate verbal processing rates contributing to short-term memory span. *Journal of Experimental Psychology: General, 127,* 141–160.

Craik, F. I. M. (1983). On the transfer of information from temporary to permanent memory. *Philosophical Transactions of the Royal Society of London, Series B, 302,* 341–359.

Crowder, R. G. (1976). *Principles of learning & memory.* Hillsdale, NJ: Erlbaum.

Cusack, R., Lehmann, M., Veldsman, M., & Mitchell, D. J. (2009). Encoding strategy and not visual working memory capacity correlates with intelligence. *Psychonomic Bulletin & Review, 16,* 641–647.

Daneman, M., & Carpenter, P. A. (1980). Individual differences in working memory and reading. *Journal of Verbal Learning & Verbal Behavior, 19,* 450–466.

Diamond, A., & Lee, K. (2011). Interventions shown to aid executive function development in children 4 to 12 years old. *Science 333,* 959–964.

Doherty, J. M., Belletier, C., Rhodes, S., Jaroslawska, A. J., Barrouillet, P., Camos, V., . . . Logie, R. H. (2019). Dual-task costs in working memory: An adversarial collaboration. *Journal of Experimental Psychology: Learning, Memory, and Cognition, 45,* 1529–1551.

Donkin, C., Nosofsky, R. M., Gold, J. M., & Shiffrin, R. M. (2013). Discrete-slots models of visual working-memory response times. *Psychological Review, 120,* 873–902.

Donkin, C., Tran, S. C., & Nosofsky, R. (2014). Landscaping analyses of the ROC predictions of discrete-slots and signal-detection models of visual working memory. *Attention, Perception, & Psychophysics, 76,* 2103–2116.

Elliott, E. M., & Cowan, N. (2001). Habituation to auditory distractors in a cross-modal, color-word interference task. *Journal of Experimental Psychology: Learning, Memory, & Cognition, 27,* 654–667.

Endress, A. D., & Potter, M. C. (2014). Large capacity temporary visual memory. *Journal of Experimental Psychology: General, 143,* 548–566.

Engle, R. W., Tuholski, S. W., Laughlin, J. E., & Conway, A. R. A. (1999). Working memory, short-term memory, and general fluid intelligence: a latent-variable approach. *Journal of Experimental Psychology: General, 128,* 309–331.

Ericsson, K. A., Chase, W. G., & Faloon, S. (1980). Acquisition of a memory skill. *Science, 208,* 1181–1182.

Frey, S. H., Vinton, D., Norlund, R., & Grafton, S. T. (2005). Cortical topography of human anterior intraparietal cortex active during visually guided grasping. *Cognitive Brain Research, 23,* 397–405.

Fukuda, K., & Vogel, E. K. (2019). Visual short-term memory capacity predicts the "bandwidth" of visual long-term memory encoding. *Memory & Cognition, 47,* 1481–1497.

Gilchrist, A. L., & Cowan, N. (2011). Can the focus of attention accommodate multiple separate items? *Journal of Experimental Psychology: Learning, Memory, and Cognition, 37,* 1484–1502.

Gilchrist A. L., Cowan, N., & Naveh-Benjamin, M. (2009). Investigating the childhood development of working memory using sentences: New evidence for the growth of chunk capacity. *Journal of Experimental Child Psychology, 104,* 252–265.

Glanzer, M., & Razel, M. (1974). The size of the unit in short term storage. *Journal of Verbal Learning & Verbal Behavior, 13,* 114–131.

Glenberg, A. M., & Swanson, N. C. (1986). A temporal distinctiveness theory of recency and modality effects. *Journal of Experimental Psychology: Learning, Memory, & Cognition, 12,* 3–15.

Graesser, A., II, & Mandler, G. (1978). Limited processing capacity constrains the storage of unrelated sets of words and retrieval from natural categories. *Journal of Experimental Psychology: Human Learning and Memory, 4,* 86–100.

Gray, S., Green, S., Alt, M., Hogan, T., Kuo, T., Brinkley, S., & Cowan, N. (2017). The structure of working memory in young school-age children and its relation to intelligence. *Journal of Memory and Language, 92,* 183–201.

Guttentag, R. E. (1984). The mental effort requirement of cumulative rehearsal: A developmental study. *Journal of Experimental Child Psychology, 37,* 92–106.

Hanley, J. R., & Young, A. W. (2019). ELD revisited: A second look at a neuropsychological impairment of working memory affecting retention of visuo-spatial material. *Cortex, 112,* 172–179.

Hardman, K., & Cowan, N. (2015). Remembering complex objects in visual working memory: Do capacity limits restrict objects or features? *Journal of Experimental Psychology: Learning, Memory, and Cognition, 41,* 325–347.

Hasher, L., & Zacks, R. T. (1988). Working memory, comprehension, and aging: A review and a new view. In G. H. Bower (Ed.), *The psychology of learning and motivation* (Vol. 22, pp. 193–225). San Diego, CA: Academic Press.

Hebb, D. O. (1949). *Organization of behavior.* New York, NY: Wiley.

Hebb, D. O. (1961). Distinctive features of learning in the higher animal. In J. F. Delafresnaye (Ed.), *Brain mechanisms and learning* (pp. 37–46). Oxford, UK: Blackwell.

Henson, R. N. A., Norris, D. G., Page, M. P. A., & Baddeley, A. D. (1996). Unchained memory: Error patterns rule out chaining models of immediate serial recall. *Quarterly Journal of Experimental Psychology (A): Human Experimental Psychology, 49,* 80–115.

James, W. (1890). *The principles of psychology.* NY: Henry Holt.

Jiang, Y., Olson, I. R., & Chun, M. M. (2000). Organization of visual short-term memory. *Journal of Experimental Psychology: Learning, Memory, & Cognition, 26,* 683–702.

Kail, R., & Salthouse, T. A. (1994). Processing speed as a mental capacity. *Acta Psychologica, 86,* 199–255.

Kane, M. J., Brown, L. H., McVay, J. C., Silvia, P. J., Myin-Germeys, I., & Kwapil, T. R. (2007). For whom the mind wanders, and when: An experience sampling study of working memory and executive control in daily life. *Psychological Science, 18,* 614–621.

Lange, E., & Engbert, R. (2013). Differentiating between verbal and spatial encoding using eye-movement recordings. *Quarterly Journal of Experimental Psychology, 66,* 1840–1857.

Lashley, K. S. (1950). In search of the engram. *Proceedings from Society for Experimental Biology, 4,* 454–482.

Lemaire, B., Pageot, A., Plancher, G., & Portrat, S. (2018). What is the time course of working memory attentional refreshing? *Psychonomic Bulletin & Review, 25,* 370–385.

Lewis-Peacock, J. A., Drysdale, A. T., Oberauer, K., & Postle, B. R. (2012). Neural evidence for a distinction between short-term memory and the focus of attention. *Journal of Cognitive Neuroscience, 24,* 61–79.

Li, D., Christ, S. E., & Cowan, N. (2014). Domain-general and domain-specific functional networks in working memory. *Neuroimage, 102,* 646–656.

Loaiza, V. M. and McCabe, D. P. (2012). Temporal–contextual processing in working memory: Evidence from delayed cued recall and delayed free recall tests. *Memory & Cognition. 40,* 191–203.

Logie, R. H. (1995). *Visuo-spatial working memory.* Hove, UK: Erlbaum.

Logie, R. H. (2016). Retiring the central executive. *Quarterly Journal of Experimental Psychology, 69,* 2093–2109.

Logie, R. H. (2019). Converging sources of evidence and theory integration in working memory: A commentary on Morey, Rhodes, and Cowan (2019). *Cortex, 112,* 162–171.

Logie, R. H., Belletier, C., & Doherty, J. D. (2021). Integrating theories of working memory. In R. H. Logie, V. Camos, & N. Cowan (Eds.), *Working memory: State of the science* (pp. 389–429). Oxford, UK: Oxford University Press.

Logie, R. H., Brockmole, J. R., & Vandenbroucke, A. R. E. (2009). Bound feature combinations in visual short-term memory are fragile but influence long-term learning. *Visual Cognition, 17,* 160–179.

Logie, R. H., & Cowan, N. (2015). Perspectives on working memory: Introduction to the special issue. *Memory & Cognition, 43,* 315–324.

Luck, S. J., & Vogel, E. K. (1997). The capacity of visual working memory for features and conjunctions. *Nature, 390,* 279–281.

Majerus, S. (2009). Verbal short-term memory and temporary activation of language representations: The importance of distinguishing between item and order information. In A. Thorn & M. Page (Eds.), *Interactions between short-term and long-term memory in the verbal domain* (pp. 244–276). Hove, UK: Psychology Press.

Majerus, S., Cowan, N., Péters, F., Van Calster, L., Phillips, C., & Schrouff, J. (2016). Cross-modal decoding of neural patterns associated with working memory: Evidence for attention-based accounts of working memory. *Cerebral Cortex, 26,* 166–179.

Majerus, S., Péters, F., Bouffier, M., Cowan, N., & Phillips, C. (2018). The dorsal attention network reflects both encoding load and top-down control during working memory. *Journal of Cognitive Neuroscience, 30,* 144–159.

Martin, R. C., Rapp, B., & Purcell, J. (2021). Domain-specific working memory: Perspectives from cognitive neuropsychology. In R. H. Logie, V. Camos, & N. Cowan (Eds.), *Working memory: State of the science* (pp. 235–281). Oxford, UK: Oxford University Press.

McClelland, J. L. (1979). On the time relations of mental processes: An examination of systems of processes in cascade. *Psychological Review, 86,* 287–330.

McClelland, J. L., & Rumelhart, D. E. (1985). Distributed memory and the representation of general and specific information. *Journal of Experimental Psychology: General, 114,* 159–188.

Morey, C. (2018). The case against specialized visual-spatial short-term memory. *Psychological Bulletin, 144,* 849–883.

Morey, C. C. (2019). Working memory theory remains stuck: Reply to Hanley and Young. *Cortex, 112,* 180–181.

Morey, C. C., & Bieler, M. (2013). Visual short-term memory always requires attention. *Psychonomic Bulletin & Review, 20,* 163–170.

Morey, C. C., Mareva, S., Lelonkiewicz, J., & Chevalier, N. (2018). Gaze-based rehearsal in children under 7: A developmental investigation of eye movements during a serial spatial memory task. *Developmental Science, 21,* e12559, 1–8.

Morey, C. C., Rhodes, S., & Cowan, N. (2019). Sensory-motor integration and brain lesions: Progress toward explaining domain-specific phenomena within domain-general working memory. *Cortex, 112,* 149–161.

Morey, C. C., Rhodes, S., & Cowan. N. (2020). Co-existing, contradictory working memory models are ready for progressive refinement: Reply to Logie. *Cortex, 123,* 200–202.

Morris, C. D., Bransford, J. D., Franks, J. J. (1977). Levels of processing versus transfer appropriate processing. *Journal of Verbal Learning and Verbal Behavior. 16:* 519–533.

Murdock, B. B. (1967). Recent developments in short-term memory. *British Journal of Psychology, 58,* 421–433.

Nairne, J. S. (1990). A feature model of immediate memory. *Memory & Cognition, 18*, 251–269.

Nairne, J. S., & Neath, I. (2001). Long term memory span. *Behavioral and Brain Sciences, 24*, 134–135.

Naveh-Benjamin, M., & Jonides, J. (1984). Maintenance rehearsal: A two component analysis. *Journal of Experimental Psychology: Learning, Memory, and Cognition, 10*, 369–385.

Naveh-Benjamin, M., Kilb, A., Maddox, G., Thomas, J., Fine, H., Chen, T., & Cowan, N. (2014). Older adults don't notice their names: A new twist to a classic attention task. *Journal of Experimental Psychology: Learning, Memory, and Cognition, 40*, 1540–1550.

Norris, D. (2017). Short-term memory and long-term memory are still different. *Psychological Bulletin, 143*, 992–1009.

Norris, D. (2019). Even an activated long-term memory system still needs a separate short-term store: A reply to Cowan (2019). *Psychological Bulletin, 145*, 848–853.

Nosofsky, R. M., & Donkin, C. (2016). Qualitative contrast between knowledge-limited mixed-state and variable-resources models of visual change detection. *Journal of Experimental Psychology: Learning, Memory, and Cognition, 42*, 1507–1525.

Nosofsky, R. M., & Gold, J. M. (2018). Biased guessing in a complete-identification visual-working-memory task: Further evidence for mixed-state models. *Journal of Experimental Psychology: Human Perception and Performance, 44*, 603–625.

Oberauer, K. (2002). Access to information in working memory: exploring the focus of attention. *Journal of Experimental Psychology: Learning, Memory, and Cognition, 28*, 411–421.

Oberauer, K. (2013). The focus of attention in working memory—From metaphors to mechanisms. *Frontiers in Human Neuroscience, 7*, Article ID 673. doi:10.3389/fnhum.2013.00673

Oberauer K., Awh E., & Sutterer D. W. (2017). The role of long-term memory in a test of visual working memory: Proactive facilitation but no proactive interference. *Journal of Experimental Psychology: Learning, Memory, and Cognition, 43*, 1–22.

Oberauer, K., & Bialkova, S. (2009). Accessing information in working memory: Can the focus of attention grasp two elements at the same time? *Journal of Experimental Psychology: General, 138*, 64–87.

Oberauer, K., & Eichenberger, S. (2013). Visual working memory declines when more features must be remembered for each object. *Memory & Cognition, 41*, 1212–1227.

Oberauer, K., & Lewandowsky, S. (2008). Forgetting in immediate serial recall: decay, temporal distinctiveness, or interference? *Psychological Review, 115*, 544–576.

Oberauer, K., & Lin, H. Y. (2017). An interference model of visual working memory. *Psychological Review, 124*, 21–59.

Oftinger, A-L., & Camos, V. (2018). Developmental improvement in strategies to maintain verbal information in children's working memory. *International Journal of Behavioral Development, 42*, 182–191.

Osth, A. F., & Dennis, S. (2015). Prior-list intrusions in serial recall are positional. *Journal of Experimental Psychology: Learning, Memory, and Cognition, 41*, 1893–1901.

Park, D. C., & Festini, S. B. (2017). Theories of memory and aging: A look at the past and a glimpse of the future. *Journals of Gerontology, Series B: Psychological Sciences and Social Sciences, 72*, 82–90.

Pashler, H. (1988). Familiarity and visual change detection. *Perception & Psychophysics, 44*, 369–378.

Peterson, D. J., Decker, R., & Naveh-Benjamin, M. (2019). Further studies on the role of attention and stimulus repetition in item-item binding processes in visual working memory. *Journal of Experimental Psychology: Learning, Memory, and Cognition, 45*, 56–70.

Postle, B. R. (2021). Cognitive neuroscience of visual working memory. In R. H. Logie, V. Camos, & N. Cowan (Eds.), *Working memory: State of the science* (pp. 333–357). Oxford, UK: Oxford University Press.

Postle, B. R., Ferrarelli, F., Hamidi, M., Feredoes, E., Massimini, M., Peterson, M., . . . Tononi, G. (2006). Repetitive transcranial magnetic stimulation dissociates working memory manipulation from retention functions in the prefrontal, but not posterior parietal, cortex. *Journal of Cognitive Neuroscience, 18*, 1712–1722.

Pratte, M. S. (2019). Swap errors in spatial working memory are guesses. *Psychonomic Bulletin & Review, 26*, 958–966.

Price, G. R., Mazzocco, M. M. M., & Ansari, D. (2013). Why mental arithmetic counts: Brain activation during single digit arithmetic predicts high school math scores. *Journal of Neuroscience, 33,* 156–163.

Redick, T. S., Shipstead, Z., Harrison, T. L., Hicks, K. L., Fried, D. E., Hambrick, D. Z., . . . Engle, R. W. (2013). No evidence of intelligence improvement after working memory training: A randomized, placebo-controlled study. *Journal of Experimental Psychology: General, 142,* 359–379.

Raye, C. L., Johnson, M. K., Mitchell, K. J., Greene, E. J., & Johnson, M. R. (2007). Refreshing: A minimal executive function. *Cortex, 43,* 135–145.

Rhodes, S., Cowan, N., Hardman, K. O., & Logie, R. H. (2018). Informed guessing in change detection. *Journal of Experimental Psychology: Learning, Memory, and Cognition, 44,* 1023–1035.

Rhodes, S., Jaroslawska, A. J., Doherty, J. M., Belletier, C., Naveh-Benjamin, M., Cowan, N., . . . Logie, R. H. (2019). Storage and processing in working memory: Assessing dual task performance and task prioritization across the adult lifespan. *Journal of Experimental Psychology: General, 148,* 1204–1227.

Ricker, T. J., & Cowan, N. (2014). Differences between presentation methods in working memory procedures: A matter of working memory consolidation. *Journal of Experimental Psychology: Learning, Memory, and Cognition, 40,* 417–428.

Ricker, T. J., Sandry, J., Vergauwe, E., & Cowan, N. (2020). Do familiar memory items decay? *Journal of Experimental Psychology: Learning, Memory, and Cognition, 46,* 60–76.

Ricker, T. J., Spiegel, L. R., & Cowan, N. (2014). Time-based loss in visual short-term memory is from trace decay, not temporal distinctiveness. *Journal of Experimental Psychology: Learning, Memory, and Cognition, 40,* 1510–1523.

Rose, N. S., LaRocque, J. J., Riggall, A. C., Gosseries, O., Starrett, M. J., Meyering, E. E., & Postle, B. R. (2016). Reactivation of latent working memories with transcranial magnetic stimulation. *Science, 354,* 1136–1139.

Rouder, J. N., Morey, R. D., Cowan, N., Zwilling, C. E., Morey, C. C., & Pratte, M. S. (2008). An assessment of fixed-capacity models of visual working memory. *Proceedings of the National Academy of Sciences of the United States of America, 105,* 5975–5979.

Rouder, J. N., Morey, R. D., Morey, C. C., & Cowan, N. (2011). How to measure working memory capacity in the change-detection paradigm. *Psychonomic Bulletin & Review, 18,* 324–330.

Rouder, J. N., Thiele, J. E., & Cowan, N. (2014, November). Evidence for guessing in working-memory judgments. Paper presented at the 55th annual meeting of the Psychonomic Society. Retrieved from https://pdfs.semanticscholar.org/2663/069179fcf08aa60db37649f4ad8456871c9d.pdf

Salthouse, T. A. (1996). The processing-speed theory of adult age differences in cognition. *Psychological Review, 103,* 403–428.

Saults, J. S., & Cowan, N. (2007). A central capacity limit to the simultaneous storage of visual and auditory arrays in working memory. *Journal of Experimental Psychology: General, 136,* 663–684.

Shallice, T., & Papagno, C. (2019). Impairments of auditory-verbal short-term memory: Do selective deficits of the input phonological buffer exist? *Cortex, 112,* 102–121.

Shimi, A., & Logie, R. H. (2019). Feature binding in short-term memory and long-term learning. *Quarterly Journal of Experimental Psychology, 72,* 1387–1400.

Simon, H. A. (1974). How big is a chunk? *Science, 183,* 482–488.

Sokolov, E. N. (1963). *Perception and the conditioned reflex.* New York, NY: Pergamon Press.

Sperling, G. (1960). The information available in brief visual presentations. *Psychological Monographs, 74,* 1–29.

Sternberg, S. (1969). The discovery of processing stages: Extensions of Donders' method. *Acta Psychologica, 30,* 276–315.

Stokes, M. G. (2015). 'Activity-silent' working memory in prefrontal cortex: A dynamic coding framework. *Trends in Cognitive Sciences, 19,* 394–405.

Surprenant, A. M., & Neath, I. (2009). The nine lives of short-term memory. In A. Thorn & M. Page (Eds.), *Interactions between short-term and long-term memory in the verbal domain* (pp. 16–43). Hove, UK: Psychology Press.

Todd, J. J., & Marois, R. (2004). Capacity limit of visual short-term memory in human posterior parietal cortex. *Nature, 428,* 751–754.

Treisman, A. M. (1964). Selective attention in man. *British Medical Bulletin, 20*, 12–16.

Tzeng, O. J. L. (1973). Positive recency effect in a delayed free recall. *Journal of Verbal Learning & Verbal Behavior, 12*, 436–439.

Unsworth, N., & Engle, R. W. (2007). The nature of individual differences in working memory capacity: Active maintenance in primary memory and controlled search from secondary memory. *Psychological Review, 114*, 104–132.

Verhaeghen, P., Cerella, J., & Basak, C. (2004). A working memory workout: How to change to size of the focus of attention from one to four in ten hours or less. *Journal of Experimental Psychology: Learning, Memory, and Cognition, 30*, 1322–1337.

Verhaeghen, P., Geierman, S., Yang, H., Montoya, A. C., & Rahnev, D. (2019). Resolving age-related differences in working memory: Equating perception and attention makes older adults remember as well as younger adults. *Experimental Aging Research, 45*, 120–134.

Wheeler, M. E., & Treisman, A. M. (2002). Binding in short term visual memory. *Journal of Experimental Psychology: General, 131*, 48–64.

Wijeakumar, S. & Spencer, J. (2021). A dynamic field theory of visual working memory. In R. H. Logie, V. Camos, & N. Cowan (Eds.), *Working memory: State of the science* (pp. 358–388). Oxford, UK: Oxford University Press.

Winkler, I., Schröger, E., & Cowan, N. (2001). The role of large-scale memory organization in the mismatch negativity event-related brain potential. *Journal of Cognitive Neuroscience, 13*, 59–71.

Wolfe, J. M. (2012). Saved by a log: How do humans perform hybrid visual and memory search? *Psychological Science, 23*, 698–703.

Yue, Q., Martin, R. C., Hamilton, A. C., & Rose, N. S. (2019). Non-perceptual regions in the left inferior parietal lobe support phonological short-term memory: Evidence for a buffer account? *Cerebral Cortex, 29*, 1398–1413.

Zaretskaya, N., Thielscher, A., Logothetis, N. K., & Bartels, A. (2010). Disrupting parietal function prolongs dominance durations in binocular rivalry. *Current Biology, 20*, 2106–2111.

Zhang, W., & Luck, S. J. (2008). Discrete fixed-resolution representations in visual working memory. *Nature, 453*, 23–35.

Zhang, W., & Luck, S. J. (2009). Sudden death and gradual decay in visual working memory. *Psychological Science, 20*, 423–428.

Zosh, J. M., & Feigenson, L. (2012). Memory load affects object individuation in 18-month-old infants. *Journal of Experimental Child Psychology, 113*, 322–336.

4

The Time-Based Resource-Sharing Model
of Working Memory

Pierre Barrouillet and Valérie Camos

As Cowan (2017) convincingly showed in a recent review, although WM is for psychological science a relatively new concept that only emerged in the late fifties of the last century
(Miller, Galanter, & Pribam, 1960), this concept has received a surprising variety of definitions reflecting a startling diversity of conceptions. The different contributions in the present volume constitute a good illustration of this diversity. However, rather than the inability
of psychologists to identify the main characteristics and functions of WM, this diversity of
definitions could reflect the complexity of this object of study. As the keystone of human
cognitive architecture, the 'hub of cognition' as Haberlandt (1997) said, WM maintains relations with almost all the cognitive systems and structures and provides a variety of functions
that defy any attempt to reach an all-encompassing definition, and possibly, theoretical
description. It is thus not so surprising that, depending on the perspective they adopt, the
function they favour, and the boundaries they draw between what does and does not belong
to WM within the cognitive system, different authors propose definitions that at first sight
do not seem to apply to one and the same object. In this chapter, we present our own conception synthesized in a model named the TBRS model. Initially inspired from the work by
John Towse and Graham Hitch (1995; Towse, Hitch, & Hutton, 1998, 2002) who stressed the
importance of temporal factors such as processing speed and temporal decay in explaining
WM development, and on the cognitive architecture proposed by John R. Anderson in
the successive versions of his ACT model (Anderson, 1983, 1993; Anderson et al., 2004;
Anderson & Lebiere, 1998), the TBRS model is intended to provide an account of WM as
a multifaceted cognitive system. As we recently argued (Camos & Barrouillet, 2018) and as
we will develop in the present chapter, the TBRS model views WM as a representational medium where representations are constructed, elaborated, and modified, an operation centre
that constitutes the seat of thought and intelligence, and ultimately as a learning device.

A Definition of Working Memory

Among the different definitions made possible by the conception of a working memory
(WM) as a multifaceted cognitive system, we propose to favour the definition of WM as a
structure where mental representations are built, maintained, or modified according to our

Pierre Barrouillet and Valérie Camos, *The Time-Based Resource-Sharing Model of Working Memory* In: *Working Memory.*
Edited by: Robert H. Logie, Valérie Camos, and Nelson Cowan, Oxford University Press (2021). © Oxford University Press.
DOI: 10.1093/oso/9780198842286.003.0004

Table 4.1 The seven designated questions and some optional questions

Question	Response
1. Definition of working memory (WM)	WM is the structure where mental representations are built, maintained, and modified according to our goals.
2. Describe and explain the methods you use, and their strengths and limitations	We have developed computer-paced complex span tasks in which each memory item is followed by a series of to-be-processed items presented at a predefined pace. This design has been generalized to the Brown–Peterson paradigm. The strength of our method is that it (a) mimics the interplay between processing and storage taking place in WM and (b) allows for a strict control of the time course of the successive cognitive operations. These tasks proved to be good predictors of school achievement and performance in high-level cognitive activities. However, they might constitute an oversimplification of the complex alternations taking place between processing and storage in real-life activities, and probably prevent us having access to the flexibility and adaptivity of human behaviour on daily dual-task situations.
3. Unitary versus non-unitary nature of working memory	The time-based resource-sharing (TBRS) model endorses a non-unitary view of memory in which WM is a separate system that interacts with LTM. Moreover, the TBRS model depicts WM as a domain-general system for both processing and storage of any kind of information supplemented by an independent domain-specific mechanism for verbal maintenance through articulatory rehearsal.
4. The role of attention and control	In the TBRS model, attention is considered as a domain-general resource shared by both processing and storage activities in a time-based manner. 'Paying attention to' is here coextensive with the fact of currently forming and manipulating a representation in the episodic buffer. Cognitive control does not require any homunculus or central executive, but is an emerging property of goal-directed WM functioning.
5. Storage, maintenance, and loss of information in working memory	The TBRS model assumes that information is encoded as composite multimodal representations (phonological, auditory, visual, spatial, ordinal, semantic, etc.) stored in an episodic buffer. These representations suffer from temporal decay and representation-based interference as soon as attention is switched away. Thus, maintenance requires a frequent attentional refreshing of decaying memory traces. Verbal information can additionally be encoded as articulatory programmes that can be maintained through articulatory rehearsal.
6. The role of long-term memory knowledge in working memory storage and processing	Declarative LTM provides tokens to build mental representations in WM, while procedural LTM provides procedures that act on these representations. Thus, LTM knowledge facilitates encoding and processing of information, increasing WM capacity. The tokens gathered within WM representations coalesce into representational units leaving footprints in LTM through associative learning.
7. Is there evidence that is not consistent with your theoretical framework, and how does your framework address that inconsistency?	Two main findings can be seen as non-consistent with the TBRS model. First, some tasks (e.g. visual search) and memoranda (e.g. unfamiliar characters, fonts, faces) proved to not lead to cognitive load effect when inserted in WM tasks. Accounting for this might require to assume different types of attention (e.g. controlled vs visual attention in the visual search) or to modulate the TBRS predictions as a function of the mode of memory assessment (recall vs recognition). Second, surprisingly good WM performance is often observed under high concurrent cognitive load. This necessitates the additional reliance on some passive maintenance in episodic LTM.

Table 4.1 Continued

Question	Response
A. Early life development	Age-related increase in WM capacity results from three main sources: increased processing speed that shortens duration of maintenance preserves WM traces from decay; increased refreshing efficiency; and availability of maintenance mechanisms (attentional refreshing and articulatory rehearsal).
C. Individual differences and limits in working memory capacity	The number of representations that can be held in WM and that define its capacity depends on the speed at which they can be refreshed, on their speed of decay, and on processing speed and pace of processing in dual-task settings. The existence of a structural upper limit in this number is not excluded. WM representations might also be limited in their maximal complexity, mainly due to attentional limits.
D. Neural correlates	We have gathered some evidence through functional magnetic resonance imaging and electroencephalography about the neural correlates for rapid switching and for the existence of attentional refreshing.
F. Working memory applications	The TBRS model has been applied in the domain of learning, stressing the importance of the rate at which information is presented. Young children's performance can be largely improved by adapting the temporal schedule of their activities. More generally, as in Chaplin's film *Modern Times*, attentional overload can become unbearable when the rhythm of even very simple tasks increases drastically.

current goals, with most of the other properties of WM resulting from this premise. These representations constitute the momentary phenomenal experience, the current content of our consciousness. Following Dulany (1991, 1997) and the self-organizing consciousness theory of Perruchet and Vinter (2002), the time-based resource-sharing (TBRS) model assumes that the only representations people create are built and stored in WM. Contrary to other prominent WM theories (Cowan, 2005; Engle, 2002; Oberauer, 2002; Shipstead, Harrison, & Engle, 2016; see chapters by Cowan, Morey, & Naveh-Benjamin, 2021; Mashburn, Tsukahara, & Engle, 2021; Oberauer, 2021), we do not think that WM contains long-term memory (LTM) representations activated above threshold. WM representations are constructed from information retrieved from LTM, but we think that this information is not representational in nature. It might be thought of as 'atoms' of representation in the same way as that our computers do not store texts, images, or music but codes that permit them to be recreated through the appropriate interfaces. Things are probably even more complex in our minds because the successive encounters with items pertaining to a same category (e.g. the myriad of cats we have seen in our life) have probably left sufficient information to create an infinity of different visual (or auditory) representations of the item 'cat' in WM, though none of these representations approaches the precision of an image recreated by our computer.

This is why WM representations are transient and ephemeral in nature, like those described by Johnson-Laird in his theory of mental models (Johnson-Laird, 1983, 2006; Johnson-Laird & Byrne, 1991). In other words, we think that there is nothing in LTM like a *representation* or even *representations* of, for example, the number 5, the letter *A*, or the word *cow*, but in each case a vast nebula of information from which some elements are used to construct ad hoc representations, the characteristics of which depend on the goal underpinning this construction and its context. This makes successive representations of a same item like a letter or a word differ from each other, each of them being constructed in a peculiar context for possibly different purposes, even if they share some characteristics that make them representations of the same entity. To use the example mentioned by Norris (2017) to illustrate the idea that short-term memory (STM) cannot be made of activated LTM representations, this would make it possible to distinguish the two tokens of the digit '1' when storing a sequence of digits such as '1, 3, 1'.

Such a conception is close to Cowan's (1988, 2005; see chapter by Cowan et al., 2021) ideas of a WM in which features activated from LTM coalesce into a WM object within the focus of attention. However, our model differs from this conception in two important ways. First, we assume that these features did not constitute a representation, or parts of representations, before their association in WM. Second, we do not believe that there exists something like an activated part of LTM surrounding the items present in the focus of attention, an activated part made of those representations that have been recently under the focus of attention and that could be retrieved even if they are no longer directly accessible (Cowan, 2005; Oberauer, 2002). Indeed, except when these associations are formed for the purpose of memorizing the resulting representation, they rapidly disappear from WM and are subsequently surprisingly difficult to retrieve, even in the short term. For example, Dagry and Barrouillet (2017) had participants memorizing series of seven letters for immediate serial recall, each letter being followed by two distractor words on which they had to perform a semantic judgement (is it an animal or not?). In some trials, after having recalled the letters, participants were asked if they remembered some of the words they had just seen. Whereas participants were able to recall a mean of 4.10 letters in the correct position, they were only able to recall 1.86 out of the 14 words they had just processed (see Carretti, Cornoldi, De Beni, & Palladino, 2004, for convergent results). This suggests that, instead of being long-term representations that could retain some activation after processing, the transient representations constructed in WM fall apart into their constituents as soon as they are no longer needed, hence the difficulty in retrieving them, even after short delays.

As we suggested earlier, several characteristics result from the definition of WM as a system for constructing, maintaining, and transforming ad hoc transient mental representations. The first is that WM is a separate system from LTM, though it interacts with it. Second, if representations result from a process of construction instead of a retrieval from LTM of ready-made mental objects, creating, maintaining, and transforming these representations might be processes very akin to each other and supported by a unique system. In the following, we will first describe this system and the cognitive architecture in which it is embedded, and then propose our own answers to the questions that have been addressed to the contributors of this volume.

Time-Based Resource Sharing in Working Memory

The intuitions at the basis of the TBRS model came initially from an observation we made while running developmental investigations. In accounting for cognitive development in children, Case (1985) assumed that cognitive operations take place in some mental space he called the Total Processing Space, the capacity of which would be limited and remain constant throughout development. This total space was assumed to be shared between a short-term storage space used for maintaining the information relevant for solving the problem at hand, and an operation space in which mental processes would operate on this information. Case's hypothesis was that, through exercise and maturation, processing would become with age increasingly efficient and less and less demanding, resulting in a progressive reduction of the operation space and a correlative increase of the short-term storage space. Being able to store more representations, children would become progressively able to deal with more and more complex problems. Case, Kurland, and Goldberg (1982) tested this hypothesis using a complex span task in which children aged from 6 to 12 years were presented with series of cards displaying sets of dots to be counted aloud while maintaining the successive cardinals for further serial recall. Case and colleagues assumed that the maximum number of cardinals children were able to correctly recall at the end of the series, called their counting span, reflected the capacity of the short term storage space. The operation space, which would be a function of processing efficiency, was assessed by independently measuring the maximum speed at which children were able to count dots, a speed that strongly increases with age from 6 to 12 years. In line with their hypothesis, Case et al. (1982) verified that the counting span was a direct and linear function of counting speed, supporting the idea that the age-related increase in short-term storage space results from a correlative decrease of the operation space needed for counting, that is, the cognitive load (CL) the counting process involves. They even demonstrated that adults have the same counting span as 6-year-old children when their counting efficiency is reduced through experimental manipulation to that of children of this age. This lent strong support to the hypothesis that processing and storage share a common resource (for Case, the total processing space resource) and that development might result from a progressive decrease of the mental space needed by less and less demanding operations.

However, Towse and Hitch (1995) called into doubt this hypothesis of resource sharing in accounting for the developmental increase in counting span. They argued that the faster counting in older children might affect counting spans not because it reveals a lower cognitive demand, but simply because it shortens the delay of retention of the successive cardinals. They assumed that in a complex span task such as the counting span task, attention is switched in an all-or-none manner on either the storage of the cardinals or the counting activity, and that memory traces of the cardinals suffer from a temporal decay when attention is switched away. Thus, the faster the counting of each card, the shorter the delay during which memory traces suffer from decay, and the better the recall performance. That would be why older children, who count faster, achieve better counting spans than younger children. After testing this prediction in counting span task, Towse and colleagues (Hitch, Towse, & Hutton, 2001; Towse et al., 1998, 2000) subsequently gathered evidence that performance in complex span tasks such as reading or operation span tasks do not depend on the CL of the processing component (i.e. reading, solving arithmetic problems), but simply on its raw duration. This led Towse and Houston-Price (2001) to conclude that it was 'increasingly apparent that both theoretical and computational accounts make the idea of limited resource-sharing capacity superfluous' (p. 246).

This conclusion constituted such a challenge for several theories of cognitive development (Case, 1985; Halford, 1993; Pascual-Leone & Johnson, 2011) that we decided to test the hypothesis that the duration of the intervening task was the unique determinant of recall performance in complex span tasks, independently of its presumed CL. For this purpose we compared children's recall performance in two complex span tasks (Barrouillet & Camos, 2001). The first was an operation span task in which children were asked to solve arithmetic problems (e.g. 6 + 7 + 8 = 22, true or false?), each problem being followed by a to-be-remembered letter. The number of problem–letter pairs was increased until failure to correctly recall the letters in correct order, the longest series of letters correctly recalled constituting the span. The second task had exactly the same structure except that, instead of solving arithmetic problems, children were asked to repeat the syllable 'ba' for periods of time equivalent to the time it took to solve the corresponding arithmetic problems in such a way that the delays of retention were equated across tasks. We called this second task the baba span task. Whereas Towse and Hitch's hypothesis did not predict any difference in recall performance between the two tasks, the delays of retention being the same, the resource-sharing hypothesis favoured by Case predicted higher baba spans than operation spans, the mere repetition of a syllable involving lower CL than solving arithmetic problems (Naveh-Benjamin & Jonides, 1984). As we expected, baba spans were higher than operation spans, lending support to the resource-sharing hypothesis. However, the effect was far smaller than we expected given the difference in cognitive demand between the two processing components (e.g. the mean baba span in 11-year-old children was 3.25 and the mean operation span 2.83, a decrease in performance of only 13%). This suggested that children's attention might not be continuously occupied when they solved arithmetic problems, and that they managed to surreptitiously switch attention back to the letters while performing the secondary task in order to maintain them, for example, when reaching some intermediary result. In other words, the lower operation spans than baba spans suggested some resource sharing, but this sharing might be time-based in nature. Such a hypothesis, if correct, would predict that a task continuously occupying attention should have a more detrimental effect on concurrent maintenance than a task allowing for frequent and prolonged attentional switches.

Such a TBRS model is based on four main assumptions. The first is that the two functions of WM, processing and storage, share a common limited attentional resource. The second is that due to a central bottleneck, cognitive processes can only take place one at a time in such a way that when attention is occupied by processing, it is no longer available for storage, and vice versa. The third is that when attention is switched away from WM traces, they suffer from temporal decay and interference. Finally, complete loss of these traces can be avoided by switching attention back and forth between processing and storage through a rapid switching process. Such a switching could take place during short pauses that can be freed during processing in order to refresh degraded memory traces.

Regarding the first assumption, it is largely agreed (but see Jones & Macken, 2018) that the kind of goal-directed processing carried on in WM requires attention. In Baddeley's model (1986), the central executive in charge of the processing function is described as an attentional system. In the ACT-R theory (Anderson, 1983; Anderson et al., 2004; Anderson & Lebiere, 1998), processing is achieved by 'if … then …' production rules that fire when the elements corresponding to their conditions of application receive source activations in WM, these source activations being conceived of as attentional resources. In the same way, other theories assume that maintaining memory items in WM requires attentional focusing (Cowan, 2005) and even creating memory traces requires attention (Logan, 1988, 1995, 1998). The idea that there is a bottleneck constraining central processes to take place one at a time has been proposed by several authors (Pashler, 1998; Welford, 1967). The sequentiality of mental operations is also at the heart of the ACT-R model already evoked because production rules can only fire one at a time (see also Newell, 1990, for the hypothesis that central cognition is serial). As we will see in the following sections of this chapter, the idea that there is a temporal decay of WM traces is more controversial and has been the topic of intense debate (Barrouillet & Camos, 2009; Barrouillet, De Paepe, & Langerock, 2012; Barrouillet, Portrat, Vergauwe, Diependaele, & Camos, 2011; Lewandowsky & Oberauer, 2009; Lewandowsky, Oberauer, & Brown, 2009; Oberauer & Lewandowsky, 2008; Portrat, Barrouillet, & Camos, 2008). However, as we will see later, findings related to the manipulation of temporal factors in WM tasks are very difficult to account for without assuming temporal decay. Finally, the idea that degraded memory traces could be reactivated through some attentional process is common to several theories (see Camos et al., 2018, for a review) and described as a covert retrieval (Cowan, 1992; Cowan et al., 1994; McCabe, 2008; Unsworth & Engle, 2007), an attentional refreshing (Raye, Johnson, Mitchell, Greene, & Johnson, 2007), or a scanning of the content of WM (Vergauwe & Cowan, 2015a, 2015b). The most recent version of the TBRS model describes refreshing as a reconstruction of WM representations (Barrouillet & Camos, 2015).

A New Conception of Cognitive Load

Barrouillet and Camos (2015) proposed to define the CL of a given activity as the impact that this activity has on other WM functions such as storage. Following the four assumptions expressed previously, the TBRS model predicts that temporal factors have a strong impact on this CL, which is not inherently dependent on the intrinsic nature of the task. As we noted earlier, a task that almost continuously occupies attention involves a high CL. It prevents the refreshing of decaying memory traces and should have a highly detrimental effect on storage. By contrast, a task that allows for frequent and prolonged pauses during which memory traces can be reactivated before their complete loss involves a low CL and should have a lower impact on storage. Taking into account the interplay between temporal decay of memory traces during processing periods and their restoration during free time, the TBRS model defines CL of a task as the ratio between the time during which this task occupies attention and the time available to perform it. It is worth noting that such a definition leads to reinterpret the relationship between CL and complexity of a task. A simple task such as reading letters can involve a higher CL than reading sentences for comprehension if it must be performed at a high rate, preventing refreshing from taking place (Lépine, Bernardin, & Barrouillet, 2005).

Testing the hypothesis that can be derived from this theoretical framework required the design of WM tasks in which temporal factors are carefully controlled. Traditional span tasks did not seem appropriate for this purpose as they are usually self-paced. For example, in the reading span task (Daneman & Carpenter, 1980), the operation span task (Turner & Engle, 1989), and the counting span task as they are usually administered, there is nothing that prevents participants from postponing some part of the task to covertly refresh memory traces. Thus, we designed computer-paced span tasks in which memoranda and items to be processed are presented on screen at a preset pace to which participants must comply and are not free to modify. Usually, these span tasks involve a series of memory items (e.g. digits, letters, words, spatial locations, movements, or symbols), each of them being followed by a series of items appearing successively on screen and on which some processing must be performed (e.g. digits for magnitude or parity judgement, for addition of 1, words for semantic categorization, or squares for spatial location judgement). Such designs are particularly appropriate for manipulating the CL of the intervening task and assess its effect on recall performance. In a computer-paced complex span task, as Fig. 4.1 illustrates, in which each memory item M is followed by a series of processing episodes P, CL can be expressed as:

$$CL = Nt \,/\, T \qquad\qquad \text{(Equation 4.1)}$$

in which N corresponds to the number of processing episodes (the number of items to be processed after each memorandum), t corresponds to the time during which each of these processing episodes occupies the central bottleneck, and T is the total time available to process these items, that is, the inter-stimulus interval between two successive memoranda. As Fig. 4.1 illustrates, increasing N or t while keeping T constant, or decreasing T while keeping N and t constant, increases CL and should thus result in poorer recall performance. However, increasing the number of items to be processed has no effect on CL if these items are processed at a constant pace. This manipulation should consequently have no effect on recall performance. Beyond constituting a laboratory for exploring WM functioning, these computer-paced complex span tasks involving very simple processing activities proved to be as good predictors of high-level cognition as traditional WM span tasks (Lépine, Barrouillet, & Camos, 2005; Lucidi, Loaiza, Camos, & Barrouillet, 2014).

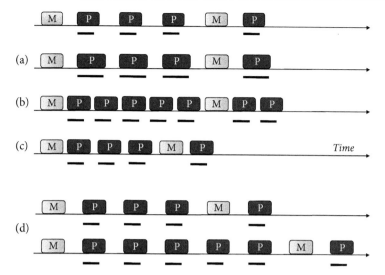

Fig. 4.1 Illustration of the temporal course of events in a trial of a typical computer-paced span task in which memory items, M, are followed by series of items to be processed, P. Black lines beneath P represent the time during which processing occupies the central bottleneck. Panels (a), (b), and (c) represent three ways of increasing CL by increasing t, N, or decreasing T, respectively. Panel (d) illustrates the fact that varying the number of items to be processed keeps CL unchanged when the pace at which these items are presented remains constant.

The Trade-Off Between Processing and Storage

The model outlined previously, which assumes that processing and storage share a common resource, predicts that a trade-off should occur between the two functions, the amount of information held in WM decreasing as the CL of processing increases. This prediction has been verified in several studies. Barrouillet, Bernardin, and Camos (2004) tested whether manipulating the parameters N and T in Equation 4.1 had the predicted effects. Using a computer-paced complex span task they called the reading digit span task, they had participants maintaining for further serial recall lists of letters of increasing length, each letter being followed by either four, eight, or ten digits to be read aloud (parameter N) within interletter intervals of either 6, 8, or 10 seconds (parameter T). This resulted in nine different values of CL that were expressed, for sake of simplicity, as the number of digits to be read per second (from 2 to 0.4). The results revealed that WM spans increased smoothly and linearly from 2.67 to 5.46 as this ratio decreased, participants being able to maintain and recall more and more letters as digits were processed at a slower pace. We verified in a subsequent study that this pace effect was not uniquely due to the faster concurrent articulation produced by reading the digits aloud, which would have prevented articulatory rehearsal, but also to the attentional capture this reading involved. Lépine, Bernardin, and Barrouillet (2005) used the same design as Barrouillet et al. (2004), except that digits were processed silently, participants having to judge their parity by pressing keys. Between four and eight digits were successively presented in each interletter interval at a rate of one digit every 800 ms or 1500 ms for the fast- and slow-pace conditions, respectively. The lower CL involved in the slow-pace condition resulted in better recall performance (mean spans of 3.81 and 5.10 for the fast- and slow-pace conditions, respectively). Note that, as it is clear in this last experiment, shorter delays of retention (i.e. shorter interletter intervals) can result in poorer recall performance if these delays of retention are filled with tasks performed at a faster pace and involving a higher CL. This suggests that, contrary to Towse and Hitch's (1995) hypothesis, participants take advantage of the time available between successive processing steps for refreshing memory traces.

As Fig. 4.1 makes clear, and as it can be deduced from Equation 4.1, increasing parameter t, the time during which each processing step captures attention, should increase CL and impair concurrent memory maintenance. We verified this hypothesis by using a reading digit span task as in Barrouillet et al. (2004), but in which reading times were varied by manipulating the way digits were displayed on screens, either as words (e.g. *four*), Arabic digits (4), or canonical dice patterns, for example :: (Barrouillet, Bernardin, Portrat, Vergauwe, & Camos, 2007). In line with the TBRS hypothesis, recall performance was an inverse function of reading times. Reading digits presented as patterns of dots took longer (507 ms) and elicited lower recall performance (75% of letters recalled in correct order) than reading the same digits in their word or Arabic format (425 ms and 424 ms of reading times, respectively, for 82% of letters correctly recalled in both conditions). Similar findings were obtained in another experiment in which the same authors varied the duration of an intervening task consisting of judging the spatial location (either in the upper or the lower part of the screen) of black squares successively displayed on screen after each letter. Response times were manipulated by varying the distance between the two possible locations, the decision taking longer when these locations were closer to each other. As expected, longer decisions were associated with lower recall performance.

It can be noted that the increase in processing time in Barrouillet et al. (2007) resulted in a correlative reduction of the free time available for refreshing memory traces, because in all conditions digits were presented for the same duration (1500 ms). However, the TBRS model predicts poorer performance with longer processing times even if the free time after each processing episode remains constant. Indeed, because memory traces suffer from decay while attention is occupied by processing, increasing processing time would result in a stronger decay for which an unchanged subsequent free time cannot compensate.[1] Poorer recall performance should follow. This prediction was verified by Barrouillet, De Paepe, and Langerock (2012) who had participants memorizing series of letters or spatial positions, each letter being followed by three multiplications for verification that were presented either in digits ($3 \times 2 = 6$) or in words (three × two = six), the latter being known to take longer. In both conditions,

---

[1] Note that increasing processing time while keeping free time constant necessarily results in higher CL because with i corresponding to the increase in processing time $(t+i)/(T+i) > t/T$.

the key press for responding to each operation initiated a constant free time of 800 ms before the next event (another operation, a letter, or the signal for recall at the end of the series). As the TBRS model predicts, longer processing times when solving word multiplications elicited lower recall performance for verbal as well as visuospatial memoranda. These results were recently replicated by Barrouillet, Uittenhove, Lucidi, and Langerock (2018) using similar tasks.

These latter studies revealed that CL affects not only verbal, but also visuospatial memory. The TBRS model acknowledges the existence of specific representation-based interference resulting from an overwriting process when representations held in WM share many common features in such a way that verbal representations should interfere more with each other than with visuospatial representations and vice versa. However, forgetting in WM should mainly be due to the decay of representations when attention is occupied by concurrent processing, a decay that affects any representation, whatever its nature, verbal or visuospatial. The effect of CL in the visual and spatial domains was investigated by Vergauwe, Barrouillet, and Camos (2009). Spatial memoranda were made of ball movements while visual memoranda were visual patterns (2 × 3 matrix with half of the cells filled in black). The intervening tasks were also either spatial or visual. The spatial tasks consisted of judging the symmetry of designs created by filling in black some squares in 6 × 6 matrices (Kane et al., 2004), or in a spatial fit task in which participants had to decide whether an horizontal line can fit into the gap between two dots (Rybash & Hoyer, 1992). The visual task was a colour discrimination task in which participants had to judge whether colours presented successively on screen were more red than blue or more blue than red. As in the previous studies, the CL induced by these tasks was varied by manipulating the number of items to be processed between two successive memoranda and the duration of these intervals. For both visual and spatial memory, WM spans were an inverse function of the CL of the intervening task, whatever its visual or spatial nature. This suggested that the TBRS model can account for visuospatial WM phenomena, but also that visual and spatial WM are not that dissociated as it had been suggested (Klauer & Zhao, 2004; Logie, 1995). This is due to the fact that in a WM in which the main source of forgetting is temporal decay, what matters is more the duration of the distracting activities than their nature. This is what we discovered when comparing the effect on verbal WM of different distracting tasks (Barrouillet et al., 2007). The computer-paced complex span tasks we used required the maintenance of letters while judging either the parity or the location of digits appearing successively either on the upper or the lower part of the screen, with either four, six, or eight digits presented in fixed interletter intervals of 6400 ms. Not surprisingly, WM spans decreased as the number of digits increased. As the TBRS model also predicted, the parity task that involved longer processing times elicited lower spans than the location task. However, when WM spans were regressed onto actual values of CL approximated by dividing the mean total processing time within interletter intervals by the duration of these intervals, it appeared that the spans from the two tasks almost fell on the same regression line. Moreover, when choice reaction time tasks as parity or location judgement were replaced by a mere simple reaction time task that does not require any representation of the stimuli on which a decision must be made, the CL effect vanished (Fig. 4.2). We concluded that the effect on recall performance of concurrent activities does not go beyond their duration, insofar as the processes are attention demanding and occupy the central bottleneck. These findings were subsequently extended to other complex span tasks with processing components involving central processes. Independently from the nature of the distracting task and the central process it involved (response selection, memory retrieval, updating, inhibition), mean spans fell onto the same regression line, CL accounting for 98% of the variance on spans (Barrouillet, Portrat, & Camos, 2011).

The hypothesis that forgetting from WM is mainly due to the duration and not the nature of the intervening activities led to the strong hypothesis that, contrary to prominent theories of WM such as Baddeley's multicomponent model (Baddeley, 1986; Baddeley & Logie, 1999), both verbal and visuospatial WM should be affected to the same extent by variation in CL of both verbal and visuospatial concurrent activities. For this purpose, Vergauwe, Barrouillet, and Camos (2010) used complex span tasks in which verbal (letters) and visuospatial storage (successive spatial locations of a red square in a 6 × 6 matrix) was associated with verbal (semantic categorization) and visuospatial processing (the spatial fit task with the horizontal line and two dots already

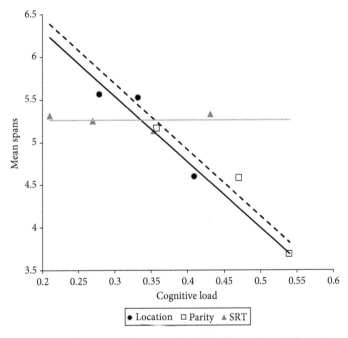

Fig. 4.2 Mean spans as a function of cognitive load for the parity, the location, and the simple reaction time (SRT) tasks with regression lines from Experiments 3 and 4 in Barrouillet et al. (2007).

described). The CL of these concurrent tasks was manipulated by varying the number of items to be processed within the inter-memoranda intervals and the duration of these intervals. As we predicted, visuospatial recall was impaired by the increase in CL of both the verbal and the visuospatial tasks, the two tasks having comparable effects. These findings are in line with the TBRS predictions and the hypothesis of a central system holding WM representations that suffer from temporal decay when concurrent activities, whatever their nature, capture attention. Verbal WM also decreased when the CL of both the verbal and the visuospatial tasks increased, but contrary to visuo-spatial recall, recall was consistently poorer when verbal storage was combined with the verbal task than when it was combined with the visuospatial task. In other words, a domain-specific interference occurred in the verbal domain that was not observed in the visuospatial domain. This suggested that verbal storage, like visuospatial storage, relies on the central system as it is affected by variation in CL of a visuospatial concurrent task, but that verbal maintenance also involves an additional domain-specific system impeded by verbal but not visuospatial concurrent activities. Our hypothesis was that verbal maintenance relies on two independent mechanisms, attentional refreshing and articulatory rehearsal, the verbal task interfering with both mechanisms whereas the visuospatial task only impeded attentional refreshing (see Camos, 2015, 2017, for review).

Mechanisms of Working Memory Maintenance

As a test of the hypothesis that verbal information can be maintained by two mechanisms, Camos, Lagner, and Barrouillet (2009) orthogonally manipulated the availability of each mechanism in complex span tasks in which participants maintained series of letters. To vary the availability of attention and hence of attentional refreshing, participants had either to judge the parity of sequentially presented digits or to react as fast as possible when digits appeared on screen. The latter being a simple reaction time task, it requires less attention, and allows the concurrent refreshing of letters. In both tasks, participants responded either silently, by pressing keys, or aloud, which prevents the use of articulatory rehearsal. As expected, impairing one of the two mechanisms resulted in poorer recall performance. Moreover, no interaction emerged, the effect of the two manipulations being additive. Similar findings were observed in two additional experiments, in which the availability of attention was varied through changes either in the pace of the parity judgement task or in the nature of the concurrent task (detection of digits vs verification of arithmetic operations). These findings were in line with Hudjetz and Oberauer (2007) who showed that besides articulatory rehearsal, a supplementary maintenance mechanism supports verbal WM.

It should be noted that some recent studies question the existence of these two mechanisms. On the one hand, doubts have been expressed on the functional role of articulatory rehearsal as a maintenance mechanism and the idea that it is a by-product of WM functioning has been put forward (e.g. Souza & Oberauer, 2018). However, some findings cannot be interpreted without the recourse to an articulatory rehearsal mechanism (Barrouillet, Gorin, & Camos, in press; Lucidi et al., 2016). On the other hand, the detrimental impact of the capture of attention on recall performance and the CL effect have been reinterpreted by Oberauer, Lewandowsky, Farrell, Jarrold, and Greaves (2012) as resulting not from the hindrance to refresh degraded WM traces, but to remove distractors. By removing interfering representations from memory, this distractor removal mechanism should improve recall (see chapter by Oberauer, 2021). However, several tests of this hypothesis failed to uncover any trace of this removal process, short-term as well as long-term memory traces of distractors being even stronger in situations assumed by Oberauer et al. (2012) to involve their more complete removal (Dagry & Barrouillet, 2017; Dagry, Vergauwe, & Barrouillet, 2017).

The existence of these two independent maintenance mechanisms is also strengthened by brain imaging studies that reported the involvement of two distinct brain regions. Whereas the regions such as Broca's area, the left premotor cortex, the left intraparietal sulcus, and the right cerebellum are activated when articulatory rehearsal is used, a network including the dorsolateral prefrontal cortex is engaged when rehearsal is impaired (Gruber, 2001; Raye et al., 2007; Smith & Jonides, 1999). Double dissociations in patients with brain lesions also support the existence of two separate mechanisms (Trost & Gruber, 2012).

As shown by Camos et al. (2009), the two maintenance mechanisms are sensitive to different task constraints, attentional refreshing being affected by any reduction in the availability of attention, while articulatory rehearsal relies on language-based processes that can be blocked by concurrent articulation. These mechanisms are in fact reflecting the existence of different maintenance systems, a central system that we conceive as an executive loop (see later) and a phonological loop, these two systems storing memory traces in different formats of representations. As a consequence, some well-known effects in verbal WM, such as the phonological similarity effect and the word length effect (i.e. reduced recall performance for lists of phonologically similar words and of long words compared to dissimilar and short words, respectively) should be specific to the use of the phonological loop and its rehearsal mechanism, while they should be immune to manipulation of the maintenance in the executive loop by the attentional refreshing. This is exactly what Camos, Mora, and Barrouillet (2013) and Mora and Camos (2013) reported. It should nevertheless be noted that the two mechanisms do not differ on all aspects of their functioning. For example, on the distinction between the maintenance of item and order information, both of them are efficient on maintaining these two aspects of verbal information (Camos, Lagner, & Loaiza, 2017).

Moreover, it can be suggested that having two maintenance systems at their disposal can lead participants, and especially adults, to make some strategic use of them. By varying the characteristics of the concurrent task in complex span tasks that could be more or less attention demanding and involve or not responses spoken aloud, Camos, Mora, and Oberauer (2011) showed that young adults favoured the articulatory rehearsal when the concurrent task was attention demanding like a location judgement task, whereas they relied on attentional refreshing when it was a low-demanding simple reaction time task. Changes in the type of maintenance strategies was reflected in the emergence or not of the phonological similarity effect, and through instructions, it was possible to make participants using one or the other maintenance mechanisms.

It remains to be explained how the coordination of different WM systems is possible to allow an efficient maintenance of information. A dual structure of verbal WM could lead to the hypothesis that several representations or copies of the same information could be simultaneously stored in WM and could lead to interference and retrieval errors. However, recent findings suggest that this dual structure does not necessarily involve the existence of several representations of a same item or the storage of several copies of a single item in different places. A recent series of experiments on the immediate serial recall of letters suggests that, under specific instructions that help individuals to strictly segregate the information maintained in the two systems, their span performance dramatically increases (Barrouillet, Gorin, & Camos, in press). It seems sufficient for this purpose to ask individuals to perform a cumulative rehearsal on the four or five first letters of the to-be-remembered list, no more, and to keep rehearsing them while they encode the subsequently presented letters. Moreover, this procedure of maintenance, which we called the maxispan procedure, makes the phonological similarity effect disappear, suggesting that the items maintained through articulatory rehearsal might not be stored under a phonological code. Our interpretation of these findings led us to slightly modify our previous conceptions of the structure of verbal WM. We would like to suggest that the existence of articulatory rehearsal does not necessarily imply the need for a phonological store, in the sense of a buffer of mental symbolic representations. On the contrary, following Baddeley, Thompson, and Buchanan (1975), we are inclined to consider what is usually called the phonological loop as 'an output buffer holding the motor programme necessary for the verbal production of the memory items', articulatory rehearsal reinstalling sensory inputs through the execution of this motor programme by the mechanisms of speech production. This cyclic articulatory production is assumed to require very little attention (Naveh-Benjamin & Jonides, 1984). It is worth noting that it constitutes one of the most basic sensorimotor cognitive processes in humans, already present in the first months of life, and described by Baldwin (1894) and Piaget (1936) as primary circular reactions in which infants cyclically repeat syllables pertaining to their repertoire, the output of the articulation triggering its repetition in a behavioural loop. Barrouillet, Gorin, and Camos (in press) assumed that, when the verbal material to be rehearsed does not exceed the capacity of this articulatory loop, the rehearsed items coalesce into an articulatory object that preserves in its structure both item and order information, resulting in their perfect recall. Moreover, we observed that these rehearsed items do not interact in the maxispan procedure with the subsequently presented, and thus non-rehearsed, items. This suggests that the two sets of information are not only stored in different systems, but are coded in different formats. The rehearsed items would be coded as motor programmes within the articulatory loop, whereas the non-rehearsed items would be stored as symbolic representations within the executive loop.

It is worth noting that the articulatory rehearsal can also be used for reactivating representations stored in the executive loop. Indeed, phonological or visual representations of verbal items in the executive loop can automatically activate through an affordance process the corresponding motor programme for the articulation of these items. This rehearsal process probably allows the number of items that can be maintained in the executive loop to be increased, as the articulatory suppression effect suggests (the fact that performance in immediate serial recall tasks is degraded by the concurrent articulation of a word, a syllable, or a sequence of syllables continuously repeated). However, this seems to lead to a suboptimal use of the dual structure of verbal WM as suggested by the fact that the maxispan procedure, which allows a strict segregation between the two loops, strongly increases immediate serial recall performance.

The idea that the articulatory loop holds concatenated motor programmes forming articulatory objects instead of discrete phonological representations stored and retrieved in some phonological store is in agreement with the view extensively promoted by Jones and colleagues (Jones, Farrand, Stuart, & Morris, 1995; Jones, Hughes, & Macken, 2007; Macken, Taylor, Kozlov, Hughes, & Jones, 2016). Nevertheless, we depart from Jones' theoretical view as we endorse the idea that along with the motor programmes that support verbal rehearsal, multimodal mental representations are created, stored, and processed in WM in the executive loop, the central component of a cognitive architecture proposed by the TBRS model.

A Cognitive Architecture

The TBRS between the two functions of processing and storage takes place within a cognitive architecture in which a central system, conceived as an executive loop, interacts with LTM and peripheral systems. This central system in which goal-directed cognition takes place can be conceived as the seat of thought as it is in charge of the construction, maintenance, and processing of multimodal transient WM representations. The TBRS model assumes that these representations are stored in an episodic buffer, as in Baddeley's (2007; see chapter by Baddeley, Hitch, & Allen, 2021) model, and are continuously read, maintained, or transformed by productions (units of procedural knowledge with an 'if *conditions* then *action*' structure) hosted in a procedural LTM. Following Baddeley (2002), these representations are said 'episodic' as they integrate inputs from the different sensory buffers as well as from LTM. Consequently, they are more than the representation of an item because they integrate a part of the context in which this item occurred, a context that can in turn modulate its meaning. For example, if we are looking at the date of a named day in the calendar, the ordinal dimension of the number we will find will be part of the representation (it is the 28th of April), whereas the representation of the same number 28 as resulting from a calculation will probably involve its cardinal rather than its ordinal meaning (the amount due is £28). These representations can also benefit from some consolidation, which makes them immune to representation-based interference but not from time-based decay (Barrouillet, Plancher, Guida, & Camos, 2013). This consolidation, which takes place just after encoding, seems to rely on the same type of attention as attentional refreshing (De Schrijver & Barrouillet, 2017). The continuous scanning and transformation by a procedural system of representations held in the episodic buffer creates what we call the executive loop (Fig. 4.3).

Peripheral systems might either provide elements for constructing these representations, as the sensory buffers and declarative LTM, or receive the outputs of the executive loop, as LTM for storage through a learning process or motor buffers for response production (e.g. pressing keys for responses, see Koechlin, Ody, & Kouneiher, 2003, for neural evidence) or for articulatory rehearsal as we explained earlier. The previous version of the TBRS model (Barrouillet & Camos, 2015) included a phonological loop inspired by Baddeley's theory, in which the articulatory mechanism is coupled with a phonological buffer. We prefer to now conceive this loop dedicated for the maintenance of verbal information as an *articulatory loop* in which the articulatory mechanism is coupled with a buffer holding motor programmes for speech production instead of phonological representations.

The Executive Loop

The TBRS model assumes that WM representations are stored in an episodic buffer. Baddeley and his colleagues focused their investigations of this cognitive structure

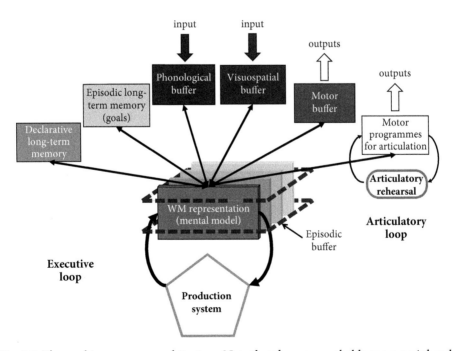

Fig. 4.3 The working memory architecture. Note that there are probably more peripheral buffers (e.g. auditory, musical, kinaesthetic, and haptic) than the visuospatial and phonological buffers represented here.

on its putative role in binding features into objects (Baddeley, Allen, & Hitch, 2010). Because they observed that the episodic buffer was not responsible for the formation of binding, they concluded that it was essentially a passive store. Our own investigation on the maintenance of cross-domain information such as letters in spatial locations revealed that this maintenance is not passive, but depends on domain-general attentional resources, something that fits perfectly with the characteristics of the central system of maintenance described by the TBRS model (Langerock, Vergauwe, & Barrouillet, 2014). In the same way as Oberauer (2002) hypothesized a region of direct access containing four items among which a single item is in the focus of attention, Barrouillet and Camos (2015) suggested that among the representations held in the episodic buffer, the content of only one of them might be available for processing or refreshing. Following Anderson's ACT-R model (Anderson, 1993; Anderson & Lebiere, 1998), we assume that a production system reads the content of this representation and, through a process of pattern matching, selects the production with a condition part that matches this content and the current goal. The most appropriate production fires, its action part being applied. Productions can reconstruct partially degraded representations for maintenance purpose, modify representations for reaching goals, switch between representations held in the episodic buffer, or retrieve information from LTM and sensory buffers for constructing new representations. The action part of the productions must be conceived as a set of instructions that trigger the action of executive functions that manipulate WM representations. Because only one production can be fired at a time and can only operate on a single representation, WM functioning is sequential in nature, including in its maintenance activities. For example, the TBRS model assumes that WM representations in the episodic buffer are refreshed in a cyclic ordered manner, though other options can be envisioned (Lemaire, Pageot, Plancher, & Portrat, 2018).

Representations in the episodic buffer are assumed to suffer from temporal decay and interference. If the factor limiting the number of representations that the episodic buffer can hold is this temporal decay remains an open question. Following Cowan (2001; Chen & Cowan, 2009), our own estimates point towards no more than four representations held in the executive loop (Langerock et al., 2014; Vergauwe et al., 2014). It is also possible that this limitation results from structural constraints if the episodic buffer is akin to an object file or slots (e.g. Cowan, 2001). The maximum complexity of WM representations might itself be limited, as it has been suggested that they cannot coordinate more than four independent elements (Halford, 1993; Halford, Cowan, & Andrews, 2007). The convergence of these two limits toward the number *four* might not be purely coincidental (Barrouillet & Camos, 2015; Camos & Barrouillet, 2018).

Goals and Control

The cyclic operation of the procedural memory on the representations stored in the episodic buffer creates an executive loop that encompasses the functions that Baddeley

(1986, 2007) attributed to the central executive for processing and the slave systems for storage. Proposing the executive loop as a theoretical alternative to the central executive hypothesized by other theories (e.g. Baddeley, 1986; Cowan, 2005) accounts for cognitive control without having recourse to any homunculus. For more clarity, we suggest to distinguish between two types of goals, the final goal of a complex protracted activity (e.g. finding the answer of an addition involving multidigit numbers), and local sub-goals, in some sense micro-goals, generated by any production and reached by the production fired in the following cognitive step (e.g. moving to the next left column without an answer digit after having written the answer of a given column).

Our proposal is that final goals are WM representations of internal or external states previously experienced or anticipated as enjoyable, useful or valuable, or constructed from received instructions. There is no need to assume that these representations of final goals must be continuously kept in WM to maintain their effectiveness. Following Anderson et al. (2004), we previously endorsed the existence of a goal module (Barrouillet & Camos, 2015). We now find it simpler to suppose that this type of goal representations rapidly leave WM after their construction without losing their effectiveness. Our hypothesis is that, when created, these goal representations would activate in LTM associated and potentially useful declarative and procedural knowledge (in the earlier example, additive facts and productions for solving additions), this activated declarative and procedural knowledge constituting the cognitive context of the task. This context allows the cognitive activity to maintain its direction and coherence without a continuous maintenance of a representation of the current goal. It could also facilitate, if needed, the retrieval from episodic LTM of the information permitting to reconstruct a representation of this goal to monitor the activity, assess the match between the reached and the desired state, update this goal if necessary, and plan further cognitive steps. As far as the micro sub-goals are concerned, and following the ACT-R model, we assume that they are generated by the action part of the production currently fired. As such, they are part of the current representation held in the executive loop and constitute one of the conditions for the selection of the next production to be fired. The prolonged maintenance of these micro-goals is consequently not needed because as the activity progresses, the representations of the previous states of the task are no longer needed and can progressively leave the episodic buffer.

From this perspective, executive control is in the TBRS model an emergent property of cognitive functioning. The control of attention, or in other words the control of the representation currently processed, would result from the construction of a precise final goal representation, the retrievability in episodic LTM of the information permitting to reconstruct this goal representation if needed, and the availability and activation of declarative and procedural knowledge providing a coherent and guiding cognitive context within which relevant knowledge and productions can easily be retrieved. This might explain why and how tasks assessing the global efficiency of the executive loop such as complex span tasks are predictive of tasks specifically requiring controlled attention such as Stroop or anti-saccade tasks, as Engle's work has demonstrated (Engle, 2002; Engle & Kane, 2004).

The Peripheral Systems

Within the proposed cognitive architecture, declarative and episodic LTM are considered as peripheral systems. Their interactions with the executive loop will be analysed in the next section. The other peripheral systems are buffers maintaining a limited amount of modality-specific information for short periods of time, a hypothesis shared with several other models (Anderson et al., 2004; Atkinson & Shiffrin, 1968; Baddeley, 1986; Hazy et al., 2006). Among them, the visuospatial and phonological buffers are of particular importance for human cognition. These peripheral buffers are passive sensory stores that provide information that can enter into the construction of WM representations. While there does not seem to be a domain-specific system for the active maintenance of visuospatial information (Vergauwe et al., 2010, 2014; see Morey, 2018 for review), we have seen that there is good evidence for such a system for verbal information and we have suggested to conceive it as an articulatory loop holding motor programmes for articulation. Like the episodic buffer, the capacity of this articulatory loop is strongly limited as it cannot hold more than four letters and only two or three multisyllabic words (Vergauwe et al., 2014). Let us now turn to the relationships between LTM components and WM.

Working Memory and Long-Term Memory

Since the modal model by Atkinson and Shiffrin (1968), the bidirectional relationships between WM and LTM constitute a central question for understanding human cognition. As we mentioned in introducing this chapter, the TBRS model can also be conceived as a learning device, the successive contents of WM leaving retrievable footprints in LTM; a hypothesis shared by several models (e.g. Cowan, 2005). This learning principle embedded in the WM architecture described earlier proved to be efficient in accounting for the acquisition and development (both typical and atypical) of a specific skill, number transcoding (Barrouillet, Camos, Perruchet, & Seron, 2004). Besides the role of WM in learning, we examined within the framework of the TBRS model how the information stored in LTM affects the functioning of the executive loop. For this purpose, the LTM effects on attentional refreshing were investigated. The TBRS model also makes specific predictions about how WM maintenance mechanisms affect the availability and retrieval of information at long term as well as its nature when stored in LTM.

Long-Term Memory Effects on Refreshing

In the last version of the TBRS model (Barrouillet & Camos, 2015), we suggested that refreshing can be considered akin to the redintegration of memory traces as described by Hulme and colleagues (Hulme et al., 1997). WM representations stored in the executive loop would degrade through decay and interference to the point that their remnants are used to reconstruct representations through the retrieval of some building blocks from LTM that would be integrated within the degrading representations to restore them.[2] As a consequence, items that benefit from easy retrieval of information from LTM would have increased probability to be reconstructed when attention is available for refreshing. To test this prediction, Camos et al. (2019) manipulated the ease of retrieval from LTM by presenting in complex span tasks lists of high- and low-frequency words, or words and non-words. They predicted that if refreshing is based on the retrieval of LTM information, the frequency and lexicality effects should interact with the CL of the secondary task, which gives more or less opportunity for refreshing. Although the frequency and lexicality effects impacted recall performance with poorer recall for low-frequency word and non-words, respectively, these LTM effects and the CL effect proved additive, contradicting Camos et al.'s (2019) predictions (see also Abadie & Camos, 2018; Campoy, Castellà, Provencio, Hitch, & Baddeley, 2015; Oberauer, 2009; Rosselet-Jordan, Mariz Elsig, Abadie, & Camos, in revision, for similar findings). Strengthening this finding, Camos et al. also established that there is no difference in refreshing speed for lists of high- and low-frequency words, or lists of words and non-words. Although further examinations are needed, this set of findings questions the conception of refreshing as a redintegration process. It would better fit with description of refreshing as the reactivation of temporary stored memory traces. Recently, Vergauwe and Langerock (2017) have provided evidence for the heightened accessibility of the just-refreshed item. This finding is consistent with the hypothesis that the executive loop processes one representation at a time, rapidly switching from one representation to the other to enhance their level of activation. In such a view, LTM effects on recall performance would originate from the encoding stage. Items for which information is easier to retrieve in LTM would be better encoded into WM, or as we proposed in the TBRS model, their mental representations would be easily constructed.

How Working Memory Impacts Long-Term Memory

Conversely to the role of LTM on WM functioning, the TBRS model makes predictions on how attentional refreshing and articulatory rehearsal differently impact recall in delayed tests aiming at assessing LTM storage, and how they create different types of representations, that may trigger false memories. In the TBRS model, the two main systems of maintenance differ in the nature of the information they manipulate. While attentional refreshing maintains mental representations that are built and stored in the executive loop, articulatory rehearsal manipulates sensorimotor patterns, the phonological loop being an output buffer holding the motor programme necessary for the verbal production of the memory items. As a consequence, LTM storage of mental

[2] Note that, as we mentioned previously, the information retrieved from LTM for constructing or refreshing WM representations does not need to be representational in nature, but provides tokens (building blocks) for this construction or reconstruction.

representations should be mostly dependent on the efficiency of attentional refreshing to maintain information and not on articulatory rehearsal. By manipulating the availability of the two maintenance mechanisms in complex span tasks in which participants memorized lists of words, Camos and Portrat (2015) tested the impact of these mechanisms on immediate and delayed recall. Replicating the deleterious effect on immediate recall of the impairment of both mechanisms, they observed that delayed recall was only reduced when attentional refreshing was impeded by a high demanding concurrent task, while blocking rehearsal by concurrent articulation did not change the level of delayed recall performance. This provides evidence of how the functioning of WM can directly impact the storage of information in LTM (see also Craik & Watkins, 1973; Glenberg, Smith, & Green, 1977), but it can also influence the emergence of false memory.

By integrating the TBRS model and the fuzzy-trace theory (Brainerd & Reyna, 2002, 2005), Abadie and Camos (2019) proposed a new theoretical account for false memory at short and long term. In the fuzzy-trace theory, the emergence of false memory depends on the balance between gist (i.e. interpretations of concepts, the meaning of the encoded information) and verbatim (i.e. surface forms) memory traces. False memory would occur when verbatim traces are not strong enough to counteract gist memory, which can trigger the retrieval of related, but not target, items. According to Abadie and Camos, refreshing reinforces gist memory traces during maintenance, and these traces can be preserved over the long term, whereas rehearsal fosters encoding and retrieval of their surface forms over the short term (i.e. their verbatim traces) independently of their meaning (see Loaiza & Camos, 2018). This predicts that using rehearsal to maintain a series of words should prevent the occurrence of false memories in immediate tests, whereas using refreshing should foster their occurrence in delayed tests. However, whether rehearsal has been used or not, verbatim memories decline over time, and remembering after a long delay could not be primarily based on the retrieval of verbatim memory, but mostly on the retrieval of gist memory or on guessing. In accordance with their predictions, results revealed that rehearsal prevents short-term false recognition of related distractors through the retrieval of verbatim memory for targets, whereas refreshing increases long-term false recognition through the retrieval of gist memory for related information. Overall, these results lend support to the architecture depicted by TBRS model, and add new evidence for the separation between WM and LTM.

Development

As we mentioned in introducing this chapter, the initial intuitions on which the TBRS model are based came from a developmental context, and we have extensively addressed the developmental aspects of WM in a recent publication (Camos & Barrouillet, 2018). Although WM plays a crucial role in cognitive development, we will here concentrate on the main factors that could account for WM development within our model, and review the main studies we conducted in this domain. Because the TBRS model conceives WM as a system for maintaining relevant information in face of temporal decay and interference, most of the factors explaining WM development must be found in the temporal aspects of its functioning and the emergence of the strategies used for preventing or counteracting forgetting.

Decay of Working Memory Traces

One of the first hypotheses that comes to mind when considering the possible sources of WM development is to suppose that the rate of decay of WM traces progressively decreases with age. A slower decay would result in WM traces remaining more accessible after equivalent delays of distraction, explaining the better WM performance exhibited by older children. Accurately assessing the pure effect of decay is a task fraught with difficulties because one must ensure that no maintenance strategies intervened to attenuate this effect. Bertrand and Camos (2021) circumvented this difficulty by studying young children aged between 4 and 6 years that are known for not spontaneously using maintenance strategies. Using game-like span tasks, Bertrand and Camos assessed the capacity of children to remember lists of fruits or the order of arrival of dolls involved in a ski race after delays of retention varying from 2 to 12 seconds. Recall performance increased with age and decreased with longer delays of retention, revealing the expected decay, but the two factors did not interact, suggesting that the better performance in older children was not due to a lower rate of decay. Another study confirmed this finding in even younger children (Bertrand, Stan-Zahno, & Camos, 2020). Variations in the rate of decay do not seem to be a strong determinant of WM development.

Processing Speed and Refreshing Efficiency

One of the main tenets of the TBRS model is that temporal decay occurs when attention is distracted from memory traces by intervening activities. In line with Towse and Hitch's (1995) hypothesis, developmental differences in WM performance might be due to faster processing in older children. All other things being equal, faster processing results in shorter periods of decay and better preserved memory traces. If developmental differences in WM performance were due to age differences in processing speed, equating processing times across ages should abolish these differences. Several of our studies followed this rationale (Barrouillet, Gavens, Vergauwe, Gaillard, & Camos, 2009; Gaillard, Barrouillet, Jarrold, & Camos, 2011; Gavens & Barrouillet, 2004). For example, Gaillard et al. (2011) asked children aged 9 and 12 years to remember series of letters while adding 1 to digits presented successively on screen after each letter. Not surprisingly, older children outperformed young children, but it appeared that they were also faster in solving the additions. In order to deprive older children of this advantage, they were asked to add 2 instead of 1 as the younger children did (we had previously observed that adding 2 took the same time in 12-year-old children as adding 1 in 9-year-old children). This manipulation strongly reduced the developmental difference, mean spans in 12-year-old children falling from 3.05 to 2.31, but they still largely outperformed their younger peers (mean spans of 2.31 and 1.72, respectively). All our studies led to the same observation, equating processing time reduces, but never abolishes, developmental differences.

Where does the residual difference come from? The digits being presented at the same pace in both age groups, equating processing time also equated the free time available for refreshing decayed memory traces after each addition. It might be that young children are not only slower for solving additions, but also less efficient in refreshing. Thus, in a last experiment, Gaillard et al. (2011) not only equated processing time across ages (older children added 2 instead of 1), but tailored free time by giving young children more free time after each addition (the extra time was computed on the basis of the difference in processing speed between the two age groups, as assessed in a pretest). This last manipulation made the developmental difference disappear, demonstrating that temporal factors are of paramount importance in understanding developmental differences. The same findings were replicated with children aged 9 and 14 years (Barrouillet, Dagry, & Gauffroy, 2021).

Use of Maintenance Strategies

Another source of WM development is the age-related changes in the use of maintenance strategies. Concerning the central mechanism of attentional refreshing, Barrouillet et al. (2009) have shown that its efficiency increases from 7 to 14 years of age, which results in the counterintuitive consequence that adolescents' recall performance is more affected by an increase in concurrent CL than young children. While this could explain at least part of the development of WM after age 7 years, things seem rather different for children younger than 7 years. Indeed, in an experiment comparing 5- to 7-year-old children, recall in young and older children proved sensitive to different parameters of the complex span task (Camos & Barrouillet, 2011). When performing a complex span task in which animal names were remembered and the colour of smileys were named, 5-year-old children's recall was not affected by variations in the CL of the naming-colour task, while it was in 7-year-olds. Five-year-olds' recall was in fact dependent on the total duration of maintenance, with a longer duration leading to poorer performance. Such a pattern is expected if children do not try to actively maintain information and wait rather passively for the recall signal to retrieve memory traces that have declined over time (see also Barrouillet et al., 2009). This speaks in favour of the idea that, before a certain age (around 7 years), attention refreshing is not at the disposal of children. It could also be possible that the mechanism is available but some tasks do not present enough incentive to use it, while game-like tasks can lead to their use (Bertrand & Camos, 2015). The goal neglect frequently reported in younger children, which is the fact that they often fail to execute the demand of the task despite being able to understand and recall it (Marcovitch, Boseovski, Knapp, & Kane, 2010), may explain why maintenance mechanisms are not triggered before 7 years of age. However, recent studies that aimed at helping children to maintain the memory goal in WM tasks failed to report any recall improvement in kindergarteners (Fitamen, Blaye, & Camos, 2019a, 2019b, 2019c).

Besides age-related changes in attentional refreshing, articulatory rehearsal could also play a role in WM development. Children aged from 6 to 9 years can jointly use attentional refreshing and articulatory rehearsal and, like adults, the impairment of these mechanisms leads to reduced performance with additive effects (Mora & Camos, 2015; Oftinger & Camos, 2016, 2017). However, what differs from adults is the strategic use of the two mechanisms. When examining when recall performance depends on the CL of the concurrent task in children, Oftinger and Camos (2018) reported that it was never the case in 6-year-olds and always the case in 8-year-olds, but it depends on the availability of rehearsal in 7-year-olds. When articulatory rehearsal was available, 7-year-olds were not sensitive to concurrent CL, which is a determinant factor when rehearsal is impaired. In other words, articulatory rehearsal is a default strategy for these children who can adaptively switch to refreshing when articulatory processes are unavailable.

Conclusion

Newell (1990) noted that, in the face of an ever-changing and often unpredictable environment, WM can be conceived as a kind of buffer necessary to obtain some temporal room for processing the elements relevant for ongoing cognition. This is due to the fact that cognitive operations are often slower than the rate at which these relevant elements are delivered to us. This calls for the short-term maintenance of some of these elements in order to re-present them to the mechanisms devoted to their processing when they are available anew. Time is consequently the main constraint of WM functioning and hence of human cognition. The TBRS model is an attempt to draw up the map of these temporal constraints and of the solutions that a slow and imperfect biological system has developed to try to overcome them.

References

Abadie, M., & Camos, V. (2018). Attentional refreshing moderates the word frequency effect in immediate and delayed recall tasks. *Annals of the New York Academy of Sciences, 1424*, 127–136.

Abadie, M., & Camos, V. (2019). False memory at short and long term. *Journal of Experimental Psychology: General, 148*, 1312–1334.

Anderson, J. R. (1983). *The architecture of cognition.* Cambridge, MA: Harvard University Press.

Anderson, J. R. (1993). *Rules of the mind.* Hillsdale, NJ: Lawrence Erlbaum Associates.

Anderson, J. R., & Lebiere, C. (1998). *The atomic components of thought.* Mahwah, NJ: Lawrence Erlbaum Associates.

Anderson, J. R., Bothell, D., Byrne, M. D., Douglass, S., Lebiere, C., & Qin, Y. (2004). An integrated theory of mind. *Psychological Review, 111*, 1036–1060.

Atkinson, R. C., & Shiffrin, R. M. (1968). Human memory: A proposed system and its control processes. *Psychology of Learning and Motivation, 2,* 89–195.

Baddeley, A. D. (1986). *Working memory.* Oxford, UK: Clarendon Press.

Baddeley, A. D. (2002). Is working memory still working? *European Psychologist, 7,* 85–97.

Baddeley, A. D. (2007). *Working memory, thought, and action.* Oxford, UK: Oxford University Press.

Baddeley, A. D., Allen, R. J., & Hitch, G. J. (2010). Investigating the episodic buffer. *Psychologica Belgica, 50,* 223–243.

Baddeley, A. D., Hitch, G. J., & Allen, R. J. (2021). A multicomponent model of working memory. In R. H. Logie, V. Camos, and N. Cowan (Eds.), *Working memory: State of the science* (pp. 10–43). Oxford, UK: Oxford University Press.

Baddeley, A. D., & Logie, R. H. (1999). Working memory: The multiple-component model. In A. Miyake, & P. Shah (Eds.), *Models of working memory: Mechanisms of active maintenance and executive control* (pp. 28–61). Cambridge, UK: Cambridge University Press.

Baddeley, A. D., Thomson, N., & Buchanan, M. (1975). Word length and the structure of short-term memory. *Journal of Verbal Learning & Verbal Behavior, 14,* 575–589.

Baldwin, J. R. (1894). *Mental development in the child and the race.* New York, NY: Macmillan.

Barrouillet, P., Bernardin, S., & Camos, V. (2004). Time constraints and resource sharing in adults' working memory spans. *Journal of Experimental Psychology: General, 133,* 83–100.

Barrouillet, P., Bernardin, S., Portrat, S., Vergauwe, E., & Camos, V. (2007). Time and cognitive load in working memory. *Journal of Experimental Psychology: Learning, Memory, and Cognition, 33,* 570–585.

Barrouillet, P., & Camos, V. (2001). Developmental increase in working memory span: Resource sharing or temporal decay? *Journal of Memory and Language, 45,* 1–20.

Barrouillet, P., & Camos, V. (2009). Interference: Unique source of forgetting in working memory? *Trends in Cognitive Sciences, 13,* 145–146.

Barrouillet, P., & Camos, V. (2015). *Working memory: Loss and reconstruction.* Hove, UK: Psychology Press.

Barrouillet, P., Camos, V., Perruchet, P., & Seron, X. (2004). A Developmental Asemantic Procedural Transcoding (ADAPT) model: From verbal to Arabic numerals. *Psychological Review, 111,* 368–394.

Barrouillet, P., Dagry, I., & Gauffroy, C. (2021). On the sources of working memory development: Manipulating temporal factors (almost) abolishes developmental differences. Manuscript submitted for publication.

Barrouillet, P., De Paepe, A., & Langerock, N. (2012). Time causes forgetting from working memory. *Psychonomic Bulletin & Review, 19,* 87–92.

Barrouillet, P. Gavens, N., Vergauwe, E., Gaillard, V., & Camos, V. (2009). Working memory span development: A time-based resource-sharing model account. *Developmental Psychology, 45,* 477–490.

Barrouillet, P., Gorin, S., & Camos, V. (in press). Simple spans underestimate verbal working memory capacity. *Journal of Experimental Psychology: General.*

Barrouillet, P., Plancher, G., Guida, A., & Camos, V. (2013). Forgetting at short term: When do event-based interference and temporal factors have an effect? *Acta Psychologica, 142,* 155–167.

Barrouillet, P., Portrat, S., & Camos, V. (2011). On the law relating processing and storage in working memory. *Psychological Review, 118,* 175–192.

Barrouillet, P., Portrat, S., Vergauwe, E., Diependaele, K., & Camos, V. (2011). Further evidence for temporal decay in working memory. *Journal of Experimental Psychology: Learning, Memory, & Cognition, 37,* 1302–1317.

Barrouillet, P., Uittenhove, K., Lucidi, A., & Langerock, N. (2018). On the sources of forgetting in working memory: The test of competing hypotheses. *Quarterly Journal of Experimental Psychology, 20,* 1–46.

Bertrand, R., & Camos, V. (2015). The role of attention in preschoolers' working memory. *Cognitive Development, 33,* 14–27.

Bertrand, R., & Camos, V. (2021). Could developmental change in forgetting rate account for working memory increase in early childhood? Manuscript submitted for publication.

Bertrand, R., Stam-Zahno, I., & Camos, V. (2020). The rate of forgetting over time in working memory during early childhood. *L'Année Psychologique, 120*, 157–174.

Brainerd, C. J., & Reyna, V. F. (2002). Fuzzy-trace theory and false memory. *Current Directions in Psychological Science, 11*, 164–169.

Brainerd, C. J., & Reyna, V. F. (2005). *The science of false memory*. New York, NY: Oxford University Press.

Camos, V. (2015). Storing verbal information in working memory. *Current Directions in Psychological Science, 24*, 440–445.

Camos, V. (2017). Domain-specific vs. domain-general maintenance in working memory: reconciliation within the time-based resource sharing model. In B. Ross (Ed.), *The Psychology of Learning and Motivation, Vol. 67* (pp. 135–171). Cambridge, MA: Academic Press.

Camos, V., & Barrouillet, P. (2011). Developmental change in working memory strategies: From passive maintenance to active refreshing. *Developmental Psychology, 47*, 898–904.

Camos, V., & Barrouillet, P. (2018). *Working memory in development*. Hove, UK: Routledge.

Camos, V., Johnson, M., Loaiza, V., Portrat, S., Souza, A., & Vergauwe, E. (2018). What is attentional refreshing in working memory? *Annals of the New York Academy of Sciences, 1424*, 19–32.

Camos, V., Lagner, P., & Loaiza, V. (2017). Maintenance of item and order information in verbal working memory. *Memory, 8*, 953–968.

Camos, V., Lagner, P., & Barrouillet, P. (2009). Two maintenance mechanisms of verbal information in working memory. *Journal of Memory and Language, 61*, 457–469.

Camos, V., Mora, G., & Barrouillet, P. (2013). Phonological similarity effect in complex span task. *Quarterly Journal of Experimental Psychology, 66*, 1927–1950.

Camos, V., Mora, G., & Oberauer, K. (2011). Adaptive choice between articulatory rehearsal and attentional refreshing in verbal working memory. *Memory & Cognition, 39*, 231–244.

Camos, V., Mora, G., Oftinger, A-L., Mariz Elsig, S., Schneider, P., & Vergauwe, E. (2019). Does long-term memory affect refreshing in verbal working memory? *Journal of Experimental Psychology: Learning, Memory, and Cognition, 45*, 1664–1682.

Camos, V., & Portrat, S. (2015). The impact of cognitive load on delayed recall. *Psychonomic Bulletin and Review, 22*, 1029–1034.

Campoy, G., Castellà, J., Provencio, V., Hitch, G. J., & Baddeley, A. D. (2015). Automatic semantic encoding in verbal short-term memory: Evidence from the concreteness effect. *Quarterly Journal of Experimental Psychology, 68*, 759–778.

Carretti, B., Cornoldi, C., De Beni, R., & Palladino, P. (2004). What happens to information to be suppressed in working-memory tasks? Short and long term effects. *Quarterly Journal of Experimental Psychology, 57*, 1059–1084.

Case, R. (1985). *Intellectual development: Birth to adulthood*. New York, NY: Academic Press.

Case, R., Kurland, D. M., & Goldberg, J. (1982). Operational efficiency and the growth of short-term memory span. *Journal of Experimental Child Psychology, 33*, 386–404.

Chen, Z., & Cowan, N. (2009). How verbal memory loads consume attention. *Memory & Cognition, 37*, 829–836.

Cowan, N. (1992). Verbal memory span and the timing of spoken recall. *Journal of Memory and Language, 31*, 668–684.

Cowan, N. (1988). Evolving conceptions of memory storage, selective attention, and their mutual constraints within the human information-processing system. *Psychological Bulletin, 104*, 163–191.

Cowan, N. (2001). The magical number 4 in short-term memory: A reconsideration of mental storage capacity. *Behavioral and Brain Sciences, 24*, 87–185.

Cowan, N. (2005). *Working memory capacity*. Hove, UK: Psychology Press.

Cowan, N. (2017). The many faces of working memory and short-term storage. *Psychonomic Bulletin & Review, 24*, 1158–1170.

Cowan, N., Keller, T., Hulme, C., Roodenrys, S., McDougall, S., & Rack, J. (1994). Verbal memory span in children: Speech timing clues to the mechanisms underlying age and word length effects. *Journal of Memory and Language, 33*, 234–250.

Cowan, N., Morey, C. C., & Naveh-Benjamin, M. (2021). An embedded-processes approach to working memory: how is it distinct from other approaches, and to what ends? In R. H. Logie, V.

Camos, & N. Cowan (Eds.), *Working memory: State of the science* (pp. 44–84). Oxford, UK: Oxford University Press.

Craik, F. I. M., & Watkins, M. J. (1973). The role of rehearsal in short-term memory. *Journal of Verbal Learning and Verbal Behavior, 12*, 599–607.

Dagry, I., & Barrouillet, P. (2017). The fate of distractors in working memory: No evidence for their active removal. *Cognition, 169*, 129–138.

Dagry, I., Vergauwe, E., & Barrouillet, P. (2017). Cleaning working memory: The fate of distractors. *Journal of Memory and Language, 92*, 327–342.

Daneman, M., & Carpenter, P. A. (1980). Individual differences in comprehending and producing words in context. *Journal of Memory and Language, 19*, 450–466.

De Schrijver, S., & Barrouillet, P. (2017). Consolidation and restoration of memory traces in working memory. *Psychonomic Bulletin & Review, 24*, 1651–1657.

Dulany, D. E. (1991). Conscious representation and thought systems. In R. S. Wyer & T. K. Srull (Eds.), *Advances in social cognition* (Vol. 4, pp. 97–120). Hillsdale, NJ: Lawrence Erlbaum Associates.

Dulany, D. E. (1997). Consciousness in the explicit (deliberative) and implicit (evocative). In J. Cohen & J. Schooler (Eds.), *Scientific approaches to consciousness* (pp. 179–211). Mahwah, NJ: Lawrence Erlbaum Associates.

Engle, R. W. (2002). Working memory capacity as executive attention. *Current Directions in Psychological Science, 11*, 19–23.

Engle, R. W., & Kane, M. J. (2004). Executive attention, working memory capacity, and a two-factor theory of cognitive control. In B. Ross (Ed.), *The Psychology of Learning and Motivation* (Vol. 44, pp. 145–199). New York, NY: Elsevier.

Fitamen, C., Blaye, A., & Camos, V. (2019a). The role of goal cueing in kindergarteners' working memory. *Journal of Experimental Child Psychology, 187*, 104666.

Fitamen, C., Blaye, A., & Camos, V. (2019b). Preschoolers' working memory benefits from transparent goal cue if children act on it. *Scientific Reports, 9*, 15342.

Fitamen, C., Blaye, A., & Camos, V. (2019c). How goal cue and motor activity modulate working memory performance in preschoolers. *PsyArXiv*. doi:10.31234/osf.io/sr8hd

Gaillard, V., Barrouillet, P. Jarrold, C., & Camos, V. (2011). Developmental differences in working memory: Where do they come from? *Journal of Experimental Child Psychology, 110*, 469–479.

Gavens, N., & Barrouillet, P. (2004). Delays of retention, processing efficiency, and attentional resources in working memory span development. *Journal of Memory and Language, 51*, 644–657.

Glenberg, A. M., Smith, S. M., & Green, C. (1977). Type I rehearsal: Maintenance and more. *Journal of Verbal Learning and Verbal Behavior, 16*, 339–352.

Gruber, O. (2001). Effects of domain-specific interference on brain activation associated with verbal working memory task performance. *Cerebral Cortex, 11*, 1047–1055.

Haberlandt, K. (1997). *Cognitive psychology* (2nd ed.). Boston, MA: Allyn & Bacon.

Halford, G. S. (1993). *Children's understanding: The development of mental models.* Hillsdale, NJ: Lawrence Erlbaum Associates.

Halford, G. S., Cowan, N., & Andrews, G. (2007). Separating cognitive capacity from knowledge: A new hypothesis. *Trends in Cognitive Sciences, 11*, 236–242.

Hazy, T. E., Frank, M. J., & O'Reilly, R. C. (2006). Banishing the homunculus: Making working memory work. *Neuroscience, 139*, 105–118.

Hitch, G., Towse, J. N., & Hutton, U. (2001). What limits children's working memory span? Theoretical accounts and applications for scholastic development. *Journal of Experimental Psychology: General, 130*, 184–198.

Hudjetz, A., & Oberauer, K. (2007). The effects of processing time and processing rate on forgetting in working memory: Testing four models of the complex span paradigm. *Memory & Cognition, 35*, 1675–1684.

Hulme, C., Roodenrys, S., Schweickert, R., Brown, G. D., Martin, S., & Stuart, G. (1997). Word-frequency effects on short-term memory tasks: evidence for a redintegration process in immediate serial recall. *Journal of Experimental Psychology: Learning, Memory, and Cognition, 23*, 1217–1232.

Johnson-Laird, P. N. (1983). *Mental models: Towards a cognitive science of language, inference, and consciousness.* Cambridge, MA: Harvard University Press.

Johnson-Laird, P. N. (2006). *How we reason*. Oxford, UK: Oxford University Press.

Johnson-Laird, P. N., & Byrne, R. M. J. (1991). *Deduction*. Hillsdale, NJ: Lawrence Erlbaum.

Jones, D. M., Farrand, P., Stuart, G., & Morris, N. (1995). Functional equivalence of verbal and spatial information in serial short-term memory. *Journal of Experimental Psychology: Learning, Memory, & Cognition, 21*, 1008–1018.

Jones, D. M., Hughes, R. W., & Macken, W. J. (2007). The phonological store abandoned. *Quarterly Journal of Experimental Psychology, 60*, 505–511.

Jones, D. M., & Macken, W. (2018). In the beginning was the deed: verbal short-term memory as object-oriented action. *Current Directions in Psychological Science, 27*, 351–356.

Kane, M. J., Hambrick, D. Z., Tuholski, S. W., Wilhelm, O., Payne, T., & W., Engle, R. W. (2004). The generality of working memory capacity: A latent-variable approach to verbal and visuospatial memory span and reasoning. *Journal of Experimental Psychology: General, 133*, 189–217.

Klauer, K. C., & Zhao, Z. (2004). Double dissociations in visual and spatial short-term memory. *Journal of Experimental Psychology: General, 133*, 355–381.

Koechlin, E., Ody, C., & Kouneiher, F. (2003). The architecture of cognitive control in human prefrontal cortex. *Science, 302*, 1181–1185.

Langerock, N., Vergauwe, E., & Barrouillet, P. (2014). The maintenance of cross-domain associations in the episodic buffer. *Journal of Experimental Psychology: Learning, Memory, and Cognition, 40*, 1096–1109.

Lemaire, B., Pageot, A., Plancher, G., & Portrat, S. (2018). What is the time course of working memory attentional refreshing? *Psychonomic Bulletin & Review, 25*, 370–385.

Lépine, R., Barrouillet, P., & Camos, V. (2005). What makes working memory span so predictive of high level cognition? *Psychonomic Bulletin & Review, 12*, 165–170.

Lépine, R., Bernardin, S., & Barrouillet, P. (2005). Attention switching and working memory spans. *European Journal of Cognitive Psychology, 17*, 329–346.

Lewandowsky, S., & Oberauer, K. (2009). No evidence for temporal decay in working memory. *Journal of Experimental Psychology: Learning, Memory, and Cognition, 35*, 1545–1551.

Lewandowsky, S., Oberauer, K., & Brown, G. D. A. (2009). No temporal decay in verbal short-term memory. *Trends in Cognitive Sciences, 13*, 120–126.

Loaiza, V., & Camos, V. (2018). The role of semantic representations in refreshing verbal information in working memory. *Journal of Experimental Psychology: Learning, Memory, and Cognition, 44*, 863–881.

Logan, G. D. (1988). Toward an instance theory of automatization. *Psychological Review, 95*, 492–527.

Logan, G. D. (1995). The Weibull distribution, the power law, and the instance theory of automaticity. *Psychological Review, 102*, 751–756.

Logan G. D. (1998). What is learned during automatization? II. Obligatory encoding of spatial location. *Journal of Experimental Psychology: Human Perception and Performance, 24*, 1720–1736.

Logie, R. H. (1995). *Visuo-spatial working memory*. Hove, UK: Psychology Press.

Lucidi, A., Langerock, N., Hoareau, V., Lemaire, B., Camos, V., & Barrouillet, P. (2016). Working memory still needs verbal rehearsal. *Memory & Cognition, 44*, 197–206.

Lucidi, A., Loaiza, V., Camos, V., & Barrouillet, P. (2014). Assessing working memory capacity through time-constrained elementary activities. *Journal of General Psychology, 141*, 98–112.

Macken, B., Taylor, J., Kozlov, M., Hughes, R., & Jones, D. (2016). Memory as embodiment: The case of modality and serial short-term memory. *Cognition, 155*, 113–124.

Marcovitch, S., Boseovski, J. J., Knapp, R. J., & Kane, M. J. (2010). Goal neglect and working memory capacity in 4- to 6-year-old children. *Child Development, 81*, 1687–1695.

Mashburn, C. A., Tsukahara, J. S., & Engle, R. W. (2021). Individual differences in attention control: Implications for the relationship between working memory capacity and fluid intelligence. In R. H. Logie, V. Camos, and N. Cowan (Eds.), *Working memory: State of the science* (pp. 175–211). Oxford, UK: Oxford University Press.

McCabe, D. P. (2008). The role of covert retrieval in working memory span tasks: Evidence from delayed recall tests. *Journal of Memory and Language, 58*, 480–494.

Miller, G. A., Galanter, E., & Pribam, K. H. (1960). *Plans and the structure of behavior*. New York, NY: Holt, Rinehart and Winston.

Mora, G., & Camos, V. (2013). Two systems of maintenance in verbal working memory: Evidence from the word length effect. *PLoS One, 8,* e70026.

Mora, G., & Camos, V. (2015). Dissociating rehearsal and refreshing in the maintenance of verbal information in 8-year-old children. *Frontiers in Psychology: Developmental Psychology, 6,* 11.

Morey, C. (2018). The case against specialized visual-spatial short-term memory. *Psychological Bulletin, 144,* 849–883.

Naveh-Benjamin, M., & Jonides, J. (1984). Maintenance rehearsal: A two-component analysis. *Journal of Experimental Psychology: Learning, Memory, and Cognition, 10,* 369–385.

Newell, A. (1990). *Unified theories of cognition.* Harvard, MA: Harvard University Press.

Norris, D. (2017). Short-term memory and long-term memory are still different. *Psychological Bulletin, 143,* 992–1009.

Oberauer, K. (2002). Access to information in working memory: Exploring the focus of attention. *Journal of Experimental Psychology: Learning, Memory, and Cognition, 28,* 411–421.

Oberauer, K. (2009). Interference between storage and processing in working memory: Feature overwriting, not similarity-based competition. *Memory & Cognition, 37,* 346–357.

Oberauer, K. (2021). Towards a theory of working memory: from metaphors to mechanisms. In R. H. Logie, V. Camos, and N. Cowan (Eds.), *Working Memory: State of the Science* (pp. 116–149). Oxford, UK: Oxford University Press.

Oberauer, K., & Lewandowsky, S. (2008). Forgetting in immediate serial recall: Decay, temporal distinctiveness, or interference? *Psychological Review, 115,* 544–576.

Oberauer, K., & Lewandowsky, S., Farrell, S., Jarrold, C., & Greaves, M. (2012). Modeling working memory: An interference model of complex span. *Psychonomic Bulletin & Review, 19,* 779–819.

Oftinger, A.-L., & Camos, V. (2016). Maintenance mechanisms in children's verbal working memory. *Journal of Educational and Developmental Psychology, 6,* 16–28.

Oftinger, A.-L., & Camos, V. (2017). Phonological similarity effect in children's working memory: Do maintenance mechanisms matter? *Journal of Child Psychology, 1,* 5–11.

Oftinger, A.-L., & Camos, V. (2018). Developmental improvement in strategies to maintain verbal information in children's working memory. *International Journal of Behavioral Development, 42,* 182–191.

Pascual-Leone, J. A., & Johnson, J. (2011). A developmental theory of mental attention: its applications to measurement and task analysis. In P. Barrouillet & V. Gaillard (Eds.), *Cognitive development and working memory* (pp. 47–68). Hove, UK: Psychology Press.

Pashler, H. E. (1998). *The psychology of attention.* Cambridge, MA: MIT Press.

Perruchet, P., & Vinter, A. (2002). The self-organizing consciousness. *Behavioral and Brain Sciences, 25,* 297–388.

Piaget, J. (1936). *La naissance de l'intelligence chez l'enfant. [Emergence of intelligence in the child].* Neuchatel: Delachaux et Nieslé.

Portrat, S., Barrouillet, P., & Camos, V. (2008). Time-decay or interference-based interference forgetting in working memory? *Journal of Experimental Psychology: Learning, Memory, and Cognition, 34,* 1561–1564.

Raye, C. L., Johnson, M. K., Mitchell, K. J., Greene, E. J., & Johnson, M. R. (2007). Refreshing: A minimal executive function. *Cortex, 43,* 135–145.

Rosselet-Jordan, F., Mariz Elsig, S., Abadie, M., & Camos, V. (in revision). Role of attention in the associative relatedness effect in verbal working memory: Behavioral and chronometric perspective.

Rybash, J. M., & Hoyer, W. J. (1992). Hemispheric specialization for categorical and coordinate spatial representations: A reappraisal. *Memory & Cognition, 20,* 271–276.

Shipstead, Z., Harrison, T. L., & Engle, R. W. (2016). Working memory capacity and fluid intelligence: Maintenance and disengagement. *Psychological Science, 11,* 771–799.

Smith, E. E., & Jonides, J. (1999). Storage and executive processes in the frontal lobes. *Science, 283,* 1657–1661.

Souza, A. S., & Oberauer, K. (2018). Does articulatory rehearsal help immediate serial recall? *Cognitive Psychology, 107,* 1–21.

Towse, J. N., & Hitch, G. J. (1995). Is there a relationship between task demand and storage space in tests of working memory capacity? *Quarterly Journal of Experimental Psychology, 48,* 108–124.

Towse, J. N., & Houston-Price, C. M. T. (2001). Reflections on the concept of central executive. In J. Andrade (Ed.), *Working memory in perspective* (pp. 240–260). Philadelphia, PA: Psychology Press.

Towse, J. N., Hitch, G. J., & Hutton, U. (1998). A reevaluation of working memory capacity in children. *Journal of Memory and Language, 39,* 195–217.

Towse, J. N., Hitch, G. J., & Hutton, U. (2000). On the interpretation of working memory spans in adults. *Memory & Cognition, 28,* 341–348.

Towse, J. N., Hitch, G. J., & Hutton, U. (2002). On the nature of the relationship between processing activity and item retention in children. *Journal of Experimental Child Psychology, 82,* 156–184.

Trost, S., & Gruber, O. (2012). Evidence for a double dissociation of articulatory rehearsal and non-articulatory maintenance of phonological information in human verbal working memory. *Neuropsychobiology, 65,* 133–140.

Turner, M. L., & Engle, R. W. (1989). Is working memory capacity task dependent? *Journal of Memory and Language, 28,* 127–154.

Unsworth, N., & Engle, R. W. (2007). The nature of individual differences in working memory capacity: Active maintenance in primary memory and controlled search from secondary memory. *Psychological Review, 114,* 104–132.

Vergauwe, E., Barrouillet, P. & Camos, V. (2009). Visual and spatial working memory are not that dissociated after all: a time-based resource-sharing account. *Journal of Experimental Psychology: Learning, Memory, and Cognition, 35,* 1012–1028.

Vergauwe, E., Barrouillet, P. & Camos, V. (2010). Verbal and visuo-spatial working memory: a case for domain-general time-based resource sharing. *Psychological Science, 21,* 384–390.

Vergauwe, E., Camos, V., & Barrouillet, P. (2014). The impact of storage on processing: Implications for structure and functioning of working memory. *Journal of Experimental Psychology: Learning, Memory, and Cognition, 40,* 1072–1095.

Vergauwe, E., & Cowan, N. (2015a). Working memory units are all in your head: Factors that influence whether features or objects are the favored units. *Journal of Experimental Psychology: Learning, Memory, and Cognition, 41,* 1404–1416.

Vergauwe, E., & Cowan, N. (2015b). Attending to items in working memory: Evidence that refreshing and memory search are closely related. *Psychonomic Bulletin and Review, 22,* 1001–1006.

Vergauwe, E., & Langerock, N. (2017). Attentional refreshing of information in working memory: Increased accessibility of just-refreshed representations. *Journal of Memory and Language, 96,* 23–35.

Welford, A. T. (1967). Single-channel operation in the brain. *Acta Psychologica, 27,* 5–22.

5

Towards a Theory of Working Memory

From Metaphors to Mechanisms

Klaus Oberauer

For the past two decades, my colleagues and I have been working towards a theory of working memory (WM). We are not there yet. What I can offer so far is a conceptual framework that integrates a number of assumptions into a coherent narrative, so that it could serve as a blueprint for a theory (Oberauer, 2009). I do not consider this framework a theory because I expect a theory to enable strong predictions of testable empirical hypotheses. By strong predictions I mean predictions that can be derived deductively from the theory with the addition of few, or ideally no, auxiliary assumptions.[1] Strong predictions are necessary to put a theory to a serious empirical test: when they succeed, we gain support for the theory, and when they fail, we obtain evidence against the theory. In contrast, weak predictions do not allow for a test that puts the theory in much jeopardy: finding a weak prediction to be false has little evidential impact on the theory because there are many ways to explain the unwelcome finding away without changing or abandoning the theory.

My framework of WM is useful for organizing ideas and questions, and for generating predictions, several of which have been confirmed and thereby provide some support for the framework, but they are weak predictions: the assumptions in the framework are to some extent vague, and they are incomplete in the sense that many auxiliary assumptions need to be added to derive any testable prediction from them deductively.

To arrive at strong predictions, I incorporated some of the assumptions from the framework in computational models of WM. A computational model expresses a theory as a mathematical function—in the form of a set of interlocking equations or a computer program—that takes the experimental conditions and the model parameters as arguments and returns predictions for the dependent variable(s). We can use such models to generate predictions through computation, a form of deduction. This is helpful for generating strong predictions. How strong they actually are depends on the flexibility that a computational model has in virtue of its form and its free parameters. At least, such a model allows us to formally determine the strength of a prediction by computing model predictions under a broad range of parameters.

---

[1] Formally, we can express the strength of a prediction as the conditional probability that the predicted hypothesis H is true if the theory T is true, $P(H|T)$.

Klaus Oberauer, *Towards a Theory of Working Memory* In: *Working Memory*. Edited by: Robert H. Logie, Valérie Camos, and Nelson Cowan, Oxford University Press (2021). © Oxford University Press. DOI: 10.1093/oso/9780198842286.003.0005

The limitation of building computational models is that they are typically useful for offering fairly detailed explanations of data patterns in a fairly narrow set of circumstances—for instance, people's behaviour in one particular test paradigm for studying WM. Therefore, so far my colleagues and I have developed a number of separate computational models for specific sub-domains in the field of WM. We have not been able yet to integrate them into one computational model that deserves to be called a theory of WM.

But let us talk about WM nonetheless. I will start with a summary of the framework because it provides a good roadmap, and then discuss three computational models that incorporate some of the framework's assumptions to apply them to three areas of research: immediate serial recall of lists, immediate recall of simple visual arrays, and switching between memory sets and between task sets. Along the way I will do my best to answer the seven questions posed by the editors of this volume (Table 5.1).

A Roadmap for a Theory of Working Memory

I find it useful to start with the question: what is the function of WM—what is it good for? In evolutionary terms, we can ask: what adaptation has it evolved for? I propose that the function of WM is to provide a medium for representations that we can manipulate and that we can use to guide our thoughts and actions in ways that are novel and potentially depart from what we have learned. For example, suppose that on your way home from work today you want to make a detour to a new shop to buy a gift for a loved one. To plan the best route for your detour you set up a representation of your usual way home in WM and change it so that it includes the detour. You might think through several alternatives in an attempt to minimize distance and traffic on the way— you manipulate your representation in WM several times until you are satisfied with the plan. After that, you can use this plan to guide your way through town, enabling you to depart from your learned routine for driving home. All this leaves your learned representation of the usual way home in long-term memory (LTM) untouched—as it should because you will need it again tomorrow.

The example illustrates a division of labour between WM and LTM: the function of LTM is to provide a relatively stable representation of what is the case (i.e. semantic LTM), what has happened in our personal past (i.e. episodic LTM), and of how to do things (i.e. procedural LTM). The function of WM is to enable us to build and manipulate temporary representations that deviate from those in LTM. It enables us, for instance, to engage in hypothetical thinking that deviates from what we know to be the case ('What if people could fly?') and from what we know happened ('Had I left home 5 minutes earlier, I would have caught the plane'). It enables us to consider alternative paths of action ('What if I take the bike to work instead of the car?') and play through multiple alternative plans (e.g. thinking through possible moves in a chess game) without distorting our representation of reality in LTM. It also enables us to act in ways that depart from our habits and routines: when presented with a list of words, our usual

Table 5.1 Summary responses to designated questions

Question	Response
1. Definition of working memory (WM)	WM is a medium for building, holding, and manipulating temporary representations that control our current thoughts and actions.
2. Methods used	In addition to behavioural experiments and individual-differences studies, I aim to build computational models to formulate theoretical ideas clearly. The strength of these models is that they enable strong predictions for behavioural data. Their main weakness is that currently they do not generalize much beyond one or two experimental paradigms. Also, computational models are so far underdeveloped for predicting data from cognitive neuroscience.
3. Unitary versus non-unitary nature of WM	(a) The relation of WM and long-term memory (LTM): WM is a medium for constructing new relational representations out of known elements. The elements are representations in LTM (i.e. learned chunks). Yet, WM is functionally distinct from LTM: WM is used for creating representations that can contradict LTM information (e.g. when we engage in hypothetical thinking, building a counterfactual mental model in WM) or countermand LTM information (e.g. when we implement an instruction as a task set in WM that contradicts a learned habit, such as saying 'red' in response to the word GREEN, and 'green' in response to RED). To enable this, WM representations must be shielded from LTM. This is accomplished by a mechanism for rapidly forming and removing temporary bindings between elements. These bindings are distinct from more slowly changing associations in LTM. (b) Content domains: I see no need to distinguish domain-specific sub-systems of WM. We can model WM as a unitary system using distributed representations in different, partially overlapping feature spaces. The degree of feature-space overlap determines the degree of interference between them. Verbal and visuospatial contents tend to be represented in feature spaces with relatively little overlap, so that they interfere less with each other than contents from the same domain.
4. The role of attention and control	The role of attention for WM depends on how we define attention. If we define attention as a limited resource, then there is no role for it in my concept of WM because I find that the concept of a limited resource creates more trouble than it is worth, for reasons explained elsewhere (Oberauer, 2019; Oberauer, Farrell, Jarrold, & Lewandowsky, 2016). If we define attention as a selection mechanism, then WM itself is a form of attention: the contents of WM are selected for being relevant for the current task. This selection is accomplished through perceptual-attention mechanisms that filter out irrelevant stimulus information, and by cue-based retrieval from LTM: relevant information in LTM is retrieved into WM with the help of appropriate retrieval cues, such as task cues in task-switching experiments, or list cues in list-switching experiments. Within WM, individual items often need to be selected for processing, and I assume a separate mechanism dedicated to this function, which I call the 'focus of attention' in WM. The contents of WM serve to control our thoughts and actions. For instance, declarative representations in WM act as search templates that guide perceptual attention to matching stimuli. Procedural WM representations—task sets—control how we respond to stimuli. In this way, cognitive control is achieved through the interplay of common mechanisms of learning, retrieval, and perceptual attention. The current search templates in WM direct attention to relevant objects in the perceived environment; the current task set in WM determines which perceptual features are relevant, and therefore encoded into WM. Information in WM serves as retrieval cue to memory sets and task sets in WM. In this way, the current contents of WM are continuously updated by new contents from perception and LTM. To avoid unnecessary interference, contents that are no longer relevant are routinely removed.

Table 5.1 Continued

Question	Response
5. Storage, maintenance, and loss	Encoding of information into WM means to create new, temporary bindings between existing content representations (e.g. words, known objects) and the contexts that are to be used as retrieval cues at test. In contrast to most theories of WM, I assume that, by default, information in WM is retained rather than lost, and therefore I see no need for a dedicated maintenance process. What is needed instead is a dedicated process for getting rid of outdated information (for instance, a removal process as implemented in the SOB-CS model).
6. Role of LTM for WM (and vice versa)	Semantic LTM provides units to be bound in WM, and helps to disambiguate retrieved representations through redintegration. Every information encoded into WM is probably also encoded into episodic LTM. This information could contribute to performance in a WM task, but whether or not it is used is controlled by a gating mechanism: the poorer the available information in WM, the more likely it is that information in episodic LTM is used. In addition to episodic information about individual events, LTM also acquires knowledge across multiple repetitions of similar events—such as when the same memory list is to be maintained in WM repeatedly. This knowledge is acquired not only by slowly changing associations but also by re-representing structures in WM as unified chunks. When the structure of future memory sets (partially) matches a learned chunk, the chunk in LTM helps to stabilize the structure in WM.
7. Inconsistent evidence	Many studies found mutual impairment of memory and concurrent processing even when the materials used in the two sub-tasks appear to have little overlap, so that we should expect little interference. Loss of visual and spatial information over unfilled retention intervals has been observed in many studies, though with some exceptions and boundary conditions. This loss could reflect a gradual drift of representations not stabilized by categorical boundaries. Behavioural and neurophysiological evidence points to a hard limit of visual WM of about three visual objects, which is inconsistent with the IM in its current form.
C. Capacity limit and individual differences	WM capacity is limited by interference, perhaps with an additional contribution of a resource limit (Oberauer et al., 2016). Individual differences arise from variations in latent variables; in computational models of WM these are the model parameters that determine performance (Oberauer, 2016).
D. Neural correlates	Neurally 'silent' WM could reflect retention of content-context bindings through rapid synaptic plasticity; neurally 'active' WM contents reflect the content of the focus of attention.

cognitive routine is to read them to extract their meaning. However, when asked by the experimenter to instead name their print colour—as in the famous 'Stroop task' (MacLeod, 1991)—we can do that by holding in WM a representation of the current task (i.e. naming the print colour), and as long as this task representation is in place, it controls what we do with printed words. Doing this task for an hour or more does not compromise our ability to read because we do not need to revise our long-term routine for processing words—rather, we temporarily override that routine by a countermanding representation in WM.

These considerations enable an answer to *Question 1* posed by the editors, which concerns the definition of WM: I propose to define WM as a medium for building, holding, and manipulating temporary representations that control our current thoughts and actions.

Starting from a functional definition of WM has the advantage that it provides guidance for the next question I want to address: how does it work? On the assumption that evolution has endowed us with fairly good (though not always optimal) solutions to adaptive problems, thinking about how a system should ideally be designed for fulfilling a certain function provides a good heuristic for how it might actually work (Anderson, 1990). What features would a WM system need to have to fulfil the function delineated earlier?

1. A first requirement is that it is possible to build new relational representations in WM. Relational representations are structures built of elements and relations between them—for instance, forming a new sentence from known words, or constructing a new mental model of a molecule from chemical elements. This functionality requires a mechanism for the rapid formation of temporary bindings between representations.

2. There needs to be a mechanism for selective access to elements within a structural representation in WM. For instance, a chess player thinking through a series of moves needs to build a representation of the configuration of chess pieces and be able to select one piece to make a hypothetical move, thereby updating the configuration.

3. Representations in WM should control our thoughts and actions. This means not only to control what we think about and act on—the objects of our thought—but also what we do with these objects. Therefore, WM needs to hold both declarative representations of the objects of thought, and procedural representations of our intended actions.

4. As our thoughts and actions progress rapidly, the information needed for guiding them changes rapidly, too. Therefore, there must be mechanisms for rapidly updating the contents of WM.

5. To function as a medium for representations that can contradict—and even countermand—more durable information in LTM, WM needs to be to some extent decoupled from LTM. This means that episodic memories and knowledge in LTM must not interfere with representations in WM. A WM system could not think through a counterfactual scenario such as 'Had I not expressed my opinion in the meeting so clearly ..', if that representation immediately suffered interference from the episodic record of how the meeting actually unfolded. Likewise, a WM system could not plan a new route between work and home if the well-learned old route interfered with it.

6. At the same time, WM must not be entirely separated from LTM, because information in LTM is an indispensable ingredient for our thinking and action planning. Conversely, new ideas and plans that are initially composed in WM are sometimes worth maintaining over the long term, so it should be possible to form

long-term representations of some—though not all—WM contents. Taking requirements (5) and (6) together, we need a system with a flexible gate between representations in WM and those in LTM, such that useful information in LTM can be selectively retrieved into WM, while currently irrelevant and potentially interfering information is blocked. Likewise, WM representations that might be useful in the future should be maintained in LTM whereas others (e.g. chess moves whose outcome has been found to be poor, or misrepresentations of heard sentences that have subsequently been corrected) are best discarded without leaving a trace in LTM, lest they interfere with more useful and accurate knowledge.

I next sketch the blueprint of a system that meets these requirements, discussing them one by one in the following five sections.

Content–Context Bindings

First, we need a mechanism for building relational representations through temporary bindings. A solution that has been proposed in several areas concerned with structural representations (for memory, e.g. Brown, Preece, & Hulme, 2000; for analogical reasoning, e.g. Hummel & Holyoak, 2003; for symbolic structures such as sentences or propositions, e.g. Smolensky, 1990) is to bind elementary *content* representations to *context* representations. Contents can be any objects of thought, including physical objects or events, people, concepts, numbers, and more. The term context is one I borrow from theories of episodic memory (e.g. Raaijmakers & Shiffrin, 1981; Sederberg, Howard, & Kahana, 2008), but I use it in a more general sense: a context can be a location in a mental coordinate system or a role in a schema.

For instance, as in episodic memory models, the context of an event could be the location on a mental time line at which it happened. It could also be the location in physical space to which we bind an object (e.g. a landmark in our mental map of a city). We can also build structural representations of relations beyond space and time by binding elements to locations in a mental coordinate system. For instance, when learning that Kate is smarter than Beth, and Beth is smarter than Joan, we can build a mental model of the rank order of the three people by binding them to successive locations on a dimension of smartness:

Joan   Beth   Kate

This mental model supports the transitive inference that Kate is smarter than Joan (Johnson-Laird, 1983). Another form of context is a role in a schema (Halford, Wilson, & Phillips, 1998). The prototypical example is the representation of a proposition through a number of role–filler bindings. For instance, the proposition expressed by 'Mary lends Anne her pen' is formed by binding 'lend' to the action role, 'Mary' to the agent role, 'Anne' to the patient role, and 'pen' to the object role. Fig. 5.1 illustrates a simple connectionist architecture for content–context bindings. There are two layers of units, one for

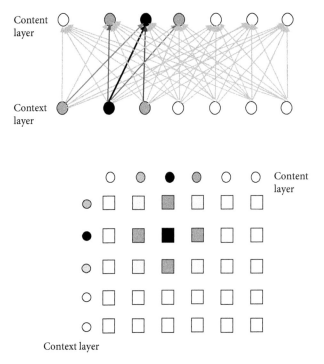

Fig. 5.1 Two-layer connectionist network for binding contents to contexts. The upper panel shows each layer as a row of units, and their connections as arrows. The bottom panel shows the same network with content and context representations as vectors of activation values across the units, together with the matrix of connection weights between them. Hebbian learning updates the connection-weight matrix by adding the outer product of content and context vectors to it.

Reproduced from Klaus Oberauer and Hsuan-Yu Lin, 'An interference model of visual working memory', *Psychological Review*, 124 (1), pp. 21–59, https://doi.org/10.1037/rev0000044 Copyright © 2017, American Psychological Association.

representing contents and one for representing contexts. A content item—for instance, the meaning of a word, or the visual appearance of an object—is represented by a pattern of activation across the units of the content layer; and a context is a pattern of activation across the context layer. The layers are interconnected by a matrix of connection weights. These weights determine how much activation flows from a given context unit to a given content unit. To bind a content (e.g. the word 'turnip') to a context (e.g. the first position in a memory list), we need to simultaneously activate the representation of 'turnip' in the content layer and the representation of 'position 1' in the context layer, then apply a Hebbian learning rule to modify the connection weights. The simplest Hebbian learning rule changes each weight w_{ij} between context unit i and content unit j as a function of the product of their activation, a_i and a_j, and a learning rate ε:

$$\Delta w_{ij} = \varepsilon a_i a_j$$

The two-layer network can represent multiple content–context bindings because the weight changes generated by successive learning events are simply added up. With more bindings, their fidelity gradually decreases, and this form of interference contributes to the capacity limit of WM.

This binding mechanism is used in many computational models of one of the most popular tasks for testing WM, the serial-recall task. In serial recall, a list of elements has to be recalled in the order of presentation (or sometimes in reverse order). The most successful models of behaviour in the serial-recall task share the assumption that the order of items in a list is represented by binding each item to a representation of its ordinal position in the list (Farrell & Lewandowsky, 2004; Hurlstone, Hitch, & Baddeley, 2014; Lewandowsky & Farrell, 2008), and the two-layer architecture sketched in Fig. 5.1, with a Hebbian learning rule, is a convenient way of implementing these content-context bindings.

The Focus of Attention

The second requirement for a functioning WM is a mechanism for selective access to its contents. I describe this mechanism as a *focus of attention* that selects a subset of the current WM contents for processing. Multiple lines of evidence converge on the conclusion that the items held in WM are not all equally accessible—the item currently held in the focus of attention can be accessed faster, and often with higher accuracy, than other items (for a review see Oberauer & Hein, 2012). The perhaps most compelling demonstration of this effect uses the retro-cue paradigm (Griffin & Nobre, 2003; Landman, Spekreijse, & Lamme, 2003). Participants in a retro-cue experiment are asked to remember a set of items—usually simple visual objects, such as an array of colour patches—and about 1 second into the retention interval, a cue points out one of these items as the one most likely to be tested. If the cued item is subsequently tested, responses are faster and more accurate than in a control condition without a cue; when one of the not-cued items is tested, it can still be reported, although typically with somewhat reduced accuracy (for a review see Souza & Oberauer, 2016). This finding demonstrates that people can direct their attention to one item in the current memory set in WM, thereby increasing its accessibility, without losing the other items in the set.

The concept of a focus of attention in WM as described here builds on similar ideas by McElree and Dosher (1993) and by Garavan (1998), but it differs from the focus of attention in the theory of Nelson Cowan (Cowan, 2005; Cowan, Morey, & Naveh-Benjamin, 2021). In Cowan's theory, the focus of attention is a limited attentional resource that can be used to maintain up to about four elements in WM. The focus of attention in my theoretical framework is not a limited resource—rather, it is a mechanism for selective access to representations in WM. Therefore, the focus of attention is not intrinsically limited to a certain number of items. The number of items held simultaneously in the focus of attention is limited by its function as a selection mechanism. In many situations it is useful to select just one item from the current memory set—for instance, when the task is to report one item, or when one item needs to be updated. In other situations, it is useful for the focus to select two or more items simultaneously, and then I expect that the focus holds multiple items.

I do assume one limitation, however: the focus of attention cannot hold multiple bindings simultaneously. This limitation arises from how I think of the focus of attention in the architecture depicted in Fig. 5.1: the representations currently active in the content layer and the context layer form the current content of the focus. When the focus holds a single content item with its context—for instance, one person in one location—then a single content is active in the content layer together with a single context in the context layer, and there is no ambiguity about them going together. However, when the focus holds two content items with their respective contexts, then the two content representations are superimposed in the content layer, and so are the two contexts.[2] In this scenario the focus of attention—the patterns of activation in the two layers—contains no information about which content belongs to which context. This information can be represented in the connection-weight matrix, but the connection weights are not part of the information in the focus. Therefore, I assume that the focus of attention holds multiple items (and their contexts) simultaneously if and only if simultaneous access to them is useful for the task at hand, and the task does not require binding information. An example is the addition of two digits in a mental-arithmetic task. When the task is to add 365 and 162, then the person could form a structural representation aligning the two digit strings in a two-dimensional coordinate system:

    3   6   5
    1   6   2.

The focus of attention could then select the two digits in the last column simultaneously, so that the patterns of activation for 5 and 2 are superimposed in the content layer. Through years of learning, the unique activation pattern generated by this superposition is associated in LTM with the sum '7', so this activation pattern can be used as a retrieval cue to retrieve the sum from semantic memory (Oberauer, 2013).

Cognitive Control by Declarative and Procedural Representations

The distinction between declarative and procedural representations has a long tradition in theories of LTM; it figures most prominently in the ACT-R theory (Anderson & Lebiere, 1998). I argue that this distinction also applies to WM. Declarative representations are about the objects of cognition: physical objects, events, people, the meaning and the sound of words, and so on. Procedural representations are representations of our intended (cognitive or overt) actions in a directly executable way. Procedural representations are a special case of structural representations that consist of bindings

---

[2] 'Superposition' is a technical term for adding two patterns of activation together.

between condition and action representations, such as [GREEN → say 'green'; RED → say 'red'] (verbally, these condition–action bindings could be expressed as if-then rules, such as "If the print colour is red, then say aloud 'red' "). In production-system architectures such as ACT-R they are called *productions*, and in the experimental literature they are referred to as *task sets* (Monsell, 2003). A task set is a set of stimulus categories, each of which is bound to a response category (Fig. 5.2). Hence, task sets are a special form of structural representation in which the stimulus category acts as a retrieval cue for the response bound to it.

Procedural representations of intended actions differ from declarative representations of the same actions in that they are directly executable. This means that when the condition is fulfilled by a representation in WM, then the action is automatically executed without the need for any further process. Some authors have therefore described them as 'prepared reflexes' (Hommel, 2000; Meiran, Liefooghe, & De Houwer, 2017). In contrast, a declarative representation of an action instruction—such as the verbal rule 'If the print colour is red, say aloud 'red''—does not make us say 'red' in response to a word printed in red (see Brass, Liefooghe, Braem, & De Houwer, 2017, for behavioural and neural evidence for the distinction between declarative and procedural WM representations).

Declarative and procedural representations in WM control our thoughts and actions. This should be obvious from the above characterization for procedural representations. The declarative representations currently in WM are, by definition, the contents of our current thoughts. They also control what we attend to in our perceived environment. This has been demonstrated by research with the attentional-capture paradigm (Olivers, Meijer, & Theeuwes, 2006; Soto, Hodsoll, Rotshtein, & Humphreys, 2008): Participants are asked to hold one (or several) stimuli in WM for a subsequent memory test. During the retention interval they do a visual-search task. On some search trials, a distractor matches the stimulus held in WM. This distractor attracts

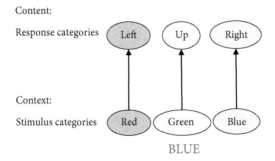

Fig. 5.2 Schematic of a task set. The example is of the task set for a three-colour Stroop task with manual responses (pressing the left, upper, or right key). The stimulus—the word BLUE printed in red—activates the stimulus category Red strongly, but also activates the stimulus category Blue to the extent that the person cannot completely avoid reading the word.

perceptual attention, slowing down search and increasing the prevalence of eye movements to the distractor.

Do representations in LTM that are not in WM also control our cognitive activity? There are reasons to believe that they do. For instance, well-practised information-processing routines such as word reading impose themselves on us even when we do not intend them, as demonstrated by the Stroop task: when the word meaning contradicts the to-be-named print colour (e.g. the word 'green' printed in red), response times and error rates increase, implying that word reading influences our response. Certainly, when instructed to ignore word meaning, we have no reason to retrieve the task set for word reading into WM, so arguably it exerts its influence on our actions directly from LTM. For the case of visual search, Woodman, Carlisle, and Reinhart (2013) have made a strong case that after just a few trials of repeatedly searching for the same target, we no longer need a representation of the target in WM—search can be directly guided from LTM. Shiffrin and Schneider (1977) have demonstrated that after practising searching for the same target over many trials, when the person is transferred to a new search task in which the former target appears as a distractor, it keeps attracting attention against the person's intention.

There are two considerations that let me hesitate endorsing the idea that LTM representations can control cognition directly. One is that we have many well-practised action routines in LTM, and yet we do not automatically execute them whenever their conditions are met. For instance, we do not go about compulsively reading every word aloud that meets our eye. Likewise, we have representations of thousands of objects in WM, and yet we do not always search for each of them in our environment. Something must distinguish between representations that are relevant for our current intentions and others that are not. Holding only the relevant ones in WM is one way of solving that problem—if LTM representations cannot control our cognitive actions in the same way as WM representations. My second reason for hesitation is the well-established finding that there is a severe limit on our ability to carry out two cognitive operations that both involve a choice between several response options at the same time, even when the operations are highly practised (Pashler, 1994). This strong competition between concurrent cognitive actions could be explained if we assume that only task sets in WM control our actions, so that when we try to carry out two actions at the same time, we need to hold two task sets in WM simultaneously, risking interference between them (Göthe, Oberauer, & Kliegl, 2016).

One way to resolve the tension between these arguments is to assume that LTM representations can influence (or bias) our thoughts and actions but not control them. For instance, attending to printed words always involves the activation of a representation of their meaning in WM (e.g. 'blue'), together with a representation of their print colour (e.g. red). If we hold a task set in WM binding print-colour categories to speaking of the corresponding colour names, as is necessary for doing the Stroop task, then the print colour in WM matches the condition RED of this task set exactly, but the word meaning also matches the condition BLUE fairly well—enough to contribute to the selection of a response, thereby creating response conflict (Fig. 5.2). If no such task set is in WM, then neither the word meaning nor the print colour makes us say a colour word.

Reflexes are an exception to this idea: a stimulus matching the condition of a reflex generates the reflexive response without the need to hold a corresponding task set in WM. For instance, we have a reflexive tendency to move our eyes towards a suddenly appearing stimulus in our visual periphery (Munoz & Everling, 2004). In the anti-saccade task, participants are instructed to suppress that reflex and instead move their eyes in the opposite direction of a flashing stimulus. People can do this, although not perfectly. The ability to overcome the pro-saccade reflex demonstrates the power of control through task sets in WM.

Rapid Updating: Control of the Contents of Working Memory

The fourth requirement is that WM must hold the information most relevant for ongoing cognitive activity at any moment in time. Our thoughts and actions progress rapidly—for instance, when reading, we take in about one new concept every 300–500 ms (Carver, 1992); when exploring a visual scene, we fixate new objects at about the same rate (Henderson & Hollingworth, 1999). Therefore, what is most relevant changes rapidly, and to keep up with that change, WM must update its contents efficiently. This involves rapid encoding of new information, and rapid removal of old, no-longer relevant contents.

The need for a process that removes outdated information from WM has long been postulated for theoretical reasons (Bjork, 1970; Hasher, Zacks, & May, 1999) but has been neglected in WM research until recently. Most WM researchers used to believe that information in WM decays over time by itself, leading them to focus on how people maintain information in WM rather than on how they get rid of it. Meanwhile, it is clear that decay—if it happens at all (more on that later)—would be too slow to clean out old information at the required pace: The best available evidence for decay suggests that it takes 5–10 seconds to cause even a modest decline of accessibility of information in WM (Lilienthal, Hale, & Myerson, 2014; Ricker, Spiegel, & Cowan, 2014). Therefore, I propose that information from WM can be removed when it is no longer relevant for the current goal.

Over the past decade, evidence for this removal process has accumulated (for a review, see Lewis-Peacock, Kessler, & Oberauer, 2018). An important question arising in this context is: how is removal controlled? In other words: how does the WM system know which information to remove when? In removal experiments participants are usually told what to remove by cues, but in everyday life we rarely get instructions to remove certain contents from WM. I think that in the wild, WM receives removal cues primarily from two sources: first, representations that are encoded (from perception) or retrieved (from LTM) into WM for a specific cognitive goal are removed as soon as that goal has been achieved. For instance, when we mentally add two numbers, reporting the result signals the completion of the task, upon which the numbers are cleared from WM. In typical WM experiments, the last response required for a trial serves as the cue to erase all information pertinent to that trial from WM. In language comprehension, the verbatim representation of the last clause is dropped shortly after a clause boundary (Jarvella, 1971), probably because at that point the goal of constructing a representation of the proposition expressed by the clause is accomplished, so the verbatim record is no longer needed. Second, when some of the current WM contents are updated, the process of encoding the new information is coupled with removal of the old information it replaces. This form of replacement can be implemented by a variant of the Hebbian learning rule called the *delta rule*. My colleagues and I have used this learning rule in one of our computational models of WM (Oberauer, Souza, Druey, & Gade, 2013).

Taking the last three sections together I can now attempt an answer to the complex of questions concerning attention and control (*Question 4*): Cognitive control means that our cognitive processes serve our current goals. To understand how the mind controls its own processes we need to characterize the representations of our goals and intentions that cause our thoughts and actions to work towards these goals. This is what the representations in WM do: declarative representations control what we think about and what we attend to in the environment, and procedural representations control our cognitive and overt actions. So what controls the contents of WM? I see three driving forces: (1) in part, the current information in WM controls the information in the next moment—for instance, when the current memory set is manipulated by the current task set, and when current information in WM guides perceptual attention to stimuli that are thereby encoded into WM. (2) Information in WM cues retrieval of new information from LTM into WM. (3) Self-generated or externally given removal cues control which information is removed from WM.

Does attention to information in WM differ from attention to stimuli in the environment? Both serve the function to select information for prioritized processing. The mechanisms underlying these functions are probably similar, but not the same: we can attend to one thing in the environment and to another in WM at the same time. A simple example for why we need this distinction is a short-term recognition or change-detection task, which requires that we compare a perceived, and presumably attended, stimulus (the probe) to a representation in WM (the target): to detect a mismatch, the two representations need to be kept separate. Directing the focus of attention to the target in WM through a retro-cue ahead of the comparison actually protects the target against interference from the probe (Souza, Rerko, & Oberauer, 2016). This would be difficult if the same attentional mechanism were responsible for prioritizing the target and the probe (see Hedge, Oberauer, & Leonards, 2015, for further evidence for separate attentional mechanisms).

Working Memory and Long-Term Memory: A Flexible Gate

The final two requirements for a functioning WM system that I outlined previously concern the relation of WM to LTM, raised in the editors' *Questions 3 and 6*. The two requirements are in tension with each other: on the one hand, WM needs to be shielded from LTM so that we can engage in novel ideas, hypothetical scenarios, and new action plans without them clashing with our knowledge and our routines in LTM. On the other hand, WM needs to be able to use LTM knowledge, and some (though not all) contents of WM should be remembered over the long term. Therefore, I think of the relation between WM and LTM as governed by a flexible gate: information from LTM is retrieved into WM when needed, but it is not retrieved automatically in response to every retrieval cue in WM that is associated to it. Automatic retrieval would lead to too much interference of LTM representations with the current contents of WM. For instance, a designer thinking of a pink banana would automatically trigger retrieval of yellow bananas from LTM that would compromise the pink-banana image.

Evidence for such a flexible gate comes from a series of experiments investigating the effects of previously acquired knowledge in LTM on performance in a WM task (Oberauer, Awh, & Sutterer, 2017). Participants first learned associations between 120 concrete objects (presented as silhouette pictures) and their randomly selected colours. Subsequently they worked on a WM test in which they saw arrays of three objects with random colours, and tried to reproduce each object's colour a few seconds later. Each array contained one old object with its old (previously learned) colour; one old object with a new colour, and a new object. When an old object's colour matched the one studied in the LTM learning phase, WM performance was improved relative to new objects, showing that people could make use of their LTM knowledge. When an old object's colour mismatched the one studied in the learning phase, WM performance was not impaired, showing that the object does not function as a retrieval cue that automatically brings back its previously learned colour—if that were the case, we should expect the object's old colour to interfere with the one we hold in WM. Yet, when people made an error in reproducing an old object's colour, they tended to pick the object's colour from the LTM learning phase. Jointly, these findings suggest that LTM knowledge about objects currently held in WM is used when it is helpful but not when it could harm performance, supporting the idea of a flexible gate.

How could such a gate work without the need for a homunculus-like gate keeper that knows when to admit information from LTM into WM? A simple heuristic could be: if the quality of a representation in WM is reasonably high, use it exclusively. Only if information in WM is so poor that it is virtually useless, try to draw on information in LTM instead. Applied to our object-colour experiment, the WM system would open the gate to LTM only when the tested object's colour representation in WM is so imprecise that retrieving the object's colour from LTM could improve performance (if that colour matched the one in the current array) but not harm it further (in case of a mismatch).

Computational Models of Working Memory

The framework sketched in the previous sections is useful for organizing our thoughts and for inspiring empirical research, but it is not sufficient to generate strong predictions. To address this limitation, my colleagues and I have worked on the development of computational models of WM that incorporate some of our theoretical ideas about how WM works. These models move us a few steps from a largely metaphorical picture of the WM system towards a characterization of the mechanisms of WM. Here I will review three of these models: (1) SOB-CS (Oberauer, Lewandowsky, Farrell, Jarrold, & Greaves, 2012) explains WM for lists in simple and complex span tasks. (2) The interference model (IM) of visual WM (Oberauer & Lin, 2017) explains maintenance of arrays of simple visual objects. (3) The set-selection model (Oberauer et al., 2013) explains how the WM system selects memory sets (i.e. sets of declarative representations) and task sets (i.e. sets of procedural representations), and how it selects elements within these sets. It accounts for how these sets are acquired in LTM, how they are retrieved into WM, and how the system switches between sets, and between elements within sets. The three models were developed to explain different sets of findings from different experimental paradigms. They share a common architecture—schematically depicted in Fig. 5.1—but differ in their details, and some of these differences so far resist their integration into one overarching model of WM.

All three models have in common that they have as their core a mechanism for binding contents to contexts. These bindings can be rapidly formed, maintained as long as needed, and rapidly removed when they are no longer needed. The contents are WM representations that can be selectively accessed by the contexts they are bound to, so the contexts serve as retrieval cues for the contents. In the SOB-CS model the contents are the list elements (e.g. letters, words, pictures, …) and the contexts are position markers, that is, representations of ordinal positions in the list. In the IM, contents are the features of visual objects (e.g. colour, orientation), and the contexts are usually the spatial locations of these objects in the visual field. Whereas these two models pertain only to declarative representations, the set-selection model is meant to also characterize procedural WM. In the procedural branch of the set-selection model, which is responsible for holding task sets, the contents are the response categories of the current task set, and the contexts are the stimulus categories (Fig. 5.2).

A Model for Simple and Complex Span Tasks: SOB-CS

The SOB-CS model grew out of the SOB family of connectionist models of immediate serial recall, also known as simple span (Farrell, 2006; Farrell & Lewandowsky, 2002; Lewandowsky & Farrell, 2008). The latest version extends the model to complex-span (CS) tasks. In the SOB model family, representations of contents and contexts are fully distributed: each list item is a pattern of activation over all units of the content layer of the network; each position marker is a pattern of activation over all units of the context layer (Fig. 5.3a). At encoding, items are bound to their positions through rapid Hebbian learning. To recall the list, position markers are reactivated one by one to act as retrieval cues for the items bound to them. In a complex-span task, presentation of each item is followed by a distractor task (e.g. reading a word aloud or verifying an equation). The distractor task involves the use of additional representations—the stimuli to

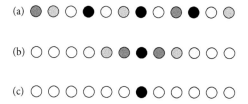

Fig. 5.3 Kinds of representations: (a) Fully distributed: each content or context is an entire pattern of activation across all units. Representations of similar entities are similar patterns. The individual units are often characterized as features, although this is not a necessary interpretation. (b) Population code: feature values are coded by a population of neurons that jointly can represent any value on a feature dimension as a specific pattern of activation across these neurons. Each neuron in the population is tuned to a particular feature value to which it responds maximally, and responds with decreasing strength to increasingly dissimilar feature values. If we order the neurons of a population according to the feature value they are tuned to along a continuous feature dimension, we can depict a population code as a symmetric, uni-modal distribution of activation over the feature dimension, centred on the represented feature. The width of that distribution reflects the width of the neurons' tuning function, that is, how steeply their activation drops off with increasing dissimilarity between the stimulus and the feature they are tuned to. (c) Localist representation: each content or context is uniquely represented by one unit which is active when that content or context is present, and inactive otherwise. Therefore, every representation is a vector of activation values over all units with only one non-zero value.

be processed, the task set for the distractor task, and the response given—that are inadvertently encoded into WM in the same way as list items: they are bound to the position marker of the preceding list item.

In SOB-CS, there are two kinds of representations in WM. On the one hand, the bindings of all items to their positions are maintained in the matrix of connection weights between content and context layer. By contrast, during encoding and during retrieval, one item and one position are activated in their respective layers at any time. These representations form the content of the focus of attention: they are the one content element, together with its context, that is selected for being encoded or retrieved at the moment. The distinction between these two kinds of representations can be tentatively mapped onto the distinction between 'neurally active' and 'neurally silent' WM that is emerging from neuroscience (Lewis-Peacock, Drysdale, Oberauer, & Postle, 2012; Stokes, 2015): information in WM that is currently attended can be decoded from the pattern of brain activity much better than unattended information in WM. This is to be expected if only the content of the focus of attention is represented as a pattern of activation across many neurons, whereas unattended contents of WM are merely represented as a pattern of connection weights between these neurons.

One problem that arises in all memory models with distributed representations is that the outcome of retrieval is not a perfect copy of the originally encoded pattern, but rather a more or less distorted approximation of the original. Therefore, the retrieved pattern needs to be disambiguated to determine the response, a process called *redintegration*. In SOB-CS, this is done by comparing the retrieved content pattern to the patterns of all representations in the set of recall candidates. For instance, if the list consists of consonants, all consonants in the alphabet form the candidate set. If the list consists of nouns, then the candidate set comprises all nouns—unless the list items all come from an easily identifiable category (e.g. all animals), in which case the candidate set can be limited to animal nouns. When the recall candidates are representations in semantic LTM, such as letters, words, or known objects, then we should expect that everything that makes such a representation more accessible—for instance, the frequency with which a word occurs in the language—should facilitate redintegration. In this way, the redintegration process affords an explanation for the many findings showing that immediate serial recall of words is influenced by characteristics of the list words in semantic memory, such as their frequency (Roodenrys, Hulme, Lethbridge, Hinton, & Nimmo, 2002), their concreteness (Campoy, Castellà, Provencio, Hitch, & Baddeley, 2015; Paivio & Csapo, 1969), and the number of other similar words in the language (Guitard, Gabel, Saint-Aubin, Surprenant, & Neath, 2018). This idea gives a partial answer to *Question 6* about the relation between WM and LTM. That said, such an explanation has not yet been worked out in the context of a computational model.

As the memory set size increases, more and more list items are blended in with the target item at retrieval. Interference between list items increases with set size, resulting in an increasing chance of confusing list items with each other (so-called order errors), and an increase in other kinds of errors as well. With larger set size, the retrieved pattern of an item becomes increasingly distorted, increasing the chance of confusing it with an extra-list item, or of a complete failure of redintegration, leading to an omission error. The accumulation of interference with larger memory sets contributes to the set-size effect which is found with all WM tests, and reflects the capacity limit of WM (Oberauer et al., 2016). In complex-span tasks, the representations involved in distractor processing add further to the interference in WM, and this explains why complex-span performance is usually worse than simple-span performance.

Another assumption in SOB-CS and its precursors, also shared with many other serial-recall models (Page & Norris, 1998), is that every item that has been recalled is removed from WM, a process referred to as *response suppression*. It serves to minimize erroneous repetitions. In SOB-CS, response suppression is implemented by removing the recalled item from WM through Hebbian anti-learning, which unbinds the currently active content (i.e. the recalled item) from its context (i.e. the current position). Response suppression is an instance of a more general removal process applied to all contents that become irrelevant for the current goal. In particular, the representations used for the distractor task in complex span are removed as soon as they are no longer needed. For instance, if the distractor task consists of reading digits aloud, each digit is encoded into WM, read aloud, and then removed again. Removal takes some time and therefore is more complete if more time is available after completion of a distractor process. Therefore, a more leisurely paced distractor task (e.g. reading digits at a pace of one every 2 seconds) allows for more complete removal of interfering representations from the distractor task than a fast-paced distractor task (e.g. reading one digit every

500 ms). With this assumption SOB-CS explains the effect of *cognitive load* in complex-span tasks: as the temporal density of the distractor demand increases, memory declines (Barrouillet, Portrat, & Camos, 2011).

Hence, SOB-CS entails the following partial answer to the editors' *Question 5* about storage, maintenance, and loss of information: in SOB-CS, once information is encoded, it stays in WM by default. We found that assuming a natural tendency of memory representations to be lost over time is neither necessary nor helpful to explain experimental data. My colleagues and I devoted several experiments to the question whether verbal information in WM declines over time when it cannot be rehearsed or refreshed, and we found that it does not (Lewandowsky, Geiger, Morrell, & Oberauer, 2010; Lewandowsky, Geiger, & Oberauer, 2008; Oberauer & Lewandowsky, 2008, 2013, 2014). Loss of information arises from interference between representations, including those used for processing of distractors.

Assuming no time-based forgetting facilitates modelling WM substantially because it removes the necessity to model maintenance processes such as rehearsal or refreshing. We found that incorporating such processes in a WM model gives rise to various complications (e.g. deciding which item is rehearsed at which point in time, and for how long) with little, if any, explanatory gain (Lewandowsky & Oberauer, 2015). We recently ran a series of experiments asking whether instructing people to engage in one or another maintenance process helps performance. Instructing people to use cumulative articulatory rehearsal increases their use of that strategy substantially without any gain for memory performance (Souza & Oberauer, 2018). Instructing people to refresh or to elaborate information in WM likewise did not yield much benefit (Bartsch, Singmann, & Oberauer, 2018). Therefore, I currently see no need to assume a functional role for any such maintenance process.

SOB-CS also explains a phenomenon that has attracted much discussion throughout the history of WM research, and motivated the second part of the editors' *Question 3*: the double dissociation of verbal and visuospatial content domains. For instance, verbal memory sets are remembered better when combined with visuospatial than verbal distractor tasks, whereas visuospatial memory sets are remembered better in the context of verbal than visuospatial distractor tasks (Chein, Moore, & Conway, 2011; Myerson, Hale, Rhee, & Jenkins, 1999). Similarly, when two memory sets are to be maintained simultaneously, performance is better when they come from different domains than when they come from the same domain (Cocchini, Logie, Della Sala, MacPherson, & Baddeley, 2002; Fougnie, Zughni, Godwin, & Marois, 2015; Oberauer & Kliegl, 2006). This double dissociation has been interpreted as evidence for separate domain-specific sub-systems in WM (Baddeley, 1986). In SOB-CS, it arises naturally from the use of distributed representations, without the need to assume separate systems or processes. This is because stimuli from different content domains usually are characterized by (to a large part) different feature dimensions. For instance, verbal stimuli have phonological features, and often semantic features. In contrast, visuospatial stimuli have visual and spatial features (e.g. colour, texture, shape, size)—but no phonological features. Hence, verbal and visuospatial contents are represented in partially non-overlapping feature spaces, defined by different feature dimensions. In distributed representations each unit (or a subset of units) is thought to code one feature. For instance, high activation of one unit could code the phonological feature 'labial' (indicating that a phoneme is produced with the lips, such as '/b'), whereas low activation of that unit would code a non-labial phoneme; high activation of another unit could code the visual feature 'red', whereas low activation could code 'green'. Because visuospatial stimuli have no phonological features, their representations do not use the phonological-feature units at all; likewise, phonological representations of verbal stimuli do not use the visuospatial feature units. More generally, representations in different content domains are patterns of activations over different sets of units in the content layer. These sets could partially overlap—for instance, both verbal and visuo-spatial stimuli often have semantic features—but also have substantial non-overlapping components. Distributed representations in non-overlapping sets of units do not interfere with each other: they are not blended together because they exist in separate media, and hence they do not distort each other.

To conclude, SOB-CS offers a parsimonious answer to the second part of the question about the unity of WM (*Question 3*): we can conceptualize WM as a unitary system, and the dissociations arise naturally from the degree of overlap of the representations it engages.

A Model of Visual Working Memory: The Interference Model

We developed the IM to account for behaviour in tests of visual WM. In a typical visual WM test, a number of simple visual objects (e.g. colour patches) are presented simultaneously in a spatial array. At test, one of the objects is chosen at random as the target to be tested. One common test method is continuous reproduction: participants are asked to reproduce the target's feature on a continuous response scale (e.g. select its colour on a colour wheel) (Blake, Cepeda, & Hiris, 1997; Wilken & Ma, 2004). Another popular test is change detection, where the target is presented again at test, and participants have to decide whether it is the same or it has changed (Vogel, Woodman, & Luck, 2001).

To do these tasks, people must keep in memory which features have been presented in which locations of the array. Therefore, the IM conceptualizes visual WM as the maintenance of temporary bindings between the features of visual objects (contents) and their array locations (contexts; Fig. 5.4).

The IM uses population-code representations for its contents and contexts (Fig. 5.3b). Like the distributed representations in SOB-CS, they are patterns of activation over a layer of units, but different from SOB-CS, the units in a layer form an ordered set, such that their proximity reflects the similarity between the feature values that each unit is tuned to. In this way, the units of a layer form a feature space, in which similar stimuli (such as red and orange) are closer to each other than more dissimilar stimuli (such as red and yellow). The representation of a feature value is not a random pattern

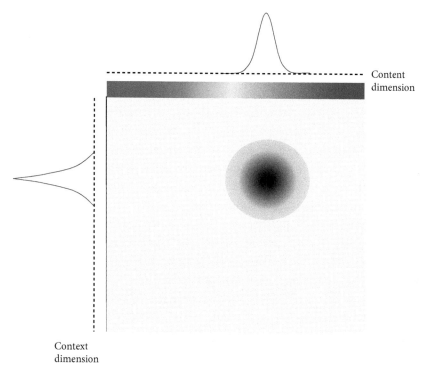

Content
dimension

Context
dimension

Fig. 5.4 IM architecture. Content and context representations are described as continuous distributions of activation over their respective feature spaces, which model population codes. Although feature spaces can have several dimensions (e.g. spatial location on the screen is two-dimensional), they are depicted here as a single dimension. The bindings between contents and contexts are bivariate distributions in binding space, modelling the distribution of connection weights in a weight matrix (see Fig. 5.1).

of activation but a unimodal distribution of activation values, centred on the unit that is maximally tuned to the represented feature. The width of these distributions reflects the precision of feature representations, and controls how confusable two feature values with a given distance on the feature dimension are. Contents are bound to contexts through rapid Hebbian learning, resulting in a change of the connection weights between the two layers that can be described as a two-dimensional distribution of binding strengths (depicted as the grey blobs in Fig. 5.4).

Access to an item in a memory array rests on cue-based retrieval exactly as in SOB-CS: the feature used to identify the target—usually its spatial location—is activated in the context layer, and this reactivates the feature units in the content layer according to how strongly they are bound to the activated context. In this way, the target feature is strongly reactivated. In addition, the features of other items in the array—so-called non-targets—are also reactivated to the extent that they are close to the target in context space because the context cue generalizes to its neighbours. For instance, in spatial arrays, features of non-targets spatially close to the target are reactivated more strongly than those further away, so that people tend to confuse the target more often with spatially close neighbours (Bays, 2016; Rerko, Oberauer, & Lin, 2014; Tamber-Rosenau, Fintzi, & Marois, 2015). In the IM we also assume that all objects in the array, regardless of their distance to the target, receive some degree of activation at test. In addition, every array item is encoded together with some background noise, modelled as a uniform distribution of activation over all units of the content and the context layer. Finally, in the IM we assign the focus of attention a role in maintenance: the population code of one visual object and its context can be maintained active throughout the retention interval with a higher degree of precision than that maintained in the bindings. If the object in the focus of attention happens to be the target, this activation pattern maintained in the focus is combined with the reactivation through cue-based retrieval, resulting in a more precise representation of the target.

When fit to data from continuous-reproduction experiments, the IM accounts for the distributions of errors at varying memory set sizes better than competing models (Oberauer & Lin, 2017). With increasing set size, the error distributions become broader, and in particular the proportion of very large errors (e.g. reproducing green when the target is red) increases. In the IM, the effect of set size on the error distribution arises from three sources: (1) with more objects in the array, an increasing number of non-targets contribute to the pattern of activation in content space that is reproduced at retrieval. (2) With a larger set size there is more background noise in the system. (3) With larger set size, the chance of the target being in the focus of attention decreases.

With its explicit assumptions about the focus of attention, the IM also explains the basic findings from experiments using pre-cues or retro-cues to direct attention to one object in an array (Griffin & Nobre, 2003; Landman et al., 2003): when the location of the target is pre-cued before the memory array is presented, precision of reproduction increases, especially at larger set sizes, so that the set-size effect is substantially reduced. When the pre-cue is invalid, so that a non-target is cued, reproduction of the target is somewhat worse than in a no-cue control condition (Fig. 5.5). In the IM, this effect is largely due to the assumption that the pre-cued object is maintained in the focus of attention, so that when it becomes the target, its reproduction is strongly improved by the high-precision information in the focus, a contribution that is independent of set size. The effect of a retro-cue presented during the retention interval is subtler: a valid retro-cue to the target improves precision, but does so about equally for all set sizes, so that the set-size effect is not reduced. An invalid retro-cue impairs reproduction, and this cost is also approximately additive with set size (Fig. 5.6). In the IM, the beneficial effect of a retro-cue arises for a different reason than that of a pre-cue: when the target is retro-cued, the focus of attention is directed to it after the perceptual input is no longer available. This cannot increase the precision of the target representation (as this would involve a magical gain of information). Therefore, focusing an object in WM in response to a retro-cue merely strengthens the bindings of that object to its context, and partially removes other objects from WM to reduce the interference arising from them. To conclude, the IM offers an explanation for the effects of pre-cues and retro-cues, and

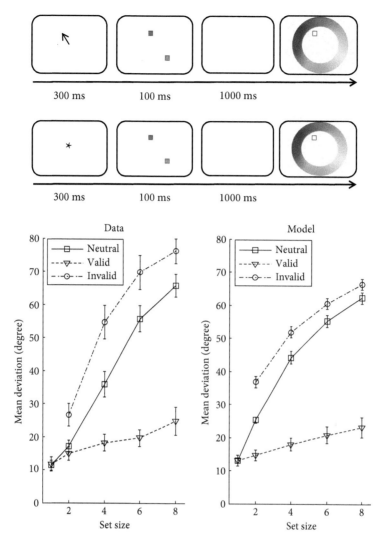

Fig. 5.5 Top panel: flow of events in a pre-cue experiment. Bottom panel: data from a pre-cue experiment (left) and predictions from the IM (right). Mean deviation of responses as a function of memory set size and cue condition; error bars are 95% confidence intervals for within-subjects comparisons.

Reproduced from Klaus Oberauer and Hsuan-Yu Lin, 'An interference model of visual working memory', *Psychological Review*, 124 (1), pp. 21–59, https://doi.org/10.1037/rev0000044 Copyright © 2017, American Psychological Association.

for the way in which they differ; this explanation provides a partial answer to *Question 4* about the role of attention in WM. That said, the pattern of experimental effects generated by pre- and retro-cues is quite complex (Souza & Oberauer, 2016), and the mechanisms incorporated in the IM presently are too coarse to account for all aspects of this rich set of findings.

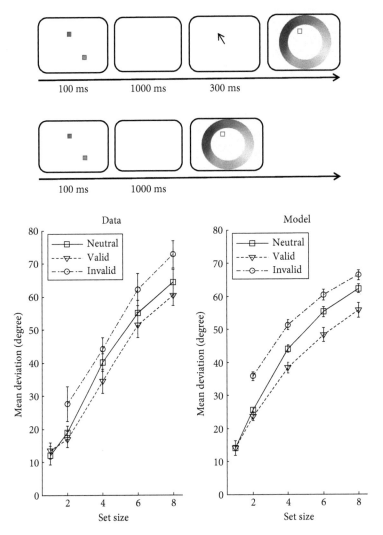

Fig. 5.6 Top panel: flow of events in a retro-cue experiment. Bottom panel: data from a retro-cue experiment (left) and predictions from the IM (right). Mean deviation of responses as a function of memory set size and cue condition; error bars are 95% confidence intervals for within-subjects comparisons.

A Model of Switching Between Memory Sets and Task Sets: The Set-Selection Model

The two models discussed previously—SOB-CS and IM—speak to how the WM system accomplishes three of the six requirements I delineated earlier: the ability to build new structural representations through temporary bindings, the ability to select individual elements from the current memory set by the focus of attention, and the ability to rapidly remove no-longer relevant information. However, these two models say nothing about cognitive control (the third requirement), and say little about the flow of information between WM and LTM (the final two requirements). My colleagues and I developed the set-selection model to start addressing these desiderata (Oberauer et al., 2013).

The set-selection model starts from the assumption that WM for declarative and for procedural representations operates by analogous principles. Declarative representations are memory sets as I have described them in the context of SOB-CS (i.e. memory lists) and IM (i.e. arrays of objects). Procedural representations are task sets. We can describe both memory sets and task sets as relational representations formed by temporary bindings between content and context elements. In the case of task sets, the contents are the response options between which the person has to choose, and the contexts are the stimulus or situation categories that the response options are bound to.

Most of the research on task sets has been concerned with how people switch between several tasks (Monsell, 2003). This research highlights the fact that control of our thoughts and actions involves selections on multiple levels. On a higher level, the cognitive system needs to select which task to do right now. Of the many task sets a person has available in LTM, one must be chosen to actually guide behaviour. This can be done by retrieving the relevant task set into WM (Mayr & Kliegl, 2000). On a lower level of selection, the appropriate response to the given situation needs to be selected—once a task set is established in WM, this selection is done according to the stimulus-response bindings in that task set. An analogous two-level selection problem arises for declarative representations as well. For instance, when we want to call someone on the phone, we need to first retrieve their phone number from LTM into WM. Once this is done, we select within that memory set the first digit to type.

The set-selection model uses the same architecture for making these selections for declarative and for procedural representations, so there are two identical copies of the network (Fig. 5.7). Each network consists of two modules, one for each selection; for instance, in declarative WM the set-selection module selects the memory set, and the item-selection module selects the item to be worked with from the current memory set. Likewise, in procedural WM the set-selection module selects the task set to be used, and the response-selection module selects the response to be given from the current task set. Each module is a two-layer neural network of the kind shown in Fig. 5.1, which serves to bind contents to contexts. The item-selection module for declarative WM is a simplified version of SOB-CS, and of the IM; it binds the items in a memory set to the contexts that are used to retrieve them, for instance, their serial position in a list, or their spatial location in an array. The model is simplified because it uses localist representations (Fig. 5.3c) for convenience. The corresponding response-selection module for procedural WM binds response categories to stimulus categories according to the instructions of a task. For instance, when a person receives the instruction to 'press the left key when you see an animal, and the right key when you see a plant', then they implement that instruction as a task set by forming bindings between 'left key' and 'animal', and

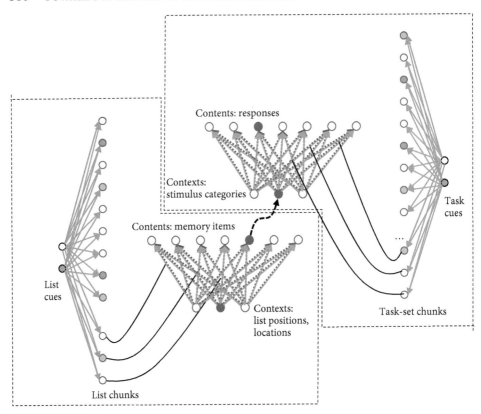

Fig. 5.7 Architecture of the set-selection model. The lower-left side shows declarative WM, and the upper-right side procedural WM. Both declarative and procedural WM consist of two modules. In declarative WM, the item-selection module is depicted by two horizontal layers of interconnected units. It represents items of a memory set in the content layer, and binds them to list positions or spatial locations in the context layer. The set-selection module is shown as two vertical layers of interconnected units; it represents memory sets (e.g. lists) as unified chunks and associates them to list cues. Connection weights of the item-selection module are mapped one-to-one onto units of the set-selection module (shown for three such mappings by the bowed continuous lines). This structure is mirrored for procedural WM, with a response-selection module (horizontal layers) binding response categories to stimulus categories (implementing the currently active task set), and a set-selection module in which task sets are represented as chunks, and associated to task cues. The inputs to the stimulus categories in the response-selection module are the outputs of the item-selection module, as shown by the broken-lined arrows: The information that the task set is applied to is the content of declarative WM that is currently in the focus of attention, which means that it is activated in the content layer.

between 'right key' and 'plant'. Once this is done, the task set acts as a prepared reflex (Cohen-Kdoshay & Meiran, 2009): when the person sees the picture of an animal or a plant, it activates the corresponding stimulus category, which in turn activates the response bound to it. Activation of each response is accumulated over time until one of them reaches a threshold, and is then selected for execution.

The set-selection module enables the model to alternate between multiple memory sets or task sets. In the set-selection module, an entire memory set or task set is represented as a distributed pattern of activation, which in turn is bound to a task cue by which it can be retrieved. Hence, a task set (or a memory set for declarative WM) is represented twice in the model: once as a set of bindings in the response-selection module, and once as a distributed pattern of activations in the set-selection module. This enables the model to re-represent a relational structure—for instance, the stimulus-response relations in a task set, or the order of items in a memory list—as a single unit (i.e. a single distributed representation) in the set-selection module, where it can in turn be used as an element in a higher-order relation, for instance, the relation between a task set and a task cue. This re-representation is accomplished by mapping the matrix of connection weights in the response-selection module into a pattern of activation in the set-selection module.

When the model learns a new task set (or a new memory set), this set is first established in the response-selection module (or item-selection module) as a pattern of connection weights. These are read out into the corresponding pattern of activation in the set-selection module, where they are bound to the retrieval cue for the task set (e.g. a representation of 'animal–plant task'). Multiple task sets can be learned in this way—for instance, the person can also learn a 'colour task' in which they press one of two buttons depending on whether the picture of an object is red or blue. After learning the task sets required for an experiment, the model can simulate people's behaviour in a task-switching experiment. The task cue at the beginning of each trial reactivates the corresponding task set as a pattern of activation in the set-selection module. This pattern is translated into changes of the connection weights in the response-selection module, thereby gradually updating the stimulus-response bindings. This updating takes longer when the task set is switched than when it is repeated.

Because the set-selection module uses the same mechanisms for selection in declarative and procedural WM, it predicts that these selection processes are reflected in analogous empirical phenomena. My colleagues and I tested this prediction with a set of experiments with a list-switch paradigm that is modelled on the classic task-switch paradigm but uses declarative memory lists instead. We found that a number of benchmark findings from task-switching research are also observed with the list-switching paradigm, and they are reproduced by simulations with the set-selection model (Gade, Souza, Druey, & Oberauer, 2017; Oberauer et al., 2013).

Apart from providing a detailed account of findings from task and list switching experiments, the set-selection model contributes to our understanding of WM in two ways. First, it offers a unified mechanism for how WM contributes to cognitive control (*Question 4*): the WM system holds the declarative and procedural representations available that are needed for our current thinking and acting. The declarative representations in WM—either retrieved from LTM or encoded through perception of the current environment—provide the input to our cognitive operations; the procedural representations control what we do with that input. Both kinds of representations are selected on the basis of retrieval cues—for instance, task cues in the environment, but also self-generated cues such as goal representations—that serve to retrieve memory sets and task sets from LTM into WM. In this way, cognitive control is ultimately governed by our learning history through which we acquired memory sets and task sets and associated them to their retrieval cues (see Verguts & Notebaert, 2009, for a similar view of cognitive control).

Second, the set-selection module provides a mechanism for unifying relational representations into chunks: by translating the connection weights in the item-selection module into a pattern of activation in the set-selection module, the entire structure of elements and their bindings in one module is re-represented as a single element in the other module. This mechanism helps to clarify one aspect of the interplay between WM and LTM (*Question 6*): a new relational representation can be composed in WM through temporary bindings, and then acquired in LTM as a chunk that can in turn be associated to other representations. Once learned, the chunk can be brought back into WM. In this way, knowledge in LTM can help holding relational representations in WM together if they match the LTM knowledge. It has been known for a long time that memory sets that match LTM knowledge—even if only partially—are maintained better than completely random memory sets. For instance, letter lists composed of known acronyms (e.g. PDFIBM) are remembered better than random lists (PIBMFD) (Cowan, Chen, & Rouder, 2004; Miller, 1956; Thalmann, Souza, & Oberauer, 2019). Repeating the same list over several trials in a sequence of serial-recall tests gradually improves performance for the repeated lists (Hebb, 1961; Page, Cumming, Norris, McNeil, & Hitch, 2013), and this so-called Hebb effect is probably due to the formation of a unified representation of the repeated list in LTM (Burgess & Hitch, 2006; Hitch, Fastame, & Flude, 2005). At present, the set-selection model has not been developed sufficiently to explain these effects, but I believe that the chunking mechanism in the model would be a good starting point for doing so.

Challenges

It is now time to address the final question on the editors' list (*Question 7*), which pertains to evidence inconsistent with the present framework. I will focus on the four empirical phenomena that I perceive as the main challenges to core assumptions of the framework.

1. Maintenance of information in WM is often seriously impaired by a processing task in the retention interval that apparently involves information from a very different content domain, so that there is arguably very little feature-space overlap between the representations in the memory set and those engaged by the distractor task. For instance, maintenance of an array of colours is impaired by the classification of tones as high or low (Morey & Bieler, 2013; Souza & Oberauer, 2017). With minimal feature-space overlap there should be minimal interference between these tasks. One way to explain this finding in SOB-CS is by assuming

that materials from different content domains are nevertheless represented in partially overlapping feature-spaces (e.g. by naming non-verbal stimuli, or by forming mental images of the meanings of words).

2. Conversely, some studies have found an effect of memory set size on the speed or accuracy of a distractor task in the retention interval, even when there is arguably little feature-space overlap between the materials of the two tasks (Chen & Cowan, 2009; Vergauwe, Camos, & Barrouillet, 2014). This effect, however, is not shown consistently (Doherty et al., 2019). Some studies have shown an effect of memory set-size on performance in a concurrent processing task if the processing task demand followed immediately after memory encoding, which disappears with a temporal gap of at least 1–2 seconds (Klapp, Marshburn, & Lester, 1983), even when the two tasks use overlapping materials, such as retention of a digit list and mental arithmetic (Oberauer, 2002; Oberauer, Demmrich, Mayr, & Kliegl, 2001). The effect of memory load on processing performance at shorter inter-task intervals could arise because it takes 1–2 seconds for consolidating a memory set in WM, and consolidation competes with other concurrent processing demands (Jolicoeur & Dell'Acqua, 1998).

3. Whereas memory for verbal WM contents is stable over time, memory for visual and spatial information has often been found to deteriorate over time even when no potentially interfering distractor activity was required during the retention interval (Lilienthal et al., 2014; Lilienthal, Hale, & Myerson, 2016; Pertzov, Bays, Joseph, & Husain, 2013; Pertzov, Manohar, & Husain, 2017). These findings invite an explanation in terms of decay, contrary to my assumption that decay does not contribute to loss of information from WM. Matters are complicated by the fact that some studies found no decline of memory over time (Blake et al., 1997; Burke, Poyser, & Schiessl, 2015; Morris, 1987; Ricker & Hardman, 2017). Some moderating variables have been identified: loss of memory for visual features over time has sometimes been reduced or even absent for smaller memory set sizes (Pearson, Raškevičius, Bays, Pertzov, & Husain, 2014; Pertzov et al., 2017). Loss of memory for spatial locations is not found when the set of possible spatial locations remains visible throughout the retention interval (Lilienthal et al., 2014; Lilienthal, Myerson, Abrams, & Hale, 2018). One possible explanation for some of these findings is that, in the absence of categorical boundaries, information in a continuous space tends to drift over time, retaining constant strength but losing precision (Schneegans & Bays, 2018).

4. A further challenge for the present framework comes from findings from visual WM that point towards an immutable maximum of about three chunks that can be held in WM. The strongest evidence for this limit comes from two sources. First, a slow electroencephalographic signal during the retention interval, the contralateral delay activity, increases with set size up to a person's individual capacity estimate, with an average of about three visual objects (Luria, Balaban, Awh, & Vogel, 2016; Vogel & Machizawa, 2004). Second, when visual WM is tested with continuous reproduction of all objects in an array, in an order chosen by

the participant, the error distributions reflect memory information only for the first three responses; subsequent responses are indistinguishable from guessing (Adam, Vogel, & Awh, 2017). These findings can so far not be explained by the IM.

Conclusion: The State of the Science of Working Memory

Where do we stand in our endeavour to understand WM? Looking at the empirical side, we know a lot about WM: over five decades, we have accumulated a wealth of well-established, replicable and reasonably general empirical phenomena (Oberauer et al., 2018). Looking at the theoretical side, we know very little about WM: we have several competing frameworks—many of which are represented in this book—that can be used to interpret these phenomena. The frameworks differ in how easy it is to tell a plausible story about different phenomena, but they are difficult to test rigorously because they make few, if any, strong predictions. To arrive at strong predictions, we need to spell out our theoretical ideas more precisely and completely, and this is best done in the form of computational models. At present, these models have very limited explanatory scope. I hope we will be able to develop more comprehensive models by building on what the existing narrow models have in common.

References

Adam, K. C. S., Vogel, E. K., & Awh, E. (2017). Clear evidence for item limits in visual working memory. *Cognitive Psychology, 97,* 79–97. doi:10.1016/j.cogpsych.2017.07.001

Anderson, J. R. (1990). *The adaptive character of thought.* Hillsdale, NJ: Erlbaum.

Anderson, J. R., & Lebiere, C. (1998). *The atomic components of thought.* Mahwah, NJ: Erlbaum.

Baddeley, A. D. (1986). *Working memory.* Oxford, UK: Clarendon Press.

Barrouillet, P., Portrat, S., & Camos, V. (2011). On the law relating processing to storage in working memory. *Psychological Review, 118,* 175–192.

Bartsch, L. M., Singmann, H., & Oberauer, K. (2018). The effects of refreshing and elaboration on working memory performance, and their contributions to long-term memory formation. *Memory & Cognition, 46,* 796–808. doi:10.3758/s13421-018-0805-9

Bays, P. M. (2016). Evaluating and excluding swap errors in analogue tests of working memory. *Scientific Reports, 6,* 19203. doi:10.1038/srep19203

Bjork, R. A. (1970). Positive forgetting: The noninterference of items intentionally forgotten. *Journal of Verbal Learning and Verbal Behavior, 9,* 255–268.

Blake, R., Cepeda, N. J., & Hiris, E. (1997). Memory for visual motion. *Journal of Experimental Psychology: Human Perception and Performance, 23,* 353–369.

Brass, M., Liefooghe, B., Braem, S., & De Houwer, J. (2017). Following new task instructions: Evidence for a dissociation between knowing and doing. *Neuroscience and Biobehavioral Reviews, 81,* 16–28. doi:10.1016/j.neubiorev.2017.02.012

Brown, G. D. A., Preece, T., & Hulme, C. (2000). Oscillator-based memory for serial order. *Psychological Review, 107,* 127–181.

Burgess, N., & Hitch, G. J. (2006). A revised model of short-term memory and long-term learning of verbal sequences. *Journal of Memory and Language, 55,* 627–652.

Burke, M. R., Poyser, C., & Schiessl, I. (2015). Age-related deficits in visuospatial memory are due to changes in preparatory set and eye-hand coordination. *Journals of Gerontology: Psychological Sciences, 70*, 682–690. doi:10.1093/geronb/gbu027

Campoy, G., Castellà, J., Provencio, V., Hitch, G. J., & Baddeley, A. D. (2015). Automatic semantic encoding in verbal short-term memory: Evidence from the concreteness effect. *Quarterly Journal of Experimental Psychology, 68*, 759–778. doi:10.1080/17470218.2014.966248

Carver, R. P. (1992). Reading rate: Theory, research, and practical implications. *Journal of Reading, 36*, 84–95.

Chein, J. M., Moore, A. B., & Conway, A. R. A. (2011). Domain-general mechanisms of complex working memory span. *NeuroImage, 54*, 550–559.

Chen, Z., & Cowan, N. (2009). How verbal memory loads consume attention. *Memory & Cognition, 37*, 829–836. doi:10.3758/MC.37.6.829

Cocchini, G., Logie, R. H., Della Sala, S., MacPherson, S. E., & Baddeley, A. D. (2002). Concurrent performance of two memory tasks: Evidence for domain-specific working memory systems. *Memory & Cognition, 30*, 1086–1095.

Cohen-Kdoshay, O., & Meiran, N. (2009). The representation of instructions operates like a prepared reflex: Flanker compatibility effects found in first trial following S-R instructions. *Experimental Psychology, 56*, 128–133.

Cowan, N. (2005). *Working memory capacity*. New York, NY: Psychology Press.

Cowan, N., Chen, Z., & Rouder, J. N. (2004). Constant capacity in an immediate serial-recall task: A logical sequel to Miller (1956). *Psychological Science, 15*, 634–640.

Cowan, N., Morey, C. C., & Naveh-Benjamin, M. (2021). An embedded-process approach to working memory: How is it distinct from other approaches, and to what ends? In R. H. Logie, V. Camos, & N. Cowan (Eds.), *Working memory: State of the science* (pp. 44–84). Oxford, UK: Oxford University Press.

Doherty, J. M., Belletier, C., Rhodes, S., Jaroslawska, A., Barrouillet, P., Camos, V., ... Logie, R. H. (2019). Dual-task costs in working memory: An adversarial collaboration. *Journal of Experimental Psychology: Learning, Memory, and Cognition, 45*, 1529–1551.

Farrell, S. (2006). Mixed-list phonological similarity effects in delayed serial recall. *Journal of Memory and Language, 55*, 587–600.

Farrell, S., & Lewandowsky, S. (2002). An endogenous distributed model of ordering in serial recall. *Psychonomic Bulletin & Review, 9*, 59–79.

Farrell, S., & Lewandowsky, S. (2004). Modelling transposition latencies: Constraints for theories of serial order memory. *Journal of Memory and Language, 51*, 115–135.

Fougnie, D., Zughni, S., Godwin, D., & Marois, R. (2015). Working memory storage is intrinsically domain specific. *Journal of Experimental Psychology: General, 144*, 30–47. doi:10.1037/a0038211

Gade, M., Souza, A. S., Druey, M. D., & Oberauer, K. (2017). Analogous selection processes in declarative and procedural working memory: N-2 list-repetition and task-repetition costs. *Memory & Cognition, 45*, 26–39. doi:10.3758/s13421-016-0645-4

Garavan, H. (1998). Serial attention within working memory. *Memory & Cognition, 26*, 263–276.

Göthe, K., Oberauer, K., & Kliegl, R. (2016). Eliminating dual-task costs by minimizing crosstalk between tasks: The role of modality and feature pairings. *Cognition, 150*, 92–108. doi:10.1016/j.cognition.2016.02.003

Griffin, I. C., & Nobre, A. C. (2003). Orienting attention to locations in internal representations. *Journal of Cognitive Neuroscience, 15*, 1176–1194.

Guitard, D., Gabel, A. J., Saint-Aubin, J., Surprenant, A. M., & Neath, I. (2018). Word length, set size, and lexical factors: Re-examining what causes the word-length effect. *Journal of Experimental Psychology: Learning, Memory, and Cognition, 44*, 1824–1844. doi:10.1037/xlm0000551

Halford, G. S., Wilson, W. H., & Phillips, S. (1998). Processing capacity defined by relational complexity: Implications for comparative, developmental, and cognitive psychology. *Behavioral and Brain Sciences, 21*, 803–864.

Hasher, L., Zacks, R. T., & May, C. P. (1999). Inhibitory control, circadian arousal, and age. In D. Gopher & A. Koriat (Eds.), *Attention and performance* (pp. 653–675). Cambridge, MA: MIT Press.

Hebb, D. O. (1961). Distinctive features of learning in the higher animal. In J. F. Delafresnaye (Ed.), *Brain mechanisms and learning* (pp. 37–46). Oxford, UK: Blackwell.

Hedge, C., Oberauer, K., & Leonards, U. (2015). Selection in spatial working memory is independent of perceptual selective attention, but they interact in a shared spatial priority map. *Attention, Perception & Psychophysics, 77*, 2653–2668. doi:10.3758/s13414-015-0976-4

Henderson, J. M., & Hollingworth, A. (1999). High-level scene perception. *Annual Review of Psychology, 50*, 243–271.

Hitch, G. J., Fastame, M. C., & Flude, B. (2005). How is the serial order of a verbal sequence coded? Some comparisons between models. *Memory, 13*, 247–258.

Hommel, B. (2000). The prepared reflex: Automaticity and control in stimulus-response translation. In S. Monsell & J. Driver (Eds.), *Attention and Performance XVIII: Control of Cognitive Processes* (pp. 247–273). Cambridge, MA: MIT Press.

Hummel, J. E., & Holyoak, J. A. (2003). A symbolic-connectionist theory of relational inference and generalization. *Psychological Review, 110*, 220–264.

Hurlstone, M. J., Hitch, G. J., & Baddeley, A. D. (2014). Memory for serial order across domains: An overview of the literature and directions for future research. *Psychological Bulletin, 140*, 339–373. doi:10.1037/a0034221

Jarvella, R. J. (1971). Syntactic processing of connected speech. *Journal of Verbal Learning and Verbal Behavior, 10*, 409–416.

Johnson-Laird, P. N. (1983). *Mental models*. Cambridge, UK: Cambridge University Press.

Jolicoeur, P., & Dell'Acqua, R. (1998). The demonstration of short-term consolidation. *Cognitive Psychology, 36*, 138–202.

Klapp, S. T., Marshburn, E. A., & Lester, P. T. (1983). Short-term memory does not involve the 'working memory' of information processing: The demise of a common assumption. *Journal of Experimental Psychology: General, 112*, 240–264.

Landman, R., Spekreijse, H., & Lamme, V. A. F. (2003). Large capacity storage of integrated objects before change blindness. *Vision Research, 43*, 149–164.

Lewandowsky, S., & Farrell, S. (2008). Short-term memory: New data and a model. In B. H. Ross (Ed.), *The psychology of learning and motivation* (Vol. 49, pp. 1–48). London, UK: Elsevier.

Lewandowsky, S., Geiger, S. M., Morrell, D. B., & Oberauer, K. (2010). Turning simple span into complex span: Time for decay or interference from distractors? *Journal of Experimental Psychology: Learning, Memory, and Cognition, 36*, 958–978.

Lewandowsky, S., Geiger, S. M., & Oberauer, K. (2008). Interference-based forgetting in verbal short-term memory. *Journal of Memory and Language, 59*, 200–222.

Lewandowsky, S., & Oberauer, K. (2015). Rehearsal in serial recall: An unworkable solution to the non-existent problem of decay. *Psychological Review, 122*, 674–699. doi:10.1037/a0039684

Lewis-Peacock, J. A., Drysdale, A. T., Oberauer, K., & Postle, B. R. (2012). Neural evidence for a distinction between short-term memory and the focus of attention. *Journal of Cognitive Neuroscience, 24*, 61–79.

Lewis-Peacock, J. A., Kessler, Y., & Oberauer, K. (2018). The removal of information from working memory. *Annals of the New York Academy of Science, 1424*, 33–44. doi:10.1111/nyas.13714

Lilienthal, L., Hale, S., & Myerson, J. (2014). The effects of environmental support and secondary tasks on visuospatial working memory. *Memory & Cognition, 42*, 1118–1129. doi:10.3758/s13421-014-0421-2

Lilienthal, L., Hale, S., & Myerson, J. (2016). Effects of age and environmental support for rehearsal on visuospatial working memory. *Psychology and Aging, 31*, 249–254. doi:10.1037/pag0000077

Lilienthal, L., Myerson, J., Abrams, R. A., & Hale, S. (2018). Effect of environmental support on overt and covert visuospatial rehearsal. *Memory, 26*, 1042–1052. doi:10.1080/09658211.2018.1462390

Luria, R., Balaban, H., Awh, E., & Vogel, E. K. (2016). The contralateral delay activity as a neural measure of visual working memory. *Neuroscience and Biobehavioral Reviews, 62*, 100–108. doi:10.1016/j.neubiorev.2016.01.003

MacLeod, C. M. (1991). Half a century of research on the Stroop effect: An integrative review. *Psychological Bulletin, 109*, 163–203.

Mayr, U., & Kliegl, R. (2000). Task-set switching and long-term memory retrieval. *Journal of Experimental Psychology: Learning, Memory, and Cognition, 26*, 1124–1140.

McElree, B., & Dosher, B. A. (1993). Serial retrieval processes in the recovery of order information. *Journal of Experimental Psychology: General, 122*, 291–315.

Meiran, N., Liefooghe, B., & De Houwer, J. (2017). Powerful instructions: Automaticity without practice. *Current Directions in Psychological Science, 26*, 509–514. doi:10.1177/0963721417711638

Miller, G. A. (1956). The magical number seven, plus or minus two: Some limits on our capacity for processing information. *Psychological Review, 63*, 81–97.

Monsell, S. (2003). Task switching. *Trends in Cognitive Sciences, 7*, 134–140.

Morey, C. C., & Bieler, M. (2013). Visual short-term memory always requires general attention. *Psychonomic Bulletin & Review, 20*, 163–170. doi:10.3758/s13423-012-0313-z

Morris, N. (1987). Exploring the visuo-spatial scratch pad. *Quarterly Journal of Experimental Psychology, 39A*, 409–430.

Munoz, D. P., & Everling, S. (2004). Look away: The anti-saccade task and the voluntary control of eye movements. *Nature Reviews Neuroscience, 5*, 218–228. doi:10.1038/nrn1345

Myerson, J., Hale, S., Rhee, S. H., & Jenkins, L. (1999). Selective interference with verbal and spatial working memory in young and older adults. *Journals of Gerontology: Psychological Sciences, 54B*, P161–P164.

Oberauer, K. (2002). Access to information in working memory: Exploring the focus of attention. *Journal of Experimental Psychology: Learning, Memory, and Cognition, 28*, 411–421.

Oberauer, K. (2009). Design for a working memory. *Psychology of Learning and Motivation: Advances in Research and Theory, 51*, 45–100.

Oberauer, K. (2013). The focus of attention in working memory—from metaphors to mechanisms. *Frontiers in Human Neuroscience, 7*. Retrieved from doi:10.3389/fnhum.2013.00673

Oberauer, K. (2016). Parameters, not processes, explain general intelligence. *Psychological Inquiry, 27*, 231–235. doi:10.1080/1047840X.2016.1181999

Oberauer, K. (2019). Working memory and attention – a conceptual analysis and review. *Journal of Cognition, 2*, 1–23. doi:10.5334/joc.58

Oberauer, K., Awh, E., & Sutterer, D. W. (2017). The role of long-term memory in a test of visual working memory: Proactive facilitation but no proactive interference. *Journal of Experimental Psychology: Learning, Memory, and Cognition, 43*, 1–22.

Oberauer, K., Demmrich, A., Mayr, U., & Kliegl, R. (2001). Dissociating retention and access in working memory: An age-comparative study of mental arithmetic. *Memory & Cognition, 29*, 18–33.

Oberauer, K., Farrell, S., Jarrold, C., & Lewandowsky, S. (2016). What limits working memory capacity? *Psychological Bulletin, 142*, 758–799. doi:10.1037/bul0000046

Oberauer, K., Farrell, S., Jarrold, C., Pasiecznik, K., & Greaves, M. (2012). Interference between maintenance and processing in working memory: The effect of item-distractor similarity in complex span *Journal of Experimental Psychology: Learning, Memory, and Cognition, 38*, 665–685. doi:10.1037/a0026337

Oberauer, K., & Hein, L. (2012). Attention to information in working memory. *Current Directions in Psychological Science, 21*, 164–169. doi:10.1177/0963721412444727

Oberauer, K., & Kliegl, R. (2006). A formal model of capacity limits in working memory. *Journal of Memory and Language, 55*, 601–626.

Oberauer, K., & Lewandowsky, S. (2008). Forgetting in immediate serial recall: Decay, temporal distinctiveness, or interference? *Psychological Review, 115*, 544–576.

Oberauer, K., & Lewandowsky, S. (2013). Evidence against decay in verbal working memory. *Journal of Experimental Psychology: General, 142*, 380–411.

Oberauer, K., & Lewandowsky, S. (2014). Further evidence against decay in working memory. *Journal of Memory and Language, 73*, 15–30. doi:10.1016/j.jml.2014.02.003

Oberauer, K., Lewandowsky, S., Awh, E., Brown, G. D. A., Conway, A. R. A., Cowan, N., . . . Ward, G. (2018). Benchmarks for models of short-term and working memory. *Psychological Bulletin, 144*, 885–958. doi:10.1037/bul0000153

Oberauer, K., Lewandowsky, S., Farrell, S., Jarrold, C., & Greaves, M. (2012). Modeling working memory: An interference model of complex span. *Psychonomic Bulletin & Review, 19*, 779–819. doi:10.3758/s13423-012-0272-4

Oberauer, K., & Lin, H. Y. (2017). An interference model of visual working memory. *Psychological Review, 124*, 21–59.

Oberauer, K., Souza, A. S., Druey, M., & Gade, M. (2013). Analogous mechanisms of selection and updating in declarative and procedural working memory: Experiments and a computational model. *Cognitive Psychology, 66*, 157–211.

Olivers, C. N. L., Meijer, F., & Theeuwes, J. (2006). Feature-based memory-driven attentional capture: Visual working memory content affects visual attention. *Journal of Experimental Psychology: Human Perception and Performance, 32*, 1243–1265.

Page, M. P. A., Cumming, N., Norris, D., McNeil, A. M., & Hitch, G. J. (2013). Repetition-spacing and item-overlap effects in the Hebb repetition task. *Journal of Memory and Language, 69*, 506–526. doi:10.1016/j.jml.2013.07.001

Page, M. P. A., & Norris, D. (1998). The primacy model: A new model of immediate serial recall. *Psychological Review, 105*, 761–781.

Paivio, A., & Csapo, K. (1969). Concrete image and verbal memory codes. *Journal of Experimental Psychology, 80*, 279–285.

Pashler, H. (1994). Dual-task interference in simple tasks: Data and theory. *Psychological Bulletin, 116*, 220–244.

Pearson, B., Raškevičius, J., Bays, P. M., Pertzov, Y., & Husain, M. (2014). Working memory retrieval as a decision process. *Journal of Vision, 14*, 1–15. doi:10.1167/14.2.2

Pertzov, Y., Bays, P. M., Joseph, S., & Husain, M. (2013). Rapid forgetting prevented by retrospective attention cues. *Journal of Experimental Psychology: Human Learning and Memory, 29*, 1224–1231. doi:10.1037/a0030947

Pertzov, Y., Manohar, S., & Husain, M. (2017). Rapid forgetting results from competition over time between items in visual working memory. *Journal of Experimental Psychology: Learning, Memory, and Cognition, 43*, 528–536. doi:10.1037/xlm0000328

Raaijmakers, J. G., & Shiffrin, R. M. (1981). Search of associative memory. *Psychological Review, 88*, 93–134. doi:10.1037/0033-295X.88.2.93

Rerko, L., Oberauer, K., & Lin, H. Y. (2014). Spatially imprecise representations in working memory. *Quarterly Journal of Experimental Psychology, 67*, 3–15. doi:10.1080/17470218.2013.789543

Ricker, T. J., & Hardman, K. O. (2017). The nature of short-term consolidation in visual working memory. *Journal of Experimental Psychology: General, 146*, 1551–1573. doi:10.1037/xge0000346

Ricker, T. J., Spiegel, L. R., & Cowan, N. (2014). Time-based loss in visual short-term memory is from trace decay, not temporal distinctiveness. *Journal of Experimental Psychology: Learning, Memory, and Cognition, 40*, 1510–1523. doi:10.1037/xlm0000018

Roodenrys, S., Hulme, C., Lethbridge, A., Hinton, M., & Nimmo, L. M. (2002). Word-frequency and phonological-neighborhood effects on verbal short-term memory. *Journal of Experimental Psychology: Learning, Memory, and Cognition, 28*, 1019–1034.

Schneegans, S., & Bays, P. M. (2018). Drift in neural population activity causes working memory to deteriorate over time. *Journal of Neuroscience, 38*, 4859–4869. doi:10.1523/JNEUROSCI.3440-17.2018

Sederberg, P. B., Howard, M. C., & Kahana, M. J. (2008). A context-based theory of recency and contiguity in free recall. *Psychological Review, 115*, 893–912.

Shiffrin, R. M., & Schneider, W. (1977). Controlled and automatic human information processing: II. Perceptual learning, automatic attending, and a general theory. *Psychological Review, 84*, 127–190.

Smolensky, P. (1990). Tensor product variable binding and the representation of symbolic structures in connectionist systems. *Artificial Intelligence, 46*, 159–216.

Soto, D., Hodsoll, J., Rotshtein, P., & Humphreys, G. W. (2008). Automatic guidance of attention from working memory. *Trends in Cognitive Sciences, 12*, 342–348.

Souza, A. S., & Oberauer, K. (2016). In search of the focus of attention in working memory: 13 years of the retro-cue effect. *Attention, Perception & Psychophysics, 78*, 1839–1860. doi:10.3758/s13414-016-1108-5

Souza, A. S., & Oberauer, K. (2017). The contributions of visual and central attention to visual working memory. *Attention, Perception & Psychophysics, 79*, 1897–1916. doi:10.3758/s13414-017-1357-y

Souza, A. S., & Oberauer, K. (2018). Does articulatory rehearsal help immediate serial recall? *Cognitive Psychology, 107*, 1–21. doi:10.1016/j.cogpsych.2018.09.002

Souza, A. S., Rerko, L., & Oberauer, K. (2016). Getting more from visual working memory: Retro-cues enhance retrieval and protect from visual interference. *Journal of Experimental Psychology: Human Perception and Performance, 42*, 890–910. doi:10.1037/xhp0000192

Stokes, M. G. (2015). 'Activity-silent' working memory in prefrontal cortex: A dynamic coding framework. *Trends in Cognitive Sciences, 19*, 394–405. doi:10.1016/j.tics.2015.05.004

Tamber-Rosenau, B. J., Fintzi, A. R., & Marois, R. (2015). Crowding in visual working memory reveals its spatial resolution and the nature of its representation. *Psychological Science.* doi:10.1177/0956797615592394

Thalmann, M., Souza, A. S., & Oberauer, K. (2019). How does chunking help working memory? *Journal of Experimental Psychology: Learning, Memory, and Cognition, 45*, 37–55. doi:10.1037/xlm0000578

Vergauwe, E., Camos, V., & Barrouillet, P. (2014). The impact of storage on processing: How is information maintained in working memory? *Journal of Experimental Psychology: Learning, Memory, and Cognition, 40*, 1072–1095.

Verguts, T., & Notebaert, W. (2009). Adaptation by binding: A learning account of cognitive control. *Trends in Cognitive Sciences, 13*, 252–257.

Vogel, E. K., & Machizawa, M. G. (2004). Neural activity predicts individual differences in visual working memory capacity. *Nature, 428*, 748–751.

Vogel, E. K., Woodman, G. F., & Luck, S. J. (2001). Storage of features, conjunctions, and objects in visual working memory. *Journal of Experimental Psychology: Human Perception and Performance, 27*, 92–114.

Wilken, P., & Ma, W. J. (2004). A detection theory account of change detection. *Journal of Vision, 4*, 1120–1135.

Woodman, G. F., Carlisle, N. B., & Reinhart, R. M. G. (2013). Where do we store the memory representations that guide attention? *Journal of Vision, 13*, 1–17. doi:10.1167/13.3.1

6

Multicomponent Working Memory System with Distributed Executive Control

André Vandierendonck

The working memory with distributed executive control (WMDEC; Vandierendonck, 2016b) model was developed in order to deal with issues of executive control in the context of working memory (WM) while avoiding explanations that invoke a homunculus. The model shares some assumptions with the multicomponent WM model (Baddeley, 1986, 1996b, 2000; Baddeley & Hitch, 1974; Baddeley & Logie, 1999; see chapter by Baddeley, Hitch, & Allen, 2021), and although that model yields a pretty good account of a number of observations regarding WM, it unfortunately continues to call on the central executive, which—even after several attempts at fractionation (e.g. Baddeley, 1996a)—remains a powerful agent. However, research has shown that it is feasible to decompose the central executive into more elementary processes, such as input monitoring, response selection, memory updating, and so on (Stuyven, Van der Goten, Vandierendonck, Claeys, & Crevits, 2000; Szmalec, Demanet, Vandierendonck, & Verbruggen, 2009; Szmalec & Vandierendonck, 2007; Szmalec, Vandierendonck, & Kemps, 2005; Szmalec et al., 2008; Szmalec, Verbruggen, Vandierendonck, & Kemps, 2011; Vandierendonck, Szmalec, Deschuyteneer, & Depoorter, 2007). Hence, a model with distributed control instead of a central executive agent is preferable and possible, as is also suggested by Logie (2016; see chapter by Logie, Belletier, & Doherty, 2021).

The WMDEC model conceptualizes WM by means of a number of maxims about the characteristics of WM as a system embedded in cognition strongly linked to goal-directed action (see also Table 6.2). The first maxim states that WM provides temporary memory storage in support of any goal-directed action, whether consciously or unconsciously planned. This idea was first proposed by Miller, Galanter, and Pribram (1960) in their thought-provoking book, *Plans and the Structure of Behavior*. On this view, WM is not only needed to store the goal (cf. findings on goal neglect; Duncan et al., 2008), but also to keep track of interim results of task execution and furthermore also to keep focus on the ways to achieve the goal and the physical and mental constraints and limitations imposed on goal attainment. Note that this maxim not only applies to deliberate conscious actions but also to actions to fulfil particular needs (hunger, thirst, curiosity, etc.) and that this concerns more than calling on prospective memory as implied by Cowan (2017).

A second maxim is rooted in the observation that language and verbal representations strongly dominate human cognition, such that all knowledge and all processes

André Vandierendonck, *Multicomponent Working Memory System with Distributed Executive Control* In: *Working Memory.*
Edited by: Robert H. Logie, Valérie Camos, and Nelson Cowan, Oxford University Press (2021). © Oxford University Press.
DOI: 10.1093/oso/9780198842286.003.0006

Table 6.1 Summary responses to designated questions

Question	Response
1. Definition of working memory (WM)	WM is the part of the memory system used to support goal-directed activities. This support includes maintaining the task goal, the selected way to achieve this goal, and the constraints or limitations of this achievement. The WM system also maintains all interim results so as to enable continuation after task interruption.
2. Methods	(a) Simulation and computational modelling to test feasibility of assumptions and to test model predictions against existing data. (b) Dual-tasking and load experiments (typically, but not exclusively Brown–Peterson or complex span designs).
3. Unitary versus non-unitary nature of WM	Non-unitary system consisting of two domain-general modules, namely the executive memory module and an episodic buffer. The former maintains task-specific information and settings; the latter is a multimodal store maintaining the currently important events. These two modules are assisted by modality-specific low-effort systems, namely the phonological buffer, and a visual/spatial memory. These systems interconnect with long-term memory (LTM; categorical and procedural) and the episodic buffer feeds episodic LTM. The phonological buffer is based on a medium for internal speech and is mainly used for rumination and self-instruction, but can also be used for verbal rehearsal as a phonological loop.
4. Role of attention and control	Attention plays a central role in goal-directed activities and by extension in WM. Control processes are the result of prior learning and are retrieved from (mainly procedural LTM) when needed.
5. Storage, maintenance, and loss of information	Executive memory is dedicated to maintenance of the current task-set and its constraints. The episodic buffer stores instances of the events as they occur by combining perceptual information, declarative knowledge, and episodic LTM. These two modules are capacity limited in terms of total amount of activation. As total activation exceeds the capacity limit, activation of the individual events in the stores is decreased proportionally. This allows for a choice between a few strongly activated traces or a larger number of traces that are less strongly activated and hence not so readily accessible. A refreshment mechanism in the episodic buffer allows selective activation increase for targeted instances (because when the capacity limit is reached, increased activation of one event has to be compensated by decreased activation in the other events). There is no such limitation to the amount of information in the modality-specific systems, but limitations are incurred due to automatic and fast decay, which can be counteracted by verbal rehearsal (in the phonological buffer), or by trace revival (in the visuospatial module). Hand in hand with the mechanisms of refreshment, the traces can be transferred to and consolidated in episodic LTM.

(Continued)

Table 6.1 Continued

Question	Response
6. Role of LTM knowledge	On the present view, WM is not the activated subset of LTM, but it heavily relies on knowledge present in LTM; namely, it relies on declarative knowledge to interpret perceptual events and create specific instances for further processing in the WM modules, and it relies on procedural knowledge to activate and select procedures to act on the WM contents.
7. Findings inconsistent with the model	At present, working memory with distributed executive control (WMDEC) cannot yet account for priming effects that are typically accounted for by spreading activation in LTM because a more complex mechanism is required within the context of the model. Although WMDEC should in principle be able to account for the Hebb learning effect, precise predictions cannot be formulated until the functioning of episodic LTM is further developed within the model.
A. Early life development	WMDEC does not pretend to explain developmental changes, but if anything, it may be assumed that some of the modules within the model come into existence at different times during development.
C. Individual differences	The model does not make any specific assumptions about individual differences. Quantitative differences can easily be handled by the model, namely differences in capacity of the different modules, and differences in speed of processing.
F. WM Applications	As the model was developed on the basis of interactions between working memory and task switching, it is evident that this model provides a basis to explain how WM is used by other cognitive tasks such as arithmetic, reasoning, and language comprehension.

using this knowledge are pervaded by language and language-based representations. This is also true in the context of memory, as shown by Morey, Morey, van der Reijden, and Holweg (2013): visuospatial task performance is dramatically disrupted by the presence of a verbal memory load, while a visual memory load has almost no effects on verbal task performance. This central role of language encoding is also evident in task execution and switching between actions. More specifically, the presence of an articulation task in a task switching sequence strongly affects performance, such that the task switch cost (slower and more error-prone task execution) is decreased when the articulatory activity supports maintenance of the task goal (e.g. repeating the task name; Goschke, 2000), whereas the switch cost becomes much larger when the articulatory task is irrelevant to the task (Baddeley, Chincotta, & Adlam, 2001; Goschke, 2000; Saeki & Saito, 2004), but other motor tasks such as foot-tapping do not affect the switch cost, showing that the concurrent articulation effect is not merely a dual-task effect (Emerson & Miyake, 2003; Liefooghe, Vandierendonck, Muyllaert, Verbruggen, & Vanneste, 2005). Furthermore, the cost of switching between arithmetic tasks is less impaired when transparent cues (+ and −) than when non-transparent cues (red and black) are provided, while the effect of articulatory suppression is not modulated by

Table 6.2 Maxims underlying the working memory with distributed executive control model

---

1. Working memory (WM) provides temporary storage space for consciously and unconsciously planned actions so as to remember the current goal, the progress towards goal attainment, the ways to attain the goal, and the physical and mental constraints and limitations imposed.

2. WM includes an inner speech mechanism that allows self-instruction, but can also be used for rehearsal, mind wandering, and rumination.

3. Control processes are an inherent part of working memory. The application of a control process can only occur if a particular condition exists. Detection of the condition triggers the autonomous execution of the process resulting in the disappearance of the triggering condition.

4. WM is a versatile and flexible system that allows different encoding formats and different levels of generality of the representations.

---

task difficulty or the number of different tasks in the switching procedure, and remains overall much stronger than the interference due to foot-tapping (Emerson & Miyake, 2003). This leads to the conclusion that self-instruction by means of inner speech is the driving factor behind these effects (see also Miyake, Emerson, Padilla, & Ahn, 2004). So, the point of importance is that language is so dominant that we, humans, speak to ourselves to give instructions, to remind ourselves what we have to do, to remind ourselves of pitfalls, and so on. In short, the second maxim states that the WM system includes an inner speech mechanism that supports self-instruction (cf. Posner & Rothbart, 2007; Vygotsky, 1962), but that can be used to support rehearsal, rumination, and mind wandering, to the extent that it is not occupied for other purposes, such as self-instruction.

The third maxim concerns the role of control processes. WM has always been conceived of as a short-term memory system endowed with control processes (e.g. Atkinson & Shiffrin, 1968, 1971; Shiffrin & Atkinson, 1969). Control processes were considered to be optional, meaning that their usage either depended on an instruction to utilize these processes, or on a decision on the part of the memorizer to do so. While some of these control processes are rather simple and straightforward, such as coding and rehearsal, others, such as decision-making or deploying rehearsal strategies may require rather elaborate processing and continuous control. With the introduction of dual-task and selective interference methods, even more complicated controls could be considered. No wonder, some theories outsourced these controls to an executive agent. Clearly, control processes are part and parcel of a WM system and without control processes WM is simply a short-term store. Hence, any model has to find a way to deal with these processes. Collecting them all in a central agent entails the danger of creating a closed box that performs the control while nobody has an idea what is going on. The only way out is to accept that control processes are bound to particular conditions that trigger a previously acquired autonomous action that resolves the issue at hand.

The fourth and final maxim holds that WM is an extremely versatile and flexible system that allows information to be stored in a modality-specific code most adapted to the current situation. These modality-specific representations allow characteristics of the perceptual input to be preserved, such as a phonological/articulatory code suitable for the inner speech mechanism or a visuospatial code for visual patterns, schematic layouts, and so on. Apart from such modality-specific or domain-specific coding, cross-modal or domain-general codes are also needed to represent information without preserving perceptual features or to bind representations from different perceptual input channels. That these encoding formats imply flexibility means that the person has a choice as to which encoding best fulfils the present needs.

These four maxims specify the conceptualization of the WM system proposed in this chapter. In terms of the various definitions reviewed by Cowan (2017), it can easily be seen that the present conception is based on a combination of the life-planning definition (Miller et al., 1960), the multicomponent definition (Baddeley, 1986, 2000; Baddeley & Hitch, 1974), and the attention-control definition (Engle, 2002; see chapter by Mashburn, Tsukahara, & Engle, 2021).

Structure of the Working Memory System

The WM system not only offers support for the control of goal-directed actions, it also provides an interface between perception and knowledge. Information coming in via the perceptual channels contacts the knowledge base stored in long-term memory (LTM) which allows the perceived events to be interpreted (apperception; Wundt, 1874). Since the work of Sperling (Averbach & Sperling, 1961; Sperling, 1960), it is known that perceptual processes leave very short-lived memory traces in so-called sensory registers, such as the iconic and echoic sensory memory for, respectively, visual and auditive processing. As these memories only yield a brief extension of the perceptual events, the WM system is used to maintain a more endurable trace of the events of interest (see also Atkinson & Shiffrin, 1968). Fig. 6.1 shows a schematic overview of all the storage modules included in the present WM model as well as the interrelations between the different modules. Table 6.1 explains the characteristics of the model according to a scheme that allows comparison of the models in the present book.

According to the present model, the WM system uses both modality-specific and domain-general storage facilities for maintaining such more endurable traces. When these memory traces include an important number of perceptual features, modality-specific storage systems are convenient. In principle, it is possible that every perceptual modality has a corresponding modality-specific storage module. Which modality-specific modules should be included is an empirical question as well as an issue of theoretical parsimony. In view of the dominant role of language in cognitive processing, a verbal-phonological module based on an inner speech mechanism that mediates self-instruction (cf. Vygotsky, 1962) is included. Furthermore, there is sufficient evidence in favour of a dissociation between modality-specific phonological storage on the one hand and visuospatial storage on the other hand (e.g. Hamilton, 2011; Logie, 2011; Logie, Zucco, & Baddeley, 1990; Parmentier, 2011). Some evidence even suggests a dissociation between visual and spatial storage (Klauer & Zhao, 2004), but some commonalities between both can still be defended because this dissociation is likely to be

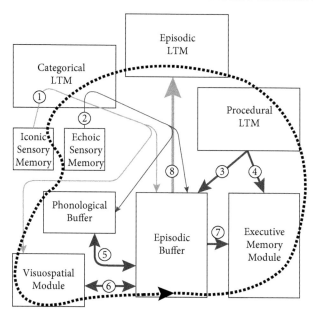

Fig. 6.1 Working memory modules and their interconnections. The procedural loop (dashed closed arrow) continuously compares iconic and echoic sensory memory and the working memory modules to condition-action rules stored in procedural long-term memory (LTM). Among the matching rules one is selected for execution (routes 3 and 4). Sensory events are interpreted with the help of categorical LTM and are instantiated in the episodic buffer via routes 1 and 2. Additionally, verbal events can be encoded in the phonological buffer (route 5) and visual events can be encoded in the visuospatial module (route 6). Over time, the contents of the episodic buffer flow over into episodic LTM via route 8. Route 7 shows the existence of interconnections between the episodic buffer and executive memory; these are realized via procedural LTM rules.

more functional than structural. In other words, according to the present state of the art, at least phonological and visuospatial WM modules should be included.

Accordingly, the *phonological buffer* maintains phonologically[1] encoded information. This maintenance is volatile as it is easily 'overwritten' by newly incoming phonemic information and by inner speech acts that are unrelated to the stored information; it is also vulnerable to decay, such that without any further action after a few seconds the phonological codes can no longer be accessed. Such automatic information loss or decay can be counteracted by verbal or articulatory *rehearsal*: by processing the

---

[1] Because the qualification 'phonological' (as in the terms 'phonological store' and 'phonological loop') is widely used, this label remains also in place for referring to the phonological buffer in the present model. However, considering that the proposed module uses inner speech, it would obviously be more convenient to call it 'articulatory buffer', in particular because it encodes in terms of articulation (output lexicon) rather than perception (input lexicon). Note however, that the term 'articulatory loop' was on some occasions also used by Baddeley and colleagues.

information in the phonological buffer via the inner speech mechanism (phonological loop), the information re-enters the phonological buffer resulting in a renewed trace.

Visuospatial information is maintained in the visuospatial module. As the term suggests, this module contains visual information linked to a particular spatial location or delimited area in surrounding space. A number of objects (minimally, shapes with a particular texture or colour) can, for example, be present in different spatial locations; these objects and locations are represented in the visuospatial module, which allows for recall of the objects (shapes or colours or both) and the location at which objects are present. Although humans are able to represent complex images of such situations at a rather global level, it is difficult to maintain all the details for all the elements of the complex image. With respect to the example of a number of objects as given here, it is difficult to maintain for every object the correct binding of shape, colour, and location. As with the phonological buffer, the information maintained in the visuospatial module can easily be disrupted by new visual images or objects changing location and the information present also suffers from decay. Although the debate as to whether a kind of rehearsal mechanism exists also for visuospatial materials, on the grounds that imagination may help to reconstitute or revive an image, in the present model, it is assumed that visuospatial information can be reprocessed and re-strengthened by means of *revival*. Such revival may be based on visual imagination but also on imagination of performing an action on an object. Hence, research on memory for action (Engelkamp, Zimmer, Mohr, & Sellen, 1994; Koriat, Ben-Zur, & Nussbaum, 1990; Mulligan & Hornstein, 2003; Yang, Gathercole, & Allen, 2014) as well as earlier work on the so-called inner scribe by Logie (1995; Logie & Pearson, 1997) is highly relevant in this context.

Episodic Buffer

Apart from these two modality-specific modules, the present model also includes two domain-general modules each with a specific purpose. The first of these is the *episodic buffer* (similar to the conception first formulated by Baddeley, 2000) which maintains domain-general or cross-modal memory traces. According to the present view, these traces start as temporary records but after consolidation[2] become part of episodic LTM, as is also shown in Fig. 6.1. The episodic buffer is the main storage module of the WM system which may be supported by the modality-specific modules in cases where maintenance of the perceptual (auditory and/or visual) features is crucial. It is the central medium for temporary maintenance of information, because this module is needed to maintain cross-modal links, and to create links to existing knowledge. Because of this mixture, this module contains representations that can easily access either of the

---

[2] The term 'consolidation' as used in the present chapter refers to long-term consolidation. This should not be confused with the same term used to refer to short-term consolidation (or transfer from sensory to working memory).

domain-specific storage systems as well as semantic or categorical LTM. As a consequence and in contrast with a number of views within the field (e.g. Atkinson & Shiffrin,
1971; Cowan, 1999; see chapter by Cowan, Morey, & Naveh-Benjamin, 2021; Oberauer,
2009, see chapter by Oberauer, 2021), this module cannot be considered as activated categorical LTM. Instead, modality-specific information and knowledge are combined into
a specific instance embodying the combination of all these features. Because the episodic
buffer consists of instances or tokens that may be linked to more general information in
categorical LTM (types), the process is called *instantiation* (see also Vandierendonck,
2016b). Within the present model, it is assumed that the episodic buffer does not suffer
from decay. However, it has a limited capacity with respect to the strength (degree of activation) of the traces being maintained, so that it is possible to keep a few items at high
strength or to keep more items at the cost of having a small activation strength for all or
almost all the items in the store. Loss of information from the episodic buffer is due to
interference and suppression of traces that are no longer useful. When this capacity limit
is reached, each time a new trace is added, the older traces lose some of their strength.
After a few new traces have been added, some of the older traces may become so weak
as to be useless; either these older traces get lost or they regain strength by applying a
strengthening mechanism similar to rehearsal and revival in the modality-specific modules, namely attentional refreshing (e.g. Camos et al., 2018; Johnson, 1992; Johnson
et al., 2005; Vergauwe & Cowan, 2015). Refreshment consists of paying attention to or
thinking of the represented information for a short time and the result is that the trace
becomes stronger; inevitably this gain of strength occurs at the expense of the strengths
of the other traces when the buffer is occupied to full capacity.

Within the present view, refreshment does not only result in a prolonged maintenance of a trace in the episodic buffer, it also involves *consolidation*, which means building
and strengthening a trace in episodic LTM. Transfer of information of short-term to
long-term storage was an attribute of rehearsal (elaborative rehearsal; Craik & Watkins,
1973) in some of the older short-term memory and WM theories (e.g. Atkinson &
Shiffrin, 1968; Broadbent, 1958; Norman, 1968), but it is at odds with views that consider WM to be essentially activated LTM. However, to the extent that WM is also considered to collaborate on the creation of episodic traces, it remains a useful idea. In the
present view, consolidation—transfer to episodic LTM—is associated with refreshment
and not with revival or rehearsal because the latter actions are assumed to run off automatically and hence do not involve attention. However, rehearsal can occur jointly with
refreshment (which would yield elaborative rehearsal) and also revival can be performed
jointly with refreshment. These joint maintenance modes ensure that not only domain-
general, but also modality-specific information can enter long-term episodic memory.

Executive Memory

The second domain-general module is specific for the maintenance of task and goal-
related information and because of its crucial role in task execution, it is referred to

as the executive module or executive memory. Unlike the central executive in some WM models (e.g. Baddeley & Hitch, 1974; Baddeley & Logie, 1999; Cowan, 1999; see chapter by Cowan et al., 2021), this module only maintains task-relevant information, such as the task set. Whereas the task goal is part of our general knowledge as maintained in categorical LTM, it can easily be instantiated in the episodic buffer with or without articulatory support from the phonological buffer, or visuospatial support from the visuospatial module. Similarly, the information which has to be processed in the task, and interim results that are obtained by task processing are represented in the episodic buffer, again with or without support from the modality-specific WM modules. A small example may clarify which representations can be maintained in the episodic buffer and which ones would have to be held in executive memory. Consider an experiment in which participants are requested to report the sum of two numbers (e.g. '27 + 35 = ?') presented in the centre of the screen, with the instruction to respond fast but correctly. As already argued, the task goal (adding numbers) will be maintained in the episodic buffer. As each sum is processed, the interim results will also be kept active in the episodic buffer until the final outcome is reached. More specifically, for the given example, the participant may decide to first sum the units (7 + 5 = 12) and maintain 12 in the episodic buffer, next sum the tens (20 + 30 = 50) and also keep this result in the buffer. Finally, these outcomes must be combined (50 + 12 = 62) before reporting this outcome and clear the interim results from the episodic buffer. In order to perform all these actions, some necessary information has to be maintained, namely to orient attention at the digits on the screen and to keep speed and accuracy of responding in balance. This information is part of the task set as it relates specifically to task execution. Therefore it is maintained in executive memory.

It could be argued that the episodic buffer as a domain-general module is perfectly equipped to maintain the latter kind of information. If the buffer would maintain the task set, a competition would be expected between task-related and content-related calls on WM capacity, but this expectation is contradicted by some findings regarding the relationship between WM and task switching. As already mentioned, some studies show that task switching relies on WM, more in particular on the phonological loop. Yet, several studies have failed to report effects of a memory load on task switching (Kiesel, Wendt, & Peters, 2007; Liefooghe, Barrouillet, Vandierendonck, & Camos, 2008; Logan, 2004). Similarly, in the opposite direction, no effect of the number of task switches on WM performance is observed when no timing constraints are imposed (Logan, 2004, 2006); it is only when the retention interval is strictly timed that the number of task switches affects WM performance (Liefooghe et al., 2008). These findings converge on the conclusion (see Vandierendonck, 2016b for a more extensive argumentation) that although task processing seems to call on WM resources, this processing does not compete for resources involved in the maintenance of content, such as the maintenance of task names in Logan (2004) or irrelevant content, as in Kiesel et al. (2007). By including a separate module for task-related information, it is ensured that task-related and content-related processes do not have to compete for storage space, and in addition, everything related to task control is available in one single module, so that information needed for proactive control of task execution is grouped within executive memory.

Because executive memory maintains task-related information, namely a representation of the action or actions that lead to goal achievement and the constraints imposed on the allowable actions, it may be concluded that this module is the same as the procedural WM module in Oberauer's WM model (Oberauer, 2009, see chapter by Oberauer, 2021). For a number of reasons executive memory must not be equated with procedural WM. First, in the present conception, when a production rule in procedural LTM matches the WM contents and is selected for execution, it is activated; this results in execution of the action part of the rule. This execution may entail a change to any of the WM modules or the initiation of a motor action, but the rule itself does not remain activated after this and does not become part of WM. In other words, there is a fundamental asymmetry between declarative (categorical, semantic, etc.) LTM and procedural LTM in that activated declarative LTM contents are maintained as part of the instances in the episodic buffer and/or in the domain-specific WM modules while activated procedural LTM elements are immediately executed and do not become part of WM contents. The contents maintained in executive memory have declarative origins, but relate to task-execution. In contrast, in Oberauer's conception, procedural WM is activated procedural LTM in symmetry to the activated declarative LTM contents that constitute declarative WM.

As the arithmetic example suggests, the task set concerns orientation of attention and speed–accuracy balance. In fact, a task set generally contains information about the means by which the goal can be attained, the modality which is used for responding, and which particular conditions constrain the execution of the actions (e.g. Logan & Gordon, 2001). The task set can best be conceived as a cognitive schema, such as a frame or a script (e.g. Abelson, 1981; Graesser & Nakamura, 1982) that is part of our acquired knowledge (categorical LTM). As is typical for such acquired cognitive structures, some of the elements of the structure are fixed, while others can vary and may or may not have a default value.

Like the episodic buffer, the executive module has a limited capacity, but does not suffer from decay. Executive memory maintains maximally a few task sets. As each task set consists of a number of components (parameters, actions, mappings, etc.), each of these components occupies some of the available capacity. If executive memory contains more than one task set, the one with the strongest activation is dominant and will be accessible to monitor task progress. When more executive memory elements are made active, the already present task sets and their components will lose some strength to allow the newly uploaded task set to consume some capacity.

Functioning of the Working Memory System

At any moment in time, the components of the WM system contain representations originating either from environmental events (represented in sensory memory) or from internal events triggered via associations between WM contents (in episodic buffer, phonological buffer, the visuospatial module, and executive memory) and LTM representations. A production system similar to that underlying ACT (Anderson, 1983; Anderson & Lebiere, 1998; Lovett, Reder, & Lebiere, 1999) governs changes to WM contents. The production system consists of a set of production rules (also known as if-then rules) stored in procedural LTM and a procedural loop (Fig. 6.1) that governs activation, selection, and execution of one rule at a time. An example of such a rule is '*IF* x is a new object in iconic sensory memory *AND* x is not present in the episodic buffer *THEN* create an instance of x in the episodic buffer'. The example shows that the IF-part (condition) may consist of several elementary conditions joined by the AND-operator. The more of such elements are included in the rule's condition, the more specific the rule is. Apart from the degree of specificity, each rule also has a strength which can change by experience. When two or more rules leading to the same action match WM contents, only the most specific of these rules will enter the competition for selection. Among the matching rules, one is selected and the rule action ('create' in the example at hand) is executed. This execution may take some time; during this interval, the rule is occupied and cannot be selected again until the creation is completed. At a fixed rate, a cycle of the procedural loop is executed. During a cycle, all production rules stored in procedural LTM are compared to the WM contents, and among the available rules that match the WM contents, at most one rule is selected for execution of its action. Each rule has a strength that determines the likelihood that it will be selected if it matches.

In order to better clarify the dynamics of this system, its operation in a few characteristic task settings will be described, namely in serial recall and in a complex span task. Each case is illustrated with the help of a concrete example so as to clarify how each part of the system contributes to WM operation.

Serial Recall

Consider a test situation where participants have to memorize consonants (W, T, Z, P, R, F, N) presented visually at a fixed rate of one per second for immediate recall in the order of presentation. A short instruction explains that the start of presentation will be announced by a visual signal, that each letter will be presented in the centre of the screen, that at the end of the list, the word 'recall' will appear, after which recall of the letters can be given orally in the same order as presented, and that the time allowed for recall is limited. This is followed by a short practice session. Focus here is on a single experimental trial, as illustrated in Fig. 6.2.

The start signal catches attention; it becomes represented in the episodic buffer (by a rule such as the one shown earlier). This signal is used as a cue to retrieve the memorization-and-recall goal from categorical LTM and to keep it active in the episodic buffer. In its turn, the goal representation will match a rule that retrieves and configures a corresponding task set in executive memory. This task-set representation includes the specifics of the task at hand, namely that recall will be oral ('Modality

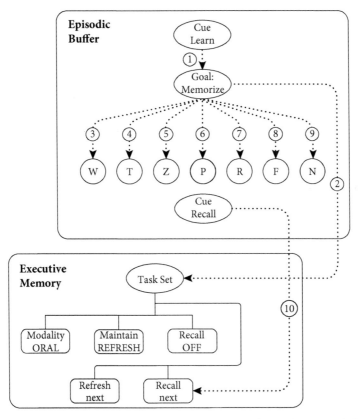

Fig. 6.2 Contents of episodic buffer and executive memory during learning and serial recall of a sequence of consonants (example explained in text). Instantiation of the cue matches a rule to load the task goal (1) which in its turn matches a rule to retrieve the task set and its components from long-term memory (2). As each letter is presented, it is instantiated in the episodic buffer (3–9) and refreshed as specified in executive memory. Finally, the recall signal triggers an adaptation (10) of the task set parameters (recall OFF to ON) so that the recall action can become active.

ORAL'), and that recall will be required later ('Recall OFF'). Typically, also other settings will be included, for example, that stimuli are presented visually, that recall will be required when the recall signal is presented. Furthermore, some self-instructed issues of importance may be included: one such element may be how received information is maintained ('Maintain REFRESH'), but this could also have been specified by instruction. When the first consonant (W) is shown, it enters iconic sensory memory and is for a short period of time available as a 'new' event (environmental change), so that it may match a rule that results in the creation of a representation. As part of the creation, categorical LTM is accessed to retrieve the meaning and relevant properties of this stimulus event; these properties are then used to create an instance in the episodic buffer. During creation, the letter will be tagged as 'to-be-remembered' and associated to the current time signal; this allows recovery of instance order in the to-be-remembered sequence. In the time remaining until the presentation of the next letter, a rule to refresh and consolidate the letter may be executed. When the next consonant is presented, it is instantiated in the same way, and in the remaining interval, both letters presented thus far will be refreshed one at a time. This continues for each letter in the sequence, but at some point, the interval will not be long enough to refresh all the letters; nevertheless refreshing continues where it left off after the previous letter. At the end of the sequence of consonants, the recall signal is presented, which becomes also encoded in the buffer as a cue to start recall. This triggers the application of rules to change the setting for the recall parameter in the task set (to 'Recall ON') and the action setting for recall is implemented changing the task action from maintenance to recall. Based on the remembered instructions, the recall setting will include the specification for the order requirement. A rule to retrieve the stored information will now match the task settings in executive memory and the oldest letter is searched for. Once the oldest letter is found, first access is attempted in the episodic buffer, and if that is not possible, episodic LTM access is tried. If either access succeeds, the instance is tagged as recalled and preparations for output are started; until this process completes, recall of the next item is not possible, but meanwhile the other letters may be refreshed. If access fails, it will be tried again. The probability that access succeeds depends on the activation strength of the stored element. On average, the lower the activation strength the more attempts for access will be needed. However, because several of the elements will have accrued strength in episodic LTM as well, recall may still be successful. After a number of attempts without success, recall will shift to the next oldest element.

The elaboration of this example was completely based on the usage of the episodic buffer as only storage medium. If the phonological buffer were used as the main storage medium, which is perfectly possible in this task, the events would be roughly the same, but instead of preparing for refreshment, a preparation for rehearsal would be in order (different setting in the task set, namely 'Maintain REHEARSE'). For maintenance, a phonological loop would be started, initially with the first consonant as single element. The maintenance would thus continuously perform the subvocal articulation of this consonant. As more letters enter storage, the loop would be extended with these consonants in the order of occurrence and rehearsal would perform subvocal articulation of each consonant in turn. When during the presentation interval between two consonants, not enough time is left to rehearse them all, rehearsal will continue, but will be selective. Note that in this case episodic buffer representations are not refreshed, unless the episodic and the phonological buffer would be used jointly. When the recall signal is presented, recall will start from the contents of the phonological buffer, consulting also the episodic buffer and episodic LTM if access does not immediately succeed.

Complex Span

In a complex span setting, the memorization and recall context is combined with execution of another task: in the intervals between the presentation of the memoranda one

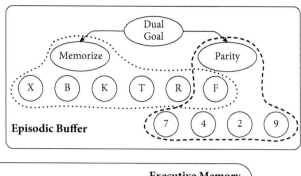

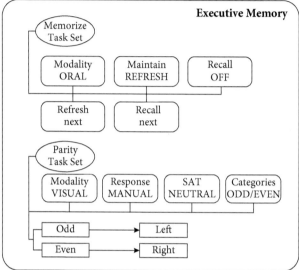

Fig. 6.3 Episodic buffer and executive memory contents in a complex span task with execution of parity task trials in the between-letter intervals of a serial memory task. Parity and memory goals are coordinated under an over-arching dual-task goal. First the memory task and the corresponding task set become active and dominant, until the parity task becomes dominant (as soon a digit is presented). If inter-digit time allows, the memory task regains dominance to allow for refreshment of the memoranda. This continues until all the digits have been presented and the next letter or the signal to recall appears. At that point, the recall parameter and action in the memory task set are adapted for this requirement.

or more simple cognitive tasks have to be performed. In other types of dual-tasking situations (also known as Brown–Peterson procedure), the tasks are presented during the overall retention interval of the memory task. In terms of WM operation, these two contexts are quite similar. Here, an example of a complex span context is considered in more detail. The participant is presented with a series of letters for later recall in the correct order. In between two letters, another task is presented. Among the many different possible tasks, such as verification of arithmetic sums (e.g. Turner & Engle, 1989), sentence comprehension (e.g. Daneman & Carpenter, 1980), simple reasoning tasks (e.g. Baddeley & Hitch, 1974), counting (e.g. Case, Kurland, & Goldberg, 1982), in the present example, a parity judgement task is used (e.g. Barrouillet, Bernardin, Portrat, Vergauwe, & Camos, 2007). The details are illustrated in Fig. 6.3.

In this type of situation the memory task and the parity task become alternately dominant within a single memory trial: the memorization task is interrupted to perform some parity trials but continues afterwards; similarly, after execution of the parity task, the parity goal should not be dismissed because more parity trials are to follow. In such a context, a coordination of the two goals is needed. This allows the goals to become dominant in turn, but remain active in WM. Thus, relevant memory information is maintained and the parity task must not be prepared and configured every time a new digit appears. In Fig. 6.3, this is shown by the representation of a dual-task goal in the episodic buffer. Although, this is not simple, humans are very well acquainted with that kind of requirement as well in dual-tasking contexts as in the context of problem solving where the main goal often requires sub-goals to be attained in order to solve the problem. Once the dual-task goal is set, the memorization goal and the parity goal are added as subsidiary goals. Presuming that a practice session has been given, at the start of the first complex span trial, the three goals (dual task, memorization, and parity) are already stored in the episodic buffer and the two task sets in executive memory are also completely prepared. The parity task set differs slightly from the memorization task set in that some of its parameters differ; additionally, the parity task set requires category-response mappings instead of stage-specific actions. As soon as a letter appears, the memorization goal is activated to become dominant over (i.e. more strongly activated than) the parity goal and the memorization task is made dominant over the parity task set. Note that if this would not be the case, letters would be treated by the parity task or in the reverse situation digits would be memorized instead of judged for parity. As long as no new information comes in, the already present letters are refreshed and consolidated. When a digit appears, the parity goal is made dominant over the memorization goal and the parity task set is activated to be stronger than the memorization task set. The settings ensure that the digit is categorized as odd or even and that the required response is initiated and emitted. As soon as the response is initiated, the memorization goal and task set will be activated to be dominant so as to enable further refreshment. When the next digit appears, dominance shifts again to the parity goal and task set. These alternations continue until the recall signal appears at which time recall is initiated and the trial finishes, with some empty time before the next trial starts.

Executive Control

The operation of the WM system in all these examples was explained without explicit reference to executive control processes. In fact, the representations in executive memory serve to support *proactive control processes*, namely to maximize the chance that the task goal is attained by the selected action sequences. The task settings in executive memory ensure that only condition-action rules matching these settings can be selected. Overall, such proactive control works quite well but not perfectly, because

WM may contain representations that are no longer relevant for the current goal. Moreover, many stimuli can be handled by several tasks (e.g. digits can be categorized on the basis of magnitude or parity) and this increases the likelihood that a lingering trace from a previous trial interferes with the processing required in the present trial. In order to avoid such processes to result in errors, *reactive executive control* can be applied.

To clarify this notion of reactive control, consider the difficulties one may encounter when performing the Stroop task, that is, identifying or naming the ink colour of printed colour words (e.g. when shown the word 'red' printed in blue, say blue). On incongruent trials, the task is difficult because reading is highly automated and produces the colour name (red) faster than the process of identifying/naming the ink colour (blue). In such a situation, a response conflict is present: a response tendency to say red as well as a response tendency to say blue become active. If there is a preference for fast responding, saying the colour name is more likely than saying the ink colour, with an incorrect response as result. With a preference for slower responding, the proactive control mechanisms allow the correct response tendency to become stronger, so that it may win the competition, resulting in a correct answer. In contrast, congruent trials do not suffer from this difficulty because there is no response conflict: both processes (colour identification and colour reading) activate the same response. In this task context, reactive executive control can come into play if the response conflict is detected (Botvinick, Braver, Barch, Carter, & Cohen, 2001). After conflict detection, reactive control can be deployed by changing the speed–accuracy balance in favour of slower and more correct responding. This results in the so-called Gratton effect (Gratton, Coles, & Donchin, 1992): the congruency effect (slower and more error-prone responses on incongruent trials) is decreased after an incongruent trial compared to a previous congruent trial. Research has shown that such reactive corrections only occur if one is aware of the presence of a response conflict, irrespective of whether a conflict was present (Desender, Van Opstal, & Van den Bussche, 2014).

Reactive executive control does not only occur to monitor and adapt response conflicts. A large amount of evidence has been collected regarding the presence of such control processes also in task switching, response inhibition, and attentional control. Because these control processes seem possible without awareness, are task or context-specific and are sensitive to reward, it has been suggested that these processes are routed in associative learning (Abrahamse, Braem, Notebaert, & Verguts, 2016). Given this associative basis, both conflict detection and reactive corrections such as changes in attention or in speed–accuracy balance can be handled by condition-action rules that result in changes to the task set parameters.

Whether this is also the case for all kinds of executive control, is at present still an open question. According to Norman and Shallice (1986), executive control is required in situations that involve planning or decision-making, involve troubleshooting, situations where responses are not well learned or contain novel action sequences, in dangerous or technically difficult situations, and situations that require overcoming of a strong habitual response or resisting temptation. The last set of situations overlaps with the control processes examined by Abrahamse et al. (2016), but the other four sets of situations seem to refer to higher cognitive processes that require some particular skills and some even require a sufficient degree of experience. An account of such processes is welcome, but requires further research.

Empirical Support

The WMDEC model was presented for the first time at the International Working Memory Conference in Cambridge, United Kingdom, in 2014, and published subsequently (Vandierendonck, 2016b). A computational version providing a proof of concept (Vandierendonck, 2012) had been published earlier. Two sources of support for the model will be considered in turn: findings from simulations with the earlier computational version of the model and predictions following from the properties of the model. Finally, also limitations and shortcomings related to the design choices will be discussed.

The model was designed in the first place to account for WM usage in task switching and other kinds of multiple task situations. The early simulation work (Vandierendonck, 2012) shows that the model accounts for the findings regarding the task span procedure (Logan, 2004) and the findings regarding the number of task switches in the strictly timed complex span and dual-task designs (Liefooghe et al., 2008). In the task-span procedure, participants are presented a series of task names they have to remember in the correct order (memory span) and which they also have to execute in the correct order (task span). Over a series of experiments that varied length of the sequence, number of task switches, and opportunities for chunking, Logan (2004) reported that the memory span (number of correctly remembered task names in the correct order) and the task span (number of correctly executed tasks in the correct order) did not differ. This was taken as evidence that task performance and memory maintenance are not mediated by the same WM resource. The strictly timed procedure used by Liefooghe et al. (2008) involved presentation of series of letters for later serial recall with digit judgements tasks intervening between letters (complex span) or in the recall interval (Brown–Peterson procedure). The number of task switches in these task sequences was varied, and it was found that when more task switches were required, memory for letters was poorer. While the Time-Based Resource-Sharing (TBRS) model obviously accounts for the latter finding, to my knowledge, WMDEC is the only model to account for the task-span findings. By design, the model can also account for findings that a task executed for the first time may show congruency effects (Liefooghe, Wenke, & De Houwer, 2012; Meiran & Cohen-Kdoshay, 2012), because also for a new task, a task set is configured in executive memory on the basis of a generic task-set schema acquired from previous experience.

Next, the focus is on showing that the model can account for a number of important findings with respect to WM performance. As the present full version of the model exists only as a verbally formulated model, it is easy to claim that it can account for many findings. For a fair test, however, it would be far more acceptable to show that a computational version of the model accounts for the findings. Currently, a computational version covering as much as possible of the present model is being developed with the aim of running a series of simulations of findings considered to be important and critical. However, for reasons exposed elsewhere (Logie, 2018; Vandierendonck, 2018) the model's predictions will not be checked against a list of so-called benchmarks (Oberauer et al., 2018). Instead, the model's predictions will be compared to findings considered relevant to the purpose of this model. The focus is on predictions that follow from the fact that WMDEC shares properties with other models and frameworks in the field.

WMDEC shares a large number of features with the multicomponent model (see chapters by, e.g. Baddeley et al., 2021; Logie et al., 2021). Therefore, the model may be expected to account for modality effects in WM, namely that a secondary task in the same modality as a primary memory task interferes more than a secondary task in a different modality. Because of the articulatory basis of the phonological buffer in the present model, like the multicomponent model, WMDEC predicts a word length effect. In a similar vein, on the basis of revival of more complex visual and spatial patterns, a complexity effect is predicted, namely that more complex visuospatial sequences are remembered less well (Kemps, 1999, 2000, 2001; Parmentier, Elford, & Mayberry, 2005; Rossi-Arnaud, Pieroni, & Baddeley, 2006). However, because the model assumes that maintenance of serial order requires the presence of a recall intention, it predicts that serial recall in a primary memory task will be more impaired by a secondary embedded memory task when it also requires ordered recall than when it requires item (unordered) recall irrespective of whether the tasks call on the same or different modalities (Depoorter & Vandierendonck, 2009; Vandierendonck, 2016a).

Although the assumptions of the present model and the TBRS model (e.g. Barrouillet, Bernardin, & Camos, 2004; Barrouillet & Camos, 2010, see chapter by Barrouillet & Camos, 2021) are substantially different, the predictions made by both models overlap to a large extent. According to TBRS, attention has to be shared in an all-or-none fashion between activities competing for attention, so that during memory refreshment, attention is not available for other tasks, and conversely while task processing is going on, attention is not available for memory maintenance resulting in decay of the WM traces. Thanks to rapid shifts of attention from one activity (e.g. memory maintenance) to another (e.g. secondary task), attention can be shared over a time interval. Within TBRS, *cognitive load* is defined as the proportion of time occupied by non-memory activity: the larger the amount of time taken up by task processing, the less time in the interval remains for attentional refreshing. Consequently, TBRS predicts that memory will suffer more, the larger the cognitive load. In fact, what happens during a maintenance or retention interval according to TBRS and according to WMDEC is very similar, so that WMDEC also predicts that when less time is available for maintenance operations (i.e. larger cognitive load), memory performance will suffer more. The only difference is in the transition between memory and task processing: whereas TBRS assumes fast switching from one to the other activity, according to the present account, these transitions have a time cost, because control has to shift from one task to another by changing the dominance relation between the two task sets in executive memory. Only a strictly quantitative test of the durations assigned to maintenance, task processing, and transitions can distinguish between the two accounts; unfortunately, such a fine-grained empirical test is presently not feasible. It may be said, therefore, that for many of the findings reported on the basis of the TBRS model, WMDEC makes the same predictions, namely the findings reported by Barrouillet and colleagues regarding the effect of cognitive load (e.g. Barrouillet et al., 2004; Barrouillet, De Paepe, & Langerock, 2012; Barrouillet, Plancher, Guida, & Camos, 2013; Camos & Portrat, 2015; Portrat, Barrouillet, & Camos, 2008; Vergauwe, Barrouillet, & Camos, 2010).

The WMDEC model assumes that apart from domain-general attentional refreshment, domain-specific rehearsal and revival is also used to protect WM representations from interference and decay. As these actions can occur independently from each other, just like TBRS, the present model predicts additive effects of refreshment and rehearsal (e.g. Barrouillet, Corbin, Dagry, & Camos, 2015; Camos, 2017), and moreover also additive effects of refreshment, rehearsal, and revival.

Within the limited scope of the present chapter, it is not possible to detail all the predictions of WMDEC, but it should be self-evident that the model predicts that as the temporary maintenance requirements of mental arithmetic tasks, reasoning tasks, problem-solving tasks, and language processing tasks increase, such maintenance would have to compete with concurrent WM maintenance resulting into performance decrements in either of the involved tasks (e.g. De Rammelaere, Stuyven, & Vandierendonck, 2001; Imbo, Vandierendonck, & De Rammelaere, 2007; Loncke, Desmet, Vandierendonck, & Hartsuiker, 2011; Vandierendonck & De Vooght, 1997).

As the model is relatively recent, findings that contradict the model haven't yet been reported. However, there are some important limitations that should be mentioned. By design, the model focuses on processes and effects that are directly related to goal-directed actions, which for memory-related actions implies a focus on explicit memory. As a consequence, it is not straightforward for the model to account for effects related to implicit memory events. In particular, the model does not predict priming effects that are typically accounted for by the mechanism of spreading activation (e.g. Collins & Loftus, 1975). In view of the model's assumption that WM contents are instantiations of mostly external events in relation to an LTM representation of the events, spreading activation among LTM representations does not directly impact WM contents. The problem of how to implement spreading activation in the model has not yet been solved.

A related concern is that the present version of the model does not predict the Hebb learning effect (e.g. Page, Cumming, Norris, Hitch, & McNeil, 2006; Stadler, 1993). Whereas the general idea for explaining this effect within the confines of the model is to assume that over trials, recurring events strengthen the recently stored event chains, a specific mechanism that achieves this has not yet been implemented. Consequently, it would be bold to claim that the model accounts for the Hebb learning effect.

In a similar vein, the current version of WMDEC makes no assumptions to account for cognitive development and inter-individual differences. No doubt, some of these differences can be captured as quantitative variations, such as speed of processing, LTM access time, and capacity limitations, for which the model could provide predictions; however, considering that developmental as well as inter-person differences are likely to depend on both structural and functional differences, some further investment in appropriate assumptions would be needed to offer proper developmental and inter-individual differences accounts.

Conclusion

The WMDEC model defines WM as a supportive system for goal-directed actions of all kinds which consists of domain-general and domain-specific modules for storage of contents and a domain-general module for storage of strictly task-related information used to maximize the chances of attaining the goal. This definition and the answers to the other standardized questions underlying this book project are shown in Table 6.1.

References

Abelson, R. P. (1981). Psychological status of the script concept. *American Psychologist, 36*, 715–729. doi:10.1037/0003-066X.36.7.715

Abrahamse, E., Braem, S., Notebaert, W., & Verguts, T. (2016). Grounding cognitive control in associative learning. *Psychological Bulletin, 142*, 693–728. doi:10.1037/bul0000047

Anderson, J. R. (1983). *The architecture of cognition.* Cambridge, MA: Harvard University Press.

Anderson, J. R., & Lebiere, C. (1998). *The atomic components of thought.* New York, NY: Lawrence Erlbaum Associates.

Atkinson, R. C., & Shiffrin, R. M. (1968). Human memory: A proposed system and its control processes. In K. W. Spence & J. T. Spence (Eds.), *The psychology of learning and motivation* (Vol. 2, pp. 89–195). New York, NY: Academic Press.

Atkinson, R. C., & Shiffrin, R. M. (1971). The control of short-term memory. *Scientific American, 225*, 82–90.

Averbach, E., & Sperling, G. (1961). Short-term storage of information in vision. In C. Cherry (Ed.), *Information theory: Proceedings of the fourth London symposium* (pp. 196–211). London, UK: Butterworth.

Baddeley, A. (1986). *Working memory.* Oxford, UK: Oxford University Press.

Baddeley, A. (1996a). Exploring the central executive. *Quarterly Journal of Experimental Psychology, 49A*, 5–28.

Baddeley, A. (1996b). The fractionation of working memory. *Proceedings of the National Academy of Sciences of the United States of America, 93*, 13468–13472.

Baddeley, A. (2000). The episodic buffer: A new component of working memory? *Trends in Cognitive Sciences, 4*, 417–423. doi:10.1016/S1364-6613(00)01538-2

Baddeley, A., Chincotta, D., & Adlam, A. (2001). Working memory and the control of action: Evidence from task switching. *Journal of Experimental Psychology: General, 130*, 641–657. doi:10.1037//0096-3445.130.4.641

Baddeley, A. D., & Hitch, G. (1974). Working memory. In G. H. Bower (Ed.), *The psychology of learning and motivation* (Vol. 8, pp. 47–89). New York, NY: Academic Press.

Baddeley, A., Hitch, G., & Allen, R. (2021). A multicomponent model of working memory. In R. H. Logie, V. Camos, & N. Cowan (Eds.), *Working memory: State of the science* (pp. 10–43). Oxford, UK: Oxford University Press.

Baddeley, A. D., & Logie, R. H. (1999). Working memory: The multiple-component model. In A. Miyake & P. Shah (Eds.), *Models of working memory. Mechanisms of active maintenance and executive control* (pp. 28–61). Cambridge, UK: Cambridge University Press.

Barrouillet, P., Bernardin, S., & Camos, V. (2004). Time constraints and resource sharing in adults' working memory spans. *Journal of Experimental Psychology: General, 133*, 83–100. doi:10.1037/0096-3445.133.1.83

Barrouillet, P., Bernardin, S., Portrat, S., Vergauwe, E., & Camos, V. (2007). Time and cognitive load in working memory. *Journal of Experimental Psychology: Learning, Memory, and Cognition, 33*, 570–585. doi:10.1037/0278-7393.33.3.570

Barrouillet, P., & Camos, V. (2010). Working memory and executive control: A time-based resource-sharing account. *Psychologica Belgica, 50*, 353–382. doi:DOI: 10.5334/pb-50-3-4-353

Barrouillet, P., & Camos, V. (2021). The time-based resource-sharing model of working memory. In R. H. Logie, N. Cowan, & V. Camos (Eds.), *Working memory: State of the science* (pp. 85–115). Oxford, UK: Oxford University Press.

Barrouillet, P., Corbin, L., Dagry, I., & Camos, V. (2015). An empirical test of the independence between declarative and procedural working memory in Oberauer's (2009) theory. *Psychonomic Bulletin & Review, 22*, 1035–1040. doi:10.3758/s13423-014-0787-y

Barrouillet, P., De Paepe, A., & Langerock, N. (2012). Time causes forgetting from working memory. *Psychonomic Bulletin & Review, 19*, 87–92. doi:10.3758/s13423-011-0192-8

Barrouillet, P., Plancher, G., Guida, A., & Camos, V. (2013). Forgetting at short term: When do event-based interference and temporal factors have an effect? *Acta Psychologica, 142*, 155–167. doi:10.1016/j.actpsy.2012.12.003

Botvinick, M. M., Braver, T. S., Barch, D. M., Carter, C. S., & Cohen, J. D. (2001). Conflict monitoring and cognitive control. *Psychological Review, 108*, 624–652. doi:10.1037//0033-295x.108.3.624

Broadbent, D. E. (1958). *Perception and communication*. London, UK: Pergamon Press.

Camos, V. (2017). Domain-specific versus domain-general maintenance in working memory: Reconciliation within the time-based resource sharing model. *Psychology of Learning and Motivation 67*, 135–171.

Camos, V., Johnson, M., Loaiza, V., Portrat, S., Souza, A., & Vergauwe, E. (2018). What is attentional refreshing in working memory? *Annals of the New York Academy of Sciences, 1424*, 19–32. doi:10.1111/nyas.13616

Camos, V., & Portrat, S. (2015). The impact of cognitive load on delayed recall. *Psychonomic Bulletin & Review, 22*, 1029–1034. doi:10.3758/s13423-014-0772-5

Case, R., Kurland, D. M., & Goldberg, J. (1982). Operational efficiency and the growth of short-term-memory span. *Journal of Experimental Child Psychology, 33*, 386–404.

Collins, A. M., & Loftus, E. F. (1975). Spreading activation theory of semantic processing. *Psychological Review, 82*, 407–428. doi:10.1037/0033-295x.82.6.407

Cowan, N. (1999). An embedded-process model of working memory. In A. Miyake & P. Shah (Eds.), *Models of working memory. Mechanisms of active maintenance and executive control* (pp. 62–101). Cambridge, UK: Cambridge University Press.

Cowan, N. (2017). The many faces of working memory and short-term storage. *Psychonomic Bulletin & Review, 24*, 1158–1170. doi:10.3758/s13423-016-1191-6

Cowan, N., Morey, C. C., & Naveh-Benjamin, M. (2021). An embedded-processes approach to working memory: How is it distinct from other approaches, and to what ends? In R. H. Logie, V. Camos, & N. Cowan (Eds.), *Working memory: State of the science* (pp. 44–84). Oxford, UK: Oxford University Press.

Craik, F. I. M., & Watkins, M. J. (1973). The role of rehearsal in short-term memory. *Journal of Verbal Learning and Verbal Behavior, 12*, 599–607. doi:10.1016/S0022-5371(73)80039-8

Daneman, M., & Carpenter, P. A. (1980). Individual differences in working memory. *Journal of Verbal Learning and Verbal Behavior, 19*, 450–466. doi:10.1016/S0022-5371(80)90312-6

De Rammelaere, S., Stuyven, E., & Vandierendonck, A. (2001). Verifying simple arithmetic sums and products: Are the phonological loop and the central executive involved? *Memory & Cognition, 29,* 267–274. doi:10.3758/BF03194920

Depoorter, A., & Vandierendonck, A. (2009). Evidence for modality-independent order coding in working memory. *Quarterly Journal of Experimental Psychology, 62,* 531–549. doi:10.1080/17470210801995002

Desender, K., Van Opstal, F., & Van den Bussche, E. (2014). Feeling the conflict: The crucial role of conflict experience in adaptation. *Psychological Science, 25,* 675–683. doi:10.1177/0956797613511468

Duncan, J., Parr, A., Woolgar, A., Thompson, R., Bright, P., Cox, S., … Nimmo-Smith, I. (2008). Goal neglect and Spearman's g: Competing parts of a complex task. *Journal of Experimental Psychology: General, 137,* 131–148. doi:10.1037/0096-3445.137.1.131

Emerson, M. J., & Miyake, A. (2003). The role of inner speech in task switching: A dual-task investigation. *Journal of Memory and Language, 48,* 148–168. doi:10.1016/S0749-596X(02)00511-9

Engelkamp, J., Zimmer, H. D., Mohr, G., & Sellen, O. (1994). Memory of self-performed tasks: Self-performing during recognition. *Memory & Cognition, 22,* 34–39. doi:10.3758/bf03202759

Engle, R. W. (2002). Working memory capacity as executive attention. *Current Directions in Psychological Science, 11,* 19–23. doi:10.1111/1467-8721.00160

Goschke, T. (2000). Intentional reconfiguration and involuntary persistence in task set switching. In S. Monsell & J. S. Driver (Eds.), *Control of cognitive processes: Attention and performance XVIII* (pp. 331–355). Cambridge, MA: MIT Press.

Graesser, A. C., & Nakamura, G. V. (1982). The impact of schema on comprehension and memory. In G. H. Bower (Ed.), *The psychology of learning and motivation* (Vol. 16, pp. 59–109). New York, NY: Academic Press.

Gratton, G., Coles, M. G. H., & Donchin, E. (1992). Optimizing the use of information: strategic control of activation of responses. *Journal of Experimental Psychology: General, 121,* 480–506. doi:10.1037/0096-3445.121.4.480

Hamilton, C. (2011). The nature of visuospatial representation within working memory. In A. Vandierendonck & A. Szmalec (Eds.), *Spatial working memory* (pp. 122–144). Hove, UK: Psychology Press.

Imbo, I., Vandierendonck, A., & De Rammelaere, S. (2007). The role of working memory in the carry operation of mental arithmetic: Number and value of the carry. *Quarterly Journal of Experimental Psychology, 60,* 708–731. doi:10.1080/17470210600762447

Johnson, M. K. (1992). MEM: Mechanisms of recollection. *Journal of Cognitive Neuroscience, 4,* 268–280. doi:10.1162/jocn.1992.4.3.268

Johnson, M. K., Raye, C. L., Mitchell, K. J., Greene, E. J., Cunningham, W. A., & Sanislow, C. A. (2005). Using fMRI to investigate a component process of reflection: Prefrontal correlates of refreshing a just-activated representation. *Cognitive Affective & Behavioral Neuroscience, 5,* 339–361. doi:10.3758/cabn.5.3.339

Kemps, E. (1999). Effects of complexity on visuo-spatial working memory. *European Journal of Cognitive Psychology, 11,* 335–356. doi:10.1080/713752320

Kemps, E. (2000). Structural complexity in visuo-spatial working memory. *Current Psychology Letters, 1,* 59–70.

Kemps, E. (2001). Complexity effects in visuo-spatial working memory: Implications for the role of long-term memory. *Memory, 9,* 13–27. doi:10.1080/09658210042000012

Kiesel, A., Wendt, M., & Peters, A. (2007). Task switching: on the origin of response congruency effects. *Psychological Research, 71,* 117–125. doi:10.1007/s00426-005-0004-8

Klauer, K. C., & Zhao, Z. M. (2004). Double dissociations in visual and spatial short-term memory. *Journal of Experimental Psychology: General, 133,* 355–381.

Koriat, A., Benzur, H., & Nussbaum, A. (1990). Encoding information for future action: Memory for to-be-performed tasks versus memory for to-be-recalled tasks. *Memory & Cognition, 18,* 568–578. doi:10.3758/bf03197099

Liefooghe, B., Barrouillet, P., Vandierendonck, A., & Camos, V. (2008). Working memory costs of task switching. *Journal of Experimental Psychology: Learning, Memory, and Cognition, 34,* 478–494. doi:10.1037/0278-7393.34.3.478

Liefooghe, B., Vandierendonck, A., Muyllaert, I., Verbruggen, F., & Vanneste, W. (2005). The phonological loop in task alternation and task repetition. *Memory, 13,* 550–560. doi:10.1080/09658210444000250

Liefooghe, B., Wenke, D., & De Houwer, J. (2012). Instruction-based task-rule congruency effects. *Journal of Experimental Psychology: Learning, Memory, and Cognition, 38,* 1325–1335. doi:10.1037/a0028148

Logan, G. D. (2004). Working memory, task switching, and executive control in the task span procedure. *Journal of Experimental Psychology: General, 133,* 218–236. doi:10.1037/0096-3445.133.2.218

Logan, G. D. (2006). Out with the old, in with the new: More valid measures of switch cost and retrieval time in the task span procedure. *Psychonomic Bulletin & Review, 13,* 139–144.

Logan, G. D., & Gordon, R. D. (2001). Executive control of attention in dual-task situations. *Psychological Review, 108,* 393–434. doi:10.1037/0033-295X.108.2.393

Logie, R. H. (1995). *Visuo-spatial working memory.* Hove, UK: Psychology Press.

Logie, R. H. (2011). The visual and the spatial of a multicomponent working memory. In A. Vandierendonck & A. Szmalec (Eds.), *Spatial working memory* (pp. 19–45). Hove, UK: Psychology Press.

Logie, R. H. (2016). Retiring the central executive. *Quarterly Journal of Experimental Psychology, 69,* 2093–2109. doi:10.1080/17470218.2015.1136657

Logie, R. H. (2018). Scientific advance and theory integration in working memory: Comment on Oberauer et al. (2018). *Psychological Bulletin, 144,* 959–962. doi:10.1037/bul0000162

Logie, R.H., Belletier, C., & Doherty, J. (2021). Integrating theories of working memory. In R. H. Logie, V. Camos, & N. Cowan (Eds.), *Working memory: State of the science* (pp. 389–429). Oxford, UK: Oxford University Press.

Logie, R. H., & Pearson, D. G. (1997). The inner eye and the inner scribe of visuo-spatial working memory: Evidence from developmental fractionation. *European Journal of Cognitive Psychology, 9,* 241–257. doi:10.1080/713752559

Logie, R. H., Zucco, G. M., & Baddeley, A. D. (1990). Interference with visual short-term memory. *Acta Psychologica, 75,* 55–74. doi:10.1016/0001-6918(90)90066-o

Loncke, M., Desmet, T., Vandierendonck, A., & Hartsuiker, R. J. (2011). Executive control is shared between sentence processing and digit maintenance: Evidence from a strictly timed dual-task paradigm. *Journal of Cognitive Psychology, 23,* 886–911. doi:10.1080/20445911.2011.586625

Lovett, M. C., Reder, L. M., & Lebiere, C. (1999). Modeling working memory in a unified architecture. In A. Miyake & P. Shah (Eds.), *Models of working memory: Mechanisms of active maintenance and executive control* (pp. 135–182). Cambridge, UK: Cambridge University Press.

Mashburn, C. A., Tsukahara, J. S., & Engle, R. W. (2021). Individual differences in attention control: Implications for the relationship between working memory capacity and fluid intelligence. In R. H. Logie, V. Camos, & N. Cowan (Eds.), *Working memory: State of the science* (pp. 175–211). Oxford, UK: Oxford University Press.

Meiran, N., & Cohen-Kdoshay, O. (2012). Working memory load but not multitasking eliminates the prepared reflex: Further evidence from the adapted flanker paradigm. *Acta Psychologica, 139,* 309–313. doi:10.1016/j.actpsy.2011.12.008

Miller, G. A., Galanter, E., & Pribram, K. H. (1960). *Plans and the structure of behavior.* New York, NY: Henry Holt and Company.

Miyake, A., Emerson, M. J., Padilla, F., & Ahn, J. C. (2004). Inner speech as a retrieval aid for task goals: the effects of cue type and articulatory suppression in the random task cuing paradigm. *Acta Psychologica, 115,* 123–142. doi:10.1016/j.actpsy.2003.12.004

Morey, C. C., Morey, R. D., van der Reijden, M., & Holweg, M. (2013). Asymmetric cross-domain interference between two working memory tasks: Implications for models of working memory. *Journal of Memory and Language, 69,* 324–348. doi:10.1016/j.jml.2013.04.004

Mulligan, N. W., & Hornstein, S. L. (2003). Memory for actions: Self-performed tasks and the reenactment effect. *Memory & Cognition, 31,* 412–421. doi:10.3758/bf03194399

Norman, D. A. (1968). Toward a theory of memory and attention. *Psychological Review, 75,* 522–536. doi:10.1037/h0026699

Norman, D. A., & Shallice, T. (1986). Attention to action: Willed and automatic control of behavior. In R. J. Davidson, G. E. Schwarts, & D. Shapiro (Eds.), *Consciousness and self-regulation* (Vol. 4, pp. 1–18). New York, NY: Plenum Press.

Oberauer, K. (2009). Design for a working memory. In B. H. Ross (Ed.), *Psychology of learning and motivation: Advances in research and theory* (Vol. 51, pp. 45–100). San Diego, CA: Elsevier Academic Press Inc.

Oberauer, K. (2021). Towards a theory of working memory: From metaphors to mechanisms. In R. H. Logie, V. Camos, & N. Cowan (Eds.), *Working memory: State of the science* (pp. 116–149). Oxford, UK: Oxford University Press.

Oberauer, K., Lewandowsky, S., Awh, E., Brown, G. D. A., Conway, A., Cowan, N., . . . Ward, G. (2018). Benchmarks for models of short-term and working memory. *Psychological Bulletin, 144*, 885–958. doi:10.1037/bul0000153

Page, M. P. A., Cumming, N., Norris, D., Hitch, G. J., & McNeil, A. M. (2006). Repetition learning in the immediate serial recall of visual and auditory materials. *Journal of Experimental Psychology: Learning, Memory, and Cognition, 32*, 716–733. doi:10.1037/0278-7393.32.4.716

Parmentier, F. B. R. (2011). Exploring the determinants of memory for spatial sequences. In A. Vandierendonck & A. Szmalec (Eds.), *Spatial working memory* (pp. 67–86). Hove, UK: Psychology Press.

Parmentier, F. B. R., Elford, G., & Maybery, M. (2005). Transitional information in spatial serial memory: Path characteristics affect recall performance. *Journal of Experimental Psychology: Learning, Memory, and Cognition, 31*, 412–427. doi:10.1037/0278-7393.31.3.412

Portrat, S., Barrouillet, P., & Camos, V. (2008). Time-related decay or interference-based forgetting in working memory? *Journal of Experimental Psychology: Learning, Memory, and Cognition, 34*, 1561–1564. doi:10.1037/a0013356

Posner, M. I., & Rothbart, M. K. (2007). Research on attention networks as a model for the integration of psychological science. *Annual Review of Psychology, 58*, 1–23. doi:10.1146/annurev. psych.58.110405.085516

Rossi-Arnaud, C., Pieroni, L., & Baddeley, A. (2006). Symmetry and binding in visuo-spatial working memory. *Neuroscience, 139*, 393–400. doi:10.1016/j.neuroscience.2005.10.048

Saeki, E., & Saito, S. (2004). Effect of articulatory suppression on task-switching performance: Implications for models of working memory. *Memory, 12*, 257–271. doi:10.1080/09658210244000649

Shiffrin, R. M., & Atkinson, R. C. (1969). Storage and retrieval processes in long-term memory. *Psychological Review, 76*, 179–193. doi:10.1037/h0027277

Sperling, G. (1960). The information available in brief visual presentations. *Psychological Monographs, 74*, 1–29.

Stadler, M. A. (1993). Implicit serial-learning: Questions inspired by Hebb (1961). *Memory & Cognition, 21*, 819–827. doi:10.3758/bf03202749

Stuyven, E., Van der Goten, K., Vandierendonck, A., Claeys, K., & Crevits, L. (2000). The effect of cognitive load on saccadic eye movements. *Acta Psychologica, 104*, 69–85. doi:10.1016/s0001-6918(99)00054-2

Szmalec, A., Demanet, J., Vandierendonck, A., & Verbruggen, F. (2009). Investigating the role of conflict resolution in memory updating by means of the one-back choice RT task. *Psychological Research, 73*, 390–406. doi:10.1007/s00426-008-0149-3

Szmalec, A., & Vandierendonck, A. (2007). Estimating the executive demands of a one-back choice reaction time task by means of the selective interference paradigm. *Quarterly Journal of Experimental Psychology, 60*, 1116–1139.

Szmalec, A., Vandierendonck, A., & Kemps, E. (2005). Response selection involves executive control: Evidence from the selective interference paradigm. *Memory & Cognition, 33*, 531–541. doi:10.3758/bf03193069

Szmalec, A., Verbruggen, F., Vandierendonck, A., De Baene, W., Verguts, T., & Notebaert, W. (2008). Stimulus ambiguity elicits response conflict. *Neuroscience Letters, 435*, 158–162.

Szmalec, A., Verbruggen, F., Vandierendonck, A., & Kemps, E. (2011). Control of interference during working memory updating. *Journal of Experimental Psychology: Human Perception and Performance, 37*, 137–151. doi:10.1037/a0020365

Turner, M. L., & Engle, R. W. (1989). Is working memory capacity task dependent? *Journal of Memory and Language, 28,* 127–154.

Vandierendonck, A. (2012). Role of working memory in task switching. *Psychologica Belgica, 52*(2-3), 229–253. doi:10.5334/pb-52-2-3-229

Vandierendonck, A. (2016a). Modality independence of order coding in working memory: Evidence from cross-modal order interference at recall. *Quarterly Journal of Experimental Psychology, 69,* 161–179. doi:10.1080/17470218.2015.1032987

Vandierendonck, A. (2016b). A working memory system with distributed executive control. *Perspectives on Psychological Science, 11,* 74–100. doi:10.1177/1745691615596790

Vandierendonck, A. (2018). Working memory benchmarks-a missed opportunity: Comment on Oberauer et al. (2018). *Psychological Bulletin, 144,* 963–971. doi:10.1037/bul0000159

Vandierendonck, A., & De Vooght, G. (1997). Working memory constraints on linear reasoning with spatial and temporal contents. *Quarterly Journal of Experimental Psychology, 50A,* 803–820.

Vandierendonck, A., Szmalec, A., Deschuyteneer, M., & Depoorter, A. (2007). Towards a multicomponential view of executive control: The case of response selection. In N. Osaka & R. Logie (Eds.), *Working memory: Behavioural and neural correlates* (pp. 247–259). Oxford, UK: Oxford University Press.

Vergauwe, E., Barrouillet, P., & Camos, V. (2010). Do mental processes share a domain-general resource? *Psychological Science, 21,* 384–390. doi:10.1177/0956797610361340

Vergauwe, E., & Cowan, N. (2015). Attending to items in working memory: evidence that refreshing and memory search are closely related. *Psychonomic Bulletin & Review, 22,* 1001–1006. doi:10.3758/s13423-014-0755-6

Vygotsky, L. S. (1962). *Thought and language.* New York, NY: Wiley.

Wundt, W. (1874). *Grundzüge der physiologischen Psychologie.* Leipzig, Germany: Engelmann.

Yang, T., Gathercole, S. E., & Allen, R. J. (2014). Benefit of enactment over oral repetition of verbal instruction does not require additional working memory during encoding. *Psychonomic Bulletin & Review, 21,* 186–192. doi:10.3758/s13423-013-0471-7

7

Individual Differences in Attention Control

Implications for the Relationship Between Working Memory Capacity and Fluid Intelligence

Cody A. Mashburn, Jason S. Tsukahara, and Randall W. Engle

In this chapter, we detail our approach to the study of individual differences in working memory capacity (WMC) and how it has contributed to understanding the mechanisms of complex cognition. Theories of working memory have primarily focused on specifying how information is represented and manipulated in a limited-capacity cognitive system. Individuals differ in the efficacy of their working memory systems, forming the basis for WMC as a psychometric construct. Decades of research have shown that WMC is predictive of a broad range of abilities and outcomes (Engle, 2002; Engle & Kane, 2004; Barrett, Tugade, & Engle, 2004). One of the most robust and, we believe, important findings is that WMC strongly predicts fluid intelligence (Gf), the ability to solve novel problems and learn new information (Kane, Hambrick, & Conway, 2005; Kyllonen & Christal, 1990). A central feature of many models of the working memory system is a domain-general executive attention, sometimes called a central executive, which regulates other components of the system (Baddeley & Hitch, 1974; Cowan, 1999). We argue that this attentional component forms the basis of the WMC–Gf relationship.

Let us begin by placing WMC within the context of a more general framework in order to understand why it is so broadly predictive. Few notions in psychology have as much theoretical utility as the distinction between automatic and controlled processing. Psychological theories that adopt this distinction are known as dual-process theories, and many theories of cognition are amenable to this outline. Norman and Shallice (1986), for example, developed a framework in which actions are automatically activated given an individual's current goals in some current context. Many action sequences can be performed this way, without need for conscious awareness or investment of conscious attention. However, situations arise in which actions selected by automatic processes are not appropriate or optimal. In such cases, the readily available response must be resisted in favour of a more effortful, controlled, and generally conscious, mode of responding. In the Norman and Shallice (1986) model, this is when the supervisory attention system becomes important. The supervisory attention system influences the selection of action schemas when the automatically activated schematic response is inappropriate, when there is conflict between activated schemas, or when a situation is novel and no schematic response is available (Norman & Shallice, 1986).

Cody A. Mashburn, Jason S. Tsukahara, and Randall W. Engle, *Individual Differences in Attention Control* In: *Working Memory.* Edited by: Robert H. Logie, Valérie Camos, and Nelson Cowan, Oxford University Press (2021). © Oxford University Press. DOI: 10.1093/oso/9780198842286.003.0007

Table 7.1 Summary responses to designated questions

Question	Response
1. Definition of working memory	We define working memory as the cognitive system that permits the maintenance of goal-relevant information. More structurally, working memory comprises domain-general executive attention coupled with domain-specific short-term memories. We regard short-term memory as those aspects of long-term memory residing above some activation threshold, making them available or potentially available to influence ongoing cognition, as well as those processes necessary to keep this activation above threshold (e.g. subvocal rehearsal).
2. Methodology	Our group has focused on the use of large, broad-ability samples to study aspects of cognition at the latent construct level. We are interested in the role of different aspects of working memory in real-world cognition and how what we learn in the laboratory can be extended to real-world tasks. The advantage of our methods is that they avoid the mistakes of thinking that a single task can reflect a construct, that 'mean performance' reflects all the people in the sample, and that data collected from college sophomores reflects cognition in all people. The disadvantage is that these methods are very time-consuming and very expensive.
3. Unitary versus non-unitary nature of working memory	Working memory is at least non-unitary to the extent that it consists of both attention and memory processes. Attention is unitary. We believe that there is one 'attention' that cannot be divided but can be switched back and forth between tasks quickly. This switching puts a premium on temporary maintenance of information from each task being switched between. Performance will be degraded when information for one task is lost/degraded while attention is directed at a different task. The resulting temporary memories are domain specific and, depending on the similarity of the domains, will vary in how they interfere with one another.
4. The role of attention and control	One possible concern with our use of 'executive attention' is that of the homunculus (in the Skinnerian sense). One might charge that we are not really saying that much about how executive attention might function, but instead are simply appealing to it as some mystical cognitive arbiter. We think that such a criticism misses the point. While we have often abstained from theorizing about the implementation and operations of executive attention, we do not regard it as remotely similar to a little man in the head. Rather, our work typically aims to understand the individual differences in cognitive abilities and what patterns of variation can tell us about the relationships between constructs. Such theorizing is thus tangential to our goal. All the same, readers of our work may suspect us of simply falling back onto a homunculus. To those readers, we point out that many explicit computational systems behave as though they might have a homunculus operating behind the scenes. For example, the computer programs Watson and Deep Blue operate as though they were inhabited by the world's best *Jeopardy!* and chess players, but the computations underlying their superb performance in these domains are completely specified. Thus, this is a good question for philosophers to sit with, but not one we are willing to become paralysed by.

Table 7.1 Continued

Question	Response
5. Storage, maintenance, and loss of information in working memory	We approach working memory via the study of attention, and so have been less interested in studying hallmark effects of working memory coding and storage, such as the word length effect, than in studying the ramifications of individual differences in executive attention for working memory and its relationship to complex cognition and real world behaviour. Indeed, the complex span tasks, which have been instrumental to the study of WMC, attempt to disrupt the rehearsal processes responsible for such effects in order to isolate the effects of executive attention. In our view, interference rather than decay is the primary reason for (unintended) loss of information in working memory. For supporting evidence, damage to the prefrontal cortex leads to impaired memory performance only when there is opportunity for interference (Della Salla, Cowan, Beschin, & Perini, 2005). Without interference, temporal delay had little effect. Our view also regards loss of information from working memory as, at times, intentional, adaptive, and requiring of attention, which we term 'disengagement'. The sensitivity of fluid intelligence (Gf) measures to disengagement processes accounts for the strong relationship between WMC and Gf.
6. What is the relationship between working memory, long-term memory, and learning?	Working memory is important for learning because it holds representations active in memory so that elaboration and integration with related representations in long-term memory can occur (c.f. Craik & Lockhart, 1972). This may create the impression that expertise increases memory capacity because 'more' can be held active in memory at one time (Chase & Simon, 1973). This has been explained via chunking, but it is less clear how 'chunking' occurs or why larger chunks do not require more resource investment despite containing more information (e.g. lists of differing length do not differ in retrieval time; Conway & Engle, 1994). Speculatively, one way this could obtain is that what is held active in memory are not representations per se but rather 'address tags' to a representation's location in long-term memory. Thus, the function of working memory would not be to contain representations, but rather to keep representations readily accessible. The result is an increase in the amount of information available to the working memory system (by virtue of more elaborated representations) without greater resource expenditure. For example, if one were tasked with summarizing their five favourite novels, the relevant information would surely exceed the limited capacity of working memory. Even so, by virtue of having a memory tag for *Crime and Punishment* active in working memory, one could report that the story follows the moral tribulations of Rodion Raskolnikov, expound upon the details, causes, and outcomes of said tribulations, and repeat the process for the other four novels. All of the pertinent information is not contained in working memory at the same time, but is made readily available by the working memory system. This notion is very different from the idea of working memory training, the idea that training working memory to have a larger capacity should increase Gf. This simply is not the case (Redick et al., 2013). This is sensible in our framework because we do not assume a causal relationship between WMC and Gf.

(*Continued*)

Table 7.1 Continued

Question	Response
7. Is there evidence that is not consistent with your theoretical framework, and how does your framework address that inconsistency?	Periodically, researchers have approached us claiming that they cannot replicate results from our studies. Upon further discussion, many of these replication attempts suffer from small samples and/or restricted ability ranges, both of which are fatal to correlational and regression-based analyses leading them to accept the null hypothesis. Other researchers who have avoided these pitfalls consistently replicate our work. At other times, we have blatantly disagreed with other researchers about how best to interpret a pattern of results. In many such cases, the difference of opinions is rooted in fundamental disagreements about how best to frame and/or measure a construct (e.g. the nature of WMC or the unitary nature of attention control). The simple fact that work is ongoing means that different researchers are in all likelihood blindly grasping at different parts of the same elephant. In dealing with this friction, we try to take seriously the criticisms of researchers with whom we respect and happen to disagree and who are working on similar topics. We try to incorporate these into ideas for future studies. In evaluating differences of opinion, we begin by considering psychometric factors associated with tasks and their use with certain samples and proceed from there.
F. Working memory applications	Our recent work has confirmed that WMC is highly predictive of success in a vast array of real-world contexts, including multitasking (Redick et al., 2016) and in detecting fatigue (Lopez, Previc, Fischer, Heitz, & Engle, 2012). However, it is important to not overstate its importance, and our recent thinking is that WMC serves a complementary function to Gf. The tasks used to measure WMC reflect primarily maintenance of information while the tasks used to measure Gf reflect the function of disengagement from information or goals no longer useful for the current task. The high correlation between WMC and Gf is due to the fact that both constructs rely on domain-general executive attention. Thus, we can better understand complex cognition by trying to understand the relative contributions of WMC and Gf to successful behaviour, and by exploring the relative predictive utility of tasks reflecting WMC, Gf, and executive attention within a domain of interest (see Martin et al., 2019 for an example of this applied to reading comprehension).

Research on the functional organization of attention in the brain also seems interpretable in a dual-process framework. Several isolable attention networks have been distinguished, namely the orienting, alerting, and executive networks (Fan, McCandliss, Sommer, Raz, & Posner, 2002). The alerting and orienting networks enact automatic stimulus selection and the executive network resolves interference or conflict between competing stimuli and/or potential responses. Other examples abound (Greenwald & Banaji, 1995; Kahneman, 2011; Spelke, Hirst, & Neisser, 1976). There are thus echoes of the automatic/controlled processing distinction in many widely known and accepted theories in cognitive psychology, cognitive neuroscience, and cognitive science.

We have argued that individual differences in WMC, defined as the ability to use attention to maintain items in memory in the face of distraction or interference, reflects individual differences in controlled processing (Feldman-Barrett et al., 2004). The fact that controlled processing becomes relevant over large swaths of human activity would thus account for the broad predictive validity of WMC. However, we now believe that it is not WMC per se that underpins variation in controlled processing. Rather, the lynchpin is the more general ability to deploy attentional resources to dynamically manage ongoing cognition.

We believe that research on the relationship between WMC and Gf suggests two broad, interacting control mechanisms: maintaining goal-relevant information in memory and disengaging from outdated or irrelevant information. Before discussing our recent theoretical advancements, we outline the development of the executive attention theory of WMC. We then summarize our recent extensions of the theory and show how it explains the relationship between WMC and Gf. Along the way, we highlight ongoing methodological and theoretical issues and some of our own missteps that should be instructive for other researchers.

Working Memory Capacity as Executive Attention

Simple and Complex Span Tasks Are Clearly Different

The executive attention theory of WMC stems from research comparing individual differences on simple memory span and complex memory span procedures. Simple memory spans, such as the digit span, present participants with a set of to-be-remembered items that must be recalled (the order of recall varies by procedure) and comprised much of the early work on short-term memory. A participant's memory span is traditionally operationalized as the list length above which memory errors occur or as the total number of correctly recalled lists of variable length (assuming that errors are fairly constrained to longer, more difficult lists). A short-term memory store, construed as a passive, limited-capacity buffer, was a core component of many early multistore models of human memory, typified by the modal model (Atkinson & Shiffrin, 1968; Engle & Oransky, 1999). Crowder (1982) attempted to retire short-term memory as a theoretically useful construct, partly based on the inability of simple span tasks to predict complex cognition (e.g. Perfetti & Lesgold, 1977; Turner & Engle, 1989). Given the centrality of the short-term store to theories of human memory, surely its limitations should be broadly predictive—that they were not was troubling. Subsequent models of working memory complicated the short-term store substantially, emphasizing not just the storage of information, but the active processing of stored information (e.g. Baddeley & Hitch, 1974). Complex spans were designed with these more complicated working memory models in mind. They, too, present participants with to-be-remembered items, except participants must perform a processing task after each item is presented (Fig. 7.1). At some point, participants are prompted to recall the presented items in their correct serial position. Compared to the simple span procedure, complex span procedures have proven immensely fruitful.

The first complex span task, the reading span, was developed by Daneman and Carpenter (1980). Daneman and Carpenter had participants read a variable number

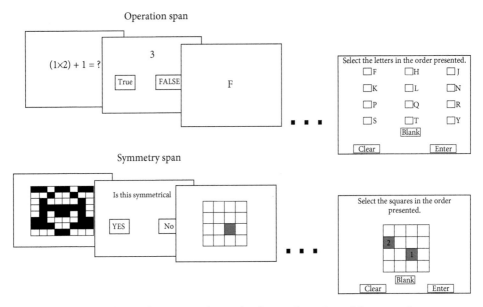

Fig. 7.1 Examples of complex span tasks. In the depicted version of the operation span (top panel), subjects solve simple equations and are given letters to remember. After a variable number of equations (usually two to eight), participants are cued to recall the letters in their correct forward serial position. The symmetry span follows the same scheme except participants make symmetry judgements about a visual pattern and are tasked with remembering highlighted cells in a 4×4 grid. The operation and symmetry spans concern memory for verbal and visuospatial material, respectively.

of sentences. Afterward, they were cued to recall the last word of each sentence in its correct serial position. In contrast to a simple word span, the number of items correctly recalled in the reading span was highly predictive of reading comprehension. Daneman and Carpenter originally attributed the correlation between reading span performance and reading comprehension to reading skill: strong readers outperformed poorer ones because they expended fewer resources while reading the sentences, leaving more resources available for actively retaining the memoranda. Turner and Engle (1989) expanded this finding, showing that the relationship between complex span performance and higher cognition is a great deal more general than Daneman and Carpenter suspected. They substituted the sentence reading task with solving simple mathematical problems (e.g. top of Fig. 7.1). This mathematical operation span predicted reading comprehension as well as the reading span did, suggesting that reading skill could not account for the reading span's predictive power. While they did not find an effect of the domain of the processing task, Turner and Engle did find that more difficult processing tasks lead to better differentiation between good and poor readers, regardless of processing domain. This suggested that the amount of processing resources available to the working memory system may be an important component of what complex spans measure. In contrast, simple spans did not correlate with reading comprehension.

Pursuing this line of thought further using latent variable analyses,[1] Engle, Tuholski, Laughlin, and Conway (1999) conducted a study differentiating short-term memory (as measured by simple span tasks) from WMC (as measured by complex span tasks) and tested their relationships with Gf. They administered numerous measures of short-term memory, WMC, and Gf to a sample of undergraduates[2] and submitted the data to a series of factor analyses and structural equation models. Prior theory fractioned the working memory system into mechanisms providing storage plus an attentional component coordinating the processing of stored information (Baddeley & Hitch, 1974; Cowan, 1988). Based on this work, Engle et al. (1999) expected substantial overlap between short-term memory and WMC latent factors due to the common influence of short-term storage, but the factors should have been distinguishable due to attention-related variance in the WMC factor. Indeed, a model positing separate short-term memory and WMC latent factors fits the data better than a model positing a single memory factor. These separate factors related differentially to Gf. In a model with WMC and short-term memory each predicting Gf, short-term memory added no predictive value above that already accounted for by WMC. Finally, under the assumption that WMC is comprised of short-term memory storage plus controlled attention, the shared variance between the WMC and short-term memory latent factors was extracted. This factor was thought to reflect short-term memory storage. The WMC residual, meanwhile, was thought to mainly reflect variance associated with executive attention. Both sources of variance were significant predictors of Gf, with the attention-related WMC residual accounting for the bulk of prediction. This suggests that attention is relatively more important for predicting Gf than short-term memory.

Engle et al.'s (1999) findings were promising, but WMC remained underspecified. Many theorists assumed that WMC was a unitary domain-general construct, but it remained possible that it could be decomposed into modality-specific control processes. For example, prior work suggested little overlap between working memory tasks of different modalities (e.g. verbal and visuospatial working memory; see Fig. 7.1; Shah & Miyake, 1996). This finding was sensible to the extent that verbal and visuospatial working memory tasks make use of different coding schemes and representational formats, and perhaps even different storage systems (Baddeley, 1986; Baddeley & Hitch, 1974; Crowder, 1982). However, methodological concerns with prior work (e.g. homogeneous sampling with regard to cognitive ability leading to likely underestimation of attentional processes) and the widely held theoretical unity of attention control led Kane et al. (2004) to test the generality of WMC. They administered a battery of verbal

---

[1] Latent variable analyses are a group of advanced statistical techniques including exploratory factor analysis, confirmatory factor analysis, and structural equation modelling (among others) that are used to study unobserved constructs based on the patterns of variation and covariation within a set of observed variables. Performance on individual tasks is determined by numerous processes, making them difficult to interpret. Latent variable analyses mitigate this problem by modelling the variance shared by a group of measures purporting to index some common construct important to each. This gives us a much better measure of the processes we are interested in measuring because variability specific to individual tasks is partialled out.

[2] Most other studies discussed in this chapter had samples consisting of individuals recruited from universities as well as the surrounding community.

and visuospatial short-term (simple span) and working memory (complex span) tasks as well as measures of verbal, spatial, and matrix reasoning. Examination of zero-order correlations suggested stronger interrelationships among their working memory tasks than among their short-term memory tasks, a finding corroborated by an exploratory factor analysis that converged on a solution with a single WMC factor and separate verbal and visuospatial short-term memory factors. A more conservative confirmatory factor analysis, meanwhile, revealed that the best-fitting solution to the data was a four-factor solution with separate but related factors for both verbal and visuospatial short-term memory and WMC. Notably, while the verbal and visuospatial short-term memory factors correlated at 0.63, the WMC factors correlated at 0.83. This confirmed that WMC is a more general concept than short-term memory, and we contend this is due to the influence of individual differences in a domain-general executive attention. The disunity in WMC we attribute to contamination by domain-specific storage processes. If we are correct, the variance common to all the measures should provide a fairly pure measure of attention control; consistent with Engle et al. (1999)'s findings, it strongly predicted Gf.

Simple and Complex Spans: Not So Different After All?

Despite many demonstrations of simple spans' failure to account for variation in complex cognition, some studies do in fact report relationships with Gf on par with complex spans (La Pointe & Engle, 1990). For example, Colom and colleagues (Colom, Abad, Quiroga, Shih, & Flores-Mendoza, 2005; Colom, Abad, Rebollo, & Shih, 2008) contend that simple and complex spans are virtually indistinguishable in the processes that they measure. These results seem difficult to square with studies showing a clear distinction (Daneman & Carpenter, 1980; Engle et al., 1999; Turner & Engle, 1989). Though initially puzzling, results from Unsworth & Engle (2006, 2007b) suggest differences across studies in simple span scoring procedures may be to blame for the discrepant findings. Plotting correlations between complex span performance and Gf as a function of memory set size, Unsworth and Engle (2006) found fairly stable correlations, even for small set sizes (see also Salthouse & Pink, 2008). Correlations between simple spans and Gf, on the other hand, were weak at smaller set sizes but rivalled complex span correlations at longer list lengths. Unsworth and Engle (2007b) argued that typical methods of scoring simple spans (e.g. summing the number of correctly recalled lists) disregard important variation in longer list lengths where errors become common. In several re-analyses of published data that initially asserted a hard distinction between simple and complex span tasks, simple spans showed correlations of similar magnitude to complex spans when the proportion of all correctly recalled memoranda was used as the estimate of memory span rather than the more stringent correctly recalled-lists criterion. Theoretically, the two methods should yield very similar correlations with Gf up to an individual's capacity for passive online memory storage. However, individuals vary with how many errors they make once this limit is surpassed. The proportion-correct method is sensitive to this variation, allowing individual differences in the recall of longer lists to contribute to the final memory span score. The correctly recalled-lists method effectively ignores this variation, since errors become common after the passive storage capacity is exceeded. When the proportion-correct scoring method was used for scoring simple spans and separate complex and simple span factors were included in a structural equation model, neither added uniquely to the prediction of Gf; the two classes of tasks were virtually isomorphic at the latent level (Unsworth & Engle, 2007b).

Outlining the processing and storage operations that occur while participants complete the tasks can help explain inconsistencies in the relationship between simple and complex spans. In recent work, we have adopted the primary memory/secondary memory terminology for discussing memory storage. Primary memory consists of currently activated portions of long-term memory that are immediately available for use by the cognitive system (a similar idea to what is usually meant by 'short-term memory'). Secondary memory is comprised of the portion of long-term memory activated below some critical threshold and not readily available for use (Conway & Engle, 1994; Shipstead, Lindsey, Marshall, & Engle, 2014; Waugh & Norman, 1965). The amount of information that can be kept active in primary memory is severely constrained (Cowan, 2001; Cowan et al., 2005; Waugh & Norman, 1965). Information in that active primary memory state will decline in activity over time due to interference or decay (primarily interference; see Nairne, 2002). Keeping it 'active' requires it be reactivated by the spotlight of attention before it falls below a threshold we think of as reflecting consciousness. In complex span tasks, to-be-remembered items compete with a processing task for activation in primary memory. As representations of memoranda lose activation, they risk being lost from primary memory though, of course, they would still be represented in secondary memory. Attentional resources must be diverted to maintain these items at some supra-threshold level of activation, or to conduct a constrained search of secondary memory based on available retrieval cues. Attention control is required to conduct this search most effectively (Unsworth & Engle, 2007a). When list length is sufficiently long to force competition among items in primary memory, simple span procedures will also place demands on primary memory maintenance and secondary memory search. This, we argue, accounts for the uniform correlation between complex spans and measures of Gf, while the relationship with simple spans varies as a function of list length.

Short-term memory and WMC measures thus exist on a continuum, a continuum which need not be graded uniformly across members of different populations. A simple span may be a short-term memory indicator for a cognitively healthy young adult, but will require significantly greater attentional resource investment from a similar young adult with executive dysfunction (Perry et al., 2001) or a cognitively healthy child (Bayliss, Jarrold, Baddeley, & Gunn, 2005). In these latter cases, a simple span may fairly be called a measure of WMC in that it involves an investment of limited-capacity attention. A similar point pertains to complex spans. For example, the operation span does a poor job discriminating between high-ability participants (Draheim, Harrison, Embretson, & Engle, 2018). One explanation for this poor differentiation is that higher-ability participants are more likely to have extensive exposure to basic mathematics and arithmetic operations. Solving simple equations may be much more automated for them than for a lower-ability participant with less mathematical proficiency (Turner & Engle, 1989). This may allow high-ability participants to direct more attentional resources to retaining memoranda, thereby limiting variability in the number of correctly reported letters (c.f. Conway, Cowan, & Bunting, 2001; Underwood, 1974). The operation span may thus tap more storage-related (i.e. short-term memory) variance than other complex spans when used in high-ability samples. None of this is to say that short-term memory and working memory are not meaningfully distinct constructs. We still regard short-term memory as providing memory storage and working memory as comprising short-term memory plus attention control. We merely wish to stress that one cannot be confident that they are measuring one construct or the other based on the class of task used alone. The crucial difference between short-term and working memory has less to do with the kind of task used and more with what participants must do to complete said task.

Though the preceding discussion fixates heavily on complex spans, the reader should not interpret this as our endorsing them as the only way of measuring WMC. As we show later, our recent theorizing has been greatly impacted by considering other more dynamic classes of measures, such as the running memory span and N-back, which sometimes show larger correlations with Gf than do complex span tasks (Broadway & Engle, 2010; Shipstead, Harrison, & Engle, 2016; Wilhelm, Hildebrandt, & Oberauer, 2013). Thus, while complex span tasks have been a fixture of our programme of research, our current theorizing also takes into account other classes of WMC measures and their relations to attention control and Gf.

Direct Evidence for the Working Memory Capacity–Attention Control Relationship

Many of these early studies assumed that variance unique to complex span tasks reflected attention control without actually measuring attention control, leaving the door open to alternative explanations of the relationship between Gf and WMC. More direct approaches were thus required to establish an association between WMC and attention control. Confirmatory evidence for this relationship initially came from quasi-experimental designs comparing the performance of individuals deemed high and low in WMC. These studies typically screened a large sample of participants on a WMC measure and divided the sample into tertiles or quartiles based on their scores. The highest and lowest scoring groups were deemed high- and low-spans, respectively, and their performance on established attention control tasks was compared. If attention control were at all predictive of WMC, span differences should be apparent whenever a task requires controlled processing.

One task featured prominently in our work and in the field at large is the anti-saccade task (Everling & Fischer, 1998). In this task, participants are presented with a central fixation cross followed by a briefly presented cue on the right or left side of the screen. A typical anti-saccade task consists of two trial types which can be presented either in separate blocks or mixed within a block. On pro-saccade trials, participants must orient their gaze towards the peripheral cue in time to identify a target presented after the cue but in the same location. The target is masked a brief time later. Orienting towards changes in the environment (e.g. movement) is an evolutionarily ingrained pre-potent response. As such, participants could presumably perform well based on reflexive responding alone. Anti-saccade trials follow the same scheme as pro-saccade trials, except the to-be-identified target appears opposite the peripheral cue. Participants must use the peripheral cue as an indication of where *not* to look. This requires them to resist the automatic predisposition to orient towards the cue, lest they miss the target appearing on the other side of the screen. Anti-saccade trials thus force controlled processing by rendering an automatic response incompatible with current goals. Attention control is necessary for overriding the automatic tendency and supplementing it with a novel goal-appropriate response (c.f. Norman & Shallice, 1986).

Kane, Bleckley, Conway, and Engle (2001) showed span differences in anti-saccade task performance. Participants were divided into upper and lower WMC quartiles based on their operation span scores and their performance on pro-saccade and anti-saccade blocks was compared. To reiterate, span differences were expected on anti-saccade trials, because performing well requires participants to avoid reflexively looking at the peripheral cue and to instead make a goal-appropriate saccade in the opposite direction. Span differences were not expected on pro-saccade trials because looking towards motion is an automatic response. The expected pattern emerged. High-spans were more accurate on anti-saccade trials and responded more quickly than low-spans. High- and low-spans did not differ on pro-saccade trials when they preceded an anti-saccade block. Interestingly, span differences *did* emerge on pro-saccade trials when the anti-saccade block came before the pro-saccade block, with low-spans being slower and more error-prone on pro-saccade trials. This pattern hinted that low-spans tended to perseverate on task goals, a common symptom of frontal lobe damage and executive dysfunction (Kane & Engle, 2002). Across every metric considered, high-spans demonstrated better attention control abilities than did low-spans.

Results from Unsworth, Schrock, and Engle (2004) replicated and extended these findings. They investigated span differences in anti-saccade performance without a target identification requirement; participants merely needed to initiate a saccade in the appropriate direction, saccades were measured with an eye tracker. Across several task configurations, they demonstrated that span differences on anti-saccade trials consistently emerge, such that high-spans were less likely to initiate a saccade towards the peripheral cue. They even found that span differences on pro-saccade trials can be induced by introducing control demands on these trials. If low-spans tend to perseverate on current goals, then requiring them to dynamically update their current task set should put them at a disadvantage; for example, switching between the goal to initiate a saccade in the opposite direction as a cue (anti-saccade) and the goal to initiate a sac-cade in the same direction as a cue (pro-saccade). Indeed, low-spans were now slower to initiate a correct pro-saccade when pro-saccade and anti-saccade trials were mixed within a single block. High-spans' consistent, systematic advantage on the anti-saccade task supports our earlier conjecture that individual differences in attention control con-tribute to variation in WMC.

The results from Kane et al. (2001) and Unsworth et al. (2004) provide some indi-cation that, at least for the anti-saccade task, differences in WMC become important whenever executive control processes are engaged. Particularly important is the instan-tiation of goals in memory (Meier, Smeekens, Silvia, Kwapil, & Kane, 2018). We have advanced similar arguments about performance in the Stroop task in which subjects must resist the automaticity of reading a colour word to name the colour in which it is printed (e.g. seeing the stimulus GREEN and having to respond with the word 'Blue'; Kane & Engle, 2003), but WMC is predictive of a wide range of attentional phenomena. For example, Heitz and Engle (2007) investigated individual differences in the ability to narrow the focus of attention to the central target in an arrow flanker task.[3] High-spans were faster to constrain their focus to the target, thereby mitigating the influence of peripheral distractors earlier than did low-spans. Bleckley, Foster, and Engle (2015) presented low- and high-span participants with parallel bars running the length of two sides of a square display. A square target was cued to appear at the end of one bar, and participants were instructed to press a key when the target appeared. However, the cue only predicted the target location 75% of the time. On the remaining 25% of trials, the cue could either appear on the opposite end of the cued bar (within an object) or on the corresponding area of the parallel bar, with both being equidistant from the actual cued location. High-spans were faster to react to the cue on invalidly cued trials when the target appeared within an object than when it appeared in the corresponding area of the other bar. For low-spans, the location of the target did not matter; they were equally slow whether the target appeared within- or between-objects relative to the invalid cue. This pattern suggests that high-spans may be more likely to attend to objects where low-spans are more likely to attend to locations. Importantly, putting high-spans under cognitive load impairs their ability to engage in object-based attention, making their performance mirror that of low-spans (Bleckley et al., 2015). High-spans thus exhibit greater efficiency and flexibility in how they allocate their attentional resources while low-spans are slower and more rigid.[4]

WMC predicts an array of attentional phenomena, lending support to the position that complex span performance is influenced by individual differences in attention control. This conclusion is made even more tenable by noting the minimal memory storage demands imposed by many attention control measures. For example, each trial

---

[3] Participants see strings of arrows and indicate the location of the central arrow. The central arrow can either be congruent with the others in the series (← ← ← ← ←) or incongruent (← ← → ← ←), and the flanker interference effect is calculated as the mean reaction time on incongruent trials minus the mean reaction time on congruent trials.

[4] Though the studies outlined thus far have been primarily concerned with visual tasks, WMC also predicts at-tention performance in various auditory domains, including dichotic listening (Conway et al., 2001).

type on the anti-saccade is defined by at most a single critical instruction, to look towards or away from the peripheral cue (Roberts et al., 1994). This is well within the limits of online memory storage (Cowan, 2001), making memory load an unlikely contributor to span differences.

The quasi-experimental studies reviewed earlier have been instrumental to our thinking about individual differences in WMC, but they have several undesirable features. For one, they ignore scores towards the middle of the WMC distribution, making it difficult to assess effect size. These studies establish an association between attention control and WMC, but they cannot speak to the magnitude of the relationship. Additionally, while these quasi-experimental results are consistent with our theoretical framework and we assume that span differences in attention control tasks map on to intelligence differences, these studies do not actually measure Gf. More importantly, the extreme-groups design suffers from a basic issue of interpretation. We grouped participants based on their scores on one or more WMC tasks, but the fact that WMC and Gf are so highly correlated means that high-WMC individuals were likely high-Gf individuals. Therefore, we do not know whether the results were due to differences in WMC, Gf, or some third variable. This difficulty is elaborated further in the later section on maintenance and disengagement theory. Although we and others have expressed reservations about the interpretive difficulties associated with extreme-groups designs (Engle, 2018; Engle & Martin, 2019; Wilhelm et al., 2013) and we instead opt for large-sample factor-analytic and structural equation modelling studies in our more recent work, the fact that high- and low-spans differ on attention control tasks despite their minimal memory load is instructive, and any theory of WMC must account for this relationship.

Relating Variation in Working Memory Capacity to Fluid Intelligence

The preceding sections outlined the theoretical account of individual differences in WMC that we have been advancing since the 1990s, and sparing a few substantial elaborations, this is how we still think about WMC. Numerous investigations all point to the conclusion that controlled attention contributes substantial variance to WMC, and accounts for WMC's broad predictive power. Though it has been challenged, we find that the major tenets of the executive attention theory remain quite tenable, and other researchers are converging on similar views (Friedman & Miyake, 2017; Gathercole et al., 2008; Gray et al., 2017; Kaufman, Schneider, & Kaufman, 2019; McCabe, Roediger, McDaniel, Balota, & Hambrick, 2010; Rueda, 2018). The theory has not remained unchanged, however and many of the revisions to our position have resulted from greater specification of the mechanisms relating WMC to Gf, predominately by their mutual dependence on attention control for regulating the contents of memory.

A study by Shipstead et al. (2014) segues nicely into our recent thinking. Shipstead et al. sought to explain the relationship between WMC and Gf by way of attention control and its interface with memory systems. They derived latent factors thought to reflect variance associated with primary memory, secondary memory, attention control, and Gf. They also formed WMC factors from several different kinds of tasks, including complex spans, running memory spans, and visual arrays tasks.

Brief treatments of the running memory span and visual arrays tasks as measures of WMC are needed before discussing Shipstead et al.'s results. Tasks like the running memory span (and others that combine storage and processing demands) typically show equivalent or slightly stronger relationships with Gf than measures that separate storage and processing (Broadway & Engle, 2010; Cowan et al., 2005; Shipstead, Redick, Hicks, & Engle, 2012). Where complex spans separate storage and processing functions, running memory spans require participants to perform storage and processing operations on the same items in memory. For example, participants may be presented with a long but variable string of letters, but will only be asked to report the last several. This requires participants to continually update the contents of primary memory. Complex span tasks, meanwhile, require participants to maintain to-be-remembered items in primary memory without further processing. Items that fall below a critical activation threshold must be retrieved from secondary memory. Complex spans thus tap primary memory to some degree, but also secondary memory. However, the running memory span's integrated storage and processing demands may provide a more comprehensive measure of a person's ability to dynamically manage the contents of primary memory. If managing and updating the contents of primary memory is important for performing well on Gf tests, this could explain their particularly strong relationship with tasks like the running memory span.

Another class of tasks used to measure WMC are the visual arrays, or change detection, tasks (Luck & Vogel, 1997). In a typical visual arrays task, participants are presented with a fixation, followed by a target array containing stimuli of differing colours, shapes, and/or orientations. This target array is removed and a test array is presented after a brief inter-stimulus interval. Depending on the version administered, participants must either indicate whether a cued item in the test array has changed from the target array or whether any item in the test array differs from the initial target. Though widely regarded as measures of static online primary memory storage capacity (Cowan et al., 2005; Luck & Vogel, 1997), evidence suggests that other processes are important for visual arrays performance. For example, visual arrays capacity estimates predict a person's susceptibility to attentional capture (Fukuda & Vogel, 2009, 2011) and varying the interval between trials modulates the build-up of proactive interference, suggesting a role for secondary memory retrieval (Shipstead & Engle, 2013). Visual arrays performance is thus more multiply determined than is typically assumed.

Shipstead et al. (2014) varied the attention control demands of their visual arrays tasks. On some versions, participants were cued to ignore a subset of items presented in the target array (Fig. 7.2c, d). For example, in Fig. 7.2d, a participant sees an assortment of red and blue rectangles in the target array with the instructions to attend to one of the colours (blue, in this case). On the test array, one of the attended elements is cued and the participant must indicate whether that element has changed in

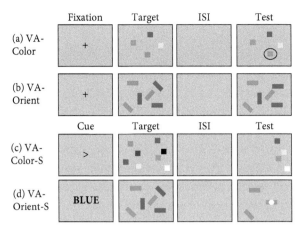

Fig. 7.2 Examples of visual array (VA) tasks used by Shipstead et al. (2014). The labelling of each task is based on the following criteria: VA-[the category of the change-based judgement]-[is there a selection component]. The two potential judgements for change are colour or orientation (i.e. has a square changed colour, or has a bar changed orientation). The selection components direct an individual to pay attention to half of the array (either one side (the right or left subset) or one subset of stimuli (blue or red bars only)). In panel (a), the test-taker must indicate whether the encircled box has changed colours. In panel (b), the test-taker must indicate whether any box has changed its orientation. Panels (c) and (d) begin with a cue that indicates which information will be relevant. This is followed by the array of to-be-remembered items, along with distractors. After the inter-stimulus interval (ISI), the probe array appears with only cued information presented. In panel (c) the test-taker must indicate whether any box has changed colour. In panel (d) the test-taker must indicate whether the box with the white dot has changed orientation.

orientation from the target array. Such manipulations introduce a filtering compo-nent to the task, increasing demands on top-down attention (Vogel, McCullough, & Machizawa, 2005). We refer to visual arrays with an attentional filtering compo-nent as *selective* visual arrays. In other visual arrays tasks no such instructions were given (Fig. 7.2a, b). Visual arrays without the filtering component were expected to mirror the complex span tasks in their relationships to primary memory, secondary memory, and Gf; we refer to them as *non-selective* visual arrays. Selective visual ar-rays were expected to show stronger relationships to attention control than their non-selective counterparts.

Shipstead et al. (2014) also derived latent factors representing attention control, primary memory, and secondary memory. Attention control was defined using anti-saccade accuracy, alongside the colour Stroop and arrow flanker interference effects. The primary memory latent factor was defined by accuracy in list recall below within the putative limits of primary memory capacity, and secondary memory capacity was defined by list recall accuracy once this limit has been exceeded (see Tulving and Colotla, 1970).

Having described their measures, we can now outline some of Shipstead et al.'s (2014) major findings. In one analysis, primary memory, secondary memory, and attention control were used to predict correlated WMC and Gf factors. When inspecting the model (Fig. 7.3), the first thing to note is that the correlation between WMC and Gf is not significant after accounting for the influences of the predictors. That is to say, the relationship between WMC and Gf is entirely explained by their relationships with attention control, primary memory, and secondary memory. The second thing to note is that the only unique predictor of both Gf and WMC is secondary memory retrieval; neither primary memory or attention control uniquely predict both WMC and Gf once the intercorrelations of predictors is taken into account. However, this does *not* suggest that attention control and primary memory are unimportant in explaining the WMC–Gf association. Rather, the bulk of the shared variance between the WMC and Gf latent variables is actually accounted for by the indirect path through primary memory and attention control, seen in bold. Substantively, this suggests that attention control and primary memory *jointly* account for much of the shared variance between WMC and Gf. This is consistent with the notion that the use of attention to manipulate the contents of primary memory is a critical aspect of the WMC–Gf relationship,

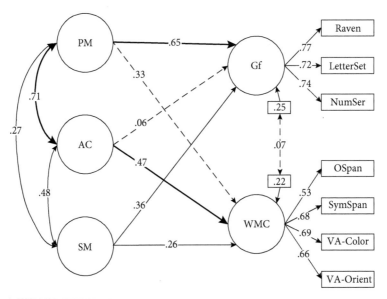

Fig. 7.3 Primary memory (PM), secondary memory (SM), and attention control (AC) predicting WMC and Gf. WMC here is defined by two complex span tasks and the nonselective visual arrays tasks without the attentional filtering component. Broken paths are not statistically significant.

which coincides with our thinking about the strong relationship between the running span (and related measures of WMC) and Gf.

This account of the relationship between WMC and Gf was further supported by models in which primary memory totally mediated the effect of attention control on Gf (Fig. 7.4a, b). Two such models were fitted, with WMC being defined either by complex and running spans (Fig. 7.4a) or by selective and non-selective visual arrays tasks (Fig. 7.4b). In Fig. 7.4a, variance unique to WMC as defined by two running spans was used to predict primary memory; all variance shared with complex span measures of WMC was used to predict attention control and secondary memory retrieval. In Fig. 7.4b, variance unique to the selective visual arrays tasks was used to predict attention control, while variance shared with non-selective visual arrays tasks was used to predict attention control and secondary memory retrieval. The substantive interpretation of both models is identical. Secondary memory retrieval once again predicted unique variance in Gf, as did primary memory. Crucially, attention control was not directly related to Gf, but exerted its entire effect indirectly through its influence on primary memory. One interpretation of these results is that attention control is related to WMC and Gf because it helps organize the contents of primary memory according to current goals. Given the strong relationship between tasks that require continual updating of primary memory and Gf, it is plausible that the ability to remove, inhibit, or otherwise disregard items in primary memory may be critical to performance on Gf tasks, whereas the ability to maintain items in memory may be more crucial to other kinds of working memory measures. Attention control would seem relevant in both cases (Shipstead et al., 2016).

Before a more extensive treatment of our current framework, we would like to address a theoretical alternative that we think is increasingly untenable. In our view, WMC and Gf are correlated because they share common cognitive mechanisms. This account of the association between WMC and Gf runs counter to the more standard view that WMC contributes causally to Gf by maintaining representations that support the generation and testing of hypotheses (Chuderski, Taraday, Neçka, & Smoleń, 2012; Oberauer, Süß, Wilhem, & Sander, 2007; Shipstead et al., 2012). However, direct tests of predictions derived from this hypothetical causal relationship provide little evidence that maintenance of information in Gf tasks drives the WMC–Gf relationship (Domnick, Zimmer, Becker, & Spinath, 2018). For example, if WMC were a causal factor in performance on Gf tasks, one would expect performance on complex reasoning items to have stronger correlations with WMC measures than simpler reasoning problems, because more complex problems should have greater storage demands. This does not occur, however (Burgoyne, Hambrick, & Altmann, 2019; Unsworth & Engle, 2005). Further, much of the research attempting to improve intelligence via working memory training is predicated on the assumed causal link between memory storage and Gf (Jaeggi, Buschkuehl, Jonides, & Perrig, 2008; Jaeggi, Buschkuehl, Jonides, & Shah, 2011). These efforts have thus far proven futile (Redick et al., 2013), bolstering the position that WMC does not causally influence Gf. In the next section, we elaborate

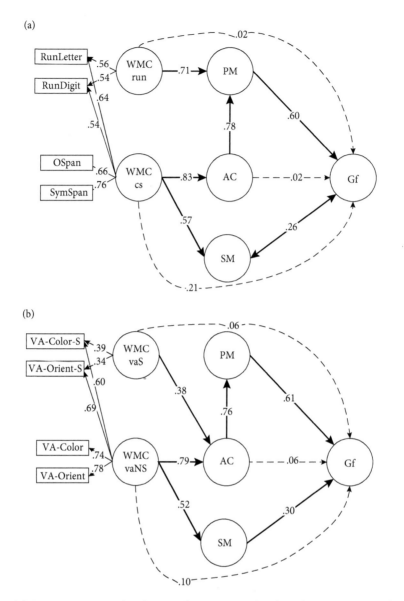

Fig. 7.4 (a) Primary memory (PM), secondary memory (SM), and attention control (AC) mediating the relationship between span measures of WMC and Gf. WMrun is a working memory capacity factor defined by variance unique to running memory span tasks and WMcs is a working memory capacity factor defined by the variance common to running memory and complex span measures. (b) PM, SM, and AC mediating the relationship between visual arrays measures of WMC and Gf. WMvaS is a working memory capacity factor defined by selective visual arrays (i.e., those with an attentional filtering component) and WMvaNS is a working memory capacity factor defined by the variance shared by both non-selective and selective visual arrays. Broken paths are non-significant.

Reproduced from Zach Shipstead, Dakota R.B. Lindsey, Robyn L. Marshall, and Randall W. Engle, 'The mechanisms of working memory capacity: Primary memory, secondary memory, and attention control', *Journal of Memory and Language*, 72, pp. 116–141, Figures 10 and 13, https://doi.org/10.1016/j.jml.2014.01.004

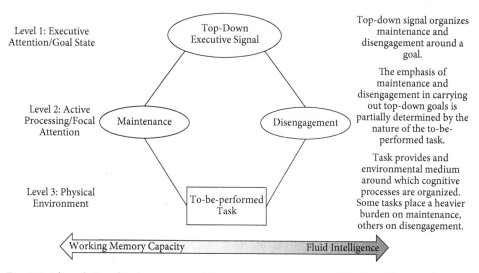

Level 1: Executive Attention/Goal State

Top-Down Executive Signal

Top-down signal organizes maintenance and disengagement around a goal.

Level 2: Active Processing/Focal Attention

Maintenance

Disengagement

The emphasis of maintenance and disengagement in carrying out top-down goals is partially determined by the nature of the to-be-performed task.

Level 3: Physical Environment

To-be-performed Task

Task provides and environmental medium around which cognitive processes are organized. Some tasks place a heavier burden on maintenance, others on disengagement.

Working Memory Capacity   Fluid Intelligence

Fig. 7.5 The relationship between working memory capacity and fluid intelligence from the maintenance and disengagement perspective.

Reproduced from Zach Shipstead, Tyler L. Harrison, Randall W. Engle, 'Working Memory Capacity and Fluid Intelligence: Maintenance and Disengagement', *Perspectives on Psychological Science*, 11, pp. 771–799. doi:10.1177/1745691616650647 Copyright © 2016, SAGE Publications.

this position and argue that WMC and Gf measures instead reflect different functions of attention.

Maintenance and Disengagement Theory

On the surface, WMC and Gf measures appear very different. WMC measures generally require participants to balance memory storage and processing demands, while Gf tasks have no explicit storage component and require participants to infer relations between the elements of a novel problem or puzzle to discover a solution. Yet, both abilities predict a broad assortment of behavioural outcomes and are highly correlated at the latent level. Given their seemingly divergent processing demands, what could account for the substantial overlap between measures of WMC and Gf? Recently, we have moved away from treating WMC and Gf as distinct cognitive processes. Instead, we regard them as patterns that emerge when common cognitive mechanisms are faced with the different constraints imposed by WMC and Gf tasks. This position is the starting point of maintenance and disengagement theory, a recently proposed generalization of the executive attention theory of WMC.

Fig. 7.5 depicts our current conception of the mechanisms underlying individual differences in WMC and Gf. Importantly, WMC and Gf themselves are not structural features of the model. Instead, we focus on the domain-general mechanisms that are constitutive of both. These are *maintenance* and *disengagement*, which, although distinct, are both executed by a top-down signal from a unitary executive attention whenever controlled processing is required. Maintenance keeps representations in an active, accessible state in the face of distraction or interference. Conversely, disengagement expunges no-longer relevant representations, preventing them from affecting ongoing cognition (c.f. Bjork, 1970; Festini & Reuter-Lorenz, 2014). Failures of maintenance lead to the premature loss of still needed memory representations and to goal-neglect (e.g. attentional capture or mind-wandering), while failures of disengagement lead to a build-up of proactive interference and perseveration on outdated hypotheses or task sets. Individual differences in WMC arise when task demands place a greater emphasis on maintenance of information, though these tasks will also require disengagement of information to some degree (e.g. mitigating proactive interference). Individual differences in Gf arise when a task places a greater emphasis on disengagement from no-longer relevant information, though maintenance of task-goals and problem sets will be required. [5] Therefore, WMC and Gf arise from similar cognitive mechanisms but are reliant on these mechanisms to different degrees. Attention control is common to both.

When referring to maintenance and disengagement as mechanisms, we do not mean that they themselves are isolable processes. Rather, they should be viewed as categories of processes that broadly serve to maintain goal-relevant information or disengage from newly irrelevant information. For instance, disengagement may be carried out by cognitive inhibition, memory updating, tagging items in episodic memory to prevent retrieval, and so on. This broad-strokes approach is a major point of departure from similar sounding positions (e.g. the memory updating function in the unity/diversity model of executive functioning; Miyake et al., 2000; see also Bialystok, 2017).

Beyond merely explaining the WMC–Gf relationship, maintenance and disengagement theory accounts for some curious findings not easily explained by its competitors. For instance, Shipstead and Engle (2013) showed that longer inter-trial intervals led to larger estimates of storage capacity on a non-selective visual arrays task. This suggests that visual arrays performance reflects more than mere capacity. Rather, scores also reflect the active removal of previously presented items to reduce proactive interference, with longer inter-trial intervals allowing more time for removal and interference reduction. Consistent with maintenance and disengagement theory, the correlation between WMC and visual arrays storage capacity did not change as a function of inter-trial interval. However, the correlation to Gf increased with longer intervals, suggesting that high-Gf individuals were actually able to take advantage of the extra time on long inter-trial intervals to *disengage* from the memory items presented in the previous trial. These results are difficult to explain with a strict maintenance perspective on the WMC–Gf relationship.[6]

---

[5] One implication pointed out by a reviewer of this chapter is that while working memory training has had little success in improving performance on Gf tasks, interventions aimed specifically at improving disengagement skills may show more promise. This is untested, but would be a useful and important test of our theory and would provide tremendous applied benefits.

[6] This also conflicts with classic temporal distinctiveness accounts of forgetting, which would predict that mere time elapsed over the course of an inter-stimulus interval is sufficient to account for forgetting. If this were the whole story, it is unclear why higher Gf would be associated with more forgetting over the course of longer inter-stimulus intervals (e.g. Crowder, 1976).

Another piece of evidence comes from the *N*-back task (Shipstead et al., 2016). The three *N*-back task is a continuous memory task in which the participant is presented with one memory item at a time and must decide if that same item was presented three items back. A critical component to *N*-back tasks is the presence of lures, items that repeat in positions other than 3-back (e.g. 2-back). Once a lure is past 3-back it is no longer relevant and retaining it in memory will create interference as evidenced by false alarming to lure items. Lures are correctly rejected with greater frequency as lure position recedes. Fig. 7.6 plots the correlation between Gf and false alarm rates (Fig. 7.6a.) and between WMC and false alarm rates (Fig. 7.6b). The raw correlations in each case follow a very similar pattern, but accounting for the influence of one ability on the other reveals a dissociation. Controlling on WMC diminishes the correlation between Gf and false alarming on the *N*-back somewhat, but there is still a discernible association. Controlling for the influence of Gf in the WMC–false alarming relationship virtually eliminates the correlation. Therefore, those higher in Gf, not WMC, are less likely to false alarm to a lure, an advantage that grows with the number of intervening

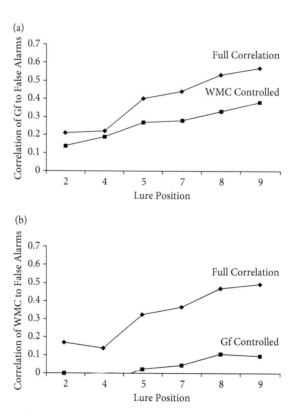

Fig. 7.6 (a) The correlation between fluid intelligence (Gf) and false alarm rates at different lure positions of the 3-back task. (b) The correlation between working memory capacity (WMC) and false alarm rates at different lure positions of the 3-back task.

Reproduced from Zach Shipstead, Tyler L. Harrison, Randall W. Engle, 'Working Memory Capacity and Fluid Intelligence: Maintenance and Disengagement', *Perspectives on Psychological Science*, 11, pp. 771–799. doi:10.1177/1745691616650647 Copyright © 2016, SAGE Publications.

items between the lure and target. The distance allows high-Gf individuals to disengage from the no longer relevant information. Low-Gf individuals are unable to similarly capitalize.

The very similar pattern observed with *N*-back performance for both WMC and Gf before imposing statistical control suggests an important lesson. Because WMC and Gf are so highly related, it is important to disentangle the two lest one misattribute an effect of WMC to Gf or vice versa. We have not always been so careful. For instance, Rosen and Engle (1997) used an extreme-groups design comparing high- and low-spans on a verbal fluency task and found that high-spans could name more exemplars of a category (e.g. types of animals) than could low-spans. Low-spans tended to re-retrieve previously generated exemplars, handicapping their performance by preventing them from retrieving new examples. High-spans did not suffer this difficulty as much, and retrieved many more exemplars as a result. Rosen and Engle concluded that WMC likely plays an important role in coordinating retrieval from long-term (i.e. secondary) memory. Shipstead et al. (2016) reached a different conclusion. Using a full range of ability and measures of both WMC and Gf, they showed that verbal fluency is uniquely predicted by Gf and not WMC, contra Rosen and Engle (1997). This is sensible in the maintenance and disengagement framework: high-Gf individuals are better able to disengage from already retrieved items, permitting the retrieval of new examples from long-term memory. WMC predicts verbal fluency only because of its correlation with Gf.

Beyond making sense of some otherwise unwieldy results, maintenance and disengagement theory also situates attention control within a broader research context. While maintenance supports the stability of our cognitive system, disengagement supports its flexibility by allowing the adoption of new patterns of thought and behaviour. The flexibility afforded by disengagement is theoretically more consistent with the way Gf has been defined and measured (i.e. the ability to reason about and solve novel problems) than a maintenance-based account of the WMC–Gf relationship. This distinction between stability and flexibility of cognition is also characteristic of other theories of cognition. For example, Smith (2003) differentiates two modes of thought: paradigmatic and revolutionary. Paradigmatic thinking is useful in routine problem-solving. Maintenance will allow for representations of routine rules to remain activated as one solves such problems (Harrison, Shipstead, & Engle, 2015). However, perseverating on routine rules when more creative or divergent thinking is required might impair reaching a correct solution. Smith (2003) referred to revolutionary thinking as being able to drop routine solutions and outdated hypotheses in favour of more creative 'out-of-the-box' thinking. We see clear parallels between this description of revolutionary and paradigmatic thought and the tenets of maintenance and disengagement theory. Thus, the theory has the potential to bridge the gap between seemingly disparate subject areas and hopefully will spawn new and fruitful investigations.

The maintenance and disengagement theory suggests that the reason WMC, Gf, and possibly other cognitive constructs are related to one another is due to their mutual reliance on attention control. One theoretical prediction derived from the theory, therefore, is that attention control should mediate, largely or completely, the relationship between WMC and Gf latent variables. One problem for maintenance and disengagement theory (and the original formulation of the executive attention theory of WMC) is that tasks typically thought to measure attention control show little in the way of convergent validity, casting doubt on the existence of a unitary attention control ability (Karr et al., 2018; Rey-Mermet, Gade, & Oberauer, 2018). An alternative conclusion is that there are widespread measurement issues in studies of attention control, leading to difficulty in forming cohesive latent factors. Indeed, we regard many of the tools currently used in the literature as problematic for individual differences research (see Draheim, Mashburn, Martin, & Engle, 2019), raising questions about how best to measure attention control.

Measuring Attention Control

Theoretical work surrounding attention control has been stymied by widespread and historically acknowledged measurement issues associated with the correlational use of experimental tasks (Draheim et al., 2019). For example, few paradigms in psychology are as recognizable and robust at the group level as the colour Stroop task, which, again, requires a person to resist the automaticity of reading the name of a colour to report the colour in which the word is printed (Stroop, 1935). The Stroop interference effect is usually calculated by subtracting the mean reaction time on congruent trials (e.g. BLUE) from the mean reaction time on incongruent trials (e.g. BLUE). Since the trials differ in one and only one regard, the presence or absence of a mismatch between the word and typeface, subtracting one reaction time from the other should yield an estimate of how long it takes to resolve the conflict from competing responses on incongruent trials, a putative function of controlled attention (Norman & Shallice, 1986).

Many other tasks in the attention control literature are variations on this basic theme. Such tasks are premised on the subtraction methodology of Franciscus Donders (1868/1969). Although groundbreaking in assuming that mental events take a quantifiable amount of time and hence are open to empirical study, several of the method's base assumptions have been vehemently criticized (e.g. Sternberg, 1969). The method can only be applied under the assumption of a serial progression of information processing steps, so parallel processing is fatal to any straightforward interpretation of reaction time difference scores. Another prerequisite is the assumption of pure insertion, whereby one assumes that by adding a single element or alteration to a base task requiring multiple processing steps, they are only affecting processing in one stage and not others. This is a tenuous assumption at best and is likely often wrong.

While subtracting reaction times from similar tasks seems a simple and appealing method for isolating effects of interest, the assumptions bounding their interpretation mean that subtraction is probably inappropriate under many experimental circumstances. This is not to say that the use of the Stroop and other interference effects should be shunned by researchers outright. After all, the effects are robust and highly replicable. It does, however, mean that interpreting such interference effects is murkier than researchers often presume, and interpreting them as pure indicators of the processes meant to be studied is often unjustified. These issues are well-known at the experimental level, but these effects are arguably more pernicious in individual differences and developmental research, and a host of other issues arise when these tasks are imported from the experimental domain to the differential (see Miller & Ulrich, 2013 for an excellent discussion of interpreting reaction time correlations).

Interpretive difficulties aside, subtractive measures pose a number of other problems for differential psychology. Experimental and differential psychology differ fundamentally in terms of the variance that they seek to explain (Cronbach, 1957). Experimental psychology seeks to understand how situational variables affect behaviour, whereas differential psychology seeks to explain factors that distinguish individuals from one another. These respective emphases lead experimental psychology to focus on within-participants variance (to the degree possible) and to strive to minimize between-participants variance. This is made explicit in the typical statistical methods employed in each tradition, with *t*-tests and ANOVAs comprising the brick-and-mortar of experimental psychology, while correlation, regression, and factor analysis, which rely on the very between-participants variance that experimentalists strive to minimize, inform much of differential psychology.

Despite this fundamental methodological and philosophical disconnect, much of our work can be seen as an attempt to achieve Cronbach's (1957) vision of a unified psychological science. We have been delighted to see others interested in bridging the gap between the two traditions, but doing so can be treacherous. The wholesale import of experimental tasks into differential research contexts presents one pervasive misstep. The impulse is laudable given the success of tasks like the Stroop task at the experimental level. However, they tend to be fairly low in between-participants variability (Hedge, Powell, & Sumner, 2018; Rouder & Haaf, 2019), which is a prerequisite for observing strong correlations, including estimates of reliability.[7] A major reason for this lack of between-participants variance is the subtraction methodology employed in calculating dependent variables in many experimental tasks. Difference scores and measures relying upon them have been criticized by psychometricians for their unreliability (Cronbach & Furby, 1970; Edwards, 2001; Paap & Sawi, 2016), which is a by-product of the correlation of their components (Chiou & Spreng, 1996). The components of an attention control task (e.g. congruent and incongruent Stroop trials) tend to be quite reliable themselves, but much of their reliable variance is subsumed by their correlation. This produces difference scores that are much less reliable than their components almost by mathematical necessity (but see Trafimow, 2015). Removing the common reliable variance also increases the proportion of error variance reflected in the score, often leading to small correlations, low reliability, and difficulty demonstrating validity

---

[7] Ironically, this homogeneity is a reason the tasks perform so well experimentally, given the logic of statistical tests.

(Hedge et al., 2018) which, in turn, often leads researchers to accept the null hypothesis that there is no correlation between variables.

Another reason to be wary of reaction time difference scores in particular is the possibility of speed/accuracy trade-offs. In many cases, speed and accuracy of responding exist in opposition, and individuals vary in their prioritizing one over the other (Heitz, 2014). For instance, cognitive ageing researchers often contend with older adults' strong bias to favour accuracy over speed of responding (Starns & Ratcliff, 2010), and those higher in cognitive ability may slow down after committing an error to avoid future errors, while lower-ability participants show no slowing in subsequent trials (Draheim, Hicks, & Engle, 2016). Differing speed/accuracy emphases can lead to spurious conclusions if not accounted for, making straightforward interpretation of correlations impossible. Given that many of the effects typically of interest in experimental attention control tasks are purely reaction-time based and do not account for one-half of the speed/accuracy dynamic, possible differences in speed/accuracy interactions are a major reason to avoid them in differential research.[8]

These measurement deficiencies are one possible reason for the widespread difficulty in forming balanced attention control factors (often operationalized using 'inhibition' tasks). This difficulty has been suggested as evidence against the existence of a unitary attentional control ability: if 'attention control' measures truly tap the same underlying construct, there should be greater cohesion in terms of task intercorrelations and factor loadings. Failure to consistently find such relationships could indicate that control processes are not unitary, and that task-specific control processes lie at the root of successful performance (Rey-Mermet et al., 2018).

This interpretation is potentially viable, but dubious given the psychometric difficulties associated with reaction time difference score measures (and difference scores more broadly). Moreover, attempts to rectify these measurement issues have yielded conflicting results. For example, a recent study by Rey-Mermet, Gade, Souza, von Bastian, and Oberauer (2019) attempted to minimize the influence of speed/accuracy trade-offs in an array of attention control tasks. They did so by instituting a response deadline that they reasoned should penalize both extremely slow accurate responding and fast error-prone responding equally. The deadline was based on speed of responding on a series of neutral trials in which attentional processes would not be expected to operate (e.g. pro-saccade trials in an anti-saccade task). The procedure was also expected to limit the influence of processing speed, which has been proposed as a possible basis of the relationship between WMC and Gf (e.g. Fry & Hale, 1996). They also took steps to minimize the influence of associative learning, episodic memory, and stimulus carryover effects. They were unable to form a coherent latent factor from the attention control measures, and individual tasks showed little relationship to WMC or

---

[8] While pure reaction time tasks are problematic in this regard, this can be less of a concern for accuracy-based tasks (see Draheim et al., 2019; Wickelgren, 1977). However, accuracy-based difference scores are also vulnerable to psychometric issues and interpretive difficulties.

Gf. They interpreted this as indicating a widespread conflation between general processing speed and attention control.

One possible reason for their null findings is their decision to use accuracy difference scores as dependent variables for their tasks. They did so in order to eliminate the possibility that different types of dependent variables might contribute to underwhelming relationships between traditionally reaction-time based executive functioning measures and accuracy-based measures of WMC and Gf. Accuracy-based difference scores suffer the same reliability concerns and are also difficult to interpret unless one is willing to assume the strictures of the subtraction methodology. Even so, we would be remiss not to note that the pattern of results for their anti-saccade task did not change when only accuracy on anti-saccade trials was used, and the reliability of their measures was uniformly very high for difference scores. This is an interesting departure from the preponderance of psychometric theory and empirical investigations of difference score reliability, although there are circumstances under which difference scores obtain acceptable reliabilities (Trafimow, 2015). Even so, there are several reasons to be cautious about their results. Their use of a thresholding procedure to account for processing speed and speed/accuracy trade-offs is novel and requires validation, especially in light of numerous macro-analytic studies which find that processing speed is unable to account for the relationships between executive control and other cognitive constructs (Cepeda, Blackwell, & Munakata, 2013; McCabe et al., 2010) or between WMC and Gf (Colom et al., 2008; Conway, Cowan, Bunting, Therriault, & Minkoff, 2002; Redick, Unsworth, Kelly, & Engle, 2012). We consider more evidence that processing speed may be a suboptimal explanation in our 'Alternative Views' section.

Draheim, Tsukahara, Martin, Mashburn, and Engle (2020) took a different approach. They tested a battery of classic, modified, and novel attention control tasks. These included standard and modified versions of the colour Stroop and arrow flanker tasks. Rather than relying on reaction time difference scores as a dependent variable, the modified versions of the tasks followed a thresholding procedure whereby a stimulus presentation rate or a response deadline was adjusted based on block-by-block response accuracy. There were also several other tasks which relied solely on accuracy as a dependent variable. These included an anti-saccade, a selective visual arrays task, and a novel task modelled on a perceptual vigilance task and the anti-saccade. These modified accuracy-based attention tasks showed stronger intercorrelations, were more reliable, and showed stronger relationships to both WMC and Gf than the reaction-time difference score measures. In fact, when defined by some of the strongest performing measures, the attention control latent factor totally mediated the relationship between WMC and Gf, consistent with predictions derived from maintenance and disengagement theory. Furthermore, these relationships were still significant even after accounting for the influence of a latent variable defined by processing speed measures. Draheim et al. (2020) took this pattern as confirmatory evidence for a unitary domain-general attention control ability.

One potential objection to the interpretation of Draheim et al. (2020) is that their so-called attention control latent factors could contain variance not associated with attention control. As their measures were not subtractive, the latent factors derived from them could contain common but process-irrelevant variance, such as that reflecting processing speed or short-term memory storage. This criticism presumes that difference scores are the only way to achieve something close to process-purity and follows from the logic of the subtraction methodology. If the strictures of the subtraction methodology are met, the criticism is approximately correct.[9] However, we have argued the subtraction methodology's assumptions are often invalid, creating difference scores that are difficult to interpret. A better means of achieving our measurement goals is to adopt latent variable methodologies and to measure constructs via broad factors comprised of structurally dissimilar tasks, which Draheim et al. attempted. The broader concern is well-taken, however. This was an overtly exploratory study and, although the results were promising, more work is required to validate the tasks before we can confidently attest to the processes they measure.

Alternative Views

Over the course of our writings, we have at various times drawn comparisons between our own work and other prominent theories of working memory and WMC. In particular, we have been sympathetic to the basic tenets of Cowan's (1988, 1999) embedded process model and Oberauer's concentric theory of WMC (Oberauer, 2002; Oberauer et al., 2007). These views share a basic scaffolding in that they assume that short-term (primary) memory consists of activated units of long-term memory. They differ in the role of attention. The embedded process model allows for about four chunks of information to be held active within the focus of attention, where they are safeguarded from the build-up of proactive interference and time-based decay (Cowan, 2001; Cowan et al., 2005). The concentric model, meanwhile, permits a single chunk to inhabit the focus of attention without proactive interference or decay, but other pieces of information can be held active outside the focus of attention by building, breaking, and updating arbitrary bindings between the item within the focus of attention and other items in secondary memory. Currently bound items are equated with primary or short-term memory. At this time, we favour the concentric model, partly based on recent data suggesting that interference occurs well within the capacity of focal attention assumed by the embedded process model (Allen, Baddeley, & Hitch, 2014; Shipstead & Engle, 2013). However, our views diverge from the concentric model in several important ways. For one, the model assumes that binding and unbinding are separable from attention processes (Wilhelm et al., 2013). In our view, binding and unbinding would putatively be classified as maintenance and disengagement processes, respectively, and would hence be regulated by attentional resources. Consistent with our characterization, binding has been shown to be disrupted by attention load (Allen et al., 2014).

---

[9] Approximately because the difference score would be a fairly pure measure (assuming highly reliable components), but we would still regard latent variable analysis as a viable and more general alternative (Donaldson, 1983).

Our theoretical framework is sufficiently general that we find relevant similarities with several theories of working memory, certainly more than we have space to discuss here. We would like to close by addressing a position that we find less amenable and that we touched upon previously: that the relationship is actually due to individual differences in processing speed.

Processing Speed

As previously noted, processing speed has been proposed as a primitive and an explanatory alternative to attention control. We and others have been addressing this criticism in various forms for years (Conway et al., 2002; Heitz & Engle, 2007; Stankov & Roberts, 1997; Unsworth et al., 2004). We believe that the popularity and persistence of processing speed as an explanatory device warrants a somewhat protracted analysis. Processing speed has been shown to relate to both WMC and Gf (although less consistently with WMC; Conway et al., 2002; Fry & Hale, 1996; Kranzler & Jensen, 1989; Redick et al., 2012). Given difficulties in deriving strong, stable latent factors using well-known attention control measures, processing speed seems a reasonable avenue for exploration. However, there are good theoretical and empirical reasons to be sceptical.

One is the sheer under-specification of what is meant by processing speed: speed of *what*, exactly? This question often goes unaddressed by researchers using processing speed to explain individual differences in higher cognition. Presumably, what is meant is a global speed difference whereby people differ similarly in the speed of all information processing, perhaps due to underlying differences in neurophysiological efficiency (Jensen, 1998; Reed & Jensen, 1992). We refer to these as global speed differences. An alternate interpretation would be that whatever processing mechanisms are involved in a given task, they operate more quickly for some people than others, but there are intra-individual speed differences across different processes. We call these local speed differences. Evidence for global processing speed differences is somewhat shakier than is immediately apparent, however. Rabbitt (1996) has argued that, even when the proportion of the speed difference between two or more individuals is variable across tasks (suggesting local speed differences), plotting these ratios can still produce strong, positive linear trends implying global speed differences. This risks masking local speed differences by erroneously creating the impression of uniform differences in a global processing speed.

Where local process-specific speed differences emerge, it surely makes more sense to deemphasize differences in speed rather than to treat them as central to theories of cognition. That is to say, if the speed of *what* matters, then it surely makes more sense to treat 'speed of processing' as a cognitive outcome rather than a causal primitive. Otherwise, one is simply capitalizing on the trivial fact that cognition unfolds over time. Rabbitt (1996) makes a similar point. Noting that speed is the only possible metric in many processing speed tasks, he writes '[to] deduce ... that individual differences in speed (which are all we can measure) must therefore necessarily be the functional bases [sic] of individual differences in ability is to weekly succumb to tautology' (p. 85). Reliable differences in the speed with which people enact mental processes emerge and relate to cognitive ability, but this fact alone is no justification for using speed as an explanatory primitive.

Jensen (1998) offers a fascinating response to the 'speed of what' question. He notes that, 'The speed of *controlled processing* and the capacity of working memory are of great importance because of their heavy contribution to variance in [general intelligence]' (p. 248, emphasis added). He asserts that many hallmark measures of processing speed work by essentially forcing controlled processing, a position that has received some empirical support (Wu et al., 2018). Thus, while some suggest executive control tasks are confounded with processing speed (e.g. Rey-Mermet et al., 2019), we submit that an alternate hypothesis, that 'processing speed' tasks may include variance better construed as reflecting attention control, is both tenable and likely.

Evidence for this position comes from a few different areas. One is the 'worst performance rule', the observation that the slowest responses on a reaction time task exhibit the strongest (negative) relationship with cognitive ability (Coyle, 2003; Schubert, 2019). One explanation for this is that the slowest responses are most diagnostic of attention capture; losing focus yields slower responses and those with better attention control abilities lose focus less often. This interpretation has been borne out by changes in response time distributions as a function of practice. As people become more skilled in a task, their mean reaction time decreases. The main driver of this decrease is not a shifting of the entire response time distribution, but rather fewer severely delayed responses (Rabbitt, 1996). This is precisely what one would expect if the slowest responses index controlled attentional processes. As the task becomes automatized, attention control is required less for responding, resulting in less positively-skewed reaction time distributions. This would imply that one reason processing speed predicts cognitive abilities is that attention control helps determine the shape of the reaction time distribution.

Another reason to suspect an executive control contribution to processing speed comes from studies indicating that more complex processing speed measures exhibit stronger relationships with cognitive ability (Ackerman, Beier, & Boyle, 2002; Cepeda et al., 2013). As complexity increases, it becomes more likely that attention control will be required for goal maintenance and manipulation of memory representations for successful task performance. This pattern has been shown to be modulated by age, with both young children and older adults exhibiting greater reliance on executive control in simpler speed tasks than do young adults (Cepeda et al., 2013), a finding consistent with proposed developmental trajectories of cognitive control (Cappell, Gmiendl, & Reuter-Lorenz, 2009; Craik & Bialystok, 2006; Jones, Rothbart, & Posner, 2003; Li, Hämmerer, Müller, Hommel, & Lindernberger, 2009). Importantly, this suggests that the relationship between processing speed and developmental change in WMC and Gf ascribed to processing speed may be, at least partly, a misattribution (Fry & Hale, 1996; Salthouse & Babcock, 1991).

Although we are sceptical of processing speed's ability to account for the covariation of WMC and Gf in any sort of theoretically interesting way, this remains an empirical question. One barrier to answering it is the sheer number of tasks that are purported to measure processing speed and the differences in their structure, demands, and implementation (see Schubert, 2019). We believe that the field would benefit from more concentrated, principled efforts to securely establish the construct validity of both processing speed and attention control (Cepeda et al., 2013).

Conclusion

The executive attention theory of WMC initially postulated that the ability to maintain goal-relevant items in memory by way of attention resources was central to many cognitive abilities and real-world outcomes and was perhaps the thread connecting all sorts of controlled cognition. We have since expanded our focus. This initial articulation of the importance of WMC is not wrong, but rather incomplete. It ignores that any goal-relevant information held active in memory will inevitably become irrelevant at some future time and prove disruptive if not removed, suppressed, blocked, or inhibited. These respective functions, maintaining and disengaging from items in memory, are uniquely indexed by measures of WMC and Gf, respectively. Executive attention coordinates maintenance and disengagement processes. The original conjecture that WMC comprises the core of individual differences in controlled cognition is more aptly rephrased by saying that the ability to dynamically and flexibly control attention is at the core of controlled cognition.

This perspective is still novel and much of the preceding is admittedly speculative (although see Martin et al., 2020 for a recent application of the theory to language ability), but the maintenance and disengagement framework has several virtues. For one, it decentres maintenance processes, encouraging a more active and dynamic view of the cognitive system. It also has the potential to organize much of the literature surrounding the relative predictive utilities of WMC and Gf while providing a general rubric for gauging the likelihood that previous work erroneously attributes an effect of Gf to WMC or an effect of WMC to Gf. Finally, it places the often ignored distinction between cognitive processes and the tasks used to measure them in the theoretical foreground.

The novelty of the maintenance and disengagement framework, coupled with extant criticisms of our work, suggests several lines of future investigation. Of immediate concern is the continued development and validation of psychometrically sound measures of attention control. The previously discussed anti-saccade task is a prime example of this, but, as we and others note, a single task is an insufficient basis for a theory of cognition (Draheim et al., 2019; Draheim et al., 2020; Rey-Mermet et al., 2018). Relatedly, more direct investigations of both attention control and processing speed, specifically aimed at construct validation, are clearly in order.

References

Ackerman, P. L., Beier, M. E., & Boyle, M. D. (2002). Individual differences in working memory within a nomological network of cognitive and perceptual speed abilities. *Journal of Experimental Psychology: General, 131*, 567–589. doi:10.1037/0096-3445.131.4.567

Allen, R. J., Baddeley, A. D., & Hitch, G. J. (2014). Evidence for two attentional components in visual working memory. *Journal of Experimental Psychology: Learning, Memory, and Cognition, 40*, 1499–1509. doi:10.1037/xlm0000002

Atkinson, R. C., & Shiffrin, R. M. (1968). Human memory: A proposed system and its control processes. In K. W. Spence (Ed.), *The psychology of learning and motivation: Advances in research and theory* (Vol. 2, pp. 89–195). New York, NY: Academic Press. doi:10.1016/S0079-7421(08)60422-3

Baddeley, A. D. (1986). *Working memory*. Oxford, UK: Oxford University Press.

Baddeley, A. D., & Hitch, G. (1974). Working memory. In G. H. Bower (Ed.), *The psychology of learning and motivation: Advances in research and theory* (Vol. 8, pp. 47–89). New York, NY: Academic Press.

Barrett, L., Tugade, M. M., & Engle, R. W. (2004). Individual differences in working memory capacity and dual-process theories of the mind. *Psychological Bulletin, 130*, 553–573. doi:10.1037/0033-2909.130.4.553

Bayliss, D. M., Jarrold, C., Baddeley, A. D., & Gunn, D. M. (2005). The relationship between short-term memory and working memory: Complex span made simple? *Memory, 13*, 414–421. doi:10.1080/09658210344000332

Bialystok, E. (2017). The bilingual adaptation: How minds accommodate experience. *Psychological Bulletin, 143*, 233–262. doi:10.1037/bul0000099

Bjork, R. A. (1970). Positive forgetting: The noninterference of items intentionally forgotten. *Journal of Verbal Learning and Verbal Behavior, 9*, 255–268. doi:10.1016/s0022-5371(70)80059-7

Bleckley, M. K., Foster, J. L., & Engle, R. W. (2015). Working memory capacity accounts for the ability to switch between object-based and location-based allocation of visual attention. *Memory & Cognition, 43*, 379–388. doi:10.3758/s13421-014-0485-z

Broadway, J. M., & Engle, R. W. (2010). Validating running memory span: Measurement of working memory capacity and links with fluid intelligence. *Behavior Research Methods, 42*, 563–570. doi:10.3758/BRM.42.2.563.

Burgoyne, A. P., Hambrick, D. Z., & Altmann, E. M. (2019). Is working memory causal factor in fluid intelligence? *Psychonomic Bulletin & Review, 26*, 1333–1339. doi:10.3758/s13423-019-01606-9

Cappell, K. A., Gmiendl, L., & Reuter-Lorenz, P.A. (2009). Age differences in prefrontal recruitment during verbal working memory depend on memory load. *Cortex, 46*, 462–473. doi:10.1016/j.cortex.2009.11.009

Cepeda, N. J., Blackwell, K. A., & Munakata, Y. (2013). Speed isn't everything: Complex processing speed measures mask individual differences and developmental changes in executive control. *Developmental Science, 16*, 269–286. doi:10.1111/desc.12024

Chase, W. G., & Simon, H. A. (1973). Perception in chess. *Cognitive Psychology, 4*, 55–81. doi:10.1016/0010-0285(73)90004-2

Chiou, J. S., & Spreng, R. A. (1996). The reliability of difference scores: A re-examination. *Journal of Consumer Satisfaction, Dissatisfaction & Complaining Behavior, 9*, 158–167.

Chuderski, A., Taraday, M., Nęcka, E., & Smoleń, T. (2012). Storage capacity explains fluid intelligence but executive control does not. *Intelligence, 40*, 278–295. doi:10.1016/j.intell.2012.02.010

Colom, R., Abad, F. J., Quiroga, M. A., Shih, P. C., & Flores-Mendoza, C. (2008). Working memory and intelligence are highly related constructs, but why? *Intelligence, 36*, 584–606. doi:10.1016/j.intell.2008.01.002

Colom, R., Abad, F. J., Rebollo, I., & Shih, P. C. (2005). Memory span and general intelligence: A latent-variable approach. *Intelligence, 33*, 623–642. doi:10.1016/j.intell.2005.05.006

Conway, A. R., Cowan, N., & Bunting, M. F. (2001). The cocktail party phenomenon revisited: The importance of working memory capacity. *Psychonomic Bulletin & Review, 8*, 331–335. doi:10.3758/bf03196169

Conway, A. R. A., Cowan, N., Bunting, M. F., Therriault, D. J., & Minkoff, S. R. (2002). A latent variable analysis of working memory capacity, short-term memory capacity, processing speed, and general fluid intelligence. *Intelligence, 30*, 163–183. doi:10.1016/s0160-2896(01)00096-4

Conway, A. R., & Engle, R. W. (1994). Working memory and retrieval: A resource-dependent inhibition model. *Journal of Experimental Psychology: General, 123*, 354–373. doi:10.1037//0096-3445.123.4.354

Cowan, N. (1988). Evolving conceptions of memory storage, selective attention, and their mutual constraints within the human information-processing system. *Psychological Bulletin, 104*, 163–191. doi:10.1037/0033-2909.104.2.163

Cowan, N. (1999). An embedded-processes model of working memory. In A. Miyake & P. Shah (Eds.), *Models of working memory: Mechanisms of active maintenance and executive control* (pp. 62–101). New York, NY: Cambridge University Press. doi:10.1017/CBO9781139174909.006

Cowan, N. (2001). The magical number 4 in short-term memory: A reconsideration of mental storage capacity. *Behavioral & Brain Sciences, 24*, 87–185. doi:10.1017/S0140525X01003922

Cowan, N., Elliott, E. M., Saults, J. S., Morey, C. C., Mattox, S., Hismjatullina, A., & Conway, A. R. A. (2005). On the capacity of attention: Its estimation and its role in working memory and cognitive aptitudes. *Cognitive Psychology, 51*, 42–100. doi:10.1016/j.cogpsych.2004.12.001

Coyle, T. (2003). A review of the worst performance rule: Evidence, theory, and alternative hypotheses. *Intelligence, 31*, 567–587. doi:10.1016/s0160-2896(03)00054-0

Craik, F. I., & Bialystok, E. (2006). Cognition through the lifespan: Mechanisms of change. *Trends in Cognitive Sciences, 10*, 131–138. doi:10.1016/j.tics.2006.01.007

Craik, F. I. M., & Lockhart, R. S. (1972). Levels of processing: A framework for memory research. *Journal of Verbal Learning and Verbal Behavior, 11*, 671–684. doi:10.1016/S0022-5371(72)80001-X

Cronbach, L. J. (1957). The two disciplines of scientific psychology. *American Psychologist, 12*, 671–684. doi:10.1037/h0043943

Cronbach, L. J., & Furby, L. (1970). How should we measure "change"—or should we? *Psychological Bulletin, 74*, 68–80. doi:10.1037/h0029382

Crowder, R. G. (1982). The demise of short-term memory. *Acta Psychologica, 50*, 291–323. doi:10.1016/0001-6918(82)90044-0

Daneman, M., & Carpenter, P. A. (1980). Individual differences in working memory and reading. *Journal of Verbal Learning & Verbal Behavior, 19*, 450–466. doi:10.1016/S0022-5371(80)90312-6

Della Sala, S. D., Cowan, N., Beschin, N., & Perini, M. (2005). Just lying there, remembering: Improving recall of prose in amnesic patients with mild cognitive impairment by minimising interference. *Memory, 13*, 435–440. doi:10.1080/09658210344000387

Domnick, F. Zimmer, H. D., Becker, N., & Spinath, H. M. (2018). Is the correlation between storage capacity and matrix reasoning driven by the storage of partial solutions? A pilot study of an experimental approach. *Journal of Intelligence, 5*, 21. doi:10.3390/jintelligence5020021

Donaldson, G. (1983). Confirmatory factor analysis models of information processing stages: An alternative to difference scores. *Quantitative Method in Psychology, 94*, 143–151. doi:10.1037/0033-2909.94.1.143

Donders, F. C. (1969). Over de snelheid van psychische processen. [On the speed of mental processes.] In W. G. Koster (Ed.), *Attention and performance II* (W. G. Koster, Trans.; pp. 412–431). Amsterdam, the Netherlands: North-Holland. (Original work published 1868.)

Draheim, C., Harrison, T. L., Embretson, S. E., & Engle, R. W. (2018). What item response theory can tell us about the complex span tasks. *Psychological Assessment, 30*, 116–129. doi:10.1037/pas0000444

Draheim, C., Hicks, K. L., & Engle, R. W. (2016). Combining reaction time and accuracy: The relationship between working memory capacity and task switching as a case example. *Perspectives on Psychological Science, 11*, 133–155. doi:10.1177/1745691615596990

Draheim, C., Martin, J. D., Tsukahara, J. S., Mashburn, C. A., & Engle, R. W. (2020). Attention control: Its measurement and nature. Manuscript submitted for publication.

Draheim, C., Mashburn, C. A., Martin, J. D., and Engle, R. W. (2019). Reaction time in differential and developmental research: A review of problems and alternatives. *Psychological Bulletin, 45*, 508–535. doi:10.1037/bul0000192

Edwards, J. R. (2001). Ten difference score myths. *Organizational Research Methods, 4*, 265–287. doi:10.1177/109442810143005

Engle, R. W. (2002). Working memory capacity as executive attention. *Current Directions in Psychological Science, 11*, 19–23. doi:10.1111/1467-8721.00160

Engle, R. W. (2018). Working memory and executive attention: A revisit. *Perspectives on Psychological Science, 13*, 190–193. doi:10.1177/1745691617720478

Engle, R. W., & Kane, M. J. (2004). Executive attention, working memorycapacity, and a two-factor theory of cognitive control. In B. Ross (Ed.), *The psychology of learning and motivation* (pp. 145–199). New York, NY: Academic Press.

Engle, R. W., & Martin, J. D. (2019). Is a science of the mind even possible? Reply to Logie (2018). *Journal of Applied Research in Memory and Cognition, 7*, 493–498. doi:10.1016/j.jarmac.2018.10.002

Engle, R. W., & Oransky, N. (1999). The evolution from short-term to working memory: Multi-store to dynamic models of temporary storage. In R. Sternberg (Ed.), *The Nature of Cognition* (pp. 514–555). Cambridge, MA: MIT Press.

Engle, R. W., Tuholski, S. W., Laughlin, J. E. & Conway, A. R. A. (1999). Working memory, short-term memory and general fluid intelligence: A latent variable approach. *Journal of Experimental Psychology: General, 128*, 309–331. doi:10.1037/0096-3445.128.3.309

Everling, S., & Fischer, B. (1998). The antisaccade: A review of basic research and clinical studies. *Neuropsychologia, 36*, 885–889. doi:10.1016/s0028-3932(98)00020-7

Fan, J., McCandliss, B. D., Sommer, T., Raz, A., & Posner, M. I. (2002). Testing the efficiency and independence of attentional networks. *Journal of Cognitive Neuroscience, 14*, 340–347. doi:10.1162/089892902317361886

Festini, S. B., & Reuter-Lorenz, P. A. (2014). Cognitive control of familiarity: Directed forgetting reduces proactive interference in working memory. *Cognitive, Affective, & Behavioral Neuroscience, 14*, 78–89. doi:10.3758/s13415-013-0231-1

Friedman, N. P., & Miyake, A. (2017). Unity and diversity of executive functions: Individual differences as a window on cognitive structure. *Cortex, 86*, 186–204. doi:10.1016/j.cortex.2016.04.023

Fry, A. F., & Hale, S. (1996). Processing speed, working memory, and fluid intelligence: Evidence for a developmental cascade. *Psychological Science, 7*, 237–241. doi:10.1111/j.1467-9280.1996.tb00366.x

Fukuda, K., & Vogel, E. K. (2009). Human variation in overriding attentional capture. *Journal of Neuroscience, 29*, 8726–8733. doi:10.1523/JNEUROSCI.2145-09.2009.

Fukuda, K., & Vogel, E. K. (2011). Individual differences in recovery time from attentional capture. *Psychological Science, 22*, 361–368. doi:10.1177/0956797611398493.

Gathercole, S. E., Alloway, T. P., Kirkwood, H. J., Elliott, J. G., Holmes, J., Hilton, K. A. (2008). Attention and executive function behaviours in children with poor working memory. *Learning and Individual Differences, 18*, 214–233. doi:10.1016/j.lindif.2007.10.003

Gray, S., Green, S., Alt, M., Hogan, T. P., Kuo, T., Brinkley, S., & Cowan, N. (2017). The structure of working memory in young children and its relation to intelligence. *Journal of Memory and Language, 92*, 183–201. doi:10.1016/j.jml.2016.06.004

Greenwald, A. G., & Banaji, M. R. (1995). Implicit social cognition: Attitudes, self-esteem, and stereotypes. *Psychological Review, 102*, 4–27. doi:10.1037//0033-295x.102.1.4

Harrison, T., Shipstead, Z., & Engle, R. W. (2015). Why is working memory capacity related to matrix reasoning tasks? *Memory & Cognition, 43*, 389–396. doi:10.3758/s13421-014-0473-3

Hedge, C., Powell, G., & Sumner, P. (2018). The reliability paradox: Why robust cognitive tasks do not produce reliable individual differences. *Behavior Research Methods, 50*, 1166–1186. doi:10.3758/s13428-017-0935-1

Heitz, R. P. (2014). The speed-accuracy tradeoff: History, physiology, methodology, and behavior. *Frontiers in Neuroscience, 8*, 150. doi:10.3389/fnins.2014.00150

Heitz, R. P., & Engle, R. W. (2007). Focusing the spotlight: Individual differences in visual attention control. *Journal of Experimental Psychology: General, 136*, 217–240. doi:10.1037/0096-3445.136.2.217

Jaeggi, S. M., Buschkuehl, M., Jonides, J., & Perrig, W. J. (2008). Improving fluid intelligence with training on working memory. *Proceedings of the National Academy of Sciences of the United States of America, 105*, 6829–6833. doi:10.1073/pnas.0801268105

Jaeggi, S. M., Buschkuehl, M., Jonides, J., & Shah, P. (2011). Short- and long-term benefits of cognitive training. *Proceedings of the National Academy of Sciences of the United States of America, 108,* 10081–10086. doi:10.1073/pnas.1103228108

Jensen, A. R. (1998). *The g factor: The science of mental ability.* Westport, CT: Praeger Publishers.

Jones, L. B., Rothbart, M. K., & Posner, M. I. (2003). Development of executive attention in preschool children. *Developmental Science, 6,* 498–504. doi:10.1111/1467-7687.00307

Kahneman, D. (2011). *Thinking, fast and slow.* New York, NY: Farrar, Straus and Giroux.

Kane, M. J., Bleckley, M. K., Conway, A. R., & Engle, R. W. (2001). A controlled-attention view of working-memory capacity. *Journal of Experimental Psychology: General, 130,* 169–183. doi:10.1037/0096-3445.130.2.169

Kane, M. J., & Engle, R. W. (2002). The role of prefrontal cortex in working-memory capacity, executive attention, and general fluid intelligence: An individual-differences perspective. *Psychonomic Bulletin & Review, 9,* 637–671. doi:10.3758/bf03196323

Kane, M. J., & Engle, R. W. (2003). Working-memory capacity and the control of attention: The contributions of goal neglect, response competition, and task set to Stroop interference. *Journal of Experimental Psychology: General, 132,* 47–70. doi:10.1037/0096-3445.132.1.47

Kane, H. J., Hambrick, D. Z., & Conway, A. R. A. (2005). Working memory capacity and fluid intelligence are strongly related constructs: Comment on Ackerman, Beier, and Boyle (2005). *Psychological Bulletin, 131,* 66–71. doi:10.1037/0033-2909.131.1.66

Kane, M. J., Hambrick, D. Z., Tuholski, S. W., Wilhelm, O., Payne, T. W. & Engle, R. W. (2004). The generality of working memory capacity: A latent variable approach to verbal and visuospatial memory span and reasoning. *Journal of Experimental Psychology: General, 133,* 189–217. doi:10.1037/0096-3445.133.2.189

Karr, J. E., Arshkenoff, C. N., Rast, P., Hofer, S. M., Iverson, G. L., & Garcia-Barrera, M. (2018). The unity and diversity of executive functions: A systematic review and re-analysis of latent variable studies. *Psychological Bulletin, 144,* 1147–1185. doi:10.1037/bul0000160

Kaufman, A. S., Schneider, W. J., & Kaufman, J. C. (2019). Psychometric approaches to intelligence. In R. J. Sternberg (Ed.), *Human intelligence: An introduction* (pp. 67–103). New York, NY: Cambridge University Press.

Kranzler, J. H., & Jensen, A. R. (1989). Inspection time and intelligence: A meta-analysis. *Intelligence, 13,* 329–347. doi:10.1016/S0160-2896(89)80006-6

Kyllonen, P. C. & Christal, R. E. (1990). Reasoning ability is (little more than) working memory capacity?! *Intelligence, 14,* 389–433. doi:10.1037/0096-3445.132.1.47

La Pointe, L. B., & Engle, R. W. (1990). Simple and complex word spans as measures of working memory capacity. *Journal of Experimental Psychology: Learning, Memory, and Cognition, 16,* 1118–1133. doi:10.1037/0278-7393.16.6.1118

Li, S., Hämmerer, D., Müller, V., Hommel, B., & Lindenberger, U. (2009). Lifespan development of stimulus-response conflict cost: Similarities and differences between maturation and senescence. *Psychological Research, 73,* 777–785. doi:10.1007/s00426-008-0190-2

Lopez, N., Previc, F. H., Fischer, J., Heitz, R. P., & Engle, R. W. (2012). Effects of sleep deprivation on cognitive performance by United States Air Force pilots. *Journal of Applied Research in Memory and Cognition, 1,* 27–33. doi:10.1016/j.jarmac.2011.10.002

Luck, S. J., & Vogel, E. K. (1997). The capacity of visual working memory for features and conjunctions. *Nature, 390,* 279–281. doi:10.1038/36846

Martin, J. D., Shipstead, Z., Harrison, T., Redick, T. S., Bunting, M., & Engle, R. W. (2020). The role of maintenance and disengagement in predicting reading comprehension and vocabulary learning. *Journal of Experimental Psychology: Learning, Memory, and Cognition, 46,* 140–154. doi:10.1037/xlm0000705

McCabe, D. P., Roediger, H. L., McDaniel, M. A., Balota, D. A., & Hambrick, D. Z. (2010). The relationship between working memory capacity and executive functioning: Evidence for a common executive attention construct. *Neuropsychology, 24,* 222–243. doi:10.1037/a0017619

Meier, M. E., Smeekens, B. A., Silvia, P. J., Kwapil, T. R., & Kane, M. J. (2018). Working memory capacity and the antisaccade task: A microanalytic-macronalytic investigation of individual differences in goal activation and maintenance. *Journal of Experimental Psychology: Learning, Memory, and Cognition, 44,* 68–84. doi:10.1037/xlm0000431

Miller, J., & Ulrich, R. (2013). Mental chronometry and individual differences: Modeling reliabilities and correlations of reaction time means and effect sizes. *Psychonomic Bulletin & Review*, *20*, 819–858. doi:10.3758/s13423-013-0404-5

Miyake, A., Friedman, N. P., Emerson, M. J., Witzki, A. H., Howerter, A., & Wager, T. D. (2000). The unity and diversity of executive functions and their contributions to complex "frontal lobe" tasks: A latent variable analysis. *Cognitive Psychology*, *41*, 49–100. doi:10.1006/cogp.1999.0734

Norman, D. A., & Shallice, T. (1986). Attention to action: Willed and automatic control of behavior. In R. J. Davidson, G. E. Schwartz & D. Shapiro (Eds.), *Consciousness and Self-Regulation: Advances in research and theory* (pp. 1–18). Boston, MA: Springer. doi:10.1007/978-1-4757-0629-1_1

Nairne, J. S. (2002). Remembering over the short-term: The case against the standard model. *Annual Review of Psychology*, *53*, 53–81. doi:10.1146/annurev.psych.53.100901.135131

Oberauer, K. (2002). Access to information in working memory: Exploring the focus of attention. *Journal of Experimental Psychology: Learning, Memory, and Cognition*, *28*, 411–421. doi:10.1037/0278-7393.28.3.411

Oberauer, K., Süß, H., Wilhelm, O., & Sander, N. (2007). Individual differences in working memory capacity and reasoning ability. *Variation in Working Memory*, 49–75. doi:10.1093/acprof:oso/9780195168648.003.0003

Paap, K. R., & Sawi, O. (2016). The role of test–retest reliability in measuring individual and group differences in executive functioning. *Journal of Neuroscience Methods*, *274*, 81–93. doi:10.1016/j.jneumeth.2016.10.002

Perfetti, C.A., & Lesgold, A.M. (1977). Discourse comprehension and sources of individual differences. In M. A. Just & P.A. Carpenter (Eds.), *Cognitive processes in comprehension* (pp. 141–183). Hillsdale, NJ: Erlbaum.

Perry, W., Heaton, R. K., Potterat, E., Roebuck, T., Minassian, A., & Braff, D. L. (2001). Working memory in schizophrenia: Transient 'online' storage versus executive functioning. *Schizophrenia Bulletin*, *27*, 157–176. doi:10.1093/oxfordjournals.schbul.a006854

Rabbitt, P. (1996). Do individual differences in speed reflect "global" or "local" differences in mental abilities? *Intelligence*, *22*, 69–88. doi:10.1016/s0160-2896(96)90021-5

Redick, T. S., Shipstead, Z., Harrison, T. L., Hicks, K. L., Fried, D. E., Hambrick, D. Z., … Engle, R. W. (2013). No evidence of intelligence improvement after working memory training: A randomized, placebo-controlled study. *Journal of Experimental Psychology: General*, *142*, 359–379. doi:10.1037/a0029082

Redick, T. S., Shipstead, Z., Meier, M. E., Montroy, J. J., Hicks, K. L., Unsworth, N., … & Engle, R. W. (2016). Cognitive predictors of a common multitasking ability: Contributions from working memory, attention control, and fluid intelligence. *Journal of Experimental Psychology: General*, *145*, 1473–1492. doi:10.1037/xge0000219

Redick, T. S., Unsworth, N., Kelly, A. J., Engle, R. W. (2012). Faster, smarter? Working memory capacity and perceptual speed in relation to fluid intelligence. *Journal of Cognitive Psychology*, *24*, 844–854. doi:10.1080/20445911.2012.704359

Reed, T., & Jensen, A. R. (1992). Conduction velocity in a brain nerve pathway of normal adults correlates with intelligence level. *Intelligence*, *16*, 259–272. doi:10.1016/0160-2896(92)90009-g

Rey-Mermet, A., Gade, M., & Oberauer, K. (2018). Should we stop thinking about inhibition? Searching for individual and age differences in inhibition ability. *Journal of Experimental Psychology: Learning, Memory, and Cognition*, *44*, 501–526. doi:10.1037/xlm0000450

Rey-Mermet, A., Gade, M., Souza, A. S., von Bastian, C. C., & Oberauer, K. (2019). Is executive control related to working memory capacity and fluid intelligence? *Journal of Experimental Psychology: General*, *148*, 1335–1372. doi:10.1037/xge0000593

Roberts, R. J., Hager, L. D., & Heron, C. (1994). Prefrontal cognitive processes: Working memory and inhibition in the antisaccade task. *Journal of Experimental Psychology: General*, *123*, 374–393. doi:10.1037/0096-3445.123.4.374

Rosen, V. M., & Engle, R. W. (1997). The role of working memory capacity in retrieval. *Journal of Experimental Psychology: General*, *126*, 211–227. doi:10.1037/0096-3445.126.3.211

Rouder, J. N., & Haaf, J. M. (2019). A psychometrics of individual differences in experimental tasks. *Psychonomic Bulletin & Review*, *26*, 452–467. doi:10.3758/s13423-018-1558-y

Rueda, M. R. (2018). Attention in the heart of intelligence. *Trends in Neuroscience and Education, 13,* 26–33. doi:10/1016/j.tine.2018.11.003

Salthouse, T. A., & Babcock, R. L. (1991). Decomposing adult age differences in working memory. *Developmental Psychology, 27,* 763–776. doi:10.1037/0012-1649.27.5.763

Salthouse, T. A., & Pink, J. E. (2008). Why is working memory related to fluid intelligence? *Psychonomic Bulletin & Review, 15,* 364–371. doi:10.3758/pbr.15.2.364

Shah, P., & Miyake, A. (1996). The separability of working memory resources for spatial thinking and language processing: An individual differences approach. *Journal of Experimental Psychology: General, 125,* 4–27. doi:10.1037/0096-3445.125.1.4

Shipstead, Z., & Engle, R. W. (2013). Interference within the focus of attention: Working memory tasks reflect more than temporary maintenance. *Journal of Experimental Psychology: Learning, Memory, and Cognition, 39,* 277–289. doi:10.1037/a0028467

Shipstead, Z., Harrison, T. L., & Engle, R. W. (2016). Working memory capacity and fluid intelligence: Maintenance and disengagement. *Perspectives on Psychological Science, 11,* 771–799. doi:10.1177/1745691616650647

Shipstead, Z., Lindsey, D. R., Marshall, R. L., & Engle, R. W. (2014). The mechanisms of working memory capacity: Primary memory, secondary memory, and attention control. *Journal of Memory and Language, 72,* 116–141. doi:10.1016/j.jml.2014.01.004

Shipstead, Z., Redick, T. S., Hicks, K. L., & Engle, R. W. (2012). The scope and control of attention as separate aspects of working memory. *Memory, 20,* 608–628. doi:10.1080/09658211.2012.691519

Schubert, A. (2019). A meta-analysis of the worst performance rule. *Intelligence, 73,* 88–100. doi:10.1016/j.intell.2019.02.003

Smith, S. M. (2003). The constraining effects of initial ideas. In P. B. Paulus & B. A. Nijstad (Eds.), *Group creativity: Innovation through collaboration* (pp. 15–31). New York, NY: Oxford University Press. doi:10.1093/acprof:oso/9780195147308.003.0002

Spelke, E., Hirst, W., & Neisser, U. (1976). Skills of divided attention. *Cognition, 4,* 215–230. doi:10.1016/0010-0277(76)90018-4

Stankov, L., & Roberts, R. D. (1997). Mental speed is not the 'basic' process of intelligence. *Personality and Individual Differences, 22,* 69–84. doi:10.1016/S0191-8869(96)00163-8

Starns, J. J., & Ratcliff, R. (2010). The effects of aging on the speed–accuracy compromise: Boundary optimality in the diffusion model. *Psychology and Aging, 25,* 377–390. doi:10.1037/a0018022

Sternberg, S. (1969). The discovery of processing stages: Extensions of Donders' method. *Acta Psychologica, 30,* 276–315. doi:10.1016/0001-6918(69)90055-9.

Stroop, J. R. (1935). Studies of interference in serial verbal reactions. *Journal of Experimental Psychology, 18,* 643–662. doi:10.1037/h0054651

Turner, M. L., & Engle, R. W. (1989). Is working memory capacity task dependent? *Journal of Memory and Language, 28,* 127–154. doi:10.1016/0749-596X(89)90040-5

Trafimow, D. (2015). A defense against the alleged unreliability of difference scores. *Cogent Mathematics, 2,* 1064626. doi:10.1080/23311835.2015.1064626

Tulving, E., & Colotla, V. A. (1970). Free recall of trilingual lists. *Cognitive Psychology, 1,* 86–98. doi:10.1016/0010-0285(70)90006-X

Underwood, G. (1974). Moray vs. the rest: The effects of extended shadowing practice. *Quarterly Journal of Experimental Psychology, 26,* 368–372. doi:10.1080/14640747408400426

Unsworth, N., & Engle, R. W. (2005). Working memory capacity and fluid abilities: Examining the correlation between operation span and Raven. *Intelligence, 33,* 67–81. doi:10.1016/j.intell.2004.08.003

Unsworth, N., & Engle, R. W. (2006). Simple and complex memory spans and their relation to fluid abilities: Evidence from list-length effects. *Journal of Memory and Language, 54,* 68–80. doi:10.1016/j.jml.2005.06.003

Unsworth, N., & Engle, R. W. (2007a). The nature of individual differences in working memory capacity: Active maintenance in primary memory and controlled search from secondary memory. *Psychological Review, 114,* 104–132. doi:10.1037/0033-295X.114.1.104

Unsworth, N., & Engle, R. W. (2007b). On the division of short-term and working memory: An examination of simple and complex span and their relation to higher order ability. *Psychological Bulletin, 133,* 1038–1066. doi:10.1037/0033-2909.133.6.1038

Unsworth, N., Schrock, J. C., & Engle, R. W. (2004). Working memory capacity and the antisaccade task: Individual differences in voluntary saccade control. *Journal of Experimental Psychology: Learning, Memory, and Cognition, 30*, 1302–1321. doi:10.1037/0278-7393.30.6.1302

Vogel, E. K., McCollough, A. W., & Machizawa, M. G. (2005). Neural measures reveal individual differences in controlling access to working memory. *Nature, 438*, 500–503.

Waugh, N. C., & Norman, D. A. (1965). Primary memory. *Psychological Review, 72*, 89–104. doi:10.1037/h0021797

Wickelgren, W. A. (1977). Speed–accuracy tradeoffs and information processing dynamics. *Acta Psychologica, 41*, 67–85. doi:10.1016/0001-6918(77)90012-9

Wilhelm, O., Hildebrandt, A., & Oberauer, K. (2013). What is working memory capacity, and how can we measure it? *Frontiers in Psychology, 4*, 433. doi:10.3389/fpsyg.2013.00433

Wu, T., Dufford, A. J., Egan, L. J., Mackie, M., Chen, C., Yuan, C., . . . & Fan, J. (2018). Hick-Hyman law is mediated by the cognitive control network in the brain. *Cerebral Cortex, 28*, 2267–2282. doi:10.1093/cerecor/bhx127

8

Working Memory and Expertise

An Ecological Perspective

David Z. Hambrick, Alexander P. Burgoyne, and Duarte Araujo

Fifty years ago, Baddeley and Hitch (1974) began their seminal *Psychology of Learning and Motivation* article by lamenting that '[d]espite more than a decade of intensive research on the topic of short-term memory (STM), we still know virtually nothing about its role in normal human information processing' (p. 47). Baddeley and Hitch were referring specifically to the *short-term store* in Atkinson and Shiffrin's (1968) stage theory of memory. Baddeley and Hitch (1974) pointed out that a number of findings contradicted the assumption that the short-term store serves as a working memory for higher-level cognition, and, as such, a bottleneck on information processing and critical determinant of performance in complex cognitive tasks. For example, drawing on the neuropsychological literature, they noted that a person with brain damage could show grossly impaired short-term memory performance, and yet have intact learning, memory, and comprehension.

To better account for such findings, Baddeley and Hitch proposed that the working memory system includes both a flexible 'workspace' and a component dedicated to information storage. Subsequently, expanding on this idea, Baddeley (1986) proposed a *multicomponent model of working memory* comprising an attention-controlling *central executive*, along with a *phonological loop* for rehearsing and storing speech-based information and a *visuospatial sketchpad* for manipulating visual images. The model had an enormous impact on the field, inspiring generations of working memory researchers. It also set the stage for research on individual differences in *working memory capacity* (WMC).[1] Daneman and Carpenter (1980) introduced the first assessment of WMC: the *reading span task*. Designed to measure the trade-off between storage and processing, the goal for participants is to read a series of sentences, judging whether each makes sense, while remembering the final word of each sentence for later recall. Daneman and Carpenter reported high positive correlations between scores in the reading span task and various measures of language comprehension. Later, Turner and Engle (1986) introduced the *operation span task* (solving mathematical equations while remembering words); in turn, Shah and Miyake (1996) introduced the *rotation span*

---

[1] A note on terminology: we use *working memory capacity* (WMC) to refer to an individual-difference construct, and *working memory* to refer to the cognitive system and to tasks used to measure WMC.

David Z. Hambrick, Alexander P. Burgoyne, and Duarte Araujo, *Working Memory and Expertise* In: *Working Memory.*
Edited by: Robert H. Logie, Valérie Camos, and Nelson Cowan, Oxford University Press (2021). © Oxford University Press.
DOI: 10.1093/oso/9780198842286.003.0008

Table 8.1 Summary responses to designated questions

Question	Response
1. How do you define working memory?	In the spirit of Boring (1923), we define working memory capacity (WMC) as whatever is measured by the psychological instruments that the field can agree to call working memory tasks. We are agnostic about which theory and definition of working memory is the 'right' one. Taking an ecological perspective, we view working memory *performance* in terms of the relationship between the person (including knowledge, skills, and abilities) and the environment (including objects and other affordances).
2. What methods do you use in your research?	We use both correlational and experimental methods in our research, and methods that combine these approaches. The strength of the correlational method is that it allows us to investigate predictors of complex cognition that are difficult, if not impossible, to experimentally manipulate (e.g. training over a decade); the weakness is that these predictors may be confounded with other variables (e.g. training with aptitude). The strength of the experimental method is that it controls for confounding variables; the weakness is that not every variable of interest can be experimentally manipulated in the laboratory.
3. Is working memory unitary or non-unitary?	We are not sure whether the working memory system should be considered unitary or non-unitary. As applied cognitive psychologists, what interests us is that WMC, as measured by tasks that require the participant to maintain information over a relatively short period of time, correlates with success in complex real-world tasks. Our goal is to understand how this attribute influences performance.
4. What is the role of attention in working memory?	We think of attention as what is measured by the broad class of tasks in which the participant must respond to one stimulus among multiple stimuli (e.g. the flanker task), and one of many hypothetical constructs that could contribute to individual differences in WMC as measured by working memory tasks.
5. How is information encoded in WM, and how is the information retained?	We do not know, exactly, but we view attention as a hypothetical construct involved in selecting information for further processing.
6. The role of long-term memory knowledge in working memory storage and processing	Knowledge stored in long-term memory supports the storage and processing of information in working memory. In a particular task domain, knowledge may, under certain conditions, enable performers to bypass performance limitations associated with temporary maintenance of task-relevant information.
7. Is there evidence that is not consistent with your perspective and how you respond to that challenge?	Our perspective assumes that WMC reflects a general cognitive ability that is important for real-world cognition. It has been argued that the influence of WMC decreases as a function of increasing expertise (e.g. Ericsson, 2014), but in reality, evidence for this possibility is weak (see, e.g. Hambrick, Burgoyne, & Oswald, 2019). We speculate that the influence of WMC on complex task performance decreases in some types of tasks (e.g. tasks with unchanging rules and predictable environments) but not in others (e.g. tasks with changing rules and unpredictable environments).
8. Working memory applications	Scores on working memory tasks may be used to predict people's future performance in applied settings such as the workplace. However, experts can also devise mechanisms to minimize the role of working memory in their workplace by strategically offloading processing demands to the environment. Prediction of real-world performance will be maximized by considering the structure of the task environment.

task (judging whether letters are mirror-imaged while remembering the orientation of each) to assess visuospatial working memory.

Measures of performance from 'complex span' tasks such as these were shown to correlate with measures of higher-level cognition, including learning, reasoning, problem-solving, and comprehension (e.g. Conway, Cowan, Bunting, Therriault, & Minkoff, 2002; Daneman & Carpenter, 1980; Engle, Carullo, & Collins, 1991). At the same time, it is difficult to say what, exactly, complex span tasks measure because they are *complex*. To put it another way, complex span tasks suffer from the 'task impurity problem'. This is the observation that no cognitive task measures only the construct of interest (Burgess, 1997; Phillips, 1997). The task *may* measure that construct, but it *will* measure other constructs. As a case in point, the operation span task measures not only the ability to simultaneously store and process information, but skill in arithmetic and perhaps even math anxiety, not to mention state-like variables such as motivation, sleep deprivation, and fatigue.

Given the task impurity problem, other procedures were designed to collect better measures of WMC. In the Luck and Vogel (1997) visual arrays task (modelled after Phillips, 1974), the participant sees an array of objects (e.g. coloured squares). The array disappears and is replaced by a visual mask, after which a new array appears, which is the same as the original array or different in one item. The participant's task is to indicate with a keypress whether the arrays are the same or different; WMC is indexed by the k parameter, representing the number of objects that the participant can successfully remember. As another example, in Cowan and colleagues' running span (modelled after Pollack, Johnson, & Knaff, 1959), the participant listens to a series of digits, presented at a rapid rate (e.g. four per second). The list stops after a random number of digits, and the participant's task is to recall as many of the digits as possible, from the end of the list backwards.

Working memory tasks are now used in laboratories around the world. As just one indication of the popularity of these tasks, a 'user's guide' to complex span tasks has been cited over twenty-three hundred times (Conway et al., 2005). As described in other chapters in this book, recent research on working memory has focused on identifying factors that give rise to individual differences in measures of performance from these tasks, and relatedly, what explains correlations between the measures and various outcomes. The Baddeley–Hitch multicomponent model has remained influential in this research (e.g. Baddeley & Logie, 1999; Logie, 2016), but other theoretical perspectives on working memory have emerged. In his *embedded-processes model*, Cowan (1988) proposed that working memory is an ensemble of components that hold information in an available state for ongoing processing (see chapter by Cowan, Morey, & Naveh-Benjamin, 2021), while Engle (2002) argued that WMC reflects the action of attention to maintain activation of goals and other information relevant to a task and to suppress activation of irrelevant information. Taking a different approach altogether, Ericsson and Kintsch (1995) proposed that the working memory system comprises long-term memory retrieval structures that enable the individual to efficiently store and retrieve information. According to this view, individual differences in WMC reflect acquired skills rather than domain-general aspects of the cognitive system.

We are agnostic about which of these theories of working memory is the 'right' one (see Table 8.1 for our answers to eight of the questions asked of contributors to this volume). In the spirit of Boring (1923), who famously wrote that 'intelligence is what the tests test', we define WMC as whatever is measured by tasks that involve maintaining information over a relatively short period of time. We are also agnostic on the question of whether the working memory system is unitary or non-unitary. As applied cognitive psychologists, what interests us is what is indisputable at this point: the diverse collection of instruments that the field calls 'working memory' tasks capture something that correlates with success in real-world tasks. Using a combination of psychometric and experimental methods, our aim is to understand how measures from these tasks predict complex task performance, in the context of other predictor variables and under different task and situational demands.

On a related note, we think that research on working memory has been myopic in two ways. First, most studies focusing on the role of WMC in complex cognition focus *only* on WMC. Yet this cognitive ability factor—however it is conceptualized and measured—cannot reasonably be expected to explain all, nearly all, or even most of the variance in the real-world outcomes that it is believed to underpin. (Single-variable explanations, while appealing in their parsimony, almost never fully account for complex phenomena.) Furthermore, the effect of WMC on complex cognition may vary depending on the level of other factors that predict performance. Thus, research that ignores these other factors oversimplifies the role of WMC in complex cognition.

The second way that research on working memory has been myopic is that it has largely ignored the environment as a determinant of complex cognition. As proposed in the 1950s by J. J. Gibson, the *ecological view* of human perception and performance argues that psychological phenomena arise from the individual's direct perception of the environment, namely *affordances*: the actions permitted by an object, place, or event, according to the characteristics (the anthropometry, the skill, etc.) of the individual (see Michaels & Carello, 1981, for an overview). This view argues that psychological phenomena can be explained without recourse to mediating mental representations. That is, in contrast to a constructivist view, in which perceivers are hypothesized to contribute substantially to perceptual processes by way of enrichment, inference, and induction (i.e. knowledge-based influences), the direct perception view holds that perceptual phenomena are rich because the information the environment provides is rich (i.e. mental elaboration is not required; Michaels & Carello, 1981). The ecological view holds that perceivers are active investigators of their environment: if the information provided is insufficient, the perceiver acts to yield more information.

We do not aim to propose a strict Gibsonian view of working memory in this chapter. Rather, in the spirit of Gibson, we argue that it is important to recognize the role of the environment in performance in tasks and situations that are assumed to involve the working memory system. Tasks and situations capture specific arrangements of the environment. As a result, the cognitive mechanisms that support performance in one task are likely to differ from those that support performance in another task, regardless of the correlation observed between performance in the two. In other words, a high correlation between tasks does not necessarily imply that the same cognitive mechanisms are responsible for performance. The relative importance of different abilities may change based on the specific task and situation at hand. To illustrate by analogy, if one wants to understand whether a particular race car is likely to win a particular race, it is not enough to know about the characteristics of the car—the engine, the suspension, the tyres, and so on. One must also know about the environment—the type of track and its conditions—and the suitability of the car's characteristics for this environment, not to mention those of the driver. The winning car will be one that is optimally configured for the track. In the same way, the level of performance that a person exhibits in the 'wild'—that is, when performing tasks in their natural habitats—reflects characteristics of the performer such as WMC, but also whether the task environment affords active perception of the particularities of the task and the use of specialized knowledge that the performer has acquired to cope with the demands of the task (for a review of an ecological approach to cognition applied to real-word tasks, specifically in sports, see Araújo, Hristovski, Seifert, Carvalho, & Davids, 2019).

In this chapter, we discuss this idea in terms of a complementary relationship between the *person* and the *environment*. We focus our discussion of the person on contents of the mind, including domain-general abilities and capacities, as well as domain-specific knowledge and skills. The environment includes the world outside of the person's mind. Our ultimate argument is simply that both the person and environment need to be considered in explaining working memory performance, even though the focus has traditionally been on the former.

The Person

A major goal of research on human intelligence is to elucidate the structure of mental abilities: their relationships to each other and their organization in a 'nomological network' of statistical factors. The most widely replicated finding in this research (and perhaps any area of psychological research) is that there is a general factor of intelligence—psychometric *g*. As first documented and described by Charles Spearman (1904) well over a century ago, *g* reflects the fact that scores on diverse tests of cognitive ability correlate positively with each other. A person who does well on one test of cognitive ability will tend to do better on other tests of cognitive ability, and when the measures are entered into a factor analysis, the first factor accounts for much more of the variance in scores than subsequent factors.

Another bedrock finding from intelligence research is that there are *group factors* 'beneath' *g*. That is, while all measures of cognitive ability tend to correlate positively with each other, certain types of cognitive measures correlate more highly with each other than with other types of cognitive measures. At the broadest level, there is a group factor for tests of reasoning, memory, visualization, problem-solving, and so on that measure the efficiency and effectiveness of cognition at the time of assessment, and a separate group factor for tests that reflect knowledge and skills acquired through experience. These group factors have been labelled, variously, as *Intelligence A* and *Intelligence B* (Hebb, 1942); *fluid ability* (Gf) and *crystallized ability* (Gc) (Cattell, 1943); *cognitive mechanics* and *cognitive pragmatics* (Baltes, 1987); *intelligence-as-process* and *intelligence-as-product* (Ackerman, 1996); and *process cognition* and *product cognition* (Salthouse, 2000).

While the basic structure of human intelligence is now firmly established—a g factor subsuming group factors (Carroll, 1993)—the question of what these factors reflect at the level of the cognitive system has never been satisfactorily answered. Beginning in the 1980s, there was a great deal of enthusiasm for the idea that WMC is the mechanism underlying individual differences in intelligence—and especially Gf. This hypothesis was supported by the finding of very high correlations between Gf and WMC from studies that used structural equation modelling to estimate these factors at the level of latent variables. Kyllonen and Christal (1990) administered reasoning tests and working memory tests to samples of military personnel, and found strong positive correlations ($rs = 0.80$–0.90) between WMC and Gf. Kyllonen and Christal concluded that 'reasoning ability is little more than working memory capacity' (p. 389). Even more boldly, Kyllonen (2002) claimed, 'we have our answer to the question of what g is. It is working memory capacity' (p. 433).

However, subsequent research revealed that the relationship between WMC and Gf was weaker than these estimates indicated, but still robust. For example, Kane et al. (2004) found that a common factor extracted from a battery of working memory and short-term memory tasks correlated 0.64 with a Gf factor comprising 12 measures of reasoning ability. Subsequently, in a meta-analysis, Ackerman, Beier, and Boyle (2005) estimated the correlation between WMC and a measure of Gf (Raven's) at 0.50, and in latent variable analyses of studies from that meta-analysis, the correlation between Gf and WMC was estimated at 0.72 (Kane, Hambrick, & Conway, 2005) and 0.85 (Oberauer, Schulze, Wilhelm, & Süß, 2005). It now seems clear that the relationship between WMC and Gf is strong, but less than 1.0.

Other research has taken a more reductionistic approach to understand the mechanisms underlying variation in WMC. Work by Engle and colleagues exemplifies this approach. In a series of studies, they showed that participants pre-selected on working memory span (typically operation span) differ under some task conditions but not others. In particular, 'high spans' (typically ≥ 75th percentile) tended to outperform 'low spans' (typically ≤ 25th percentile) under conditions that placed a premium on controlled attention to manage distraction or interference, but less so under conditions in which the task could be performed via automatic processes. For example, Unsworth, Schrock, and Engle (2004) found that high spans were better able than low spans to control their saccadic eye movements in a task in which the goal was to direct eye movements away from a salient stimulus (a flash on the screen). By comparison, high spans and low spans did not differ when told to direct eye movements towards the stimulus. As another example, Kane and Engle (2000) found that high spans and low spans performed equivalently when recalling list items after a filled delay, but only on the first trial. On successive trials, and as proactive interference built up, low spans showed progressively worse recall.

In one of our own studies (Burgoyne, Hambrick, & Altmann, 2019), we tested the hypothesis that people high in WMC are more successful at solving complex problems because they can temporarily maintain more problem-relevant information (e.g. goals, hypotheses, and partial solutions) in an active state (Unsworth, Fukuda, Awh, & Vogel, 2014). This hypothesis predicts that as the capacity demand of reasoning problems increases, the correlation between WMC and reasoning performance will also increase. Participants ($N = 256$) completed tests of WMC (operation span, symmetry span, and visual arrays) and a test of reasoning ability (Raven's Advanced Progressive Matrices). The reasoning problems were categorized by their capacity demand (i.e. the number of rule tokens required to solve them; Carpenter, Just, & Shell, 1990).

The results revealed that the association between WMC and reasoning performance did not increase as the capacity demand of the reasoning problems increased (Fig. 8.1). This was true even after accounting for restriction of range on the reasoning problems and separately examining the complex span measures (operation span and symmetry span) and visual arrays. Similar results were found by Unsworth and Engle (2005) and Wiley, Jarosz, Cushen, and Colflesh (2011), suggesting that the shared variance between working memory and Gf is not attributable to the number of goals or partial solutions that can be held in working memory.

Another perspective on individual differences in WMC was proposed by Ericsson and Kintsch (1995). They argued that when performing tasks such as reading or mathematics, people maintain access to task-relevant information not by holding it in the

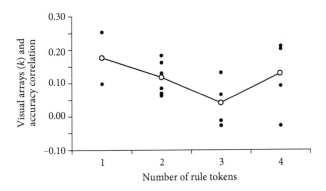

Fig. 8.1 The correlation between WMC (k from the visual arrays task) and reasoning performance as a function of the capacity demand of the reasoning items. Open circles (connected by the solid line) represent the average point-biserial correlations between visual arrays (k) and solution accuracy for Raven's items. The filled circles represent individual point-biserial correlations between visual arrays (k) and accuracy on each Raven's item.

Reproduced from Alexander P. Burgoyne, David Z. Hambrick, and Erik M. Altmann, 'Is working memory capacity a causal factor in fluid intelligence?', *Psychonomic Bulletin & Review*, 26, pp. 1333–1339, https://doi.org/10.3758/s13423-019-01606-9 Copyright © 2019, Springer Nature.

capacity-limited 'transient portion' of working memory (i.e. short-term working memory), but by encoding it into *retrieval structures* (i.e. long-term working memory (LT-WM)). Thus, in this theory, the limiting factor in complex cognition is assumed to be acquired skills rather than general capacities.

Inconsistent with this skill-based account of WMC, scores on working memory tasks that use different procedures and stimuli correlate moderately and positively with each other (e.g. Cowan et al., 2005). It should also be noted that LT-WM theory is under-specified, posing issues for falsifiability. That is, Ericsson and Kintsch (1995) were vague on important aspects of their theory, such as the nature of the hierarchical retrieval structures that are posited to support expert memory, the amount of time needed to encode information within retrieval structures, and the probability of elaborating on schemas stored in long-term memory (Gobet, 1998). These ambiguities have led some researchers to supply their own specifications for these parameters (e.g. Gobet, 2000), discovering from simulations that substantively different predictions emerge depending on the parameters used.

Furthermore, recent empirical findings directly contradict predictions of the LT-WM theory, as well as those predictions that can be divined from the theory. For example, Ericsson and Kintsch (1995) claimed that the transient portion of working memory is unnecessary for text comprehension, stating that 'reading can be completely disrupted for over 30 s with no observable impairment of subsequent text comprehension' (Ericsson & Kintsch, 1995, p. 232). Foroughi, Werner, Barragán, and Boehm-Davis (2015) tested this claim and found that interruptions were disruptive to comprehension. Subsequently, Foroughi, Barragán, and Boehm-Davis (2016) found that the degree of interruption was significantly larger for low- than for high-WMC participants, as assessed by operation span. Thus, contrary to Ericsson and Kintsch's (1995) LT-WM theory, there is now evidence that maintaining information in the 'transient' (i.e. active) portion of working memory is important for comprehension.

The current state of research on individual differences in WMC can be summed by stating that working memory tasks measure domain-general factors (mental processes and/or components) that are important for a wide range of higher-level cognitive tasks. It remains unclear what these factors are, but there are a few viable possibilities. One is the ability to control attention (see Mashburn, Tsukahara, & Engle, 2021); another is the amount of information one can maintain in an active state; and another is the retrieval from secondary memory of information (Unsworth et al., 2014). Any (or all) of these factors may contribute to individual differences in WMC and its relationship with outcomes. Less viable is the view that scores on assessments of WMC derive their predictive power from domain-specific skills, applicable to a narrow range of tasks.

What Else Matters?

Research aimed at elucidating primitives underlying individual differences in WMC is critical for a mechanistic understanding of the construct. However, as we already mentioned, this research has seldom considered the influence of other factors that may influence performance. The issue here is analogous to the assumption underlying subtractive factors logic in experimental design, which is that factors influence the dependent variable independently (Donders, 1969; Friston et al., 1996). In the same way, when a researcher focuses on the effect of a single predictor variable (e.g. working memory capacity) on an outcome variable (e.g. problem-solving), the implicit assumption is that the predictor–outcome relationship will be unaffected by other potential predictor variables. Yet, this assumption may not be reasonable, on either theoretical or empirical grounds—which is to say that there may be ample reason to think that these other factors will influence the predictor–outcome relationship.

In our own research, we have focused on the interplay between WMC and another major determinant of performance: *domain-specific knowledge.* As distinct from *cultural knowledge* (e.g. knowledge of the history of one's country) and *everyday knowledge* (e.g. how to brew a pot of coffee), domain knowledge refers to the perceptions, skills, heuristics, and strategies that people acquire through experience with a particular task (or class of task). As an example, in piano, domain knowledge includes the declarative and procedural knowledge that pianists use to read and interpret music, and place and move their hands on the keyboard to produce music.

Domain knowledge is an important determinant of expertise: a person's stable level of skill in some task. In fact, many tasks cannot be performed *at all* without some amount of domain-specific knowledge. A person must have learned the rules of chess to play the game. Similarly, as the first author of this chapter learned while visiting Great Britain, a game of cricket is incomprehensible for the spectator who knows nothing about the sport. Not surprisingly, then, domain knowledge is an important predictor of individual differences in performance on complex tasks. To put it another way, a major factor in explaining why some people perform better on complex cognitive tasks than others is simply knowledge.

As the classic example of this point, Chase and Simon (1973) had a novice, intermediate, and master chess player attempt to reproduce chess positions after memorizing them for only 5 seconds. The master chess player demonstrated superior memory for legal game positions, but when random (i.e. scrambled) game positions were used, the master's memory performance was only negligibly better than the novice's. In one of our own studies, we found that knowledge of obscure terms such as *aril* (a seed covering) and *etui* (a needle case), which are frequently referenced in crossword puzzles (but seldom elsewhere), accounted for a very large amount of the variance in people's success in solving crossword puzzles in *The New York Times* (e.g. Hambrick, Salthouse, & Meinz, 1999).

In short, knowledge is 'power' in complex cognition. Our research has focused on characterizing the interplay between WMC and domain knowledge in complex cognitive tasks using two methodological approaches. The first approach is a *differential approach*, which asks how WMC and domain-specific knowledge interact with each other in the prediction of performance in some task. We have focused specifically on testing

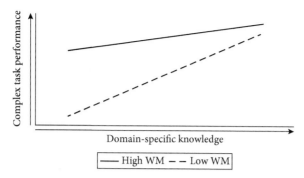

Fig. 8.2 The interaction between WMC and domain-specific knowledge on complex task performance predicted by the circumvention-of-limits hypothesis. WM, working memory.

what we call the *circumvention-of-limits hypothesis* (Hambrick & Meinz, 2011). This hypothesis holds that as performers acquire domain knowledge through training, it becomes possible to circumvent or 'bypass' general constraints on performance such as WMC. As illustrated in Fig. 8.2, the hypothesis predicts an under-additive interaction between WMC and domain knowledge, such that the effect of WMC on performance is smaller at high levels of domain knowledge than at lower levels. Alternatively, if domain knowledge is treated as a group variable (i.e. low knowledge vs high knowledge), then the prediction is a larger correlation between WMC and performance in the low knowledge group than in a high knowledge group.

The circumvention-of-limits hypothesis is appealing because it implies that performance limitations stemming from WMC can be overcome with training. That said, there is little evidence to support this hypothesis (see a summary of evidence in Table 8.2). Hambrick and Engle (2002) had participants with a wide range of knowledge about the game of baseball listen to and attempt to remember information from fictitious (but realistic sounding) radio broadcasts of baseball games, including the sequence of events in each half-inning (i.e. which bases were occupied after each at-bat), as well as game-relevant details (e.g. the batting averages of the players) and non-game-relevant details (e.g. the size of the crowd). Effects of WMC and baseball knowledge were additive when predicting memory for game sequences, and over-additive when predicting memory for game-relevant details. Thus, there was no evidence that a high level of domain-specific knowledge attenuated, much less eliminated, the effect of WMC on memory performance.

A few studies have tested the circumvention-of-limits hypothesis in the domain of aviation. In a sample of 86 pilots with a wide range of experience and skill, Morrow, Menard, Stine-Morrow, Teller, and Bryant (2001) found that a cognitive ability composite based on WMC, perceptual speed, and visuospatial ability positively predicted aviation-related performance (i.e. accuracy in recalling and understanding air traffic control commands), accounting for 29% of the variance. An expertise composite based on air traffic control knowledge and flight hours accounted for an additional 37% of the variance, but the expertise × cognitive ability interaction was non-significant for all

Table 8.2 Summary of evidence for the circumvention-of-limits hypothesis

Study	Domain	N	Evidence for WMC circumvention?
Morrow et al. (2001)	Aviation	182	No
Hambrick & Engle (2002)	Memory	181	No
Sohn & Doane (2003)	Aviation	50	Yes
Sohn & Doane (2004)	Aviation	52	Mixed
Taylor et al. (2005)	Aviation	97	No
Kopiez & Lee (2008)	Music	52	No
Meinz & Hambrick (2010)	Music	57	No
Meinz et al. (2012)	Poker	155	No

performance measures, indicating that the effect of cognitive ability on performance was similar across levels of expertise.

In another study of pilots ($N = 92$), Morrow et al. (2003) found that cognitive ability accounted for an average of 22% of the variance in air traffic control tasks; expertise accounted for an additional 28% of the variance on average (expertise × cognitive ability interactions were not reported for this study.) Consistent with these findings, in a study of 97 licensed pilots with a wide range of flight experience, Taylor, O'Hara, Mumenthaler, Rosen, and Yesavage (2005) found that performance in an aviation communication task correlated significantly with WMC ($r = 0.76$), but the interaction between WMC and expertise (flight rating) was non-significant.

Using a sample with 25 novice and 25 expert pilots, Sohn and Doane (2003) found that WMC predicted success in an aviation situational awareness task, but only in pilots who scored low on an aviation-specific test measuring skilled access to long-term memory (i.e. LT-WM; Ericsson & Kintsch, 1995), as evidenced by a significant interaction between LT-WM and WMC. In another study, Sohn and Doane (2004) found that two measures of WMC (spatial span and verbal span) correlated more strongly with situational awareness in 25 novice pilots ($rs = 0.52$, $p < 0.01$, and 0.30, $p > 0.14$, respectively) than in 27 expert pilots ($rs = 0.10$ and 0.10, $ps > 0.61$, respectively). However, these correlations are not significantly different from each other across skill groups ($zs < 1.5$). Sohn and Doane (2004) did not test the LT-WM × WMC interaction using the full sample (as in their earlier study), but instead tested it separately in each skill group, finding significance only in the expert group.

Other studies have used music as the venue for testing the circumvention-of-limits hypothesis. Meinz and Hambrick (2010) had pianists provide estimates of deliberate practice and perform tests of both WMC and sight-reading. Deliberate practice accounted for 45% of the variance in sight-reading performance and WMC accounted for an additional 7.4% of the variance. However, the deliberate practice × WMC interaction was non-significant, indicating that the effect of WMC on performance was similar across levels of deliberate practice. Using a sample of 52 pianists with a more uniform level of skill (piano majors at a music university), Kopiez and Lee (2008) estimated the contribution of practice and cognitive ability to sight-reading performance. Using their data, we found that when sight-reading experience and WMC were entered into a regression analysis predicting sight-reading performance, only the contribution of sight-reading experience was significant ($\beta = 0.32$, $p = 0.02$). By contrast, the contribution of WMC ($\beta = 0.22$, $p = 0.10$) and the WMC × sight-reading experience interaction were non-significant ($\beta = 0.18$, $p = 0.18$).[2]

The second approach that we use in our research to investigate the circumvention-of-limits hypothesis is to experimentally manipulate the activation of domain knowledge in a laboratory task. The goal with this *knowledge-activation* approach is to 'add knowledge' to the mind of a participant in a tractably short amount of time before his or her performance is assessed. In the study that introduced this approach (Hambrick & Oswald, 2005), participants performed a memory task in which they attempted to remember the movements of spaceships that 'flew' from planet to planet in a solar system. Unbeknownst to participants, the spaceships flew in the same manner that baseball players run around a baseball diamond. Participants then performed an isomorphic task in which a baseball diamond replaced the solar system and baseball players replaced the spaceships. Finally, participants completed tests of WMC and knowledge of baseball. The relationship between baseball knowledge and performance was greater in the baseball condition than in the spaceship condition, indicating activation of domain knowledge in the baseball condition. However, the relationship between WMC and performance did not differ across conditions. That is, contrary to the circumvention-of-limits hypothesis, the relationship between WMC and performance was as large in the baseball condition, where task-relevant knowledge was activated, as in the spaceship condition, where it was not.

In a more recent study, we used the knowledge activation approach to test the circumvention-of-limits hypothesis in a 'placekeeping' task (Hambrick, Altmann, & Burgoyne, 2018). We define placekeeping as the ability to perform a sequence of operations in a specified order. The placekeeping task we used is called UNRAVEL; each letter in the acronym UNRAVEL corresponds to a different two-alternative forced choice task that the participant must perform. Every so often, the participant is interrupted by a distractor task. Afterwards, they must return to the UNRAVEL procedure at the place where they left off. Performance is measured based on participants' accuracy and response time for each two-alternative forced choice trial.

In the knowledge-activated condition of the placekeeping task, we instructed participants to use the mnemonic 'UNRAVEL' to remember the order of the steps/tasks in the procedure. In the knowledge-not activated condition, no mnemonic was given, and the use and discovery of mnemonics was frustrated by reversing the terms of some of the two-alternative forced choice tasks so that their first letters spelled the non-word 'UNRBCEL'. We also had participants complete tests of fluid intelligence, perceptual speed, and crystallized intelligence. The key finding was that the positive effect of cognitive ability on placekeeping performance did not differ across conditions. That is, contrary to the

---

[2] We are grateful to Reinhard Kopiez for sharing data from this study with us so we could perform these analyses.

circumvention-of-limits hypothesis, cognitive ability was as predictive of performance when domain knowledge was activated as when it was not.

Taken together, findings from these two lines of research—one using a differential approach and the other an experimental approach—converges on the conclusion that domain knowledge does not necessarily mitigate performance limitations associated with WMC, or cognitive ability, in general. In more concrete terms, this evidence indicates that WMC appears to influence complex cognition even at high levels of domain knowledge (in the differential approach) or when domain knowledge is activated in a task (in the experimental approach). However, another important consideration is the external environment of a task—the degree to which the environment affords strategies for task performance that offload processing demands of the performer.

The Environment

An assumption in the traditional approach to research on working memory is that the internal cognitive processes and structures that constitute the working memory system exist apart from the external environments in which these mental entities are applied to accomplishing various tasks. Working memory paradigms such as the operation span, N-back, and running span tasks are designed to be unfamiliar to participants to capture these factors without the influence of skills and knowledge specific to some particular task (i.e. expertise). Moreover, the tasks are administered under controlled conditions to minimize the influence of external factors that may aid or otherwise influence performance. For example, while performing the operation span task, participants are not allowed to use paper and pencil to remember the words. The task is designed to capture internal ('inside the head') factors bearing on people's ability to remember the words.

However, as Logie (2018) recently observed, 'people may use their cognition in different ways to perform the same task in the laboratory and in everyday life' (p. 471; see also Logie, Belletier, & Doherty, 2021). That is, they may use different strategies. One major reason for this is that cognition does not unfold in a vacuum in the real-world. Rather, it unfolds in an environment replete with objects and information of various types that may influence how a person performs a particular task. This includes artefacts associated with some specific task: tools and instruments; devices, displays, and controls; and so on. It may also include other people, such as team members, opponents, evaluators, and observers. The environment also includes a myriad of stressors and other contextual factors, such as temperature, precipitation, and atmospheric conditions. It also includes what can be called *distractors*: objects and information that are irrelevant to the task and which may even lead to competing (and incorrect) responses.

Consider the task of piloting an aircraft. The pilot's (person's) characteristics include all the knowledge, skills, and abilities that he or she can bring to bear on flying the aircraft. The environment, on the other hand, is the aircraft's cockpit, which includes monitors that display information about the performance and position of the aircraft (e.g. altitude, airspeed), the location of other aircraft, and a communication system for interacting with air traffic control. The environment also includes the physical environment of the aircraft (e.g. whether the flight is at night or during the day, whether there is cloud cover) and may also include a flight crew. Finally, the environment includes many different types of distractors, including everything from personal text messages on the crew's phones to incidents involving passengers. Any (or all) of these objects may influence the pilot's ability to fly the aircraft.

Hutchins' (1995) analysis of how a 'cockpit remembers its speeds' provides a concrete example of the concept of distributed cognition. A critical task for a flight crew is to set airspeeds for the descent, approach, and landing phases of the flight, which must take into account factors such as the expected weight of the plane upon landing, the length of the runway, and energy dissipated by braking. (As Hutchins noted, pilots call this a 'killer' task: if a mistake is made, the consequence can be a crash.) The ideal landing speed is one that is slow enough that the plane is losing lift as the wheels touch down, but fast enough that control can be maintained during the approach and the plane can regain altitude if there is an emergency. To this end, during descent and approach, the plane is slowed in stages, requiring the crew to manipulate devices called slats and flaps, which change the shape of the wings and thus lift.

A crucial subtask in the process is setting 'speed bugs'—the speeds at which the configuration of the slats and flaps should be changed. As Hutchins (1995) explains, the cockpit's long-term memory in setting speed bugs is a printed or digital table containing correspondence between weights and speeds—how fast the plane must be travelling at a given weight. The cockpit's working memory is created by the pilots physically marking the speed bugs on the airspeed indicator, and also by verbalizations among the crew members: as the co-pilot sets the speed bugs, he or she announces them to the pilot, who repeats them back. Thus, as Hutchins (1995) explained, 'The cockpit system remembers its speeds, and the memory process emerges from the activity of the pilots' (p. 286).

An observational study by Kirlik (1998) further illustrates how the environment influences working memory performance. The Majestic Diner is one of the most popular restaurants in Atlanta, Georgia, United States. During busy times, a short-order cook at the Majestic is responsible for a dozen or more orders, which must be managed simultaneously. Kirlik identified three strategies that the cooks used for cooking steaks to order (rare to well-done). In the *brute force* strategy, the cook places steaks on the grill in random locations and attempts to remember how each should be cooked. In the *position control* strategy, the cook places steaks on areas of the grill designated for different temperatures (right for rare, middle for medium, left for well-done). Finally, in the *position + velocity control* strategy, the cook partitions the grill both horizontally and vertically. The back of the grill is for well-done, the middle for medium, and the front for rare; in addition, within each horizontal band, left is for well-done, the middle for medium, and right for rare. Within each horizontal band, the cook keeps the steaks moving right to left at a constant velocity, flipping each at the middle of the grill and removing it when it reaches the left edge.

Kirlik (1998) noted that 'each of the three strategies above are (approximately) functionally equivalent: to the extent they are implemented satisfactorily, each cook will succeed at the task' but that 'the cognitive demands associated with implementing the various strategies are quite different' (p. 22; see Fig. 8.3). Using the brute force strategy, the cook's task is not unlike performing a laboratory working memory task; the goal is to remember some unstructured information. However, the nature of the task changes when the other strategies are used. Using the position control strategy, the cook must remember the temperature of each position on the grill and how long each steak has been cooking for. However, using the position + velocity strategy, there is no need to remember how a steak is to be cooked once it is placed on the grill. The cook need only keep the steaks moving from the right to left at a constant velocity.

Thus, an account of how cooks at the Majestic Diner perform their job must include an analysis of the way in which they interact with the external environment. Fisk and Kirlik (1996) summarized this critical point in general terms as follows:

The endeavor of understanding the environment in which cognitive activity will take place may be as important as understanding the overarching task in which the

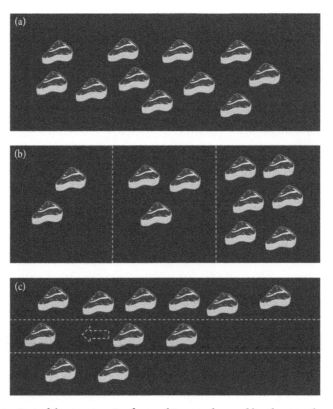

Fig. 8.3 Illustration of three strategies for cooking steaks used by short-order cooks at the Majestic Diner (Kirlik, 1998). (a) Brute force strategy, (b) position control strategy, and (c) position + velocity control strategy.

cognitive activity of interest is embedded. Thus, one must focus on determining under what environmental conditions various cognitive activities will be activated, and required, for effective task performance. The issue is not only to understand cognitive processes such as problem solving, working memory, or skill acquisition but also to determine in what context problems must be solved, when decisions must be made and what factors affect their outcome, what task characteristics lead to working memory demands, or what skills must be acquired given various environmental constraints. (p. 6)

In another study that illustrates the importance of considering the structure of the environment in accounting for working memory performance, Beach (1993) investigated how bartenders use the environment in the real-world working memory task of taking and filling drink orders. Using a mock bar set up at a bartending school, Beach compared the performance of bartending students (novices) and recent graduates (experts) in filling simulated drink orders. In each trial, the participants were given four drink orders; their task was to fill them as quickly and accurately as possible. In the first three trials, the glasses were shaped differently for different drinks (Collins, cocktail, rock, and champagne), as they would be in a real bar. In the last three trials, the glasses were black, opaque, and of the same shape for all drinks. As expected, the expert bartenders outperformed the novices in the first condition. However, in the second condition, the experts made substantially more errors than before, whereas novices' performance was unaffected.

Beach's (1993) study uncovered a strategy used by expert bartenders that offloaded working memory demands of drink orders to the environment. As an order was placed, experts could select the appropriate glass and use it as a retrieval cue for the drink order. With a transparent glass, a bartender could keep track of which ingredients had already been added by judging the colour and amount of liquid in the glass. However, this strategy was stymied when the participants were forced to use black, opaque, identical glasses for all drinks, and the experts' bartending advantage was reduced as a result. Thus, for the skilled bartender, working memory for drink orders is supported by both internal representations and external representations. Internal representations include knowledge about how to mix particular drinks and what glasses to use for the drinks. External representations include cues created by the glasses as the bartender sets them out, and possibly other cues, including 'regulars' who always order certain drinks. Just as the cockpit remembers its speeds, a bar remembers its drinks.

A final illustration of how environmental cues bear on working memory performance comes from a study by Wright, Logie, and Decker (1995). Experienced burglars—people with skill at the art of gaining illegal entry to people's homes—and homeowners rate houses, as shown in photographs, on how attractive they were as break-in targets. In a surprise recognition test, the participants were again shown a series of photographs, some that were the same as before but others that had been changed on details relevant to a burglar (e.g. an open window was now shut) or to a homeowner (e.g. the appearance of the garden). The participants' task was to indicate whether the photographs had been changed. The major finding was that the burglars detected more changes in burglary-relevant features than the homeowners did (58% vs 50%), whereas there was no difference between the groups in memory for non-burglary-relevant features (48% vs 51%). Environmental cues direct attention to certain information depending on a person's expertise, prioritizing that information in working memory for further processing.

The preceding studies illustrate how the structure of the environment bears on working memory performance in real-world tasks. Patsenko and Altmann (2010) demonstrated that the structure of the environment is also important to consider in laboratory cognitive tasks, including even a task such as the Tower of Hanoi that is far removed from any real-world task. The Tower of Hanoi is a puzzle task in which performers must move discs of different sizes across three pegs. There are three rules constraining performance: only one disc can be moved per turn; larger discs cannot be placed on smaller discs; and only the top disc can be moved off of a peg. The typical explanation for how people perform this task is that they plan ahead or work their way backwards from a solution, in both cases storing a sequence of moves in working memory that will allow them to transform the initial problem state into the goal state (see, e.g. Welsh, Satterlee-Cartmell, & Stine, 1999).

However, Patsenko and Altmann (2010) used eye tracking during problem-solving to demonstrate that planned behaviour may be more apparent than real. Specifically, they used gaze-contingent display manipulations to alter problem states in a computerized version of the Tower of Hanoi task while participants made saccades (i.e. rapid eye-movements during which visual input is not processed; Rayner, 1998). Across three experiments, discs in Tower of Hanoi problems were moved or removed by the computer program. If participants were problem-solving using a planned sequence of actions stored in working memory, one might expect them to notice the change in the problem state, which was designed to require a different solution sequence. Surprisingly, however, most participants did not notice that the problem had been altered by the computer program during the task. Furthermore, participants' actions, response latencies, and eye movements suggested performance was not dependent on planned behaviour, but instead on 'rule-based representations interacting with the environment through perception and attention' (Patsenko & Altmann, 2010, p. 112). Thus, performance on what many consider to be a flagship task capturing 'planful' problem-solving can be explained simply in terms of rule-based responses to environmental conditions.

To sum up, the structure of the environment is critical to consider in accounting for cognitive performance, in general, and working memory performance, in particular. In many real-world tasks, performers can strategically use the environment to offload processing demands to their surroundings. Thus, performance of the same task be it bartending, cooking, or flying a plane, can invoke a different constellation of cognitive processes and environmental affordances depending on the knowledge and strategies brought to bear on the task by the performer. This observation has important implications for applied cognitive science. For example, if strategies change as performers acquire expertise, the cognitive mechanisms supporting performance will also change, and cognitive abilities that support performance early in training may differ from those that support performance later on. Relatedly, the predictive validity of cognitive ability may differ across groups of individuals with similar knowledge and experience if they use different strategies to accomplish the same task. For researchers, the challenge is to capture these relevant sources of variance: individual factors, environmental factors, strategy use, and their interaction.

Towards an Ecological Theory of Working Memory

We have made two major points so far. The first is that WMC is only one potential predictor of individual differences in complex cognition, even though research most often focuses on WMC as if it were the only predictor. The second point is that whether and to what extent WMC might be expected to influence performance in some complex task depends on the environment. People can—and readily do—develop strategies for performing tasks that are inextricably tied to the environment, and this person-environment relationship must be considered if the goal is to understand working memory performance in the real world.

What would an ecological theory of working memory look like? At the most general level, it would include two features. First, it would represent both the person and the environment in some way. Second, it would be dynamic, to capture changes in influences of the person and environment on task performance over time and situations. By definition, a beginner in a domain has no domain-specific knowledge. Through training, the person acquires not only declarative knowledge and procedural knowledge relevant to the task, but strategic knowledge of how to use the external environment to manage the cognitive demands of the task. That is, the person becomes *attuned* to the environment.

One way to think about attunement relies on the idea of mental representations. However, it may also possible to think of it in Gibsonian terms (for a contrast between these perspectives, see Raab & Araújo, 2019). According to the ecological approach (Gibson, 1979), the person and the environment are mutual (i.e. one implies the other) and reciprocal (i.e. one could not exist without the other). In other words, the influence of an organism on its environment and the influence of an environment on an organism are both equivalent and complementary (Gibson, 1979; Richardson, Shockley, Fajen, Riley, & Turvey, 2008). More than just mutual and reciprocal, however, organism and environment are considered a combined whole (Turvey, 2009), such that the organism-in-its-environment (i.e. the organism-environment system) is the preferred unit of analysis for studying behaviour (Turvey & Shaw, 1999).

Järvilehto (1998) suggests that from this perspective, behaviour is a reorganization of the organism-environment system, not an interaction between the organism and the environment. Furthermore, cognitive processes are different aspects of the organization and dynamics of the organism-environment system, not local processes of the organism. This is why from an ecological approach, there is no need for a part of the system (the organism) to represent another part of the system (the environment), itself (the body), or interactions between the two (e.g. see Vicente & Wang, 1998, or Turvey & Shaw, 1979, for memory without mental representations; see Turvey & Carello, 2012, for intelligence without mental representations). As traditionally conceptualized, working memory is an inherently representational construct, but at the very least, this perspective emphasizes that working memory performance emerges from characteristics of both the person and the environment, and their interplay.

Conclusion

Working memory has been a vital area of research in cognitive psychology for nearly half a century. Workhorse measures of WMC are both theoretically and practically useful. They have shed light on the nature of cognitive limitations, and they predict performance in complex real-world tasks. At the same time, working memory research has been myopic in that the focus is typically on WMC as the sole predictor of (or mechanism underlying) performance in such tasks. Here, we have argued that a more profitable approach is to think about working memory performance from a person-environment perspective. Whatever the real-world task, WMC is one of many possible predictors of performance, any one of which may alter the importance of WMC as a predictor variable. Furthermore, the importance of WMC can only be understood in the context of the specific features of the environment in which a task is performed. We believe that taking this person-environment perspective is critical for advancing both scientific understanding of working memory in real-world cognition and for using measures of WMC for applied purposes.

References

Ackerman, P. L. (1996). A theory of adult intellectual development: Process, personality, interests, and knowledge. *Intelligence*, *22*, 227–257.

Ackerman, P. L., Beier, M. E., & Boyle, M. O. (2005). Working memory and intelligence: The same or different constructs? *Psychological Bulletin*, *131*, 30–60.

Araújo, D., Hristovski, R., Seifert, L., Carvalho, J., & Davids, K. (2019). Ecological cognition: Expert decision-making behaviour in sport. *International Review of Sport and Exercise Psychology*, *12*, 1–25.

Atkinson, R. C., & Shiffrin, R. M. (1968). Human memory: A proposed system and its control processes. In K. Federmeier & E. Schotter (Eds.), *Psychology of Learning and Motivation* (Vol. 2, pp. 89–195). New York, NY: Academic Press.

Baddeley, A. D. (1986). *Working memory*. Oxford, UK: Oxford University Press.

Baddeley, A. D., & Hitch, G. (1974). Working memory. In G. H. Bower (Ed.), *Psychology of Learning and Motivation* (Vol. 8, pp. 47–89). New York, NY: Academic Press.

Baddeley, A. D., & Logie, R. H. (1999). Working memory: The multiple-component model. In A. Miyake & P. Shah (Eds.), *Models of working memory: Mechanisms of active maintenance and executive control* (pp. 28–61). New York, NY: Cambridge University Press.

Baltes, P. B. (1987). Theoretical propositions of life-span developmental psychology: On the dynamics between growth and decline. *Developmental Psychology*, *23*, 611–626.

Beach, K. (1993). Becoming a bartender: The role of external memory cues in a work-directed educational activity. *Applied Cognitive Psychology, 7*, 191–204.

Boring, E. G. (1923). Intelligence as the tests test it. *New Republic, 35*, 35–37.

Burgess, P. W. (1997). Theory and methodology in executive function research. In P. Rabbitt (Ed.), *Methodology of frontal and executive function* (pp. 81–116). Hove, UK: Psychology Press.

Burgoyne, A. P., Hambrick, D. Z., & Altmann, E. M. (2019). Is working memory capacity a causal factor in fluid intelligence? *Psychonomic Bulletin & Review, 26*, 1333–1339.

Carpenter, P. A., Just, M. A., & Shell, P. (1990). What one intelligence test measures: A theoretical account of the processing in the Raven Progressive Matrices Test. *Psychological Review, 97*, 404–431.

Carroll, J. B. (1993). *Human cognitive abilities: A survey of factor-analytic studies.* New York, NY: Cambridge University Press.

Cattell, R. B. (1943). The measurement of adult intelligence. *Psychological Bulletin, 40*, 153–193.

Chase, W. G., & Simon, H. A. (1973). Perception in chess. *Cognitive Psychology, 4*, 55–81.

Conway, A. R., Cowan, N., Bunting, M. F., Therriault, D. J., & Minkoff, S. R. (2002). A latent variable analysis of working memory capacity, short-term memory capacity, processing speed, and general fluid intelligence. *Intelligence, 30*, 163–183.

Conway, A. R., Kane, M. J., Bunting, M. F., Hambrick, D. Z., Wilhelm, O., & Engle, R. W. (2005). Working memory span tasks: A methodological review and user's guide. *Psychonomic Bulletin & Review, 12*, 769–786.

Cowan, N. (1988). Evolving conceptions of memory storage, selective attention, and their mutual constraints within the human information-processing system. *Psychological Bulletin, 104*, 163–191.

Cowan, N., Elliott, E. M., Saults, J. S., Morey, C. C., Mattox, S., Hismjatullina, A., & Conway, A. R. (2005). On the capacity of attention: Its estimation and its role in working memory and cognitive aptitudes. *Cognitive Psychology, 51*, 42–100.

Cowan, N., Morey, C., & Naveh-Benjamin, N. (2021). An embedded-processes approach to working memory: How is it distinct from other approaches, and to what ends? In R. H. Logie, V. Camos, & N. Cowan (Eds.), *Working memory: State of the science* (pp. 44–84). Oxford, UK: Oxford University Press.

Daneman, M., & Carpenter, P. A. (1980). Individual differences in working memory and reading. *Journal of Verbal Learning and Verbal Behavior, 19*, 450–466.

Donders, F. C. (1969). On the speed of mental processes. *Acta Psychologica, 30*, 412–431.

Engle, R. W. (2002). Working memory capacity as executive attention. *Current Directions in Psychological Science, 11*, 19–23.

Engle, R. W., Carullo, J. J., & Collins, K. W. (1991). Individual differences in working memory for comprehension and following directions. *The Journal of Educational Research, 84*, 253–262.

Ericsson, K. A. (2014). Why expert performance is special and cannot be extrapolated from studies of performance in the general population: A response to criticisms. *Intelligence, 45*, 81–103.

Ericsson, K. A., & Kintsch, W. (1995). Long-term working memory. *Psychological Review, 102*, 211–245.

Fisk, A. D., & Kirlik, A. (1996). Practical relevance and age-related research: Can theory advance without application. In W. A. Rogers, A. D. Fisk, & N. Walker (Eds.), *Aging and skilled performance: Advances in Theory and Applications* (pp. 1–15). Mahwah, NJ: Lawrence Erlbaum Associates.

Foroughi, C. K., Barragán, D., & Boehm-Davis, D. A. (2016). Interrupted reading and working memory capacity. *Journal of Applied Research in Memory and Cognition, 5*, 395–400.

Foroughi, C. K., Werner, N. E., Barragán, D., & Boehm-Davis, D. A. (2015). Interruptions disrupt reading comprehension. *Journal of Experimental Psychology: General, 144*, 704–709.

Friston, K. J., Price, C. J., Fletcher, P., Moore, C., Frackowiak, R. S. J., & Dolan, R. J. (1996). The trouble with cognitive subtraction. *Neuroimage, 4*, 97–104.

Gibson, J. J. (1950). *The perception of the visual world.* Oxford, UK: Houghton Mifflin.

Gibson, J. J. (1979). *The ecological approach to visual perception.* Boston, MA: Houghton, Mifflin and Company.

Gobet, F. (1998). Expert memory: A comparison of four theories. *Cognition, 66*, 115–152.

Gobet, F. (2000). Long-term working memory: A computational implementation for chess expertise. In *Proceedings of the 3rd International Conference on Cognitive Modelling* (pp. 142–149).
Veenendaal, The Netherlands: Universal Press.

Hambrick, D. Z., Altmann, E. M., & Burgoyne, A. P. (2018). A knowledge activation approach to
testing the circumvention-of-limits hypothesis. *American Journal of Psychology, 131*, 307–321.

Hambrick, D. Z., & Engle, R. W. (2002). Effects of domain knowledge, working memory capacity, and
age on cognitive performance: An investigation of the knowledge-is-power hypothesis. *Cognitive
Psychology, 44*, 339–387.

Hambrick, D. Z., & Meinz, E. J. (2011). Limits on the predictive power of domain-specific experience
and knowledge in skilled performance. *Current Directions in Psychological Science, 20*, 275–279.

Hambrick, D. Z., & Oswald, F. L. (2005). Does domain knowledge moderate involvement of working
memory capacity in higher-level cognition? A test of three models. *Journal of Memory and
Language, 52*, 377–397.

Hambrick, D. Z., Burgoyne, A. P., & Oswald, F. L. (2019). Domain-general models of expertise: The
role of cognitive ability. In P. Ward, J. M. Schraagen, J. Gore, & E. Roth (Eds.) *The Oxford Handbook
of Expertise* (pp. 1–40). Oxford, UK: Oxford University Press.

Hambrick, D. Z., Salthouse, T. A., & Meinz, E. J. (1999). Predictors of crossword puzzle proficiency
and moderators of age–cognition relations. *Journal of Experimental Psychology: General, 128*,
131–164.

Hebb, D. O. (1942). The effect of early and late brain injury upon test scores, and the nature of normal
adult intelligence. *Proceedings of the American Philosophical Society, 85*, 275–292.

Hutchins, E. (1995). How a cockpit remembers its speeds. *Cognitive Science, 19*, 265–288.

Järvilehto, T. (1998). The theory of the organism-environment system: I. Description of the theory.
Integrative Physiological and Behavioral Science, 33, 321–334.

Kane, M. J., & Engle, R. W. (2000). Working-memory capacity, proactive interference, and divided
attention: Limits on long-term memory retrieval. *Journal of Experimental Psychology: Learning,
Memory, and Cognition, 26*, 336–358.

Kane, M. J., Hambrick, D. Z., & Conway, A. R. (2005). Working memory capacity and fluid intelligence
are strongly related constructs: Comment on Ackerman, Beier, and Boyle (2005). *Psychological
Bulletin, 131*, 66–71.

Kane, M. J., Hambrick, D. Z., Tuholski, S. W., Wilhelm, O., Payne, T. W., & Engle, R. W. (2004). The
generality of working memory capacity: A latent-variable approach to verbal and visuospatial
memory span and reasoning. *Journal of Experimental Psychology: General, 133*, 189–217.

Kirlik, A. (1998). The ecological expert: Acting to create information to guide action. In *Proceedings of
the Fourth Annual Symposium on Human Interaction with Complex Systems* (pp. 15–27). Hillsdale,
NJ: IEEE Computer Society.

Kopiez, R., & Lee, J. (2008). Towards a general model of skills involved in sight reading music. *Music
Education Research, 10*, 41–62.

Kyllonen, P. C. (2002). 'g:' Knowledge, speed, strategies, or working-memory capacity? A systems perspective. In R. J. Sternberg & E. L. Grigorenko (Eds.), *The general factor of intelligence: How general
is it?* (pp. 415–445). Mahwah, NJ: Erlbaum.

Kyllonen, P. C., & Christal, R. E. (1990). Reasoning ability is (little more than) working-memory capacity?! *Intelligence, 14*, 389–433.

Logie, R. H. (2016). Retiring the central executive. *Quarterly Journal of Experimental Psychology, 69*,
2093–2109.

Logie, R. H. (2018). Human cognition: Common principles and individual variation. *Journal of
Applied Research in Memory and Cognition, 7*, 471–486.

Logie, R. H., Belletier, C., & Doherty, J. M. (2021). Integrating theories of working memory. In R. H.
Logie, V. Camos, & N. Cowan (Eds.), *Working memory: State of the science* (pp. 389–429). Oxford,
UK: Oxford University Press.

Luck, S. J., & Vogel, E. K. (1997). The capacity of visual working memory for features and conjunctions. *Nature, 390*, 279–281.

Mashburn, C. A., Tsukahara, J. S., & Engle, R. W. (2021). Individual differences in attention control: Implications for the relationship between working memory capacity and fluid intelligence.

In R. H. Logie, V. Camos, & N. Cowan (Eds.), *Working memory: State of the science* (pp. 175–211). Oxford, UK: Oxford University Press.

Meinz, E. J., & Hambrick, D. Z. (2010). Deliberate practice is necessary but not sufficient to explain individual differences in piano sight-reading skill: The role of working memory capacity. *Psychological Science, 21*, 914–919.

Meinz, E. J., Hambrick, D. Z., Hawkins, C. B., Gillings, A. K., Meyer, B. E., & Schneider, J. L. (2012). Roles of domain knowledge and working memory capacity in components of skill in Texas Hold'Em poker. *Journal of Applied Research in Memory and Cognition, 1*, 34–40.

Michaels, C. F., & Carello, C. (1981). *Direct perception*. Englewood Cliffs, NJ: Prentice-Hall.

Morrow, D. G., Menard, W. E., Stine-Morrow, E. A., Teller, T., & Bryant, D. (2001). The influence of expertise and task factors on age differences in pilot communication. *Psychology and Aging, 16*, 31–46.

Morrow, D. G., Ridolfo, H. E., Menard, W. E., Sanborn, A., Stine-Morrow, E. A., Magnor, C., . . . & Bryant, D. (2003). Environmental support promotes expertise-based mitigation of age differences on pilot communication tasks. *Psychology and Aging, 18*, 268–284.

Oberauer, K., Schulze, R., Wilhelm, O., & Süß, H.-M. (2005). Working memory and intelligence—their correlation and their relation: Comment on Ackerman, Beier, and Boyle (2005). *Psychological Bulletin, 131*, 61–65.

Patsenko, E. G., & Altmann, E. M. (2010). How planful is routine behavior? A selective-attention model of performance in the Tower of Hanoi. *Journal of Experimental Psychology: General, 139*, 95–116.

Phillips, W. A. (1974). On the distinction between sensory storage and short-term visual memory. *Perception & Psychophysics, 16*, 283–290.

Phillips, L. H. (1997). Do "frontal tests" measure executive function? Issues of assessment and evidence from fluency tests. In P. Rabbitt (Ed.), *Methodology of frontal and executive function* (pp. 191–213). Hove, UK: Psychology Press.

Pollack, I., Johnson, L. B., & Knaff, P. R. (1959). Running memory span. *Journal of Experimental Psychology, 57*, 137–146.

Raab, M., & Araújo, D. (2019). Embodied cognition with and without mental representations: The case of embodied choices in sports. *Frontiers in Psychology, 10*, 1825.

Rayner, K., & Pollatsek, A. (1997). Eye movements, the eye-hand span, and the perceptual span during sight-reading of music. *Current Directions in Psychological Science, 6*, 49–53.

Rayner, K. (1998). Eye movements in reading and information processing: 20 years of research. *Psychological Bulletin, 124*, 372–422.

Richardson, M. J., Shockley, K., Fajen, B. R., Riley, M. A., & Turvey, M. T. (2008). Ecological psychology: Six principles for an embodied–embedded approach to behavior. In P. Calvo & T. Gomila (Eds.), *Handbook of cognitive science: An embodied approach* (pp. 159–187). Amsterdam, The Netherlands: Elsevier.

Salthouse, T. (2000). *A theory of cognitive aging* (Vol. 28). Amsterdam, The Netherlands: Elsevier.

Shah, P., & Miyake, A. (1996). The separability of working memory resources for spatial thinking and language processing: An individual differences approach. *Journal of Experimental Psychology: General, 125*, 4–27.

Sohn, Y. W., & Doane, S. M. (2003). Roles of working memory capacity and long-term working memory skill in complex task performance. *Memory & Cognition, 31*, 458–466.

Sohn, Y. W., & Doane, S. M. (2004). Memory processes of flight situation awareness: Interactive roles of working memory capacity, long-term working memory, and expertise. *Human Factors, 46*, 461–475.

Spearman, C. (1904). 'General Intelligence,' objectively determined and measured. *The American Journal of Psychology, 15*, 201–292.

Taylor, J. L., O'Hara, R., Mumenthaler, M. S., Rosen, A. C., & Yesavage, J. A. (2005). Cognitive ability, expertise, and age differences in following air-traffic control instructions. *Psychology and Aging, 20*, 117–133.

Turner, M. L., & Engle, R. W. (1986). Working memory capacity. In *Proceedings of the Human Factors Society Annual Meeting* (Vol. 30, No. 13, pp. 1273–1277). Los Angeles, CA: SAGE Publications.

Turvey, M. T. (2009). On the notion and implications of organism-environment system. *Ecological Psychology, 21,* 97–111.

Turvey, M. T., & Carello, C. (2012). On intelligence from first principles: Guidelines for inquiry into the hypothesis of physical intelligence (PI). *Ecological Psychology, 24,* 3–32.

Turvey, M. T., & Shaw, R. E. (1979). The primacy of perceiving: An ecological reformulation of perception for understanding memory. In L. G. Nilsson (Ed.), *Perspectives on memory research: Essays in honor of Uppsala University's 500th anniversary* (pp. 167–222). Hillsdale, NJ: Erlbaum.

Turvey, M. T., & Shaw, R. E. (1999). Ecological foundations of cognition. I: Symmetry and specificity of animal-environment systems. *Journal of Consciousness Studies, 6,* 95–110.

Unsworth, N., & Engle, R. W. (2005). Working memory capacity and fluid abilities: Examining the correlation between Operation Span and Raven. *Intelligence, 33,* 67–81.

Unsworth, N., Fukuda, K., Awh, E., & Vogel, E. K. (2014). Working memory and fluid intelligence: Capacity, attention control, and secondary memory retrieval. *Cognitive Psychology, 71,* 1–26.

Unsworth, N., Schrock, J. C., & Engle, R. W. (2004). Working memory capacity and the antisaccade task: Individual differences in voluntary saccade control. *Journal of Experimental Psychology: Learning, Memory, and Cognition, 30,* 1302–1321.

Vicente, K. J., & Wang, J. H. (1998). An ecological theory of expertise effects in memory recall. *Psychological Review, 105,* 33–57.

Welsh, M. C., Satterlee-Cartmell, T., & Stine, M. (1999). Towers of Hanoi and London: Contribution of working memory and inhibition to performance. *Brain and Cognition, 41,* 231–242.

Wiley, J., Jarosz, A. F., Cushen, P. J., & Colflesh, G. J. (2011). New rule use drives the relation between working memory capacity and Raven's Advanced Progressive Matrices. *Journal of Experimental Psychology: Learning, Memory, and Cognition, 37,* 256–263.

Wright, R., Logie, R. H., & Decker, S. H. (1995). Criminal expertise and offender decision making: An experimental study of the target selection process in residential burglary. *Journal of Research in Crime and Delinquency, 32,* 39–53.

9

Domain-Specific Working Memory

Perspectives from Cognitive Neuropsychology

Randi C. Martin, Brenda Rapp, and Jeremy Purcell

Our primary objective with this chapter is to review the neuropsychological evidence that is relevant to our understanding of working memory (WM). We also report on behavioural and neuroimaging studies with healthy individuals, but these have been selected either because they have been motivated by findings from cognitive neuropsychology or they provide converging evidence for the neuropsychological findings we discuss. This review will illustrate the richness of the neuropsychological evidence and the extent to which it provides novel, convergent, or confirmatory evidence relative to studies of healthy individuals. In doing so, we expect to communicate the importance of the neuropsychological approach as a method for advancing our understanding of the normal operations of WM.

Our discussion is organized in terms of our response to the questions that all authors in this volume were asked to address, with summaries of the answers shown in Table 9.1.

1. Definition of Working Memory

The model of WM that we endorse assumes specialized storage systems which are each dedicated to the maintenance of different types of information (e.g. phonological vs visuospatial) and which are critical for processing in these domains. Here we focus on the systems involved in maintaining verbal representations (i.e. orthographic, phonological, and semantic). The approach lies somewhere between embedded-processes models (Cowan, 1999; Cowan, Morey, & Naveh-Benjamin, 2021) and standard buffer models (Baddeley & Hitch, 2019; Baddeley, Hitch, & Allen, 2021). While buffer models assume the existence of storage systems dedicated to the maintenance of specific types of information, embedded-processes models assume that WM consists of the activated portion of long-term memory (LTM) and that a domain-general attentional mechanism serves to keep information activated. In our approach, we assume that buffers exist which are separate from LTM representations in a given domain, but that these buffers are integral parts of processing in that domain (they are domain specific) and, in that sense, they can be thought to be embedded in a domain-specific processing system. Our position is consistent

Randi C. Martin, Brenda Rapp, and Jeremy Purcell, *Domain-Specific Working Memory* In: *Working Memory*. Edited by: Robert H. Logie, Valérie Camos, and Nelson Cowan, Oxford University Press (2021). © Oxford University Press. DOI: 10.1093/oso/9780198842286.003.0009

Table 9.1 Summary responses to designated questions

Question	Response from domain-specific working memory approach
1. Definition of working memory (WM)	Storage systems dedicated to maintenance of specific types of information that are crucial for operation of the system.
2. Methods of multicomponent model	All methods are relevant, including standard behavioural paradigms, neuropsychological case studies and case series, structural and functional brain imaging, and computational modelling.
3. Unitary versus non-unitary nature of WM	The system is non-unitary with different WM systems for different types of information. These storage capacities are embedded within domain-specific processing systems. We assume different systems not only for verbal versus non-verbal information but within the verbal system, separate storage for phonological, semantic, and orthographic information. These distinctions are supported by neuropsychological dissociations and by the differentiated distribution of brain activity in healthy individuals.
4. The role of long-term memory (LTM) knowledge in working-memory storage, processing	Domain-specific WM and LTM systems are separable and may be independently affected by brain damage. Additionally, direct interactions exist between WM representations and LTM representations such that LTM representations stabilize the representations in WM and maintenance in WM increases the likelihood of formation of new LTM representations. The bidirectional connectivity between LTM and WM systems is assumed to be domain specific.
5. The role of attention and control	While attentional processes may serve to boost the activation of representations in WM, domain-specific WM processes can be differentiated from attentional or executive processes.
6. Storage, maintenance, and loss of information from WM	Both decay and interference play a role in forgetting in WM. Neuropsychological evidence indicates that these are dissociable process such that disruption of the temporal stability of WM representations results in overly rapid decay while disruption of representational distinctiveness results in exaggerated interference.
7. Limitations of the approach and accounting for inconsistencies	Some evidence from healthy individual suggests only domain-general WM processes whereas other evidence supports domain-specific capacities. These differences may relate to whether simple or complex span measures are used. While domain-general approaches appear to be more parsimonious, they have difficulty accounting for dissociations in neuropsychological cases.
8. Applications of WM to sentence processing	Semantic but not phonological WM plays a crucial role in sentence comprehension although phonological WM is critical for verbatim repetition. On the production side, semantic WM supports the elaboration of the content of sentences whereas phonological WM is related to speech rate. Neither semantic nor phonological WM is critical for maintaining the syntactic aspects of sentences in either comprehension or production.

with the Caramazza, Miceli, Villa, and Romani (1987) proposal that a WM buffer is computationally motivated whenever there is a 'mismatch' between the size of the computational units processed by a component and the unit size processed by the component that provides input to it. Thus, for example, we assume an orthographic

WM buffer that interfaces between the whole word representations of word spellings stored in LTM and the motor processes involved in writing or typing, that are executed in a serial, letter-by-letter fashion (Rapp, Purcell, Hillis, Capasso, & Miceli, 2016). This WM buffer is assumed to be specialized to orthography and thus separate from buffers maintaining other verbal information (e.g. phonological). As will become evident in the following sections, neuropsychologically based WM research considers not only the existence of WM buffers but also the structure and functioning of these buffers—including the nature of the relation between the LTM and WM components in these models and the processes involved in forgetting and selection from the buffers (Costa, Fischer-Baum, Capasso, Miceli, & Rapp, 2011; Martin, Lesch, & Bartha, 1999).

In our approach, we assume that information can be maintained simultaneously in different storage buffers. Fig. 9.1a provides the model put forward by Martin and colleagues (Martin et al., 1999) that shows the knowledge system on the left for spoken words, with levels representing semantic, lexical, and phonological information. As spoken words are perceived, they activate their phonological representations, which then spread activation to lexical and semantic levels. As several words are presented, the representations for the set of words are associated with slots in the phonological and semantic buffers on the right. In production, semantic representations are selected first, which then activate lexical and phonological representations. If more than one word is planned prior to articulation, then the semantic and phonological representations are buffered until articulation is executed. In fact, such simultaneous maintenance is assumed to be critical during language processing, where, for instance, one may be maintaining several semantic representations while planning the phonological form of a phrase prior to its utterance. In order to accommodate written word processing, Fig. 9.1b shows the same model but includes letter representations and a graphemic buffer.

It should be acknowledged that while the models shown in Fig. 9.1 may seem complex, they do not capture all of the distinctions that have been made regarding the representations involved in verbal WM. These models show a domain-neutral lexical representation connected to both phonemes and letters. However, one could add in domain-specific lexical representations for spoken and written words (Caramazza, 1997). In the phonological domain, some have assumed that the same phonological maintenance system is used for maintaining the phonemes within a word and for maintaining several lexical phonological representations (Gupta & Tisdale, 2009; Martin & Saffran, 1997), whereas others have argued that the phonemes within a word can be maintained purely via activation in the lexical system prior to output (Romani, Galluzzi, & Olson, 2011). Most research on phonological WM has used words or numbers as the stimuli and has not focused on the distinction between the maintenance of lexical and sublexical phonological representations (though see Burgess & Hitch, 1999) and that is the case for the research reviewed here. In the orthographic domain, in contrast, the research has focused on maintenance of the letters within a single word rather than across a series of words. In either case, however, we assume that both decay

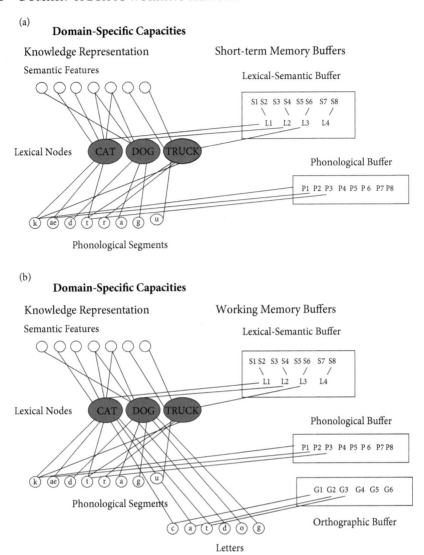

Fig. 9.1 Model of Verbal WM showing separable LTM and WM components and A) separable phonological WM and semantic WM buffers, B) separable phonological WM, semantic WM, and orthographic WM buffers.

and interference may affect the maintenance of or access to the information in the WM components.

Finally, we assume that there are domain-general processes, such as attention, control, and others (that are sometimes referred to as 'executive functions') that can affect the functioning of the WM components. However, for example, although attention can be allocated differentially to the information in these different storage buffers, we assume that information can persist even though attention is allocated elsewhere.

Although the assumption of domain-general executive processes is shared with an embedded-processing account, critically, we do not assume that these processes substitute for distinct domain-specific WM systems.

Summary

We argue for domain-specific WM storage systems that are critical for processing in that domain. As such, they are tightly linked to LTM representations in that domain, though separable from them. We assume that attentional processes may enhance the maintenance of information in a particular domain but storage may persist without attention, allowing for representations in different domains to be maintained simultaneously.

2. Methods of Investigation

Our methods include behavioural approaches with healthy and brain-damaged individuals, neuroimaging approaches using structural and functional magnetic resonance imaging (fMRI) and also computational modelling research specifically directed at testing hypotheses of WM.

Behavioural Studies of Neurologically Healthy Individuals

Behavioural studies of healthy individuals have examined the contributions of the maintenance of phonological and semantic representations to list recall (Romani, McAlpine, & Martin, 2008; Romani, McAlpine, Olson, Tsouknida, & Martin, 2005) as well as to language production and comprehension (Martin & Romani, 1994; Martin, Yan, & Schnur, 2014; Tan & Martin, 2018). In the spelling domain, studies with healthy individuals have primarily focused on spelling errors that do not reflect lack of knowledge of word spellings but are instead, the result of transient WM failures (Wing & Baddeley, 1980) that give rise to slips of the pen (Jones, Folk, & Rapp, 2009).

Case Studies and Case Series

Publications from many researchers during the 1980s laid out the logic of the case study approach (Caramazza, 1986; Caramazza & McCloskey, 1988; Coltheart, 2001), and we do not wish to reiterate all of those lines of argumentation here. Briefly, the approach assumes that the cognitive system is modular and that brain damage may selectively affect some components (e.g. phonological WM) while sparing others (speech perception). In order to establish that a particular component is spared or impaired, it is necessary to administer several tasks each of which draws on a given component, because performance on a single task may be influenced by factors unrelated to the cognitive function of interest (e.g. word list recall would be impaired by an articulatory disorder and thus phonological WM tests should be assessed with recognition measures in addition to those involving verbal output). Although it is sometimes claimed that a double dissociation is required to identify independent components, establishing a double dissociation may be impossible in certain instances, given the organization of the cognitive system. For example, although semantic WM may be severely impaired for those showing no or minimal semantic knowledge deficits (Martin & He, 2004), the opposite would not be expected to occur—that is, a severe deficit in semantic knowledge but preserved semantic WM—because preserved semantic knowledge would be required in order to have some content to maintain in WM. Those supporting the case study approach argue against group studies which average performance across individuals classified on the basis of syndrome or lesion localization, pointing out that individuals within such groups may differ in theoretically important ways, making averaging unjustified. In the case study approach, generalization from the single case is not to some group of individuals but rather to some theoretical model that accounts for the pattern of performance. The model is then tested against future case studies as well as through studies of healthy individuals.

In the context of evidence of dissociations, case studies typically report those individuals showing the clearest dissociations between the components of interest (Buchwald & Rapp, 2009). Some researchers may object that presentation of these cases is somehow misleading in that the bulk of individuals may show impairment in both components. However, an association of deficits would be expected even if the components are independent given that nearby and closely interconnected brain regions may underlie the components. For instance, considerable evidence supports the contention that the left superior temporal gyrus is critically involved in speech perception (Turkeltaub & Coslett, 2010) whereas the left supramarginal gyrus in the parietal lobe is involved in phonological WM (Shallice & Papagno, 2019; Yue, Martin, Hamilton, & Rose, 2019). These regions are adjacent and, given the nature of vascular damage, both might be expected to be damaged following stroke due to a left middle cerebral artery infarct (i.e. the most common site for those with language deficits following stroke). However, damage is variable and some individuals may have damage to only one of these regions. Thus, the existence of many cases showing both speech perception deficits and phonological WM deficits does not undermine the claim that these functions are separable, provided that individual cases exist where the dissociation can be demonstrated.

In more recent years, a case series approach has developed, which makes it possible to draw on the data from a wider range of brain damaged individuals (Schwartz & Dell, 2010). This approach is similar to the individual differences approach taken with healthy subjects, which assumes that even though performance on tasks tapping different cognitive components may be correlated (e.g. as for verbal and performance IQ), one can establish that these make independent contributions to performance through a regression or factor-analytic approach. In the case series approach, a set of individuals that meet some screening criteria are tested on measures designed to tap the cognitive functions of interest. One can then examine how these functions relate in a theoretically motivated fashion to behavioural or neural outcomes (e.g. Fischer-Baum & Rapp, 2012; Schwartz, Dell, Martin, Gahl, & Sobel, 2006). Because of this regression or covariance approach, case series studies are distinguished from other group studies which involve averaging of performance.

The case study and case series approaches have different strengths and weaknesses (see Rapp, 2011, for discussion). The case study approach allows for an intensive examination of the domain of interest, allowing one to carry out many tests to rule out alternative interpretations of patterns of spared and impaired function. However, any one laboratory may have only a few individuals demonstrating a clear pattern of dissociations. For the case series approach, a much broader range of patients can be tested and one can more easily map behavioural performance onto brain damage using multivariate techniques. However, because of the large numbers of subjects, the amount of testing for any one individual is bound to be limited. Other important issues arise regarding how one determines the selection criteria and how one deals with outliers in a regression approach.

Lesion–Symptom Mapping

In this approach, one examines the brain regions that support different cognitive functions. If cognitive modules may be separately affected by brain damage, one would expect an underlying neural modularity, with different brain regions supporting these functions (Coltheart, 2001). To carry out lesion–symptom mapping, detailed analysis of the performance of several individuals is carried out and those who show strong evidence of impairment to one cognitive component but not another and vice versa are selected. Then, using lesion overlap methods, one can determine if there are regions of brain damage that are uniquely related to each of the components of interest. For instance, Rapp et al. (2016) took this approach in identifying regions associated with orthographic WM and LTM. A different lesion–symptom mapping method, more aligned with the case series approach, is voxel-based lesion–symptom mapping (Bates et al., 2003) in which continuous variation on cognitive measures tapping functions of interest is correlated with brain damage on a voxel-by-voxel basis (Schwartz, Faseyitan, Kim, & Coslett, 2012).

Functional Neuroimaging

Using fMRI, one can examine whether different brain regions support LTM versus WM processing (Rapp & Dufor, 2011; Yue et al., 2019). One may also investigate whether different brain regions are activated to support WM in different domains such as visual, orthographic, phonological, or semantic (Martin, Wu, Freedman, Jackson, & Lesch,

2003). Studies identifying the regions involved in WM have often examined whether activation persists in a given region during a delay period in a WM task and/or whether activation is related to WM load (Rapp & Dufor, 2011). However, given an embedded-processes perspective, one might argue that these activation patterns reflect the engagement of attention to enhance the activation of those items in the focus of attention. More recent approaches allow one to address such claims by examining whether one can decode the content of the representations presumably being maintained in these regions by using pattern analysis techniques like multivoxel pattern analysis (Norman, Polyn, Detre, & Haxby, 2006) and representational-similarity analysis (Kriegeskorte, Mur, & Bandettini, 2008). The rationale would be that if these regions correspond to domain-general attentional mechanisms, decoding of representational content should not be possible.

Computational Modelling of Working Memory

Computational modelling approaches have been used quite extensively in testing theories of WM, primarily in the phonological domain, and especially in the specific context of serial recall and phonological learning (e.g. Burgess & Hitch, 1999, 2006; Gupta & MacWhinney, 1997). Whereas all such models have attempted to replicate standard WM findings from healthy individuals, some have been explicitly motivated to account for neuropsychological findings, such as the effects of disruption of articulatory, phonemic, and lexical representations on serial recall (Burgess & Hitch, 1999; Gupta & MacWhinney, 1997). Some computational models have incorporated semantic as well as phonological WM (e.g. Martin, Saffran & Dell, 1996). Models presented by Burgess and Hitch (1999) and Gupta and Tisdale (2009) incorporate a separate phonological store that allows for the encoding of order information, thus providing a means of accounting for phonological WM deficits without disruptions of phonological LTM.

In the orthographic domain, Houghton and colleagues (Houghton, Glasspool, & Shallice, 1994) carried out foundational work with their development of a competitive queuing model of orthographic WM, which was largely tested on neuropsychological data. Also in the orthographic domain, Goldberg and Rapp (2008) used a computational modelling approach to specifically examine the nature of the serial order processing mechanism in orthographic WM. Using simple recurrent networks (Elman, 1990), they simulated deficits and tested the model outputs with neuropsychological data to evaluate if (compound) chaining was a plausible account of the serial order mechanism in orthographic WM.

Summary

Our methods have consisted predominantly of neuropsychological approaches. Our goal is to understand the organization of the cognitive system and thus to develop models that accommodate not only the patient data but also those from healthy individuals. As a consequence, behavioural and neuroimaging approaches with healthy individuals as well as computational and lesion–symptom mapping approaches are relevant and we have employed these to provide converging evidence or expand on the neuropsychological findings.

3. The Unitary or Non-Unitary Nature of Working Memory

As indicated in the preceding discussion, we posit a non-unitary organization of WM. The origin of this claim dates back to neuropsychological findings from the 1960–1970s, in which case studies identified individuals who showed very restricted verbal WM capacity for digits and words despite showing preserved speech perception and word production (e.g. as evidenced by the ability to accurately repeat single words and monitor for a word or digit in a long list) and preserved LTM for verbal materials (Warrington, Logue, & Pratt, 1971; Warrington & Shallice, 1969). Investigations of performance on phonological WM tasks like word list recall provided evidence that these individuals relied on visual coding for such tasks (Warrington & Shallice, 1972) and that they performed at the control level on tasks tapping visuospatial short-term memory, such as the Corsi blocks task (Basso, Spinnler, Vallar, & Zanobio, 1982). Other studies documented individuals showing a complementary pattern of impaired visuospatial WM but preserved verbal WM (Hanley, Young, & Pearson, 1991). Thus, these findings have been taken as consistent with the Baddeley WM model which assumes specialized phonological and visuospatial WM storage buffers, with the case studies demonstrating that they can be independently affected by brain damage. While some researchers have recently argued that these reported dissociations are not compelling when the data are examined closely (Morey, 2018; Morey, Rhodes, & Cowan, 2019), others have provided convincing counter-arguments to these claims (Hanley & Young, 2019; Logie, 2019).

Separable Buffers for Phonological and Semantic Information

The model of verbal WM put forward by Martin et al. (1999), with some modifications, provides the framework for the domain-specific approach (Fig. 9.1). Based on case study data, we proposed that there are different buffers for maintaining semantic and phonological information. Individuals with damage to the phonological WM buffer showed very reduced span, better performance with visual than auditory presentation, and reduced or absent effects of phonological variables on span, particularly with visual presentation (see also Vallar & Baddeley, 1984). In contrast, those with semantic WM deficits, while also showing reduced span, showed the normal pattern of better performance with auditory than visual presentation and effects of phonological variables on span, indicating better preservation of phonological WM capacities (Martin & He, 2004; Martin, Shelton, & Yaffee, 1994). The two types of patients differed also in the effects of lexical status, with those with a phonological WM deficit showing substantially better performance for words than non-words (in line with the control pattern), whereas those with semantic WM deficits showed no advantage for words over non-words, suggesting that they did not benefit from the semantic information in the words (Martin & He, 2004; see also Hoffman, Jefferies, & Lambon Ralph, 2011; Wong & Law, 2008). Martin et al. (1994) developed two tasks to contrast phonological versus semantic maintenance using a probe paradigm: (1) rhyme probe, in which participants judge whether a probe word rhymes with one of words on a previously presented list, and (2) category probe, in which participants judge whether a probe word is in the same semantic category as one of the words in the previously presented list. The patients with phonological WM deficits did better than those with semantic WM deficits on the category probe task, whereas the reverse was true for the rhyme probe task.

In order to establish that these individuals' phonological and semantic WM deficits could not be attributed to other phonological or semantic processing deficits, they were tested on speech perception and single word comprehension and production. For example, Martin and He (2004) showed that a patient with a phonological WM deficit (EA) and two with semantic WM deficits (AB, ML) scored above the control mean on word comprehension and scored at a high level within the control range on picture naming. However, some have argued that these standardized comprehension tests typically do not require fine phonological distinctions and if the patients were tested on difficult speech discrimination tasks they would show deficits (Allport, 1984; Belleville, Caza, & Peretz, 2003). Martin and Breedin (1992) showed, however, that even though a patient with a severe phonological WM deficit (EA) scored slightly below the control range on difficult tests of speech perception, this was not the source of her phonological WM difficulties as other patients who showed similar mild speech perception deficits did much better on phonological WM.

At times, researchers whose work is limited to studying non-brain damaged individuals question why so few cases have been reported showing particular dissociations (Morey, 2018; Morey et al., 2019). As others have indicated (Logie, 2019), this often results because neuropsychological researchers consider the issue closed and further report of the same dissociation would be unenlightening. Nonetheless, particularly given the current emphasis on replication, it is valuable to determine the extent to which these dissociations can be replicated across a large sample of individuals with brain damage. In an ongoing large-scale study of individuals at the acute stage of left-hemisphere stroke (Martin & Schnur, 2019), 70 individuals have been tested on the single word processing and WM tasks. The category probe task discussed earlier was used to tap semantic WM and a digit matching span task was used to tap phonological WM. (In the digit matching span task, participants judge whether pairs of digit strings are the same or different, with non-matching

Relations between Sem-WM and Sem LTM, Ph-WM and Ph-LTM, and Sem WM and Ph-WM

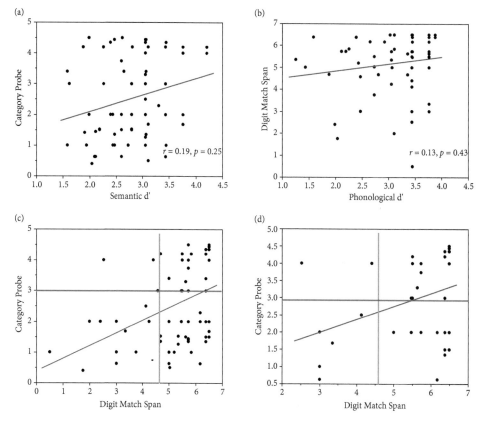

Fig. 9.2 Relation between semantic and phonological processing and WM for acute stroke cases (a) relation between semantic WM and semantic processing measure, (b) relation between phonological WM and phonological processing measure, (c) dissociations between semantic WM and phonological WM for whole sample, (d) dissociations between semantic WM and phonological WM for those within control range on both phonological and semantic processing measures.

strings differing in the order of two adjacent digits.) Single word processing was assessed via a word–picture matching test, computing d's for their ability to discriminate matching pictures from semantically related (d' semantic) or phonologically related pictures (d' phonological). Fig. 9.2a, b show the relation between these measures and the category probe and digit matching span values, respectively. These relations were quite weak, making it unlikely that semantic or phonological processing deficits are the source of their WM deficits (consistent with Martin and Breedin, 1992). Fig. 9.2c shows the relation between performance on the semantic and phonological WM measures. Even though the correlation between these is significant, a sizeable number (18) showed performance within the control range on digit span matching but performance below the control range for semantic category probe. A smaller number showed the opposite dissociation (three). Even if one restricts the sample to those who scored within the control range on both d′ measures (Fig. 9.2d), nine individuals showed preserved phonological but impaired semantic WM and two showed the opposite pattern.

A similar approach has been taken with a sample of 23 chronic patients who are part of the Rice chronic aphasia database, for whom we have more extensive background measures (Martin, 2017). Among these, four showed a semantic WM deficit without a phonological WM deficit and two showed the reverse, based on performance on the category probe and digit matching tests. All scored within normal limits on speech perception and word processing tasks (i.e. minimal pairs syllable discrimination, word–picture matching with phonologically and semantically related foils, standardized vocabulary (Peabody Picture Vocabulary Test; Dunn & Dunn, 2007)) and a test of semantic association using picture stimuli (Pyramids and Palm Trees Test; Howard, 1992). Thus, it is certainly possible to find individuals who show WM deficits in one of the two domains without concomitant speech processing or LTM deficits.

The distinction between phonological and semantic WM was also supported by Martin et al. (1994) and Martin and Romani (1994) who reported on the first case studies demonstrating the differential relations of domain-specific WM deficits to sentence processing deficits. Martin et al. (1994) reported better comprehension for a patient with a phonological WM deficit but better sentence repetition for a patient with a semantic WM deficit. Martin and Romani (1994) (see also Martin & He, 2004) showed that those with semantic WM deficits were impaired in judging the semantic acceptability of sentences in which word meanings had to be maintained prior to integration across some intervening words but did better when the information could be integrated immediately (Martin & He, 2004; Martin & Romani, 1994). That is, when detecting the anomaly in sentences in which one to three adjectives appeared before a noun (e.g. 'The rusty swimsuit', 'The rusty, old, red swimsuit', …) versus after a noun (e.g. 'The swimsuit was rusty …', 'The swimsuit was old, red, and rusty'), the performance of individuals with semantic WM impairment was at a high level when there was only one adjective before or after the noun, but declined substantially to a near chance level as the number of adjectives before the noun increased, but remained at a high level as the numbers of adjectives after the noun increased. These results can be explained if we assume that in the 'before' condition, the meanings of the adjectives had to be maintained in semantic WM until the noun was processed, whereas in the 'after' condition, each adjective could be integrated with the preceding noun as it was heard. In contrast to the findings for those with a semantic WM deficit, the patient with a phonological WM deficit showed an effect of the immediate versus delayed integration conditions that was within the range of controls.

Further discussion of more recent results on the role of semantic WM and phonological WM in sentence comprehension and production will be presented in the later section on applications of WM to sentence processing.

Neuroimaging Evidence for the Distinction Between Semantic and Phonological Working Memory

In an early fMRI study, Martin et al. (2003) contrasted the brain regions involved during the delay period in a recognition probe paradigm involving either semantic retention (synonym probe) or phonological retention (rhyme probe). During the delay period, greater activation in a left inferior parietal region (the supramarginal gyrus) was seen for the phonological than the semantic retention task. Greater activation was seen in a left frontal region for the semantic than the phonological task, though this difference was only marginally significant. Hamilton, Martin, and Burton (2009) provided stronger evidence for a frontal localization of semantic retention in a phrase comprehension test modelled on the sentence comprehension task reported by Martin and Romani (1994). In the delayed integration (or 'before') condition, subjects saw three adjectives (green, bright, shining) preceding a semantically congruent (emerald) or incongruent (sun) noun, whereas in the immediate integration (or 'after') condition, the adjectives followed the noun. Three left middle/inferior frontal regions showed increasingly greater activation over time in the delayed versus immediate integration conditions. No regions previously identified to be involved with phonological retention or rehearsal showed an effect of this manipulation.

Neuropsychological Evidence for Separable Orthographic, Phonological, and Visuospatial Working Memory

Our approach assumes distinct and dissociable phonological, orthographic, and visuospatial WM components. Table 9.2 reports six individuals with clear orthographic WM deficits (with significant letter length effects in word spelling indexing orthographic WM impairment) in the context of performance within normal limits on tests of phonological WM (digit span or digit matching span) and visuospatial WM (Corsi blocks). In contrast, there are four individuals with significant phonological WM deficits, as measured by digit span and digit matching span,[1] but with no evidence of orthographic WM deficits (non-significant letter length effects in word spelling) or visuospatial span limitations. Furthermore, the individuals with orthographic WM deficits also do not show orthographic LTM impairment: word length significantly affects error probability while word frequency does not. (The evidential role of length and frequency effects is discussed in more detail in Section 4 on the relationship between WM and LTM). Similarly, those with phonological WM deficits show no indications of phonological LTM impairment, as evidenced by performance within normal limits on speech perception, requiring discriminating phonologically related words in

---

[1] MLB's digit matching span was only marginally below that of controls, but he was significantly below controls on both digit span and on a non-word probe task.

Table 9.2 Dissociations of orthographic and phonological WM and LTM showing significance of word length (reflecting orthographic WM) and word frequency (reflecting orthographic LTM) and performance relative to controls on tests of phonological WM and phonological LTM.

Patient	Type of WM deficit	Orthographic WM — Spelling: length effect (short, long)	Orthographic LTM — Spelling: frequency effect (HF, LF)	Phonological WM — Digits forward	Phonological WM — Digit matching	Phonological WM — Non-word probe span	Phonological LTM — Consonant discrimination	Phonological LTM — WPM - phon foils	Phonological LTM — Auditory LDT Palpa 5 freq effect	Auditory comp. — PPVT or word pic. matching overall	Visuospatial WM — Corsi or WMS spatial span
DTE	Ortho	64% vs 0% *p* < 0.0001	36% vs 29% *p* < 0.58	5 WNL	5.77 *p* < 0.95	6.24 *p* < 0.328	97% (PALPA 1)			91st %ile (PPVT)	5 (Corsi)
LPO	Ortho	89% vs 46% *p* < 0.0005	75% vs 61% *p* < 0.26	4.5 WNL	n/a		100% (PALPA 1)			73rd %ile (PPVT)	5 (Corsi)
JRE	Ortho	25% vs 0% *p* < 0.005	29% vs 26% *p* < 0.78	5 WNL	n/a		94% (PALPA 1)			94th %ile (PPVT)	4 (WMS)
SDI	Ortho	8% vs 0% *p* < 0.008	8% vs 8% *p* < 1	4.5/5.0 WNL	n/a					98% (WPM)	
CRI	Ortho	74% vs 0% *p* < 0.0001	55% vs 65% *p* < 0.36	4.5/5.0 WNL	n/a					97% (WPM)	5 (Corsi)
PQS	Ortho	92% vs 74% *p* < 0.001	83% vs 78% *p* < 0.26	5 WNL	4.72 *p* < 0.094	5 *p* < 0.939	99% (PALPA 1)			99th %ile (PPVT)	5 (Corsi)
LC	Phon+Sem	75% vs 60 *p* < 0.31	75% vs 60% *p* < 0.62	3 *p* < 0.002	3 *p* < 0.002		93% WNL	98% WNL	87% vs 80% *p* < 0.33	98% (WPM) 42nd %ile (PPVT)	5 (Corsi)

PP	Phon	86% vs 71%	93% vs 64%	3.5	3.68	94%	100%	97% vs 97%	100% (WPM)	6
		p < 0.35	p < 0.07	p < 0.006	p < 0.009	WNL	WNL	p < 1.0	77th %ile (PPVT)	(Corsi)
MK	Phon+Sem	11% vs 36%	43% vs 43%	3.5	3.76	94%	98%	97% vs 90%	94% (WPM)	
		p < 0.36	p < 1	p < 0.006	p < 0.011	WNL	WNL	p < 0.14	4th %ile (PPVT)	
MLB	Phon+Sem	86% vs 86%	93% vs 79%	3.5	4.72 2.59	85	98%	98% vs 92%	97% (WPM)	
		p < 1	p < 0.28	p < 0.006	p < 0.094	p < 0.005	WNL	p < 0.10	47th %ile (PPVT)	

Notes: HF, high frequency; LF, low frequency; LDT, lexical decision task; Corsi Blocks (Mueller & Piper, 2014); PALPA, Psycholinguistic Assessments of Language Processing in Aphasia (Kay, Lesser, & Coltheart, 1996); PPVT, Peabody Picture Vocabulary Test (Dunn & Dunn, 2007); WMS, Wechsler Memory Scale (Wechsler, 2008); WPM, word-picture matching (from Rapp et al., 2016, or Allen et al., 2012).

word–picture matching and the absence of lexical frequency effects in auditory lexical decision.[2] These latter findings reinforce the assumption of the independence of WM and LTM systems (Norris, 2017, 2019), an issue we discuss in detail in the later section on the relationship between WM and LTM.

Neuroimaging and Lesion Evidence of Domain-Specific Orthographic and Phonological Working Memory

Neuroimaging findings with healthy controls and neuropsychological evidence indicate that the left parietal lobe supports WM in both phonological and orthographic domains, suggesting that either (1) the left parietal lobe instantiates multiple domain-specific WM components or (2) The left parietal lobe instantiates domain-general processes that support the maintenance of both phonological and orthographic information (Cowan et al., 2005, 2011; Kane et al., 2004).

To evaluate these hypotheses, we present a novel lesion overlap analysis that included individuals with left-hemisphere strokes diagnosed with only either phonological WM or orthographic WM deficits. The phonological WM deficit group (four individuals; zero female) had well-documented phonological WM deficits, without deficits in LTM for phonology or in orthographic WM. The orthographic WM deficit group (five individuals; three females) had well-documented orthographic WM deficits in spelling, without deficits in LTM for orthography or in phonological WM. The neuroimaging modalities included one computed tomography scan and eight T1-weighted MRI scans. MRIcron software (https://www.nitrc.org/projects/mricron) was used to draw each lesion, and enantiomorphic normalization was used to warp the lesions to a standard brain with coordinates reported in Montreal Neurological Institute (MNI) space (Nachev, Coulthard, Jäger, Kennard, & Husain, 2008).

As reported in Fig. 9.3, the lesion overlays reveal non-overlapping brain regions for the two groups in the parietal lobe and elsewhere. The parietal region for the phonological WM group was in the inferior supramarginal gyrus while the region for orthographic WM group was more posterior and superior. These parietal regions showed good convergence with regions activated in fMRI studies with neurotypical individuals that showed domain-specific neurotopography: phonological WM (−55, −36, 23; Martin et al., 2003) and orthographic WM (−28, −54, 57; Rapp & Dufor, 2011).

These findings are clearly consistent with the hypothesis that distinct parietal regions support domain-specific phonological and orthographic WM processes. Of course, this does not rule out the possibility that there are also additional parietal regions that support a shared, domain-general process WM process.

---

[2] MLB was significantly below control range on speech perception (consonant discrimination) but was within normal limits on the other two measures involving word perception.

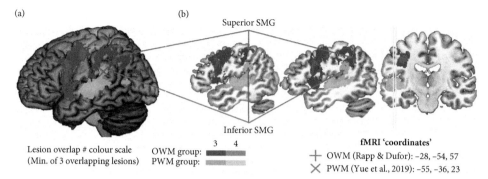

(a)   (b)

Superior SMG

Inferior SMG

	3 4	
Lesion overlap # colour scale	OWM group:	fMRI 'coordinates'
(Min. of 3 overlapping lesions)	PWM group:	+ OWM (Rapp & Dufor): -28, -54, 57
		✕ PWM (Yue et al., 2019): -55, -36, 23

Fig. 9.3 Overlay of orthographic WM and phonological WM deficit lesions. OWM lesions are in violet/pink and PWM lesions are in green. (a) Rendered lesions affecting PWM and OWM. The x is centred on the reported coordinate (MNI: −55 −36 23) from an fMRI study of PWM (Yue et al., 2019; original peak reported in Talaraich coordinates as −52.5, −34.5, 23.5 in Table 9.2 and was converted to MNI via http://sprout022.sprout.yale.edu/mni2tal/mni2tal.html). The + is centred the reported (MNI −28 −54 57) from an fMRI study of OWM (Rapp & Dufor, 2011). (b) Slices through −50 and -47 z-slices (MNI). The colour scale is at the bottom (min = 3, max =4); there were no locations with greater than 4 lesions overlapping. This constitutes converging findings that there is a domain-specific WM topography: whereas PWM is in the more anterior/inferior portion of the supramarginal gyrus (SMG) extending inferiorly to the posterior superior temporal gyrus, OWM is in the more posterior/superior portion of the SMG extending superiorly to the intraparietal sulcus.

Summary

We argue that WM is non-unitary with separable WM systems specialized for maintaining phonological, semantic, orthographic, and visuospatial information. For all of these domains, we present behavioural dissociations in patient performance on WM tasks tapping these different domains, which cannot be accounted for by LTM deficits in the respective domains. For the contrast of phonological and semantic WM, we report differential effects of deficits in these domains on sentence processing and also different brain regions that support retention in these domains based on functional neuroimaging with healthy young adults. Finally, for the phonological and orthographic domains, we present lesion–symptom mapping findings showing distinct brain regions supporting WM performance.

4. The Relationship Between Working Memory and Long-Term Memory

As stated in the first section of this chapter and depicted in Fig. 9.1, we assume that the domain-specific WM systems are distinct from the LTM knowledge components that may be associated with each domain. Thus, there are direct connections between LTM and WM in each domain (Fig. 9.1). In Martin et al. (1999), we suggested that feedforward and feedback connections between the knowledge representations and the buffer would support activation in the buffer and serve to maintain the stability of representations in the lexical system. As a result of this organization, lexical effects may be propagated to the buffer. For instance, higher-frequency words (with greater activation in the knowledge representation) would transmit greater activation to the buffer, resulting in better recall for high than low-frequency words.

The proposed interaction between LTM and WM should not, however, be interpreted as opening the door to collapsing the distinction between them. Yue et al. (2019; see also Yue, 2018) used a multivariate decoding approach (Norman et al., 2006) to examine the brain regions involved in speech perception and phonological WM. Note that the brain regions involved in speech perception are not purely auditory sensory regions, but also include regions that instantiate the LTM representations for phonemes, syllables, and spoken words onto which incoming acoustic information can be mapped (Mesgarani, Cheung, Johnson, & Chang, 2014; Price, 2012). The main issue was whether phonological WM would be reflected in persisting activation in the speech perception region (localized to the left superior temporal gyrus as would be predicted by an embedded-processes approach or instead in a different region outside of the speech perception regions as predicted by a buffer approach (postulated to be the left supramarginal gyrus, based on prior imaging and neuropsychological results). In the WM task, subjects were presented with a list of either one or three nonsense syllables or one or three chords and, after a 10-second delay, indicated whether a probe item (syllable or chord) was in the preceding list. As shown in Fig. 9.4, standard univariate fMRI analyses showed no significant activation in the perception region (superior temporal gyrus) during the delay period but activation was observed in the WM region (supramarginal gyrus).

Yue et al. (2019) used multivoxel pattern analysis to determine whether speech versus music could be distinguished in the superior temporal gyrus and supramarginal gyrus during the delay. Greater evidence for distinguishing speech versus music during the delay was obtained in the supramarginal gyrus than in the superior temporal gyrus. Furthermore, Yue et al. (2019, supplementary materials) showed that while individual differences in decoding success in the supramarginal gyrus were correlated with accuracy on the WM task for the speech stimuli, decoding success in the superior temporal gyrus was unrelated to WM performance.

Yue (2018) followed up on these findings using representational similarity analysis, which, in contrast to multivoxel pattern analysis, allows one to examine the content of the information represented (Kriegeskorte et al., 2008). Representational similarity analysis was carried out by comparing a theoretical matrix of similarities of stimuli (i.e. phonological or semantic similarity) to the obtained similarity of patterns of neural activation. In this task, participants maintained a single word in WM over a delay and judged either the degree of phonological or semantic similarity of a probe word to the memory word. As shown in Fig. 9.5, Yue found that phonological information could be decoded in the superior temporal gyrus during the encoding period of the phonological WM task, but not during the delay period. In contrast, phonological

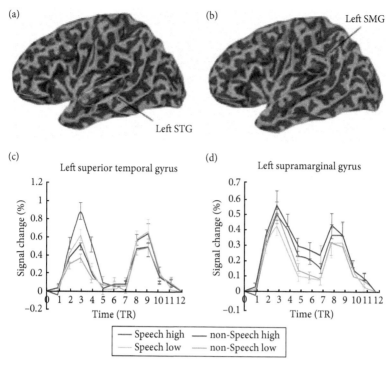

Fig. 9.4 Univariate activation results in Yue et al. (2018). (a) The activation map for speech versus non-speech in the perception task shows a speech perception region in the left superior temporal gyrus (STG). (b) The activation map for high versus low memory load conditions during the delay period of the STM task show a set of dorsal frontoparietal regions, including one in the left supramarginal gyrus (SMG). Average signal changes from univariate analyses for the STM task in (c) the left STG and (d) the left SMG as shown in (a) and (b). Error bars represent the standard error of the mean.

information could not be decoded in the supramarginal gyrus during the encoding period but could during the delay period and semantic information could not be decoded in either region for any time point during the phonological WM task, but could be decoded elsewhere during the semantic task (not shown).

The ability to decode phonological information in the supramarginal gyrus but not the superior temporal gyrus during a WM delay (Yue, 2018) provided strong evidence that the supramarginal gyrus serves as a buffer for maintaining phonological information, rather than instantiating more general attentional processes.

Code-Specific Transfer From Working Memory to Long-Term Memory in Learning

The early findings of Warrington and Shallice (1969) and Warrington et al. (1971) showed that patients could have very reduced verbal span but show normal

(a)

SMG

STG

(b)

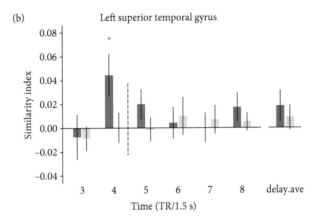

Left superior temporal gyrus

Similarity index

Time (TR/1.5 s)

(c)

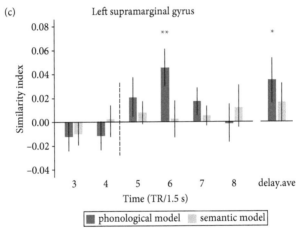

Left supramarginal gyrus

Similarity index

Time (TR/1.5 s)

■ phonological model ▨ semantic model

Fig. 9.5 Regions of interest and representational similarity analysis results for phonological WM task. (a) Two functional regions of interest derived from a study on phonological STM (Yue et al. 2018) shown on an inflated surface of a brain template. (b, c) The graphs show the average neural-model similarity index (i.e., Spearman correlation coefficient) at each time point spanning the encoding period to the delay period, with the one calculated based on the average activation pattern (delay.ave) across the delay period (i.e. TR 6–8) on the rightmost side of the x-axis in (a) the left superior temporal gyrus (STG) and (B) the left supramarginal gyrus (SMG). The dark blue represents the correlations with the target phonological model whereas the light blue represent the correlations with the semantic models. Error bars represent the standard error of the mean. Dashed lines indicate the typical boundaries between the encoding period and the delay period. pho: phonological; sem: semantic. Asterisks indicate the significance of one-sample t-test: * $p < 0.05$, ** $p < 0.01$.

long-term learning. While this dissociation supported the distinction between WM and LTM, it caused problems for theories assuming that information had to be held in WM in order to be transferred to LTM (e.g. Atkinson & Shiffrin, 1968). Freedman and Martin (2001) suggested that these findings might be accommodated if one assumed domain-specific WM systems and domain-specific transfer from WM to LTM, rather than a single WM capacity as was implicit in standard memory models (Atkinson & Shiffrin, 1968; Waugh & Norman, 1965). That is, whereas recall in the verbal WM tasks administered to these patients (digit and word list recall) depends to a large extent on phonological maintenance, recall in standard verbal LTM tasks such as free recall and paired associate learning depend on the use of semantic codes (Crowder, 1976). Thus, patients with a WM deficit on word and digit lists may have impaired phonological retention but a preserved ability to retain semantic information in WM which supported their long-term learning on standard word recall tasks. If so, then one might predict that their long-term learning of phonological information would be impaired. (See Baddeley, Papagno, & Vallar, 1988, for supportive findings.) By contrast, patients that have a semantic WM deficit should show impaired long-term learning of semantic information but better preserved learning of phonological information. Freedman and Martin (2001) tested this notion of domain-specific transfer from WM to LTM by assessing learning of new phonological information (i.e. a foreign translation of a known word) and learning of new semantic information (i.e. a new definition of a known word) for patients with phonological or semantic WM deficits. They found that a patient with a phonological WM deficit (EA) showed worse performance for learning the foreign translations than learning the new definitions, whereas a patient with a semantic WM deficit (ML) showed the opposite pattern. Thus, Freedman and Martin concluded that storage in WM was required for transfer to LTM, but storage in WM depended on code-specific (i.e., phonological, semantic) WM buffers.

Freedman and Martin's (2001) findings might lead one to predict that a patient with semantic WM deficit would show symptoms like those of an amnesic individual with difficulty in learning any new semantic information. However, Romani and Martin (1999) showed that this was not the case for patient AB, who had a semantic WM deficit. They found that while he was very impaired on LTM tasks for random word lists (the typical materials used in such tasks), he showed preserved long-term learning for pictures and shapes and even for the propositional information in spoken stories. Romani and Martin suggested that his WM deficit was specific to maintaining semantic representations for words. Once he was able to integrate semantic information into larger propositional units and map information onto coherent information in LTM, he was able to retain that information in a normal fashion. Consequently, the semantic WM deficit that we are describing should not be seen as a general deficit in maintaining and transferring any type of conceptual information to LTM, but a deficit specific to word meanings.

The Distinction Between Working Memory and Long-Term Memory in the Orthographic Domain

In the orthographic domain, patterns of dysgraphic impairment support the existence of structurally distinct orthographic LTM and WM processing components. Selective disruption of orthographic LTM was first described by Beauvois and Dérouesné (1981), for a French speaking patient RG. Although RG had no difficulties in speaking words, he showed greater overall difficulty in spelling low- compared to high-frequency words, regardless of their length. Virtually all of his errors consisted of phonologically plausible spellings for irregular words with low predictability phoneme-grapheme mappings (e.g. 'photo' → FAUTO,) and he was able to generate plausible spellings for pseudowords, regardless of their length. He exhibited the same performance pattern across output modalities (written and oral spelling) and input modalities (spelling to dictation or written picture naming). (See Rapp & Fischer-Baum, 2015, for a review of numerous similar cases.) The performance pattern is interpreted as resulting from disruption in the processing or retrieval of the learned representations of word spellings stored in orthographic LTM, a system that is especially sensitive to the frequency of the learned representations. When the orthographic LTM system is unable to process a word, phonologically plausible spelling responses may be generated by the sublexical phoneme–grapheme conversion system (Fig. 9.6).

A contrasting dysgraphic pattern attributed to disruption to orthographic WM was first reported by Miceli and colleagues (Caramazza et al., 1987; Miceli, Silveri, & Caramazza, 1985) in Italian and, subsequently, many other cases have been described involving different languages. These cases all exhibit significant word length effects such that the probability of making an error on any given letter increases depending on the number of letters in the word, precisely what would be expected from disruption to a limited capacity WM system. The dysgraphic difficulties are manifested in spelling both words and pseudowords, regardless of the output modality (written or oral spelling or typing). Error rates are generally unaffected by lexical factors (word frequency, part of speech, and concreteness), although mild effects of lexical variables have been reported (Sage & Ellis, 2004, see Buchwald and Rapp, 2009, for discussion). In contrast to LTM deficits, errors consist of letter substitutions, deletions, transpositions, and additions as would be expected from WM failures. Serial position effects are typically reported consisting of either U-shaped or decreasing accuracy functions (see later section on decay and interference in WM for more details).

In summary, two distinct patterns of dysgraphic performance have been reported with contrasting sensitivities to word frequency and letter length as well as with distinctive patterns of errors. These performance patterns have been shown to doubly dissociate and they provide the key empirical foundations for the distinction between LTM and WM in spelling that is supported by lesion and neuroimaging evidence (discussed in a later section). Furthermore, there are recent reports of developmental difficulties in

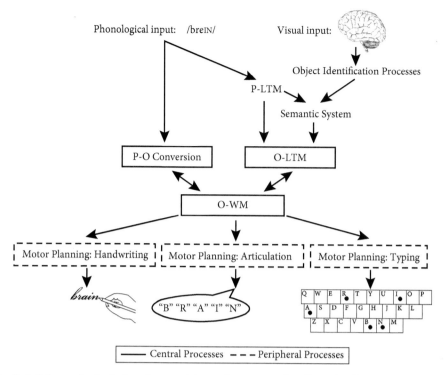

Fig. 9.6 Schematic depicting the cognitive architecture of spelling, highlighting central (core) and peripheral processes. P = phonological/phonology; O = orthographic/ orthography; WM = working memory.

Reproduced from Brenda Rapp, Jeremy Purcell, Argye E. Hillis, Rita Capasso, and Gabriele Miceli, 'Neural bases of orthographic long-term memory and working memory in dysgraphia', *Brain*, 139 (4), p. 590, Figure 1. doi:10.1093/brain/awv348 Copyright © The Authors (2015).

children selectively affecting the learning of orthographic LTM (Hepner, McCloskey, & Rapp, 2017) or orthographic WM (Barisic, Kohnen, & Nickels, 2017).

Interaction Between Long-Term Memory and Working Memory in the Orthographic Domain: Neuropsychological Evidence

Although the evidence for structurally distinct orthographic LTM and orthographic WM processing components is strong, this does not preclude interaction between the two systems. In fact, McCloskey, Macaruso, and Rapp (2006) argued for bi-directional feedforward/feedback interaction between orthographic WM and orthographic LTM based on the error pattern produced by patient CM who suffered from damage to orthographic WM. Although, as expected, most of CM's errors were non-lexical (e.g., letter substitutions, deletions, transpositions, and additions), about one-quarter of them were lexical substitutions (e.g. solid spelled as SOLAR, method as MOTHER, etc.). These errors were primarily orthographically but not semantically or phonologic-ally related to the target, and the same error pattern was observed with written or typed responses and in writing with eyes open or eyes closed, ruling out more peripheral sources of the errors either in terms of visual feedback or motor processes. McCloskey et al. suggested these lexical errors arose because, following retrieval from orthographic LTM, the unstable representations in orthographic WM were fed back to orthographic LTM, activating words that shared letters still available in orthographic WM. In this way, AMBER might be produced in response to the stimulus 'arm' even though CM was not confused about the identity of the stimulus (e.g. even after writing AMBER he could report that the stimulus had been 'arm').

However, because lexical responses can occur by chance based on the letter errors (substitutions, deletions, additions, transpositions) that occur with orthographic WM disruption, the key challenge for the feedback account was determining if the observed lexical responses occurred at rates higher than would be expected by chance.[3] On the basis of a complex analysis that considered multiple possible sources of lexical errors, McCloskey and colleagues concluded that the lexical errors could be understood only by positing bi-directional connectivity between orthographic WM and orthographic LTM that may serve to stabilize representations (Dell, 1986; Dell & Gordon, 2003). This bi-directional connectivity also accounts for a number of other previously reported findings (see Folk, Rapp, & Goldrick, 2002).

Evidence From Lesion and Neuroimaging Studies for the Distinction Between Orthographic Working Memory and Long-Term Memory

Rapp et al. (2016) examined the distribution of lesions of 33 individuals with ac-quired dysgraphia: 17 with orthographic LTM impairment, 10 with orthographic WM impairment, and 6 with both (O-Mixed). The individuals were selected for the study based only on their behavioural profiles, with no consideration of lesion characteristics. A voxel-based lesion mapping analysis was carried out in order to determine if there were voxels specifically associated with orthographic LTM but not orthographic WM impairment and vice versa. The results (Fig. 9.7a) reveal a distinct, non-overlapping lesion distribution such that lesions selectively associated with orthographic WM impairments overlapped in the left superior parietal lobe (centred on the intraparietal sulcus, −39, −50, 36) and there were two sites associ-ated with orthographic LTM deficits, in the left ventral temporal lobe and the pos-terior inferior frontal gyrus with lesion densities centred on −49, −39, −19 and −52, −19, 18 respectively.

---

[3] It is worth noting that similar conclusions have been reached by researchers working with spoken phoneme errors produced by healthy and aphasic individuals, where lexical errors have been argued to be produced more often than would be expected by chance (Dell, Schwartz, Martin, Saffran, & Gagnon, 1997; Goldrick & Rapp, 2001).

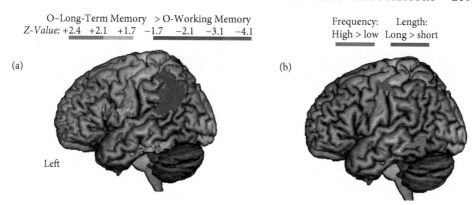

O–Long-Term Memory > O-Working Memory
Z-Value: +2.4 +2.1 +1.7 −1.7 −2.1 −3.1 −4.1

Frequency: Length:
High > low   Long > short

(a)

(b)

Left

Fig. 9.7 Brain regions involved in orthographic LTM and orthographic WM from lesion analysis (A) and functional neuroimaging (B). (A) Voxel-based lesion mapping comparison of the lesions of individuals with orthographic LTM and WM deficits, from Rapp et al. (2016). Depicted are the results of testing (at each voxel) for differences in presence/absence of lesion for individuals with deficits affecting orthographic LTM or orthographic WM. Clusters of significant difference are rendered on a left hemisphere standard brain template. All clusters are FDR (false discovery rate) corrected for multiple comparisons at a p < 0.05. The colour scale reflects the z-values of the significant clusters. Positive z-values (orange/red) indicate the orthographic LTM deficit clusters; negative z-values (blue/pink) indicate orthographic WM deficit clusters. (B) Results of voxelwise analysis of word frequency and letter length effects from a spelling task administered during fMRI (corrected p < 0.05). Violet: length effect (Long > Short). Red: frequency effect (Low > High frequency words). Clusters were adapted with permission from Table 3/ Figure 4 in Rapp and Dufor (2011).

(a) Adapted from Brenda Rapp, Jeremy Purcell, Argye E. Hillis, Rita Capasso, and Gabriele Miceli, 'Neural bases of orthographic long-term memory and working memory in dysgraphia', *Brain*, 139 (4), p. 600, Figure 3. doi:10.1093/brain/awv348 Copyright © The Authors (2015). (b) Adapted with permission from Brenda Rapp and Olivier Dufor, 'The Neurotopography of Written Word Production: An fMRI Investigation of the Distribution of Sensitivity to Length and Frequency', *Journal of Cognitive Neuroscience*, 23 (12), pp. 4067–4081, Table 3/ Figure 4 © 2011 by the Massachusetts Institute of Technology.

While it is perhaps not surprising that distinct behavioural patterns arise from distinct lesion sites, the finding of non-overlapping neurally distant lesion sites, provides strong confirmation that the behavioural patterns are, in fact, reliable indicators that although orthographic LTM and orthographic WM are computationally 'proximal', they are supported by structurally distinct systems (for converging results, see also Hillis-Trupe et al., 2002, and Rapcsak & Beeson, 2004).

In neuroimaging studies of healthy individuals, the general parietal region associated with orthographic WM (and especially its right hemisphere homologue) has been associated with spatial and/or visual WM/attentional processes (Todd & Marois, 2004; Wager & Smith, 2003). It has also been associated with mechanisms supporting attentional switching in visual (Serences & Yantis, 2006) and auditory (Shomstein & Yantis, 2006) displays as well as in task switching (Shomstein & Yantis, 2004). This association with attentional processes raises the question of whether or not orthographic WM is specifically a WM component or whether, as would be predicted by an embedded-processes account, WM is more appropriately conceptualized as the contents of orthographic LTM that are in spotlight of attention at any given moment. Under that view, the parietal lesions would reflect damage to domain-general attentional processes. However, as we discuss in more detail in upcoming section on the role of attention and control, the evidence is at odds with that position. Thus, for example, the individuals with orthographic WM deficits in Rapp et al. (2016), performed within the normal range on visuospatial WM, with spatial spans on the Corsi blocks task (Kessels, van Zandvoort, Postma, Kappelle, & de Haan, 2000) averaging 4.75 (range = 4–5).

Importantly, the locations identified with orthographic LTM and orthographic WM lesions are also highly consistent with fMRI findings obtained with healthy participants. In an fMRI study during which participants carried out written spelling while being scanned, Rapp and Dufor (2011) identified a left parietal region that was associated with sensitivity to word length but not frequency (orthographic WM) as well as frontal and ventral sites associated with the complementary pattern of sensitivity to frequency but not length (orthographic LTM). In fact, as can be seen in Fig. 9.7b, the areas identified by Rapp and Dufor (2011) were in close proximity to the centres of high-density lesion overlap depicted in Fig. 9.7a (for additional converging findings, see also Planton, Jucla, Roux, & Démonet, 2013; Purcell, Turkeltaub, Eden, & Rapp, 2011; Rapp & Lipka, 2011).

In sum, the neural data—both lesion and neuroimaging results—provide strong and convergent evidence for substantially independent WM and LTM mechanisms in the orthographic domain.

Summary

Within our domain-specific WM framework, we argue that although WM and LTM interact in each domain, they are distinct. In the phonological domain, evidence for the distinction comes from neuroimaging results showing different regions are involved in matching incoming input to LTM representations of speech sounds and words and the regions involved in maintaining those representations in WM. Although WM and LTM are distinct, we argue that information is maintained in domain-specific WM storage systems to support transfer to LTM in that domain. In the orthographic domain, both patient lesion data and functional neuroimaging data point to anatomically distinct regions involved in WM and LTM. Interactions between orthographic WM and LTM can be seen in the error types produced by an individual with an orthographic WM deficit where the interaction with orthographic LTM resulted in the substitution of orthographically similar words in WM.

5. Role of Attention and Control

As indicated in the first section, while we assume that there are centralized domain-general processes, such as attention, control, and other functions that may enhance the availability of information stored in buffers, attention is not necessary for maintenance. This view contrasts with that from the embedded-processes approach which assumes that, rather than dedicated WM mechanisms, attention is used to maintain a subset of items in LTM within the focus of attention (Cowan, 1999). Thus, according to the embedded-processes approach, one might hypothesize that patients such as those described in earlier sections with WM deficits actually have difficulty allocating attention to the target representations and not with WM per se.

Attention and Control Processes in Semantic Working Memory Disorders

With regard to the possible role of attention and control in WM in neuropsychological deficits, Lambon Ralph and Jefferies and their colleagues have put forward the Controlled Semantic Cognition (CSC) framework which assumes two major components of semantic processing: the semantic knowledge system and semantic control (Lambon Ralph, Jefferies, Patterson, & Rogers, 2017). Semantic control has been argued to be related to executive function abilities that involve selecting appropriate semantic representations and inhibiting inappropriate representations (Jefferies & Lambon Ralph, 2006; Jefferies, Patterson, & Ralph, 2008). The claims for the separation of semantic knowledge and control in the CSC framework derive largely from what are argued to be distinctive patterns of semantic disruption in two neuropsychological syndromes: semantic dementia, characterized by a disruption of the semantic knowledge component, and semantically impaired stroke aphasia, characterized by a disruption of the semantic control component (though see Chapman, Hasan, Schulz, & Martin, 2020). Hoffman et al. (2011) have argued that patients with semantic WM deficits but excellent performance on single word semantic tasks actually have a mild deficit in semantic control. On semantic tasks with minimal control requirements (e.g. picture naming or picture-word matching), their performance may not be impaired. However, on tasks requiring a high degree of control (e.g. selecting a synonym for a word while ignoring a highly related but non-synonymous alternative) they demonstrate striking deficits. They argue that performance on semantic WM tasks such as the category probe task simply requires a high degree of control. If the CSC account is correct, it could be interpreted as an embedded-processes approach to semantic WM that does not require positing specific semantic WM mechanisms. However, embedded processes accounts typically assume a domain general attentional control system, whereas in the CSC, it is unclear whether the control component is hypothesized to be specific to semantics or part of more general executive function abilities (Jefferies & Lambon Ralph, 2006; Hoffman, Jefferies, Haffey, Littlejohns, & Lambon Ralph, 2013).

Martin and colleagues (Allen, Martin, & Martin, 2012; Hamilton & Martin, 2005, 2007) examined the cognitive control deficit hypothesis as an explanation for a semantic WM deficit. Case studies of one individual with a semantic WM deficit (Hamilton & Martin, 2005, 2007) seemed to provide some support for this view as he showed an inhibition deficit on verbal tasks (Stroop; recent negatives task), though not on non-verbal inhibition tasks (non-verbal Stroop; anti-saccade). However, Allen et al. (2012) examined whether semantic WM deficits were necessarily associated with inhibition deficits or more general executive function deficits. They examined, in 20 individuals with aphasia, the degree to which semantic or phonological WM deficits were associated with executive function deficits, separately assessing inhibition, shifting, and updating components of executive function (Miyake et al., 2000). Contrary to the inhibition hypothesis, they found that neither semantic nor phonological WM was related to inhibition or task switching measures. Only the phonological WM measure correlated with the updating component of executive function and with a complex executive function task (Wisconsin Card Sort Task; Heaton et al., 1993). They argued that these correlations were due to the role of phonological WM in supporting performance on the updating tasks (N-back and keep track tasks) and in the Wisconsin Card Sort Task, rather than the causation running in the opposite direction, with executive function deficits causing the WM deficits.

In addition, findings from Tan, Martin, and Van Dyke (2017) and Tan and Martin (2018) also argued against the equivalence of semantic WM and control functions as they reported that semantic WM measures predicted semantic aspects of sentence comprehension whereas measures related to control (inhibition and other executive function measures) did not.

The Relationship between Working Memory and General Attentional/Executive Processes

We have recently examined attentional/executive abilities in patients showing WM deficits in phonological and orthographic domains. Table 9.3 presents previously unreported data showing performance on several executive function tasks, including components of the Attention Networks Task (ANT; Fernandez-Duque & Black, 2006) and a non-verbal Stroop task involving spatial conflict (Hull, Martin, Beier, Lane, & Hamilton, 2008), for patients classified as showing WM deficits without processing/LTM deficits in that domain. As can be seen, most of the patients showed effects within the normal range across most/all tasks. These findings thus lend little support to the notion that their WM deficits might be attributed or reduced to attentional deficits. The natural counterargument is that these are not the appropriate tasks with which to evaluate the attentional hypothesis of WM. However, these are fairly standard executive function/attention tasks

Table 9.3 Attentional processing for individuals with orthographic WM and phonological WM deficits on components of the ANT and non-verbal Stroop task. (Probability values reflect whether individual patient effects differed significantly from controls; WNL = within normal limits)[a]

| Patient | Type of WM deficit | Attention networks test | | | Nonverbal Stroop |
| | | Executive control effect (flankers) | Alerting effect | Orienting/validity effect | Interference effect |
		Incongruent–congruent (ms)	No cue–alert (ms)	Invalid–valid (ms)	Incongruent–neutral (ms)**
DTE	Ortho	209 p<0.13	-55 p<0.001	237 p<0.44	n/a
PQS	Ortho	117 p<0.96	45 p<0.79	20 p<0.68	n/a
MWE	Ortho	113 p<0.43	-87 p<0.001	167 p<0.99	n/a
LC	Phon+Sem	181 p<0.16	44 p=0.92	49 p=0.83	91 WNL
PP	Phon	169 p<0.21	53 p=0.86	38 p=0.72	71 WNL
MK	Phon+Sem	n/a			117 WNL
MLB	Phon+Sem	17* WNL			44 WNL
RF	Phon+Sem+Ortho	68* WNL			60 WNL
RK	Phon+Sem+Ortho	262 p<0.03	23 p=0.49	29 p=0.64	107 WNL

[a] Normative data are from Fernandez-Duque & Black (2006) for the ANT task and significance was calculated using the Crawford & Howell (1998) modified t-test for small samples. Normative data for the nonverbal Stroop task were from Hull et al. (2008) (N=100, μ=63.2, σ=60.9).

that are used to assess what are widely assumed to be central attentional/executive processes. Thus, a critic would need to motivate the choice of other tasks.

Working Memory and Attentional Mechanisms

A patient reported by Hillis and Caramazza (1989) provides important insights into the relationship between domain-specific WM and (at least certain) domain-general attentional mechanisms. Patient NG suffered visuospatial neglect subsequent to a left-hemisphere parietal stroke that manifested itself in lack of perception and/or awareness of items on the right side of space. The deficit apparently affected a domain-general mechanism of spatial attention operating in an object-centred frame of reference that disrupted processing of a wide range of spatial stimuli: visually presented real objects, line drawings and, importantly, written words and pseudowords in *both* reading and in spelling. In reading and spelling, the deficit affects orthographic WM (Caramazza, Capasso, & Miceli, 1996) and NG omitted or substituted letters on the right side of words or pseudowords, regardless of the modality of input or output (visual, written, oral, picture) and, regardless of the orientation of the input stimulus in reading (horizontal, vertical or mirror-reversed). For example, she read: HUMID → 'hman' DRING → 'drill' and spelled: 'normal' → NORMANT; 'ground' → GROU.

With respect to our understanding of the relationship between domain-general attentional mechanisms and WM, this case (see also Baxter & Warrington, 1983; Moscovitch & Behrmann, 1994) supports two conclusions: (1) domain-general processes such as those involved in spatial attention contribute to successful processing in orthographic WM, but also (2) orthographic WM cannot be 'reduced' to a domain-general spatial attention mechanisms because it is also the case that the vast majority of individuals with orthographic WM do not exhibit visuospatial neglect and, thus, do not suffer from disruption to mechanisms of spatial attention. These findings illustrate that while domain-general processes may contribute significantly or even critically to WM, they are not the sole basis of WM.

While embedded-processes approaches assume a domain-general system that directs attention to representations in different domains, one might propose instead that there are domain-specific attentional systems (Tamber-Rosenau & Marois, 2016) and it is the disruption of these domain-specific attentional systems that accounts for selective WM deficits. However, several arguments can be raised against this proposal. For one, findings reviewed earlier from Allen et al. (2012) showed that executive function measures like Stroop that have a semantic component did not correlate with semantic WM deficits. Such correlations would be expected if the two reflected the same attentional processes. Fougnie and Marois (2006) presented evidence from healthy young subjects for the separation of WM and attention in the visuospatial domain. They demonstrated greater disruption on a visual WM task from increasing load of a second visual WM task during the delay period than from increasing load from a visuospatial attentional task (multiple-object tracking). Finally, in the neuroimaging work of Yue (2018), the supramarginal region that was shown to be sensitive to phonological WM load (Yue et al., 2019) allowed for the representational similarity analysis decoding of phonological codes, which would not be expected if the region solely served to direct attention to phonological codes stored elsewhere. Furthermore, if the role of this purported domain-specific attentional system was to maintain activation of LTM representations of speech in the superior temporal gyrus, one would have predicted that phonological decoding would have been possible in that temporal region, which was not the case.

Summary

Considerable neuropsychological data argues for a separation between attentional processes and WM. Little relation has been found between executive function abilities and WM deficits in phonological or semantic domains. New data presented here demonstrate that patients with phonological or orthographic WM deficits may perform at normal levels on attentional and executive function tasks. Other data supporting the distinction of WM and attentional processes come from sentence processing studies that show an effect of WM but not executive function in predicting sentence comprehension findings for patients and for healthy young adults.

6. Storage, Maintenance, and Loss of Information From Working Memory

A key question is: why does forgetting happen in WM? Thus far, we have focused this review on the structural organization of WM, however, answering this question requires understanding the internal functions of WM. Research with healthy individuals has largely converged on two sources of forgetting: decay and interference. Decay refers to the limitations of WM systems with regard to the temporal maintenance of the contents of WM (items and their order) during (serial) recall. As a result of decay, items whose representations have not been maintained may be forgotten at the time of recall (Baddeley, 1986; Burgess & Hitch, 1992, 1999; Cowan, 1992; Page & Norris, 1998). By contrast, interference is often conceptualized as arising from competition for shared but limited resources among the items held in WM themselves or between them and/or other relevant (e.g. LTM) representations. The fact that similar items typically show greater interference and distinctive items are less likely to be forgotten suggests that the competition could be considered to involve a competition for representational resources such that differentiating similar compared to dissimilar items requires more resources (Brown, Neath, & Chater, 2007; Farrell & Lewandowsky, 2002; Nairne, Thompson, & Pandeirada, 2007). Much research has pitted decay and interference accounts against one another (Lewandowsky, Geiger, & Oberauer, 2008; Oberauer, 2021). However, it is also possible that both mechanisms contribute to forgetting in WM (Anderson & Matessa, 1997; Barrouillet, Plancher, Guida, & Camos, 2013; Henson,

1998). In the following section, we discuss neuropsychological evidence for the separability of the cognitive functions that give rise to decay and interference, respectively.

Decay and Interference in Orthographic Working Memory

In Wing and Baddeley's (1980) analysis of a large spelling error corpus they distinguished between 'slips' and 'convention' errors arguing that the latter were due to lack of knowledge of a word's spelling and, thus, were not relevant to their goal of understanding the WM processes of spelling. They assumed that, by contrast, 'slips' (errors which were either self-corrected or correctly spelled in some other place in the essay) largely arose in a 'temporary storage buffer'. These constituted about 80% of the errors and consisted of letter substitutions, omissions, insertions, and reversals. Wing and Baddeley had expected that slips would increase in frequency from the beginning to the end of words due to decay between the time that the letters entered the buffer until when they were produced serially in writing but found that, instead, there was a bow-shaped accuracy function, with lower accuracy for letters in the middle positions of words. They attributed the bow shape to the effects of lateral interference between neighbouring items, with letters on the ends having fewer neighbors and, hence, less interference.

Individuals with damage to orthographic WM commonly exhibit bow-shaped accuracy functions although decreasing accuracy functions have also been reported. The fact that both have been observed suggests that both interference and decay may be operating in orthographic WM. Costa et al. (2011) specifically evaluated this possibility in their investigation of two (Italian) patients with the profile of orthographic WM deficit whose impairments were largely limited to consonants (see also Kay & Hanley, 1994; Miceli, Capasso, Benvegnù, & Caramazza, 2004). Despite these similarities, the two differed in the shape of their consonant accuracy functions, with GSI exhibiting a decreasing accuracy function across consonant position, while CRI exhibited a bow shaped accuracy function.

Costa et al. (2011) hypothesized that the decreasing accuracy function was caused by abnormal decay affecting the buffer's capacity to maintain *temporal stability* of the consonant representations. In contrast, they hypothesized that the bow-shaped function arose from interference among consonant representations due to a deficit affecting the buffer's ability to maintain the *representational distinctiveness* of the consonants. The consonant specificity of the deficits allowed for testing a number of predictions of these hypotheses. For a decay deficit they predicted that consonant accuracy should be affected by the total number of letters in a word because, regardless of whether the elements are consonants or vowels, they both contribute to the time elapsed during the serial production of the letters in spelling. In contrast, for the representational distinctiveness deficit, consonant accuracy should be affected only by the number of consonants in a word as only these are affected by the deficit. Costa et al. (2011) reported evidence that conformed with this and various other predictions. On that basis, they concluded that, within the orthographic WM system, there are distinct mechanisms responsible for maintaining temporal stability and representational distinctiveness and that these can be selectively affected by brain damage, resulting in abnormal decay and abnormal interference, respectively. This study not only advances our understanding of the mechanisms operating within orthographic WM, but also illustrates that neuro-psychological data can be used to test highly detailed hypotheses regarding cognitive processes.

Summary

We suggest that both decay and interference play a role in forgetting. Different patterns of loss from orthographic WM have been reported which suggest that these are dissociable processes as some patients demonstrate an exaggerated effect of interference whereas others suffer from overly rapid decay.

7. Applications of Working Memory to Sentence Processing

An often-cited reason for studying verbal WM is its presumed importance in sentence processing (Camos, 2017; Fougnie & Marois, 2011) which necessarily involves inter-action with multiple LTM and other cognitive systems. However, this claim is actually quite controversial. Beginning with the early studies of Baddeley and Hitch (1974), a number of studies with healthy participants found little detrimental effect on comprehension from an external verbal memory load (see Caplan & Waters, 1999). In addition, correlations between performance on standard short-term memory span tasks and comprehension performance are low (ranging from 0.18 to 0.30 for digit or word span for age-homogeneous samples; Daneman & Merikle, 1996). Further, Caplan and Waters (1999) presented a good deal of evidence arguing against the claim that even the WM capacity reflected in complex span measures (see Daneman & Carpenter, 1980) plays a role in online sentence processing, as have more recent studies by McElree, Lewis, and Van Dyke and their colleagues (Lewis, Vasishth, & Van Dyke, 2006; McElree, Foraker, & Dyer, 2003; Van Dyke, Johns, & Kukona, 2014).[4] In fact, a review paper by Baddeley, Gathercole, and Papagno (1998) argued that the principal role of the phonological buffer was in supporting phonological learning (i.e. in learning new words), rather than in supporting sentence comprehension

---

[4] Caplan and Waters (1999, 2013) have argued that while WM is not involved in automatic online aspects of sentence processing, it does support conscious, controlled aspects such as those that involve encoding linguistic information in memory in order to carry out a task. This proposal might account for observed relations between WM and performance on tasks requiring acting out a sequence of events for sentences with arbitrary combinations of words, such as 'touch the large red circle with the small green square' (e.g., Jaroslawska, Gathercole, Logie, & Holmes, 2016).

Table 9.4 Example of stimulus materials in Tan et al. (2017) and Tan and Martin (2018)

Sentence region		Example stimulus
Introduction		The critic
Intervening region	LoSyn/LoSem	who had enjoyed the memorable *play*
	LoSyn/HiSem	who had enjoyed the memorable *actress*
	HiSyn/LoSem	who mentioned that the *play* was memorable
	HiSyn/HiSem	who mentioned that the *actress* was memorable
Adverbial phrase		at the new theatre
Critical region		will visit
Spillover region		the director.

Note: 'Lo-' and 'Hi-' refer to low and high interference condition, while '-Syn' and '-Sem' refer to syntactic interference and semantic interference condition.

Our findings from the case studies reported earlier concur with these negative conclusions at least with respect to phonological WM and sentence comprehension (Martin & He, 2004; Martin & Romani, 1994), with patients with phonological WM deficits doing well on sentence comprehension tests (see also, Butterworth, Campbell, & Howard, 1986; Caplan & Waters, 1999). By contrast, we have argued that semantic WM capacity does play a role in comprehension, supporting comprehension for sentences which require maintaining several words' semantic representations prior to integration (Hanten & Martin, 2000; Martin & He, 2004; Martin & Romani, 1994). Two recent studies with neurologically healthy participants (Tan & Martin, 2018; Tan et al., 2017) have added to these case study findings in supporting a role for semantic but not phonological WM in sentence comprehension. These studies manipulated the degree of semantic and syntactic interference in the sentences (Table 9.4). In these sentences, when an individual hears the main verb (e.g. in this example, 'visit'), we assume that s/he attempts to locate the subject for the verb based on semantic and syntactic cues, finding a memory representation for a prior noun that is semantically consistent with the verb and which was previously encoded as a syntactic subject. In the sentences with high semantic interference, an intervening noun ('actress') in the subordinate clause is semantically plausible as the subject of the verb whereas in the low semantic interference condition, the intervening noun ('play') is not. In the sentences with high syntactic interference, the intervening noun is a subject (e.g. 'the *play* was memorable') whereas in the low syntactic interference condition, it is not a subject but a prepositional object or direct object (e.g. 'enjoyed the memory play'). Tan et al. (2017) found that for 126 undergraduate subjects, individuals' semantic WM measure (category probe) predicted reaction times involved in resolving semantic interference during question answering even after controlling for their vocabulary and their performance on composite complex WM measure (i.e. combining reading span and operation span), whereas their phonological WM (digit span) did not predict any of the sentence comprehension outcomes.[5] In the Tan and Martin (2018) study of ten aphasic individuals, their semantic WM capacity again predicted the ability to resolve semantic interference in sentence reading times, after controlling for semantic knowledge, whereas phonological WM did not. Both studies showed that individuals' degree of syntactic interference was unrelated to either their semantic or phonological WM capacities. Results from both of these studies provide further evidence against a role for phonological WM in comprehension and a specific role for semantic WM in maintaining semantic representations.

The differing patterns of WM deficits and associated sentence processing deficits contribute to the evidence supporting the distinction between semantic and phonological WM stores. The generally good comprehension of those with phonological WM deficits strongly implies that some WM capacity beyond that tapped by phonological WM is involved during comprehension. To account for this, it has been argued that phonological retention per se does not play a critical role because integration of information across parts of a sentence cannot be made on the basis of phonological representations. For example, when hearing 'Mary often flirts with John and sometimes embarrasses herself', linkage of 'herself' with 'Mary' cannot be made on the basis of phonological information but instead on the basis of knowing that 'herself' refers semantically to a female person and syntactically to the subject of the sentence, which is consistent with linking to 'Mary'. To carry out this linkage those features would have to have been encoded when 'Mary' was processed (Lewis et al., 2006). Thus, what individuals need to maintain is the semantic and syntactic information derived from each word and the constituent structure and interpretation that is built as each word is processed rather than the phonology of the words.

While a considerable body of research has been directed at studying the role of WM in comprehension, relatively few studies have been carried out on its role in language production. Case studies of patients with a semantic WM deficit demonstrated that they were impaired in language production when producing phrases containing several content words (e.g. producing 'short blonde hair' to describe a picture) even though they could produce the individual words in isolation (Martin & Freedman, 2001; Martin, Miller, & Vu, 2004), which was congruent with their difficulty in comprehending similar phrases (Martin & He, 2004; Martin & Romani, 1994). Patients with phonological WM deficits, by contrast, were unimpaired in producing such phrases (see also Martin et al., 1994; Shallice & Butterworth, 1977).

The neuropsychological findings for language production were a bit more unexpected than those for comprehension, as one might have anticipated that a phonological WM buffer is used in planning the phonological forms of an utterance prior to articulation. Recently, Martin and Schnur (2019) carried out a case-series study examining the relation of phonological and semantic WM capacities to language production in a relatively large sample of individuals at the acute stage of stroke. They recruited all individuals with left hemisphere

---

[5] The exception was one relation to digit span that went in the opposite direction predicted, which was attributed to a suppressor effect.

stroke and only excluded those scoring more than 2.5 standard deviations below the patient mean on auditory word recognition. The intent was to determine whether the case study findings for individuals with chronic aphasia would extend to spontaneous speech involved in storytelling for those at the acute stage. Patient narrative production was obtained by having them tell the Cinderella story after viewing a picture book with the words covered up. Narratives were scored using the quantitative production analysis (Rochon, Saffran, Berndt, & Schwartz, 2000). Based on the case study findings, they predicted that the degree of semantic WM deficit would predict patients' ability to produce multiple content words in phrases and sentence whereas the degree of phonological WM deficit would not. Using a multiple regression approach, they assessed the independent contributions of semantic and phonological WM to narrative measures, after controlling for semantic and phonological single word processing abilities.[6] They found that semantic WM capacity but not phonological WM capacity, made a unique contribution in predicting the degree of sentence elaboration and mean length of utterance. By contrast, their phonological WM capacity but not their semantic WM capacity made a unique contribution to predicting speech rate (words per minute). A measure of their ability to produce grammatical words in utterances was unrelated to both WM measures. The results imply that semantic capacity is crucial for planning the semantic content of phrases, but not their grammatical structure, and suggests that once these phrases have been constructed, phonological WM capacity, but not semantic, affects the rate at which speech is uttered, with greater phonological capacity allowing for more fluent and rapid production.[7]

Thus, the results for language production, like those for comprehension, support the contention that there are separable phonological WM and semantic WM capacities that play different roles in language processing.

Summary

Considerable data from both patients and healthy individuals imply a greater contribution from semantic than phonological WM in sentence comprehension. Semantic WM is needed when maintaining word meanings prior to their integration and when resolving interference from semantic, but not syntactic representations. On the production side, semantic working memory is important in planning the lexical-semantic representations within a phrase and thus supports sentence elaboration. Recent evidence suggest that phonological WM capacity is related to speech rate in terms of words per minute, with greater capacity resulting in more rapid, fluent speech.

---

[6] In a multiple regression approach, the significance of the weights for each predictor reflects the unique contribution of that variable while controlling for the other predictors.

[7] The role of phonological capacity in speech rate was surprising given previous case studies revealing a normal speech rate for patients with a phonological WM deficit (Martin et al., 1994; Shallice & Butterworth, 1977). A possible explanation relies on a distinction between input and output phonological buffers, involved in perception and production, respectively (Martin et al., 1999). That is, it is possible that the chronic cases had purely input phonology buffer deficits whereas these acute cases had a mix of input and output phonological buffer deficits, and the output buffer deficits were the source of the relation to speech rate.

8. Limitations of the Approach and Accounting for Inconsistencies

The WM approach that we are advocating assumes multiple domain-specific resources, which are separate from perceptual processes and LTM systems in these domains, and separable from general attentional/executive function mechanisms. The approach thus contrasts with many WM theories based primarily on findings from healthy adults, that typically postulate only domain-general capacities (McElree et al., 2003; Oberauer, 2009). Part of the evidence used to support the role of domain-general resources are findings from paradigms requiring the simultaneous maintenance of information across different domains, where intermodal costs are observed (i.e., the amount recalled is less than would be expected based on the addition of different capacities). When, however, the two domains are phonological and visuospatial, the costs are greater for recall of the visuospatial information than the phonological, leading some to argue for specialized resources for phonological storage but general attentional mechanisms supporting retention and refreshing of information in all other domains (Barrouillet & Camos, 2021; Camos, 2017; Cowan & Morey, 2007). Important exceptions to the claims of domain-generality have come from studies by Fougnie and Marois and colleagues (Fougnie & Marois, 2011; Fougnie, Zughni, Godwin, & Marois, 2015; see also Soemer & Saito, 2016). Fougnie and Marois (2011) showed that when retaining both visual and auditory verbal information, intermodal costs were reduced when the demand on WM capacities were more similar across the two tasks and, under those conditions, more items were retained across the two modalities than was possible from one modality alone, supporting the existence of separate storage capacity across modalities; in addition, there was no evidence for greater costs for visual than verbal information, arguing against a domain-specific capacity solely for phonological information. Moreover, Fougnie et al. (2015) showed no dual-task costs in a short-term recognition paradigm involving both visual and auditory verbal information when procedures were implemented to minimize differences between single-task and dual-task execution demands and the possibility of shared representations across domains (e.g. the possibility of encoding a visual array in terms of a verbal description—'red square on left'). Recently, however, Uittenhove, Chaabi, Camos, and Barrouillet (2019) found that when employing the procedures of Fougnie et al. but requiring recall rather than recognition, dual-task costs were obtained, though the effects of increasing load in the other modality were often quite small. Their findings would seem to leave open the possibility of domain-specific capacities along with domain-general capacities, though they discuss arguments against that claim.

Another challenge to the multiple capacities approach comes from large-scale studies using factor analytic approaches which show that complex WM tasks such as reading span, operation span, and symmetry span load on the same latent factor, despite their differences in the domain being tapped (verbal vs mathematical vs spatial) (Unsworth, Fukuda, Awh, & Vogel, 2014). However, these studies used complex tasks that required switching between different components of the task (e.g. reading sentences while re-membering sets of letters) and thus one might expect a large contribution of executive function abilities which may be domain general. Also, one might expect a great deal of interference between the representations in the two components of a task. For instance, in reading span, one might expect interference between the phonological codes derived from reading sentences and the phonological codes used to maintain letter lists. Thus, modality-specific representations may be obscured by the interference between these representations. In contrast to the findings for complex span tasks, studies taking a latent variable approach which have focused on simple span tasks such as digit or word span or recall of spatial arrays have shown much more domain specificity (Alloway, Gathercole, & Pickering, 2006; Kane et al., 2004; Tian, Fischer-Baum, & Beier, 2017). In neuropsychological studies, the focus has been on simple span tasks, and thus the domain specificity that is evidenced is in line with these findings from healthy individuals.

A more general critique of the domain-specific capacities approach that might be levelled is that it is unparsimonious in that additional buffers (i.e. semantic and graphemic) have been postulated beyond the phonological and visuospatial stores in the Baddeley approach and one might question whether there is any limit to the number of buffers that might be proposed. An embedded-processes approach may appear more parsimonious in that any type of information can be maintained in WM as long as it is represented in LTM. However, while simplicity may be attractive, it is necessary to be able to account for how one maintains repetitions of items (as for words in lists and sentences). Moreover, there is a need to account for the body of evidence demonstrating dissociations between different WM capacities—for example, between maintenance of graphemic versus visuospatial information—which cannot be accounted for by LTM or attentional deficits.

While our approach allows for the postulation of multiple buffers, we would not suggest that they exist for all types of information and can be postulated willy-nilly. As discussed earlier, Caramazza et al. (1987) proposed that buffers are computationally motivated when there is a mismatch between unit sizes at the interface between processes. For example, in spelling, one can retrieve the letters and their positions simultaneously for a lexical representation, but then one needs to access the letters one at a time for output. A buffer is needed to maintain the representation of the whole word while this serial output process occurs. The need for a semantic buffer arises when there is a mismatch in the other direction in comprehension, with single word meanings being maintained until they can be integrated to form a propositional unit. One can imagine that as expertise develops in any domain, storage systems and procedures for acting on these systems are developed to increase efficiency and automaticity in those domains.

Summary

Empirical challenges to the domain-specific capacities framework come from studies of healthy individuals suggesting shared capacities across different domains—that is, under-additive capacities when retaining information simultaneously across domains and a common underlying factor in individual differences studies of working memory capacities assessed across multiple domains. However, there are exceptions to these findings under certain conditions and thus the conclusions to be drawn from these studies are still up for debate. At a more theoretical level, there is a concern that the domain-specific capacities approach is unparsimonious. We suggest, however, that there are findings that are difficult to accommodate in an embedded-processes approach. Moreover, we propose a limitation on the existence of capacities to processing systems where there is a mismatch between the size of the units at one level and those required at subsequent levels.

Conclusion

Our aim in this chapter was to provide an overview of neuropsychological evidence on WM in the verbal domain, to demonstrate the robustness and richness of the findings and the challenges or new directions they present for current theorizing on WM. We hope that the material and ideas presented here will serve to spur a lively and constructive discussion on the means of integrating these findings and theoretical perspectives with those obtained from other approaches.

Acknowledgements

The authors would like to acknowledge the contributions of Jennifer Shea, Rachel Mis, Elizabeth Baca, and Giulia Campana for their assistance in collecting and analysing patient data. Preparation of this manuscript was supported in part by NIH DC014976 grant to Baylor College of Medicine and NIH DC012283 to Johns Hopkins University.

References

Allen, C. M., Martin, R. C., & Martin, N. (2012). Relations between short-term memory deficits, semantic processing, and executive function. *Aphasiology, 26*, 428–461. doi:10.1080/02687038.2011.617436

Alloway, T. P., Gathercole, S. E., & Pickering, S. J. (2006). Verbal and visuospatial short-term and working memory in children: are they separable? *Child Development, 77*, 1698–1716. doi:10.1111/j.1467-8624.2006.00968.x

Allport, D. A. (1984). Speech production and comprehension: one lexicon or two? In W. Prinz & A. F. Sanders (Eds.), *Cognition and motor processes* (pp. 209–228). Berlin: Springer. doi:10.1007/978-3-642-69382-3_15

Anderson, J. R., & Matessa, M. (1997). A production system theory of serial memory. *Psychological Review, 104*, 728–748. doi:10.1037/0033-295X.104.4.728

Atkinson, R. C., & Shiffrin, R. M. (1968). Human memory: a proposed system and its control processes. In K. W. Spence & J. T. Spence (Eds.), *Psychology of learning and motivation* (Vol. 2, pp. 89–195). New York, NY: Academic Press. doi:10.1016/S0079-7421(08)60422-3

Baddeley, A. (1986). *Working memory*. New York, NY: Oxford University Press.

Baddeley, A. D., & Hitch, G. (1974). Working memory. In G. H. Bower (Ed.), *Psychology of learning and motivation* (Vol. 8, pp. 47–89). New York, NY: Academic Press. doi:10.1016/S0079-7421(08)60452-1

Baddeley, A. D., & Hitch, G. J. (2019). The phonological loop as a buffer store: An update. *Cortex, 112*, 91–106. doi:10.1016/j.cortex.2018.05.015

Baddeley, A. D., Hitch, G. J., & Allen, A. (2021). A multicomponent model of working memory. In R. H. Logie, V. Camos, and N. Cowan (Eds.), *Working memory: State of the science* (pp. 10–43). Oxford, UK: Oxford University Press.

Baddeley, A., Gathercole, S., & Papagno, C. (1998). The phonological loop as a language learning device. *Psychological Review, 105*, 158–173.

Baddeley, A., Papagno, C., & Vallar, G. (1988). When long-term learning depends on short-term storage. *Journal of Memory and Language*, I, 586–595.

Barisic, K., Kohnen, S., & Nickels, L. (2017). Developmental graphemic buffer dysgraphia in English: A single case study. *Cognitive Neuropsychology, 34*, 94–118. doi:10.1080/02643294.2017.1359154

Barrouillet, P., & Camos, V. (2021). The time-based resource sharing model of working memory. In R. H. Logie, V. Camos, and N. Cowan (Eds.), *Working memory: State of the science* (pp. 85–115). Oxford, UK: Oxford University Press.

Barrouillet, P., Plancher, G., Guida, A., & Camos, V. (2013). Forgetting at short term: When do event-based interference and temporal factors have an effect? *Acta Psychologica, 142*, 155–167.

Basso, A., Spinnler, H., Vallar, G., & Zanobio, M. E. (1982). Left hemisphere damage and selective impairment of auditory verbal short-term memory. A case study. *Neuropsychologia, 20*, 263–274. doi:10.1016/0028-3932(82)90101-4

Bates, E., Wilson, S. M., Saygin, A. P., Dick, F., Sereno, M. I., Knight, R. T., & Dronkers, N. F. (2003). Voxel-based lesion–symptom mapping. *Nature Neuroscience, 6*, 448–450. doi:10.1038/nn1050

Baxter, D. M., & Warrington, E. K. (1983). Neglect dysgraphia. *Journal of Neurology, Neurosurgery, and Psychiatry, 46*, 1073–1078. doi:10.1136/jnnp.46.12.1073

Beauvois, M. F., & Dérouesné, J. (1981). Lexical or orthographic agraphia. *Brain: A Journal of Neurology, 104*, 21–49. doi:10.1093/brain/104.1.21

Belleville, S., Caza, N., & Peretz, I. (2003). A neuropsychological argument for a processing view of memory. *Journal of Memory and Language, 48*, 686–703. doi:10.1016/S0749-596X(02)00532-6

Brown, G. D. A., Neath, I., & Chater, N. (2007). A temporal ratio model of memory. *Psychological Review, 114*, 539–576. doi:10.1037/0033-295X.114.3.539

Buchwald, A., & Rapp, B. C. (2009). Distinctions between orthographic long-term memory and working memory. *Cognitive Neuropsychology, 26*, 724–751. doi:10.1080/02643291003707332

Burgess, N., & Hitch, G. J. (1992). Toward a network model of the articulatory loop. *Journal of Memory and Language, 31*, 429–460. doi:10.1016/0749-596X(92)90022-P

Burgess, N., & Hitch, G. J. (1999). Memory for serial order: A network model of the phonological loop and its timing. *Psychological Review, 106*, 551–581. doi:10.1037/0033-295X.106.3.551

Burgess, N., & Hitch, G. J. (2006). A revised model of short-term memory and long-term learning of verbal sequences. *Journal of Memory and Language, 55*, 627–652. doi:10.1016/j.jml.2006.08.005

Butterworth, B., Campbell, R., & Howard, D. (1986). The uses of short-term memory: a case study. *Quarterly Journal of Experimental Psychology Section A, 38*, 705–737. doi:10.1080/14640748608401622

Camos, V. (2017). Domain-specific versus domain-general maintenance in working memory. In B. H. Ross (Ed.), *Psychology of learning and motivation* (Vol. 67, pp. 135–171). New York, NY: Academic Press. doi:10.1016/bs.plm.2017.03.005

Caplan, D., & Waters, G. S. (1999). Verbal working memory and sentence comprehension. *Behavioral and Brain Sciences, 22*, 77–94. doi:10.1017/S0140525X99001788

Caplan, D., & Waters, G. S. (2013). Memory mechanisms supporting syntactic comprehension. *Psychonomic Bulletin & Review, 20*, 243–268.

Caramazza, A. (1986). On drawing inferences about the structure of normal cognitive systems from the analysis of patterns of impaired performance: The case for single-patient studies. *Brain and Cognition, 5*, 41–66. doi:10.1016/0278-2626(86)90061-8

Caramazza, A. (1997). How many levels of processing are there in the mental lexicon? *Cognitive Neuropsychology, 14*, 177–208. doi:10.1080/026432997381664

Caramazza, A., Capasso, R., & Miceli, G. (1996). The role of the graphemic buffer in reading. *Cognitive Neuropsychology, 13*, 673–698. doi:10.1080/026432996381881

Caramazza, A., & McCloskey, M. (1988). The case for single-patient studies. *Cognitive Neuropsychology, 5*, 517–527. doi:10.1080/02643298808253271

Caramazza, A., Miceli, G., Villa, G., & Romani, C. (1987). The role of the graphemic buffer in spelling: evidence from a case of acquired dysgraphia. *Cognition, 26*, 59–85.

Chapman, C., Hasan, O., Schulz, P. E., & Martin, R. C. (2020). Evaluating the distinction between semantic knowledge and semantic access: Evidence from semantic dementia and comprehension-impaired stroke aphasia. *Psychonomic Bulletin & Review*. doi:10.3758/s13423-019-01706-6. Advance online publication.

Coltheart, M. (2001). Assumptions and methods in cognitive neuropsychology. In B. Rapp (Ed.), *The handbook of cognitive neuropsychology: What deficits reveal about the human mind* (pp. 3–21). New York, NY: Psychology Press.

Costa, V., Fischer-Baum, S., Capasso, R., Miceli, G., & Rapp, B. (2011). Temporal stability and representational distinctiveness: Key functions of orthographic working memory. *Cognitive Neuropsychology, 28*, 338–362. doi:10.1080/02643294.2011.648921

Cowan, N. (1992). Verbal memory span and the timing of spoken recall. *Journal of Memory and Language, 31*, 668–684. doi:10.1016/0749-596X(92)90034-U

Cowan, N. (1999). An embedded-processes model of working memory. In A. Miyake, & Shah, P. (Eds.), *Models of working memory: Mechanisms of active maintenance and executive control* (pp. 62–101). Cambridge, UK: Cambridge University Press. doi:10.1017/CBO9781139174909.006

Cowan, N., Elliott, E. M., Saults, J. S., Morey, C. C., Mattox, S., Hismjatullina, A., & Conway, A. R. A. (2005). On the capacity of attention: its estimation and its role in working memory and cognitive aptitudes. *Cognitive Psychology, 51*, 42–100. doi:10.1016/j.cogpsych.2004.12.001

Cowan, N., Li, D., Moffitt, A., Becker, T. M., Martin, E. A., Saults, J. S., & Christ, S. E. (2011). A neural region of abstract working memory. *Journal of Cognitive Neuroscience, 23*, 2852–2863. doi:10.1162/jocn.2011.21625

Cowan, N., & Morey, C. C. (2007). How can dual-task working memory retention limits be investigated? *Psychological Science, 18*, 686–688. doi:10.1111/j.1467-9280.2007.01960.x

Cowan, N., Morey, C. C., & Naveh-Benjamin, N. (2021). An embedded-processes approach to working memory: how is it distinct from other approaches, and to what ends? In R. H. Logie, V. Camos, and N. Cowan (Eds.), *Working memory: State of the science* (pp. 44–84). Oxford, UK: Oxford University Press.

Crowder, R. G. (1976). *Principles of learning & memory*. Hillsdale, NJ: Erlbaum.

Daneman, M., & Carpenter, P. A. (1980). Individual differences in working memory and reading. *Journal of Verbal Learning and Verbal Behavior, 19*, 450–466. doi:10.1016/S0022-5371(80)90312-6

Daneman, M., & Merikle, P. M. (1996). Working memory and language comprehension: A meta-analysis. *Psychonomic Bulletin & Review, 3*, 422–433. doi:10.3758/BF03214546

Dell, G. S. (1986). A spreading-activation theory of retrieval in sentence production. *Psychological Review, 93*, 283–321. doi:10.1037/0033-295X.93.3.283

Dell, G. S., & Gordon, J. (2003). Neighbors in the lexicon: Friends or foes? In N. O. Schiller & A. S. Meyer (Eds.), *Phonetics and phonology in language comprehension and production: Differences and similarities* (pp. 9–38). New York, NY: Mouton de Gruyter.

Dell, G. S., Schwartz, M. F., Martin, N., Saffran, E. M., & Gagnon, D. A. (1997). Lexical access in aphasic and nonaphasic speakers. *Psychological Review, 104*, 801–838.

Dunn, L. M., & Dunn, D. M. (2007). *PPVT-4: Peabody picture vocabulary test*. Minneapolis, MN: Pearson Assessments.

Elman, J. L. (1990). Finding structure in time. *Cognitive Science, 14*, 179–211. doi:10.1207/s15516709cog1402_1

Farrell, S., & Lewandowsky, S. (2002). An endogenous distributed model of ordering in serial recall. *Psychonomic Bulletin & Review, 9*, 59–79.

Fernandez-Duque, D., & Black, S. E. (2006). Attentional networks in normal aging and Alzheimer's disease. *Neuropsychology, 20*(2), 133–143. https://doi.org/10.1037/0894-4105.20.2.133

Fischer-Baum, S., & Rapp, B. (2012). Underlying cause(s) of letter perseveration errors. *Neuropsychologia, 50*, 305–318. doi:10.1016/j.neuropsychologia.2011.12.001

Folk, J. R., Rapp, B., & Goldrick, M. (2002). The interaction of lexical and sublexical information in spelling: What's the point? *Cognitive Neuropsychology, 19*, 653–671. doi:10.1080/02643290244000184

Fougnie, D., & Marois, R. (2006). Distinct capacity limits for attention and working memory: evidence from attentive tracking and visual working memory paradigms. *Psychological Science, 17*, 526–534. doi:10.1111/j.1467-9280.2006.01739.x

Fougnie, D., & Marois, R. (2011). What limits working memory capacity? Evidence for modality-specific sources to the simultaneous storage of visual and auditory arrays. *Journal of Experimental Psychology: Learning, Memory, and Cognition, 37*, 1329–1341. doi:10.1037/a0024834

Fougnie, D., Zughni, S., Godwin, D., & Marois, R. (2015). Working memory storage is intrinsically domain specific. *Journal of Experimental Psychology: General, 144*, 30–47. doi:10.1037/a0038211

Freedman, M. L., & Martin, R. C. (2001). Dissociable components of short-term memory and their relation to long-term learning. *Cognitive Neuropsychology, 18*, 193–226. doi:10.1080/02643290126002

Goldberg, A. M., & Rapp, B. (2008). Is compound chaining the serial-order mechanism of spelling? A simple recurrent network investigation. *Cognitive Neuropsychology, 25*, 218–255. doi:10.1080/02643290701862332

Goldrick, M., & Rapp, B. (2001). What makes a good neighbor? Evidence from malapropisms. *Brain and Language, 79*, 141–143.

Gupta, P., & MacWhinney, B. (1997). Vocabulary acquisition and verbal short-term memory: computational and neural bases. *Brain and Language, 59*, 267–333. doi:10.1006/brln.1997.1819

Gupta, P., & Tisdale, J. (2009). Word learning, phonological short-term memory, phonotactic probability and long-term memory: Towards an integrated framework. *Philosophical Transactions of the Royal Society B: Biological Sciences, 364*, 3755–3771. doi:10.1098/rstb.2009.0132

Hamilton, A. C., & Martin, R. C. (2005). Dissociations among tasks involving inhibition: A single-case study. *Cognitive, Affective & Behavioral Neuroscience, 5*, 1–13. doi:10.3758/CABN.5.1.1

Hamilton, A. C., & Martin, R. C. (2007). Proactive interference in a semantic short-term memory deficit: role of semantic and phonological relatedness. *Cortex, 43*, 112–123. doi:10.1016/S0010-9452(08)70449-0

Hamilton, A. C., Martin, R. C., & Burton, P. C. (2009). Converging functional magnetic resonance imaging evidence for a role of the left inferior frontal lobe in semantic retention during language comprehension. *Cognitive Neuropsychology, 26*, 685–704. doi:10.1080/02643291003665688

Hanley, J. R., & Young, A. W. (2019). ELD revisited: A second look at a neuropsychological impairment of working memory affecting retention of visuo-spatial material. *Cortex, 112*, 172–179. doi:10.1016/j.cortex.2018.10.029

Hanley, J. R., Young, A. W., & Pearson, N. A. (1991). Impairment of the visuo-spatial sketch pad. *Quarterly Journal of Experimental Psychology Section A, 43*, 101–125. doi:10.1080/14640749108401001

Hanten, G., & Martin, R. C. (2000). Contributions of phonological and semantic short-term memory to sentence processing: evidence from two cases of closed head injury in children. *Journal of Memory and Language, 43*, 335–361. doi:10.1006/jmla.2000.2731

Heaton, R. K., Chelune, G. J., Talley, J. L., Kay, G. G., & Curtiss, G. (1993). *Wisconsin Card Sorting Test manual: Revised and expanded.* Lutz, FL: Psychological Assessment Resource.

Henson, R. N. A. (1998). Short-term memory for serial order: the start-end model. *Cognitive Psychology, 36*, 73–137. doi:10.1006/cogp.1998.0685

Hepner, C., McCloskey, M., & Rapp, B. (2017). Do reading and spelling share orthographic representations? Evidence from developmental dysgraphia. *Cognitive Neuropsychology, 34*, 119–143. doi:10.1080/02643294.2017.1375904

Hillis-Trupe, A., Kane, A., Tuffiash, E., Beauchamp, N. J., Barker, P. B., Jacobs, M., & Wityk, R. J. (2002). Neural substrates of the cognitive processes underlying spelling: Evidence from MR diffusion and perfusion imaging. *Aphasiology*, *16*, 425–438. doi:10.1080/02687030244000248

Hillis, A. E., & Caramazza, A. (1989). The graphemic buffer and attentional mechanisms. *Brain and Language*, *36*, 208–235. doi:10.1016/0093-934X(89)90062-X

Hoffman, P., Jefferies, E., & Lambon Ralph, M. A. (2011). Explaining semantic short-term memory deficits: Evidence for the critical role of semantic control. *Neuropsychologia*, *49*, 368–381. doi:10.1016/j.neuropsychologia.2010.12.034

Hoffman, P., Jefferies, E., Haffey, A., Littlejohns, T., & Lambon Ralph, M. A. (2013). Domain-specific control of semantic cognition: A dissociation within patients with semantic working memory deficits. *Aphasiology*, *27*(4), 740–764. doi:10.1080/02687038.2012.751578

Houghton, G., Glasspool, D. W., & Shallice, T. (1994). Spelling and serial recall: Insights from a competitive queuing model. In G. D. A. Brown & N. C. Ellis (Eds.), *Handbook of spelling: Theory, process and intervention* (pp. 365–404). Chichester, UK: John Wiley and Sons.

Howard, D. (1992). *The pyramids and palm trees test: A test of semantic access from words and pictures*. Bury St Edmunds, UK: Thames Valley Test Company.

Hull, R., Martin, R. C., Beier, M. E., Lane, D. L., & Hamilton, A. C. (2008). Executive function in older adults: A structural equation modeling approach. *Neuropsychology*, *22*, 508–522.

Jaroslawska, A. J., Gathercole, S. E., Logie, M. R., & Holmes, J. (2016). Following instructions in a virtual school: Does working memory play a role? *Memory & Cognition*, *44*, 580–589.

Jefferies, E., & Lambon Ralph, M. A. (2006). Semantic impairment in stroke aphasia versus semantic dementia: A case-series comparison. *Brain*, *129*, 2132–2147. doi:10.1093/brain/awl153

Jefferies, E., Patterson, K., & Ralph, M. A. L. (2008). Deficits of knowledge versus executive control in semantic cognition: Insights from cued naming. *Neuropsychologia*, *46*, 649–658. doi:10.1016/j.neuropsychologia.2007.09.007

Jones, A. C., Folk, J. R., & Rapp, B. (2009). All letters are not equal: subgraphemic texture in orthographic working memory. *Journal of experimental psychology: Learning, Memory, and Cognition*, *35*, 1389–1402.

Kane, M. J., Hambrick, D. Z., Tuholski, S. W., Wilhelm, O., Payne, T. W., & Engle, R. W. (2004). The generality of working memory capacity: A latent-variable approach to verbal and visuospatial memory span and reasoning. *Journal of Experimental Psychology: General*, *133*, 189–217. doi:10.1037/0096-3445.133.2.189

Kay, J., & Hanley, J. R. (1994). Peripheral disorders of spelling: The role of the graphemic buffer. In G. D. A. Brown & N. C. Ellis (Eds.), *Handbook of spelling: theory, process and intervention* (pp. 295–318). New York, NY: John Wiley and Sons.

Kay, J., Lesser, R., & Coltheart, M. (1996). Psycholinguistic assessments of language processing in aphasia (PALPA): An introduction. *Aphasiology*, *10*(2), 159–180. https://doi.org/10.1080/02687039608248403

Kessels, R. P., van Zandvoort, M. J., Postma, A., Kappelle, L. J., & de Haan, E. H. (2000). The Corsi Block-Tapping Task: Standardization and normative data. *Applied Neuropsychology*, *7*, 252–258. doi:10.1207/S15324826AN0704_8

Kriegeskorte, N., Mur, M., & Bandettini, P. (2008). Representational similarity analysis—connecting the branches of systems neuroscience. *Frontiers in Systems Neuroscience*, *2*, 4. doi:10.3389/neuro.06.004.2008

Lambon Ralph, M. A. L., Jefferies, E., Patterson, K., & Rogers, T. T. (2017). The neural and computational bases of semantic cognition. *Nature Reviews Neuroscience*, *18*, 42–55. doi:10.1038/nrn.2016.150

Lewandowsky, S., Geiger, S. M., & Oberauer, K. (2008). Interference-based forgetting in verbal short-term memory. *Journal of Memory and Language*, *59*, 200–222. doi:10.1016/j.jml.2008.04.004

Lewis, R. L., Vasishth, S., & Van Dyke, J. A. (2006). Computational principles of working memory in sentence comprehension. *Trends in Cognitive Sciences*, *10*, 447–454. doi:10.1016/j.tics.2006.08.007

Logie, R. H. (2019). Converging sources of evidence and theory integration in working memory: A commentary on Morey, Rhodes, and Cowan (2019). *Cortex*, *112*, 162–171. doi:10.1016/j.cortex.2019.01.030

Martin, N., & Saffran, E. M. (1997). Language and auditory-verbal short-term memory: Evidence for common underlying processes. *Cognitive Neuropsychology*, *14*, 641–682.

Martin, N., Saffran, E. M., & Dell, G. S. (1996). Recovery in deep dysphasia: Evidence for a relation between auditory—verbal STM capacity and lexical errors in repetition. *Brain and Language*, *52*, 83–113. doi:10.1006/brln.1996.0005

Martin, R. C. (2017). Buffer vs. embedded process models of working memory: Evidence from neuropsychology. Paper presented at the 58th Annual Meeting of the Psychonomic Society, Vancouver, BC, Canada, November.

Martin, R. C., & Breedin, S. D. (1992). Dissociations between speech perception and phonological short-term memory deficits. *Cognitive Neuropsychology*, *9*, 509–534. doi:10.1080/02643299208252070

Martin, R. C., & Freedman, M. L. (2001). Short-term retention of lexical-semantic representations: Implications for speech production. *Memory*, *9*, 261–280. doi:10.1080/09658210143000173

Martin, R. C, & He, T. (2004). Semantic short-term memory and its role in sentence processing: A replication. *Brain and Language*, *89*, 76–82. doi:10.1016/S0093-934X(03)00300-6

Martin, R. C., Lesch, M. F., & Bartha, M. C. (1999). Independence of input and output phonology in word processing and short-term memory. *Journal of Memory and Language*, *41*, 3–29. doi:10.1006/jmla.1999.2637

Martin, R. C., Miller, M., & Vu, H. (2004). Lexical-semantic retention and speech production: further evidence from normal and brain-damaged participants for a phrasal scope of planning. *Cognitive Neuropsychology*, *21*, 625–644. doi:10.1080/02643290342000302

Martin, R. C., & Romani, C. (1994). Verbal working memory and sentence comprehension: A multiple-components view. *Neuropsychology*, *8*, 506–523. doi:10.1037/0894-4105.8.4.506

Martin, R. C., & Schnur, T. T. (2019). Independent contributions of semantic and phonological working memory to spontaneous speech in acute stroke. *Cortex*, *112*, 58–68. doi:10.1016/j.cortex.2018.11.017

Martin, R. C., Shelton, J. R., & Yaffee, L. S. (1994). Language processing and working memory: neuropsychological evidence for separate phonological and semantic capacities. *Journal of Memory and Language*, *33*, 83–111. doi:10.1006/jmla.1994.1005

Martin, R. C., Wu, D., Freedman, M., Jackson, E. F., & Lesch, M. (2003). An event-related fMRI investigation of phonological versus semantic short-term memory. *Journal of Neurolinguistics*, *16*, 341–360. doi:10.1016/S0911-6044(03)00025-3

Martin, R. C., Yan, H., & Schnur, T. T. (2014). Working memory and planning during sentence production. *Acta Psychologica*, *152*, 120–132. doi:10.1016/j.actpsy.2014.08.006

McCloskey, M., Macaruso, P., & Rapp, B. (2006). Grapheme-to-lexeme feedback in the spelling system: Evidence from a dysgraphic patient. *Cognitive Neuropsychology*, *23*, 278–307. doi:10.1080/02643290442000518

McElree, B., Foraker, S., & Dyer, L. (2003). Memory structures that subserve sentence comprehension. *Journal of Memory and Language*, *48*, 67–91. doi:10.1016/S0749-596X(02)00515-6

Mesgarani, N., Cheung, C., Johnson, K., & Chang, E. F. (2014). Phonetic feature encoding in human superior temporal gyrus. *Science*, *343*, 1006–1010. doi:10.1126/science.1245994

Miceli, G., Capasso, R., Benvegnù, B., & Caramazza, A. (2004). The categorical distinction of vowel and consonant representations: Evidence from dysgraphia. *Neurocase*, *10*, 109–121. doi:10.1080/13554790409609942

Miceli, G., Silveri, M. C., & Caramazza, A. (1985). Cognitive analysis of a case of pure dysgraphia. *Brain and Language*, *25*, 187–212. doi:10.1016/0093-934X(85)90080-X

Miyake, A., Friedman, N. P., Emerson, M. J., Witzki, A. H., Howerter, A., & Wager, T. D. (2000). The unity and diversity of executive functions and their contributions to complex "frontal lobe" tasks: a latent variable analysis. *Cognitive Psychology*, *41*, 49–100. doi:10.1006/cogp.1999.0734

Morey, C. C. (2018). The case against specialized visual-spatial short-term memory. *Psychological Bulletin*, *144*, 849–883. doi:10.1037/bul0000155

Morey, C., Rhodes, S., & Cowan, N. (2019). Sensory-motor integration and brain lesions: Progress toward explaining domain-specific phenomena within domain-general working memory. *Cortex*, *112*, 149–161. doi:10.1016/j.cortex.2018.11.030

Moscovitch, M., & Behrmann, M. (1994). Coding of spatial information in the somatosensory system: Evidence from patients with neglect following parietal lobe damage. *Journal of Cognitive Neuroscience, 6,* 151–155. doi:10.1162/jocn.1994.6.2.151

Mueller, S. T., & Piper, B. J. (2014). The Psychology Experiment Building Language (PEBL) and PEBL Test Battery. *Journal of Neuroscience Methods, 222,* 250–259. doi:10.1016/j.jneumeth.2013.10.024

Nachev, P., Coulthard, E., Jäger, H. R., Kennard, C., & Husain, M. (2008). Enantiomorphic normalization of focally lesioned brains. *NeuroImage, 39,* 1215–1226. doi:10.1016/j.neuroimage.2007.10.002

Nairne, J. S., Thompson, S. R., & Pandeirada, J. N. S. (2007). Adaptive memory: Survival processing enhances retention. *Journal of Experimental Psychology: Learning, Memory, and Cognition, 33,* 263–273. doi:10.1037/0278-7393.33.2.263

Norman, K. A., Polyn, S. M., Detre, G. J., & Haxby, J. V. (2006). Beyond mind-reading: Multi-voxel pattern analysis of fMRI data. *Trends in Cognitive Sciences, 10,* 424–430. doi:10.1016/j.tics.2006.07.005

Norris, D. (2017). Short-term memory and long-term memory are still different. *Psychological Bulletin, 143,* 992–1009.

Norris, D. (2019). Even an activated long-term memory system still needs a separate short-term store: A reply to Cowan (2019). *Psychological Bulletin, 145,* 848–853.

Oberauer, K. (2009). Design for a working memory. In B. H. Ross (Ed.), *The psychology of learning and motivation: The psychology of learning and motivation* (Vol. 51, pp. 45–100). New York, NY: Academic Press. doi:10.1016/S0079-7421(09)51002-X

Oberauer, K. (2021). Towards a theory of working memory: From metaphor to mechanism. In R. H. Logie, V. Camos, and N. Cowan (Eds.), *Working memory: State of the science* (pp. 116–149). Oxford, UK: Oxford University Press.

Page, M. P. A., & Norris, D. (1998). The primacy model: A new model of immediate serial recall. *Psychological Review, 105,* 761–781. doi:10.1037/0033-295X.105.4.761-781

Planton, S., Jucla, M., Roux, F.-E., & Démonet, J.-F. (2013). The "handwriting brain": A meta-analysis of neuroimaging studies of motor versus orthographic processes. *Cortex, 49,* 2772–2787. doi:10.1016/j.cortex.2013.05.011

Price, C. J. (2012). A review and synthesis of the first 20 years of PET and fMRI studies of heard speech, spoken language and reading. *Neuroimage, 62,* 816–847. doi:10.1016/j.neuroimage.2012.04.062

Purcell, J. J., Turkeltaub, P. E., Eden, G. F., & Rapp, B. (2011). Examining the central and peripheral processes of written word production through meta-analysis. *Frontiers in Psychology, 2,* 239. doi:10.3389/fpsyg.2011.00239

Rapcsak, S. Z., & Beeson, P. M. (2004). The role of left posterior inferior temporal cortex in spelling. *Neurology, 62,* 2221–2229. doi:10.1212/01.WNL.0000130169.60752.C5

Rapp, B. (2011). Case series in cognitive neuropsychology: promise, perils and proper perspective. *Cognitive Neuropsychology, 28,* 435–444. doi:10.1080/02643294.2012.697453

Rapp, B., & Dufor, O. (2011). The neurotopography of written word production: an fMRI investigation of the distribution of sensitivity to length and frequency. *Journal of Cognitive Neuroscience, 23,* 4067–4081. doi:10.1162/jocn_a_00109

Rapp, B. & Fischer-Baum, S. (2015). Uncovering the cognitive architecture of spelling. In A. Hillis (Ed.), *Handbook on adult language disorders: Integrating cognitive neuropsychology, neurology and rehabilitation* (2nd edn). Philadelphia, PA: Psychology Press.

Rapp, B., & Lipka, K. (2011). The literate brain: the relationship between spelling and reading. *Journal of Cognitive Neuroscience, 23,* 1180–1197. doi:10.1162/jocn.2010.21507

Rapp, B., Purcell, J., Hillis, A. E., Capasso, R., & Miceli, G. (2016). Neural bases of orthographic long-term memory and working memory in dysgraphia. *Brain, 139,* 588–604. doi:10.1093/brain/awv348

Rapp, B., Shea, J., Mis, R., & Martin, R. (2016). Domain specificity in orthographic long-term and working memory. *Frontiers in Psychology, 95.* Conference Abstract: 54th Annual Academy of Aphasia Meeting. doi:10.3389/conf.fpsyg.2016.68.00095

Rochon, E., Saffran, E. M., Berndt, R. S., & Schwartz, M. F. (2000). Quantitative analysis of aphasic sentence production: further development and new data. *Brain and Language, 72,* 193–218. doi:10.1006/brln.1999.2285

Romani, C., Galluzzi, C., & Olson, A. (2011). Phonological–lexical activation: A lexical component or an output buffer? Evidence from aphasic errors. *Cortex*, *47*, 217–235. doi:10.1016/j.cortex.2009.11.004

Romani, C., & Martin, R. (1999). A deficit in the short-term retention of lexical-semantic information: Forgetting words but remembering a story. *Journal of Experimental Psychology: General*, *128*, 56–77. doi:10.1037/0096-3445.128.1.56

Romani, C., McAlpine, S., & Martin, R. C. (2008). Concreteness effects in different tasks: implications for models of short-term memory. *Quarterly Journal of Experimental Psychology*, *61*, 292–323. doi:10.1080/17470210601147747

Romani, C., McAlpine, S., Olson, A., Tsouknida, E., & Martin, R. (2005). Length, lexicality, and articulatory suppression in immediate recall: Evidence against the articulatory loop. *Journal of Memory and Language*, *52*, 398–415. doi:10.1016/j.jml.2005.01.005

Sage, K., & Ellis, A. W. (2004). Lexical influences in graphemic buffer disorder. *Cognitive Neuropsychology*, *21*, 381–400. doi:10.1080/02643290342000438

Schwartz, M. F., & Dell, G. S. (2010). Case series investigations in cognitive neuropsychology. *Cognitive Neuropsychology*, *27*, 477–494. doi:10.1080/02643294.2011.574111

Schwartz, M. F., Dell, G. S., Martin, N., Gahl, S., & Sobel, P. (2006). A case-series test of the interactive two-step model of lexical access: Evidence from picture naming. *Journal of Memory and Language*, *54*, 228–264. doi:10.1016/j.jml.2005.10.001

Schwartz, M. F., Faseyitan, O., Kim, J., & Coslett, H. B. (2012). The dorsal stream contribution to phonological retrieval in object naming. *Brain*, *135*, 3799–3814. doi:10.1093/brain/aws300

Serences, J. T., & Yantis, S. (2006). Selective visual attention and perceptual coherence. *Trends in Cognitive Sciences*, *10*, 38–45. doi:10.1016/j.tics.2005.11.008

Shallice, T., & Butterworth, B. (1977). Short-term memory impairment and spontaneous speech. *Neuropsychologia*, *15*, 729–735. doi:10.1016/0028-3932(77)90002-1

Shallice, T., & Papagno, C. (2019). Impairments of auditory-verbal short-term memory: Do selective deficits of the input phonological buffer exist? *Cortex*, *112*, 107–121. doi:10.1016/j.cortex.2018.10.004

Shomstein, S., & Yantis, S. (2004). Control of attention shifts between vision and audition in human cortex. *Journal of Neuroscience*, *24*, 10702–10706. doi:10.1523/JNEUROSCI.2939-04.2004

Shomstein, S., & Yantis, S. (2006). Parietal cortex mediates voluntary control of spatial and nonspatial auditory attention. *Journal of Neuroscience*, *26*, 435–439. doi:10.1523/JNEUROSCI.4408-05.2006

Soemer, A., & Saito, S. (2016). Domain-specific processing in short-term memory in short-term serial order memory. *Journal of Memory and Language*, *88*, 1–17. doi:10.1016/j.jml.2015.12.003

Tamber-Rosenau, B., & Marios, R. (2016). Central attention is serial, but midlevel and peripheral attention are parallel: A hypothesis. *Attention, Perception and Psychophysics*, *78*, 1784–1868.

Tan, Y., & Martin, R. C. (2018). Verbal short-term memory capacities and executive function in semantic and syntactic interference resolution during sentence comprehension: Evidence from aphasia. *Neuropsychologia*, *113*, 111–125. doi:10.1016/j.neuropsychologia.2018.03.001

Tan, Y., Martin, R. C., & Van Dyke, J. A. (2017). Semantic and syntactic interference in sentence comprehension: a comparison of working memory models. *Frontiers in Psychology*, *8*, 198. doi:10.3389/fpsyg.2017.00198

Tian, Y., Fischer-Baum, S., & Beier, M. (2017, November). The domain-specific capacity for serial order in working memory: An individual differences approach. Poster Session presented at the Psychonomic Society Annual Meeting, Vancouver, BC.

Todd, J. J., & Marois, R. (2004). Capacity limit of visual short-term memory in human posterior parietal cortex. *Nature*, *428*, 751–754. doi:10.1038/nature02466

Turkeltaub, P. E., & Coslett, H. B. (2010). Localization of sublexical speech perception components. *Brain and Language*, *114*, 1–15. doi:10.1016/j.bandl.2010.03.008

Uittenhove, K., Chaabi, L., Camos, V., & Barrouillet, P. (2019). Is working memory storage intrinsically domain-specific? *Journal of Experimental Psychology: General*, *148*, 2027–2057. doi:10.1037/xge0000566

Unsworth, N., Fukuda, K., Awh, E., & Vogel, E. K. (2014). Working memory and fluid intelligence: Capacity, attention control, and secondary memory retrieval. *Cognitive Psychology, 71*, 1–26. doi:10.1016/j.cogpsych.2014.01.003

Vallar, G., & Baddeley, A. D. (1984). Fractionation of working memory: Neuropsychological evidence for a phonological short-term store. *Journal of Verbal Learning and Verbal Behavior, 23*, 151–161.

Van Dyke, J. A., Johns, C. L., & Kukona, A. (2014). Low working memory capacity is only spuriously related to poor reading comprehension. *Cognition, 131*, 373–403. doi:10.1016/j.cognition.2014.01.007

Wager, T. D., & Smith, E. E. (2003). Neuroimaging studies of working memory: A meta-analysis. *Cognitive, Affective & Behavioral Neuroscience, 3*, 255–274.

Warrington, E. K., & Shallice, T. (1969). The selective impairment of auditory-verbal short-term memory. *Brain, 92*, 885–896. doi:10.1093/brain/92.4.885

Warrington, E. K., & Shallice, T. (1972). Neuropsychological evidence of visual storage in short-term memory tasks. *Quarterly Journal of Experimental Psychology, 24*, 30–40. doi:10.1080/14640747208400265

Warrington, E. K., Logue, V., & Pratt, R. T. C. (1971). The anatomical localisation of selective impairment of auditory verbal short-term memory. *Neuropsychologia, 9*, 377–387. doi:10.1016/0028-3932(71)90002-9

Waugh, N. C., & Norman, D. A. (1965). Primary memory. *Psychological Review, 72*, 89–104.

Wechsler, D. (2008). *WMS-IV administration and scoring manual*. San Antonio, TX: Pearson.

Wing, A. M., & Baddeley, A. (1980). Spelling errors in handwriting: A corpus and a distributional analysis. In U. Frith (Ed.), *Cognitive processes in spelling* (pp. 251–285). New York, NY: Academic Press.

Wong, W., & Law, S. P. (2008). The relationship between semantic short-term memory and immediate serial recall of known and unknown words and nonwords: Data from two Chinese individuals with aphasia. *Journal of Experimental Psychology: Learning, Memory, and Cognition, 34*, 900–917. doi:10.1037/0278-7393.34.4.900

Yue, Q. (2018). Evaluating the buffer vs. Embedded processes accounts of verbal short-term memory by using multivariate neuroimaging and brain stimulation approaches [Unpublished doctoral dissertation]. Rice University.

Yue, Q., Martin, R. C., Hamilton, A. C., & Rose, N. S. (2019). Non-perceptual regions in the left inferior parietal lobe support phonological short-term memory: evidence for a buffer account? *Cerebral Cortex, 29*, 1398–1413. doi:10.1093/cercor/bhy037

10

Remembering Over the Short and Long Term

Empirical Continuities and Theoretical Implications

Patricia A. Reuter-Lorenz and Alexandru D. Iordan

Working memory (WM) is among the most influential constructs in cognitive psychology and cognitive neuroscience. The term WM is attributed to Miller, Galanter, and Pribram (1960). Drawing on the computer-analogy of mind, they viewed WM as a temporary storage mental system with quick and easy access to support and coordinate information needed to execute higher-order plans and intentions. Baddeley and his colleagues (Baddeley, 1986; Baddeley & Hitch, 1974) elaborated the construct of WM extensively, both theoretically and empirically, laying the foundation for many of the agreements and the debates that persist to this day. The view of WM described in this chapter likely aligns well with others in this volume, at least on some points (Table 10.1), but there will surely be points of contention as well, where data either lend themselves to multiple interpretations, or do not yet exist in sufficient form to settle the matter. We will begin by articulating what we recognize to be the defining features of WM, and then we will go on to review the behavioural and neuroscientific evidence that has shaped our view.

Cognitive Definition of Working Memory: Representations, Maintenance, Manipulation

WM refers to the short-term maintenance and mental manipulation of limited amounts of information held actively in mind. We use the term 'information' to refer to representations—representations of incoming stimuli being processed by sensory systems, representations of interoceptive signals of feeling states, or representations of an idea or a memory from the past that is brought to the mind's forefront. Such representations may be unimodal (e.g. a spoken word), multimodal (e.g. a word spoken on camera), simple (e.g. a short string of letters or numbers), or complex (e.g. a short meaningful utterance).

To the extent that a representation can be maintained at the forefront of one's mind when the sensory input is no longer present, that representation resides in a state we consider to be 'WM' (see also, e.g. Cowan, 2001; Oberauer, 2009; Rose, Buchsbaum, & Craik, 2014). This is in contrast to the 'latent' state of representations in long-term memory (LTM), representations of past experiences, personal events (episodic

Patricia A. Reuter-Lorenz and Alexandru D. Iordan, *Remembering Over the Short and Long Term* In: *Working Memory*. Edited by: Robert H. Logie, Valérie Camos, and Nelson Cowan, Oxford University Press (2021). © Oxford University Press. DOI: 10.1093/oso/9780198842286.003.0010

Table 10.1 Summary responses for seven core questions set for this volume and two additional applications

Question	Response
1. Definition of working memory (WM)	WM is a capacity-limited system for the short-term maintenance and manipulation of (domain-specific) information held actively in mind, and commensurate with the notion of the 'activated portion of long-term memory (LTM)'. We advocate for better integration of psychologically and neurally informed construct development.
2. Methods	We use behavioural and neuroimaging methods to investigate semantic influences on WM (e.g. Atkins & Reuter-Lorenz, 2008; Atkins & Reuter-Lorenz, 2011), the effects of healthy ageing on WM (e.g. Cappell, Gmeindl, & Reuter-Lorenz, 2010; Iordan et al., 2020), and the interaction of emotion and WM (e.g. Iordan, Dolcos, & Dolcos, 2013; Iordan & Dolcos, 2017; Iordan, Dolcos, & Dolcos, 2019; Mikels & Reuter-Lorenz, 2019). In this chapter we focus on our research examining verbal WM, semantic errors, their theoretical implications, and relevant human neuroscience evidence. This line of our research uses variants of the Sternberg item-recognition task, where small sets of items are presented, followed by a brief delay, that may or may not include a distractor task. Memory is tested with recognition or recall. The hybrid paradigm, first reported by Flegal, Atkins, and Reuter-Lorenz (2010) tests WM and subsequent long-term recognition. This paradigm equates encoding of several words probed within seconds of presentation and subject to minimal retroactive interference, relative to items probed 10+ minutes later and following substantial interference. This methodology can address questions about the nature of representations held in memory over a brief delay, putatively within WM, for comparison with memory representations available after a long, filled delay, putatively drawing from LTM, while assuming equivalent initial encoding conditions.
3. Unitary/non-unitary WM	WM representations include sensory/perceptual features that are represented in modality/domain-specific brain regions. The hybrid paradigm, and related methods from the Reuter-Lorenz laboratory, have generated evidence consistent with the unitary nature of memory. That is, short-term and long-term recognition tests demonstrate effects typically thought to characterize LTM exclusively, including depth of processing (Flegal & Reuter-Lorenz, 2014); encoding specificity (Olszewska et al., 2015); semantic/associative errors in recognition or recall with or without an intervening processing task (Atkins & Reuter-Lorenz, 2008; Dimsdale-Zucker et al., 2019; Festini & Reuter-Lorenz, 2014; Flegal et al., 2010; MacDuffie, Atkins, Flegal, Clark, & Reuter-Lorenz, 2012; Olszewska et al., 2015); and value-directed memory effects (Jantz, 2018; Jantz & Reuter-Lorenz, 2016) for immediate recall of three to six items, suggesting associative/evaluative encoding typically attributed to LTM.
4. Role of LTM knowledge	WM representations are distributed in nature and include perceptual as well as semantic/conceptual information associated with the stimulus input and activated from LTM/knowledge.

(Continued)

Table 10.1 Continued

Question	Response
5. The role of attention and control	There are both top-down and bottom-up attentional signals/mechanisms whose continuous coordination determines which representations are selected and maintained.
	The greater the WM load the more attentional control is needed to maintain information in an active state (Reuter-Lorenz & Jonides, 2007).
	The top-down (dorsal) network is governed by goals that determine which representations will be selected/prioritized at any given moment, and is aligned with executive/attentional control.
	The bottom-up (ventral) network can interrupt and reset ongoing activity in the dorsal network in response to salient cues that may summon and redirect attentional resources.
	The current focus on attention may be limited to a single item conferring privileged access relative to other items in WM (activated elements of LTM).
6. Storage, maintenance, and loss of information in WM	WM representations are maintained in an activated state by frontoparietal–sensory cortex interactions (attentional control) and this interplay confers resistance to distraction.
	Unintended loss of information in WM could be due to interference from newly arriving information or an interruption of control processes needed to maintain information in an activated state.
7. Inconsistent evidence	Dissociations among conditions, including modality effects, effects of different maintenance operations, encoding strategies, or dual-task effects are typically taken to indicate separate stores, separate memory processes, or separate memory systems. We propose that such manipulations alter the activational state, reveal differences in the time course of different representational features, or varying attentional priority of representations or nodes within representations, and need not implicate dissociable processes or systems.
	Neuropsychological evidence from patients suggests separate WM stores, including semantic WM. We propose that selective disruption may reflect attentional or activation-related deficits that render relevant components of representations inaccessible to maintenance or access over the short term and do not necessitate the inference of separate localized stores or buffers.
B. Adult ageing	For tasks ostensibly requiring maintenance-only item recognition, older adults are more likely to require greater contribution of top-down control for any given load compared to younger adults (i.e. CRUNCH: Compensation-Related Utilization of Neural Circuits Hypothesis; Reuter-Lorenz & Cappell, 2008).
	At the neural level, CRUNCH manifests as a tendency for older adults to over-activate prefrontal regions at lower loads, while performing equivalently to younger adults, and to under-activate these regions at higher loads, while performing more poorly than younger adults (Iordan et al., 2020).
	Other age-related compromises of executive control processes could interfere with more complex WM tasks independently or in addition to the increased requirement for top-down control needed for maintenance.
D. Neural correlates	WM is characterized by the interplay between 'lower-level' domain/modality-specific sensory regions and 'higher-level' multimodal frontoparietal regions.
	WM content/representation (like LTM content) is highly distributed across the brain, which likely reflects distinct functional roles for these representations, from representing rich details (sensory regions) and meaning, to representing goals, rules, and action plans (frontoparietal regions).

memory), or memory for facts, meanings, and world knowledge (i.e. semantic memory) that are accessible but not currently active. The nature of the representations (i.e. their modality, complexity, etc.), however, influences the mechanisms required to maintain them in an active state. As we discuss subsequently, the nature of these representations and their encoded properties may also determine the features or cues that are accessible for 'read out' and thus available for subsequent recollection (Nairne, 1990, 2002). This view is in accord with recent cognitive neuroscience perspectives and in contrast to initial views of WM that assigned representations to dedicated 'stores'. As we emphasize later, in the section pertaining to the neural bases of WM, our view is that WM representations are distributed across the specialized brain areas in which they are processed. Thus, WM refers to specific states of these representations (i.e. temporary availability) and functions for which they are used (i.e. maintenance over a short delay) to guide goal-directed behaviour.

Focused attention is widely assumed to be the primary means by which (non-verbal) representations are actively maintained—a sort of internal spotlight that can be allocated voluntarily to mental contents. Similar to attention focused on external things in the world around us, the internal focus of attention is limited in scope, resolution, and staying power, thereby limiting the capacity of WM (i.e. the amount of information that can be actively maintained). Several prominent theories of WM argue that only one item (i.e. representation) can be held in the focus of attention thus enjoying 'privileged' access, while an additional limited number (approximately three) are maintained in an accessible, but less active state (e.g. McElree, 2006; Oberauer, 2002, 2009). The data we review does not bear directly on this point, so we, like others (e.g. Jonides et al., 2008), consider the capacity limits of WM to be approximately four to six items, recognizing that within this set, the state of activation may be non-uniform.

In the verbal domain, (subvocal) rehearsal is the primary means by which information is maintained in an active state. Rehearsal is typically accompanied by the subjective experience of silently repeating the to-be-remembered words, and indeed decades of research suggest that verbal maintenance entails a time-consuming articulatory loop, influenced by word length and phonological properties of the memoranda. More recently, the operation referred to as 'refreshing' has been proposed as an alternative means of reactivating representations by applying punctate bursts of attention. By its initial formulation (e.g. see Johnson, Reeder, Raye, & Mitchell, 2002), refreshing is applied to a currently activated representation to bring it back to the current focus, and therefore is different from the operation of 'reactivating' which refers to the process of bringing a representation from an inactive to an active state (i.e. presumably when retrieved from LTM). Since Johnson et al.'s proposal, the refreshing operation has taken on additional significance and has been the subject of considerable research and theoretical development (e.g. Barrouillet & Camos, 2015, 2021; Souza & Vergauwe, 2018; see also Camos et al., 2018), which we revisit later in this chapter.

The manipulation aspect of WM refers to the idea that active representations can be readily accessed by control processes and used in higher-order cognition. For example, one can hold a small set of numbers in mind, and apply mathematical operations to do mental arithmetic, or one can mentally devise a seating arrangement for several guests arriving for dinner later that evening. These examples involve using (working with) active representations to accomplish mental goals, hence WM. In laboratory assessments of WM, the 'working' aspect is engaged by requiring that people maintain representations in an active state, while also completing an additional task that may or may not use the maintained representations. For example, the operation span task requires that one holds a set of words in mind, while performing an unrelated task of mental arithmetic. These dual, or distractor, tasks presumably introduce operations and strategies beyond simple maintenance, while also competing for attention, thereby reducing the number of items that can be maintained in an activated state. Another example is the N-back task, where a continuous string of items is presented and the current item must be compared with the one presented 'N' items prior in the list. This task requires continuous updating, comparison, and 'discarding' of memory contents. According to some researchers, tasks of these types (maintenance plus processing, or complex span tasks) are the only ones that actually measure WM (e.g. Engle, 2002, 2018). The additional operations invoked by these 'maintenance plus processing' tasks are thought to be executive in nature, meaning that they rely on modality-general, prefrontal processes that can be flexibly applied to representations regardless of sensory modality or complexity. Our view is that, even simple maintenance tasks that lack explicit dual-task/manipulation requirements tap WM in that they can invoke executive processes, depending on, for example, the capacity of the individual, the encoding strategies they employ, the magnitude of interference, and the nature/complexity of the memoranda.

Behavioural Methods to Measure Working Memory Versus Episodic Memory

As this overview suggests, numerous laboratory tasks have been developed to assess WM since the construct was first proposed (see, e.g. Oberauer et al., 2018). Their most common features include (1) small sets of memoranda ranging from one to six items—larger set sizes are thought to exceed capacity of most individuals and thus rely on episodic memory; (2) relatively brief retention intervals extending anywhere from 1 to 10 seconds. Longer intervals are also thought to rely on episodic memory, based on the supposition that 10 seconds is approximately the upper limit of the average individual's ability to maintain representations in an active state. Memory is tested by recall, where all items held in memory are reported (with recall order sometimes scored as well), or by recognition, where a probe item is presented with the requirement to indicate whether or not the probe matches an item in the memory set. Tasks presenting one to six items for several seconds, followed by a delay, and then a probe, are variants of the 'item-recognition' task first developed by Sternberg (1966). We consider this to be a 'canonical' WM task, because it is characterized by the temporal and load parameters used to define WM. Sternberg variants are also the tasks used most frequently in our own research, as we review in this chapter.

It is useful at this point to underscore the properties of WM tasks that distinguish them from measures of long-term, episodic memory. Tasks that measure LTM will typically use set sizes larger than seven, and retention intervals longer than 10 seconds, or more typically, on the order of minutes, hours, or days. However, as with WM tests, recall and recognition are used as the dependent measures. Nevertheless, a critical difference resides in the type of instructions given to the remember. Even in a typical Sternberg-like task, if participants are instructed that the items will be tested later in the session, and not simply a few seconds after presentation, people will likely use intentional memory strategies used for remembering over the long term. In this respect, a canonical WM task could be used to probe LTM. Likewise, if people are given long lists of 12 or more words (i.e. exceeding the capacity of WM), and asked to recall them immediately, words presented most recently and recalled first (recency items) are thought to be retrieved from short-term or WM, whereas words recalled from earlier portions of the list are thought to come from LTM. These examples illustrate that task parameters provide basic guidelines for investigating particular properties of memory but do not solely determine the aspects of memory that will be tapped in any given paradigm.

Nevertheless, list-learning tasks of this type helped establish some of the long-standing dichotomies in the memory literature (Atkinson & Shiffrin, 1968). Finding that recall errors from the recency portion of the serial position curve were more likely to be phonological (e.g. mistakenly recalling 'bride' instead of 'bribe') whereas errors from the primacy portion of this list were more likely to be semantic (e.g. mistakenly recalling 'horse' instead of 'pony') contributed to the characterization of short-term memory/WM as phonological and sensory in nature, whereas LTM represents semantic, associative, conceptual properties of the input. According to this traditional, multi-store view (Baddeley, 1986; see also Cowan, 2017), information represented and retrieved from WM would be characterized primarily by surface-level, perceptual features of the input. Semantic and associative information is the province of long-term, episodic memory, and distinct from the nature of information held in short-term, WM stores. This constitutes an excellent starting point for the consideration of semantic distortions of memory over the short versus long term.

False Memories Over the Short Term

It started with a simple question: could semantic false memories occur in WM to produce so-called false working memories? When Alexandra Atkins first posed this question for her doctoral work in 2004, there were no published data available to provide a clear answer. Randi Martin's group had reported considerable neuropsychological evidence indicating that semantic information could be retained in WM, and that some patients with focal lesions had deficits that could be explained by inferring a selective deficit in the short-term maintenance of semantic information. Further, Martin's group showed that semantic confusions occur under some circumstances in WM tasks (Bartha, Martin, & Jensen, 1998). Nevertheless, there had yet to be the frank demonstration of the false memory illusion, where people report words they had not studied and claim with high confidence to *remember* studying the word, in a canonical WM task.

In episodic memory, the false memory effect works when people try to remember a long list of words associated with a theme word, like 'sleep', for example. So, they will study 'dream, slumber, bed, pillow, snore', and so on, and then when asked to recall the words they studied, people will generate the word 'sleep', or in a recognition test they will falsely recognize 'sleep' as a word they studied. This is the *false memory*. Further, when asked about confidence, or phenomenology (i.e. do you clearly recollect the experience of studying that word?), people report vivid memory of studying the word even though they didn't.

There are good reasons to doubt that false memory errors of this kind would occur in a canonical WM task. First, false memories are generally considered to be LTM phenomena (e.g. Gallo, 2006). They require semantic associative processing which, as noted earlier, is widely viewed as the province of LTM. Second, these errors would also seem to require long, supra-span word lists that exceed WM capacity and render 'monitoring' processes at retrieval insufficient to review the entire list. Finally, some reasonable delay would need to be interposed to compromise the fidelity of the veridical memory signal to allow errors to occur. Indeed, *The Science of False Memory* by Brainerd and Reyna (2005) indexes neither the terms 'short-term memory' nor 'WM'. For these reasons, false 'working' memories would seem unlikely to be a real 'thing'. We thought that testing this idea was important because it could shed new light on the question of whether short- and LTM are separate systems, or whether there is continuity in memory processes across delay.

We started with a canonical Sternberg-like, item-recognition task using short lists of four associatively related words (drawn from the Roediger–McDermott lists; Roediger & McDermott, 1995) presented for 1.2 seconds, followed by a 3–4-second delay, and then a yes/no recognition task: is this probe one of the items you were asked to remember? The stimulus lists were formed according to all of the paradigmatic criteria, with theme words serving as all probe types to prevent response bias, associative strength appropriately balanced across lists, and so on. That is, following the solid tradition of false memory experimentation in LTM, we needed to dot all the 'i's and cross all the 't's to ensure that we produced a WM version of the Deese–Roediger–McDermott (DRM) task (Deese, 1959; Roediger & McDermott, 1995).

Our first report (Atkins & Reuter-Lorenz, 2008) of false working memories included four experiments, two testing recall, two testing recognition, with either a filled or unfilled retention interval. For the filled condition, a mathematical verification task was performed during the 3–4-second retention interval. This condition should suffice to satisfy theorists who require a processing component for tasks to measure 'WM'. For the unfilled condition, participants were free to rehearse the four items throughout the brief delay. Regardless of the condition, false recall and false recognition of associatively related theme words were reliably greater than for unrelated theme words—which has also been the main criterion for establishing the existence of false long-term memories.

That is, false memories occurred 4 seconds after studying a four-word list, whether or not people performed a distracting mathematical problem during the 4-second delay.

The range of experimental conditions included in this first report (Atkins & Reuter-Lorenz, 2008; see also Coane, McBride, Raulerson, & Jordan, 2007) would seem to satisfy most people's definition of a canonical WM task. Moreover, our laboratory has replicated these false recall effects in a serial list learning variant that permitted the attribution of false memories to the recency or primacy portions of the list (Dimsdale-Zucker, Flegal, Atkins, & Reuter-Lorenz, 2019). In this version of the task, lists of 12 words were composed of three semantically distinct quartets of words that were associatively related to a unique theme word (e.g. the list for theme words BAKE–KING–ROOF would be: broil, oven, cook, cake, throne, queen, crown, reign, shingle, ceiling, tar, tin). We found that false recall from the final, most recent quartet was reliable whether or not recall was immediate or followed a mathematical verification task. As we discuss later, list length, retention interval, and the presence or absence of a processing task may influence the accuracy of memory, as well as the frequency of false memories. Nevertheless, false recall and false recognition occur under experimental conditions that satisfy the canon of WM.

These demonstrations, therefore, indicate that semantic-associative processing can be brought to bear immediately within the context of a canonical WM task. At least on the face of it, such demonstrations challenge the idea that false memories are exclusively a 'LTM' phenomenon. Of course semantic memory, a form of LTM, would need to be involved in false memory errors regardless of the timescale over which they emerge, but given our task parameters—which fit the definition of WM—one would have to argue that people are using episodic memory processes in the context of a simple maintenance WM task, or alternatively, that semantic-associative encoding processes and the retrieval operations they support are ubiquitous in memory regardless of delay—and that these are the processes that give rise to false memories.

The Hybrid Paradigm: Phenomenology of False Memories Over the Short and Long Term

These demonstrations of so-called false working memories would seem to be problematic for memory theories that subscribe to the view that short-term memory and LTM depend on separate systems. However, several arguments could be mounted in an effort to salvage the dual-system view in the face of these false memory results. For example, it could be argued that short- and long-term false memories arise from different operations—short-term distortions are more like priming effects, in that they rely more on automatic processes and therefore should lack the recollective phenomenology that characterizes false memories that emerge over the long term. To address this possibility our laboratory developed a task now known as the *hybrid paradigm* (Flegal et al., 2010). In this task (Fig. 10.1), each trial presents short lists of four associatively related words followed by a delay that is typically filled with a brief distractor task. As

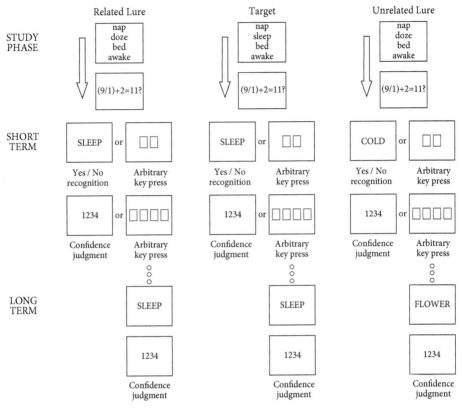

Fig. 10.1 This figure depicts the design for Experiment 1 in Flegal et al. (2010). Each list consists of four associatively related words that converge upon a theme word, which served as the probe on all trial types. The three probe/trial types were: *related lures*, the unstudied theme word associated with a studied list; *unrelated lures*, an unstudied theme word associated with a non-presented list; and *targets*, the theme word associated with and presented in a studied list. Once the WM phase of the experiment was completed there was a 2-minute break, followed by a surprise test of long-term recognition in which lists that were studied but not probed during the WM phase were tested with related lures, unrelated lures, and studied theme words, and confidence judgements were obtained.

in the standard item-recognition procedure, participants then decide whether or not a probe word was in the studied list. However, on a random half of the trials, rather than making a recognition decision, participants are instructed to make an arbitrary response. Unbeknownst to them, the lists on these trials are then probed later in a subsequent, surprise LTM recognition test that (like the short-term test) includes related and unrelated theme words. We also obtained meta-memory judgements where participants reported their confidence in having previously studied each probe word, and in a replication experiment, 'remember/know/new' judgements were obtained to assess the quality of recognition decisions (e.g. Rajaram, 1993).

Across both experiments included in the Flegal et al. (2010) report, false recognition was reliably evident regardless of delay. Unsurprisingly, veridical memory for words that were actually studied was better in the short than long term, and quantitatively false recognition errors were greater following an approximately 20-minute (filled) delay. However, corrected false recognition rates that normalize performance based on veridical memory were equivalent regardless of delay. Furthermore, memory phenomenology was indistinguishable over the short and long term: false memories were experienced as 'real' with high confidence and with recollective detail whether they occurred 4 seconds or 20 minutes after the study episode. In other words, like memory distortions evident over the long term, false working memories feel as if they actually happened.

These delay-invariant false memory results provoke the argument that participants engage episodic memory processes during the short-term trials in the hybrid paradigm, even though these trials conform to the canonical requirements of a WM task. In other words, what looks like a canonical WM task in fact relies on episodic memory thereby tapping associative processes and semantic representations of items considered to be part of LTM. Against this interpretation we retort that participants have *no* reason to approach this task like they would approach an episodic memory task or to engage episodic encoding strategies. In our hands in the hybrid task, participants are completely naïve about the delayed (long-term) memory test (in contrast to the related method used by Abadie & Camos, 2019, where participants are informed at the outset that they will be tested immediately and after a delay). Further, the fact that only a random half of the trials are probed in the short term (the other half requiring an arbitrary non-memory based response) should discourage any tendency to engage strategic, long-term encoding processes. These features of our design were intended to maximize the likelihood that the same short-term *encoding* operations would be brought to bear on all memory lists, regardless of whether retention was probed immediately or after a delay. In fact, the long-term distortions we have documented indicate that false memories readily occur despite incidental encoding of multiple short lists.

Depth of Processing Effects on False Memories Over the Short and Long Term

Nonetheless, memory encoding strategies were not explicitly controlled in the hybrid task used by Flegal et al. (2010), leaving open the possibility that participants engaged episodic encoding strategies, despite the immediate nature of the memory test. This prompted a follow-up investigation (Flegal & Reuter-Lorenz, 2014) that manipulated the level of processing engaged during list encoding (Craik & Lockhart, 1972). In this version, four associatively related items were presented sequentially, and participants were instructed to judge the visual features of each word (number of ascending and descending letters, such as 'b's and 'p's, respectively) or to judge the extent to which they liked or disliked each word. The former 'orienting' task engages shallow, feature-level processing, which leads to poor long-term retention, whereas the latter task engages deep processing because it requires consideration of word meanings, thereby promoting long-term memorability. As in the previous versions of the hybrid task, a mathematical verification task was required during the 4-second retention interval between the study items and the short-term memory probe. Likewise, in both encoding conditions for a random 50% of the trials, only long-term retention was tested with a surprise recognition test that, like the short-term test, included related and unrelated theme words along with studied probes.

As expected, depth of processing had minimal effects on memory performance over the short term: true recognition was relatively stable ranging from 82% to 87% (Experiment 1). Also, short-term false recognition effects were robust regardless of processing depth, occurring on 16% and 18% of the trials, respectively. In contrast, depth of processing had a pronounced effect on LTM, with true recognition rates as low as 53% in the shallow condition and as high as 84% in the deep condition. Likewise, long-term false recognition rates varied considerably due to processing depth (from 32% to 53%).

These results challenge the view that episodic encoding operations per se are the source of false short-term memories. If they were, then these operations should have been curtailed with shallow orienting, and enhanced by deep orienting, leading to variation in the magnitude of true and false recognition in the short term, just like in the long term—but this did not happen. While false memories were robust regardless of delay, processing depth led to a clear dissociation in recognition performance when tested over the short and long term. This experiment therefore presents us with a paradox: semantic distortions can occur under conditions that satisfy the canonical requirements of WM, consistent with continuity of memory processes across delay and unitary models of memory (Cowan, 1999; Nairne, 2002; Ranganath & Blumenfeld, 2005). Concurrently, we find that canonical WM conditions are relatively unaffected by processing depth, a result that simultaneously challenges the claim that false working memories arise from episodic memory, while also suggesting that WM and LTM are separable systems or at minimum differentially affected by processing depth. We return to this paradox after considering additional paradoxical evidence consistent with both unitary and separable systems.

Modality and Encoding Specificity Effects on False Memories Over the Short and Long Term

In the classic literature on short-term memory, verbal information presented in the auditory modality has a clear advantage relative to information presented in the visual modality. Short lists of spoken words are retained in WM more accurately than short lists of written words, an advantage referred to as the 'modality effect' (e.g. Penney, 1989). This advantage is explained by the idea that the auditory modality is more feature-rich than the visual modality, and greater feature-richness renders representations of spoken words more distinctive, and thus more memorable than representations of visual words, which by this account have fewer distinctive features (Gallo, 2006). This modality difference leads to an interesting prediction about false working memories: they should be more prevalent in the visual than in the auditory modality where memory is expected to be more accurate. Olszewska, Reuter-Lorenz, Munier, and Bendler (2015) provide support for this prediction across a series of experiments comparing the prevalence of false working memories in the visual and auditory modalities.

In an initial experiment, the traditional modality effect was extended to the domain of false WM by demonstrating that true recognition was more accurate and false recognition more rare in the auditory than in the visual modality (auditory: 0.95, 0.05, respectively; visual: 0.91, 0.13, respectively). A second experiment replicated this pattern, while also indicating that the advantage is conferred by auditory encoding: words presented in the auditory modality but tested visually were better recalled and less subject to distortion than words presented in the visual modality and tested auditorily. Overall, when words were studied in one modality and tested in the other there was lower accuracy and more false memory errors than when the study and test conditions were in the same modality, as predicted by the principle of encoding specificity (Tulving & Thomson, 1973). In sum, the work of Olszewska and her colleagues indicates that words presented auditorily are less susceptible to semantic distortion than words presented visually, at least over the short term (see also Lim & Goh, 2019).

Yet this modality effect is *opposite* to the pattern typically observed with long-term testing (for reviews, see Gallo, 2006; Olszewska et al., 2015). In LTM, the visual modality tends to be more robust against memory distortions than the auditory modality, an effect that has been attributed to the idea that false memories are more likely to be auditory-like (a voice in the head) than visual in nature, and therefore more likely to occur in the context of an auditory task than a visual one, where such auditory 'illusions' can be distinguished from items that were studied visually. This well-established long-term modality advantage clearly contrasts with the well-established short-term modality advantage and suggests that opposite patterns of false memory prevalence should emerge depending on both input modality and delay. To test this idea, in a further experiment Olszewska and her colleagues (2015) used the hybrid task of Flegal et al. (2010) in both visual and auditory study-test conditions, and found the predicted cross-over interaction: in the short term, visual false memories prevailed over auditory distortions (auditory: 6%; visual 14%), whereas in the long term, the opposite pattern emerged (auditory: 43%; visual 33%).

Once again, we are confronted with a paradox. Semantic false memories are evident under canonical WM conditions (including those in the hybrid task) that produce the well-known modality effect (an auditory modality advantage) considered a signature of WM (Olszewska et al., 2015). The auditory modality advantage corroborates the inference that the task engages WM, as does the relative lack of a levels-of-processing effect observed by Flegal and Reuter-Lorenz (2014). Nevertheless, semantic distortions (i.e. false working memories) occurred reliably in both studies. Likewise, in the corresponding LTM conditions of the hybrid tasks (i.e. supra-capacity lists, long delays), the Olszewska et al. (2015) study documents a visual modality advantage and the Flegal et al. (2010) study demonstrates the characteristic levels-of-processing effect, with patterns of false memory. Within the circumscribed range of studies reviewed here, this leaves us with two important commonalities across delay, namely semantic distortions, and encoding specificity, as well as two striking dissociations: opposite modality effects in the short versus long term, and levels of processing effects only in the long term. How can these paradoxical patterns be reconciled?

Maintenance Operations in Working Memory

One potential way to reconcile these effects is to hypothesize that a canonical WM task may or may not give rise to false semantic memories depending on how the representations are maintained in an active state. That is, whether they occur in the short or long term, false memories indicate the use of the episodic memory system, which is otherwise separable and independent from WM. According to this account (Loaiza & Camos, 2018), maintenance through rote rehearsal is the sine qua non of the WM system, and should *not* give rise to semantic distortions because rehearsal emphasizes phonology. Alternatively, conditions that promote refreshing, and diminish reliance on rehearsal, will engage episodic memory processes within the structure of a WM task, because refreshing entails repeated retrievals from outside to inside the focus of attention (also referred to as episodic reinstatements, see, e.g. Hoskin, Bornstein, Norman, & Cohen, 2019). Therefore, according to this account, the occurrence of false memories in the short term is due to reliance on refreshing and an episodic memory phenomenon (Abadie & Camos, 2019).

Despite the evidence marshalled in support of this account (see Abadie & Camos, 2019), it cannot explain the paradoxes delineated previously. If false memories occurred only in the short term when episodic memory is engaged, then levels of processing and visual superiority should also co-occur with false memories in the short term—but neither effect co-occurs. As described earlier, we have shown the opposite: false memories in the short term are evident under conditions that give rise to the auditory modality advantage that is characteristic of verbal WM, and when levels of processing effects are minimal, which is also characteristic of WM. Moreover, in contrast with Abadie and Camos (2019) we and others have documented reliable false memories in the short term under conditions where rote rehearsal is unimpeded (Atkins & Reuter-Lorenz, 2008, Experiments 2A and 2B; see also Macé & Caza, 2011; see also McBride, Coane, Xu, & Yu, 2019, and Dimsdale-Zucker et al., 2019, Experiment 1), where rote rehearsal is promoted (Festini & Reuter-Lorenz, 2013) and when LTM contributions are minimal (e.g. Sikora-Wachowicz et al., 2019).

We believe these co-occurring effects and the paradoxes they pose are incompatible with the dual-system view whereby WM consists of short-term storage modules or buffers that are dissociable from a LTM system (e.g. Baddeley, Hitch, & Allen, 2021; Barrouillet & Camos, 2021; Logie, Belletier, & Doherty, 2021; Martin, Rapp, & Purcell, 2021). Instead, we advocate for a unitary view whereby memoranda are 'in' WM when their representations are in an activated state and accessible for on-line processing. According to this view, memoranda are processed and represented in a distributed manner that includes sensory/perceptual, associative (LTM-semantic properties) and contextual features, and ultimately action-based codes. While these codes accrue during encoding processes, the time course is sufficiently rapid that such rich, multifaceted representations are accessible in canonical WM tasks. Critically, the fidelity and durability of different representational features can vary depending on encoding instructions (i.e. memory goals), the stimulus modality, stimulus novelty, and complexity, among other things. Moreover, sensory level, modality-specific features likely have a shorter half-life than other features (i.e. semantic associations), a property that distinguishes these perceptual or so-called verbatim features from more abstract codes pertaining to meaning and gist, which are more enduring (fuzzy-trace theory; Brainerd & Reyna, 2002). Differences in fidelity and durability will in turn influence which features of the representation are available at retrieval, as will the processing demands of the retrieval task itself (e.g. Nairne, 2002). Thus, according to our view, memory representations are distributed across the various sensory/perceptual, conceptual and action-related networks recruited at encoding, and accessed or operated upon by various control (top-down, strategic) processes determined by ongoing cognitive and behavioural goals. We believe this view accords with considerable cognitive neuroscience evidence pertaining to the neural bases of WM, and inter-relations with LTM and semantic processing, to which we now turn.

Cognitive Neuroscience of Working Memory: Specialized Systems and Distributed Representations

Recent trends in cognitive neuroscience distinguish between short-term retention of information as a 'neurobiological phenomenon' and WM as a 'class of behaviour' (e.g. Buchsbaum & D'Esposito, 2019; Christophel, Klink, Spitzer, Roelfsema, & Haynes, 2017; Eriksson, Vogel, Lansner, Bergström, & Nyberg, 2015; Hasson, Chen, & Honey, 2015; Jonides et al., 2008; Lee & Baker, 2016; Nee & D'Esposito, 2020; Postle, 2006, 2016; Zimmer, 2008). Specifically, short-term retention of information is generally viewed as an 'intrinsic property' of brain circuitry that affords a state of temporary enhanced accessibility of neural representations. This state can be assessed more or less directly in the brain using decoding techniques able to determine whether the representation of a certain stimulus is maintained over a delay or not (e.g. multivoxel pattern analysis (MVPA)). At the same time, the term 'WM' is typically used to denote a class of behaviour that involves short-term retention but also other processes such as perception, attention, inhibition, and is typically discussed in the context of representative tasks, such as Sternberg-like tasks or N-back tasks (Christophel et al., 2017; Postle, 2006, 2016). In line with this view, the evidence reviewed in this section comes from studies that have examined brain states elicited when a sensory percept is no longer present in the environment and the participant is instructed to maintain the representation of that percept in mind for a short period of time. In accord with the prior sections of this chapter, this activated state of a representation is what we are referring to as 'WM'.

Over the past decade, neuroscientific evidence has portrayed the brain as a complex system of interacting networks (e.g. Bassett & Sporns, 2017; Power et al., 2011) that is hierarchically organized and accommodates various representational gradients, for instance from 'simple' representations that code for sensory features to more 'abstract' representations that code for task goals and serve control functions (e.g. Christophel, Iamshchinina, Yan, Allefeld, & Haynes, 2018; Hasson et al., 2015; Huntenburg, Bazin, & Margulies, 2018). In our view, this perspective is more compatible with the so-called state models of WM (e.g. Cowan, 1988, 1995; Oberauer, 2002, 2009) that propose a unitary basis of memory (or at least permeable boundaries between WM and LTM) than with the so-called store models of WM that postulate dedicated stores with presumed neural implementation (e.g. phonological loop) and hard boundaries between WM and LTM. We will articulate this perspective and present recent supporting evidence.

Recent research in cognitive neuroscience supports the idea that WM emerges from the coordination between 'general purpose' frontal control systems and 'specialized' more posterior systems that are engaged according to the particular type of processing that they support: for example, sensory-perceptual, verbal-semantic, and sensorimotor (Fig. 10.2). Thus, representations supporting WM performance are thought to be highly distributed across the brain, spanning 'high-level' prefrontal, parietal, and temporal association cortices, as well as 'low-level' unimodal (i.e. visual, auditory, motor) cortex. For instance, a visual object maintained in WM would elicit the coordinated representation of its visual features (e.g. pattern, colour, shape) in primary and secondary visual cortices along the ventral visual pathway, its spatial context and modes of interacting with it in frontoparietal areas, and its current behavioural significance in prefrontal cortex (PFC). Similarly, a word or sentence held in WM would elicit the coordinated representation of its sensory-perceptual properties according to input modality, its phonological structure in the superior temporal gyrus, auditory-motor integration in the temporoparietal cortex, and motor-articulatory representations in the ventral PFC (Brodmann area 44). In addition, what we typically denote by 'meaning' would be represented by the 'semantic system', a distributed network of cortical areas including superior, inferior, and medial prefrontal, lateral and ventral temporal, and lateral and medial parietal regions (Binder, Desai, Graves, & Conant, 2009; Huth, de Heer, Griffiths, Theunissen, & Gallant, 2016; Xu, Lin, Han, He, & Bi, 2016; see later).

While both 'high-level' association and 'low-level' unimodal cortices are thought to possess the neurobiological properties required to maintain neural representations over short periods of time, it is the distributed and hierarchical nature of WM

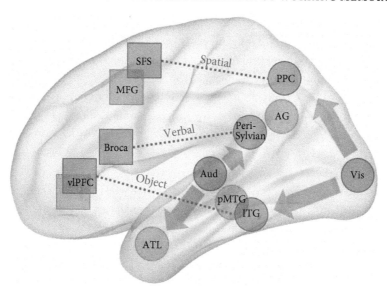

Fig. 10.2 Schematic representation of interactions between working memory, sensory, and semantic networks. Frontal regions are depicted as squares, whereas more posterior regions are depicted as circles. Frontoparietal/temporal networks linked to the maintenance of spatial, verbal, and object WM representations are depicted in blue (see Buchsbaum & D'Esposito, 2019; Nee & D'Esposito, 2020). Primary visual and auditory sensory regions are depicted in red. The red-to-blue arrows indicate progressively more complex (abstract) perceptual representations (see Christophel et al., 2017; Hasson et al., 2015). A subset of hubs of the semantic network representing points of intersection with the other networks are displayed in yellow (see Binder et al., 2009; Xu et al., 2016). Hippocampal interactions between perceptual, working memory, and semantic regions are not depicted. AG, angular gyrus; ATL, anterior temporal lobe; Aud, auditory cortex; Broca, Broca's area; ITG, inferior temporal gyrus; MFG, middle frontal gyrus; Peri-Sylvian, peri-Sylvian cortex; pMTG, posterior middle temporal gyrus; PPC, posterior parietal cortex; SFS, superior frontal sulcus; Vis, visual cortex; vlPFC, ventrolateral prefrontal cortex.

representations that allow them to take on different functional roles. Given the specific computations associated with different parts of the brain, sensory regions encode 'low-level' features that support fine discrimination whereas prefrontal regions encode 'high-level' information that generalizes across modalities (or 'abstract' information). Thus, posterior cortices have greater specificity for representing different types of stimuli, whereas frontal regions represent goals, rules, and action plans. Further, representational gradients have been identified both within sensory-driven processing of posterior regions and at more abstract processing of frontal regions, as detailed in the next section.

Critically, the specialized systems contributing to WM support various other functions as well, including perception, LTM, and action planning. As such, the same neural systems responsible for visual perception and action, and for language perception and production, respectively, are also recruited for the temporary maintenance of the specialized information that they can represent. Despite this overlap, the sensory features that support perception, for example, may differ from those available to support WM. This implies that the neural representations that support perception are partially, but not entirely isomorphic with the representations that support WM. Nevertheless, frontal representations contribute to the maintenance of representations in sensory regions. This obviates the necessity of invoking separate storage systems in the brain and is supported by recent computational models of WM (Bouchacourt & Buschman, 2019; see also Adam & Serences, 2019).

In particular, contextual information encoded by the PFC interacts with perceptual areas to guide task-relevant processing, with frontoparietal attentional signals acting as gating mechanisms that segregate memory from perceptual representations (Knight, Staines, Swick, & Chao, 1999; Scimeca, Kiyonaga, & D'Esposito, 2018). Consistent with this formulation, it has been shown that WM representations can be biased by distractors similar to the memoranda: the greater the similarity between distractor and WM contents, the greater the biasing of WM representations towards the distractor (e.g. Lorenc, Sreenivasan, Nee, Vandenbroucke, & D'Esposito, 2018; Teng & Kravitz, 2019). Thus, whereas irrelevant distraction (which is more readily ignored) is less consequential, because perceptual representations supporting WM can be reinstated in a top-down fashion, distraction that engages attentional processing is more impactful because it alters frontoparietal WM representations. This is further illustrated by the ability of PFC to resist interference during WM and the more severe consequences of PFC perturbation on performance, for a larger array of behaviours, including WM, attention, and motor responses (see Katsuki & Constantinidis, 2012).

In sum, from a cognitive neuroscience perspective, what we typically denote as 'WM' is not a single phenomenon but a complex mental state, involving not only the maintenance of neural representations in a state of enhanced accessibility but also the recruitment of various brain systems as a function of the specialized types of processing that they support. Current evidence suggests that WM is implemented via coordination of hierarchically organized representations distributed across multiple networks, including frontoparietal control and sensory circuits. Because the neural implementation of these processes is partially shared, the contents of WM is bound to interact with perceptual, language and LTM mechanisms, being influenced by them and exerting its own influence upon them, as we elaborate in the next section.

Neural Mechanisms of Maintenance and Manipulation: Overlaps with Perceptual, Language, and Long-Term Memory Mechanisms

In cognitive neuroscience research, the study of WM maintenance typically focuses on the delay activity, that is, brain activity recorded during the delay (i.e. retention) interval between the memoranda and the probes. Initially, delay activity was described in the lateral PFC using single-cell recordings (e.g. Fuster & Alexander, 1971). However, subsequent technological advances allowing brain-wide recordings (e.g. positron emission tomography and later, functional magnetic resonance imaging) and new analytic techniques enabling decoding from brain activity (e.g. MVPA) led to identification of changes in delay activity spanning not only frontoparietal cortices but also sensory, temporoparietal, and medial temporal lobe regions commonly associated with perception, language, and LTM, respectively. Evidence indicating overlaps of WM mechanisms with neural correlates of other processes supports the distributed representation perspective, whereby brain networks implementing computations specific to the type of information that they represent are flexibly recruited as a function of task goals and demands.[1]

The lateral PFC and posterior parietal cortex are the main hubs of the so-called frontoparietal control network which is recruited in a wide spectrum of tasks requiring cognitive control (Bressler & Menon, 2010; Hugdahl, Raichle, Mitra, & Specht, 2015; Power & Petersen, 2013). Although the two regions share many functional properties, they are considered to play distinct roles in WM maintenance. Specifically, whereas lateral PFC is thought to support a multidimensional representation of WM content as well as the task goals, posterior parietal cortex has been linked to selective attentional control, as well as representation of lower-level stimulus information and preferentially encoding visual category information (Sreenivasan & D'Esposito, 2019). In addition, current evidence suggests that the lateral PFC is organized based on representational content rather than specific process types (e.g. Nee & D'Esposito, 2016). Specifically, evidence points to a gradient of abstraction following the rostral/caudal axis of the PFC, with representation of maximally abstract goals and task rules in the frontopolar cortex and gradually more specific and context-dependent representations posteriorly, toward the premotor cortex. Within this organization, the mid-lateral PFC—a region typically associated with WM maintenance—lays in the optimal position to integrate abstract and concrete information in order to guide behaviour (Nee & D'Esposito, 2016).

A central tenet of the distributed or 'sensorimotor' WM perspective is that sustained activity in the PFC during WM delay is linked to the active maintenance of high-level representations and *not* to the storage of maintained information per se, which is implemented by more posterior regions (D'Esposito & Postle, 2015; Eriksson et al., 2015; Sreenivasan & D'Esposito, 2019). Although lower-level WM content is not stored in the prefrontal regions, PFC representations exert the top-down influence necessary to maintain the represented patterns in sensory areas. Thus, the sensory recruitment model of visual WM posits that 'low-level' sensory delay activity, in conjunction with influence from 'high-level' regions, is important for representing detailed WM information (Serences, 2016; Sreenivasan & D'Esposito, 2019).

In support of the sensory-recruitment model of WM, brain imaging studies have found evidence for maintenance of content-specific visual information (e.g. orientation, motion direction, patterns, objectual information) in both early and higher-order

---

[1] Of note, other regions commonly involved in WM processing include the basal ganglia, conceptualized as a gating mechanism for PFC representations (Chatham & Badre, 2015; O'Reilly, 2006) and the cerebellum, usually linked to performance monitoring (Peterburs & Desmond, 2016). A review of these additional regions exceeds the scope of this section and the interested reader is pointed to the cited reviews.

visual areas. Recent evidence also suggests bi-directional interactions between the contents of visual WM and perception of ongoing stimuli, consistent with the idea of shared WM and sensory representations within visual areas (e.g. Rademaker, Chunharas, & Serences, 2019; Teng & Kravitz, 2019). Consistent with the idea of a gradient of representation, delay activity in sensory cortices has been shown to be highly specific for individual WM items or features, whereas representations in parietal areas (i.e. intraparietal sulcus) reflect maintained information in a transformed and presumably lower-dimensional format (Rademaker et al., 2019). Also, consistent with the idea of a hierarchy of processing, research has shown that content-selective delay activity in sensory cortices is susceptible to interference by irrelevant input and can be reinstated via top-down modulation; at the same time, mnemonic representations in the parietal cortex are relatively more stable in the face of distraction (Katsuki & Constantinidis, 2012).

Similarly, in the verbal domain, recent evidence points to overlap between verbal WM and language circuits, and suggests that verbal WM is critically dependent on the same sensorimotor brain regions that form the core of the language network. According to a sensorimotor view of verbal WM (Buchsbaum & D'Esposito, 2019), the putative function of the 'articulatory loop' is implemented by a network connecting the auditory and motor speech systems. Within this network, the Sylvian-parietal-temporal region serves as an interface binding acoustic and motor representations of speech. This hypothesis is supported by univariate, MVPA, and transcranial magnetic stimulation evidence showing that activity in the Sylvian-parietal-temporal region is sensitive to WM load and codes phonemic information, and when disrupted, affects not only WM maintenance but also reading of non-words (for a review, see Buchsbaum & D'Esposito, 2019). Thus, the functionality of a dedicated 'phonological loop' could be accomplished by coordinated activity in a network comprising the auditory phonological zone of the superior temporal gyrus, the auditory–motor interface in the Sylvian-parietal-temporal regions, and motor-articulatory structures in the PFC (Brodmann area 44). However, in this view, the Sylvian-parietal-temporal region is *not* a 'store' per se because it does not just hold information but actively transforms it, whereas active maintenance is distributed across all components of the network rather than being concentrated in one region (Buchsbaum & D'Esposito, 2019).

Regarding overlap between WM and LTM mechanisms, neuroimaging evidence points to a dynamic interplay between the frontal cortex and the medial temporal lobe during WM tasks, at least under certain circumstances (Ranganath & Blumenfeld, 2005). Although neuropsychological evidence showing impaired LTM but apparently normal short-term memory in patients with medial temporal lobe resection or damage has originally contributed to the view that short-term memory and LTM are mediated by separate systems, more recent neuroimaging evidence has shown that the hippocampal complex is recruited in contexts that match or approximate canonical WM tasks. For instance, evidence shows that the hippocampus is recruited not only for retention intervals that exceed a few seconds but also contributes to brief (e.g. 900 ms) maintenance of visual information, although it does not necessarily contribute to the quality of the maintained information (Warren, Duff, Cohen, & Tranel, 2014). Engagement of the hippocampus in WM tasks has been reported also when stimuli to be encoded are complex (Kaminski et al., 2017; Kornblith, Quian Quiroga, Koch, Fried, & Mormann, 2017) and/or novel (Hasselmo & Stern, 2006), and even if task irrelevant (Ranganath & D'Esposito, 2001); when WM load is high and/or approaches the upper limits of individuals' WM capacity (Jeneson & Squire, 2012; Rissman, Gazzaley, & D'Esposito, 2008); and when the task requires forming new associations (Olson, Page, Moore, Chatterjee, & Verfaellie, 2006). These findings suggest that factors such as task goals, informational content, and processing demands (rather than cognitive taxonomies or task parameters such as the number of items to be remembered or duration of the delay interval) dictate more whether certain brain structures will be recruited by a task or not (Henke, 2010; Jeneson & Squire, 2012). Such results are at odds with the traditional double-dissociation between WM and LTM, and provide support for theories that postulate continuities between WM and LTM (Cowan, 1988, 1995; Oberauer, 2002, 2009).

In sum, recent neuroscientific evidence supports the distributed nature of WM mechanisms and the idea that specialized neural systems, including sensorimotor and semantic systems, are recruited to support goal-oriented performance in the context of WM tasks. While it is still a matter of debate to what degree the role played by early sensory areas is critical for WM maintenance (e.g. Xu, 2017, 2018), current evidence strongly suggests that higher-level perceptual regions and regions involved in LTM are also implicated in WM maintenance. We turn next to the neural bases of semantic representations and false memories and highlight overlaps with WM mechanisms.

Neural Bases of Semantic Representations and False Memories

Similar to evidence revealing close links between sensorimotor processing and WM, an accumulating body of neuroimaging evidence highlights overlap between semantic representations and WM. Although this has led some researchers to postulate the existence of a specialized semantic WM store (see Martin et al., 2021), we advocate a more parsimonious explanation whereby verbal WM can recruit semantic circuits. While recent evidence generally supports a distinction between 'language-based semantic' and 'general-purpose control' systems, it also emphasizes the connections and reciprocal influences between semantic, perceptual, and control regions (e.g. Lambon Ralph, Jefferies, Patterson, & Rogers, 2017). Thus, current evidence does not restrict semantic knowledge to LTM, but instead suggests that phonological and semantic codes can be dynamically engaged as a function of task demands and the participant's own expectations. In other words, semantic processing is essentially available in the context of tasks thought to elicit not only LTM but also WM processing.

The 'semantic', 'high-level' or 'core' language processing system (Binder et al., 2009; Fedorenko, Behr, & Kanwisher, 2011; Fedorenko & Thompson-Schill, 2014; Friederici, 2011; Xu et al., 2016) overlaps with a mainly left-lateralized perisylvian network,

spanning temporal (middle temporal gyrus), temporoparietal (supramarginal and anterior angular gyri), and prefrontal (middle and inferior frontal gyri and dorsal medial
frontal gyrus) brain areas. Although this network has been identified as a distinct
system at rest, it interacts with other large-scale brain networks (e.g. default-mode,
frontoparietal, sensorimotor networks) at the level of multiple 'hubs' that it shares
with these other networks (Xu et al., 2016). For instance, the anterior temporal lobe
(ATL) has been identified as the hub for semantic coding and merging of information represented in other modality- or category-specific regions (i.e. 'hub and spokes'
theory; Lambon Ralph et al., 2017; Rogers et al., 2004). This integratory function of
the ATL has been supported by functional connectivity analyses demonstrating intrinsic connectivity between ATL and modality-specific brain areas, as well as MVPA
and electrocorticographic evidence suggesting a gradient of functional specialization
within the ATL region (reviewed in Lambon Ralph et al., 2017). Specifically, while the
ventrolateral ATL is maximally recruited by semantic tasks irrespective of input modality, engagement of adjacent cortical regions becomes weaker and more stimulus
specific as one moves away from this focal point and toward more medial and superior
areas responding preferentially to pictures/concrete concepts and words/abstract concepts, respectively (see also Chiou & Lambon Ralph, 2019).

Thus, similar to other cognitive functions (e.g. perception), the semantic function
is supported not only by its own specialized network, but also by interactions with a
'control system' represented by the (mainly left) frontoparietal network and a 'memory-
based simulation system' represented by the default-mode network (Xu et al., 2016).
Regarding its interactions with the frontoparietal network, the semantic network is
thought to require executive input mainly under special circumstances (e.g. weakly
encoded information, suppression of over-learned responses, emphasis on unchar-
acteristic features) rather than in well-practised contexts. Thus, prefrontal regions
are deemed essential for accessing and manipulating representations within the semantic system, rather than being responsible for coding the semantic representations
per se, paralleling the role ascribed by the sensorimotor view on WM (Lambon Ralph
et al., 2017).

Although verbal WM tasks are typically thought to involve rehearsal of only phonological codes, there is now substantial behavioural, neuropsychological, and neuroimaging evidence that semantic codes and their representational cortical areas do support
WM performance (e.g. Rose et al., 2014; Rose, Craik, & Buchsbaum, 2015). According
to the 'processing view' of the distinction between WM and LTM (Rose & Craik, 2012),
whether words are maintained in WM as either phonological or semantic features is
determined by task demands and the participant's goals or expectations, rather than the
duration of the retention interval or the memory load. For instance, Rose et al. (2015)
showed that recalling of even a single word after a 10-second delay demonstrated behavioural and neural signatures of retrieval from LTM (i.e. levels-of-processing effect
and greater recruitment of ventrolateral PFC, ATL, and medial temporal lobe regions, respectively) when participants solved mathematical equations during the delay
interval, compared to when they were allowed to rehearse the word. This suggests that

the type of neural code that is maintained in WM may dynamically change with task goals and expectations, in line with a large body of neuroimaging evidence showing overlaps between regions typically recruited during WM and LTM tasks (see earlier).

Interestingly, a recent study by Yue et al. (2019) identified a dissociation between regions in the left superior temporal gyrus and left supramarginal gyrus, with the former supporting speech perception, and the latter showing both sustained delayed activity and a load effect, and successful decoding of the memoranda during the delay interval. The authors interpreted these results as evidence supporting a buffer rather than an embedded model of phonological STM. However, Buchsbaum and D'Esposito (2019) point to the spatial proximity of the supramarginal region identified by Yue et al. to the Sylvian-parietal-temporal area previously implicated in both speech production and WM maintenance (e.g. Fegen, Buchsbaum, & D'Esposito, 2015). While such overlaps and dissociations between adjacent regions remain to be further clarified, they are compatible with the idea of gradients of representation, which has been repeatedly demonstrated in the visual domain (e.g. Rademaker et al., 2019).

In sum, consistent with the distributed WM perspective, the semantic system is thought to enable simultaneous reactivation of multiple modality-specific representations that are distributed across the cortex and is controlled by the same multipurpose frontoparietal executive control network as WM. Given these similarities, it is likely that semantic representations could be recruited in the service of WM, both directly, as higher-level representations of previously encoded sensorimotor content and/or by virtue of their inherent links with 'lower-level' sensorimotor representations. Next, we turn to neuroimaging evidence supporting the idea that false memories are a functional expression of the operation of language/semantic mechanisms.

Recent meta-analytical evidence from univariate activation studies indicates that false memories reliably elicit greater activity than veridical memories mainly in prefrontal (e.g. bilateral ventrolateral and medial frontal cortices) and parietal cortices (e.g. inferior parietal), consistent with the involvement of top-down cognitive control mechanisms (Kurkela & Dennis, 2016). However, there is also evidence for the role of stimulus-specific processing in false memory, with activity in verbal processing regions (i.e. left ventrolateral PFC) linked to retrieval of semantic false memories and activity in visual processing regions (i.e. left occipital cortex) linked to false memories in perceptual relatedness tasks. Thus, although frontal cortex generally shows greater activation for false than true memories, results suggest that early sensory cortex can also mediate the retrieval of distorted memories, although this may vary with stimulus modality and the type of employed baseline (Kurkela & Dennis, 2016). Interestingly, though, meta-analytic evidence failed to identify a consistent contribution of medial temporal lobe regions to false memories.

This evidence is generally consistent with the results of our investigation of the neural mechanisms of semantic interference and false recognition in a short-term version of the DRM task (Atkins & Reuter-Lorenz, 2011). Our analyses identified greater left ventrolateral PFC (Brodmann area 45) activity associated with the correct rejection of probes related in meaning to the current memoranda (i.e. related lures) compared with unrelated probes (i.e. unrelated lures), consistent with the interpretation that the ventrolateral PFC responds to selection demands associated with multiple semantic competitors. Interestingly, activity in the ventrolateral PFC did not distinguish between semantic interference that was resolved correctly or not, as indicated by similar increase in probe-related activity for both correct rejections of and false alarms to related lures. By contrast, activity in the left dorsolateral PFC did distinguish between correct rejections and false alarms to related lures, suggesting that monitoring operations mediated by this region might be critical for accurate task performance. Finally, our study identified greater left parahippocampal gyrus activation associated with true versus false recognition, which suggests that a bias toward perceptual regions may be associated with better veridical retrieval under canonical WM conditions.

Computational models of semantic cognition have proposed that similarity of neural representations in the ATL semantic hub might reflect the semantic relatedness between the DRM words and could predict both true and false memories. Consistent with this hypothesis, Chadwick et al. (2016) have provided evidence that false memories are related to partially overlapping neural representations of related concepts, reflected by the similarity-based neural code in the ATL, and that each individual has a partially unique semantic code within the temporal pole, which can predict patterns of memory errors. Thus, the level of neural overlap in the ATL may predict the probability that a false memory will be constructed for a given DRM list. Similarly, a recent investigation manipulating the sensory modalities (visual and auditory) at learning and test in the standard DRM task (Zhu et al., 2019) showed that the auditory-learning visual-test (AV) group produced more false memories that the other three groups (i.e. VV, AA, and VA). This outcome is consistent with the encoding specificity principle and the advantage for visual memory at long delays (e.g. Gallo, 2006; Olszewska et al., 2015). At the same time, the AV's group proneness to false memories was associated with greater neural similarity for semantically related words in the ATL, greater prefrontal recruitment, and reduced representational match between the tested item versus studied items in the visual cortex, as a result of auditory learning. Overall, these results support the idea that domain-specific semantic features are distributed across a wide range of cortical regions and false memories are more related to functional mechanisms of semantic representation rather than expressing a unique characteristic for LTM.

In summary, evidence from cognitive neuroscience research supports a distributed representations perspective that is more in line with a unitary view of memory. Although this evidence is currently dominated by studies of visual WM, there is little reason to believe that visual and verbal WM function in fundamentally different ways. In respect to verbal WM, the distributed perspective postulates that the same neural systems that are responsible for language perception and production are also employed for the maintenance of phonological sequences in mind (Buchsbaum & D'Esposito, 2019). Thus, false verbal memories could be viewed more as a by-product of language/semantic processing, rather than a phenomenon characteristic for LTM. This is consistent with the idea that WM representations are stored in multiple codes, and this promotes semantic influences on phonological WM content. In the distributed perspective, the demarcations between LTM and WM, and between retention and processing become more fluid: memory can be conceived as a unitary entity that is either active or inactive (latent) and activated representations reflect both the accumulation of information in a specific system/circuit during an event as well as the subset of latent representations (LTM) that are activated concurrently with the processing of incoming information (Hasson et al., 2015).

Conclusion

In this chapter we review behavioural evidence from the Reuter-Lorenz laboratory and from other laboratories that documents the occurrence of (semantic) false memories under experimental conditions widely recognized to define WM: few memoranda (four or less) retained for only several seconds. Immediate false memories occur under conditions of recall or recognition, with or without rehearsal, with or without distraction, and whether processing is deep or shallow. We argue that these behavioural phenomena are inconsistent with separate short-term memory and LTM stores that are structurally and functionally distinct. Instead, these results contribute to the body of evidence demonstrating continuity of memory over the short and long term, such that mnemonic representations are distributed across a network of feature nodes, that vary in their time course, and are influenced by task goals and top-down strategic processes at encoding and retrieval. The cognitive neuroscience evidence reviewed in this chapter is largely consistent with this interpretation, and inconsistent with an architecture that posits separate representational, storage, and retrieval processes for remembering over the short versus long term.

References

Abadie, M., & Camos, V. (2019). False memory at short and long term. *Journal of Experimental Psychology: General, 148*, 1312–1334.

Adam, K. C. S., & Serences, J. T. (2019). Working memory: Flexible but finite. *Neuron, 103*, 184–185.

Atkins, A. S., & Reuter-Lorenz, P. A. (2008). False working memories? Semantic distortion in a mere 4 seconds. *Memory & Cognition, 36*, 74–81.

Atkins, A. S., & Reuter-Lorenz, P. A. (2011). Neural mechanisms of semantic interference and false recognition in short-term memory. *Neuroimage, 56*, 1726–1734.

Atkinson, R. C., & Shiffrin, R. M. (1968). Human memory: A proposed system and its control processes. In K. W. Spence & J. T. Spence (Eds.), *The psychology of learning and motivation: Advances in research and theory* (Vol. 2, pp. 89–195). New York, NY: Academic Press.

Baddeley, A. D. (1986). *Working memory*. Oxford, UK: Oxford University Press.

Baddeley, A. D., & Hitch, G. J. (1974). Working memory. In G. A. Bower (Ed.), *The psychology of learning and motivation: Advances in research and theory* (Vol. 8, pp. 47–89). New York, NY: Academic.

Baddeley, A. D., Hitch, G. J., & Allen, R. J. (2021). A multicomponent model of working memory. In R. H. Logie, V. Camos, & N. Cowan (Eds.), *Working memory: State of the science*, (pp. 10–43). Oxford, UK: Oxford University Press.

Barrouillet, P., & Camos, V. (2015). *Working memory: Loss and reconstruction*. Hove, UK: Psychology Press.

Barrouillet, P., & Camos, V. (2021). The time-based resource-sharing model of working memory. In R. H. Logie, V. Camos, & N. Cowan (Eds.), *Working memory: State of the science* (pp. 85–115). Oxford, UK: Oxford University Press.

Bartha, M. C., Martin, R. C., & Jensen, C. R. (1998). Multiple interference effects in short-term recognition memory. *American Journal of Psychology*, *111*, 89–118.

Bassett, D. S., & Sporns, O. (2017). Network neuroscience. *Nature Neuroscience*, *20*, 353–364.

Binder, J. R., Desai, R. H., Graves, W. W., & Conant, L. L. (2009). Where is the semantic system? A critical review and meta-analysis of 120 functional neuroimaging studies. *Cerebral Cortex*, *19*, 2767–2796.

Bouchacourt, F., & Buschman, T. J. (2019). A flexible model of working memory. *Neuron*, *103*, 147–160.e148.

Brainerd, C. J., & Reyna, V. F. (2002). Fuzzy-trace theory and false memory. *Current Directions in Psychological Science*, *11*, 164–169.

Brainerd, C. J., & Reyna, V. F. (2005). *The science of false memories*. Oxford, UK: Oxford University Press.

Bressler, S. L., & Menon, V. (2010). Large-scale brain networks in cognition: Emerging methods and principles. *Trends in Cognitive Sciences*, *14*, 277–290.

Buchsbaum, B. R., & D'Esposito, M. (2019). A sensorimotor view of verbal working memory. *Cortex*, *112*, 134–148.

Camos, V., Johnson, M., Loaiza, V., Portrat, S., Souza, A., & Vergauwe, E. (2018). What is attentional refreshing in working memory? *Annals of the New York Academy of Sciences*, *1424*, 19–32.

Cappell, K. A., Gmeindl, L., & Reuter-Lorenz, P. A. (2010). Age differences in prefontal recruitment during verbal working memory maintenance depend on memory load. *Cortex*, *46*, 462–473.

Chadwick, M. J., Anjum, R. S., Kumaran, D., Schacter, D. L., Spiers, H. J., & Hassabis, D. (2016). Semantic representations in the temporal pole predict false memories. *Proceedings of the National Academy of Sciences of the United States of America*, *113*, 10180–10185.

Chatham, C. H., & Badre, D. (2015). Multiple gates on working memory. *Current Opinion in Behavioral Sciences*, *1*, 23–31.

Chiou, R., & Lambon Ralph, M. A. (2019). Unveiling the dynamic interplay between the hub- and spoke-components of the brain's semantic system and its impact on human behaviour. *Neuroimage*, *199*, 114–126.

Christophel, T. B., Iamshchinina, P., Yan, C., Allefeld, C., & Haynes, J. D. (2018). Cortical specialization for attended versus unattended working memory. *Nature Neuroscience*, *21*, 494–496.

Christophel, T. B., Klink, P. C., Spitzer, B., Roelfsema, P. R., & Haynes, J. D. (2017). The distributed nature of working memory. *Trends in Cognitive Sciences*, *21*, 111–124.

Coane, J. H., McBride, D. M., Raulerson, B. A., 3rd, & Jordan, J. S. (2007). False memory in a short-term memory task. *Experimental Psychology*, *54*, 62–70.

Cowan, N. (1988). Evolving conceptions of memory storage, selective attention, and their mutual constraints within the human information-processing system. *Psychological Bulletin*, *104*, 163–191.

Cowan, N. (1995). *Attention and memory: An integrated framework*. New York, NY: Oxford University Press.

Cowan, N. (1999). An embedded-processes model of working memory. In A. Miyake & P. Shah (Eds.), *Models of working memory: Mechanisms of active maintenance and executive control* (pp. 62–101). Cambridge, UK: Cambridge University Press.

Cowan, N. (2001). The magical number 4 in short-term memory: A reconsideration of mental storage capacity. *Behavioral and Brain Sciences*, *24*, 87–114.

Cowan, N. (2017). The many faces of working memory and short-term storage. *Psychonomic Bulletin and Review*, *24*, 1158–1170.

Craik, F. I. M., & Lockhart, R. S. (1972). Levels of processing: A framework for memory research. *Journal of Verbal Learning and Verbal Behavior*, *11*, 671–684.

D'Esposito, M., & Postle, B. R. (2015). The cognitive neuroscience of working memory. *Annual Review of Psychology*, *66*, 115–142.

Deese, J. (1959). On the prediction of occurrence of particular verbal intrusions in immediate recall. *Journal of Experimental Psychology, 58*, 17–22.

Dimsdale-Zucker, H. R., Flegal, K. E., Atkins, A. S., & Reuter-Lorenz, P. A. (2019). Serial position-dependent false memory effects. *Memory, 27*, 397–409.

Engle, R. W. (2002). Working memory capacity as executive attention. *Current Directions in Psychological Science, 11*, 19–23.

Engle, R. W. (2018). Working memory and executive attention: A revisit. *Perspectives on Psychological Science, 13*, 190–193.

Eriksson, J., Vogel, E. K., Lansner, A., Bergström, F., & Nyberg, L. (2015). Neurocognitive architecture of working memory. *Neuron, 88*, 33–46.

Fedorenko, E., Behr, M. K., & Kanwisher, N. (2011). Functional specificity for high-level linguistic processing in the human brain. *Proceedings of the National Academy of Sciences of the United States of America, 108*, 16428–16433.

Fedorenko, E., & Thompson-Schill, S. L. (2014). Reworking the language network. *Trends in Cognitive Sciences, 18*, 120–126.

Fegen, D., Buchsbaum, B. R., & D'Esposito, M. (2015). The effect of rehearsal rate and memory load on verbal working memory. *Neuroimage, 105*, 120–131.

Festini, S. B., & Reuter-Lorenz, P. A. (2013). The short- and long-term consequences of directed forgetting in a working memory task. *Memory, 21*, 763–777.

Festini, S. B., & Reuter-Lorenz, P. A. (2014). Cognitive control of familiarity: Directed forgetting reduces proactive interference in working memory. *Cognitive, Affective and Behavioral Neuroscience, 14*, 78–89.

Flegal, K. E., Atkins, A. S., & Reuter-Lorenz, P. A. (2010). False memories seconds later: The rapid and compelling onset of illusory recognition. *Journal of Experimental Psychology: Learning, Memory, and Cognition, 36*, 1331–1338.

Flegal, K. E., & Reuter-Lorenz, P. A. (2014). Get the gist? The effects of processing depth on false recognition in short-term and long-term memory. *Memory & Cognition, 42*, 701–711.

Friederici, A. D. (2011). The brain basis of language processing: From structure to function. *Physiological Reviews, 91*, 1357–1392.

Fuster, J. M., & Alexander, G. E. (1971). Neuron activity related to short-term memory. *Science, 173*, 652–654.

Gallo, D. A. (2006). *Associative illusions of memory: False memory research in DRM and related tasks.* New York, NY: Psychology Press.

Hasselmo, M. E., & Stern, C. E. (2006). Mechanisms underlying working memory for novel information. *Trends in Cognitive Sciences, 10*, 487–493.

Hasson, U., Chen, J., & Honey, C. J. (2015). Hierarchical process memory: Memory as an integral component of information processing. *Trends in Cognitive Sciences, 19*, 304–313.

Henke, K. (2010). A model for memory systems based on processing modes rather than consciousness. *Nature Reviews. Neuroscience, 11*, 523–532.

Hoskin, A. N., Bornstein, A. M., Norman, K. A., & Cohen, J. D. (2019). Refresh my memory: Episodic memory reinstatements intrude on working memory maintenance. *Cognitive, Affective, & Behavioral Neuroscience, 19*, 338–354.

Hugdahl, K., Raichle, M. E., Mitra, A., & Specht, K. (2015). On the existence of a generalized non-specific task-dependent network. *Frontiers in Human Neuroscience, 9*, 430.

Huntenburg, J. M., Bazin, P. L., & Margulies, D. S. (2018). Large-scale gradients in human cortical organization. *Trends in Cognitive Sciences, 22*, 21–31.

Huth, A. G., de Heer, W. A., Griffiths, T. L., Theunissen, F. E., & Gallant, J. L. (2016). Natural speech reveals the semantic maps that tile human cerebral cortex. *Nature, 532*, 453–458.

Iordan, A., Dolcos, S., & Dolcos, F. (2013). Neural signatures of the response to emotional distraction: A review of evidence from brain imaging investigations. *Frontiers in Human Neuroscience, 7*, 200.

Iordan, A. D., Cooke, K. A., Moored, K. D., Katz, B., Buschkuehl, M., Jaeggi, S. M., . . . Reuter-Lorenz, P. A. (2020). Neural correlates of working memory training: Evidence for plasticity in older adults. *NeuroImage, 217*, 116887.

Iordan, A. D., & Dolcos, F. (2017). Brain activity and network interactions linked to valence-related differences in the impact of emotional distraction. *Cerebral Cortex*, *27*, 731–749.

Iordan, A. D., Dolcos, S., & Dolcos, F. (2019). Brain activity and network interactions in the impact of internal emotional distraction. *Cerebral Cortex*, *29*, 2607–2623.

Jantz, T. (2018). *Value-directed memory: Investigating effects of list length and working memory capacity* [Unpublished doctoral dissertation]. University of Michigan, Ann Arbor, MI.

Jantz, T., & Reuter-Lorenz, P. A. (2016). *Value influences immediate recall of sub- and supra-span memory loads*. Poster presented at the 57th Annual Meeting of the Psychonomics Society, Boston, MA.

Jeneson, A., & Squire, L. R. (2012). Working memory, long-term memory, and medial temporal lobe function. *Learning and Memory*, *19*, 15–25.

Johnson, M. K., Reeder, J. A., Raye, C. L., & Mitchell, K. J. (2002). Second thoughts versus second looks: An age-related deficit in reflectively refreshing just-activated information. *Psychological Science*, *13*, 64–67.

Jonides, J., Lewis, R. L., Nee, D. E., Lustig, C. A., Berman, M. G., & Moore, K. S. (2008). The mind and brain of short-term memory. *Annual Review of Psychology*, *59*, 193–224.

Kaminski, J., Sullivan, S., Chung, J. M., Ross, I. B., Mamelak, A. N., & Rutishauser, U. (2017). Persistently active neurons in human medial frontal and medial temporal lobe support working memory. *Nature Neuroscience*, *20*, 590–601.

Katsuki, F., & Constantinidis, C. (2012). Unique and shared roles of the posterior parietal and dorso-lateral prefrontal cortex in cognitive functions. *Frontiers in Integrative Neuroscience*, *6*, 17.

Knight, R. T., Staines, W., Swick, D., & Chao, L. L. (1999). Prefrontal cortex regulates inhibition and excitation in distributed neural networks. *Acta Psychologica*, *101*, 159–178.

Kornblith, S., Quian Quiroga, R., Koch, C., Fried, I., & Mormann, F. (2017). Persistent single-neuron activity during working memory in the human medial temporal lobe. *Current Biology*, *27*, 1026–1032.

Kurkela, K. A., & Dennis, N. A. (2016). Event-related fMRI studies of false memory: An activation likelihood estimation meta-analysis. *Neuropsychologia*, *81*, 149–167.

Lambon Ralph, M. A., Jefferies, E., Patterson, K., & Rogers, T. T. (2017). The neural and computational bases of semantic cognition. *Nature Reviews Neuroscience*, *18*, 42–55.

Lee, S. H., & Baker, C. I. (2016). Multi-voxel decoding and the topography of maintained information during visual working memory. *Frontiers in Systems Neuroscience*, *10*, 2.

Lim, L. C. L., & Goh, W. D. (2019). False recognition modality effects in short-term memory: Reversing the auditory advantage. *Cognition*, *193*, 104008.

Loaiza, V. M., & Camos, V. (2018). The role of semantic representations in verbal working memory. *Journal of Experimental Psychology: Learning, Memory, and Cognition*, *44*, 863–881.

Logie, R. H., Belletier, C., & Doherty, J. M. (2021). Integrating theories of working memory. In R. H. Logie, V. Camos, & N. Cowan (Eds.), *Working memory: State of the science* (pp. 389–429). Oxford, UK: Oxford University Press.

Lorenc, E. S., Sreenivasan, K. K., Nee, D. E., Vandenbroucke, A. R. E., & D'Esposito, M. (2018). Flexible coding of visual working memory representations during distraction. *Journal of Neuroscience*, *38*, 5267–5276.

MacDuffie, K. E., Atkins, A. S., Flegal, K. E., Clark, C. M., & Reuter-Lorenz, P. A. (2012). Memory distortion in Alzheimer's disease: Deficient monitoring of short- and long-term memory. *Neuropsychology*, *26*, 509–516.

Macé, A.-L., & Caza, N. (2011). The role of articulatory suppression in immediate false recognition. *Memory*, *19*, 891–900.

Martin, R. C., Rapp, B., & Purcell, J. (2021). Domain-specific working memory: Perspectives from cognitive neuropsychology. In R. H. Logie, V. Camos, & N. Cowan (Eds.), *Working memory: State of the science* (pp. 235–281). Oxford, UK: Oxford University Press.

McBride, D. M., Coane, J. H., Xu, S., Feng, Y., & Yu, Z. (2019). Short-term false memories vary as a function of list type. *Quarterly Journal of Experimental Psychology*, *72*, 2726–2741.

McElree, B. (2006). Accessing recent events. In B. H. Ross (Ed.), *Psychology of learning and motivation* (Vol. 46, pp. 155–200). San Diego, CA: Academic Press.

Mikels, J. A., & Reuter-Lorenz, P. A. (2019). Affective working memory: An integrative psychological construct. *Perspectives on Psychological Science, 14*, 543–559.

Miller, G. A., Galanter, E., & Pribram, K. H. (1960). *Plans and the structure of behavior.* New York, NY: Henry Holt.

Nairne, J. S. (1990). A feature model of immediate memory. *Memory & Cognition, 18*, 251–269.

Nairne, J. S. (2002). Remembering over the short-term: The case against the standard model. *Annual Review of Psychology, 53*, 53–81.

Nee, D. E., & D'Esposito, M. (2016). The hierarchical organization of the lateral prefrontal cortex. *eLife, 5*, e12112.

Nee, D. E., & D'Esposito, M. (2020). Working memory. In J. T. Wixted (Ed.), *Stevens' handbook of experimental psychology and cognitive neuroscience* (pp. 1–26). Retrieved from https://onlinelibrary.wiley.com/doi/abs/10.1002/ 9781119170174.epcn112. doi:10.1002/9781119170174.epcn112

Oberauer, K. (2002). Access to information in working memory: Exploring the focus of attention. *Journal of Experimental Psychology: Learning, Memory, and Cognition, 28*, 411–421.

Oberauer, K. (2009). Design for a working memory. In B. H. Ross (Ed.), *The psychology of learning and motivation* (Vol. 51, pp. 45–100). San Diego, CA: Elsevier Academic.

Oberauer, K., Lewandowsky, S., Awh, E., Brown, G. D. A., Conway, A., Cowan, N., . . . Ward, G. (2018). Benchmarks for models of short-term and working memory. *Psychological Bulletin, 144*, 885–958.

Olson, I. R., Page, K., Moore, K. S., Chatterjee, A., & Verfaellie, M. (2006). Working memory for conjunctions relies on the medial temporal lobe. *Journal of Neuroscience, 26*, 4596–4601.

Olszewska, J. M., Reuter-Lorenz, P. A., Munier, E., & Bendler, S. A. (2015). Misremembering what you see or hear: Dissociable effects of modality on short- and long-term false recognition. *Journal of Experimental Psychology: Learning, Memory, and Cognition, 41*, 1316–1325.

O'Reilly, R. C. (2006). Biologically based computational models of high-level cognition. *Science, 314*, 91–94.

Penney, C. G. (1989). Modality effects and the structure of short-term verbal memory. *Memory & Cognition, 17*, 398–422.

Peterburs, J., & Desmond, J. E. (2016). The role of the human cerebellum in performance monitoring. *Current Opinion in Neurobiology, 40*, 38–44.

Postle, B. R. (2006). Working memory as an emergent property of the mind and brain. *Neuroscience, 139*, 23–38.

Postle, B. R. (2016). How does the brain keep information 'in mind'? *Current Directions in Psychological Science, 25*, 151–156.

Power, J. D., Cohen, A. L., Nelson, S. M., Wig, G. S., Barnes, K. A., Church, J. A., . . . Petersen, S. E. (2011). Functional network organization of the human brain. *Neuron, 72*, 665–678.

Power, J. D., & Petersen, S. E. (2013). Control-related systems in the human brain. *Current Opinion in Neurobiology, 23*, 223–228.

Rademaker, R. L., Chunharas, C., & Serences, J. T. (2019). Coexisting representations of sensory and mnemonic information in human visual cortex. *Nature Neuroscience, 22*, 1336–1344.

Rajaram, S. (1993). Remembering and knowing: Two means of access to the personal past. *Memory & Cognition, 21*, 89–102.

Ranganath, C., & Blumenfeld, R. S. (2005). Doubts about double dissociations between short- and long-term memory. *Trends in Cognitive Sciences, 9*, 374–380.

Ranganath, C., & D'Esposito, M. (2001). Medial temporal lobe activity associated with active maintenance of novel information. *Neuron, 31*, 865–873.

Reuter-Lorenz, P. A., & Cappell, K. A. (2008). Neurocognitive aging and the compensation hypothesis. *Current Directions in Psychological Science, 17*, 177–182.

Reuter-Lorenz, P. A., & Jonides, J. (2007). The executive is central to working memory: Insights from age, performance and task variations. In R. A. Conway, C. Jarrold, M. J. Kane, A. Miyake, & J. Towse (Eds.), *Variations in working memory* (pp. 250–270). Oxford, UK: Oxford University Press.

Rissman, J., Gazzaley, A., & D'Esposito, M. (2008). Dynamic adjustments in prefrontal, hippocampal, and inferior temporal interactions with increasing visual working memory load. *Cerebral Cortex, 18*, 1618–1629.

Roediger, H. L., & McDermott, K. B. (1995). Creating false memories: Remembering words not presented in lists. *Journal of Experimental Psychology: Learning, Memory, and Cognition, 21*, 803–814.

Rogers, T. T., Lambon Ralph, M. A., Garrard, P., Bozeat, S., McClelland, J. L., Hodges, J. R., & Patterson, K. (2004). Structure and deterioration of semantic memory: A neuropsychological and computational investigation. *Psychological Review, 111*, 205–235.

Rose, N. S., Buchsbaum, B. R., & Craik, F. I. M. (2014). Short-term retention of a single word relies on retrieval from long-term memory when both rehearsal and refreshing are disrupted. *Memory & Cognition, 42*, 689–700.

Rose, N. S., Craik, F. I., & Buchsbaum, B. R. (2015). Levels of processing in working memory: Differential involvement of frontotemporal networks. *Journal of Cognitive Neuroscience, 27*, 522–532.

Rose, N. S., & Craik, F. I. M. (2012). A processing approach to the working memory/long-term memory distinction: Evidence from the levels-of-processing span task. *Journal of Experimental Psychology: Learning, Memory, and Cognition, 38*, 1019–1029.

Scimeca, J. M., Kiyonaga, A., & D'Esposito, M. (2018). Reaffirming the sensory recruitment account of working memory. *Trends in Cognitive Sciences, 22*, 190–192.

Serences, J. T. (2016). Neural mechanisms of information storage in visual short-term memory. *Vision Research, 128*, 53–67.

Sikora-Wachowicz, B., Lewandowska, K., Keresztes, A., Werkle-Bergner, M., Marek, T., & Fafrowicz, M. (2019). False recognition in short-term memory—age-differences in confidence. *Frontiers in Psychology, 10*, 2785.

Souza, A. S., & Vergauwe, E. (2018). Unravelling the intersections between consolidation, refreshing, and removal. *Annals of the New York Academy of Sciences, 1424*, 5–7.

Sreenivasan, K. K., & D'Esposito, M. (2019). The what, where and how of delay activity. *Nature Reviews Neuroscience, 20*, 466–481.

Sternberg, S. (1966). High-speed scanning in human memory. *Science, 153*, 652–654.

Teng, C., & Kravitz, D. J. (2019). Visual working memory directly alters perception. *Nature Human Behaviour, 3*, 827–836.

Tulving, E., & Thomson, D. M. (1973). Encoding specificity and retrieval processes in episodic memory. *Psychological Review, 80*, 352–373.

Warren, D. E., Duff, M. C., Cohen, N. J., & Tranel, D. (2014). Hippocampus contributes to the maintenance but not the quality of visual information over time. *Learning and Memory, 22*, 6–10.

Xu, Y. (2017). Reevaluating the sensory account of visual working memory storage. *Trends in Cognitive Sciences, 21*, 794–815.

Xu, Y. (2018). Sensory cortex is nonessential in working memory storage. *Trends in Cognitive Sciences, 22*, 192–193.

Xu, Y., Lin, Q., Han, Z., He, Y., & Bi, Y. (2016). Intrinsic functional network architecture of human semantic processing: Modules and hubs. *Neuroimage, 132*, 542–555.

Yue, Q., Martin, R. C., Hamilton, A. C., & Rose, N. S. (2019). Non-perceptual regions in the left inferior parietal lobe support phonological short-term memory: Evidence for a buffer account? *Cerebral Cortex, 29*, 1398–1413.

Zhu, B., Chen, C., Shao, X., Liu, W., Ye, Z., Zhuang, L., … Xue, G. (2019). Multiple interactive memory representations underlie the induction of false memory. *Proceedings of the National Academy of Sciences of the United States of America, 116*, 3466–3475.

Zimmer, H. D. (2008). Visual and spatial working memory: From boxes to networks. *Neuroscience and Biobehavioral Reviews, 32*, 1373–1395.

11

Manifold Visual Working Memory

Nicole Hakim, Edward Awh, and Edward K. Vogel

Working memory (WM) maintains information in an 'online' and easily accessible state for use in ongoing cognition. It allows us to perform complex cognitive tasks, such as computing a derivative, composing a symphony, and writing a book. It has a clear connection to intelligent behaviours (Ackerman, Beier, & Boyle, 2005; Conway, Kane, & Engle, 2003; Engle, Laughlin, Tuholski, & Conway, 1999; Unsworth, Fukuda, Awh, & Vogel, 2014), and modern views of WM explicitly characterize it within the context of its interaction with long term memory (LTM) (Cowan, 2001). These embedded-processes models (also see Cowan, Morey, & Naveh-Benjamin, 2021) describe memory representations as existing in three potential states: *inactivated LTM*, including all representations stored in LTM; *activated LTM*, which are latent representations that can quickly be brought into an active state due to contextual priming or recency; and the *focus of attention*, an active but sharply limited state in which only a small number of items can be represented simultaneously. These embedded-processes models define WM as any processing mechanism that allows information to be temporarily available. This functional definition of WM highlights that an array of different mechanisms (e.g. the focus of attention, activated LTM, and inactivated LTM) can contribute to performance in WM tasks. However, this definition of WM makes it difficult to maintain the important theoretical distinction between WM and LTM, and previous research has provided strong empirical evidence that WM and LTM are functionally distinct. For example, WM and LTM account for distinct variance in overall cognitive abilities (Unsworth, Brewer, & Spillers, 2009; Unsworth et al., 2014; Unsworth, Spillers, & Brewer, 2011), and neuropsychology studies have shown a double dissociation between performance on WM and LTM tasks (Scoville & Milner, 1957; Shallice & Warrington, 1969). Therefore, a taxonomy of memory that dissociates WM and LTM mechanisms is motivated by strong empirical evidence.

How can this dissociation between WM and LTM be maintained when many complex cognitive tasks rely on a careful collaboration between these two processes? In this case, behavioural measures alone may not be sufficient because they reflect the end product of multiple memory processes. For example, many studies have shown that learned associations, such as between colours, letters, or words, lead to significant increases in performance on WM recall tasks (Brady, Konkle, & Alvarez, 2008; Chen & Cowan, 2005, 2009; Ngiam et al., 2018; Ngiam et al., 2019). This type of task is typically associated only with WM. However, even though the amount of information that participants recalled increases, this may not necessarily indicate that the amount of

Nicole Hakim, Edward Awh, and Edward K. Vogel, *Manifold Visual Working Memory* In: *Working Memory.*
Edited by: Robert H. Logie, Valérie Camos, and Nelson Cowan, Oxford University Press (2021). © Oxford University Press.
DOI: 10.1093/oso/9780198842286.003.0011

Table 11.1 Summary of responses to the designated questions

Question	Response
1. Definition of working memory	We endorse the embedded-processes model, which puts working memory (WM) in the context of other types of memory. However, we define WM as the processes that maintain a limited amount of information via active neural firing. Therefore, our view of WM closely aligns with the embedded-processes model's definition of the focus of attention.
2. Methods	In our research, we primarily use behavioural and electroencephalographic (EEG) techniques to understand WM and attention. EEG is a time-resolved measure of neural activity that allows us to track information processing in 'real time' in the brain. One downside of EEG is that we have to average over hundreds of trials because of the relatively low signal-to-noise ratio. Without further technological advances, averaging over hundreds of trials impedes our ability to answer fundamental questions on the single-trial level.
3. Unitary versus non-unitary nature of working memory	Overall, we endorse the embedded-processes model framework with the additional fragmentation of the focus of attention. Therefore, our view of WM is less unitary than the original embedded-processes model to the extent that different neural processes contribute to the active maintenance of information in the focus of attention. Additionally, our view of WM is also less unitary than other models that propose that there is one single set of mechanisms and rules that account for all of memory (Brown, Neath, & Chater, 2007; Surprenant & Neath, 2006). However, we also believe that information held in the focus of attention can come in various forms and can be from different modalities. Therefore, in this way, our view of WM is unitary.
4. The role of attention and control	Across the population there are large differences in performance on WM tasks. There is a growing body of evidence that suggests that these individual differences in WM performance are due to variability in controlled attention (Adam, Mance, Fukuda, & Vogel, 2015; Vogel & Fukuda, 2009; Vogel, McCollough, & Machizawa, 2005). For example, individuals who perform poorly on WM tasks tend to score lower on measures of controlled and sustained attention (Adam et al., 2015; deBettencourt, Keene, Awh, & Vogel, 2019). Therefore, the ability to control attention is essential for the storage and maintenance of information in WM and is likely the primary source of variance between individuals in WM capacity measurements.
5. Storage, maintenance, and loss of information in working memory	Previous research that has manipulated maintenance demands while controlling for encoding demands has found that the precision of information and the probability of completely losing information from WM are both mechanisms by which information can be lost. However, the contribution of each of these processes to the loss of information may be dependent upon strategies such as verbalization.

Table 11.1 Continued

Question	Response
6. The role of long-term memory knowledge in working memory storage and processing	Many (if not all) complex cognitive tasks rely on a careful collaboration between WM and long-term memory (LTM). Previous research has shown that LTM can boost behavioural performance on tasks typically associated only with WM (Chen & Cowan, 2005, 2009; Ngiam, Brissenden, & Awh, 2019; Ngiam, Khaw, Holcombe, & Goodbourn, 2018). However, such boosts in WM performance do not necessarily indicate that the amount of information in WM has also increased. One alternate explanation is that information maintained in WM activates the relevant associations in LTM. Therefore, LTM performance may boost behavioural performance without necessarily increasing the amount of information maintained in WM. We maintain the dissociation between WM and LTM by defining these two processes neurally. We define WM as those processes that are maintained via active (online) neural firing, whereas LTM is maintained via passive (offline) neural signatures.
7. Evidence that is not consistent with our theoretical framework	In our framework, we provide evidence that contralateral delay activity (CDA) and lateralized alpha power support storage of information in WM. However, some research suggests that these active neural signatures of memory could be epiphenomenal (Lundqvist, Herman, & Miller, 2018; Mongillo, Barak, & Tsodyks, 2008; Stokes, 2015). Specifically, this research proposes that on single trials, neural firing occurs in sparse transient bursts, and averaging across time and trials causes these sparse transient bursts to appear as though there is consistent neural firing. Along the same line, other work proposes that storage of information can be done with 'activity-silent' WM, which maintains information via changes in synaptic weights, rather than via active neural firing (Rose, in press). Nevertheless, the idea of 'activity-silent' WM is still relatively new, and further research should be done that investigates the distinction between these types of memories and representations stored in long-term memory.

information held in WM also increases. One alternate explanation is that performance is boosted by maintenance of the relevant associations (or 'chunks') in LTM (Huang & Awh, 2018; Ngiam et al., 2019). Thus, using behavioural measures alone, we cannot determine whether performance on these types of tasks increases due to increases in WM storage or due to LTM activation.

To gain leverage on this issue, we propose that active representations in WM should be defined operationally based on neural activity. Previous research has shown that WM generates persistent neural activity that tracks stimulus-specific information (Curtis & D'Esposito, 2003; Harrison & Tong, 2009; Vogel & Machizawa, 2004). These processes are functionally distinct from LTM, as LTMs are thought to be maintained via changes in synaptic weights, not active neural processes (Lamprecht & LeDoux,

2004). Therefore, we define WM as active neural firing that supports the maintenance of information. Other types of memory that are supported by passive neural representations may be better understood as types of LTM. Thus, our neural definition of WM most closely aligns with how the embedded-processes model defines the focus of attention because both are active processes that are sharply limited in capacity. In this chapter, we will use the terms 'WM' and 'focus of attention' synonymously.

Though the operational definition of WM that is endorsed by the embedded-processes model distinguishes between actively (focus of attention) and passively (LTM) stored information, it essentially treats the active maintenance of information as a monolithic process. That is, information is simply either within the focus of attention or not. However, there is growing evidence that suggests that multiple distinct processes may contribute to successfully maintaining information in an active state. In this chapter, we will argue that the focus of attention is manifold and should be thought of as a compilation of multiple processes that support the active representation of relevant information. Specifically, we will provide empirical evidence that suggests that the focus of attention is comprised of an index of prioritized space and an item-based index (Fig. 11.1). This dissection of the focus of attention into multiple subcomponent processes diverges from other models that propose that there is one single set of mechanisms and rules that account for all of memory (Brown et al., 2007; Surprenant & Neath, 2006). Nevertheless, we believe that a common ensemble of processes may maintain

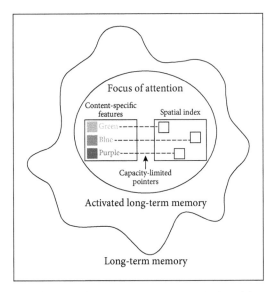

Fig. 11.1 Depiction of the embedded processes model with the additional subcomponents. The focus of attention is a limited capacity system that maintains information in a neurally active state. It is comprised of at least two subcomponent processes, content-specific features, and a spatial index. The focus of attention is situated in a larger memory system, which includes activated long-term memory and long-term memory.

multiple types of information in the focus of attention, such that there is a unitary or domain-general aspect of WM.

In the following sections, we will first discuss the evidence in support of the focus of attention construct. Then, we will dissect the focus of attention into these two subcomponent processes.

Behavioural Evidence for the Focus of Attention

The most notable feature of the focus of attention is that it is capacity limited (Cowan, 1999). There is an array of cognitive evidence that has found such a limit (Cowan, 2001; Luck & Vogel, 1997; Miller, 1956). Much of this research has used colour change detection tasks, which require participants to remember a series of objects over a brief delay (Luck & Vogel, 1997). In this type of task, accuracy declines as a function of the number of presented items. Accuracy is close to 100% when participants are presented with one or two items, and begins to decline thereafter. Based on this, the average amount of information that can be maintained in the focus of attention has been calculated to be approximately three items, with some variability across individuals (Cowan, 2001).

Though there is a general consensus in the WM literature that the focus of attention is strongly limited in scope, the nature of this limit has been hotly debated. On one side, the limit in the focus of attention is best explained by a limited pool of resources that can be flexibly distributed among all relevant items, regardless of how many items are presented (Bays & Husain, 2008; Ma, Husain, & Bays 2014; Wilken & Ma, 2004). On the other side, it has been proposed that WM storage is limited to a fixed number of items, such that no further online storage is possible once that limit has been reached (Cowan, 2001; Fukuda, Awh, & Vogel, 2010; Luck & Vogel, 1997). Zhang and Luck (2008) took a key step forward in this debate by using a continuous recall procedure that used the distribution of errors during recall to obtain separate estimates of the number of items stored in WM and the precision of those representations. Thus, while past behavioural work had not been able to distinguish between pure guessing and errors made due to limited mnemonic resolution, Zhang and Luck provided the first compelling evidence that observers fail to store more than about three simple items from a visual display. This interpretation, however, has been contested based on the observation that the same data can be closely fit using a so-called variable precision model that presumes storage of all items, while allowing wide variations in mnemonic precision across items (e.g. van den Berg, Awh, & Ma, 2014; van den Berg, Shin, Chou, George, & Ma, 2012). In this case, participants have at least some information about all of the items from the original array, and, thus, their responses are never true guesses.

While these no-guessing models provide strong fits with aggregate error distributions, more recent work by Adam, Vogel, and Awh (2017) has provided compelling evidence for a sharp limit in the number of items that can be recalled. Adam et al. (2017) used a whole report procedure that provided a richer characterization of WM performance by measuring recall performance for every memorandum in each display. They found that with six memoranda, the modal subject had no information about three of six items. Indeed, while variable precision models that denied guessing argued for storage of all six items, formal model comparisons showed that the worst of these 'memories' was better described by a model—with zero free parameters—that presumed completely random responses. Thus, recent data have disconfirmed continuous resource models that argue for storage of all items, regardless of set size. Therefore, the focus of attention has been empirically shown to be limited by a fixed number of item representations, not the number of available resources.

A related, but distinct question that has also been debated is whether the number of item representations that can be maintained in the focus of attention varies across individuals. Across the population, there are large differences in performance on WM tasks (Conway et al., 2003; Shipstead, Harrison, & Engle, 2016; Unsworth et al., 2015). These differences have real-world implications, as they are related to differences in general fluid intelligence and academic achievement (Gonthier, 2015; Johnson et al., 2013). Some previous research has proposed that individuals who perform well on WM tasks are able to store more information in the focus of attention than individuals who perform poorly on these tasks (Cowan, 2010). However, these studies have not dissociated the contribution of controlled attention and storage capacity to performance. There is a growing body of evidence that suggests that individual differences in WM performance are actually due to variability in controlled attention, rather than variability in the number of item representations that are able to be maintained in the focus of attention (Adam et al., 2015; Vogel & Fukuda, 2009; Vogel et al., 2005).

One recent study that investigated the relationship between WM performance and controlled attention showed that the plurality of individuals, regardless of performance, were able to maximally store the same number of item representations (Adam et al., 2015). Thus, strong variations in performance across observers were driven by differences in the frequency with which individuals achieved this maximum capacity. Therefore, they conclude that the maximum number of item representations that are able to be maintained in the focus of attention is stable across individuals. However, the ability to hold such information is variable over time and predictive of individual differences in performance. This and other studies that have dissociated attention and storage have focused on how fluctuations of attention at encoding influence performance. Nevertheless, attention is also critically implicated in active maintenance of information in the focus of attention (Hülür, Keye-Ehing, Oberauer, & Wilhelm, 2019; Souza & Oberauer, 2017; Souza, Rerko, Lin, & Oberauer, 2014). Therefore, it is also plausible that fluctuations of attention during maintenance could also influence performance. Currently, this is an underexplored question that should be the focus of future research. Overall, the above-mentioned research provides strong behavioural evidence that suggests that the focus of attention is an active process that is limited by a fixed number of item representations.

Encoding, Maintenance, and Loss of Information from the Focus of Attention

The focus of attention is sharply limited to about three to four pieces of information (Cowan, 2001). Therefore, displays that contain more information than can be held in the focus of attention (supra-capacity displays) present a problem for this system. Given this limit, we may expect that only the most relevant information should be encoded into the focus of attention. However, there are individual differences in the ability to select relevant information and ignore irrelevant information (Cowan & Morey, 2006; Vogel et al., 2005). In fact, previous research has shown that the ability to filter relevant information is related to measures of WM performance (Vogel et al., 2005). Individuals who perform better on WM tasks are better able to selectively encode relevant information and ignore irrelevant information. People who perform worse on these tasks may actually be maintaining more information than the high-performance individuals, but this extra information tends to be irrelevant. Therefore, many failures of WM arise from failures of encoding. Nevertheless, once information is encoded into the focus of attention, other failures may also occur during maintenance.

One productive route to study how information is maintained in the focus of attention is to vary the retention interval of a WM task. This manipulation controls for encoding demands while selectively varying maintenance demands. When the retention interval is longer, maintenance demands are higher, as participants have to maintain information in the focus of attention for longer amounts of time. Most studies that have varied retention interval length have found that performance gets worse after long (~10-second) than short (~1-second) retention intervals (Donkin, Nosofsky, Gold, & Shiffrin, 2015; Rademaker, Park, Sack, & Tong, 2018; Zhang & Luck, 2009). This suggests that higher maintenance demands cause information to be lost from the focus of attention. But, how and why is information lost? One of these studies had participants do a single-probe WM task with varying retention intervals (1, 4, and 10 seconds), which required participants to report the precise colour or shape of one of three presented items (Zhang & Luck, 2009). They found that WM representations could be maintained for several seconds without changes in precision. However, these representations could be lost suddenly and completely during this same time. These results suggest that higher maintenance demands cause individual items to be dropped from the focus of attention without any perceivable changes in precision.

Other published studies, however, have found that the precision of representations in the focus of attention actually does change over time (Donkin et al., 2015; Rademaker et al., 2018). One such study had participants perform a one-item precision task for oriented gratings, colours, and faces over 1-, 3-, 6-, and 12-second retention intervals (Rademaker et al., 2018). They found that the precision of the memory item declined as a function of time for all three types of stimuli. They propose that previous papers that have found no change in precision over time have had high levels of guessing rates, which could distort changes in precision. However, another study proposed that decrements in precision of visual information may only occur when participants are able to verbally label visual information (Donkin et al., 2015). When participants are not able to verbalize, these decrements in performance were better explained by the sudden loss of information than by decrements in precision. These results suggest that verbalization strategies may be able to boost WM performance. Therefore, changes in precision and the probability of completely losing information from the focus of attention are both mechanisms by which information can be lost. However, the contribution of each of these processes to the loss of information may be dependent upon strategies, such as verbalization.

Neural Signals that Track the Focus of Attention

While the focus of attention can actively represent only a few items at a time, it can quickly and flexibly change contents as task goals or the environment change. This is particularly evident in retro-cue paradigms. In these types of tasks, participants are presented with an array of items and are later told which items will be relevant. When this retro-cue correctly indicates the object that will be tested, participants respond more quickly and accurately (Makovski, Sussman, & Jiang, 2008; Souza & Oberauer, 2016). This boost in performance is proposed to happen because the retro-cued object is more likely to be actively maintained in the focus of attention, rather than passively maintained in activated LTM. However, when you probe an item that was not retro-cued, participants respond more slowly, suggesting that this information is stored more passively than the item that was retro-cued. These results suggest that memory representations may change fluidly between 'active' and 'passive' states in service of performing any complex cognitive task. However, even though reaction times can be used to estimate whether information is actively or passively stored, the mere fact that an individual can accurately report a piece of information does not diagnose which state of memory was driving the behaviour. This challenge for interpreting behavioural responses has motivated many to establish neural markers of actively represented information in WM.

Single-unit neurophysiological studies in non-human primates have found that there is sustained delay-period activity in individual neurons in prefrontal cortex during WM tasks (Fuster, 1973; Fuster & Alexander, 1971; Niki, 1974). This delay-period activity has been shown to be an essential aspect of active information processing. For example, this delay activity is highly selective such that cells in different parts of the brain selectively respond to specific featural information that is maintained in the focus of attention (Kobatake & Tanaka, 1994). The inferotemporal cortex contains neurons that are selective for particular feature dimensions, such as shape and colour (Wang, Fujita, & Murayama, 2000). This means that when participants are maintaining a specific feature value in WM, neural activity that is selective for that feature is sustained throughout the memory period. This prediction has also been confirmed in functional magnetic resonance imaging studies with humans (Curtis & D'Esposito, 2003; Harrison & Tong, 2009; Serences, Ester, Vogel, & Awh, 2009). Thus, persistent neural firing maintains stimulus-specific feature information that is actively maintained in the focus of attention.

In our research, we primarily use EEG in conjunction with behavioural methods to answer questions about WM and attention. Behavioural methods allow us to measure the end result of different WM processes. EEG, by contrast, has sufficient temporal resolution to track information flowing into and out of an active state during a trial. Without this time-resolved measure of these WM processes, it would be very difficult to dissociate the unique contributions of WM and LTM to behavioural performance. In the rest of this section, we will discuss various productive univariate EEG methods that have been shown to track information in the focus of attention. However, we would like to note that, recently, multivariate analyses have also become a productive and popular way to analyse EEG and functional magnetic resonance imaging data. Multivariate techniques allow us to use the relationship between multiple variables to understand and quantify a specific process. For example, in EEG, multivariate pattern analyses allow us to use the pattern of neural activity across multiple electrodes to answer questions about a variety of cognitive processes. These analyses have been applied to answer questions, such as can more than one piece of information be maintained in the focus of attention at any one moment (Sutterer, Foster, Adam, Vogel, & Awh, 2019), how is information retrieved from LTM (Sutterer, Foster, Serences, Vogel, & Awh, 2019), and what are the trade-offs between attention and WM (van Moorselaar et al., 2017)? These types of analyses allow us to understand more complex relationships than some univariate methods and, thus, might help enhance empirical and theoretical advances in future WM research.

One limit of both multivariate and univariate EEG analyses is that they often require averaging over hundreds of trials in each condition. When you average over trials, you are not able to answer fundamental questions on the single-trial level, such as whether activity is continuous, and it can make it difficult to do experiments with real-time EEG-based feedback and triggering. Additionally, collecting hundreds of trials is costly and time consuming, and there are very few studies that have empirically investigated the appropriate number of trials to obtain high levels of reliability and reproducibility. One recent study investigated the reliability and stability of change detection performance on a behavioural task and found that both the number of trials and the sample size can influence the reliability and stability of this task (Z. Xu, Adam, Fang, & Vogel, 2018). For example, if an experiment has 10 participants and 150 trials, the average reliability of change detection performance is about 75%. However, the worst iteration, akin to the worst expected experiment out of 100, only had a reliability of 42%. This study provides a useful criterion for deciding sample size and trial number for a behavioural paradigm, but does not address the reliability and stability of EEG measures. Therefore, future research should provide empirical evidence for the number of trials and sample size that EEG experiments should have in order to obtain reliable and replicable results.

Despite these limitations, a large body of EEG research using univariate and multivariate methods has advanced our empirical and theoretical understanding of WM. Given that WM is flexible, fast, and capacity limited, we should expect that EEG signals that track active representations in WM should share these properties. Within the EEG literature, two candidate neural signals have been productive indices of WM storage: alpha power and the contralateral delay activity (CDA).

Alpha power (8–12 Hz) is an oscillatory signal that is typically measured at electrodes located at posterior parts of the head. This signal shows sustained reductions in power during delay periods of WM tasks. It is modulated by memory array set size, shows limits at typical capacity levels, and predicts individual differences in WM performance (Fukuda, Mance, & Vogel, 2015). Moreover, further work has shown that it contains precise spatial information about remembered and attended stimuli, and dynamically and flexibly tracks updating of spatial information (Foster, Bsales, Jaffe, & Awh, 2017; Foster, Sutterer, Serences, & Awh, 2016; van Moorselaar et al., 2017). It can be measured in a number of ways. One popular way to measure alpha power is to take the difference between contralateral and ipsilateral electrodes at posterior parts of the brain. By taking the difference between activity from the two hemispheres, we are able to control for the effect of visual stimulation on this signal. This type of analysis is best for tracking coarse changes in visual attention, such as whether the participant is covertly attending to the left or right side of their visual field. A similar signal, global alpha power, is also measured at posterior electrode sites, but is not a difference between hemispheres. Instead, this signal tracks overall changes in power at the back of the head and has been shown to track the number of attended items. More fine-grained multivariate analyses of alpha power (Fig. 11.2) have been done using inverted encoding models. These types of analyses take into account the topography of alpha power across the entire scalp, and have been shown to track the precise location of attended and maintained stimuli (Foster et al., 2016; Foster, Sutterer, Serences, Vogel, & Awh, 2017; Samaha, Sprague, & Postle, 2016). Overall, lateralized, global, and the topography of alpha power all seem to represent actively maintained spatial information.

The *CDA* is a signal that appears to track the number of items maintained in the focus of attention. Just like lateralized alpha power, this signal is computed as a difference in amplitude between contralateral and ipsilateral electrodes with respect to the attended side of the display. By taking the difference between activities from the two hemispheres, this approach isolates the neural correlates of WM activity by controlling for the effect of visual stimulation. The CDA is a sustained negativity over the hemisphere contralateral to the positions of to-be-remembered items. Its amplitude is modulated by the number of items held in WM, asymptotes at WM capacity, dynamically tracks adding and dropping of information, and predicts both trial-by-trial variations in memory storage and stable individual differences in WM capacity (Adam et al., 2015; Vogel & Machizawa, 2004; Vogel et al., 2005; Williams & Woodman, 2012). If one doesn't eliminate the sensory response, a non-lateralized variation of the same activity can be measured as a negative slow wave, which is measured at the same electrodes as the CDA. However, the negative slow wave is a measure of mean amplitude at

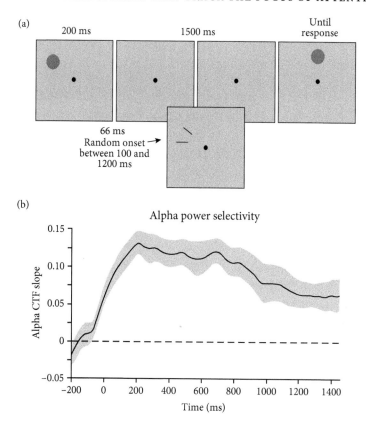

Fig. 11.2 Alpha power selectivity. (a) Attention task during which participants had to attend the location of an object over a brief delay. In this task, participants were first shown one circle. They were told to attend the location of that circle over the delay in order to detect a rare target line that would appear in the circle's location. This target line was always accompanied by a distractor line, which appeared somewhere else on the screen. The circle on the final screen indicated that it was time for the participant to report the orientation of the target line, if it was present. If no line was present, the participant clicked 'b' to indicate that the screen remained blank the entire delay. (b) Alpha CTF slope is a measure of the amount of location-specific activity (selectivity) in the topographic distribution of alpha power over time. Higher CTF slopes indicate greater location-specific activity. CTF slope is calculated in inverted encoding model analyses.

posterior electrodes, rather than a difference between the two hemispheres. Just like the CDA, this signal has been shown to track the number of items stored in WM.

Both alpha power and CDA are delay-period signals with high temporal resolution that dynamically track information that is actively maintained in the focus of attention. The dissociation between these two neural signals is central to the argument that the focus of attention is manifold. If alpha power and CDA co-occur, yet track distinct cognitive constructs, this would suggest that actively maintained information in the focus of attention is supported by at least two dissociable processes. In the next sections, we will discuss the debate about whether CDA and alpha power track distinct cognitive constructs and how this debate relates to the fractionation of the focus of attention.

Do Alpha Power and Contralateral Delay Activity Reflect Isomorphic Mechanisms of the Focus of Attention?

From the previous summary, it is clear that one can make a case for both alpha power and CDA as neural candidates for the focus of attention construct. Both the CDA and alpha power are flexible, dynamic, predict performance, and track trial-by-trial fluctuations. Indeed, motivated in part by these overlapping properties, some research has suggested that these two measures of brain activity can be explained by a common neural process, and, thus, track a single cognitive process. For example, van Dijk, van der Werf, Mazaheri, Medendorp, and Jensen (2010) proposed that the CDA is generated by changes in alpha power. CDA analyses average over a series of trials and are time-locked to stimulus onset. Typically, it is assumed that oscillatory activity is averaged out of such a signal because oscillatory activity should not be consistently aligned to the onset of a jittered stimulus. However, previous research has found that alpha has 'amplitude fluctuation asymmetry' (Nikulin et al., 2007), which means that amplitude changes are reflected more in either the peak or trough of the oscillation. Thus, Nikulin et al. suggest that it is at least possible for asymmetric amplitude asymmetry to generate a sustained change in the amplitude of an event-related potential component. Based on this and other observations, van Dijk et al. (2010) concluded that the CDA may be a by-product of alpha oscillations, and, thus, the CDA and alpha power may index a common neural process. Van Dijk et al.'s study simulated this type of neural data and concluded that alpha power and the CDA are isomorphic. However, follow-up research has found evidence against this hypothesis by showing that alpha power and the negative slow wave (a global signal that is analogous to the CDA) had dissociable time courses, and explained distinct variance in WM performance (Fukuda, Kang, & Woodman, 2016).

Another study also came to the conclusion that CDA and alpha power are isomorphic, but took a slightly different approach (Berggren & Eimer, 2016). This study sought to determine whether the CDA also tracked spatial attention (in a manner consistent with alpha power) or whether it tracked the number of concurrently stored representations in WM. In order to determine whether the CDA tracks items or space, Berggren and Eimer presented participants with sequential displays that either appeared in the same or different hemifield. Since the CDA is a difference wave between contralateral and ipsilateral electrodes, they proposed that if the CDA tracks the number of items held in WM, the amplitude of the CDA should be additive when the two sequential displays are presented in the same hemifield. However, if the CDA actually reflects the current allocation of spatial attention, then the amplitude of the CDA should only reflect the number of items presented in the current display. Berggren and Eimer found the latter result, and thus they argued that the CDA tracked the current focus of attention, rather than the number of maintained representations. However, an alternative explanation for this pattern is that subjects may have shifted the items in the first array into activated LTM rather than storing them concurrently with the second array. Feldmann-Wüstefeld, Vogel, and Awh (2018) speculated that subjects may have offloaded the first array because the format of the test display was not conducive to maintaining a concurrent representation of both arrays. Using a test display with a different format, Feldmann-Wüstefeld et al. (2018) showed that the CDA tracked the total amount of information stored across both arrays. This is consistent with the hypothesis that the CDA tracks the number of representations maintained in WM rather than the current focus of spatial attention.

Further evidence in support of a dissociation between alpha power and CDA came from a study that investigated event-related potential and oscillatory correlates of WM performance (Fukuda, Mance, & Vogel, 2015). In this study, participants did a whole-field WM task while EEG activity was recorded. Fukuda et al. found that alpha power and the slow wave (a global signal that is analogous to the CDA) both tracked the amount of presented information and showed characteristics associated with the focus of attention. However, while the two signals both correlated with performance, they were not correlated with each other. A regression analysis additionally revealed that each explained unique variance in individual differences in WM performance. Furthermore, in a separate experiment that manipulated retention interval, the study authors observed that the two components have different durations, again, supporting a clear dissociation between these two neural measures. Together, these results suggest that these two neural signals, the slow wave and alpha power, reflect dissociable neural and cognitive processes that both uniquely contribute to the maintenance of information in the focus of attention.

Manifold Focus of Attention: Item-Based and Spatial Indices

More recent research provides further evidence for the dissociation of CDA and alpha power while also motivating a refined account of the link between CDA activity and WM storage (Hakim, Adam, Gunseli, Awh, & Vogel, 2019). In this study (Fig. 11.3), participants performed two tasks that had identical displays, but varied the relative demands for the maintenance of item-based representations while EEG activity was recorded. In the item-based storage task, participants had to remember the colour or location of objects over a brief delay. In the spatial index task, participants had to monitor the locations marked by those objects over a brief delay to determine the orientation of a rare target line that could appear during the delay. Although both tasks required maintenance of spatial information, only the item-based storage task encouraged participants to maintain active representations of the items in the sample display. Critically, Hakim et al. found a robust CDA that was sensitive to mnemonic load only in the item-based storage task. However, they found that alpha power was significantly lateralized in both tasks. Based on these findings, they concluded that the CDA tracks

(a)

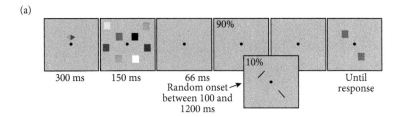

300 ms   150 ms   66 ms
                    Random onset
                    between 100 and
                    1200 ms

90%

10%

Until
response

(b)

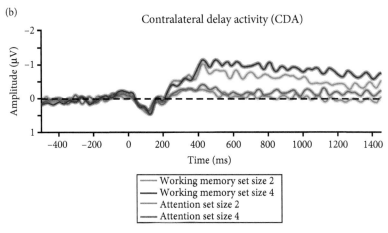

Contralateral delay activity (CDA)

Working memory set size 2
Working memory set size 4
Attention set size 2
Attention set size 4

Fig. 11.3 Evidence that suggests that item and spatial indices are neurally dissociable. (a) Experiment 1a task design from Hakim et al. (2019). In this series of experiments, participants performed two tasks, an 'attention' and a 'WM task' with two set sizes (2 and 4). In both tasks, the visual stimuli were exactly the same. The only thing that differed was the instructions. In the 'WM' task, participants performed a typical lateralized change detection task. They were cued to one side of the screen and told to remember the colours and locations of the objects on that side of the screen over the brief delay. Following the delay, participants had to determine whether the object that reappeared on the cued side changed colours. They were told to ignore any lines that appeared during the delay. In the 'attention task', participants were cued to one side of the screen and told to attend the locations of the objects on that side of the screen in order to detect a rare target line during the blank delay. At the end of the delay, if there was a target on that trial, participants had to report the orientation of the line (tilted left or right). If there was no target present, participants pressed 'space'. (b) Contralateral delay activity (CDA) amplitude over time shown separately for each condition in the WM and attention tasks collapsed across all four experiments from Hakim et al. (2019). Time 0 represents the onset of the memory array, and time 1450 marks the onset of the response array. In each plot, the thick line represents the mean of the sample, and the shaded bars around these lines are error bars that show the standard error of the mean.

Adapted from Nicole Hakim, Kirsten C. S. Adam, Eren Gunseli, Edward Awh, and Edward K. Vogel, 'Dissecting the Neural Focus of Attention Reveals Distinct Processes for Spatial Attention and Object-Based Storage in Visual Working Memory', *Psychological Science*, 30 (4), pp. 526–540. https://doi.org/10.1177/0956797619830384

the *number* of item-based indices maintained in the focus of attention and lateralized alpha power tracks the prioritized spatial positions. This study, in conjunction with Fukuda et al. (2016), show that the CDA and lateralized alpha power are neurally dissociable processes. Additionally, these results suggest that the CDA tracks the number of individuated representations (independent of featural content), whereas lateralized alpha power tracks prioritized regions of space (independent of the number of individuated representations).

Further evidence for a dissociation between the CDA and lateralized alpha power, and thus item-based and spatial indices, comes from a study that had participants memorize a lateralized item which was either currently relevant for an upcoming task, or prospectively relevant for a future task (de Vries, van Driel, & Olivers, 2017). In both the currently relevant and prospectively relevant tasks, participants had to maintain information in WM as that information would be relevant in the near future. However, in the prospectively relevant task, participants had to maintain that information while performing an unrelated, intervening task. They found that the CDA did not differ between the currently and prospectively relevant tasks, suggesting that participants actually were actively maintaining information in WM for use in the near future. However, alpha power was more lateralized for the current than for the prospective task. From this, they concluded that the CDA tracked the number of item-based representations, whereas lateralized alpha power tracked the spatial index of current attentional selection. These results further emphasize the dissociation between the CDA, which tracks the number of individuated representations, and alpha power, which tracks prioritized regions of space.

Another study found that CDA and alpha power had distinct responses to task-irrelevant interruption by during WM maintenance (Hakim, Feldmann-Wüstefeld, Awh, & Vogel, 2020). In this study (Fig. 11.4), interrupters were presented on the midline on a subset of trials. Importantly, when distractors are presented on the vertical midline and targets are presented laterally, as is the case in this experiment, the neural signature of target processing can be isolated. Reductions in CDA amplitude can be interpreted as dropping memory items, and reductions in lateralized alpha power can be interpreted as a shift of attention away from the laterally presented memory arrays. Following interruption, lateralized alpha power immediately shifted towards baseline, but recovered by the end of the trial. However, the CDA sustained for a few hundred milliseconds, but was gone by the end of the trial. This dissociable pattern of activity suggests that item-based and spatial indices distinctly respond to interruption.

Taken together, these studies show that alpha power and CDA uniquely contribute to WM performance, have dissociable time courses, and distinctly track the number of item-based representations and relevant spatial information. Thus, we argue that the focus of attention is comprised of at least two subcomponent processes that index item-based storage and currently prioritized spatial locations. The separation of spatial from object-based information is broadly consistent with results from Y. Xu and Chun (2006), which argued that the visual system uses spatial information to select a fixed number of items (object individuation) and then encode their details (object

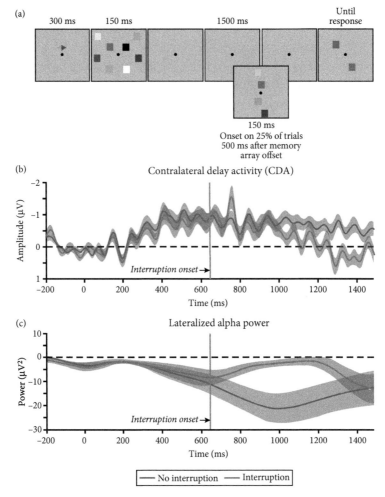

Fig. 11.4 The influence of task-irrelevant interruption on the CDA and lateralized alpha power. (a) Lateralized change detection task with interruption on a subset of trials. In this type of task, participants are first cued to attend one side of the screen. Following this cue, a series of coloured squares briefly appear on both sides of the screen. Participants are told to remember the colours and locations of the squares on the cued side of the screen. Then, the screen goes blank and either remains blank until the response screen (75% of trials), or a series of new squares appear on the midline 500 ms after the offset of the memory array (25% of trials). Participants are told that they should always ignore the interrupting squares. After this delay period, one square on each side of the screen reappears and participants have to determine whether the square that reappears on the cued side is the same or different colour as the original square in that location. (b) CDA amplitude over time shown separately for each condition (interruption in green and no interruption in purple). Time 0 represents the onset of the memory array, time 650 represents the onset of the interruption (if there was interruption on that trial) and time 1450 marks the onset of the response array. In each plot, the thick line represents the mean of the sample, and the shaded bars around these lines are error bars that show the standard error of the mean. (c) Lateralized alpha power over time shown separately for each condition (interruption in green and no interruption in purple). Time 0 represents the onset of the memory array, time 650 represents the onset of the interruption (if there was interruption on that trial), and time 1450 marks the onset of the response array. In each plot, the thick line represents the mean of the sample, and the shaded bars around these lines are error bars that show the standard error of the mean.

identification). Thus, their proposal that spatial information aids the individuation of item-based indices implicitly suggests that spatial and item-based information are separate. They additionally provide neural evidence for the separation of these two processes by showing that spatial and item-based information are processed in distinct sections of intraparietal sulcus: inferior intraparietal sulcus represents item-based information and superior intraparietal sulcus represents spatial information and current goals. Thus, multiple lines of evidence converge on the idea that the focus of attention is supported by distinct indices of item-based storage and spatial priority.

We would like to highlight that the distinction we make between spatial and item-based indices is not the same as the previously proposed distinction between visual and spatial information (Logie, 1995). Previous research has shown a double dissociation between visual and spatial memory, such that impairments in remembering spatial locations do not always co-occur with impairments in remembering visual appearances of stimuli and vice versa (Darling, Della Sala, Logie, & Cantagallo, 2006; Klauer & Zhao, 2004). This distinction between spatial and visual information (also see: Logie, Belletier, & Doherty, 2021) is based on the featural content of memory, and a large body of research has shown that different features can be behaviourally and neurally dissociated. We propose an orthogonal distinction between signals that index the number of individuated representations (independent of featural content) and signals that track prioritized regions of space (independent of the number of individuated representations). The item-based index (e.g. CDA) is content-free and could be thought of as a pointer-based index that tracks the total number of objects maintained in WM. The spatial index (e.g. alpha power), by contrast, tracks the locations of relevant objects without regard to the number of item-based representations. Both of these indices are independent from the featural content of memory.

Other Components of the Focus of Attention

Our view that the focus of attention is manifold is a relatively new development in this field of research. Therefore, future research should further investigate whether other distinct subcomponents contribute to maintenance of information in the focus of attention. For example, previous research has suggested that content-specific information, such as colour and orientation, is also maintained in the focus of attention and, thus, should also be decodable from neural activity. In line with this, Bae and Luck (2018) were able to decode feature-specific orientation information from the topography of raw EEG data. In this study, they had participants remember the orientation of a teardrop over a brief delay. Using inverted encoding models during the delay period, they found that alpha power carried clear information about the location of the stimulus, as had previously been found, and raw EEG amplitude tracked the orientation of the remembered stimulus. These results suggest that there are also feature-specific neural signals that can be broadly picked up from EEG activity. Therefore, understanding the relationship between how content-independent (e.g. CDA and alpha power) and content-specific information is represented in the brain would provide a valuable extension of the neural underpinnings of the focus of attention.

Conclusion

There has been a long-standing effort to understand what exactly WM is and how it is represented in the brain. Most contemporary theories of WM have embraced the embedded-processes model, which proposes that information in WM is maintained in three distinct layers: the focus of attention, activated LTM, and LTM. Here, we offer a new hypothesis regarding the distinct subcomponents of the focus of attention by providing evidence for dissociable delay-period activity that separately tracks spatial and item-based information. The dissociation between these two subprocesses further elucidates how information is maintained within the focus of attention, and our hope is that this will provide further traction for understanding this central component of intelligent human behaviour.

Acknowledgement

Research was supported by NIMH grant ROIMH087214 and Office of Naval Research grant N00014-12-1-0972.

References

Ackerman, P. L., Beier, M. E., & Boyle, M. O. (2005). Working memory and intelligence: The same or different constructs? *Psychological Bulletin*, *131*, 30–60. doi:10.1037/0033-2909.131.1.30

Adam, K. C. S., Mance, I., Fukuda, K., & Vogel, E. K. (2015). The contribution of attentional lapses to individual differences in visual working memory capacity. *Journal of Cognitive Neuroscience*, *27*, 1601–1616. doi:10.1162/jocn_a_00811

Adam, K. C. S., Vogel, E. K., & Awh, E. (2017). Clear evidence for item limits in visual working memory. *Cognitive Psychology*, *97*, 79–97. doi:10.1016/j.cogpsych.2017.07.001

Bae, G. Y., & Luck, S. J. (2018). Dissociable decoding of spatial attention and working memory from EEG oscillations and sustained potentials. *Journal of Neuroscience*, *38*, 409–422. doi:10.1523/JNEUROSCI.2860-17.2017

Bays, P. M., & Husain, M. (2008). Dynamic shifts of limited working memory resources in human vision. *Science (New York, N.Y.)*, *321*, 851–854. doi:10.1126/science.1158023

Berggren, N., & Eimer, M. (2016). Does contralateral delay activity reflect working memory storage or the current focus of spatial attention within visual working memory? *Journal of Cognitive Neuroscience*, *28*, 2003–2020. doi:10.1162/jocn_a_01019

Brady, T. F., Konkle, T., Alvarez, G. A., & Oliva, A. (2008). Visual long-term memory has a massive storage capacity for object details. *Proceedings of the National Academy of Sciences of the United States of America*, *105*, 14325–14329. doi:10.1073/pnas.0803390105

Brown, G. D. A., Neath, I., & Chater, N. (2007). A temporal ratio model of memory. *Psychological Review*, *114*, 539–576. doi:10.1037/0033-295X.114.3.539

Chen, Z., & Cowan, N. (2005). Chunk limits and length limits in immediate recall: A reconciliation. *Journal of Experimental Psychology. Learning, Memory, and Cognition, 31*, 1235–1249. doi:10.1037/0278-7393.31.6.1235

Chen, Z., & Cowan, N. (2009). How verbal memory loads consume attention. *Memory & Cognition, 37*, 829–836. doi:10.3758/MC.37.6.829

Conway, A. R. A., Kane, M. J., & Engle, R. W. (2003). Working memory capacity and its relation to general intelligence. *Trends in Cognitive Sciences, 7*, 547–552. doi:10.1016/j.tics.2003.10.005

Cowan, N. (1999). An embedded-processes model of working memory. In A. Miyake & P. Shah (Eds.), *Models of working memory: Mechanisms of active maintenance and executive control* (pp. 62–102). Cambridge, UK: Cambridge University Press.

Cowan, N. (2001). The magical number 4 in short term memory: A reconsideration of storage capacity. *Behavioral and Brain Sciences, 24*, 87–186. doi:10.1017/S0140525X01003922

Cowan, N. (2010). The magical mystery four: How is working memory capacity limited, and why? *Current Directions in Psychological Science, 19*, 51–57. doi:10.1177/0963721409359277

Cowan, N., & Morey, C. C. (2006). Visual working memory depends on attentional filtering. *Trends in Cognitive Sciences, 10*, 139–141. doi:10.1016/j.tics.2006.02.001

Cowan, N., Morey, C., & Naveh-Benjamin, M. (2021). An embedded-processes approach to working memory: How is it distinct from other approaches, and to what ends? In R. H. Logie, V. Camos, & N. Cowan (Eds.), *Working memory: State of the science* (pp. 44–84). Oxford, UK: Oxford University Press.

Curtis, C. E., & D'Esposito, M. (2003). Persistent activity in the prefrontal cortex during working memory. *Trends in Cognitive Sciences, 7*, 415–423. doi:10.1016/S1364-6613(03)00197-9

Darling, S., Della Sala, S., Logie, R. H., & Cantagallo, A. (2006). Neuropsychological evidence for separating components of visuo-spatial working memory. *Journal of Neurology, 253*, 176–180. doi:10.1007/s00415-005-0944-3

de Vries, I. E. J., van Driel, J., & Olivers, C. N. L. (2017). Posterior alpha EEG dynamics dissociate current from future goals in working memory-guided visual search. *Journal of Neuroscience, 37*, 1591–1603. doi:10.1523/JNEUROSCI.2945-16.2016

deBettencourt, M. T., Keene, P. A., Awh, E., & Vogel, E. K. (2019). Real-time triggering reveals concurrent lapses of attention and working memory. *Nature Human Behaviour 3*, 808–816. doi:10.1038/s41562-019-0606-6

Donkin, C., Nosofsky, R., Gold, J., & Shiffrin, R. (2015). Verbal labeling, gradual decay, and sudden death in visual short-term memory. *Psychonomic Bulletin & Review, 22*, 170–178. doi:10.3758/s13423-014-0675-5

Engle, R. W., Laughlin, J. E., Tuholski, S. W., & Conway, A. R. A. (1999). Working memory, short-term memory, and general fluid intelligence: A latent-variable approach. *Journal of Experimental Psychology: General, 128*, 309–331. doi:10.1037/0096-3445.128.3.309

Feldmann-Wüstefeld, T., Vogel, E. K., & Awh, E. (2018). Contralateral delay activity indexes working memory storage, not the current focus of spatial attention. *Journal of Cognitive Neuroscience, 30*, 1185–1196. doi:10.1162/jocn_a_01271

Foster, J. J., Bsales, E. M., Jaffe, R. J., & Awh, E. (2017). Alpha-band activity reveals spontaneous representations of spatial position in visual working memory. *Current Biology, 27*, 3216–3223.e6. doi:10.1016/j.cub.2017.09.031

Foster, J. J., Sutterer, D. W., Serences, J. T., & Awh, E. (2016). The topography of alpha-band activity tracks the content of spatial working memory. *Journal of Neurophysiology, 115*, 168–177. doi:10.1152/jn.00860.2015

Foster, J. J., Sutterer, D. W., Serences, J. T., Vogel, E. K., & Awh, E. (2017). Alpha-band oscillations enable spatially and temporally resolved tracking of covert spatial attention. *Psychological Science, 28*, 929–941. doi:10.1177/0956797617699167

Fukuda, K., Awh, E., & Vogel, E. K. (2010). Discrete capacity limits in visual working memory. *Current Opinion in Neurobiology, 20*, 177–182. doi:10.1016/j.conb.2010.03.005

Fukuda, K., Kang, M. S., & Woodman, G. F. (2016). Distinct neural mechanisms for spatially lateralized and spatially global visual working memory representations. *Journal of Neurophysiology, 116*, 1715–1727. doi:10.1152/jn.00991.2015

Fukuda, K., Mance, I., & Vogel, E. K. (2015). Alpha power modulation and event-related slow wave provide dissociable correlates of visual working memory. *Journal of Neuroscience, 35,* 14009–14016. doi:10.1523/JNEUROSCI.5003-14.2015

Fuster, J. M. (1973). Unit activity in prefrontal cortex during delayed-response performance: Neuronal correlates of transient memory. *Journal of Neurophysiology, 36,* 61–78. doi:10.1152/jn.1973.36.1.61

Fuster, J. M., & Alexander, G. E. (1971). Neuron activity related to short-term memory. *Science, 173,* 652–654. doi:10.1126/science.173.3997.652

Gonthier, C. (2015). Strategy use fully mediates the relationship between working memory capacity and performance on Raven's matrices. *Journal of Experimental Psychology. General, 144,* 916–924. doi:10.1037/xge0000101

Hakim, N., Adam, K. C. S., Gunseli, E., Awh, E., & Vogel, E. K. (2019). Dissecting the neural focus of attention reveals distinct processes for spatial attention and object-based storage in visual working memory. *BioRxiv,* 347518. doi:10.1101/347518

Hakim, N., Feldmann-Wüstefeld, T., Awh, E., & Vogel, E. K. (2020). Perturbing neural representations of working memory with task-irrelevant interruption. *Journal of Cognitive Neuroscience, 32,* 558–569. doi:10.1162/jocn_a_01481

Harrison, S. A., & Tong, F. (2009). Visual areas. *Nature, 458,* 632–635. doi:10.1038/nature07832

Huang, L., & Awh, E. (2018). Chunking in working memory via content-free labels. *Scientific Reports, 8,* 23. doi:10.1038/s41598-017-18157-5

Hülür, G., Keye-Ehing, D., Oberauer, K., & Wilhelm, O. (2019). The effect of stimulus-response compatibility on the association of fluid intelligence and working memory with choice reaction times. *Journal of Cognition, 2,* 1–19. doi:10.5334/joc.66

Johnson, M. K., McMahon, R. P., Robinson, B. M., Harvey, A. N., Hahn, B., Leonard, C. J., . . . Gold, J. M. (2013). The relationship between working memory capacity and broad measures of cognitive ability in healthy adults and people with schizophrenia. *Neuropsychologia, 27,* 220–229. doi:10.1037/a0032060

Klauer, K. C., & Zhao, Z. (2004). Double dissociations in visual and spatial short-term memory. *Journal of Experimental Psychology: General, 133,* 355–381. doi:10.1037/0096-3445.133.3.355

Kobatake, E., & Tanaka, K. (1994). Neuronal selectivities to complex object features in the ventral visual pathway of the macaque cerebral cortex. *Journal of Neurophysiology, 71,* 856–867. doi:10.1152/jn.1994.71.3.856

Lamprecht, R., & LeDoux, J. (2004). Structural plasticity and memory. *Nature Reviews Neuroscience, 5,* 45–54. doi:10.1038/nrn1301

Logie, R. H. (1995). *Visuo-spatial working memory.* Hove, UK: Erlbaum.

Logie, R. H., Belletier, C., & Doherty, J. D. (2021). Integrating theories of working memory. In R. H. Logie, V. Camos, & N. Cowan (Eds.), *Working memory: State of the science* (pp. 389–429). Oxford, UK: Oxford University Press.

Luck, S., & Vogel, E. K. (1997). The capacity of visual working memory for features and conjuctions. *Nature, 390,* 279–281.

Lundqvist, M., Herman, P., & Miller, E. K. (2018). Working memory: Delay activity, yes! persistent activity? Maybe not. *Journal of Neuroscience, 38,* 7013–7019. doi:10.1523/JNEUROSCI.2485-17.2018

Ma, W. J., Husain, M., & Bays, P. M. (2014). Changing concepts of working memory. *Nature Neuroscience, 17,* 347–356. doi:10.1038/nn.3655

Makovski, T., Sussman, R., & Jiang, Y. V. (2008). Orienting attention in visual working memory reduces interference from memory probes. *Journal of Experimental Psychology: Learning, Memory, and Cognition, 34,* 369–380. doi:10.1037/0278-7393.34.2.369

Miller, G. A. (1956). The magical number seven, plus or minus two: Some limits on our capacity for processing information. *Psychological Review, 63,* 81–97. doi:10.1037/h0043158

Mongillo, G., Barak, O., & Tsodyks, M. (2008). Synaptic theory of working memory. *Science, 319,* 1543–1546. doi:10.1126/science.1150769

Ngiam, W. X. Q., Brissenden, J. A., & Awh, E. (2019). 'Memory compression' effects in visual working memory are contingent on explicit long-term memory. *Journal of Experimental Psychology: General, 148,* 1373–1385. doi:10.1037/xge0000649

Ngiam, W. X. Q., Khaw, K. L. C., Holcombe, A. O., & Goodbourn, P. T. (2018). Visual working memory for letters varies with familiarity but not complexity. *Journal of Experimental Psychology: Learning, Memory, and Cognition, 45,* 1761–1775. doi:10.1037/xlm0000682

Niki, H. (1974). Differential activity of prefrontal units during right and left delayed response trials. *Brain Research, 70,* 346–349. doi:10.1016/0006-8993(74)90324-2

Nikulin, V. V., Linkenkaer-Hansen, K., Nolte, G., Lemm, S., Müller, K. R., Ilmoniemi, R. J., & Curio, G. (2007). A novel mechanism for evoked responses in the human brain. *European Journal of Neuroscience, 25,* 3146–3154. doi:10.1111/j.1460-9568.2007.05553.x

Rademaker, R. L., Park, Y. E., Sack, A. T., & Tong, F. (2018). Evidence of gradual loss of precision for simple features and complex objects in visual working memory. *Journal of Experimental Psychology. Human Perception and Performance, 44,* 925–940. doi:10.1037/xhp0000491

Rose, N. S. (in press). The dynamic processing model of working memory. *Current Directions in Psychological Science.*

Samaha, J., Sprague, T. C., & Postle, B. R. (2016). Decoding and reconstructing the focus of spatial attention from the topography of alpha-band oscillations. *Journal of Cognitive Neuroscience, 28,* 1090–1097. doi:10.1162/jocn_a_00955

Scoville, W. B., & Milner, B. (1957). Loss of recent memory after bilateral hippocampal lesions. *Journal of Neurology, Neurosurgery, and Psychiatry, 20,* 11–21. doi:10.1136/jnnp.20.1.11

Serences, J. T., Ester, E. F., Vogel, E. K., & Awh, E. (2009). Stimulus-specific delay activity in human primary visual cortex. *Psychological Science, 20,* 207–214. doi:10.1111/j.1467-9280.2009.02276.x

Shallice, T., & Warrington, E. k. (1969). The selective impairment of auditory verbal short-term memory. *Brain, 92,* 885–896. doi:10.1093/brain/92.4.885

Shipstead, Z., Harrison, T. L., & Engle, R. W. (2016). Working memory capacity and fluid intelligence: Maintenance and disengagement. *Perspectives on Psychological Science, 11,* 771–799. doi:10.1177/1745691616650647

Souza, A. S., & Oberauer, K. (2016). In search of the focus of attention in working memory: 13 years of the retro-cue effect. *Attention, Perception, and Psychophysics, 78,* 1839–1860. doi:10.3758/s13414-016-1108-5

Souza, A. S., & Oberauer, K. (2017). The contributions of visual and central attention to visual working memory. *Attention, Perception, and Psychophysics, 79,* 1897–1916. doi:10.3758/s13414-017-1357-y

Souza, A. S., Rerko, L., Lin, H. Y., & Oberauer, K. (2014). Focused attention improves working memory: Implications for flexible-resource and discrete-capacity models. *Attention, Perception, and Psychophysics, 76,* 2080–2102. doi:10.3758/s13414-014-0687-2

Stokes, M. G. (2015). 'Activity-silent' working memory in prefrontal cortex: A dynamic coding framework. *Trends in Cognitive Sciences, 19,* 394–405. doi:10.1016/j.tics.2015.05.004

Surprenant, A. M., & Neath, I. A. N. (2006). The 9 lives of short-term memory. In A. Thorn & M. Page (Eds.), *Interactions between short-term and long-term memory in the verbal domain* (pp. 16–43). Hove, UK: Psychology Press. Retrieved from https://memory.psych.mun.ca/pubs/chapters/reprints/Surprenant & Neath (2009).pdf

Sutterer, D. W., Foster, J. J., Adam, K. C. S., Vogel, E. K., & Awh, E. (2019). Item-specific delay activity demonstrates concurrent storage of multiple active neural representations in working memory. *PLoS Biology, 17,* e3000239. doi:10.1371/journal.pbio.3000239

Sutterer, D. W., Foster, J. J., Serences, J. T., Vogel, E. K., & Awh, E. (2019). Alpha-band oscillations track the retrieval of precise spatial representations from long-term memory. *Journal of Neurophysiology, 122,* 539–551. doi:10.1152/jn.00268.2019

Unsworth, N., Brewer, G. A., & Spillers, G. J. (2009). There's more to the working memory capacity-fluid intelligence relationship than just secondary memory. *Psychonomic Bulletin and Review, 16,* 931–937. doi:10.3758/PBR.16.5.931

Unsworth, N., Fukuda, K., Awh, E., & Vogel, E. K. (2014). Working memory and fluid intelligence: Capacity, attention control, and secondary memory retrieval. *Cognitive Psychology, 71,* 1–26. doi:10.1016/j.cogpsych.2014.01.003

Unsworth, N., Fukuda, K., Awh, E., & Vogel, E. K. (2015). Working memory delay activity predicts individual differences in in cognitive abilities. *Journal of Cognitive Neuroscience, 27,* 853–865. doi:10.1162/jocn_a_00765

Unsworth, N., Spillers, G. J., & Brewer, G. A. (2011). Variation in verbal fluency: A latent variable analysis of clustering, switching, and overall performance. *Quarterly Journal of Experimental Psychology, 64*, 447–466. doi:10.1080/17470218.2010.505292

van den Berg, R., Awh, E., & Ma, W. J. (2014). Factorial comparison of working memory models. *Psychological Review, 121*, 124–149. doi:10.1037/a0035234

van den Berg, R., Shin, H., Chou, W.-C., George, R., & Ma, W. J. (2012). Variability in encoding precision accounts for visual short-term memory limitations. *Proceedings of the National Academy of Sciences of the United States of America, 109*, 8780–8785. doi:10.1073/pnas.1117465109

van Dijk, H., van der Werf, J., Mazaheri, A., Medendorp, W. P., & Jensen, O. (2010). Modulations in oscillatory activity with amplitude asymmetry can produce cognitively relevant event-related responses. *Proceedings of the National Academy of Sciences of the United States of America, 107*, 900–905. doi:10.1073/pnas.0908821107

van Moorselaar, D., Foster, J. J., Sutterer, D. W., Theeuwes, J., Olivers, C. N. L., & Awh, E. (2017). Spatially selective alpha oscillations reveal moment-by-moment trade-offs between working memory and attention. *Journal of Cognitive Neuroscience, 30*, 256–266. doi:10.1162/jocn_a_01198

Vogel, E. K., & Fukuda, K. (2009). In mind and out of phase. *Proceedings of the National Academy of Sciences of the United States of America, 106*, 21017–21018. doi:10.1073/pnas.0912084107

Vogel, E. K., & Machizawa, M. G. (2004). Neural activity predicts individual differences in visual working memory capacity. *Nature, 428*, 748–751. doi:10.1038/nature02447

Vogel, E. K., McCollough, A. W., & Machizawa, M. G. (2005). Neural measures reveal individual differences in controlling access to working memory. *Nature, 438*, 500–503. doi:10.1038/nature04171

Wang, Y., Fujita, I., & Murayama, Y. (2000). Neuronal mechanisms of selectivity for object features revealed by blocking inhibition in inferotemporal cortex. *Nature Neuroscience, 3*, 807–813. doi:10.1038/77712

Wilken, P., & Ma, W. J. (2004). A detection theory account of change detection. *Journal of Vision, 4*, 1120–1135. doi:10.1167/4.12.11

Williams, M., & Woodman, G. F. (2012). Directed forgetting and directed remembering in visual working memory. *Journal of Experimental Psychology: Learning, Memory, and Cognition, 38*, 1206–1220. doi:10.1037/a0027389

Xu, Y., & Chun, M. M. (2006). Dissociable neural mechanisms supporting visual short-term memory for objects. *Nature, 440*, 91–95. doi:10.1038/nature04262

Xu, Z., Adam, K. C. S., Fang, X., & Vogel, E. K. (2018). The reliability and stability of visual working memory capacity. *Behavior Research Methods, 50*, 576–588. doi:10.3758/s13428-017-0886-6

Zhang, W., & Luck, S. J. (2008). Discrete fixed-resolution representations in visual working memory. *Nature, 453*, 233–236. doi:10.1038/nature06860

Zhang, W., & Luck, S. J. (2009). Sudden death and gradual decay in visual working memory. *Psychological Science, 20*, 423–428. doi:10.1111/j.1467-9280.2009.02322.x

12

Cognitive Neuroscience of Visual Working Memory

Bradley R. Postle

Memory refers to the influence of past experience on current thought and behaviour. Although all sentient humans have an intuition about what memory is, and what it feels like to remember something, understanding how memory relates to other aspects of cognition requires careful definition of constructs, and explicit articulation of assumptions. For example, although memory is often thought of as a (or many) cognitive system(s), the word *memory* can also be used to refer to a property of a system whose primary function is not mnemonic. For example, the gill withdrawal reflex of *Aplysia* demonstrates habituation when the tenth instance of touching it with a probe produces a slower and smaller withdrawal motion than had the otherwise-identical first instance of touching it. The molecular events and physiological processes that underlie this experience-dependent change in the functioning of the sensorimotor circuitry that innervates the gill and its musculature are understood in exquisite detail. Importantly, however, these are best construed as elements of the gill-withdrawal system that endow it with mnemonic properties, not as the mechanisms of a memory system per se. This chapter will be guided by the perspective that behaviour on visual working memory tasks arises from intrinsic properties of the visual system, of the oculomotor and skeletomotor systems, and of frontoparietal control systems, including those that function as sources of attentional control. That is, working memory may not involve any discrete *systems*, whether considered from a cognitive or a neural perspective, whose primary function is working memory. Rather, it may be a functionality resulting from the control of sensorimotor and representational systems.

1. Definition of Working Memory

Working memory is the ability to hold information in an accessible state—in the absence of relevant sensory input—to transform it when necessary, and to use it to guide behaviour in a flexible, context-dependent manner.

Bradley R. Postle, *Cognitive Neuroscience of Visual Working Memory* In: *Working Memory*. Edited by: Robert H. Logie, Valérie Camos, and Nelson Cowan, Oxford University Press (2021). © Oxford University Press. DOI: 10.1093/oso/9780198842286.003.0012

Table 12.1 Summary responses to designated questions

Question	Response
1. Definition of working memory	The ability to hold information in an accessible state—in the absence of relevant sensory input—to transform it when necessary, and to use it to guide behaviour in a flexible, context-dependent manner
2. Methods	Human behaviour, functional magnetic resonance imaging, and electroencephalography, with an emphasis on multivariate analysis methods.
3. Unitary versus non-unitary	An ill-posed question, because there is no working memory 'system'.
4. Attention and control	The same mechanisms and principles that apply to visual cognition apply to visual working memory (because the latter is just a subset of the former); the control of priority among items held in working memory can result in representational transformation, possibly via a mechanism of rotational remapping.
5. Storage	Information is held in visual working memory by the same systems/circuits involved in the perception of, and guidance of action with, that information; this can include covert motor planning.
6. Long-term memory	Long-term memory influences working memory in two ways: (a) in recognition of and representation of presented stimulus information; (b) in the biasing of that information with prior knowledge about the statistical properties of the world.
7. Inconsistent evidence	The existence of memory buffers, per se, in parietal and frontal cortex would be evidence for a working memory system; however, it need not be the case that every instance of stimulus-specific delay-period activity supports a buffering function.

2. Describe and Explain the Methods You Use

I am interested in the neural bases of human cognition—*how does the brain give rise to the mind?* One important development in cognitive neuroscience over the past two decades has been the development of methods for applying multivariate information-based analyses to neuroimaging data. This has allowed for assessment of the neural representation of information in ways that simply weren't possible previously, and has resulted in re-evaluation of several earlier findings.

Multivariate Analyses of Neural Data

Fundamentally, what multivariate methods make possible is the assessment of distributed representations, an important advance beyond the assumption implicit in most univariate analyses, which is that fluctuations in regional aggregations of signal intensity correspond to varying levels of engagement of a single mechanism or process. For example, in the first decade-and-a-half following the earliest studies of human working memory with neuroimaging (Cohen et al., 1994; Jonides et al., 1993), memory load-related changes in delay-period signal intensity pooled across tens—if not hundreds or more—of voxels were assumed to index varying demands on information storage (e.g. Braver et al., 1997; Postle, 2006; Todd & Marois, 2004). More recently, however, studies using multivariate pattern analysis (MVPA) have demonstrated that stimulus-specific information cannot always be decoded from regions whose activity shows load sensitivity and, conversely, stimulus-specific information can be decoded from regions that show neither load sensitivity nor, indeed, elevated levels of activity during the delay (Emrich, Riggall, Larocque, & Postle, 2013; Gosseries et al., 2018; Harrison & Tong, 2009; Riggall & Postle, 2012; Serences, Ester, Vogel, & Awh, 2009). Such findings have provided important evidence for sensorimotor-recruitment models of visual working memory (e.g. D'Esposito & Postle, 2015; Postle, 2015; Serences, 2016).

Multivariate inverted encoding modelling

Although most readers of this volume will be familiar with MVPA (e.g. Norman, Polyn, Detre, & Haxby, 2006; Pereira, Mitchell, & Botvinick, 2009), a summary of a second type of multivariate analysis method, inverted encoding modelling (IEM), will be useful, both because much of the work to be described here relies on this method, and because there exist misconceptions about how results generated with IEM are typically interpreted. IEM is a forward modelling approach that implements a dimensionality reduction on neural data to track population-level representation of stimulus characteristics. In the case of line orientation, for example, one can hypothesize that any given angular value can be represented in a unique pattern of weightings across several hypothetical broadly tuned information channels. These channels are represented in the analysis with a basis set of overlapping broadly tuned basis functions, typically half-wave rectified sinusoids, each centred at a different angular value such that they span the full possible range of 180° of rotation. The model is then trained by regressing against it neural data (in our case, functional magnetic resonance imaging (fMRI) or electroencephalography (EEG)) acquired while a subject was performing visual working memory for line orientation. For fMRI, for example, the basis set's representation of the angular value of each stimulus presented to the subject is entered as a regressor into a general linear model that estimates the orientation tuning function of each voxel (sometimes referred to as the 'population receptive field'; Dumoulin & Wandell, 2008) in a region of interest. Testing of the model is carried out by inverting the matrix that maps from channel space to voxel space, then determining whether data from trials that the model has never seen generate reconstructions, in channel space, of the stimulus values used for these test trials. Successful reconstructions of test stimulus values are interpreted as reconstructions of population-level representations of these stimuli. Importantly, because the shape of the basis functions was determined a priori and used in the training of the model, quantitative values from stimulus reconstruction can be interpreted as indices of, for example, the magnitude and the precision of a neural representation (indexed by the amplitude and width of the reconstruction, respectively; Brouwer & Heeger, 2009; Serences & Saproo, 2012).

Recently, some critiques of the IEM approach have appeared in the literature, and although these contain mistaken assumptions and, indeed, outright misconceptions about the assumptions underlying IEM and how IEM reconstructions are interpreted, addressing some of these will be helpful for clarifying some of the useful features of this approach. One point raised by Gardner and Liu across two papers (Gardner & Liu 2019; Liu, Cable, & Gardner, 2018) is that the results from IEM cannot be used to draw inferences about the tuning properties of individual neurons. Although this assertion is true, it has no bearing on the results that will be described here, because our experiments with fMRI and EEG are simply not intended to address this level of neural functioning, a point made with more elaboration elsewhere (Sprague et al., 2018; Sprague, Boynton, & Serences, 2019). A second concern raised by Gardner and Liu (2019) gets to a fundamental issue of studying the neural representation of information. They frame this concern with the observation that IEM differs from more direct reporting of neurophysiological measures in that 'the ordinate of the graph [produced by testing an IEM] is no longer a direct measure of neural activity' (p. 3). Examples of direct measures that the authors raise include firing rate, membrane potential, reflectance changes from intrinsic signals, and fluorescence changes from voltage sensitive dyes. 'Even for BOLD [blood oxygenation level-dependent] activity averaged across a visual area', they note, 'parametric sensitivity to the strength of a visual stimulus can be assessed by plotting response magnitude as a function of stimulus properties like contrast ... or motion coherence' (p. 3). Although these statements are true, what they don't acknowledge is that to limit oneself to analyses of data formatted such that they can be expressed as a direct measure of neural activity is to preclude the ability to study much of cognition, because the neural coding of most kinds of information that one would want to study is high dimensional. That is, firing rate, membrane potential, and other first-order summaries of neural activity are inherently univariate measures, and analyses that are limited to such measures are blind to information that is represented in high-dimensional patterns of activity distributed across multiple processing units. To be concrete, if one were to average BOLD signals across a 500-voxel region of interest that included the foveal representation of V1, it is true that one would expect to observe a monotonic increase in BOLD signal intensity in conjunction with parametric increases in contrast of a sinusoidal grating of a particular orientation— let's say 0°. The limitation of this approach, however, is clear as soon as one considers that the same pattern of monotonically increasing BOLD signal intensity would also be observed from this 500-voxel region of interest for a sinusoidal grating of 30°, for one of 60°, and so on. That is, univariate measures are rarely informative about the neural representation of stimulus-specific information. Indeed, we have already considered the fact that cognitive neuroscience research on working memory has established that univariate measures can lack sensitivity (e.g. they fail to detect delay-period stimulus representation in early visual cortex) and they can lack specificity (e.g. load-sensitive activity need not contain stimulus-related information). IEM, like any other dimension-reducing approach to data analysis (e.g. principal component analysis, independent component analysis), necessarily cannot retain the units in which levels of activity measured at individual sensors are acquired.

The goal of measuring stimulus information also motivates the choice of IEM over multivariate *decoding* approaches, such as MVPA. Although MVPA can provide important information about where in the brain stimulus- or category-level information is represented, its results are typically evaluated in terms of decoder performance, not with reference to the stimulus representation, per se. Thus, for example, when varying memory load from one to two to three items is seen to result in a decrease in delay-period stimulus decodability from roughly 80% to 70% to 65%, as is the case for subject #6 from Figure 5 of Emrich et al. (2013), one can't know what aspect of the neural representation of the stimulus is changing to produce this pattern. (Is it a decline in precision? In the strength of the representation? In both? Or in some other factor?) IEM, in contrast, provides quantification of parameters that can be interpreted in terms of the properties of a stimulus representation. An instructive example comes from Sprague and Serences (2013), who explored the effects of attention on the representation of locations in retinotopic space by flashing a flickering checkerboard stimulus at each of 36 distinct locations while subjects either attended to the fixation point or to the flickering checkerboard (while maintaining central fixation). Two 'sanity checks' indicated that IEM reproduced known facts about the visual representation of space: the size of neural representations of space increased as location of the checkerboard moved further from central fixation; and the size of the representation of any given retinotopic location was larger (i.e. coarser) in higher-level areas such as V4, MT+, intraparietal sulcus (IPS), and superior frontal sulcus, than in early visual areas. Importantly, with regard to the effects of attention, IEM revealed that univariate and population-level measures diverged. When attention was allocated to a region away from central fixation, the size of the population receptive fields of voxels in higher-level brain areas that represented the attended region increased. This trend, alone, would be difficult to reconcile with the fact that allocating attention to a location in the periphery is known to improve the precision of visual perception at that location, for the simple reason that larger receptive fields are less spatially precise. In contrast to the univariate effects at the level of individual voxels, however, IEM indicated that allocating spatial attention to a region in space resulted in an increase in the amplitude of the population-level representation of that location, but not in a change in the precision of these representations. Thus, at a population level—the level that we assume to be most important for guiding behaviour and for determining subjective experience—the effect of covert attention to a region in space is to strengthen the neural representation of that location.

Neural Network Modelling

One point highlighted by the recent debate about the assumptions underlying the IEM approach (see 'Multivariate Analyses of Neural Data'; Gardner & Liu, 2019; Liu et al., 2018; Sprague et al., 2018; Sprague et al., 2019) is that IEM reconstructions are models of neural representations, but not direct measurements of representations themselves. As can be the case in many other domains of science, unexpected or atypical behaviour of a model can lead one to address the same question with a different method that does not make the same assumptions as the model. Of particular relevance here, this chapter will consider studies in which the manipulation of priority between two items concurrently held in working memory has produced a systematic, but heretofore rarely reported, change in the IEM reconstruction of the unprioritized item. To better understand the factors that underlie this effect, we have turned to neural network models.

Masse and colleagues have recently noted that 'recurrent neural network (RNN) models have opened a new avenue to study the putative neural mechanisms underlying various cognitive functions. Crucially, RNNs have successfully reproduced the patterns of neural activity and behavioural output that are observed in vivo, generating insights into circuit function that would otherwise be unattainable through direct experimental measurement' (Masse, Yang, Song, Wang, & Freedman, 2019, p. 1159). In our case, it is not circuit-level function, but the dynamics of population-level stimulus representation for which we seek insights. Important details of implementation will be described later (see 'Priority-based remapping: evidence from neural network modelling'), but the general logic is to train a RNN to perform a working memory task, then examine how the hidden layer of the RNN represents stimulus information during the delay period of the task. Although such an exercise cannot, alone, provide 'proof' about how the human brain accomplishes working memory performance, it can reveal candidate processes whose biological reality can then be tested with human data.

3. Unitary Versus Non-Unitary Nature of Working Memory

This strikes me as an ill-posed question, because it presupposes that working memory *is* a system, and the question to be sorted is what kind of system. To elaborate on the perspective laid out in the preamble, consider this example of a parent spectating at a gymnastics competition. His challenge is to track the activity of his daughter and her teammates among the churning melee of adolescent girls, all sporting similar-looking ponytail hair styles and spangly leotards. This is not a behaviour that makes overt demands on memory, although it certainly does require guidance from a priority map, believed to be instantiated in recurrent activity between the IPS and the frontal eye fields (FEFs; located in the superior frontal cortex in humans), as well as the superior colliculus (e.g. Bisley & Mirpour, 2019). In this scenario, if the spectator's priority map can temporarily retain information about the locations of the athletes of interest while he briefly averts his eyes to read a text message on his mobile phone, there is no need to assert that an additional system, nor that a qualitatively different neural computation, needs to be engaged for him to successfully return his gaze to the targets of interest gathered around the uneven parallel bars, halfway across the crowded gymnasium. Luck and Vogel (2013) have made a similar argument, noting that 'visual working memory may not be a memory system per se, but may instead be a general-purpose visual representation system that can, when necessary, maintain information over short delays' (p. 394). (At the risk of sounding churlish, though, I would insist that there does not exist a 'general-purpose visual representation system' that's different from the visual system and the oculomotor system that are also engaged in tasks not considered to require working memory.)

Neural data are also consistent with this perspective. Neurons in the FEFs of non-human primates (NHPs) encode information about recent saccade targets during free viewing behaviour (Mirpour, Bolandnazar, & Bisley, 2019), and MVPA of fMRI activity from superior frontal cortex and from IPS in humans indicates that the neural encoding of egocentric location is highly similar whether subjects are engaged in planning a delayed saccade to a visible stimulus ('intention'), covertly attending to this stimulus in order to detect a change in its luminance ('attention'), or preparing a delayed response to the same location when it must be remembered across a delay ('retention'; Jerde, Merriam, Riggall, Hedges, & Curtis, 2012). Damage to (Mackey, Devinsky, Doyle, Meager, & Curtis, 2016) and repetitive transcranial magnetic stimulation of (Hamidi, Tononi, & Postle, 2008) prefrontal cortex (PFC) in humans only disrupts spatial working memory performance when the FEFs are affected.

4. The Role of Attention and Control

Spatial Attention and Spatial Working Memory

Top-down control of mental activity arises from the dynamic interplay between dorsal (endogenous) and ventral (exogenous) attentional circuits. The strong overlap between neural systems that support oculomotor control, spatial attention, and visuospatial working memory has been thoroughly documented in several previous studies and reviews (one recent authoritative review being Jonikaitis & Moore, 2019), and provides a compelling basis for the long-standing idea that working memory performance may reflect '"nothing more" than the preparation to perform an action, whether it be oculomotor, manual, verbal, or otherwise' (Theeuwes, Olivers, & Chizk, 2005) (pp. 198–199). This perspective receives further support from the fMRI study of Jerde et al. (2012), as reviewed earlier, as well as from demonstrations that eye movements executed in the dark selectively disrupt visual working memory for locations (e.g. Postle, Idzikowski, Sala, Logie, & Baddeley, 2006).

Feature- and Object-Based Attention and Visual Working Memory for Features and Objects

Real-time visual object recognition requires interactive signalling between neural circuits at multiple levels of the visual hierarchy, from primary visual cortex to high-level distributed representations that underlie categorization and semantic memory.

Importantly, feedback from higher levels to primary cortex, and even to sensory thalamus, is critical for visual perception and its attentional control (e.g. Cudeiro & Sillito, 2006; Sillito, Jones, Gerstein, & West, 1994; Sillito, Cudeiro, & Jones, 2006), and this has also been shown to be important for visual working memory (van Kerkoerle, Self, & Roelfsema, 2017). Because one can see the effects of object-based attention at all levels of processing involved in object perception and categorization (e.g. Çukur, Nishimoto, Huth, & Gallant, 2013; Ester, Sutterer, Serences, & Awh, 2016), the sensorimotor-recruitment framework predicts that working memory for objects and features of objects would also entail the top-down modulation of these circuits. (The constructs of feature-based attention and object-based attention are closely linked and, indeed, it is unclear if the two differ other than in the grain of detail at which elements in the visual scene must be analysed in any given task or situation (e.g. Scolari, Ester, & Serences, 2014). Therefore, for simplicity, this chapter will use 'object-based attention' to refer generally to the two constructs, and similarly it will use 'object working memory' to refer in general to working memory for visually presented objects and to working memory for the features of visually presented objects.)

Although object-based attention is ostensibly 'non-spatial', the fact that visual perception is inherently grounded in spatial reference frames provides a rationale for why there may be important links between the workings of frontoparietal gaze control circuitry and feature-based attention (e.g. Bisley & Mirpour, 2019; Moore & Zirnsak, 2017). A compelling empirical example comes from the fact that subthreshold microstimulation of the FEFs (i.e. at an amplitude that does not generate a saccade) produces an attention-like enhancement of the visually driven response of V4 neurons with receptive fields overlapping with the stimulated FEF motor field, enhancements that are greater for stimuli for which the V4 neuron is optimally tuned and/or when a distractor is present elsewhere in the visual field (Moore & Armstrong, 2003). Saccade planning has also been shown to influence object working memory. For example, preparing a saccade to a stimulus location improves the subsequent recognition of the shape that had been presented at that location, even if the planned saccade is never performed (Hanning, Jonikaitis, Deubel, & Szinte, 2016). Furthermore, within this same experimental context, an intervening saccade can negate the attentional benefits that are otherwise produced by a retrocue: when sample offset is followed by a retrocue indicating which of two sample stimuli will be tested, this retrocue does not benefit recognition performance on trials for which subjects know that they will first need to make a saccade to the location that had been occupied by the uncued sample (Hanning et al., 2016).

The linkage between oculomotor control and object working memory may help explain the results from a recent fMRI study of delayed recall of orientations, which showed evidence that individual differences in the precision of behavioural performance were predicted, in part, by the representation of stimulus location, even though this contextual information was not needed to perform the task (Cai, Sheldon, Yu, & Postle, 2019). One-item trials on this task began with the presentation of a sample at one of four locations, followed by a delay, followed by a recall dial that appeared at the same location as had the sample. Across subjects, the strength of the representation of sample location (indexed by MVPA) at encoding and at recall was positively related to the behavioural precision of recall. Furthermore, IEM estimates of the neural representation of orientation in occipital cortex were higher in amplitude, and more closely related to recall precision, when the IEM models that generated them included information about location context.

The role of microsaccades in visual attention and visual working memory

An additional factor that has recently been gaining prominence in the literature is the linkage between object-based attention, object working memory, and microsaccades. Microsaccades are small saccadic deviations from the point of fixation, typically smaller in amplitude than 1° of visual angle, that occur during fixation of a stable target. Although there are many proposed functions for microsaccades relating to possible roles in optimizing foveal vision, they have received relatively little consideration in attention research. Recently, however, it has been reported that the attentional effects of cuing are strongly tied to microsaccades, with the neurophysiological enhancement of the representation of the cued stimulus only observed when preceded by a microsaccade in the direction of the cued stimulus. Furthermore, the precise timing of the onset of this attentional enhancement was more closely tied to the execution of this microsaccade than to the onset of the attentional cue (Lowet et al., 2018). Interestingly, the periodicity of the attention-related microsaccadic activity described by Lowet et al. (2018) is in the same 3–4 Hz range that is associated with the periodic attentional sampling of the visual scene that is characteristic of the behaviour and the neurophysiology of NHP and human visual cognition (e.g. Fiebelkorn & Kastner, 2019). The importance of understanding the relation of microsaccades to object working memory has recently been highlighted by the demonstration that subtle but systematic differences in location of gaze can be used to decode the delay-period representation of line orientation (Mostert et al., 2018). We will return later in the chapter to the question of whether such effects in eye-tracking data—and, indeed, whether microsaccade-related signals in neural data—are best treated as a potential empirical confounds in studies of working memory, or, alternatively, as factors reflecting an inherently functional role that microsaccades may play in encoding the contents of non-spatial visual working memory (Dotson, Hoffman, Goodell, & Gray, 2018).

The Top-Down Control of Attention and Working Memory

Several explicit computational models can produce controlled attention without resorting to a homunculus. One model that accounts in considerable detail for the empirical findings that motivated the biased competition model of visual attention (Chelazzi, Duncan, Miller, & Desimone, 1998; Chelazzi, Miller, Duncan, & Desimone, 1993), and that's also relevant to considerations of the overlap between gaze control and attention (e.g. Bisley & Mirpour, 2019; Moore & Zirnsak 2017), is

Hamker's (2005) model of biased competition in visual search, which relies on recurrent activity between feature-selective neurons in IT cortex and the FEF. In this model, top-down control emerges from the complex interaction between the representation of the search template in IT, feedforward signalling by IT, and feedback signalling from the subpopulation of 'movement neurons' in FEF. (Note that although our understanding of some specific details about FEF circuitry, cell types, and connectivity with other brain areas have evolved during the ensuing years (e.g. Merrikhi et al., 2017), the principles underlying the Hamker (2005) model continue to be relevant.) A second model that's highly relevant to concerns about control without a homunculus was developed by Rougier and colleagues, in part to address the fact that 'a major challenge for theories of the neural bases of cognitive control ... [is] how it can be explained in terms of self-organizing mechanisms that develop on their own, over time, without recourse to unexplained sources of influence or intelligence' (Rougier et al., 2005, p. 7338). The authors used a connectionist framework with many biologically inspired properties, including synaptic learning rules (O'Reilly & Munakata, 2000), and an architecture that included a 'posterior cortex' hidden layer, and a separate 'PFC' context layer that could influence both the hidden layer and the 'response' (i.e. output) layer. Units in the 'PFC' had two unique and also biologically inspired properties: an 'up' state of sustained, elevated activity that was robust against interfering signals, and a readily triggered bistability between this sustained 'up' state and a 'down' state that enabled rapid updating of patterns of activity in the PFC. The final critical element was a dopamine-mediated reward prediction error signal that could trigger transitions in the bistable state of PFC units, a biologically inspired element (in that dopamine has this influence on PFC pyramidal neurons) that incorporated principles of reinforcement learning into the simulation. With this architecture, the authors used trial-and-error learning to first train the model to perform naming and same-different comparisons of stimuli that could vary according to shape, size, egocentric location, and colour. This stage of training taught the 'posterior cortex' to reliably represent the different stimulus domains and the relations between ordinal levels within each (e.g. small < medium small < medium large < large), and the 'PFC' to represent rules (e.g. how to decide if a medium small-sized, yellow, vertically striped square located in the upper-right quadrant is the same as or different from a small, green, vertically striped square located in the upper-right if the matching dimension is size). Finally, they introduced a Wisconsin Card-Sorting Task, and the network learned to perform it at a high level of proficiency, staying on one sorting rule as long as that rule produced positive feedback, and switching rules upon receiving negative feedback (the incorrect choice generating a reward prediction error signal, which transiently shunted the PFC from its up to its down state). Interestingly, if one considers the simulated role of the reward prediction error signal in the Rougier et al. (2005) model, together with empirical evidence for the role of dopamine in controlling the influence of the FEF on visual attention and working memory (e.g. Merrikhi et al., 2017; Noudoost & Moore, 2011), one can see how the Hamker (2005) model might be modified to support the flexible and context-sensitive selection of rules to guide oculomotor behaviour.

Whereas the Rougier et al. (2005) model illustrated the power of incorporating principles of reinforcement learning into neural models, more recently it has been suggested that PFC has a property of 'meta reinforcement learning' in which dynamic adaptations of behaviour that follow the principles of reinforcement learning can be implemented by on a trial-by-trial basis by patterns of activity in the PFC (Wang et al., 2018). The gist is that unique physiological properties and anatomical connectivity of the PFC allow for dopamine-based reinforcement learning to train this region, over time, to be able to operate as a 'learning system' that implements principles of reinforcement learning in patterns of activity. Although 'conventional' reinforcement learning is slow, based, as it is, on incremental changes in synaptic weights, 'meta reinforcement learning' can change behaviour on a moment-by-moment basis, because such constructs as reward, choice history, object value, and prediction error can be represented dynamically in distributed patterns of activity (rather than in patterns of weights that bias connection strengths between different neurons). Importantly, because reinforcement learning is unsupervised, this scheme endows the PFC with the ability to control behaviour without needing the 'supervision' of a homunculus.

The neural bases of the source of object-based attention (and of object working memory?)

Mapping theoretical models like those summarized in the previous subsection onto neural systems is an important goal for cognitive neuroscience moving forward. One region that is emerging as an important node in the control of object-based attention is in posterior ventrolateral PFC, a region known as the inferior frontal junction (at the intersection of the inferior frontal and precentral sulci) in the human, and the ventral pre-arcuate area (VPA) in the NHP. In humans, Baldauf and Desimone (2014) observed with magnetoencephalography that alternating attention between superimposed streams of translucent images of faces and of houses produced the expected alternations of attention-related boosts of signal intensity in stimulus-related activity in posterior face- and house-sensitive regions, and these were tightly linked to alternations in the strength of coherence in the upper gamma band (roughly 60–100 Hz) between the inferior frontal junction and these posterior regions. In the NHP, Bichot, Heard, DeGennaro, and Desimone (2015) have demonstrated that, in a visual search task, neurons in VPA showed selectivity for the search target and showed feature-based attentional modulation earlier than did neurons in FEF. Furthermore, local inactivation of VPA neurons produced marked deficits in search performance, and abolished the feature-based attention modulation of FEF that was observed prior to the inactivation (Bichot et al., 2015). It remains to be determined how closely the feature-based attention-related functions of VPA may correspond the involvement of VPA in the control of visuo-object working memory, as has been described in separate research (Mendoza-Halliday, Torres, & Martinez-Trujillo, 2014).

5. Storage, Maintenance, and Loss of Information in Working Memory

Evidence for Where Influences Models of How

In cognitive neuroscience, questions of *how* information is retained for working memory task performance are often closely tied to *where* in the brain one can find evidence for the delay-period representation of trial-relevant information. Historically, evidence for stimulus-selective delay-period activity has often been interpreted as evidence for a storage function in that region, and such evidence, in turn, has been influential in the development of models of visual working memory and visual cognition. For example, reports of stimulus-selective delay-period activity in the dorsolateral PFC, at the level of single-unit recordings (e.g. Funahashi, Bruce, & Goldman-Rakic, 1989, 1990; Wilson, O'Scalaidhe, & Goldman-Rakic, 1993) or MVPA decoding from population recordings (Mendoza-Halliday et al., 2014), has influenced theories on a wide range of questions, including the role of working memory in high-level cognition (e.g. Davachi, Romanski, Chafee, & Goldman-Rakic, 2004; Goldman-Rakic, 1992), the functional organization of cortical contributions to high-level cognition (Katsuki and Constantinides, 2012; Leavitt, Mendoza-Halliday, & Martinez-Trujillo, 2018), and principles of neural coding (Constantinidis et al., 2018; Murray et al., 2017). Another important example is that the observation of patterns of load-sensitive delay-period activity measured with fMRI in IPS (Todd & Marois, 2004, 2005; Xu & Chun, 2006), and with EEG at occipitoparietal scalp electrodes (Vogel and Machizawa, 2004; Vogel, McCollough, & Machizawa, 2005), has led to the codification of an EEG component, the contralateral delay activity, that has been an influential tool for developing models of individual differences in working memory abilities (also known as capacity limitations; e.g. Luck & Vogel, 2013; Luria, Balaban, Awh, & Vogel, 2016), of visual search (Woodman, 2013), of automaticity (Servant, Cassey, Woodman, & Logan, 2018), and for inferring roles for working memory in a wide variety of cognitive tasks that do not make overt demands on the short-term retention of information (Balaban & Luria, 2019).

Caveats about inferring function from activity
As discussed earlier (see 'Multivariate analyses of neural data'), the application of multivariate analyses to neuroimaging data sets has led to important advances in our understanding of the neural bases of many cognitive functions. The impressive sensitivity of these methods has also highlighted the challenge of how to go about assessing, when multiple regions can be shown to represent stimulus-specific information, whether these regions are all supporting the same function, or perhaps different functions that nonetheless all entail the active representation of the same information.

Not long after the power of MVPA for working memory research was demonstrated by delay-period decoding of stimulus information from V1 (despite the absence of elevated activity; Harrison & Tong, 2009; Serences et al., 2009), Christophel and col-leagues (Christophel & Haynes, 2014; Christophel, Hebart, & Haynes, 2012) and Bettencourt and Xu (2016) published evidence for delay-period stimulus representa-tion in parietal cortex, and Ester and colleagues published IEM evidence that 'Parietal and frontal cortex encode stimulus-specific mnemonic representations during visual working memory' for the orientation of square-wave gratings (Ester, Sprague, & Serences, 2015; see also Cai et al., 2019). Similarly, the remembered direction of motion is decodable with MVPA from delay period signal across multiple subregions of the IPS (Gosseries et al., 2018). Although some have interpreted these and similar find-ings as evidence for working memory buffers operating in IPS and frontal cortex (e.g. Christophel, Klink, Spitzer, Roelfsema, & Haynes, 2017; Leavitt et al., 2018; Riley & Constantinidis, 2016; Xu, 2017), other interpretations are possible. In data from this author's group, for example, the measures of delay-period stimulus information that we have observed in IPS and PFC differ from those simultaneously measured in ven-tral occipitotemporal regions in several ways. IPS and PFC representations tend to be weaker and less robust, as indexed by lower decoding scores and the failure to decode or reconstruct at memory loads higher than 1 (e.g. Gosseries et al., 2018). Furthermore, in Gosseries et al. (2018), we operationalized memory load with trials presenting one mo-tion patch (*1M*) versus one motion patch and two colour patches (*1M2C*), and context-binding load with *1M* versus *3M*. (On three-item trials (i.e. *1M2C* and *3M*) samples were presented serially, and a digit indicated the item to recall, thereby requiring the binding of each sample to its ordinal context.) In this study, MVPA-decoded delay-period representations in IPS coexisted with patterns of BOLD signal whose sensitivity to context-binding load covaried with *1M-to-3M* declines in behavioural precision, and with *1M-to-3M* declines in decoding from ventral occipitotemporal regions; no such relations were observed in comparison to analogous patterns of variation across *1M-to-1M2C*. Therefore, it is possible that delay-period representations in IPS had a more important role in the control of context binding than in stimulus representation per se. In the study by Cai et al. (2019), IPS and PFC representations did not show evi-dence for an influence of location context, and variation in their strength did not relate to behaviour, suggesting that these representations may have been more abstract than those carrying information specific to the current trial.

Dynamic Representations Supporting Working Memory Function

One argument that is made for the need for working memory buffers in non-sensory regions the brain is that this scheme would avoid the potential problem of working memory storage interfering with ongoing perception. For example, it has been argued that 'the content of VWM [visual working memory] is fairly resistant to distraction. This is at odds with an intuitive understanding of the sensory account, which would predict a large interference between VWM storage and sensory processing of the dis-tractor as a result of shared neural resources' (Xu, 2017, p. 799). Where intuition fails, however, information theory, dynamical systems theory, and computational modelling offer promising ways forward.

At a general level, one solution to the intuited problem of interference between memory storage and ongoing perception is to re-represent the to-be-remembered information in a format that does not interfere with perceptual codes. One scheme that could accomplish this would be to encoding to-be-remembered information into an 'activity-silent' state (Stokes, 2015), possibly supported by patterns of oscillatory synchrony and/or transient changes in synaptic weights (e.g. Barak & Tsodyks, 2014; Erickson, Maramara, & Lisman, 2010; Mongillo, Barak, & Tsodyks, 2008; Toda et al., 2012). Empirical evidence consistent with this idea has been generated with perturb-and-measure studies that reveal the otherwise-subthreshold representation of information in the multivariate readout of responses evoked by the delay-period perturbation (Rose et al., 2016; Wolff, Ding, Myers, & Stokes, 2015; Wolff, Jochim, Akyürek, & Stokes, 2017), as well as with computer simulations (Manohar, Zokaei, Fallon, Vogels, & Husain, 2019; Masse et al., 2019). A second possibility (that is not incompatible with an activity-silent mechanism, c.f. Masse et al., 2019) would be to recode to-be-remembered information it into a format that is different from, and perhaps more robust than, the perceptual code. In this scheme, the recoded information could later be decoded back into its original format (e.g. Koyluoglu, Pertzov, Manohar, Husain, & Fiete, 2017), or used in its transformed state to influence thought and/or guide behaviour (e.g. Myers, Stokes, & Nobre, 2017; van Ede, Chekroud, Stokes, & Nobre, 2019). Importantly, a recoding scheme does not require engaging circuits that were not involved in the initial encoding of the information in question. In the next section I'll consider empirical and computational evidence for one candidate recoding mechanism: priority-based remapping.

Priority-based remapping as a candidate mechanism for storage in working memory
Evidence for priority-based remapping was first observed by the author's group in a two-item dual serial retrocuing study of delayed recall (Yu, Teng, & Postle, 2020) but here we will focus on a 2-back working memory task with which this phenomenon has been studied in the greatest detail to date. In the 2-back study of Wan, Cai, Samaha, and Postle (2020), subjects viewed the serial presentation of oriented grating stimuli, and indicated for each, with a button press, whether it matched or non-matched the item that had appeared two positions previously in the series. In this way, each item n transitions through multiple states of priority: first as a recognition probe for the item $n - 2$; then as an 'unprioritized memory item' (UMI) while the subject compares item $n + 1$ against $n - 1$; then as a 'prioritized memory item' (PMI) in anticipation of its comparison with $n + 2$. The EEG data from Wan et al. (2020) were analysed with an IEM that was trained on data from the delay period of an independent one-item delayed-recognition task. The principal empirical finding of interest, which replicated Yu, Teng, and Postle (2020), was that the IEM estimate of the neural representation of the UMI took on a value that was the opposite of its true value, then returned to its true value

when it transitioned to PMI. To make this concrete, let's take the example of a hypothetical grating stimulus of orientation 30° (from a stimulus set where 0° corresponded to a horizontal orientation and 90° to a vertical one). While this 30° stimulus grating was a UMI, its neural representation was reconstructed by the IEM as most similar to the neural representation of 120°, then, when a PMI, its neural representation was once again reconstructed by the IEM as 30°.

There are two important points to emphasize about this finding. The first is to acknowledge that this pattern of IEM reconstruction of the UMI suggests an active memory trace, a finding at variance with previous studies that have failed to find evidence for an active trace of the UMI (LaRocque, Lewis-Peacock, Drysdale, Oberauer, & Postle, 2013; LaRocque, Riggall, Emrich, & Postle, 2017; Lewis-Peacock, Drysdale, Oberauer, & Postle, 2012; Rose et al., 2016). The second is that this pattern would be more consistent with a remapping of how stimuli are represented within neural code than an actual recoding operation. This because an IEM trained to learn one code should fail when tested on data corresponding to a different code. A neural operation that preserved the learned neural states but changed the neural-pattern-to-stimulus-value mapping (e.g. flipping the mappings, or rotating them), however, could produce the pattern similar to what we have observed with the IEM reconstruction of the UMI (Wan et al.,2020; Yu, Teng & Postle, 2020).

Priority-based remapping: evidence from neural network modelling
To explore the mechanism that may underlie the transformation of the neural representation of the UMI, Wan, Cai, Rogers, and Postle (2019) trained a RNN with a hidden layer of 16 so-called "long short-term memory" (LSTM) units to perform the 2-back task (Fig. 12.1a, b). (For the present purposes, LSTM can be understood as a kind of architecture that allows artificial neural networks to process information during time steps when no new information is being fed to the network.) Once the network was trained, the representational dynamics of the network could be observed by tracking the shifting patterns of activity over the course of an item's evolution from probe to UMI to PMI. More specifically, the dimensionality of the 16-unit hidden layer was reduced using principal component analysis and the trajectory of the first two principal components tracked. As illustrated in Fig. 12.1c, the network's representation of each stimulus item underwent a dynamic trajectory while held in working memory: when initially presented to the RNN, the RNN's representation of item n was aligned along an axis that separated 'match' from 'non-match' responses; during the ensuing delay period, when its status in the task transitioned to UMI, its representation by the RNN rotated until, during the presentation of $n + 1$, it was orthogonal to the decision axis; then, when its status in the task transitioned to PMI, it continued its rotation along the same high-dimensional manifold (i.e. along the same 'plane'), re-aligning with the decision axis during the presentation of $n + 2$. As calculated across multiple simulations, the average distance between the axis of alignment of the UMI versus the PMI was 134°.

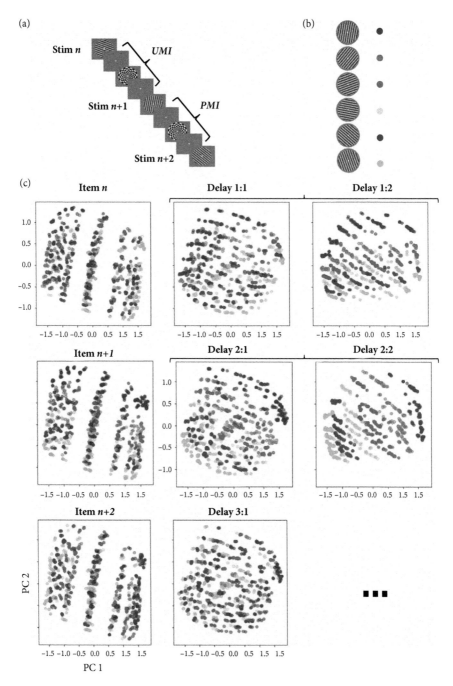

Fig. 12.1 Rotational remapping as a mechanism to represent priority in working memory. (a) Cartoon of a sequence of stimuli from the 2-back task as administered by Wan et al. (2020). (b) Correspondence between stimulus labels (left-hand column) and colour codes used for RNN simulation by Wan et al. (2019). (c) Multidimensional scaling of the first two principal components extracted from activation patterns of the hidden layer of the RNN, at multiple successive time steps of simulated 2-back performance. The plot labelled 'Item *n*' corresponds to the presentation of 'Stim *n*' in panel (a); the plots labelled 'Delay

Priority-based remapping: evidence from human EEG

The previous subsection reviewed evidence, from a neural network simulation, that rotational remapping may be a process whereby information can be held in working memory in a format that doesn't interfere with behaviour. Is there, however, any evidence that a similar mechanism might be deployed by the human brain? To address this, Wan et al. (2019) applied the analysis that had been applied to the RNN to the EEG data in which IEM reconstructions of stimulus orientation differed as a function of the item's priority status (Wan et al., 2020). Conceptually, they treated the data from the 60 channels of the EEG in the same way as they had the activation values of the 16 units from the hidden layer of the RNN. (Some of the processing steps were necessarily different; before performing the principal component analysis, temporal covariance matrices were first computed from the EEG data, then these covariance matrices eigendecomposed, following Cohen (2014).) The results produced a qualitative replication of the results with the RNN, with the UMI rotated relative to the PMI by 177°.

The putative priority-based mechanism described here may also account for the findings of van Loon, Olmos-Solis, Fahrenfort, and Olivers (2018), who acquired fMRI while subjects performed a visual search task in which each trial began with the sequential presentation of two search targets, followed by the sequential presentation of two search arrays, one corresponding to each of the two targets. Because the order of appearance of the search arrays would not be known until after the offset of the second target, each trial was assumed to entail the sequential prioritization of the working-memory representation of the two targets. Analyses with MVPA revealed that although a classifier trained on epochs when a stimulus category corresponded to the impending search array (i.e. when it was the prioritized item) could also decode evidence for that same category from epochs when it did not correspond to the impending search array (i.e. when it was the unprioritized item), the pattern of activity when this category was the unprioritized differed from when it was prioritized. This manifested in two ways: first, decoding of the unprioritized category with a decoder trained on information in the prioritized state was significantly below chance; and second, the

---

1:1' and 'Delay 1:2' correspond to the two time steps while item n is a UMI; and so on. Each coloured dot represents a simulated trial in which that item progressed through the states of recognition probe ('Item n'), UMI ('Delay 1:1', 'Delay 1:2', and 'Item $n + 1$'); and PMI ('Delay 1:1', 'Delay 1:2', and 'Item $n + 2$'). In the 'Item n' plot, trials for which n required a match response occupy the manifold (i.e., the 'stripe') that aligns with the value of 0.0 of the first principal component, and trials for which n required a non-match response occupy the manifolds that appear to the left and to the right of the 'match' manifold in this plot. Note that, across the time that n is processed in working memory, its representation rotates clockwise in the image plane, such that when item $n + 1$ is presented, n is aligned with an axis that is orthogonal to the decision axis, and that when $n + 2$ is presented, n is again aligned with the decision axis. The rotated state of the representation of n at the time when the network is assessing the match between $n + 1$ and $n - 1$ may reduce the likelihood that the identity of n will interfere with the decision about $n + 1$.

high-dimensional representation of each category projected into opposite regions of multidimensional scaling space during epochs when it was prioritized versus when it was unprioritized.

Priority-based remapping in working memory: a specific case of a more general mechanism?

Together, the results from IEM of neural data from two experiments using two different tasks (Wan et al., 2020; Yu, Teng, & Postle, 2020) and the principal component analysis-based analyses of 2-back data from an RNN simulation and from human EEG (Wan et al., 2019) suggest that the phenomenon of priority-based remapping may be implemented as a rotational remapping that is emergent from the dynamics of high-dimensional distributed representations. In keeping with the idea that working memory performance does not depend on specialized systems, a qualitatively similar phenomenon has been observed in populations of neurons in primary auditory cortex in mice exposed to sequences of tones. Although the animals were not trained on any specific task, stimuli that deviated from predictable sequences produced a transformation of the representation of previous stimuli from their perceptual codes into an orthogonal dimension. The authors propose that 'This rotational dynamic may be a general principle, by which the cortex protects memories of prior events from interference by incoming stimuli' (Libby & Buschman, 2019). Future research will need to assess the mechanism whereby rotational remapping can be triggered by top-down signals, which must be the case when it is observed in retrocuing tasks (Sahan, Sheldon, & Postle, 2020; Yu, Teng, & Postle, 2018).

6. The Role of Long-Term Memory Knowledge in Working Memory Storage and Processing

Every domain of cognition, including object recognition, depends on long-term memory (LTM). Without access to pre-existing representations of meaning, an individual viewing a scene would experience associative agnosia (Farah, 1990). Indeed, it may not be possible for humans to perceive, nor to hold in working memory, a novel, abstract object or shape without associating it with prior knowledge and applying a verbal label to it (Postle, D'Esposito, & Corkin, 2005, Postle & Hamidi, 2007). It follows from this that visual working memory necessarily entails the representation of information from semantic LTM, in addition to sensory and motoric representations. One recent article that makes a thorough and compelling set of arguments consistent with this line of thinking is from Cowan (2019).

One recent and exciting demonstration of an influence of LTM on working memory has come from the application of ideas from dynamical systems theory. Panichello, DePasquale, Pillow, and Buschman (2019) tested 90 human subjects and two NHPs on short-term recall (also known as delayed estimation) of colour from arrays of one versus three (for humans) or two (for NHPs) coloured squares. For both species, even though stimuli were drawn evenly from the full 360° of possible colours, responses were markedly biased away from some colours and toward others. Attractor dynamics accounted for the frequency, bias, and precision of behaviour better than standard mixture modelling. In particular, the greater imprecision in responses on high-load trials was shown to reflect both a drift of remembered stimulus representations toward stable attractor states and a greater influence of random diffusion (i.e. noise). The authors framed this as evidence for an error-correcting mechanism, whereby increased internal noise (manipulated here by varying load) is counteracted by drift toward stable long-term representations of colour space. (From a Bayesian perspective, one could construe this as drawing on prior knowledge to counteract uncertainty about the recently presented stimuli.) Evidence that the inferred attractor landscape reflected knowledge acquired prior to the presentation of sample stimuli on any given trial of the task came from the fact that the attractor landscape could be made to shift systematically to reflect new environmental statistics, as implemented by changing from a flat distribution of sample stimuli to a strongly biased distribution (Panichello et al., 2019).

To investigate the neural bases of these attractor dynamics, we have re-analysed data from an fMRI study in which subjects had performed delayed recall of one versus three line orientations (Cai, Yu, Sheldon, & Postle, 2018). Analysis of the behavioural data from Cai et al. (2018) with the discrete attractor model developed by Panichello et al. (2019) provided a much better account of the data than did the classical three-factor mixture model (Bays, Catalao, & Husain, 2009): the discrete attractor model was estimated to be 2.9×10^6 times more likely than the mixture model by cross-validated log-likelihood estimation. Furthermore, the drift and diffusion parameters from the discrete attractor model also related closely to load-related changes in IPS. We used within-subject correlation to relate individual differences in load-related changes in behaviour to individual differences load-related changes in fMRI signal, and whereas using only the concentration parameter from the classical mixture model produced an adjusted r^2 of 0.25, adding the parameters from the discrete attractor model increased the adjusted r^2 to 0.69.

The question of whether or not working memory necessarily draws on LTM is often approached with logical argumentation, with reasonable people disagreeing over the strength of various arguments (e.g. Cowan, 2019; Norris, 2017). The findings reviewed here, in contrast, provide a quantitative demonstration that a model that incorporates an influence of LTM on working memory performance does a far superior job of accounting for individual differences, both in behaviour and in task-related neural activity, than does a model that does not.

7. Is There Evidence That Is Not Consistent with Your Theoretical Framework, and How Does Your Framework Address That Inconsistency?

Within the domain of visual working memory, the evidence that would be most prominently inconsistent with my theoretical framework would be evidence for working memory storage-related functions in circuits that are not associated with visual perception and/or the representation of visual knowledge. Prominent claims of such evidence come from findings of stimulus-specific delay-period activity in the IPS (e.g. Bettencourt & Xu, 2016; Christophel, Iamshchinina, Yan, Allefeld, & Haynes, 2018; Christophel, Klink, Spitzer, Roelfsema, & Haynes, 2017; Xu, 2017, 2018) and the PFC (Constantinidis et al., 2018; Leavitt et al., 2017; Mendoza-Halliday et al., 2014; Mendoza-Halliday & Martinez-Trujillo, 2017; Riley & Constantinidis, 2015; Riley, Qi, & Constantinidis, 2017). Importantly, I do not question the veracity of the data contained in these reports, but, rather, the interpretation often given to these data. Stated most broadly, I believe that many of the instances of delay-period stimulus-specific activity in IPS and PFC may reflect the operation of control processes rather than the operation of storage buffers per se. Alternative explanations for the functions supported by these findings appeal to the same roles in controlling behaviour that these neural systems play in situations that don't make overt demands on working memory. These include protection from the influence of external interference (e.g. Chao & Knight, 1995; Malmo 1942); control of perseveration and/or proactive interference (e.g. Tsujimoto & Postle, 2012); and the need to manipulate remembered information prior to using it to guide behaviour (e.g. D'Esposito, Postle, Ballard, & Lease, 1999; Masse et al., 2019).

References

Balaban, H., & Luria, R. (2019). Using the contralateral delay activity to study online processing of items still within view. *Neuromethods, 151,* 107–128.

Baldauf, D., & Desimone, R. (2014). Neural mechanisms of object-based attention. *Science, 344,* 424–427.

Barak, O., & Tsodyks, M. (2014). Working models of working memory. *Current Opinion in Neurobiology, 25,* 20–24.

Bays, P. M., Catalao, R. F., & Husain, M. (2009). The precision of visual working memory is set by allocation of a shared resource. *Journal of Vision, 9,* 7.1–7.11.

Bettencourt, K. C., & Xu, Y. (2016). Decoding the content of visual short-term memory under distraction in occipital and parietal areas. *Nature Neuroscience, 19,* 150–157.

Bichot, N. P., Heard, M. T., DeGennaro, E. M., & Desimone, R. (2015). A source for feature-based attention in prefrontal cortex. *Neuron, 88,* 832–844.

Bisley, J. W., & Mirpour, K. (2019). The neural instantiation of a priority map. *Current Opinion in Psychology, 29,* 108–112.

Braver, T., Cohen, J. D., Nystrom, L. E., Jonides, J., Smith, E. E., & Noll, D. C. (1997). A parametric study of prefrontal cortex involvement in human working memory. *NeuroImage, 5,* 49–62.

Brouwer, G. J., & Heeger, D. J. (2009). Decoding and reconstructing color from responses in human visual cortex. *Journal of Neuroscience, 29,* 13992–14003.

Cai, Y., Sheldon, A. D., Yu, Q., & Postle, B. R. (2019). Overlapping and distinct contributions of stimulus location and of spatial context to nonspatial visual short-term memory. *Journal of Neurophysiology, 121,* 1222–1231.

Cai, Y., Yu, Q., Sheldon, A. D., & Postle, B. R. (2018). The role of location-context binding in nonspatial visual working memory. *bioRxiv,* 352435. doi.org/10.1101/352435

Chao, L. L., & Knight, R. T. (1995). Human prefrontal lesions increase distractibility to irrelevant sensory inputs. *NeuroReport, 6,* 1605–1610.

Chelazzi, L., Duncan, J., Miller, E. K., & Desimone, R. (1998). Responses of neurons in inferior temporal cortex during memory-guided visual search. *Journal of Neurophysiology, 80*, 2918–2940.

Chelazzi, L., Miller, E. K., Duncan, J., & Desimone, R. (1993). A neural basis for visual search in inferior temporal cortex. *Nature, 363*, 345–347.

Christophel, T. B., & Haynes, J. D. (2014). Decoding complex flow-field patterns in visual working memory. *NeuroImage, 91*, 43–51.

Christophel, T. B., Hebart, M. N., & Haynes, J. D. (2012). Decoding the contents of visual short-term memory from human visual and parietal cortex. *Journal of Neuroscience, 32*, 2983–12989.

Christophel, T. B., Iamshchinina, P., Yan, C., Allefeld, C., & Haynes, J. D. (2018). Cortical specialization for attended versus unattended working memory. *Nature Neuroscience, 21*, 494–496.

Christophel, T. B., Klink, P. C., Spitzer, B., Roelfsema, P. R., & Haynes, J. D. (2017). The distributed nature of working memory. *Trends in Cognitive Sciences, 21*, 111–124.

Cohen, J. D., Forman, S. D., Braver, T. S., Casey, B. J., Servan-Schreiber, D., & Noll, D. C. (1994). Activation of the prefrontal cortex in a nonspatial working memory task with functional MRI. *Human Brain Mapping, 1*, 293–304.

Cohen, M. X. (2014). *Analyzing neural time series data: Theory and practice.* Cambridge, MA: MIT Press.

Constantinidis, C., Funahashi, S., Lee, D., Murray, J. D., Qi, X.-L., Wang, M., & Arnsten, A. F. T. (2018). Persistent spiking activity underlies working memory. *Journal of Neuroscience, 38*, 7020–7028.

Cowan, N. (2019). Short-term memory based on activated long-term memory: A review in response to Norris (2017). *Psychological Bulletin, 145*, 822–847.

Cudeiro, J., & Sillito, A. M. (2006). Looking back: corticothalamic feedback and early visual processing. *Trends in Neuroscience, 29*, 298–306.

Çukur, T., Nishimoto, S., Huth, A. G., & Gallant, J. L. (2013). Attention during natural vision warps semantic representation across the human brain. *Nature Neuroscience, 16*, 763–770.

D'Esposito, M., & Postle, B. R. (2015). The cognitive neuroscience of working memory. *Annual Review of Psychology, 66*, 115–142.

D'Esposito, M., Postle, B. R., Ballard, D., & Lease, J. (1999). Maintenance versus manipulation of information held in working memory: an event-related fMRI study. *Brain & Cognition, 41*, 66–86.

Davachi, L., Romanski, L. M., Chafee, M. V., & Goldman-Rakic, P. S. (2004). Domain specificity in cognitive systems. In M. S. Gazzaniga (Ed.), *The Cognitive Neurosciences III* (pp. 665–678). Cambridge, MA: MIT Press.

Dotson, N. M., Hoffman, S. J., Goodell, B., & Gray, C. M. (2018). Feature-based visual short-term memory is widely distributed and hierarchically organized. *Neuron, 99*, 215–226.e4.

Dumoulin, S. O., & Wandell, B. A. (2008). Population receptive field estimates in human visual cortex. *NeuroImage, 39*, 647–660.

Emrich, S. M., Riggall, A. C., Larocque, J. J., & Postle, B. R. (2013). Distributed patterns of activity in sensory cortex reflect the precision of multiple items maintained in visual short-term memory. *Journal of Neuroscience, 33*, 6516–6523.

Erickson, M. A., Maramara, L. A., & Lisman, J. (2010). A single brief burst induces glur1-dependent associative short-term potentiation: A potential mechanism for short-term memory. *Journal of Cognitive Neuroscience, 22*, 2530–2540.

Ester, E. F., Sprague, T. C., & Serences, J. T. (2015). Parietal and frontal cortex encode stimulus-specific mnemonic representations during visual working memory. *Neuron, 87*, 893–905.

Ester, E. F., Sutterer, D. W., Serences, J. T., & Awh, E. (2016). Feature-selective attentional modulations in human frontoparietal cortex. *Journal of Neuroscience, 36*, 8188–8199.

Farah, M. (1990). *Visual agnosia.* Cambridge, MA: MIT Press.

Fiebelkorn, I. C., & Kastner, S. (2019). A rhythmic theory of attention. *Trends in Cognitive Sciences, 23*, 87–101.

Funahashi, S., Bruce, C. J., & Goldman-Rakic, P. S. (1989). Mnemonic coding of visual space in the monkey's dorsolateral prefrontal cortex. *Journal of Neurophysiology, 61*, 331–349.

Funahashi, S., Bruce, C. J., & Goldman-Rakic, P. S. (1990). Visuospatial coding in primate prefrontal neurons revealed by oculomotor paradigms. *Journal of Neurophysiology, 63*, 814–831.

Gardner, J. L., & Liu, T. (2019). Inverted encoding models reconstruct an arbitrary model response, not the stimulus. *eNeuro, 6*, ENEURO.0363-18.2019.

Goldman-Rakic, P. S. (1992). Working memory and the mind. *Scientific American, 267*, 110–117.

Gosseries, O., Yu, Q., LaRocque, J. J., Starrett, M. J., Rose, N., Cowan, N., & Postle, B. R. (2018). Parieto-occipital interactions underlying control- and representation-related processes in working memory for nonspatial visual features. *Journal of Neuroscience, 38*, 4357–4366.

Hamidi, M., Tononi, G., & Postle, B. R. (2008). Evaluating frontal and parietal contributions to spatial working memory with repetitive transcranial magnetic stimulation. *Brain Research, 1230*, 202–210.

Hamker, F. H. (2005). The reentry hypothesis: The putative interaction of the frontal eye field, ventrolateral prefrontal cortex, and areas V4, IT for attention and eye movement. *Cerebral Cortex, 15*, 431–447.

Hanning, N. M., Jonikaitis, D., Deubel, H., & Szinte, M. (2016). Oculomotor selection underlies feature retention in visual working memory. *Journal of Neurophysiology, 115*, 1071–1076.

Harrison, S. A., & Tong, F. (2009). Decoding reveals the contents of visual working memory in early visual areas. *Nature, 458*, 632–635.

Jerde, T., Merriam, E. P., Riggall, A. C., Hedges, J. H., & Curtis, C. E. (2012). Prioritized maps of space in human frontoparietal cortex. *Journal of Neuroscience, 32*, 17382–17390.

Jonides, J., Smith, E., Koeppe, R., Awh, E., Minoshima, S., & Mintum, M. (1993). Spatial working memory in humans as revealed by PET. *Nature, 363*, 623–625.

Jonikaitis, D., & Moore, T. (2019). The interdependence of attention, working memory and gaze control: behavior and neural circuitry. *Current Opinion in Psychology, 29*, 126–134.

Katsuki, F., & Constantinides, C. (2012). Unique and shared roles of the posterior parietal and dorsolateral prefrontal cortex in cognitive functions. *Frontiers in Integrative Neuroscience, 6*, 17.

Koyluoglu, O. O., Pertzov, Y., Manohar, S. M., Husain, M., & Fiete, I. R. (2017). Fundamental bound on the persistence and capacity of short-term memory stored as graded persistent activity. *eLife, 6*, e22225.

LaRocque, J. J., Lewis-Peacock, J. A., Drysdale, A., Oberauer, K., & Postle, B. R. (2013). Decoding attended information in short-term memory: An EEG study. *Journal of Cognitive Neuroscience, 25*, 127–142.

LaRocque, J. J., Riggall, A. C., Emrich, S. M., & Postle, B. R. (2017). Within-category decoding of information in different states in short-term memory. *Cerebral Cortex, 17*, 4881–4890.

Leavitt, M. L., Mendoza-Halliday, D., & Martinez-Trujillo, J. C. (2018). Sustained activity encoding working memories: not fully distributed. *Trends in Neurosciences, 40*, 328–346.

Lewis-Peacock, J. A., Drysdale, A. T., Oberauer, K., & Postle, B. R. (2012). Neural evidence for a distinction between short-term memory and the focus of attention. *Journal of Cognitive Neuroscience, 24*, 61–79.

Libby, A., & Buschman, T. J. (2019). Rotational dynamics reduce interference between sensory and memory representations. *bioRxiv*, 641159. doi.org/10.1101/641159

Liu, T., Cable, D., & Gardner, J. L. (2018). Inverted encoding models of human population response conflate noise and neural tuning width. *Journal of Neuroscience, 38*, 398–408.

Lowet, E., Gomes, B., Srinivasan, K., Zhou, H., Schafer, R. J., & Desimone, R. (2018). Enhanced neural processing by covert attention only during microsaccades directed toward the attended stimulus. *Neuron, 99*, 207–214.

Luck, S. J., & Vogel, E. K. (2013). Visual working memory capacity: from psychophysics and neurobiology to individual differences. *Trends in Cognitive Sciences, 17*, 391–400.

Luria, R., Balaban, H., Awh, E., & Vogel, E. K. (2016). The contralateral delay activity as a neural measure of visual working memory. *Neuroscience and Biobehavioral Reviews, 62*, 100–108.

Mackey, W., Devinsky, O, Doyle, W., Meager, M., & Curtis, C. E. (2016). Human dorsolateral prefrontal cortex is not necessary for spatial working memory. *Journal of Neuroscience, 36*, 2847–2856.

Malmo, R. B. (1942). Interference factors in delayed response in monkey after removal of the frontal lobes. *Journal of Neurophysiology, 5*, 295–308.

Manohar, S. G., Zokaei, N., Fallon, S. J., Vogels, T. P., & Husain, M. (2019). Neural mechanisms of attending to items in working memory. *Neuroscience and Biobehavioral Reviews, 101*, 1–12.

Masse, N. Y., Yang, G. R., Song, H. F., Wang, X.-J., & Freedman, D. J. (2019). Circuit mechanisms for the maintenance and manipulation of information in working memory. *Nature Neuroscience, 22,* 1159–1167.

Mendoza-Halliday, D., & Martinez-Trujillo, J. C. (2017). Neuronal population coding of perceived and memorized visual features in the lateral prefrontal cortex. *Nature Communications, 8,* 15471.

Mendoza-Halliday, D., Torres, S., & Martinez-Trujillo, J. C. (2014). Sharp emergence of feature-selective sustained activity along the dorsal visual pathway. *Nature Neuroscience, 17,* 1255–1262.

Merrikhi, Y., Clark, K., Albarran, E., Parsa, M., Zirnsak, M., Moore, T., & Noudoost, B. (2017). Spatial working memory alters the efficacy of input to visual cortex. *Nature Communications, 8,* 15041.

Mirpour, K., Bolandnazar, S., & Bisley, J. W. (2019). Neurons in FEF keep track of items that have been previously fixated in free viewing visual search. *Journal of Neuroscience, 39,* 2114–2124.

Mongillo, G., Barak, O., & Tsodyks, M. (2008). Synaptic theory of working memory. *Science, 319,* 1543–1546.

Moore, T., & Armstrong, K.M. (2003). Selective gating of visual signals by microstimulation of frontal cortex. *Nature, 421,* 370–373.

Moore, T., & Zirnsak, M. (2017). Neural mechanisms of selective visual attention. *Annual Review of Psychology, 68,* 47–72.

Mostert, P., Albers, A. M., Brinkman, L., Todorova, L., Kok, P., & de Lange, F. P. (2018). Eye movement-related confounds in neural decoding of visual working memory representations. *eNeuro, 5,* ENEURO.0401-17.2018.

Murray, J. D., Bernacchia, A., Roy, N. A., Constantinidis, C., Romo, R. X., & Wang, X. J. (2017). Stable population coding for working memory coexists with heterogeneous neural dynamics in prefrontal cortex. *Proceedings of the National Academy of Sciences of the United States of America, 114,* 394–399.

Myers, N. E., Stokes, M. G., & Nobre, A. C. (2017). Prioritizing information during working memory: Beyond sustained internal attention. *Trends in Cognitive Sciences, 21,* 449–461.

Norman, K. A., Polyn, S. M., Detre, G. J., & Haxby, J. V. (2006). Beyond mind-reading: Multi-voxel pattern analysis of fMRI data. *Trends in Cognitive Sciences, 10,* 424–430.

Norris, D. (2017). Short-term memory and long-term memory are still different. *Psychological Bulletin, 143,* 992–1009.

Noudoost, B., & Moore, T. (2011). Control of visual cortical signals by prefrontal dopamine. *Nature, 474,* 372–375.

O'Reilly, R. C., & Munakata, Y. (2000). *Computational explorations in cognitive neuroscience: Understanding the mind by simulating brains.* Cambridge, MA: MIT Press.

Panichello, M. F., DePasquale, B., Pillow, J. W., & Buschman, T. J. (2019). Error-correcting dynamics in visual working memory. *Nature Communications, 10,* 3366.

Pereira, F., Mitchell, T., & Botvinick, M. M. (2009). Machine learning classifiers and fMRI: a tutorial overview. *NeuroImage, 45,* S199–S209.

Postle, B. R. (2006). Working memory as an emergent property of the mind and brain. *Neuroscience, 139,* 23–38.

Postle, B. R. (2015). The cognitive neuroscience of visual short-term memory. *Current Opinion in Behavioral Sciences, 1,* 40–46.

Postle, B. R., D'Esposito, M., & Corkin, S. (2005). Effects of verbal and nonverbal interference on spatial and object visual working memory. *Memory & Cognition, 33,* 203–212.

Postle, B. R., & Hamidi, M. (2007). Nonvisual codes and nonvisual brain areas support visual working memory. *Cerebral Cortex, 17,* 2134–2142.

Postle, B. R., Idzikowski, C., Della Salla, S., Logie, R. H., & Baddeley, A. D. (2006). The selective disruption of spatial working memory by eye movements. *Quarterly Journal of Experimental Psychology, 59,* 100–120.

Riggall, A. C., & Postle, B. R. (2012). The relationship between working memory storage and elevated activity as measured with funtional magnetic resonance imaging. *The Journal of Neuroscience, 32,* 12990–12998.

Riley, M. R., & Constantinidis, C. (2016). The role of prefrontal persistent activity in working memory. *Frontiers in Systems Neuroscience, 9,* 181.

Riley, M. R., Qi, X.-L., & Constantinidis, C. (2017). Functional specialization of areas along the anterior-posterior axis of the primate prefrontal cortex. *Cerebral Cortex, 27*, 3683–3697.

Rose, N., Larocque, J. J., Riggall, A. C., Gosseries, O., Starrett, M. J., Meyering, E., & Postle, B. R. (2016). Reactivation of latent working memories with transcranial magnetic stimulation. *Science, 354*, 1136–1139.

Rougier, N. P., Noelle, D. C., Braver, T. S., Cohen, J. D., & O'Reilly, R. C. (2005). Prefrontal cortex and flexible cognitive control: Rules without symbols. *Proceedings of the National Academy of Sciences of the United States of America, 102*, 7338–7343.

Sahan, M. I., Sheldon, A. D., & Postle, B. R. (2020). The neural consequences of attentional prioritization of internal representations in visual working memory. *Journal of Cognitive Neuroscience, 32*, 917–944.

Scolari, M., Ester, E. F., & Serences, J. T. (2014). Feature- and object-based attentional modulation in the human visual system. In A. C. Nobre and S. Kastner (Eds.), *The Oxford Handbook of Attention* (pp. 573–600). Oxford: Oxford University Press.

Serences, J. T. (2016). Neural mechanisms of information storage in visual short-term memory. *Vision Research, 128*, 53–67.

Serences, J. T., Ester, E. F., Vogel, E. K., & Awh, E. (2009). Stimulus-specific delay activity in human primary visual cortex. *Psychological Science, 20*, 207–214.

Serences, J. T., & Saproo, S. (2012). Computational advances towards linking BOLD and behavior. *Neuropsychologia, 50*, 435–446.

Servant, M., Cassey, P., Logan, G. D., & Woodman, G. F. (2018). The neural bases of automaticity. *Journal of Experimental Psychology: Learning, Memory, and Cognition, 44*, 440–464.

Sillito, A. M., Cudeiro, J., & Jones, H. E. (2006). Always returning: feedback and sensory processing in visual cortex and thalamus. *Trends in Neuroscience, 29*, 307–316.

Sillito, A. M., Jones, H. E., Gerstein, G. L., & West, D. C. (1994). Feature-linked synchronization of thalamic relay cell firing induced by feedback from the visual cortex. *Nature, 369*, 479–482.

Sprague, T. C., Adam, K. C. S., Foster, J. J., Rahmati, M., Sutterer, D. W., & Vo, V. A. (2018). Inverted encoding models assay population-level stimulus representations, not single-unit neural tuning. *eNeuro, 5*, ENEURO.0098-18.2018.

Sprague, T. C., Boynton, G. M., & Serences, J. T. (2019). Inverted encoding models estimate sensible channel responses for sensible models. *bioRxiv*, 642710; doi: https://doi.org/10.1101/642710

Sprague, T. C., & Serences, J. T. (2013). Attention modulates spatial priority maps in the human occipital, parietal and frontal cortices. *Nature Neuroscience, 16*, 1879–1887.

Stokes, M. G. (2015). 'Activity-silent' working memory in prefrontal cortex: a dynamic coding framework. *Trends in Cognitive Sciences, 19*, 394–405.

Theeuwes, J., Olivers, C. N. L., & Chizk, C. L. (2005). Remembering a location makes the eyes curve away. *Psychological Science, 16*, 196–199.

Toda, K., Sugase-Miyamoto, Y., Mizuhiki, T., Inaba, K., Richmond, B. J., & Shidara, M. (2012). Differential encoding of factors influencing predicted reward value in monkey rostral anterior cingulate cortex. *PLoS One, 7*, e30190.

Todd, J. J., & Marois, R. (2004). Capacity limit of visual short-term memory in human posterior parietal cortex. *Nature, 428*, 751–754.

Todd, J. J., & Marois, R. (2005). Posterior parietal cortex activity predicts individual differences in visual short-term memory capacity. *Cognitive, Affective, & Behavioral Neuroscience, 5*, 144–155.

Tsujimoto, S., & Postle, B. R. (2012). The prefrontal cortex and delay tasks: a reconsideration of the 'mnemonic scotoma'. *Journal of Cognitive Neuroscience, 24*, 627–635.

van Ede, F., Chekroud, S. R., Stokes, M. G., & Nobre, A. C. (2019). Concurrent visual and motor selection during visual working memory guided action. *Nature Neuroscience, 22*, 477–483.

van Kerkoerle, T., Self, M. W., & Roelfsema, P. R. (2017). Layer-specificity in the effects of attention and working memory on activity in primary visual cortex. *Nature Communications, 8*, 13804.

van Loon, A. M., Olmos-Solis, K., Fahrenfort, J. J., & Olivers, C. N. L. (2018). Current and future goals are represented in opposite patterns in object-selective cortex. *eLife, 7*, e38677.

Vogel, E. K., & Machizawa, M. G. (2004). Neural activity predicts individual differences in visual working memory capacity. *Nature, 428*, 748–751.

Vogel, E. K., McCollough, A. W., & Machizawa, M. G. (2005). Neural measures reveal individual differences in controlling access to working memory. *Nature, 438*, 368–387.

Wan, Q., Cai, Y., Rogers, T. T., & B. R. Postle, B. R. (2019). Rotational remapping as a candidate mechanism for priority-based recoding in visual working memory: empirical and computational evidence. Unpublished manuscript.

Wan, Q., Cai, Y., Samaha, J., & Postle, B. R. (2020). Tracking stimulus representation across a 2-back visual working memory task. *Royal Society Open Science*.

Wang, J. X., Kurth-Nelson, Z., Kumaran, D., Tirumala, D., Soyer, H., Leibo, J. Z., . . . Botvinick, M. (2018). Prefrontal cortex as a meta-reinforcement learning system. *Nature Neuroscience, 21*, 860–868.

Wilson, F. A. W., O'Scalaidhe, S. P., & Goldman-Rakic, P. S. (1993). Dissociation of object and spatial processing domains in primate prefrontal cortex. *Science, 260*, 1955–1958.

Wolff, M. J., Ding, J., Myers, N. E., & Stokes, M. G. (2015). Revealing hidden states in visual working memory using electroencephalography. *Frontiers in Systems Neuroscience, 9*, 123.

Wolff, M. J., Jochim, J., Akyürek, E. G., & Stokes, M. G. (2017). Dynamic hidden states underlying working-memory-guided behavior. *Nature Neuroscience, 20*, 864–871.

Woodman, G. F. (2013). Viewing the dynamics and control of visual attention through the lens of electrophysiology. *Vision Research, 80*, 7–18.

Xu, Y. (2017). Reevaluating the sensory account of visual working memory storage. *Trends in Cognitive Sciences, 27*, 794–815.

Xu, Y. (2018). Sensory cortex is nonessential in working memory storage. *Trends in Cognitive Sciences, 22*, 192–193.

Xu, Y., & Chun, M. M. (2006). Dissociable neural mechanisms supporting visual short-term memory for objects. *Nature, 440*, 91–95.

Yu, Q., Teng, & Postle, B. R. (2020). Different states of priority recruit different neural representations in visual working memory. *PLoS Biology, 18*, e3000769. doi.org/10.1371/journal.pbio.3000769

13

A Dynamic Field Theory of Visual Working Memory

Sobanawartiny Wijeakumar and John Spencer

Working memory is a key cognitive system that is responsible for maintaining and manipulating information and detecting changes when they occur (Luck & Vogel, 2013). Examples from everyday functions include maintaining and manipulating numbers during a complex set of calculations, storing the words before a conjunction until the rest of the sentence is read to comprehend the meaning, or even continually maintaining and updating information from a dynamic visual scene while driving.

In the four decades since the proposition of the influential model of working memory (WM) by Baddeley and Hitch, behavioural and neuroimaging findings have paved the way for the development of multiple theoretical accounts of WM. Specifically, the advent of micro- and macro-scale neuroimaging techniques have afforded the possibility of 'peeking' into brains while humans and animals engage in experimental tasks. It is now possible to associate encoding, maintenance, and retrieval processes with levels of activation in specialized cortical networks, map these functions across age, and examine the extent of spatial overlap with other cognitive functions. Further, it is possible to spatially overlay regions of activation from WM tasks, inhibitory control tasks, and cognitive flexibility tasks to examine similar and unique mechanisms.

Our research group employs behavioural and neuroimaging methods to investigate how a specific type of WM—visual working memory (VWM)—emerges in infancy (Wijeakumar, Kumar, Reyes, Tiwari, & Spencer, 2019) and early childhood (Buss, Fox, Boas, & Spencer, 2014), and develops across the lifespan (Wijeakumar, Magnotta, & Spencer, 2017). Research across the lifespan emphasizes the importance of creating theories that can explain age-related changes in VWM processing. To this end, we have used experimental tasks such as change detection (CD; Colbert & Bo, 2017; Luck & Vogel, 1997; Phillips, 1974; Read, Rogers, & Wilson, 2016) and preferential looking (Ross-Sheehy, Oakes, & Luck, 2003) that can be scaled across the lifespan by manipulating load (one to six items) and trial types (same/different). We refer to the chapter by Hakim, Awh and Vogel (2021) in this volume that describes some of the research conducted using variants of the CD task. To record brain activation across the lifespan, we rely on functional near-infrared spectroscopy, a neuroimaging technique where near infrared light is shone through the scalp and differentially absorbed by oxy- and deoxyhaemoglobin. This technique can be used in studies with infants, children, and older adults because

Sobanawartiny Wijeakumar and John Spencer, *A Dynamic Field Theory of Visual Working Memory* In: *Working Memory*. Edited by: Robert H. Logie, Valérie Camos, and Nelson Cowan, Oxford University Press (2021). © Oxford University Press. DOI: 10.1093/oso/9780198842286.003.0013

Table 13.1 Summary responses to designated questions

Question	Response
1. Definition of working memory (WM)	In dynamic field theory (DFT), WM is an attractor state where representations are self-sustained through strong recurrent interactions between excitation and inhibition.
2. Describe and explain the methods you use, and their strengths and limitations	Behavioural measures are used to tune model performance. Neuroimaging methods explain activation in cortical networks across the lifespan and across cognitive functions to understand the processes that underlie behaviour. Computational modelling to investigate causality and the link between behaviour and brain.
3. Unitary versus non-unitary nature of working memory	The implementation of WM in DFT is a domain-general system that interacts with long-term memory (LTM). It can be engaged within any cognitive function, because, in DFT, WM is an attractor state that emerges from the interactions between excitation and inhibition. That said, DFT is strongly committed to the grounding of cognition in sensorimotor systems. This requires understanding the domain-specific nature of the task and the sensorimotor systems engaged.
4. The role of attention and control	There is no central homunculus/executive controller. Instead, its role emerges from the interactions between perceptual, WM, and decision-making fields. However, larger DF architectures have feature/spatial attention fields that build activation when fixation moves to a particular item/location.
5. Storage, maintenance and loss of information in WM	Encoding occurs when a peak of activation responsive to a stimulus, enters a stabilized attractor state. Maintenance occurs when this peak of activation enters a self-sustaining state as a result of the interaction between excitation and inhibition. Loss of information occurs as a result of competition between multiple peaks of activation (representations)—under some conditions, a peak can be de-stabilized (forgotten).
6. The role of LTM knowledge in WM storage and processing	Peaks of activation in WM can form sub-threshold memory traces that are likened to LTM traces. Conversely, these memory traces can speed up encoding and/or strengthen WM maintenance.
7. Is there evidence that is not consistent with your theoretical framework	The key challenging topics for DFT are: (1) incorporating differences in strategies (e.g. verbal strategies employed by older adults during change detection). (2) Capturing differences in LTM processing (declarative versus procedural memory). (3) The representation of temperament, affect, gender, and motivation, purported to influence WM processing.
A. WM development	Changes in WM across development are explained by changes in the strength and width of excitation and inhibition within and/or between fields in the DF model.
C. Individual differences and limits in WM capacity	Limits in WM capacity occur due to an increase in inhibition from multiple competing peaks of activation. Manipulating self-excitation, lateral inhibition, neural noise, and/or resting level in the fields of the DF model can potentially capture individual differences.
D. Neural correlates of WM	Local field potentials (LFPs) can be computed from trial-by-trial estimates of each field of the DF model. These LFPs can be convolved with canonical impulse response functions to create regressors for each experimental condition to be used in a general linear model—synonymous with statistical analyses used in fMRI.

it does not require that participants remain still. Further, it is less susceptible to motion artefacts. More recently, portable systems have also become available affording the possibility of conducting home assessments. Recent innovations in methodology also allow for the spatial overlap of regions of activation to compare neural correlates across the lifespan (Wijeakumar, Huppert, Magnotta, Buss, & Spencer, 2017). Concretely, it is possible to spatially overlay brain activation from a 6-month-old infant engaging in a preferential looking VWM task with an 80-year-old adult engaging in a CD VWM task. In addition to behaviour and brain function, our research employs the use of computational models to pursue a mechanistic and causative approach to understanding VWM processing. Specifically, we aim to develop models that can capture behaviour and brain activation, are constrained by manipulations to task parameters, and can make specific predictions.

In this chapter, we introduce the computational framework that we use in our research—dynamic field theory (DFT). We begin by providing an overview of this framework and the neurophysiological basis for its foundation. Then, we present a step-by-step guide to the development of a three-field dynamic field (DF) model of VWM. In doing so, we demonstrate how this computational framework instantiates a neural basis for VWM via a self-sustained state of activation in a cortical field. Further, we explain how this model can explain encoding, consolidation, maintenance, and comparison of items while being implemented within a real-time neural system. Finally, we demonstrate how the three-field DF model can be used to capture age-related changes in VWM processing across the lifespan.

Overview of Dynamic Field Theory

DFT refers to a class of continuous attractor neural network models used to capture the dynamics involved in neural and behavioural processes of perception, cognition, and action (Schöner, Spencer, & The DFT Research Group, 2016). Its emergence is heavily rooted in work by Esther Thelen and Linda Smith (Thelen & Smith, 1994, 2007). They adopted a dynamical systems perspective to studying early development, and in doing so, highlight two valuable points: (1) development occurs as a result of micro-scale, moment-to-moment changes (e.g. moving the hand in response to a painful stimulus), but also, as a result of macro-scale changes (chronic exposure to life stress) across years; and (2) these changes unfold as a consequence of the complex, mutual, and continuous interactions between the brain, body, and environment. Within this complexity, changes will occur across multiple spatial scales—cellular to cultural. The principle of 'change' is captured through the use of differential equations in DFT (Spencer & Schöner, 2003). Moreover, DF models capture interactions between systems by integrating perceptual, memory, and decision-making systems. Finally, DF models have been implemented using autonomous robotic systems, showing how the concepts of DFT span across the body, brain, and the environment (Lipinski, Schneegans, Sandamirskaya, Spencer, & Schöner, 2012; Milde et al., 2017).

In DFT, behaviour is 'softly assembled' via the integration and disintegration of multiple processes, instead of being centrally controlled by a single entity. In dynamical systems, local neural populations that constitute these processes move in and out of attractor states. Neural systems can exist in at least three attractor states: a 'resting' attractor state where it can be activated following input, a 'stabilized' state where the system is anchored to external input, and a 'self-sustaining' state wherein interactions within the system and interactions with other systems can sustain activation even after input is removed. This self-sustaining state creates a form of WM, which as we discuss in later sections, is a product of the balance between local excitation and surround inhibition in populations of neurons. Note that in our DF models, we label particular fields as 'WM' fields. This reflects that these fields have neural interactions that are 'tuned' to operate in the self-sustaining state with strong local excitation and strong surround inhibition. Within our DFT models, the WM field is modelled separately to imply functional differences from perceptual fields and decision nodes. More generally, we adopt the view that the WM field represents the instantiation of a property that might exist in all of the cortex.

More broadly within the DFT framework, moving in and out of these attractor states is conceptualized as the formation of thoughts. The refinement of these patterns is conceptualized as learning. Finally, cementing these patterns through repeated engagement over time is conceptualized as development. In general, every attractor system can be represented by an activation variable moving in and out of these states. However, this view does not take into consideration differences in representational states. Consider this example: you reach out to grab a cup that contains coffee, placed on the right side of a table. A perception activation variable should activate to a stable 'on' state, a long-term memory activation variable should activate to recognize the presence of coffee, and a motor preparation and movement variable should activate before the arm actually starts to move. Now, consider differences in the same example: reaching out to a red cup on the table versus reaching out to the red cup, among blue cups on the right side of the table versus reaching out to a red cup placed on the left side of the table. Capturing these different representational states require (1) splitting single activation variables into multiple fields (colour, orientation, location, etc.) and further, (2) allowing for continuous metric representation of dimensions (left to right for location, blue to yellow for colour, etc.). Such metric dimension fields can be coupled together to provide potential architectures for experimental manipulations.

DFT was first used to study motor planning and spatial category biases from childhood to early adulthood (Smith, Thelen, Titzer, & McLin, 1999; Thelen, Schöner, Scheier, & Smith, 2001). In the last decade, DFT has been used to capture the working of higher-order functions such as VWM (J. S. Johnson, Simmering, & Buss, 2014; J. S. Johnson, Spencer, & Schöner, 2008), inhibitory control (Wijeakumar, Ambrose, Spencer, & Curtu, 2017), word learning (Samuelson, Smith, Perry, & Spencer, 2011) and executive functions (Buss & Spencer, 2018).

The properties of DF architectures are anchored to properties of neural populations (see Jancke et al., 1999; Schöner et al., 2016). However, these models do not represent single neuronal synapses or capture neuron-to-neuron signalling, instead, their properties reflect activation from populations of neurons. These properties are synonymous with observations from an electrophysiological analyses technique called distribution of population activation. In this technique, firing rates of each neuron to a particular stimulus feature is plotted on a continuous metric scale by centring a Gaussian function of fixed width and shape over the centre of the cell's receptive field (point of maximum spike rate). When plotted in the XY plane, the x-axis corresponds to the parameters of the dimension and the y-axis refers to the spike rate of each neuron, thus, resulting in a 'tuning curve'. Then, the tuning curves for the pool of neurons are weighted by each individual neuron's spike rate, summed, and normalized to obtain distributed population activation (DPA) of a population of neurons. This approach increases stability by creating a decision not based on single neurons, but pools of neurons. Further, a single neuron is likely to respond to parameters across more than one dimension, therefore, computing a population distribution based on multiple neurons reduces ambiguity. Thus, a Gaussian peak of activation in a colour metric field (as an example) of a DF architecture is based on DPA estimated from pools of neurons responding to the red colour of a cup.

Neural systems are not stand-alone—they are constantly triggered by external inputs, are inherently noisy, and densely interconnected with neighbouring systems through excitatory and inhibitory interactions. Any activation in a neural system is a result of the summation of all these processes. Indeed, DFT fields encapsulate these processes. Thus, in a DFT field, the rate of change of activation $\dot{u}_j(y,t)$ with time constant τ_e is formally specified with the following equation:

$$\tau_e \dot{u}_j(x,t) = -u_j(x,t) + h_j + [c_j \times g_j(u_j)](x,t) + \sum_k [c_{jk} \times g_k(u_k)](y,t) + \eta_j(x,t) + s_j(x,t).$$

Here, $-u_j(x,t)$ represents activation within the neural field; y is a point along the metric field. h_j is the resting level of the field, which represents a systematic restoring force that is capable of pulling increased or decreased activation back to a 'starting point'. This starting point is the constant value specified by h_j. External input provided to the system is specified by $s_j(x,t)$. The neural system is subject to random perturbations that cause activation to fluctuate in small quantities. These random perturbations are modelled as Gaussian white noise η_j. Interactions between fields can be excitatory or inhibitory. Generally, interactions are implemented as the convolution between the field output $g(u(y,t))$ and a connectivity kernel $c(x)$ within or between the fields. The field output $g(u(x,t))$ is calculated using a sigmoid function $g(u) - 1 / (1 + \text{Exp}[-\beta u])$ $g(u) - 1 / (1 + \text{Exp}[-\beta u])$ with threshold set to zero and steepness parameter β $g(u)$ has a value close to zero for low activation. As activation approaches a soft threshold, $g(u)$ starts to rise and, reaches saturation (a value of 1) when activation is well above the 0 threshold. The connectivity kernel $c(x)$ is defined as a Gaussian function:

$$c_i(x - x') = a_i Exp\left[-\frac{(x - x')^2}{2\sigma_i^2} \right],$$

where, a_i represents the amplitude of the Gaussian function and σ_i^2 represents the width of the Gaussian function.

An external input to this field stabilizes a peak of activation at a location in the neural field. Local excitation within the field prevents the peak from decaying and pushes it into a self-sustaining state even after input is removed. However, under just these circumstances, the boundary of the peak will continue expanding and grow out of control. To prevent the peak from growing out of control, this 'excitatory' field is reciprocally coupled to an 'inhibitory' field. This field receives excitation from the excitatory field and projects inhibition back to the excitatory field. These inhibitory projections create surround inhibition around the peak in the excitatory field and prevent it from growing out of control. This two-layer model is analogous to the connectivity between pyramidal cells, which are excitatory by nature, and inhibitory interneuron cells. Jancke and colleagues elegantly demonstrated the importance of the two-field model (Fig. 13.1) (Jancke et al., 1999). They compared DPAs constructed from the cat visual cortex when it was stimulated by simultaneous presentations of two squares of light to the linear superposition of DPAs in response to separate presentations of the two squares of light. In both cases, one square of light was presented at a nasal position and the position of the other square of light was varied across six locations. The authors also constructed a DF model to replicate the effects they observed in the cat visual cortex. Both sets of DPAs showed peaks of activation around the area of stimulation. However, DPA from the simultaneous presentations showed lower activation levels, or rather, an overall suppressed effect when compared to the DPA from the separate presentations, implying the role of strong

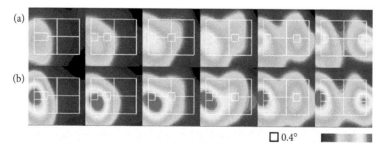

$\square$ 0.4°

Fig. 13.1 (a) Distribution population activation (DPA) measured from cat primary visual cortex when two squares of light were presented simultaneously at varying distances (left to right). (b) Superposition of DPAs from separate presentations of the two squares of light, at varying distances (left to right).

Reproduced from Dirk Jancke, Wolfram Erlhagen, Hubert R. Dinse, Amir C. Akhavan, Martin Giese, Axel Steinhage, and Gregor Schöner, 'Parametric Population Representation of Retinal Location: Neuronal Interaction Dynamics in Cat Primary Visual Cortex', *The Journal of Neuroscience*, 19 (20), pp. 9016–9028, Figure 6. DOI: 10.1523/JNEUROSCI.19-20-09016.1999 Copyright © 1999, Society for Neuroscience.

laterally inhibitory interactions across the cortical field. They also showed that there was an earlier rise in activation in the simultaneous DPA when a small distance separated the squares of light. This effect vanished when larger distances separated the squares of light. The authors captured this early rise in activation via local excitation in the DF model. They also observed that the peaks of activation showed a more rapid drop in activation. This effect was captured in the DF model by connecting the excitatory field to an inhibitory field, wherein local excitation causes the initial rise in activation. Excitation to the inhibitory field resulted in projecting inhibition back to the excitatory field, resulting in a delayed onset to suppression. Finally, if a moderate distance separated both peaks, surround inhibition was particularly strong in the area between the peaks. This inhibitory effect is larger than the inhibition on the other side of the peaks and resulted in moving the peaks further apart. This is evident in the DPA recorded from stimuli positioned some distance away in the simultaneous presentations. The inhibitory field also projects global inhibition to the excitatory field. In global inhibition, each site in the inhibitory field projects inhibition uniformly to every respective site in the excitatory field. Global inhibition prevents the formation of spurious peaks of activation at uninhibited sites, for instance, under the influence of noise.

Building a Dynamic Field Model of Visual Working Memory

In the previous section, we have discussed that WM is an attractor state where peaks of activation can be maintained even after stimulus input has been removed. Peaks are maintained through the balance achieved between local excitatory and inhibitory interactions in the field. For this section, we focus on the CD task because it has been used to measure VWM processing in children (Simmering, 2012), young adults (Ambrose, Wijeakumar, Buss, & Spencer, 2016; Todd & Marois, 2004; Wijeakumar, Magnotta, & Spencer, 2017) and older adults (Wijeakumar, Magnotta, & Spencer, 2017). We review previous work and use an integrative DF model to capture performance in a colour CD task and shed light on current debates surrounding capacity limitations, production of errors, development of VWM processing across the lifespan, and the association between brain and behaviour.

Each trial in a colour CD task begins with the presentation of a memory array of coloured objects followed by a short delay and finally, a test array of coloured objects. At the end of the test array, participants have to indicate if the colours of the objects in the memory and test arrays were 'same' or 'different'. Under the 'different' condition, the colour of one of the objects differs between the memory and test arrays. VWM load is typically varied between one and six items. Based on participants' responses, four trial types can be estimated—Hits (H—correct different trials), Misses (incorrect different trials), Correct rejections (CR—correct same trials), and False alarms (FA—incorrect same trials). We use an updated version of Grier's formula by Aaronson and Watts (1987) to calculate Accuracy (A'):

$$\text{If } H \geq FA: A' = \frac{1}{2} + \left\{ \left[(H - FA) \times (1 + H - FA) \right] / \left[4 \times H \times (1 - FA) \right] \right\}.$$

$$\text{If } H < FA: A' = \frac{1}{2} - \left\{ \left[(FA - H) \times (1 + FA - H) \right] / \left[4 \times FA \times (1 - H) \right] \right\}.$$

According to this formula, A' of 1 indicates perfect performance and a score of 0.5 indicates chance performance. Work from our research group and others have shown that in young adults, A' decreases as VWM load increases from one to six items.

We estimate capacity (K) at each load using Pashler's formula given by:

$$K = \text{load} \times (H - FA) / (1 - FA).$$

In young adults, capacity increases as VWM load increases. However, the maximum capacity (Max K) estimates tend to vary between three and six items.

Our VWM DF model has three continuous metric fields (CON, WM, and Inh), two decision-making nodes (Same and Different nodes), and one Gating node (Fig. 13.3) (J. S. Johnson et al., 2014; J. S. Johnson, Spencer, Luck, & Schöner, 2009; Simmering, 2016). The CON or contrast field is an excitatory field that mainly receives afferent external input and serves two roles. First, it acts as a perceptual field that encodes visual stimuli and second, it is also responsible for comparison by providing a 'contrast' between stored items and novel items. The WM field is also an excitatory field that allows peaks of activation to stabilize and become self-sustaining to capture how items are stored in WM. The Inh or inhibitory field assumes the function of inhibitory interneurons and is responsible for projecting inhibition to the WM and CON fields. The Gate node gates activation from the WM and CON fields to the decision-making Same and Different nodes respectively. WM, CON, Same, Different, and Gate nodes have local excitatory interactions that are depicted by circular green arrows in Fig. 13.2. Longer-range excitatory and inhibitory connections are shown in green and red in Fig. 13.2, respectively. The CON field is the site of afferent external input and this mechanism is likened to perceptual mechanisms that encode stimuli.

Projections from CON field: the CON field projects excitation to the WM field and this process is likened to the transition from encoding to WM processes. It also projects excitation to the Inh field and the Different node and inhibits the Same node.

Projections from WM field: the WM field projects excitation to the Inh field and the Same and Gate nodes and inhibits the Different node.

Projections from nodes: the Same and Different nodes are reciprocally coupled and inhibit one another. The Same node passes excitation to the WM field and inhibition to the CON field. By contrast, the Different node passes excitation to the CON field and inhibits the WM field. In the model, the strength of the connection from the CON field to the Different node is set to be much higher than the strength of the connection between the WM field and the Same node. This difference in connection

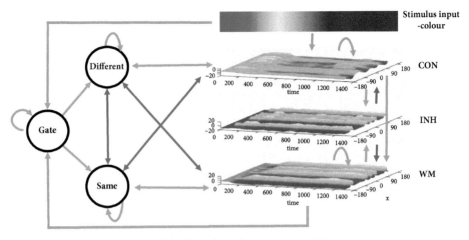

Fig. 13.2 Three-field DFT model of visual working memory. Green arrows represent excitatory connections and red arrows represent inhibitory connections.

strengths causes the model to overcome the same bias that occurs because the WM field will always have greater activation at comparison (due to the presence of multiple peaks at higher loads) than the CON field. Interestingly, evidence for this bias is also evident in behavioural data, where accuracy for same trials is greater than accuracy for different trials.

Next, we present exemplar equations for the WM field and Same node. The full set of equations (CON field, Inh field, Different node, and Gate node) is available elsewhere (J. S. Johnson et al., 2014).

The activation in the WM field is given by:

$$\tau_e \dot{u}_{wm}(x,t) = -u_{wm}(x,t) + h_{wm} + \int c_{wm}(x-x')g_{wm}(u_{wm}(x',t))dx'$$
$$- \int c_{wm,Inh}(x-x')g_{wm,inh}(u_{inh}(x',t))dx'$$
$$+ \int c_{wm,con}(x-x')g_{wm,con}(u_{con}(x',t))dx' + a_{wm}g_{wm}(r_n(t)) + (c_{ws} \times r_s)$$
$$- (c_{wd} \times r_d) + S(x,t) + noise.$$

Here, $-u_{wm}(x,t)$ specifies rate of change of activation along space x as a function of time, t. h_s represents the resting level. In addition, each field contains spatially correlated noise created by convolving a field of independent noise sources with a Gaussian kernel:

$$noise = q \int dy' g_{noise}(x-x')\xi(y',t)$$

$$g_{noise}(x-x') = \frac{1}{\sqrt{2\sigma_{noise}}} Exp\left[-\frac{(x-x')^2}{2\sigma_{noise}^2}\right]$$

External input $S(x,t)$ is projected as a Gaussian with strength c. These inputs are turned on for a time interval specified by the pulse function $\chi^{(t)}$.

$$S(x,t) = c\, Exp\left[-\frac{(x - x_{center})^2}{2\sigma^2}\right]\chi^{(t)}$$

Local and long-range interactions are specified by the convolution of a connectivity Gaussian kernel $c(x - x')$ with a sigmoidal threshold function $g(u_{to\ field}(x',t))dx'$. The Gaussian kernel is specified by $c(x - x') = c\, Exp\left[-\frac{(x - x')^2}{2\sigma^2}\right] - k$, where, c is the strength and σ is the width of the connectivity, and, k is global inhibition. The sigmoidal threshold function is given by $g(u(x',t))dx' = 1/(1 + Exp[-\beta u])$.

The activation in the Same node is given by:

$$\begin{aligned}\dot{v}_s(t) = &-r_s + h_s + c_{s,s}g_s(r_s) - c_{s,d}g_{s,d}(r_d) + a_{s,g}g_{s,g}(g(t)) \\ &+ g_{sg}(g(t))\int c_{s,wm}g_{wm}(u_{wm}(x',t))dx' \\ &+ g_{sg}(g(t))\int c_{s,con}g_{con}(u_{con}(x',t))dx' + noise.\end{aligned}$$

Interactions within and between the nodes have a similar representation, $a\,g(g(t))$, where $g(g(t))$ is a sigmoidal threshold function and a is the node-to-node connection strength. The connection strength between both nodes and the Gate node is weighted by the sigmoidal threshold of the Gate node $(g_{dg}(g(t))\int c_{d,con}g_{con}(u_{con}(y',t))dx')$. Long-range interactions from a field to node are represented by the summed excitation or inhibition projected to the node (e.g. the projection from the WM field to the same node:

$$g_{sg}(g(t))\int c_{s,wm}g_{wm}(u_{wm}(x',t))dx'.$$

Spencer, Johnson, Simmering, Buss, and colleagues have previously used this three-layer model to demonstrate how Hits, Correct rejections, False alarms, and Misses occur (Costello & Buss, 2018; J. S. Johnson et al., 2014; Simmering, 2016). They have also used this model to explore the origin of capacity limitations. We review their work in the following sections. Further, we present findings from new quantitative simulations to bring together work in early childhood with young and older adulthood. To run quantitative simulations, we used the same parameters as those used by Costello and Buss to simulate behavioural data from a colour CD task from young adults (Costello & Buss, 2018). We simulated 50 same and 50 different trials across 20 runs (equivalent to 20 participants) for each of the VWM loads (one to six items). We compared model fits to the behavioural data from another study from our lab (Ambrose et al., 2016). In later sections, we modify the base 'young adult' model parameters to capture behavioural data from early childhood using behavioural data from Simmering (2012) and McKay et al. (in preparation) and late adulthood (Wijeakumar, Magnotta, & Spencer, 2017).

How Does the Three-Layer Dynamic Field Model Capture Visual Working Memory Behaviours?

To demonstrate the working of the three-layer model, we begin by showing how the model explains Correct rejections and Hits for a load of three items. Fig. 13.3 shows snapshots of the state of the CON, Inh, and WM fields at the end of the memory array, delay, and test array for a Correct rejection trial. It also shows the activation of the Same and Different nodes throughout the duration of the trial. During the presentation of the memory array, afferent input is projected to the CON field at three different locations causing peaks of activation to form; this process is encoding in the model (Fig. 13.3a). Weak external input is also projected to the WM field. This weak input combined with the excitatory projections from the CON field causes peaks of activation to form in the WM field; this process is consolidation in the model (Fig. 13.3a). WM and CON fields project excitation to the Inh field. Peaks of activation in the Inh field project strong inhibition to the WM and CON fields. During the delay phase in the absence of external input, low levels of local excitation and strong inhibition from the Inh field diminishes peaks in the CON field and builds troughs at those locations. By contrast, higher local excitation and inhibition from the Inh field allow peaks in WM to become

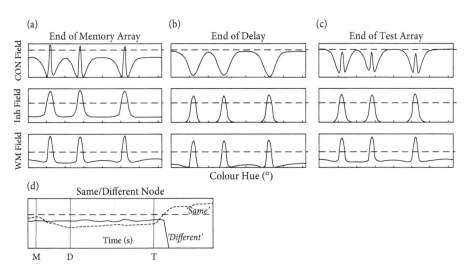

Fig. 13.3 Working of the model during a Correct rejection trial. Dotted line across the snapshots indicates the baseline (value of 0). (a) Activation in the three fields at the end of the memory array. (b) Activation in the three fields at the end of the delay phase. (c) Activation in the three fields at the end of the test array. (d) Activation in the Same (dashed line) and Different (solid line) nodes throughout the trial. Vertical red lines indicate the onset of the memory array (M), delay (D), and test array (T).

self-sustained; this process is maintenance in the model (Fig. 13.3b). Essentially, at this state, memory representations are being actively maintained in WM. In a same trial, the items in the test array match the memory array. Thus, at the onset of the test array, external input is projected to the CON field, but activation is unable to pass threshold because of the strong inhibition from the Inh field at the same locations (Fig. 13.3c). After the presentation of the test array, the Gate node receives the necessary activation from the WM field and the external input from the presentation of the test array, to allow the WM/CON fields to communicate with the decision-making nodes. In this instance, the WM field has greater activation than the CON field and projects excitation to the Same node, resulting in the system correctly identifying a same trial; this process is comparison in the model (Fig. 13.3d).

During a Hit trial, the model should correctly identify that one of the items in the test array is different from the memory array. The function of the model is identical to the function during a correct rejection trial during the presentation of the memory array (Fig. 13.4a) and the delay phase (Fig. 13.4b). During the presentation of the test array, the novel item generates a peak in an uninhibited part of CON field (shown by a red '*' in Fig. 13.4c). The CON field projects excitation to the Different node and the system correctly identifies that it was a different trial (Fig. 13.4d). Note that the connection strength between the WM field and Same node is set lower than the connection

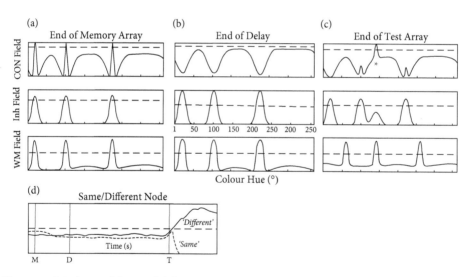

Fig. 13.4 Working of the model during a Hit trial. Dotted line across the snapshots indicates the baseline (value of 0). (a) Activation in the three fields at the end of the memory array. (b) Activation in the three fields at the end of the delay phase. (c) Activation in the three fields at the end of the test array. The peak of activation for the novel item built in the CON layer during the presentation of the test array is shown by a red '*'. (d) Activation in the Same (dashed line) and Different (solid line) node throughout the trial. Vertical red lines indicate the onset of the memory array (M), delay (D), and test array (T).

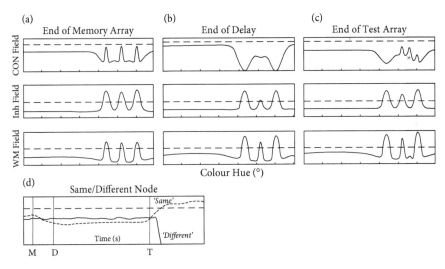

Fig. 13.5 Working of the model during a Miss trial. Dotted line across the snapshots indicates the baseline (value of 0). (a) Activation in the three fields at the end of the memory array. (b) Activation in the three fields at the end of the delay phase. (c) Activation in the three fields at the end of the test array. The peak that failed to build in the CON field following the presentation of the test array has been shown by a red '*'. (d) Activation in the Same (dashed line) and Different (solid line) node throughout the trial. Vertical red lines indicate the onset of the memory array (M), delay (D), and test array (T).

strength between the CON field and Different node to overcome a greater same bias from having more peaks of activation in the WM field.

The model can also explain how errors occur. During Misses, items in the sample array build peaks in the CON field, and eventually in the WM field (Fig. 13.5a). During the delay phase, the CON field receives inhibition from the Inh layer and develops troughs at the colour locations (Fig. 13.5b). During the presentation of the test array, if the novel item is close to the colour of one of the other items in the array and falls within the inhibited region, it can fail to build a peak in the CON layer (see red '*' in Fig. 13.5c). Activation from the WM field is greater than activation in the CON field, and in this case, the model will incorrectly decide that it was a same trial (Fig. 13.5d).

During False alarm trials, peaks of activation build in the CON and WM fields, following the presentation of the memory array. However, competition between peaks in the WM field could prevent a peak from consolidating (i.e. forming a peak) or could destabilize one of the peaks during the delay phase (see red '*' in Fig. 13.6a). At the onset of the test array presentation, a new peak builds in the CON field at the location of the old item since this area is no longer inhibited. The CON field projects excitation to the Different node and the model incorrectly decides that it was a different trial (Fig. 13.6d). Thus, in the DFT model, false alarms occur as a result of the loss of peaks due to competition with other peaks.

By contrast, Misses are mostly a result of the inability to form peaks in the CON field in locations that receive strong inhibition. Our quantitative simulations revealed that the three-layer model was able to capture the percentage of Hits (Fig. 13.7a) and Correct rejections (Fig. 13.7b) across loads one to six items from Ambrose et al. (2016).

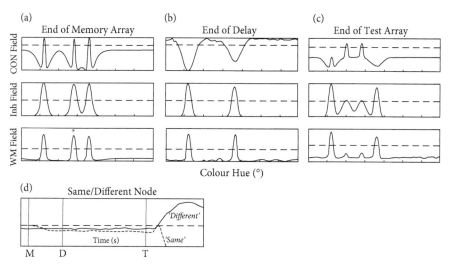

Fig. 13.6 Working of the model during a Correct rejection trial. Dotted line across the snapshots indicates the baseline (value of 0). (a) Activation in the three fields at the end of the memory array. (b) Activation in the three fields at the end of the delay phase. (c) Activation in the three fields at the end of the test array. The disappearance of a peak from the WM field due to competition between peaks is shown by a red '*'. (d) Activation in the Same (dashed line) and Different (solid line) node throughout the trial. Vertical red lines indicate the onset of the memory array (M), delay (D), and test array (T).

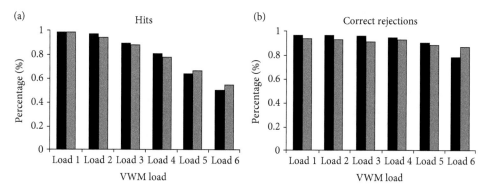

Fig. 13.7 (a) Percentage of Hits across loads of one to six items. (b) Percentage of Correct rejections across loads of one to six items. Behavioural data is adapted from Ambrose et al. (2016; shown as grey bars) and modelled using the three-layer VWM DF model (shown as black bars).

Data from Ambrose JP, Wijeakumar S, Buss AT and Spencer JP (2016), 'Feature-Based Change Detection Reveals Inconsistent Individual Differences in Visual Working Memory Capacity', *Frontiers in Systems Neuroscience*. 10:33. doi: 10.3389/fnsys.2016.00033.

The Origin of Capacity Limitations in the Dynamic Field Model

In the three-layer model of VWM, capacity limitations occur as a result of two contributions: (1) neighbourhood effects and (2) increase in global inhibition. First, local excitation in the WM field helps build peaks of activation. As the number of peaks increase, WM projects stronger excitation to the Inh field, which in turn, projects strong inhibition back to the same locations in the WM field. These projections result in stronger surround inhibition around each peak, resulting in the sharpening of the peak and reduction in overall amplitude. As a result, the WM field projects weaker activation to the Inh layer and so on. Thus, the nature of the interactions between the excitation and inhibition keeps the peaks in the WM field active. As the numbers of peaks start to increase, the area between peaks are heavily inhibited because of overlap from two sources of surround inhibition. Greater inhibition prevents new peaks from forming, limiting the storage of items in the WM field. The second contribution comes from global inhibition; each new peak adds some global inhibition. As the number of peaks builds, this global inhibition reaches a point that it is not possible to build another peak without destabilizing an old peak. Metric similarity of stimuli can also influence capacity limitations. If two peaks of activation are very closely separated, then they might fuse together, or one peak might 'kill' the other peak (as we discuss in the previous section on Miss trials). Quantitative simulations showed that the model showed decreasing A' with increasing VWM load from one to six items (shown in black in Fig. 13.8a). These results agree with findings from Ambrose et al. (2016; shown in grey in Fig. 13.8a). Further, Max K estimates were similar across the model and data from Ambrose et al. (2016; Fig. 13.8b). The root mean-squared error (RMSE) between this model performance and the behavioural data was 0.05.

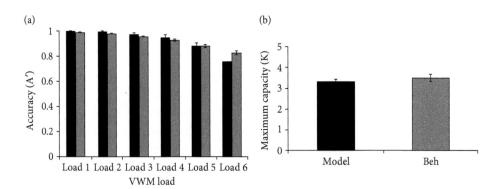

Fig. 13.8 (a) Accuracy (A') across loads of one to six items. (b) Max K across all loads. Note that behavioural data is adapted from Ambrose et al. (2016; shown as grey bars) and modelled using the three-layer VWM DF model (shown as black bars).

Data from Ambrose JP, Wijeakumar S, Buss AT and Spencer JP (2016), 'Feature-Based Change Detection Reveals Inconsistent Individual Differences in Visual Working Memory Capacity', *Frontiers in Systems Neuroscience*. 10:33. doi: 10.3389/fnsys.2016.00033.

In an elegant review, Johnson and colleagues explored how this DF model ad-dresses the 'slots' versus 'resource' theories on capacity and resolution of items (J. S. Johnson et al., 2014). Briefly, the 'slots' theory posits that capacity is fixed and items stored have high-resolution representations. By contrast, the 'resources' theory posits that VWM capacity is unlimited; however, as the number of representations increase, their resolution decreases. Johnson and colleagues argue that the DF model offers a unique account that captures properties of both theories. Concretely, in the DF model, peak formation is a discrete, all-or-none phenomenon that occurs only if the peak reaches threshold. If the peak does not pass the threshold, it does not become self-sustained. In this respect, the DF model is similar to the 'slots' account. However, the number of peaks that can be maintained (capacity) is not fixed and is variable depending upon the excitatory and inhibitory interactions and noise within the field. Variability is also introduced by the possibility of a peak merging with an-other peak or the destabilization of a neighbouring peak due to competition with other peaks. Finally, the resolution of the representations is also variable in the DF model depending on the interactions within the field—more peaks in the WM field result in more inhibition from the Inh field, thus sharpening peaks and reducing overall amplitude.

Visual Working Memory Processing Across the Lifespan Using the Dynamic Field Model

In this section, we will investigate how the DF model might be used to understand VWM processing across the lifespan. Capturing changing dynamics across the life-span provides a different perspective to manipulating conditions of a task; to under-stand VWM processing through the lens of age-related changes such as individual differences in early childhood, and deficits in older adults. We have pooled data from three studies conducted by our research group to test model performance across the lifespan (Ambrose et al. 2016 and Simmering, 2012; Wijeakumar et al., 2017). In early childhood, the Max K estimate is around one to two items, and this estimate in-creases to four to six items in young adulthood. In late adulthood, Max K drops back to about two items. Fig. 13.9 shows accuracy estimates across load for each of these studies. Accuracy estimates across load are highest for young adults (shown in black and grey). Children between the ages of 3 and 5 years show the lowest accuracy esti-mates across load (shown in hues of blue). Accuracy estimates for older adults lie be-tween estimates for children and young adults (shown in hues of red). Thus, a robust model of VWM is one that should be able to capture performance as a manipulation of load and age.

The balance between excitation and inhibition in neurons is important for maintaining stability in the neocortex (Yizhar et al., 2011). Mouse models have shown that the disruption of excitation and inhibition (referred to as the E/I ratio) is associated with the development of neurodevelopmental disorders such as

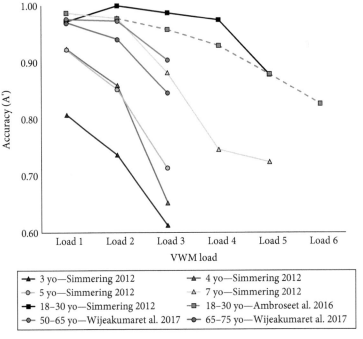

Fig. 13.9 Accuracy estimates from studies using a colour CD task. Data points from childhood are shown in hues of blue, data points from young adults are shown in grey and black, and data points from older adults are shown in hues of red.

autism (E. Lee, Lee, & Kim, 2017). On the other end of the lifespan, senescence is associated with reduction in the number of dopamine D2 receptors from the age of 20 (D. F. Wong et al., 1984; D. F. Wong, Young, Wilson, Meltzer, & Gjedde, 1997). In general, the role of the dopamine system is conceptualized as regulating neurons' sensitivity through the signal-to-noise ratio. In a neurobiological computational model, Li and colleagues reduced the G parameter of the sigmoidal activation function (likened to reducing the unit's average responsivity to excitatory and inhibitory signals) and found that it reduced the distinctiveness of internal representations (Li, Lindenberger, & Sikstrom, 2001). Specifically, internal representations were less distinctive in the 'old' adult model than in the 'young' adult model. Accounts of age-related loss of distinction in representations reported from neurobiological models is also evident in literature employing macro-scale neuro-imaging methods; this account is termed de-differentiation (Fandakova, Sander, Werkle-Bergner, & Shing, 2014). Other accounts of ageing include compensation-related utilization hypothesis (CRUNCH), and hemispheric asymmetry reduction (HAROLD) hypothesis (Cabeza, 2002; Schneider-Garces et al., 2010). Both these accounts specify the recruitment of 'extra' neural resources to fulfil the less complex demands of a cognitive task in ageing. Indeed, it is still possible that recruitment of compensatory resources is a product of the loss of precision in maintained representations.

In DFT, it is possible to represent excitatory–inhibitory interactions discussed previously for modelling developmental changes, by altering the properties of the projections between the WM/CON field and the Inh field. It is important to recall, however, that the mapping between neuromodulation and population dynamics as employed by DFT is somewhat speculative. Previous work from our research group has shown that in DFT, early developmental changes occur as a result of strengthening neural interactions over time—referred to as the spatial precision hypothesis. Schutte, Spencer, and colleagues first tested this hypothesis exploring developmental changes in spatial cognition (Schutte & Spencer, 2009; Simmering, Schutte, & Spencer, 2008). Next, Simmering showed that increasing the strength of connectivity of excitation and inhibition resulted in sharper, more stable peaks that can explain increasing performance (accuracy and capacity) with increasing age in VWM tasks (Simmering, 2016). More recently, Costello and Buss used the three-layer DF model to investigate the parameters that would need to be modulated to capture changes in behavioural performance in older adults (Costello & Buss, 2018). They tested ten different models manipulating strength and width of excitation and inhibition, and strength and width of noise. Most of their models show comparable performance. However, they emphasize that increasing the width of both excitation and inhibition was able to best capture behavioural performance in older adults.

Here, we use the same three-layer model to capture behavioural performance from Ambrose et al. (2016), described previously, to re-demonstrate how manipulating excitation and inhibition can capture behaviour across the lifespan. To do this, we collated data from the studies shown in Fig. 13.9 to create three age groups: early childhood (3-, 4-, and 5-year-olds from Simmering, 2012), young adulthood (18- to 30-year-olds from Ambrose et al., 2016), and older adulthood (> 60 years from Wijeakumar et al., 2017). Fig. 13.10 shows Hits and Correct rejections for these three age categories. Children

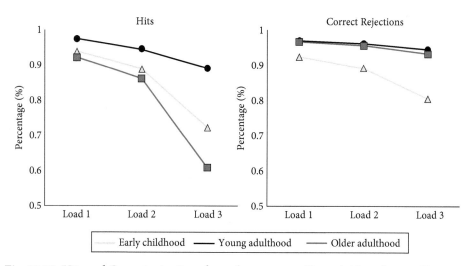

Fig. 13.10 Hits and Correct rejections for early, young, and late adulthood created by pooling data from the studies shown in Fig. 13.9.

demonstrated a lower percentage of Hits and Correct rejections than young adults. However, older adults only showed a lower percentage than young adults in Hit trials. Interestingly, older adults 'behaved' like young adults during the 'same' trials, whereas, during different trials, their behaviour was similar to that of children. We used this critical difference between the three groups to 'age' our model.

It is possible to randomly vary model parameters to test model performance, but we adopted a systematic theory-driven approach by anchoring our model to neurobiological evidence that we discussed at the start of this section. We varied two key parameters of the model: (1) strength of local excitation in CON and WM and inhibition from Inh field to WM and CON (spatial precision hypothesis reported by Simmering et al., 2008) and (2) width of local excitation in CON and WM and inhibition from Inh field to WM and CON (reported by Costello and Buss). Note that Simmering and colleagues only varied the strength, and not the width of connectivity, so we tested whether the latter could also capture changes in early development.

The parameters that were used to capture behaviour from children are shown in blue, young adults are shown in black, and older adults are shown in red (Width model) and orange (Strength model), in Table 13.2. In line with findings from Simmering et al., we varied the strength of local excitation in CON and WM, and, the inhibition between Inh and CON and Inh and WM, from 10% to 100% of the estimates used for young adults. Model performance approached behavioural performance when the strength of excitation and inhibition was reduced to 60% to 70% of the estimates used for young adults. However, the model did not perform as poorly on different trials because the strength of the excitation from the CON field to the Different node was strong. When this strength of excitation from the CON field to the Different node was reduced (to 60% of the estimates used for young adults), the model captured behavioural performance in early childhood (RMSE = 0.09). Decreasing the strength of excitation and inhibition reduced the robustness of the peaks in the CON and WM fields, allowing them to become de-stabilized relatively quickly. Losing stability increased the possibility of errors across both same and different trials. These findings are in agreement with those from Simmering (2012).

By contrast, two versions of the DF model captured behavioural data from the older adults. In the Width model, the width of local excitation and lateral inhibition in CON and WM field was increased by 12% of the estimates used in young adults. In the Strength model, the strength of local excitation and lateral inhibition was increased by 90% of the estimates used in young adults. Both the Width model (RMSE = 0.1) and Strength model (RMSE = 0.11) were able to capture the trend in behavioural performance following quantitative simulations. Fig. 13.11a shows the working of both models during a load 3 different trial. In the Strength model, increased strength of local excitation in the WM field creates large robust peaks of activation. Strong excitation is projected to the Inh field, which in turn, projects strong and broad inhibition to the CON field to form small peaks in broadly inhibited regions. In the Width model, similar but less pronounced effects are observed in the CON field. Fig. 13.11b shows summed output activation from the WM and CON fields throughout a trial duration

Table 13.2 Parameters used for the three-layer VWM model. Parameters shown in black were used to capture performance from Ambrose et al. (2016) for VWM load of one to six items, and the 'young adulthood' category. The parameters that were scaled to capture performance in early childhood are shown in blue. The parameters that were scaled to capture performance in older adulthood are shown in red (Width model) and orange (Strength model). Note that the parameters shown only in black were unchanged across the lifespan. The slope of the activation β = 5.0 for all terms.

Layer/node	Tau	h	Self-excitation		Excitatory projections		Inhibitory projection			Target input		Noise	
			Strength	Sigma	Strength	Sigma	Strength	Sigma	Global Inhibition	Strength	Sigma	Strength	Sigma
u(CF)	80	−5	uu = 1.5 (1.05) (2.85)	uu = 3 (3.375)	ud = 4		uv = 1.35 (0.945) (2.565) us = 0.15	uv = 14 (15.75)	Uv = 0.005	tar = 30	tar = 3	u = 0.04	q = 1
v(Inh)	10	−12			vu = 1.7 vw = 1.95	vu = 10 vw = 5						v = 0.04	q = 1
w(WM)	80	−4.5	ww = 3.75 (2.375) (7.125)	ww = 3 (3.375)	wu = 1.6 ws = 1	wu = 5	wv = 0.325 (0.2275) (0.6175) wd = 1	wv = 35 (39.375)	uv = 0.06	tar = 6 wS = 0.2	tar = 3	w = 0.04	q = 1
Gate	80	−4.9	gg = 4.8		gw = 0.03					tar = 0.03 transient = 18 gS = 0.01		g = 0.025	
Different	80	−8	dd = 3.7		du = 2.8 (1.6) dg = 4.75		ds = 100					d = 0.065	
Same	80	−5	ss = 3.7		sw = 0.5 sg = 4.75		sd = 100 sv = 0.2					s = 0.065	

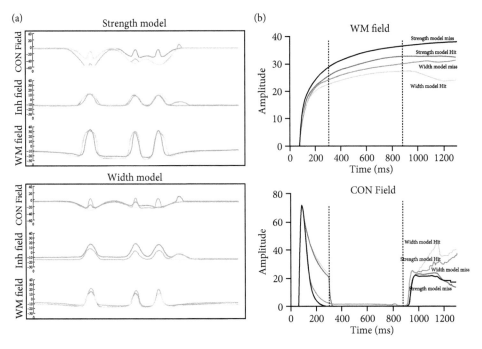

Fig. 13.11 (a) Working of the Width model and Strength model on a load 3 different trial. Blue line represents activation at the end of the sample array. Cyan line represents activation at the end of delay. Black line represents activation at the end of the test array. (b) Summed activation in the WM and CON fields for the Width model and the Strength model for hit and miss trials at load 3. First dashed line indicates the end of sample array and second dashed line indicates the end of the delay period.

during load 3 Hits and Misses. As expected, across both models, summed activation is higher for Hits than for Misses in the CON field. The converse is true for the WM field. One big functional difference is evident between both models. Both models begin encoding in the CON field around the same time; however, it takes longer for these peaks to decay (or be supressed by Inh field) in the Width model. Therefore, in the Width model, activation in the WM field is kept supressed throughout the trial. Thus, the Strength model elicits greater activation than the Width model in the WM field during Hit trials. Both variants of the DF model could be informative in exploring individual differences. The Strength model might represent brain mechanisms in older adults who recruit verbal strategies, resulting in quicker consolidation of items in the WM field. However, in general, such reliance is still indicative of age-related decline because it relies on extra resources to complete the task (Forsberg, Johnson, & Logie, 2019; Wijeakumar, Magnotta, & Spencer, 2017). By contrast, the Width model might represent a different form of age-related decline, where deficits in perceptual processes result in longer decay times for peaks in the CON field. Such model variations might also be used to understand age-related changes across other types of WM (Brockmole & Logie, 2013; W. Johnson, Logie, & Brockmole, 2010; Maylor & Logie, 2010).

Fig. 13.12 shows the percentage of Hits and Correct rejections, and A' for behavioural data and the quantitative simulations for children (blue), young (black), and older adults (red).

Using the DF Model to Make Haemodynamic Predictions of Brain Activation?

In recent work, our research group adapted a model-based fMRI approach from Deco and colleagues (Deco, Rolls, & Horwitz, 2004) to make haemodynamic predictions in an inhibitory control Go/Nogo task (Buss, Wifall, Hazeltine, & Spencer, 2013; Wijeakumar et al., 2017). We used the same approach to make haemodynamic predictions using the three-layer VWM model. First, we created a local field potential (LFP) from every field and node by summing t absolute value of all the terms in this equation that contribute to the rate of change of activation, with the exception of the stability terms $-u(y,t)$ and h. Here, we show the equation for calculating LFPs from the WM field:

$$u_{LFP}(t) = \frac{1}{n}\left|\int c_{wm,wm}(x-x')g_{wm}(u_{wm}(x',t))dx'\right|$$
$$+\frac{1}{n}\left|\int c_{wm,Inh}(x-x')g_{wm}(u_{wm}(x',t))dx'\right|$$
$$+\frac{1}{n}\left|\int c_{wm,con}(x-x')g_{wm}(u_{wm}(x',t))dx'\right|$$
$$+\left|a_{wm}g_{wm}(r_n(t))\right|+\left|(c_{ws}\times r_s)\right|-\left|(c_{ws}\times r_d)\right|+\frac{1}{n}\left|s(x)\right|+\frac{1}{n}\left|\text{noise}\right|$$

where, n is the number of units in each field. Since each field in the model has different contributions, the LFP measures are unique. LFPs are generated for each model component, condition, trial (100 trials) and run (20 runs in total). Then, they are averaged across each trial and run to create a predicted LFP per condition (e.g. load 3 same trial). Next, to obtain a predicted haemodynamic response, we convolve the average LFPs with a canonical impulse response function specified by:

$$u_{LFP}(t) = \frac{t^{n-1}}{\lambda^n(n-1)!}Exp\left(-\frac{t}{\lambda}\right),$$

where, $\lambda = 1.3$ and $n = 4$. Note that this process is similar to what is described in the fMRI literature.

We used this approach to create an average haemodynamic response function for each load, trial type, and component of the model. This process was repeated for early childhood, young adulthood, and older adulthood models. We compare these haemodynamic response functions to findings from two studies that used functional near-infrared spectroscopy to record brain activation (McKay et al., in preparation; Wijeakumar, Magnotta,

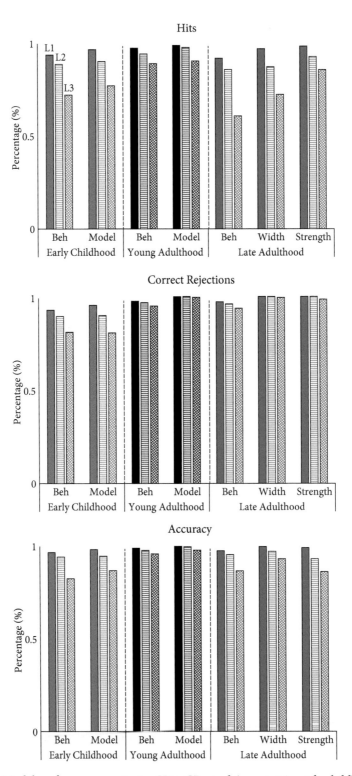

Fig. 13.12 Model performance capturing Hits, CRs, and Accuracy in early childhood (blue), young adulthood (black), and late adulthood (red). Note that two potential 'older adulthood' models have been discussed. The parameters for the Width model are shown in red in Table 13.2 and the parameters for the Strength model are shown in orange in Table 13.2.

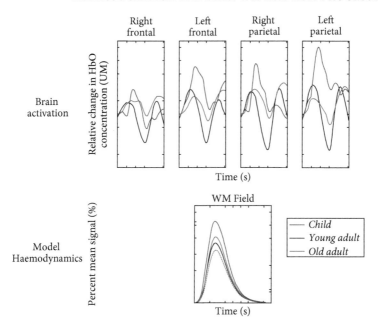

Fig. 13.13 Recorded brain activation (top) and predicted haemodynamic activation from the WM field of the model (bottom) from children (shown in blue), young adults (shown in black), and older adults (shown in red).

& Spencer, 2017). We averaged activation across channels from the functional near-infrared spectroscopy system to obtain an exemplar haemodynamic response function from the left frontal, right frontal, left parietal, and right parietal cortices, for each condition and age group. Note that we report only on the frontoparietal network for both studies because we did not record from the occipito-temporal cortices in McKay and colleagues. Fig. 13.13 shows haemodynamic response functions for load 3 (averaged across same and different trials) from recorded brain activation (top row) and predicted haemodynamic activation from the WM field (bottom row) for early childhood, young adulthood and older adulthood. We highlight two observations. First, predictions from the WM field of the three-layer model match trends in brain activation across age group. Specifically, the model predicted that children would recruit greater activation than young or older adults at load 3. Second, this neural signature is pronounced in the left frontal cortex and bilateral parietal cortex suggesting that the WM field might be distributed across these cortical areas, in accordance with a distributed or integrated account of VWM processing (we discuss our stance on this in an upcoming section).

The Association Between Working Memory and Long-Term Memory Processes

A central issue in the memory literature is whether WM is essentially reactivated LTM (Atkinson & Shiffrin, 1971; Cameron, Haarmann, Grafman, & Ruchkin, 2005; Cowan,

1988; Lewis-Peacock & Postle, 2008; Oberauer, 2002; Öztekin, Davachi, & McElree, 2010). Recent studies have reported that neural activation recruited by LTM processes were also observed in WM processing. A notable example is work from Lewis-Peacock and Postle who trained a classifier to first identify brain activity from LTM processes involved in making judgements about pictures of famous people, locations, and objects (Lewis-Peacock & Postle, 2008). Then, outside the scanner, participants learnt the association between stimuli (e.g. a person with a location). Finally, participants engaged in a delayed paired-association recognition task, where they were required to indicate whether the first and second stimuli presentations were associated. This LTM-trained classifier was able to successfully decode delay-period activity from a network of regions for stimuli that were associated through the learning phase. This work showed that retention of information during WM processing could be supported by LTM representations. In reviewing all of this evidence, Norris makes a valid observation—both WM tasks and LTM tasks are likely to recruit both processes, so merely observing LTM-related activation in a WM task does not imply the absence of WM processing (Norris, 2017). Lifespan studies might add value to this discussion which has, thus far, been fuelled by findings from young adults and lesion patients. On one end of the lifespan spectrum, in infancy, VWM processing can be measured as early as 4 months of age using the preferential-looking task (Ross-Sheehy et al., 2003). This demonstration questions the veracity of the account that WM is essentially reactivated LTM processing. On the other end of the spectrum, older adults reportedly employ verbal strategies to successfully detect changes in VWM tasks. Specifically, work from our group found that older adults associated labels based on their familiarity to abstract shapes in the memory array of a shape CD task and relied on rehearsal to compare shapes across the memory and test arrays (Wijeakumar, Magnotta, & Spencer, 2017). Our findings are supported by recent work from Logie and colleagues, who suggest that age-related changes in VWM might reflect the difficulty in actively engaging cognitive systems required to employ strategies to successfully perform the task (Forsberg, Johnson, & Logie, 2019; Logie, 2018; see chapter by Logie, Belletier, & Doherty, 2021). These findings in older adults defend the dependence of WM processes on LTM. Our experience with implementing LTM in DF models allows us to deviate from the discussion of whether WM is essentially activated LTM, and instead posit that both processes are inextricably linked and share bi-directional properties; in infancy, LTM processes are built through sufficiently maintained WM traces, and in late adulthood, WM processing is reliant in LTM processes. Concretely, in DFT, LTM is implemented through the creation and strengthening of 'sub-threshold' memory traces in Hebbian fields within the DF architecture. These Hebbian fields are coupled to their respective main neural fields (e.g. WM and CON). Simmering, Perone, and colleagues modified the standard three-layer DFT architecture to capture looking behaviour in infants and children in a preferential-looking task (Perone, Simmering, & Spencer, 2011; Simmering, 2016). They added a fixation system that would stochastically look at two side-by-side flashing displays of coloured squares, where one side contained a square that constantly changed its colour. Here, peaks of activation were encoded in the CON field and, consolidated in the WM field as the model passively viewed each display. Those peaks that were successfully encoded and maintained also built memory traces in the associated Hebbian fields. When the model stochastically returned back to attended displays, these memory traces were strengthened if the items were successfully encoded and maintained. Conversely, strengthening memory traces also sped up encoding in the CON field and strengthened maintenance of the peaks of activation in the WM field. This work highlights the how LTM traces can be formed from mounting WM peaks, and conversely, how suitably strengthened LTM traces can influence future encoding and maintenance in future WM peaks.

A Distributed Account of Visual Working Memory Processing

WM processing has been shown to recruit a distributed network of areas across the visual, parietal, temporal, and frontal cortices. The significance of the term 'distribution' within the context of WM processing is multifold. First, conventional load-dependent effects have been observed across the intraparietal sulcus, inferior parietal lobule, superior parietal lobule, dorsolateral prefrontal cortex, and frontal eye fields (Druzgal & D'Esposito, 2003; Linden et al., 2003; Ma, Husain, & Bays, 2014; Pessoa & Ungerleider, 2004; Postle, 2015; Rypma, Prabhakaran, Desmond, Glover, & Gabrieli, 1999; Todd & Marois, 2004). Second, different stimuli dimensions have been shown to recruit a wide distribution of cortical regions during the delay period. For instance, lower-level features such as colour and orientation have been decoded from the visual cortex (Harrison & Tong, 2009; Serences, Ester, Vogel, & Awh, 2009), whereas, complex shapes have been decoded from the frontal eye fields (Ester, Sprague, & Serences, 2015; Wijeakumar, Magnotta, & Spencer, 2017). Further, more complex stimuli such as natural objects (S. H. Lee, Kravitz, & Baker, 2013) have been decoded from the prefrontal cortex. Third, WM subprocesses of encoding, maintenance, and retrieval recruit some common, but mostly unique areas in the frontal, parietal, and motor areas (Linden et al., 2003). This evidence has inspired theoretical accounts that subscribe to the view that WM processes are distributed and integrative by nature.

Christophel and colleagues argue for moving away from a modular perspective of WM processing, where areas perform specialized functions, towards the distribution of cortical networks working together to transform sensory information to behaviour (Christophel, Klink, Spitzer, Roelfsema, & Haynes, 2017). Their account acknowledges the likelihood of a posterior-to-anterior gradient of information processing in the brain, where the posterior cortex is involved in processing sensory information and the anterior cortex is involved in processing information that is abstract or categorical. This view is supported by Postle and colleagues, who advocate that WM emerges through the recruitment and coordination of cortical areas that have evolved to process sensory and action-related functions (Postle, 2006; see chapter by Postle, 2021). This account further proposes that a representation held in WM will recruit as many resources as necessary. An example that anchors both accounts to our work is the engagement of a distributed network of areas in the posterior and anterior cortices in older adults as they employ strategies to successfully attend to complex shapes in a shape CD task and (Wijeakumar, Magnotta, & Spencer, 2017). Here, older adults reported assigning labels to the abstract shapes, to complete the VWM task. We posit that employing these strategies might have resulted in recruiting as many resources as possible, and the classical posterior to anterior shift in activation observed in older adults.

Neuro-computational modelling accounts from Hazy and colleagues define WM as an emergent process that stems from the interactions between a posterior cortex system, a hippocampal system and a prefrontal cortex/basal ganglia system (Hazy, Frank, & O'Reilly, 2006, 2007). In their model, the posterior cortex system is responsible for sensory and motor processing, the hippocampal system is responsible for rapid learning, and, the prefrontal cortex/basal ganglia system is necessary for active maintenance of internal contextual information. Concretely, they argue that their model builds on existing mechanisms in motor control where the basal ganglia modulates frontal motor representations in inhibitory control, to the current model where it modulates the maintenance of more abstract frontal representations in WM processing.

In accordance with these accounts, we also posit the instantiation of WM in DFT anchored to encoding and decision-making is distributed across cortical networks in the brain. In one sense, the implementation of WM in DFT is domain general, wherein the activation as a result of scaling of interactions within and between fields and in some cases, other parameters such as noise and resting level will determine the nature and type of distribution across cortical networks. Recall, however, that in its core principles and origin, DFT grounds cognition in the sensorimotor processing; in this sense, our model cannot be strictly domain general. To come full circle, our account appears to deviate away from, but not necessarily disagree with the popular notion of a central executive or homunculus as described in the Baddeley and Hitch model (Baddeley, 1996; Baddeley, Hitch, & Allen, 2021). Indeed, in the DFT account and the interpretation of the accounts described earlier, the role of the homunculus is subsumed by the properties of the systems, instead of assuming the highest, and somewhat mysterious role in a hierarchical model.

Conclusion

In DFT, WM is a self-sustaining attractor state attained through strengthened interactions between self-excitation and lateral inhibition. This state is represented in a WM field and coupled with fields that have stabilized attractor states representing encoding and comparison, and decision-making processes, to implement performance in a CD task. Capacity limitations are demonstrated through competition between neighbouring peaks and greater global inhibition preventing the formation of new peaks without destabilizing an existing peak. Under the framework, improvements in VWM processing from early childhood to young adulthood is a result of strengthening interactions between excitation and inhibition—referred to as the spatial precision hypothesis. Strengthened interactions create more distinct and precise peaks of activation, and by extension, more precise representations of the stimuli. By contrast, the model captures performance in older adults by increasing the width and strength of excitatory and inhibitory projections in the fields; creating less distinct representations and/or interfering in the comparison process. Lastly, our model predictions are in line with haemodynamic activation recorded from the frontoparietal network across the lifespan, advocating for a distributed perspective of VWM processing in the brain.

References

Aaronson, D., & Watts, B. (1987). Extensions of Grier's computational formulas for A′ and B″ to below-chance performance. *Psychological Bulletin, 102*, 439–442.

Ambrose, J. P., Wijeakumar, S., Buss, A. T., & Spencer, J. P. (2016). Feature-based change detection reveals inconsistent individual differences in visual working memory capacity. *Frontiers in Systems Neuroscience, 10*, 1–10. doi:10.3389/fnsys.2016.00033

Atkinson, R. C., & Shiffrin, R. M. (1971). The control of short-term memory. *Scientific American, 225*, 82–90.

Baddeley, A. D. (1996). Exploring the central executive. *Quarterly Journal of Experimental Psychology A: Human Experimental Psychology, 49A*, 5–28.

Baddeley, A. D., Hitch, G. J., & Allen, R. J. (2021). A multicomponent model of working memory. In R. H. Logie, V. Camos, & N. Cowan (Eds.), *Working memory: State of the science* (pp. 10–43). Oxford: Oxford University Press.

Brockmole, J. R., & Logie, R. H. (2013). Age-related change in visual working memory: A study of 55,753 participants aged 8-75. *Frontiers in Psychology, 4*, 1–5. doi:10.3389/fpsyg.2013.00012

Buss, A. T., Fox, N., Boas, D. A., & Spencer, J. P. (2014). Probing the early development of visual working memory capacity with functional near-infrared spectroscopy. *NeuroImage, 85*, 314–325. doi:10.1016/j.neuroimage.2013.05.034

Buss, A. T., & Spencer, J. P. (2018). Changes in frontal and posterior cortical activity underlie the early emergence of executive function. *Developmental Science, 21*, 1–14. doi:10.1111/desc.12602

Buss, A. T., Wifall, T., Hazeltine, E., & Spencer, J. P. (2013). Integrating the behavioral and neural dynamics of response selection in a dual-task paradigm: A dynamic neural field model of Dux et al. (2009). *Journal of Cognitive Neuroscience, 26*, 334–351. doi:10.1162/jocn_a_00496

Cabeza, R. (2002). Hemispheric asymmetry reduction in older adults: the HAROLD model. *Psychology and Aging, 17*, 85–100. doi:10.1037/0882-7974.17.1.85

Cameron, K. A., Haarmann, H. J., Grafman, J., & Ruchkin, D. S. (2005). Long-term memory is the representational basis for semantic verbal short-term memory. *Psychophysiology, 42*, 643–653. doi:10.1111/j.1469-8986.2005.00357.x

Christophel, T. B., Klink, P. C., Spitzer, B., Roelfsema, P. R., & Haynes, J. D. (2017). The distributed nature of working memory. *Trends in Cognitive Sciences, 21*, 111–124. doi:10.1016/j.tics.2016.12.007

Colbert, A., & Bo, J. (2017). Evaluating working memory: Comparing change-detection tasks and Wechsler working memory subtests in school-age children. *Journal of Clinical and Experimental Neuropsychology, 39*, 636–645. doi:10.1080/13803395.2016.1252726

Costello, M. C., & Buss, A. T. (2018). Age-related decline of visual working memory: behavioral results simulated with a dynamic neural field model. *Journal of Cognitive Neuroscience, 30*, 1532–1548. doi:10.1162/jocn_a_01293

Cowan, N. (1988). Evolving conceptions of memory storage, selective attention, and their mutual constraints within the human information-processing system. *Psychological Bulletin, 104*, 163–191. doi:10.1037/0033-2909.104.2.163

Deco, G., Rolls, E. T., & Horwitz, B. (2004). "What" and "Where" in visual working memory: A computational neurodynamical perspective for integrating fMRI and single-neuron data. *Journal of Cognitive Neuroscience, 16*, 683–701. doi:10.1162/089892904323057380

Druzgal, T. J., & D'Esposito, M. (2003). Dissecting contributions of prefrontal cortex and fusiform face area to face working memory. *Journal of Cognitive Neuroscience, 15*, 771–784. doi:10.1162/089892903322370708

Ester, E. F., Sprague, T. C., & Serences, J. T. (2015). Parietal and frontal cortex encode stimulus-specific mnemonic representations during visual working memory. *Neuron, 87*, 893–905. doi:10.1016/j.neuron.2015.07.013

Fandakova, Y., Sander, M. C., Werkle-Bergner, M., & Shing, Y. L. (2014). Age differences in short-term memory binding are related to working memory performance across the lifespan. *Psychology and Aging, 29*, 140–149. doi:10.1037/a0035347

Forsberg, A., Johnson, W., & Logie, R. H. (2019). Aging and feature-binding in visual working memory: The role of verbal rehearsal. *Psychology and Aging, 34*, 933–953. doi:10.1037/pag0000391

Hakim, N., Awh, E., & Vogel, E. K. (2021). Manifold visual working memory. In R. H. Logie, V. Camos, & N. Cowan (Eds.), *Working memory: State of the science* (pp. 311–332). Oxford, UK: Oxford University Press.

Harrison, S. A., & Tong, F. (2009). Decoding reveals the contents of visual working memory in early visual areas. *Nature, 458*, 632–635. doi:10.1038/nature07832

Hazy, T. E., Frank, M. J., & O'Reilly, R. C. (2006). Banishing the homunculus: Making working memory work. *Neuroscience, 139*, 105–118. doi:10.1016/j.neuroscience.2005.04.067

Hazy, T. E., Frank, M. J., & O'Reilly, R. C. (2007). Towards an executive without a homunculus: Computational models of the prefrontal cortex/basal ganglia system. *Philosophical Transactions of the Royal Society B: Biological Sciences, 362*, 1601–1613. doi:10.1098/rstb.2007.2055

Jancke, D., Erlhagen, W., Dinse, H. R., Akhavan, A. C., Giese, M., Steinhage, A., & Schöner, G. (1999). Parametric population representation of retinal location: neuronal interaction dynamics in cat primary visual cortex. *Journal of Neuroscience, 19*, 9016–9028. doi:10.1523/JNEUROSCI.19-20-09016.1999

Johnson, J. S., Simmering, V. R., & Buss, A. T. (2014). Beyond slots and resources: Grounding cognitive concepts in neural dynamics. *Attention, Perception, and Psychophysics, 76*, 1630–1654. doi:10.3758/s13414-013-0596-9

Johnson, J. S., Spencer, J. P., Luck, S. J., & Schöner, G. (2009). A dynamic neural field model of visual working memory and change detection. *Psychological Science, 20*, 568–577. doi:10.1111/j.1467-9280.2009.02329.x

Johnson, J. S., Spencer, J. P., & Schöner, G. (2008). Moving to a higher ground: the dynamic field theory and the dynamics of visual cognition. *New Ideas in Psychology, 26*, 227–251.

Johnson, W., Logie, R. H., & Brockmole, J. R. (2010). Working memory tasks differ in factor structure across age cohorts: Implications for dedifferentiation. *Intelligence, 38*, 513–528. doi:doi:10.1016/j.intell.2010.06.005

Lee, E., Lee, J., & Kim, E. (2017). Excitation/inhibition imbalance in animal models of autism spectrum disorders. *Biological Psychiatry, 81*, 838–847. doi:10.1016/j.biopsych.2016.05.011

Lee, S. H., Kravitz, D. J., & Baker, C. I. (2013). Goal-dependent dissociation of visual and prefrontal cortices during working memory. *Nature Neuroscience, 16*, 997. doi:10.1038/nn.3452

Lewis-Peacock, J. A., & Postle, B. R. (2008). Temporary activation of long-term memory supports working memory. *Journal of Neuroscience, 28*, 8765–8771. doi:10.1523/JNEUROSCI.1953-08.2008

Li, S. C., Lindenberger, U., & Sikström, S. (2001). Aging cognition: From neuromodulation to representation. *Trends in Cognitive Sciences, 5*, 479–486. doi:10.1016/S1364-6613(00)01769-1

Linden, D. E. J., Bittner, R. A., Muckli, L., Waltz, J. A., Kriegeskorte, N., Goebel, R., . . . Munk, M. H. J. (2003). Cortical capacity constraints for visual working memory: Dissociation of fMRI load effects in a fronto-parietal network. *NeuroImage, 20*, 1518–1530. doi:10.1016/j.neuroimage.2003.07.021

Lipinski, J., Schneegans, S., Sandamirskaya, Y., Spencer, J. P., & Schöner, G. (2012). A neurobehavioral model of flexible spatial language behaviors. *Journal of Experimental Psychology: Learning, Memory, and Cognition, 38*, 1490–1511. doi:10.1037/a0022643

Logie, R. (2018). Human cognition: Common principles and individual variation. *Journal of Applied Research in Memory and Cognition, 7*, 471–486. doi:10.1016/j.jarmac.2018.08.001

Logie, R. H., Belletier, C., & Doherty, J. M. (2021). Integrating theories of working memory. In R. H. Logie, V. Camos, & N. Cowan (Eds.), *Working memory: State of the science* (pp. 389–429). Oxford, UK: Oxford University Press.

Luck, S. J., & Vogel, E. K. (1997). The capacity of visual working memory for features and conjunctions. *Nature, 390,* 279–281.

Luck, S. J., & Vogel, E. K. (2013). Visual working memory capacity: from psychophysics and neurobiology to individual differences. *Trends in Cognitive Sciences, 17,* 391–400. doi:10.1016/j.tics.2013.06.006

Ma, W. J., Husain, M., & Bays, P. M. (2014). Changing concepts of working memory. *Nature Neuroscience, 17,* 347–356. doi:10.1038/nn.3655

Maylor, E. A., & Logie, R. H. (2010). A large-scale comparison of prospective and retrospective memory development from childhood to middle age. *Quarterly Journal of Experimental Psychology, 63,* 442–451. doi:10.1080/17470210903469872

Milde, M. B., Blum, H., Dietmüller, A., Sumislawska, D., Conradt, J., Indiveri, G., & Sandamirskaya, Y. (2017). Obstacle avoidance and target acquisition for robot navigation using a mixed signal analog/digital neuromorphic processing system. *Frontiers in Neurorobotics, 11,* 1–17. doi:10.3389/fnbot.2017.00028

Norris, D. (2017). Short-term memory and long-term memory are still different. *Psychological Bulletin, 143,* 992–1009. doi:10.1037/bul0000108

Oberauer, K. (2002). Access to information in working memory: exploring the focus of attention. *Journal of Experimental Psychology: Learning, Memory, and Cognition, 28,* 411–421.

Öztekin, I., Davachi, L., & McElree, B. (2010). Are representations in working memory distinct from representations in long-term memory?: Neural evidence in support of a single store. *Psychological Science, 21,* 1123–1133. doi:10.1177/0956797610376651

Perone, S., Simmering, V. R., & Spencer, J. P. (2011). Stronger neural dynamics capture changes in infants' visual working memory capacity over development. *Developmental Science, 14,* 1379–1392. doi:10.1111/j.1467-7687.2011.01083.x

Pessoa, L., & Ungerleider, L. G. (2004). Neural correlates of change detection and change blindness in a working memory task. *Cerebral Cortex, 14,* 511–520. doi:10.1093/cercor/bhh013

Phillips, W. A. (1974). On the distinction between sensory storage and short-term visual memory. *Perception & Psychophysics, 16,* 283–290.

Postle, B. (2015). The cognitive neuroscience of visual short-term memory. *Current Opinion in Behavioral Sciences, 1,* 40–46. doi:10.1016/j.cobeha.2014.08.004

Postle, B. R. (2006). Working memory as an emergent property of the mind and brain. *Neuroscience, 139,* 23–38. doi:10.1016/j.neuroscience.2005.06.005

Postle, B. R. (2021). Cognitive neuroscience of visual working memory. In R. H. Logie, V. Camos, & N. Cowan (Eds.), *Working memory: State of the science* (pp. 333–357). Oxford, UK: Oxford University Press.

Read, C. A., Rogers, J. M., & Wilson, P. H. (2016). Working memory binding of visual object features in older adults. *Aging, Neuropsychology, and Cognition, 23,* 263–281. doi:10.1080/13825585.2015.1083937

Ross-Sheehy, S., Oakes, L. M., & Luck, S. J. (2003). The development of visual short-term memory capacity in infants. *Child Development, 74,* 1807–1822. doi:10.1046/j.1467-8624.2003.00639.x

Rypma, B., Prabhakaran, V., Desmond, J. E., Glover, G. H., & Gabrieli, J. D. E. (1999). Load-dependent roles of frontal brain regions in the maintenance of working memory. *Neuroimage, 9,* 216–226.

Samuelson, L. K., Smith, L. B., Perry, L. K., & Spencer, J. P. (2011). Grounding word learning in space. *PloS One, 6,* E28095.

Schneider-Garces, N. J., Gordon, B. A., Brumback-Peltz, C. R., Shin, E., Lee, Y., Sutton, B. P., . . . Fabiani, M. (2010). Span, CRUNCH, and beyond: working memory capacity and the aging brain. *Journal of Cognitive Neuroscience, 22,* 655–669. doi:10.1162/jocn.2009.21230

Schöner, G., Spencer, J. P., & The DFT Research Group. (2016). *Dynamic thinking: A primer on dynamic field theory.* New York, NY: Oxford University Press.

Schutte, A. R., & Spencer, J. P. (2009). Tests of the dynamic field theory and the spatial precision hypothesis: capturing a qualitative developmental transition in spatial working memory. *Journal* of *Experimental Psychology: Human Perception and Performance*, 35, 1698–1725. doi:10.1037/a0015794

Serences, J. T., Ester, E. F., Vogel, E. K., & Awh, E. (2009). Stimulus-specific delay activity in human primary visual cortex. *Psychological Science*, 20, 207–214. doi:10.1111/j.1467-9280.2009.02276.x

Simmering, V. R. (2012). The development of visual working memory capacity during early childhood. *Journal of Experimental Child Psychology*, 111, 695–707. doi:10.1016/j.jecp.2011.10.007

Simmering, V. R. (2016). Working memory capacity in context: Modeling dynamic processes of behavior, memory, and development. *Monographs of the Society for Research in Child Development*, 81, 7–24. doi:10.1111/mono.12249

Simmering, V. R., Schutte, A. R., & Spencer, J. P. (2008). Generalizing the dynamic field theory of spatial cognition across real and developmental time scales. *Brain Research*, 1202, 68–86. doi:10.1016/j.brainres.2007.06.081

Smith, L. B., Thelen, E., Titzer, R., & McLin, D. (1999). Knowing in the context of acting: The task dynamics of the A-not-B error. *Psychological Review*, 106, 235–260.

Spencer, J. P., & Schöner, G. (2003). Bridging the representational gap in the dynamical systems approach to development. *Developmental Science*, 6, 392–412.

Thelen, E., Schöner, G., Scheier, C., & Smith, L. B. (2001). The dynamics of embodiment: A field theory of infant perseverative reaching. *Behavioral & Brain Sciences*, 24, 1–86.

Thelen, E., & Smith, L. B. (1994). A dynamic systems approach to the development of cognition and action. *Journal of Cognitive Neuroscience*, 7, 512–514. doi:10.1162/jocn.1995.7.4.512

Thelen, E., & Smith, L. B. (2007). Dynamic systems theories. In W. Damon & R. M. Lerner (Eds.), *Handbook of Child Psychology* (6th edn, pp. 258–312). Hoboken, NJ: John Wiley & Sons. doi:10.1002/9780470147658.chpsy0106

Todd, J. J. J., & Marois, R. (2004). Capacity limit of visual short-term memory in human posterior parietal cortex. *Nature*, 428, 751–754. doi:10.1038/nature02466

Wijeakumar, S., Ambrose, J. P., Spencer, J. P., & Curtu, R. (2017). Model-based functional neuroimaging using dynamic neural fields: An integrative cognitive neuroscience approach. *Journal of Mathematical Psychology*, 76, 212–235. doi:10.1016/j.jmp.2016.11.002

Wijeakumar, S., Huppert, T., Magnotta, V., Buss, A., & Spencer, J. (2017). Validating an image-based fNIRS approach with fMRI and a working memory task. *NeuroImage*, 147, 204–218. doi:10.1016/j.neuroimage.2016.12.007

Wijeakumar, S., Kumar, A., Reyes, L. D., Tiwari, M., & Spencer, J. P. (2019). Early adversity in rural India impacts the brain networks underlying visual working memory. *Developmental Science*, 22, e12822. doi:doi:10.1111/desc.12822

Wijeakumar, S., Magnotta, V. A., & Spencer, J. P. (2017). Modulating perceptual complexity and load reveals degradation of the visual working memory network in ageing. *NeuroImage*, 157, 464–475. doi:10.1016/j.neuroimage.2017.06.019

Wong, D. F., Wagner, H. N., Dannals, R. F., Links, J. M., Frost, J. J., Ravert, H. T., . . . et, al. (1984). Effects of age on dopamine and serotonin receptors measured by positron tomography in the living human brain. *Science*, 226, 1393–1396. doi:10.1126/science.6334363

Wong, D. F., Young, D., Wilson, P. D., Meltzer, C. C., & Gjedde, A. (1997). Quantification of neuroreceptors in the living human brain: III. D2-like dopamine receptors: theory, validation, and changes during normal aging. *Journal of Cerebral Blood Flow & Metabolism*, 17, 316–330. doi:10.1097/00004647-199703000-00009

Yizhar, O., Fenno, L. E., Prigge, M., Schneider, F., Davidson, T. J., O'Shea, D. J., . . . Deisseroth, K. (2011). Neocortical excitation/inhibition balance in information processing and social dysfunction. *Nature*, 477, 171–178. doi:10.1038/nature10360

14

Integrating Theories of Working Memory

Robert H. Logie, Clément Belletier, and Jason M. Doherty

Introduction

There are multiple theories of working memory (WM), many of which are described in the contributions to this book. A previous, highly influential edited book on WM (Miyake and Shah, 1999) covered ten different theories of WM, and Cowan (2017) listed nine, but this does not reflect the multiple variants of each type that have been developed over the last 50 years. This proliferation of theories is by no means new, nor is it restricted to WM. Watkins (1984) famously likened theories of cognition to toothbrushes: we all need one, but we would rather not use one belonging to someone else. Developing one's own theory of cognition can mark a researcher as an independent and creative scientist, whereas building (even with substantial modifications) on a theory originally developed by someone else might be seen, at best, as indicating a lack of originality or an inability to think for oneself, and at worst might be viewed as a form of plagiarism. However, is this expansion in the number of theories making a positive contribution to our field of research, or is it scientifically counterproductive and driven primarily by the pragmatics of academic career development?

In other sciences, the norm is to build on what has gone before, and a major breakthrough involves substantial development and extension of existing theory. In physics, Stephen Hawking built on and extended the work of Albert Einstein, who built on the work of Isaac Newton, who built on work by Nicolaus Copernicus among others. In biology, DNA was first identified in 1860 by Miescher, building on previous work by Mulder accredited with first describing proteins. Miescher's work led to Kossel providing the chemical name DNA, then to Mendel's work on inheritance followed by a wide range of scientists building on previous theory and discoveries before Franklin, Wilkins, Crick, and Watson identified the structure of DNA, leading eventually to work by Sanger and others on DNA sequencing.

There were numerous steps along the way between these major developments in physics and biology by renowned and less well-known scientists, each building on what had gone before. There were and are few rival theories, and each tends to be linked with very large groups of scientists rather than small groups or individuals. In these fields, researchers around the world tend to work on common large problems, using established or novel methodologies to seek solutions on which all might agree. Debates have led to development and extension of previous theory rather than multiple new theories to explain multiple individual phenomena.

Robert H. Logie, Clément Belletier, and Jason M. Doherty, *Integrating Theories of Working Memory* In: *Working Memory.*
Edited by: Robert H. Logie, Valérie Camos, and Nelson Cowan, Oxford University Press (2021). © Oxford University Press.
DOI: 10.1093/oso/9780198842286.003.0014

Table 14.1 Summary responses to assigned questions

Question	Response
1. Definition of working memory (WM)	Our hypothesis is that WM is a collection of domain-specific temporary memory stores and cognitive functions that work in concert to support task performance. Detailed definitions vary according to the research questions and the level of explanation being addressed rather than because of fundamental theoretical differences.
2. Methods	Multiple methods are used to explore converging evidence from different sources. These include cognitive experimental approaches in the laboratory and via the Internet across the healthy human adult lifespan, cognitive assessments of individuals and groups with cognitive impairments following focal brain damage or neurodegenerative disease, brain imaging, and clinical and other applications such as design of digital technologies for human use.
3. Unitary versus non-unitary	This depends on the research question. The multiple stores and functions act in an integrated way in healthy adults. A non-unitary cognitive architecture that is fully integrated with effective lines of communication between cognitive components can function as if it is a unitary system. Specific impairments following brain damage demonstrate that some aspects of cognition can be damaged leaving others intact, providing evidence for a non-unitary system.
4. Attention/control	Control arises from local interactions among multiple components, not from a central controller. Attention refers to processes and representations of which the individual currently is aware and are prioritized, but many cognitive functions are assumed to be outside of awareness, including passive retention of information in domain-specific temporary memory systems.
5. Storage, maintenance, loss	Multiple memory codes may be used to retain representations of stimuli regardless of presentation modality. For example, visually presented words may be retained phonologically, visually as letter/word shape, as word meaning, or as a visual image of the object to which the word refers. Maintenance is passive over one or two seconds, but can be extended by rehearsal. There can be visual and motor as well as verbal rehearsal. Forgetting arises from a combination of decay and interference.
6. Role of long-term memory	Long-term memory is assumed to be activated by sensory input, and it is the products of that activation that are then available within WM. The contents of WM are not raw sensory images, but include links to stored knowledge. Although WM is assumed to be multiple components separate from long-term memory, the cognitive system as a whole contributes to task performance, including episodic and semantic long-term memory, and components of WM that can form novel associations for the performance of any task.
7. Contrary evidence	There are multiple sources of evidence described as contrary to our view. We argue that this challenge is more apparent than real. The components of WM operate in concert to support task performance so can give the impression of a single, domain-general system in healthy adults. Contrary evidence from brain imaging may be difficult to interpret unless it is clear how participants are performing tasks in the scanner. There is no guarantee that domain-specific cognitive functions will directly map on to specific brain structures, and they may reflect different modes of operation of the same network. This remains consistent with a multiple domain-specific cognitive system.

If we were to try to follow the same historical scientific pathway for WM (e.g. Logie, 1996; Logie & Cowan, 2015), we might start with Locke (1690) who referred to 'contemplation' as distinct from the 'storehouse of ideas'. Then William James (1890) referred to 'the specious present' as 'primary memory', distinct from the storehouse of 'secondary memory'. Broadbent (1958) referred to 'immediate memory' coupled with shifting attention. Atkinson and Shiffrin (1968) built on Broadbent's ideas for their proposal of a short-term store coupled with control processes. In this process of building upon previous theoretical work, Baddeley and Hitch (1974) published their empirical exploration of the concept of WM as a verbal short-term store coupled with a central executive. Baddeley (1986) suggested that there might also be a visuospatial store, and this multiple component (MC) theoretical framework dominated research on the topic across Europe, incorporating empirical studies of brain-damaged individuals as well as of healthy individuals from childhood through to late adulthood. The ideas were tested in a wide range of clinical and everyday applications as well as in laboratory studies (for reviews, see Baddeley, 2007; Logie & Morris, 2015; Osaka, Logie, & D'Esposito, 2007). The approach in our own laboratory has built on that body of research.

In parallel, in North America, a range of different approaches to the topic built on the Atkinson and Shiffrin model leading to computational models of cognition that incorporated the concept of WM such as ACT-R (Anderson, 1996), SOAR (Newell, 1990), and EPIC (Meyer & Kieras, 1997). Other conceptual, theoretical frameworks built on studying individual differences in performance on proposed measures of WM capacity (Daneman & Carpenter, 1980; Engle, Kane, & Tuholski, 1999), or viewed WM as the currently activated area of long-term memory plus a limited capacity focus of attention (Cowan, 1988, 1995, 2005, 2019), or as a set of knowledge and highly practised skills comprising expertise in specific domains (e.g. Ericsson & Kintsch, 1995). Subsequent developments were fuelled by use of experimental cognitive, behavioural methods with both healthy and brain-damaged individuals, by rapid expansion in use of brain imaging techniques, by computational modelling, and by mapping of WM function onto functional and structural brain organization, discussed in other chapters of this volume.

In addition to the expansion in diversity of theories and methodologies, there has been an expansion in definitions of WM (Cowan, 2017). For some researchers it is a conceptual, theoretical framework to understand important aspects of cognition, or it is a theory to understand conscious control of behaviour, or it is the overall cognitive capacity of individuals to perform a wide range of everyday and laboratory tasks. For others, it is a network of connections and structures in the brain coupled with temporary activation of those networks, or is a framework for understanding the impact on cognitive function associated with specific brain damage, or it is a set of parameters and processes in a computational model. Finally, there has also been proliferation of empirically observed phenomena and of what might be considered 'micro-theories' for sets of very specific empirical findings (e.g. Oberauer et al., 2018; for commentaries see Logie, 2018; see chapter by Vandierendonck, 2021). This might lead us to question whether there have been genuine advances in knowledge since Watkins' (1984) admonishment of theory proliferation in cognitive psychology. Does this expansion of research volume and fractionation of theory reflect building on what has gone before, or a diaspora of theory and research effort that fuels ever more debates that are never resolved?

We approached the assigned questions from our own conceptual framework that was inspired by Baddeley's (1986; Baddeley & Logie, 1999) proposal of a WM system comprising MCs that work in concert to support task performance. However, our current view differs from Baddeley's in important ways. In summary, control within WM is assumed to arise from local interactions between components each of which fulfils specific functions, and integrated representations arise from those interactions. So there is no central executive which was described as a placeholder for aspects of cognition that had yet to be explored (Baddeley, 1996), but which now might be better described as a set of executive functions (e.g. Hazy, Frank, & O'Reilly, 2006, 2007; Miyake et al., 2000). There is also no episodic buffer (Baddeley, 2000; see chapter by Baddeley, Hitch, & Allen, 2021), the functions of which are assumed to arise from the local interactions between domain-specific components (Logie, 2016).

We discuss whether differences between theories are fundamental or arise from different research questions, or different levels of explanation, or because participants may perform WM tasks using different strategies. In doing so, we offer potential approaches to resolving apparent theoretical differences and a framework for integrated theory development rather than theory fractionation. Responses to the supplementary questions on ageing, individual differences, cognitive neuropsychology, neural correlates, and clinical applications are incorporated within our responses to the assigned questions. There is then a brief section outlining non-clinical applications that have been investigated within a MC framework. Summary responses are presented in Table 14.1.

1. Definition of Working Memory

Our starting point for defining WM is to consider the specific research question being addressed. Most WM researchers agree that it refers to the temporary retention and ongoing processing of information to support moment-to-moment cognition. However, the research question can determine the more precise definition that is assumed for a specific research programme. For most of the research questions in our laboratory, our hypothesis is that WM comprises MCs: a collection of specialized (domain-specific) temporary memory stores and processes that act together in different combinations to meet task demands, drawing on the lifetime of accumulated knowledge and experiences as well as on the capacities and characteristics of each WM component. We further assume that participants may use the components they have available in different combinations for performing the same tasks but in different ways, that is, using different strategies. For example, visually presented shapes and colours might be retained in terms of visual appearance, verbal labels, or their semantic associates. There is no guarantee that a given task will be performed in the same way by different participants, or even the same way by the same participant on different trials (e.g. Logie, Della Sala, Laiacona, Chalmers, & Wynn, 1996; for a discussion see Logie, 2018). For example, there is often reference in the literature to 'a short-term memory task'. However, unless we know how participants are performing the task, this label makes a very strong assumption that might be misleading. Any 'short-term memory task' inevitably relies on knowledge in long-term memory about the stimuli as well as other aspects of cognition, such as language to understand instructions. Few, if any tasks are pure measures of a single conceptual construct or aspect of cognition. Nevertheless, there is a strong, although not universal, tendency in the research literature to develop theories of tasks rather than theories of the cognition that can be used to perform tasks. We will expand on this claim throughout the chapter.

We assume that overall WM capacity is derived from the capacities of the different components and the efficiency with which they can work in concert. When asking research questions about individual differences in WM capacity (see chapter by Mashburn, Tsukahara, & Engle, 2021) the measure derived from the task performance of each individual will reflect the combination of components that they deploy to perform the task or tasks used in the study. The more tasks there are in a given test battery, then the more cognitive components will be deployed that contribute to the overall score and the more complete will be the assessment of the overall mental ability. If the research question is concerned with how overall WM capacity correlates with other measures, such as a score for fluid intelligence, then the extent to which they correlate will be determined by which cognitive components contributed to the WM measure, and which contributed to the tasks used to measure fluid intelligence. It is widely assumed that intelligence is what is measured by intelligence tests (e.g. Boring, 1923; see chapter by Hambrick, Burgoyne, & Araujo, 2021). For example, intelligence might be viewed as the ability to process information to reach sound conclusions, the ability to think effectively in novel situations, or the ability to use whatever information is available to best advantage. It may be misleading to assume that a single score for general fluid intelligence (Gf) that is derived from multiple measures, accurately reflects each of those abilities (Kovacs & Conway, 2016). The same applies to any concept of mental capacity. In particular, WM capacity is what is measured by tasks assumed to measure the capacity of WM, and the choice of tasks will be driven by the assumed definition of the WM concept, that is, whether it is a general mental capacity to retain information in an activated state, or a collection of multiple systems that act in concert. An overall measure of WM capacity will predict performance on academic and life success insofar as the cognitive components required for the WM measures will be helpful for addressing the challenges during an individual's lifetime. Notably different tasks thought to measure WM capacity do not necessarily correlate highly with one another (e.g. Daneman & Hannon, 2007; Kane, Conway, Miura, & Colflesh, 2007; Logie & Duff, 2007; Waters & Caplan, 2003). So, a measure that includes several different measures of WM function would give a more complete assessment of overall WM capacity than any single measure.

If, instead, the research question is concerned with the capacity of the focus of attention (see chapter by Cowan, Morey, & Naveh-Benjamin, 2021), the results from any given experiment will reflect the specific combination of components that are required to function most intensively or at their capacity limits to perform a specific experimental task. This might well be mostly constant across different tasks, and generate data patterns that suggest a single, limited capacity focus of attention, but nevertheless reflect different combinations of components, depending on the task requirements (e.g. Cowan, Saults, & Blume, 2014).

In both of these scenarios, the contributions of different components of WM will be invisible in the patterns of results because the research questions are concerned with observing how the overall cognitive system functions in an integrated fashion to support task performance. However, if the research question is concerned with an investigation into whether there are different components, and if so what they are and how they function individually and in concert, then there is more likelihood that such components will be identified. Whether it is useful to view WM as domain-general cognitive capacity with a focus of attention, or as MCs will depend on the research questions being addressed. So seemingly contrasting theoretical frameworks might be addressing different research questions and different levels of explanation rather than being inherently incompatible.

Our focus is on understanding the characteristics and interactions among a range of different cognitive functions that healthy adult participants have available as a form of 'cognitive toolbox'. This includes memory stores that retain specific kinds of representations that are subject to loss over 2 or 3 seconds, or when displaced by new representations. There can be multiple different forms of representation for the same items. It also includes processes that can act to maintain the contents of each store to prevent decay and to reduce the likelihood of displacement. The maintenance process differs according to each memory store. Overall control arises from the accumulation of local interactions between system components, and not from a central controller. The domain-specific memory stores are largely passive and their contents are not in conscious awareness, but an individual may be aware of individual items when they are retrieved from a store. There is also awareness of some, but not all aspects of executive functions when they are implemented. Our general assumption is that conscious experience is the result of activities in the brain, and not necessarily the cause of those activities. A schematic illustration is shown in Fig. 14.1.

Sensory input is thought to activate stored knowledge in episodic and semantic memory, and then some of that activated knowledge is retained on a temporary basis and processed within a separate, MC WM system. Task performance reflects the use of activated stored knowledge, together with different combinations of the MCs of WM (Logie, 1995, 2003, 2011, 2016, 2018). Temporary binding within a single domain-specific system arises from how representations are formed within that system. For example, the representation of a 'red triangle' may be stored as a combination of the two words within a temporary verbal store, and/or as the visual appearance of the coloured object in a visuospatial store. In addition, there will be activation of semantic and episodic

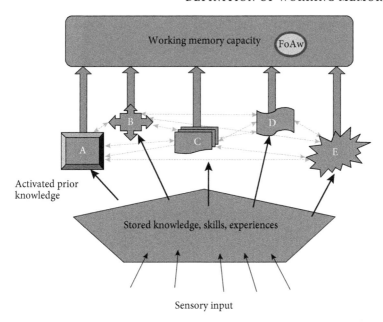

Fig. 14.1 A schematic illustration of a multiple component WM system, developed from Logie (1995, 2003, 2011, 2016, 2018). Sensory input activates stored knowledge, skills, and experiences. The activated information is made available to a range of domain-specific memory systems and cognitive functions in working memory (A to E in the figure). Control within WM (see text and response to Question 4) arises from local interactions (dotted arrows) between domain-specific systems that function in concert in different combinations as required to support task performance. Measures of overall WM capacity assess the cumulative contributions of the interacting domain-specific systems. FoAw = focus of awareness, that refers to conscious experience of current cognitive functions, not as the locus of control.

knowledge associated with red triangles, for example, as road warning signs. Temporary binding between different domain-specific systems and with activated knowledge arises from the local interactions that form temporary links between these systems. Which information is used to support performance in a task will depend on the task require-ments, and participants will produce a pattern of performance that reflects their inter-pretation of how they are expected to respond. So, if the task requires detecting whether a visual feature has changed between a study array and a test array, then the temporary visual representation will be the primary support for performance. If the task requires immediate, serial ordered verbal recall, then the temporary verbal storage system will be the primary source of support for performance, and so on. Moreover, if a task requires participants to remember the precise colour of a previously presented stimulus, there will be support from the temporary visual system, and performance will reflect the pre-cision or accuracy with which the colour is represented. If the task requires retrieval of individual items or objects, then performance will suggest that objects are the basis for the representation. The Focus of Awareness in Fig. 14.1 is thought to reflect conscious experience that may not have direct access to the MCs that work together to support overall WM capacity. The shift in focus of awareness may be driven by a cognitive function component, set by the goals of the current demands on cognition to inhibit some components and activate others for refreshing, task switching, updating, or to have two sets of components running concurrently to perform dual tasks. Dual-task interference then arises from the degree of overlap between the components required for each of two tasks that are performed concurrently.

The hypothesis of a MC WM is difficult to study in healthy adults simply because the components are assumed to function in an integrated fashion and, as such, give the strong impression of being a single system, both in the personal conscious experience of the experimenter, and in observed data patterns. However, the hypothesis of MCs becomes easier to study when attempting to understand very specific cognitive impairments in individuals with very specific brain damage. We will return to this issue when discussing methods in the next section.

An alternative, but related approach asks questions about how a limited capacity attention system is directed to, and swapped between, different cognitive functions, notably in the time-based resource sharing (TBRS) framework for WM (see chapter by Barrouillet & Camos, 2021). However, this can also be seen as entirely compatible with a MC view. Indeed, the most recent version of TBRS incorporates MCs and multiple memory buffers, several of which, such as an articulatory loop for retention and rehearsal of a verbal sequence, map on to components that have been identified within the MC framework (see chapter by Baddeley et al., 2021). A major additional and important feature of TBRS is the detailed exploration and specification of how material is retained within memory buffers other than the articulatory loop. In this sense, TBRS offers a theoretical bridge between levels of explanation.

One view that has been presented as a further alternative eschews the concept of memory and attempts to describe the functions of WM as reflecting links between perception and preparation for action (e.g. Buchsbaum & D'Esposito, 2019; Jones & Macken, 2018). For our theoretical assumptions, it does not matter if what we refer to as a memory buffer can also be described as a sensory input buffer or a motor programme in preparation for output. These concepts can equally be considered respectively as systems for supporting temporary memory after a stimulus has been removed and before a response is generated. Indeed, Buchsbaum and D'Esposito (2019) specifically refer to the concept of a phonological loop, and Postle (2021) in his chapter in this volume refers to representations when expressing support for the perception–action view of WM. It seems difficult to consider what these representations comprise if not some form of temporary memory. We view this argument primarily as a difference in labelling for the different research questions being addressed. If the questions concern the links between sensory input and action, then there may be references to representations that support those links. If we are interested in the nature of the temporary representations, then we call that WM. There are no contemporary views of WM that view it as functioning completely independently of perception and action in the healthy brain. So too, unless actions are completely automated in response to a stimulus, the link between perception and action cannot function in isolation from WM. As we argue in response to designated Questions 2 and 4, the MC view has proved to be particularly useful in the interpretation of specific cognitive impairments following brain damage (e.g. Della Sala & Logie, 1993; Logie & Della Sala, 2005; MacPherson & Della Sala, 2019; Parra, Della Sala, Logie, & Abrahams, 2009; Shallice & Papagno, 2019; see chapters by Baddeley et al., 2021, and Martin, Rapp, & Purcell, 2021). It seems unlikely that a sensory-motor perspective would have generated the same insights or have had the same clinical value (for a discussion see Logie, 2019).

In summary, our core argument is that the definition of WM and the associated theoretical assumptions depend on the research questions being asked, and the level of explanation that drives those research questions. Empirical attempts to demonstrate that there is one 'winning' theoretical framework might not be helpful for advancing understanding, because understanding can function at multiple levels.

2. Describe and Explain the Methods You Use, and Their Strengths and Limitations

Our core methods are cognitive, behavioural experiments, assessing the impact of experimental manipulations on error rates, error types, and response times, in laboratory settings and with data collected via the Internet. We study changes across healthy adult ageing, and as sequelae of focal brain damage (e.g. from stroke or neurosurgery) or neurodegenerative disease, particularly Alzheimer's disease. Some of our work has combined cognitive, behavioural experiments with brain imaging using functional magnetic resonance imaging (fMRI). Our approach is to seek converging evidence from different sources using different methods. The disadvantage is that collating evidence from a range of different sources is challenging and time-consuming. This is particularly true for collecting data from special groups such as individuals with Alzheimer's disease or with more focal brain damage resulting in specific verbal or visual short-term memory impairments. As is often the case for research on any special group, this approach depends on collaboration with researchers who have access to the relevant participants (for reviews, see Della Sala & Logie, 1993; Logie & Della Sala, 2005; Logie et al., 2015; Shallice & Papagno, 2019).

Experimental Methods for Multiple Components: An Example

One example of our use of experimental techniques to explore the MC hypothesis in healthy young adults was reported by Saito, Logie, Morita, and Law (2008). In immediate verbal serial recall, it is well established that participants show poorer performance when items to be recalled are phonologically similar than when they are phonologically distinct, even when the items are presented visually (Conrad, 1964). This suggests that participants form phonological representations from the visually, as well as from aurally presented verbal items. However, participants may also store information about the visual appearance of the items, and there is evidence of poorer performance for visually similar than for visually distinct items (e.g. Connor & Hoyer, 1976; Logie, Della Sala, Wynn, & Baddeley, 2000; Logie, Saito, Morita, Varma, & Norris, 2016). Saito et al. (2008) explored whether both visual similarity effects and phonological similarity effects might appear at the same time, with written recall of a visually presented list. This would indicate that both visual and phonological codes support immediate serial recall of visually presented verbal lists. It is very difficult factorially to manipulate phonological and visual similarity in English, but is easier with Japanese kanji. Japanese participants were visually presented with sequences of six kanji characters for immediate, written, serial recall. There were four sets of kanji in which the visual similarity and phonological similarity of the materials were manipulated.

Fig. 14.2 shows the results from one of the Saito et al. (2008) experiments. It is clear that there were effects both of phonological similarity and visual similarity, consistent with the interpretation that participants encoded both the visual appearance of the kanji characters and their phonological representations, and both types of code contributed to recall performance. There was no interaction, suggesting that these effects are independent. We discuss further how information is encoded in WM in response to designated Question 5.

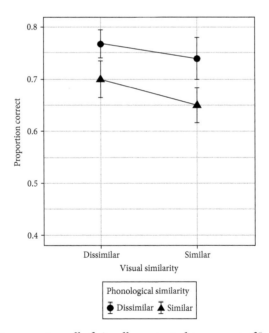

Fig. 14.2 Proportion correct recall of visually presented sequences of Japanese kanji characters varying in phonological and visual similarity.

Data from Saito, S., Logie, R.H., Morita, A. & Law, A. 'Visual and phonological similarity effects in verbal immediate serial recall: A test with kanji materials', *Journal of Memory and Language*, 59, pp. 1–17, 2008.

Internet Data Collection

Our use of the Internet has facilitated collection of data from very large numbers of participants, many of whom would not normally volunteer to come into a psychology laboratory. Johnson, Logie, and Brockmole (2010) reported data from over 95,000 participants collected via the Internet, whereas Maylor and Logie (2010) reported data on prospective and retrospective memory from over 318,000 participants. These large numbers were possible because the study was conducted in collaboration with and promoted by the British Broadcasting Corporation (BBC).[1] These data required careful scrutiny to ensure that they were of high quality and not subject to artefacts associated with the method of data collection. For example, we compared the patterns of data collected over the Internet with data collected from the same experiments conducted in a laboratory setting. The very large dataset allowed us to answer questions that would be difficult to address with much smaller laboratory-based samples alone. Fig. 14.3 shows Z-scores from 111,188 of these participants on five different WM tests. These comprised recall by reconstruction of the colour, shape (e.g. square, circle, triangle), and location of up to four objects shown in arrays (feature binding), typed serial recall of visually presented digit sequences (digit span), recall of visual square matrix patterns (visual pattern span), recall of the final words from a series of simple sentences with true/false judgements for each (WM sentence span), and deciding on whether a human figure presented in different orientations held a ball in their left or right hand (spatial orientation).

From Fig. 14.3 it is clear that the age-related trajectories during child development look very similar, but the trajectories across adult ageing look dramatically different. The peak level of performance is around 20 years, but performance on visual pattern span, and visual feature binding decline throughout adulthood. WM sentence span and spatial orientation also decline during adulthood but less dramatically. In contrast, digit span remains stable during adulthood, and only starts to decline from around the age of 65 years onwards. These results suggest that the cognitive functions required to perform each of these tasks decline at very different rates across adult ageing. This pattern of results is highly consistent with multiple cognitive functions contributing to task performance, but with the functions that are most important for remembering visual material declining much more rapidly with age than do other functions. However, the cognitive functions for digit span are preserved throughout most of adulthood.

Johnson et al. (2010) carried out additional analyses to consider the concept of measurement invariance. That is, did the pattern of variance across tests and across individuals change according the age of the participants? What Johnson et al. (2010) found was that among young adults, the visual pattern span had more task-specific variance and digit span had more common variance with other tests. The analysis showed the opposite pattern for older participants, with more common

[1] The full set of data from over 408,000 participants is available via a link at http://womaac.psy.ed.ac.uk/.

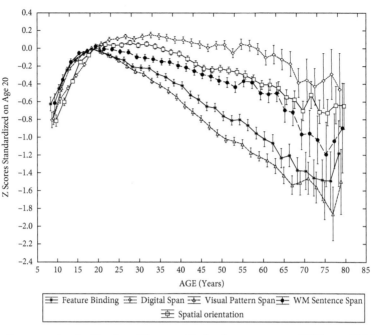

Fig. 14.3 Z-scores standardized on 20-year-olds for five measures of different WM functions collected via the Internet from 111,188 participants aged 8–80 years.

Reproduced from Logie, R.H., Horne, M.J. & Pettit, L.D., 'When cognitive performance does not decline across the lifespan', in Robert H. Logie and Robin G. Morris, *Working Memory and Ageing*, p. 25, Figure 2.1 Copyright © 2015 Psychology Press.

variance for visual pattern span and more task-specific variance for digit span. These results (Fig. 14.4) suggested that younger participants appeared to be relying more on domain-specific cognitive resources for the visual pattern task, and more on domain-general resources for digit span. Conversely, older participants were relying more on domain-general resources for visual pattern span and more on domain-specific resources for digit span. In other words, the older and the younger participants were attempting to perform the tasks in different ways. So, as argued earlier, we cannot assume that different individuals will perform the same task in the same way, and may choose different combinations of cognitive functions to do so (Logie, 2018).

It is difficult to interpret these results in terms of a single, domain-general WM that depends on a limited capacity focus of attention, such as argued in the chapter by Cowan et al. (2021). If this were the case, we might expect performance on the most attention-demanding tasks to decline most rapidly with age, but it is difficult to argue in advance of seeing the data, that remembering square matrix patterns is more attention demanding than WM sentence span. For example, several variations of this last measure have been shown to correlate highly with Gf. The domain-general view could only account for these results by claiming post hoc that the tasks showing the greatest age-related decline were those that are most attention-demanding. However, this argument is entirely circular and so not convincing.

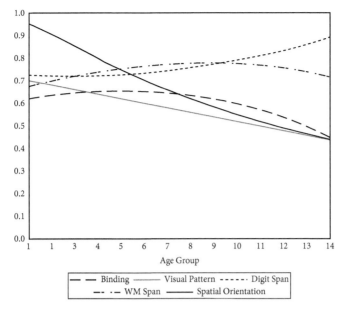

Fig. 14.4 Residual variances from fitted regression lines for 95,199 participants across five WM tests and 14 age groups. Age Group 1 = 18–20 years, with other groups in 5-year age bands, for example, Group 2 = 21–25 years and so on to Group 13 = 75–79 years.

Reproduced from Wendy Johnson, Robert H. Logie, and James R. Brockmole, 'Working memory tasks differ in factor structure across age cohorts: Implications for dedifferentiation', *Intelligence*, 38 (5), pp. 513–528, Figure 2. https://doi.org/10.1016/j.intell.2010.06.005 Copyright © 2010 Elsevier Inc. All rights reserved.

Finally, because of the large numbers of participants, age was a continuous, not a grouping variable, so the data suggest continuous, but differential age-related trajectories across different cognitive abilities required to perform each of the five tasks.

Brain Imaging

We would argue that brain imaging techniques can only be used to confirm a cognitive theory, not to refute it (Coltheart, 2006, 2013). There is no guarantee that a psychological, cognitive concept that is effective for predicting and explaining behavioural data patterns in healthy and brain-damaged individuals will map directly onto the organization or structure of neurobiology. A cognitive concept (domain-specific system) could reflect a specific mode of operation of a network in the brain, or a specific combination of brain structures and the interaction among them (see chapter by Wijeakumar & Spencer, 2021). The neurobiological principles that govern activation of a set of synaptic connections will be very different from the neurobiological principles that govern the formation of new synaptic connections, and each set of principles of the biological function could be compromised differentially by different forms of brain damage or dysfunction and map on to conceptually different cognitive constructs. For example, epilepsy disrupts electrical activation (e.g. Nair & Szaflarski, 2020), Alzheimer's disease comprom- ises white matter connectivity or conductivity through degrading of the myelin sheath around nerve cells (e.g. Charlton & Morris, 2015), and a stroke may damage a key structure in a network of structures that support a particular cognitive func- tion (see chapter by Martin et al., 2021). So, suggesting that WM is activated long- term memory is actually no different from saying that WM and long-term memory reflect different neurobiological mechanisms, and so are theoretically distinct at a cognitive level of explanation. That is, brain activation patterns and understanding of the neurobiology need not constrain the development of conceptual theories of cognition (e.g. Coltheart, 2006, 2013; Page, 2006).

We would argue further that brain activation patterns derived from performance of the cognitive task in a scanner can only be interpretable with respect to a cogni- tive theory if there is a clear understanding of how participants are performing tasks in the scanner (Logie, Pernet, Buonocore, & Della Sala, 2011; Logie, Venneri, Della Sala, Redpath, & Marshall, 2003; Zacks, 2008). Given our arguments that different par- ticipants might perform any given cognitive task in different ways, it is essential that there is clear behavioural evidence for how each participant is performing a task be- fore attempting to interpret the results from a brain imaging study, regardless of the technique for recording neural correlates. Without such an understanding of the cog- nition involved, then any interpretation is highly speculative, and could be extremely misleading.

Variability in how each participant attempts to perform a task raises the possibility that using aggregate data across participants might not reflect the neural correlates as- sociated with a given task for any one participant. The aggregate data give an average pattern of results for a task, and do not necessarily reflect the different networks that might be deployed to perform the task in different ways. For example, in a meta- analysis of brain imaging studies of mental rotation, Zacks (2008) noted inconsistency in patterns of brain activation across studies, and reported that virtually every area of the brain had been shown to be involved. This lack of replicability across studies could arise from different protocols for the brain imaging, different methods of analyses, or different participants in different laboratories performing mental rotation in different ways, that is, using different brain networks to perform the same task (for a similar ar- gument, see Sanfratello et al., 2014).

One of our own brain imaging studies followed up on Zacks (2008). Logie, Pernet, et al. (2011) selected two groups of participants who scored respectively high or low on the Vividness of Visual Imagery Questionnaire (Marks, 1973, 1995). These two groups then performed mental rotation in fMRI, deciding whether pairs of depicted three- dimensional block figures (Shepard & Metzler, 1971) were identical or not, and the angle of rotation between the items in each pair varied from 20° to 140°. The patterns of fMRI blood oxygen level-dependent (BOLD) responses are shown in Fig. 14.5 for contrasts between the two groups and across different angles of rotation. It is clear from the figure, that although there was some overlap in the activation patterns for the two groups, there were also striking differences, suggesting that different, but overlapping

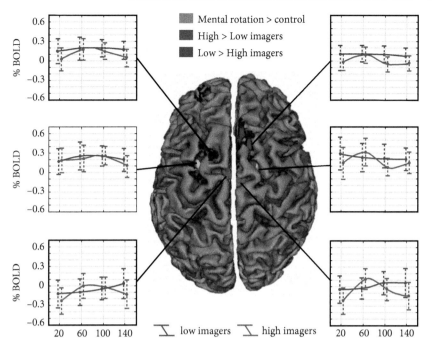

Fig. 14.5 Percentage of BOLD variation for each rotation angle (20°, 60°, 100°, 140°) relative to 0° control condition for low (blue), and high (red) imagers. Dashed lines show 95% confidence intervals.

networks were being used by the two groups, and that the two groups were attempting to perform the mental rotation task in different ways.

The conclusion from the contrasts in BOLD responses was reinforced by group differences in behavioural data. Fig. 14.6 shows the accuracy and correct response times for the high-imagery and low-imagery groups. From the figure it is clear that the patterns for the two groups look very different.

An Example From Neuropsychology

Zeman et al. (2010) described the case of MX, aged 65 years, who lost his ability to experience mental imagery that he had used throughout his personal and professional life as a building surveyor. He rated himself as experiencing almost no imagery on standard questionnaires, yet performed normally on standard tests of perception and visual memory. However, when tested with mental rotation MX showed a complete lack of the increase in response time with increasing angle of rotation that is typical of healthy individuals (e.g. Fig. 14.6 for high imagers), with no change in response time between

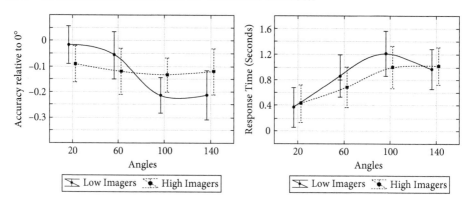

Fig. 14.6 Mean percentage accuracy relative to 0° control and mean accurate response time for each rotation angle (20°, 60°, 100°, 140°) for high imagers (dashed line) and low imagers (solid line). Error bars represent 95% confidence intervals.

Reproduced from Robert H. Logie, Cyril R. Pernet, Antimo Buonocore, and Sergio Della Sala, 'Low and high imagers activate networks differentially in mental rotation', *Neuropsychologia*, 49 (11), pp. 3071–3077, Figure 1. https://doi.org/10.1016/j.neuropsychologia.2011.07.011 Copyright © 2011 Elsevier Ltd. All rights reserved.

40° and 180°. The typical healthy adult response time pattern was shown by healthy control participants matched with MX on age and occupation, and controls generated more errors on the task than did MX. He reported that he was performing the task by perceptual comparisons, and that he had no mental experience of visual imagery. That is, his impairment was specific to the use of visual imagery, but his visual perception, visual short-term memory, and other cognitive abilities were all intact. These results illustrate one of our core arguments, that individuals may perform the same task in different ways, using different combinations of WM. In the case of individuals with specific brain damage, they can use the components of WM that remain intact to perform tasks in a different way from healthy controls, using different strategies that are supported by brain networks unaffected by the damage.

Summary on Methodologies

Taken together, the example studies previously described provide converging evidence using different approaches and methodologies to ask the general question whether WM function, and cognitive function more generally, is supported by multiple domain-specific resources that can be used in different combinations to support task performance. We have described only a small number of example studies to illustrate the use of each methodology. We describe additional studies in response to the other assigned questions in the following sections. However, the accumulated evidence from these different approaches has all been consistent with the MC view. The major advantage from using multiple methods, is that we do not rely on a single paradigm or method, and if the same theoretical framework can account for evidence from a range of different sources, using a range of different methodologies, this gives us more confidence in the adequacy of that framework for the level of explanation that we have attempted to address.

3. Unitary Versus Non-Unitary Nature of Working Memory

We have found that the account that most readily incorporates the broad range of findings from multiple approaches and methods is offered by viewing WM as comprising a range of cognitive functions, each with different characteristics, that act together to support moment to moment cognition. This theoretical perspective also has advantages for clinical application. If we assume that there are multiple cognitive functions in the healthy brain, then we can expect that any one or any combination of those functions may be impaired by brain damage, while other functions remain intact. This allows identification of the pattern of cognitive impairment and sparing in each individual with neurological damage. Therefore, professional clinical and carer support may be targeted to support the impairment by capitalizing on identifying what remains unimpaired. This can be invaluable for managing the impairments day to day, and can offer an assessment of whether clinical interventions are reducing the impact of the impairment (e.g. Logie et al., 2015). If an individual is found to have a specific verbal short-term memory deficit, they may be taught to use their intact visuospatial abilities, and to acquire new cognitive skills and strategies that can allow them to circumvent their impairment (e.g. Haslam & Kessels, 2018; Wilson, 1987). A similar approach has been taken to understand the development of cognitive strategies and recruitment of additional networks in the brain to compensate for age-related decline in cognition (e.g. Baltes & Baltes, 1990; Park & Reuter-Lorenz, 2009).

Participants may respond in different ways depending on task requirements, and to compensate for cognitive impairments. Because these different cognitive functions act in concert, and rarely in isolation, then there are few, if any, cognitive tasks that are pure measures of a single function. The vast majority of cognitive tasks used in laboratory experiments will require the use of several functions within WM. Therefore, performance patterns on any given task may give the impression of a unified system (WM capacity in Fig. 14.1), and evidence for a unified system does not undermine the view that overall capacity of WM arises from multiple systems acting in concert. Nor does the concept of multiple systems undermine the value of viewing WM at the level of explanation of a unified system.

4. The Role of Attention and Control

Control within our theoretical framework arises from the accumulation of local interactions between components of WM that are recruited for any given task. As illustrated in Fig. 14.1, there is no assumption of a central controller or central executive, and temporary binding between different sources of information arises from the accumulation of these local interactions. This concept of 'self-organizing systems' without a central controller (e.g. Willshaw, 2006) has been shown to account for the coordinated action of colonies of insects through to groups of baboons (e.g. Eisenreich, Akaishi, & Hayden, 2017), and has been a long-standing principle for understanding social organization among humans such as the behaviour of crowds (e.g. Morgan, 1986). Recently, self-organizing principles have been applied to control within the 'Internet of things' (e.g. Nascimento, & Lucena, 2017), a development for domestic technology that does not lend itself to centralized control.

A major advantage of this form of distributed control is graceful degradation in response to damage. With a centralized control system, if the control component is damaged, the rest of the system cannot function. With distributed control, only the damaged components are affected while the rest of the system can function, even if its overall efficiency is degraded. When the brain is damaged, there is rarely catastrophic and complete loss of control unless the damage is very extensive or results in coma or death. This is true even when the damage is in areas of the brain that have been identified with cognitive control or control of attention such as the prefrontal cortex (e.g. Stuss, 2011). The impairments tend to affect a specific set of cognitive functions. For example, there can be severe impairments of episodic memory without a noticeable impact on language, and with largely intact ability to retain information over short periods of time. There are many such cases in the literature (for reviews, see MacPherson & Della Sala, 2019), but the best known is patient HM (Scoville & Milner, 1957) who suffered a dense anterograde amnesia as a result of damage to the hippocampi from surgery intended to control epilepsy. Yet, he had intact WM function. A more recent case, JB (Baddeley, Allen, & Vargha-Khadem, 2009), had hippocampal damage from infancy, and as an adult his long-term memory impairment contrasted sharply with his intact WM ability. These patients have impairments in retaining new information for more than a few minutes, but there is not catastrophic loss of cognitive control.

Damage to the frontal lobes is often associated with what has been referred to as the 'dysexecutive syndrome' in which there is loss of the ability to form and implement plans, suggesting a loss of 'executive control'. However, it is worth noting that the frontal lobes comprise a very large proportion of the brain, and damage to this area also damages the connectivity with other brain areas. So any cognitive function that, for example, relies on a network involving connections between the frontal lobes and other brain networks will be impaired by frontal lobe damage (e.g. Tullberg et al., 2004). In other words, it could be very misleading to suggest that any one area of the brain is associated with a specific cognitive concept such as executive function. Moreover, tests of so-called frontal lobe function in healthy adults often show small positive correlations, and not all so-called frontal functions are disrupted by frontal lobe damage (for reviews, see Duncan, 2005; Rabbitt, 2005).

Within WM, there are multiple cases of individuals with specific impairments in their ability to retain verbal sequences, with intact ability to retain sequences of movement, or the appearance of visual patterns (for reviews, see Della Sala & Logie, 1993;

Vallar & Shallice, 1990). Moreover, such patients show severely impaired immediate serial-ordered verbal recall when lists are presented aurally, and performance is often too poor (span of one or two items) to detect phonological similarity effects (Wang, Logie, & Jarrold, 2016). However, they show much better verbal recall for visually presented lists (e.g. Basso, Spinnler, Vallar, & Zanobio, 1982; Tree & Playfoot, 2019; Warrington & Shallice, 1972; Vallar, 2019; for a review, see Shallice & Papagno, 2019). Other patients have been described with intact episodic memory and verbal short-term memory, but with impaired ability to retain visual and/or spatial information for short periods (e.g. De Renzi & Nichelli, 1975; Hanley & Young, 2019; Hanley, Young, & Pearson, 1991; Parra, Della Sala, et al., 2009; Warrington & Rabin, 1971; for reviews, see Logie, 1995; Logie & Della Sala, 2005). In all these cases, the patients have largely intact episodic long-term memory for both new and previous experiences, as well as unimpaired access to acquired knowledge and experiences, and there is no indication of a major loss of cognitive control.

In the cases of brain damage cited thus far, the damage is typically very localized to an identified brain area or structure, and the impairments are quite specific. In the case of neurodegenerative disease, and in particular Alzheimer's disease, the damage is more widespread, and spreads further as the disease progresses. In most cases, the initial damage is in the temporal cortex, associated with episodic memory impairments, although prefrontal areas and the occipital cortex can also be affected in some patients. Patients with this form of more widespread and progressive damage offer the opportunity to investigate more severe loss of cognitive control. Insights from such investigations may also have clinical value for everyday management of the cognitive impairments associated with the disease.

Some early research on WM impairments in individuals in the relatively early stages of the disease showed that they had digit spans that were slightly lower than expected for their age, but not dramatically so (Baddeley, Logie, Bressi, Della Sala, & Spinnler, 1986; Morris, 1986; Morris & Baddeley, 1988), indicating that their verbal short-term memory was only minimally impaired. However, when asked to perform digit recall while tracking a moving target around the computer screen, individuals with Alzheimer's disease showed a very substantial drop in performance of around 40–45% compared with performing either task on its own. In contrast, healthy older and younger individuals showed a 15–20% drop when performing tracking together with digit recall (Baddeley et al., 1986). This dual-task impairment became more marked as the disease progressed (Baddeley, Bressi, Della Sala, Logie, & Spinnler, 1991). In a later study (Logie, Cocchini, Della Sala, & Baddeley, 2004), Alzheimer patients showed this dual-task impairment even when the demands of digit recall and of tracking were set at very easy levels (Fig. 14.7, centre plot). Crucially, the size of this dual-task impairment did not change as the demands of each task increased above their span. There was a clear main effect of dual task in the Alzheimer group relative to the healthy older and younger participants, but no interaction between group and increasing demand of the tasks. The left plot in Fig. 14.7 shows identical decline for all three groups in single-task tracking performance with increased tracking speed. The right plot shows that when tracking speed was fixed, changing the length of the concurrent digit sequences for recall did not affect tracking performance. Similar results were found for digit recall although the main effect of group was less clear.

The finding of a specific dual-task performance impairment in patients with Alzheimer's disease has been replicated in multiple other studies (e.g. Della Sala, Baddeley, Papagno, & Spinnler, 1995; Della Sala, Cocchini, Logie, & MacPherson, 2010; Holtzer, Burright, & Donovick, 2004; Kaschel, Logie, Kazén, & Della Sala, 2009; MacPherson, Della Sala, Logie, & Willcock, 2007; Sebastian, Menor, & Elosua, 2006). These results suggest a specific impairment in carrying out two tasks at the same time, and that this impairment was not driven by overall task demand. This further suggested that performing two tasks concurrently might reflect a specific ability in healthy adults that is independent of the ability to perform single tasks as task demand increases, and which appears relatively intact in Alzheimer's disease.

The ability to perform two tasks concurrently could be identified as one of several executive functions. Perry and Hodges (1999) review evidence for deficits in switching and dual task in Alzheimer's disease, but note that sustained attention is relatively well preserved (Baddeley, Cocchini, Della Sala, Logie, & Spinnler, 1999). Crawford et al. (2005) reported Alzheimer-related impairments in inhibitory control. More recently, several studies have demonstrated that Alzheimer patients have a specific deficit in temporary memory for colour–shape feature binding, but have relatively intact ability to retain individual colours or shapes (e.g. Logie et al., 2015; Parra, Abrahams, et al., 2009; Parra et al., 2010). One hypothesis is that performing two tasks concurrently, or temporary binding of colours and shapes, requires communication between different

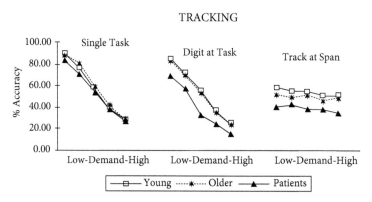

TRACKING

Fig. 14.7 Percentage time on target below, at, and above span with younger and older healthy participants and Alzheimer patients for perceptuo-motor tracking as a single task, when combined with digit recall at span, or with tracking speed fixed and digit sequence length increased.

components of the cognitive system more so than does performing a single task or temporary retention of single visual features. There is considerable evidence that the white matter tracts in the brain that serve to transmit signals between different brain structures are severely compromised by the disease, and this has been clearly linked with cognitive decline (e.g. Charlton & Morris, 2015), offering support for the suggestion that a major problem in Alzheimer's disease is the interaction between different cognitive systems.

The results from the Alzheimer studies demonstrate that not all executive functions are impaired, at least in the early stages of the disease. Moreover, there is not catastrophic failure of the cognitive system, with some functions remaining relatively intact such as sustained attention and coping with increased cognitive demand, as well as immediate memory for single-digit sequences and individual visual features such as colours. This offers evidence for our earlier argument that there is a range of different executive functions as well as domain-specific temporary memory systems in the healthy brain, and that some executive functions rely on intact communication between domain-specific systems. It also illustrates that there is not a single overall controlling mechanism, damage to which would cause complete breakdown of the whole system. It is clear that as the disease progresses, there is indeed overall breakdown in control, but this is a gradual process. Complete loss of control only occurs when the disease is very advanced, so that most of the brain is affected, and the individual is close to the end of their life.

From these differential patterns of impairment and sparing, it is clear that the cognitive impact of brain damage can be very specific, and cannot readily be explained in terms of impaired control of general attention or of a domain-general central executive.

At a theoretical level, the assumption of distributed control avoids the need to assume an ill-defined homunculus as a central controller, or the logical problem that arises when considering what controls the homunculus, what controls that controller and so on ad infinitum (Hazy et al., 2006, 2007; Logie, 2016). Subjective mental experience may suggest centralized control closely linked with consciousness. However, as noted by Pylyshyn (1973), not all that is functional in cognition is necessarily conscious, and what is experienced in consciousness does not necessarily reflect what is functional in cognition. So, it is possible that what we experience are those components of a distributed control system that are core to the current task, with other components functioning to support task performance but not at a level that enters conscious awareness.

5. Storage, Maintenance, and Loss of Information in Working Memory

Information from sensory input activates stored knowledge related to the stimulus, and so multiple codes are generated from any given stimulus, with different levels of activation for each type of code. Activated codes are held in modality-specific passive temporary stores in addition to their activation in long-term memory, and loss from those stores is assumed to result from decay over a few seconds of activated long-term memory and from disruption by new material displacing the previous content in the passive stores (Logie, Brockmole, & Vandenbroucke, 2009; Shimi and Logie, 2019; see responses to Question 6). Both decay and interference are assumed to drive forgetting, but from different systems that support temporary memory. However, the modality of input does not guarantee that a specific code will be the most highly activated, and what representations are held in the passive stores will depend on the components of cognition that the participant deploys to support task performance as well as from the requirements of the task. For example, a visually presented word will activate visual, phonological, lexical, and semantic information. The visual information may be a mental visual image depicting an object or scene, or it could be a visual representation of the shapes of the letters in the word held in a passive visual store. The phonological information is held in a passive phonological store. Forgetting may be prevented by rehearsing the phonological code, or by reactivating a visual image or codes in the passive visual store. An action sequence or pathway may be rehearsed by repeatedly imagining the movement sequence (Logie, 1995; 2011; Logie & Della Sala, 2005).

As noted earlier, a visually presented word list tends to be encoded phonologically, and this code dominates retention and recall (Conrad, 1964). However, as noted in response to Question 2, more recent studies have shown that participants form both visual codes for the letter/word shape and phonological codes for visually presented word lists in serial recall tasks (Logie et al., 2000, 2016; Saito et al., 2008). In contrast, we have also known for a long time that if the task is to recall longer lists without regard to their serial order of presentation, both a verbal code and a visual image of the meaning of each word can support recall (e.g. Paivio, 1971; Paivio & Csapo, 1969). There is also evidence for visual representations of letters and words, as well as visual images of named objects and their locations when attempting to retain and recall aurally presented verbal material and verbal descriptions of spatial layouts of objects (e.g. Borst, Niven, & Logie, 2012; Brooks, 1967; Della Sala, Logie, Beschin, & Denis, 2004).

In a similar fashion, it was established some time ago that non-verbal material presented visually, such as shapes, colours, pictures, square matrix patterns, or abstract shapes, results in a range of codes including visual appearance of the stimuli, associated verbal labels or a verbal description, semantic associates, or visual mental images (e.g. Brandimonte, Hitch, & Bishop, 1992; Broadbent & Broadbent, 1981; Brown, Forbes, & McConnell, 2006; Logie, 1996; Paivio, 1971; Schooler, & Engstler-Schooler, 1990; for reviews, see Cornoldi, Logie, Brandimonte, Kaufman, & Reisberg, 1996).

In other words, which codes are used as the basis for encoding, retention, retrieval, and report of material will depend on the task requirements and how participants choose to perform a task, not on the modality of presentation.

6. The Role of Long-Term Memory Knowledge in Working Memory Storage and Processing

Within our theoretical framework, episodic and semantic memory, both declarative and procedural, contribute to any WM task in addition to the various components of WM. Early work by Hulme, Maughan, and Brown (1991) and Hulme, Roodenrys, Brown, and Mercer (1995) reported evidence that immediate memory for a short list of familiar words in a memory span task is better than memory for unfamiliar words or non-words. Baddeley, Hitch, & Allen (2009) showed that participants could re-call many more words in a meaningful sentence than they could recall from a list of random words. These findings strongly suggest that lexical, syntactic, and semantic memory contribute to a simple memory span task, in addition to the phonological and visual codes.

The fact that healthy participants can recall a random verbal list in sequential order has been shown in a very large number of studies since the late nineteenth century (Jacobs, 1887). This demonstrates that procedural knowledge about what it means to recall in serial order also contributes to memory span. Other evidence comes from studies demonstrating that within a domain of expertise, substantially more informa-tion can be retained than is widely assumed to be within the capacity of WM (Ericsson, 2014; Ericsson et al., 2017; see chapter by Hambrick et al., 2021). Some of the best known findings have arisen from studies of expert chess players who can retain details of multiple chess positions based on storage in long-term memory (e.g. Charness, 1976; Saariluoma, 1989). There is also the classic study of Steve Faloon (Ericsson, Chase & Faloon, 1980) who started with an average memory span of seven, but learned to use his knowledge of athletics to group short sequences of numbers, eventually being able to recall 80 random digits. The current world record of 4620 digits memorized in 1 hour was achieved during the World Memory Championships in 2019 by Ryo Song I of North Korea. However, these skills are specific to the domain of expertise and do not generalize to other aspects of memory ability. This expertise effect on memory has been shown in a wide range of domains, including remembering dinner orders (Ericsson & Polson, 1988) and soccer scores (P. E. Morris, Tweedy, & Gruneberg, 1985), and even in burglars remembering burglary-related details of houses (Logie, Wright, & Decker, 1992; Wright, Logie, & Decker, 1995).

Our core assumption in response to this question is that WM serves to hold novel information long enough to form new associations. For example, the finding that par-ticipants can recall non-words and retain abstract patterns, even if at a relatively low level of performance (e.g. Broadbent & Broadbent, 1981; Della Sala, Gray, Baddeley, Allamano, & Wilson, 1999; Phillips & Christie, 1977) suggests that performance on these tasks cannot rely solely on activated knowledge in semantic or episodic memory. The initial activation of representations of the sensory characteristics of these novel stimuli may be held in WM while there is additional activation of some relevant, but limited prior knowledge about the likely pronunciation of a non-word, or of familiar shapes that might resemble a presented abstract pattern. So WM can support new learning, and can form new associations between apparently disconnected aspects of existing knowledge (e.g. Cornoldi et al., 1996; Helstrup & Logie, 1999; see also chapter by Barrouillet & Camos, 2021).

In addition, WM can hold information on a temporary basis until a current task is complete, when new information replaces the contents of WM. Here, the assumption is that there is no residual trace of what was previously held in WM. For example, Logie et al. (2009) demonstrated that participants could be shown exactly the same array of six coloured shapes on 60 trials for detecting a swap in colour and shape in a test array, and yet fail to learn the array, with performance at around 75% at the end and the start of the experiment (equivalent to remembering four of the six items). Shimi and Logie (2019) showed a small improvement in performance when the same six-item array was presented on every one of 120 trials. However, with four-item arrays, they were close to ceiling performance from trial 1, suggesting a WM system with a capacity of four items, allowing almost perfect performance on every trial. However, when six item arrays were presented, this was beyond the capacity of the temporary visual passive store, but that around four of the six items in the array could be retained. The lack of learning with repeated presentation suggested that the contents of the store were over-written when the array for the next trial was presented, and there was no residual trace in the passive store from one trial to the next. This conclusion was supported by the lack of a build-up of proactive interference across trials in another experiment in which the target array occurred only on every third trial, and the interpretation accounts for the lack of learning in Logie et al. (2009). The very slow learning with 120 repetitions of the same six-item array in Shimi and Logie (2019) suggested that, in addition to temporary representation in a passive visual store, there was a weak episodic trace from trial to trial that could support learning, but at a very slow rate. In contrast, when participants were asked to recall the names of the colour–shape combinations in response to a location cue (Logie et al., 2009), or were asked to reconstruct colour–shape–location combinations (Shimi & Logie, 2019), learning was rapid and substantial. Being required to reproduce (recall) the items in the repeated visual array led to learning whereas detecting changes in the repeated array did not. This is consistent with research showing that recalling recently presented information enhances learning, whereas repeated presentation of information does not (e.g. Karpicke & Roediger, 2008; Thomas, Weywadt, Anderson, Martinez-Papponi, & McDaniel, 2018).

In summary, WM can hold on to a small amount of new information, and its contents can also be updated moment to moment. When assessing performance on a task, there are multiple contributions, from episodic and semantic memory as well as from several WM components, and it is the combination of these various contributions that results in overall performance.

7. Is There Evidence That Is Not Consistent with Your Theoretical Framework, and How Does Your Framework Address That Inconsistency?

There are multiple studies suggesting inconsistency with the MC framework. These are reviewed in detail in several of the other chapters in this volume. The general argument from these other studies is that WM is limited by general attention. For Cowan et al. (2021), this is a limited capacity focus of attention that can hold approximately four items. For Barrouillet and Camos (2021), this is a limitation on how long attention can be focused on refreshing the contents of WM when there are other tasks to complete, with attention switching between concurrent tasks and memory refreshing.

Cowan et al. (2021) review evidence that when the capacity of the assumed focus of attention is exceeded, performance is impaired, and this occurs regardless of whether the stimuli for retention are, or are not in the same presentation modality. Whether disruption of performance occurs is determined by the extent to which the demands on attention exceed its capacity. The MC framework addresses this kind of evidence by noting that there are both domain-general and domain-specific effects (Baddeley, 1986; Baddeley & Hitch, 1974; Baddeley & Logie, 1999; Endress, 2019; Logie, 1995; Logie et al., 1990). For example, there are several studies showing that when two demands on WM come from different domains, e.g. remembering a visual pattern concurrent with an aurally presented random list of numbers, there is disruption of performance but that disruption is much smaller than when the two demands come from the same domain, such as remembering a visual pattern while tracking a randomly moving object or undertaking visual processing (Cocchini, Logie, Della Sala, & MacPherson, 2002; see also Allen, Marcell, & Anderson, 1978; Farmer, Berman, & Fletcher, 1986; Logie, Zucco, & Baddeley, 1990; Tresch, Sinnamon, & Seamon, 1993; see reviews in Logie, 1995, 2003, 2011). As noted earlier, no given task requires only one component of the cognitive system. Therefore, the smaller amount of disruption from combining tasks thought to be from different domains, could be explained by overlap in the components, and potentially the underlying networks in the brain (Nijboer, Borst, van Rijn, & Taatgen, 2014) required for each task. For example, in Cocchini et al. (2002), participants might have relied partly on verbal labels for remembering matrix patterns (e.g. Broadbent & Broadbent, 1981; Brown et al., 2006) in addition to a visual representation. This partial use of verbal representations would then interfere with the verbal codes for the number list.

Each component within the MC cognitive system is thought to have its own domain-specific capacity. The more demanding the task, the more components of cognition will be involved. If a task depends heavily on a given component, and the capacity of that component is exceeded, other components may support performance. If those other components might be required for some other concurrent task, then overall performance is compromised. An illustration of this comes from a study by Doherty and Logie (2016) who investigated the effects of titrating task demands on dual-task costs to memory span. They found that if the demand of a visuospatial processing task was set according to each participant's individually measured span, then participants' dual-task memory spans were no different from single-task spans. They also found that processing accuracy was affected only when the demand of the memory task exceeded participants' span, suggesting that participants were able to maintain memory items (digit sequences) along with visuospatial processing so long as the demands of both tasks were set according to each participant's single-task ability.

In a follow up study, Doherty (2016—Experiment 5) showed participants a random letter sequence for subsequent serial recall. During a retention interval of 6000 ms there was either a fixation cross or a 1000 ms fixation cross followed by 5000 ms filled with a visuospatial processing task in which a series of boxes appeared one at a time on the screen. The participant had to decide whether each box was above or below the horizontal centre of the screen. As for Doherty and Logie (2016), each participant was assessed for their memory span for letter sequences, and for how many boxes they could respond to accurately within five seconds. Each participant then performed the two tasks together, with the demand for the memory and processing tasks varied below, at, and above single-task span. The procedure is illustrated in Fig. 14.8.

Fig. 14.9 shows that memory accuracy was affected by increases in memory load but was only affected by the processing task when processing task load was above span. Importantly, when memory load was at span, participants' performance remained at 80% (the level used to set span) under dual-task conditions until processing load exceeded participants' single-task ability. Similar results were found for the processing performance which was only affected by the memory task when the memory load was set above each participant's span.

Doherty (2016) concluded that participants were able to perform verbal memory and spatial processing tasks without dual-task costs until the demand of the processing task exceeded their span, when there was a cost to memory and to processing.

In summary, Doherty (2016) and Doherty and Logie (2016) supported the idea that memory and visuospatial processing do not rely entirely on the same cognitive resource: participants were able to maintain single-task levels of performance until task demands were set above span. Note that this does not imply that there is just a single, limited capacity system for supporting memory for a verbal sequence at or below span, nor does it imply that there is a single system that supports visuospatial processing. As noted earlier, our assumption is that multiple cognitive systems will support task performance on most tasks, with some of those systems used more heavily than others, depending on task requirements. The results described earlier suggest that cognitive systems used for deciding if a box is above or below the horizontal midline of a screen can also be used to support temporary memory for aurally presented numbers, but not vice versa.

These conclusions were further tested across three experiments by Doherty et al. (2019), using the same general design as Doherty (2016) except that during the

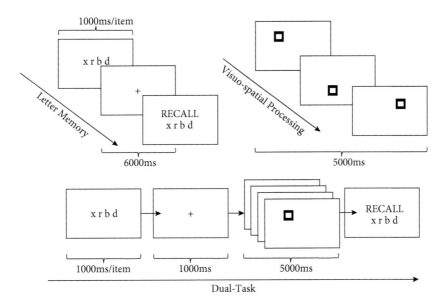

Fig. 14.8 Span and dual-task procedures from Doherty (2016). Memory (top left) and processing (top right) spans for each participant were used to titrate the dual-task conditions (bottom). Dual-task memory and processing accuracy were then measured with each task load, at 'Span – 1', 'Span', and 'Span + 1'.

Reproduced from Doherty, Jason M., 'What limits dual-tasking in working memory? An investigation of the effect of sub-task demand on maintenance mechanisms employed during dual-tasking', Unpublished PhD thesis, University of Edinburgh, 2016.

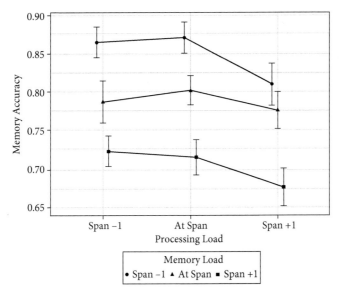

Fig. 14.9 Mean memory span scores (with standard errors) across memory and processing load levels varied from span – 1 through span + 1.

Reproduced from Doherty, Jason M., 'What limits dual-tasking in working memory? An investigation of the effect of sub-task demand on maintenance mechanisms employed during dual-tasking', Unpublished PhD thesis, University of Edinburgh, 2016.

retention interval participants performed visually presented simple arithmetic verification (e.g. 4 + 5 = 8, true or false). For illustration, we summarize Experiment 1 from that set.

Memory span for letter sequences was assessed for each participant, with a retention interval of 10,000 ms. Processing span was based on how many sums could be accurately completed within 10,000 ms. For both memory and verification, span was defined as the highest load at which the participant achieved 80% correct. Participants completed memory and verification as single tasks, then with a memory preload and verification during the 10,000 ms retention interval. These three conditions were completed in silence or with articulatory suppression (repeating ba–ba–ba aloud at two per second). The memory items were presented visually and participants recalled the letters by typing on the computer keyboard.

Data were collected in two different laboratories, one that favoured the MC view (the Logie laboratory in the United Kingdom) and the other that favoured the TBRS view (TBRS laboratory in Switzerland—see chapter by Barrouillet and Camos, 2021). Each of these laboratories plus a third laboratory that favoured the embedded-processes (EP) view (see chapter by Cowan et al., 2021) generated different sets of predictions for experimental outcomes. The details of these predictions are described in Doherty et al. (2019).

Barrouillet and Camos (TBRS) and Cowan (EP) predicted a medium effect size for the dual-task impact on memory performance, a medium effect size for the dual-task impact on processing performance, and large effects of articulatory suppression on memory. However, TBRS predicted a small effect of articulatory suppression on processing whereas EP predicted a large effect. The EP predictions were based on the assumption that the memory task and the processing task share limited capacity attention. TBRS assumes that articulatory suppression does not require attention, but does have an impact on a specific verbal memory store. In contrast, MC predicted that the effect of dual task on memory performance would be small, and that there would be no effect of dual task on processing. Articulatory suppression was predicted to have a medium-sized effect on memory but no effect on processing. These predictions were based on the Doherty and Logie (2016; Doherty, 2016) conclusions that memory performance might rely on a specific memory system that can be supported in part by the cognitive resources that are required for processing. However, the processing task does not rely on a specific memory system, and so performance should be unaffected by a concurrent memory load. Like TBRS, the MC view assumes a specific verbal memory store that is disrupted by articulatory suppression.

Results for memory are shown in Fig. 14.10, and for processing in Fig. 14.11.

From Fig. 14.10, it is clear that memory performance dropped when arithmetic verification occurred during the retention interval, and that articulatory suppression also resulted in poorer memory performance. Both of these were large effects statistically. There was a small, but significant interaction across laboratories, but this was in the opposite direction to the predictions respectively from each laboratory, so did not reflect any theoretical bias. The main effects were very similar across test sites. All three

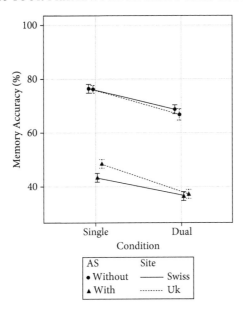

Fig. 14.10 Mean memory accuracy under single-task conditions and with a processing load (arithmetic verification) during a 10,000 ms retention interval, without and with articulatory suppression. Data are shown separately for the laboratory in which they were collected.

Reproduced from Jason M. Doherty, Clement Belletier, Stephen Rhodes, Agnieszka Jaroslawska, Pierre Barrouillet, Valerie Camos, Nelson Cowan, Moshe Naveh-Benjamin, and Robert H. Logie, 'Dual-Task Costs in Working Memory: An Adversarial Collaboration', *Journal of Experimental Psychology: Learning, Memory, and Cognition*, 45 (9), pp. 1529–1551, Figure 2. http://dx.doi.org/10.1037/xlm0000668, Copyright © 2018 The Author(s)/CC BY-SA (https://creativecommons.org/licenses/by-sa/3.0).

theoretical perspectives predicted reductions in memory under these conditions, but the results for dual task were larger than any of the theoretical views predicted. Only EP predicted a large effect for articulatory suppression.

From Fig. 14.11, it is clear that there was no effect of a memory preload or of articulatory suppression on arithmetic verification, and no differences across laboratories. This is consistent with the expectations of the MC theoretical perspective, and contrasts with the expectations of TBRS and EP, although TBRS did predict a small effect of articulatory suppression.

In the context of differential predictions for statistical effect size, none of the three theoretical perspectives can account for all of the data. TBRS and EP essentially predicted the results for memory, and MC predicted the results for processing.

However, were the predictions really that different? An additional key difference between the theoretical perspectives that was not a basis for the predictions in Doherty et al. (2019), is that MC focuses on the size of the residual performance under dual-task conditions, and previous references to small, medium, or large effects have been based on the proportional drop in performance rather than statistical effect size. So, a drop of 5–10% in performance under dual-task conditions would be considered small, even if this might be a large statistical effect size. In contrast, the TBRS and EP theoretical

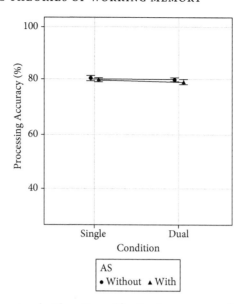

Fig. 14.11 Mean processing (arithmetic verification) accuracy under single-task conditions and with an at-span memory preload, without and with articulatory suppression. Data are collapsed across sites since there were no interactions.

Reproduced from Jason M. Doherty, Clement Belletier, Stephen Rhodes, Agnieszka Jaroslawska, Pierre Barrouillet, Valerie Camos, Nelson Cowan, Moshe Naveh-Benjamin, and Robert H. Logie, 'Dual-Task Costs in Working Memory: An Adversarial Collaboration', *Journal of Experimental Psychology: Learning, Memory, and Cognition*, 45 (9), pp. 1529–1551, Figure 3. http://dx.doi.org/10.1037/xlm0000668, Copyright © 2018 The Author(s)/CC BY-SA (https://creativecommons.org/licenses/by-sa/3.0).

perspectives focus on the statistically significant reduction in performance under dual-task conditions, even if there is substantial residual performance.

The proportional dual-task drops in memory performance under dual task were around 10%, so were consistent with previous MC experiments that interpreted this as small. This result was also consistent with previous results from the TBRS and EP laboratories in showing statistically significant dual-task effects. However, although an effect size is large statistically, it is questionable whether a 10% drop in performance under dual-task conditions, leaving 90% of single-task performance, is strong evidence that the two concurrent tasks rely entirely on the same shared cognitive resource.

Results for processing performance might seem more promising for selecting a 'winning' theory with results predicted by MC but not by TBRS or EP. However, again, we should be careful about drawing strong theoretical conclusions. Whereas the results for processing are entirely consistent with the MC perspective, it is possible, post hoc to interpret the lack of a dual-task effect within the EP and TBRS perspective by assuming that participants focused on processing performance, reducing rehearsal or refreshing of the memory items, leading to a drop in memory performance.

There was a similar pattern of results for statistical effect sizes that were not wholly consistent with any of the three theoretical perspectives in the other experiments reported in Doherty et al. (2019), and in another study by the same research group that explored age-related changes in dual-task performance (Rhodes et al., 2019). In both articles, the agreed consensus conclusion was that each of the three theoretical perspectives was partly correct and partly incorrect but about different aspects of the data, and none was a clear 'winner'.

So should we completely revise our theoretical assumptions? Maybe, maybe not. Different empirical bases generated these different predictions, and it could be argued that all three predictions were correct from their own perspective. From an MC perspective, the effects on memory were small with a large residual level of performance under dual-task conditions. From a TBRS and EP perspective, the effects were statistically significant. This points to the suggestion that the contrasts between the empirical expectations were more a question of emphasis on residual performance or emphasis on the statistically significant presence of an effect, rather than reflecting fundamental differences between predictions and empirical outcomes. This further highlights that it is very difficult to use quantitative contrasts in statistical effect sizes to distinguish between theories that make essentially qualitative predictions.

One approach to accounting for the observed results, and to attempt theory integration would be to suggest that participants use multiple cognitive functions to perform most if not all demanding tasks in laboratory experiments, and that any tasks that are combined in dual-task studies will almost inevitably draw on overlapping cognitive functions, resulting in dual-task costs. On this scenario, there could be rapid swapping between the use of a given set of overlapping functions for performing a memory or a processing task, as assumed by TBRS. However, because the cognitive functions required for memory and for processing do not completely overlap, there is still some residual support for memory during processing, and some residual support for processing when holding items in memory. That is, the switching is not 'all-or-none', and this is why the size of dual-task costs vary depending on which cognitive functions are required when two tasks are combined, and why rarely, if ever, does performance on one or other task drop to zero under dual-task conditions. For the same reasons, this account could also be used for a synergy between EP and the MCs theoretical perspective. This integrated approach could account for all of the data that we observed in Doherty et al. (2019) and Rhodes et al. (2019) by viewing the three theoretical frameworks as offering different levels of explanation that are required for each aspect of the data. We can view performance patterns as reflecting a single, global cognitive function referred to as attention, and for many research questions, this works extremely well. Alternatively, we can view performance patterns as reflecting integrated functioning of multiple cognitive functions acting in concert to support performance, giving the impression of a single, global cognitive function. Combining these two levels of explanation also could offer substantial new insight into contrasting data patterns that have fuelled debate in this field for several decades, with no resolution in sight. We fully acknowledge that this account is post hoc and speculative, although see discussions in Logie (2016, 2018), and see chapter by Vandierendonck (2021) for a possible implementation. However, we would argue that it provides a possible pathway to theoretical integration.

F. Working Memory Applications

A major theme in our laboratory has been to consider potential applications of theory. Not only might this generate potential solutions to applied problems, but we can test the applicability and utility of a theory and possibly refine a theory as a result. There is not scope within the current chapter for detailed discussion of all of these applications, but in summary, in addition to the applications to effects of brain damage discussed earlier, this approach has been found to be particularly useful in healthy early-age language and WM development (e.g. Gathercole & Baddeley, 1989; Logie & Pearson, 1997), healthy adult ageing (e.g. Johnson et al., 2010; Logie & Morris, 2015), developmental learning disorders (e.g. Gathercole et al., 2016), WM training (e.g. Gathercole, Dunning, Holmes, & Norris, 2019; Logie, 2012), following instructions (Jaroslawska, Gathercole, Logie, & Holmes, 2016), acquisition of complex cognitive and motor skills (e.g. Logie, Baddeley, Mane, Donchin, & Sheptak, 1989; Wickens & Liu, 1988), counting and mental arithmetic (e.g. Hitch, 1978; Logie & Baddeley, 1987; Logie, Gilhooly, & Wynn, 1994), planning and plan implementation in virtual environments (e.g. Logie, Trawley, & Law, 2011), creative thinking (e.g. Cornoldi et al., 1996), syllogistic reasoning (e.g. Gilhooly, Logie, Wetherick, & Wynn, 1993), managed remembering and forgetting in digital storage (Logie, Wolters, & Niven, 2018; Niederee, Kanhabua, Gallo, & Logie, 2015), and design of 'digital cognitive assistants' (e.g. Belletier et al., 2019; van der Meulen et al., 2010).

Conclusion: An Approach to Theory Integration

We have discussed a wide range of arguments and studies within the context of a MC framework for WM, and suggested that differences with alternative frameworks might reflect differences in research questions, in levels of explanation, and in labels used for very similar concepts and functions, rather than fundamental differences in underlying assumptions. We considered in detail three of the frameworks that are addressed within this volume, namely EP (Cowan et al., 2021), TBRS (Barrouillet & Camos, 2021), and a version of the MCs framework (Logie, 1995, 2003, 2011, 2016, 2018). In so doing, we suggested an approach to synergy rather than conflict between theories.

We have emphasized the value of converging operations for theory development, using a range of methodologies, including cognitive experimental work with healthy and brain-damaged individuals across adult ageing, and practical applications, for example, in clinical settings, that arise from, and help refine our theoretical framework. We have argued that participants within or across experiments will not necessarily perform the same task in the same way. So, there may be no common principles that govern how all participants perform a given task, and it is misleading to seek a 'winning' theory of how a task is performed. However, there may be common principles that determine the range of cognitive functions and systems that healthy participants have available to support task performance. If the research goal is to address the functional organization of human cognition, greater insight may be achieved by exploring the different ways in which participants perform tasks rather than treating all individual variability as statistical noise, or as reflecting only overall cognitive ability. If the research goal is to explore the limits of overall cognitive ability, then a theoretical framework that assumes domain-general cognitive capacity and attentional control can do so very effectively. These different approaches are not incompatible or in conflict. They are simply asking different research questions at different levels of explanation.

A similar approach was proposed by Reuchlin (1978), who also argued that all healthy individuals will not necessarily perform a task in the same way. If the aggregate data suggest considerable variability across participants, a common conclusion is that the results are ambiguous or very difficult to interpret. Reuchlin (1978) also argued that there may be different cognitive functions that can compensate for each other when one of them is damaged, or otherwise unavailable because of experimental manipulations. This appears common in biology, possibly because it gives a selective advantage to organisms that have this form of flexibility. With human cognition, different combinations of cognitive functions may be available, and a given response can result from different processes within and across individuals. Reuchlin's ideas have only been published in French, and there has been limited direct follow-up (e.g. Barrouillet & Camos, 2017; Belletier et al., 2019; Lautrey, 2018). The first author of this chapter only became aware of Reuchlin's work from the second author. However, the ideas are strikingly similar to those developed independently in our laboratory.

The conception of cognitive flexibility and adaptive selection of different combinations of tools from the cognitive toolbox might give the impression that studying WM is an insurmountable challenge (Engle & Martin, 2018), because results are inherently ambiguous. However, one approach to this challenge is to consider whether different theoretical assumptions and interpretations of data reflect different levels of explanation and different research questions. A second approach is to explore the different ways in which participants attempt to perform their assigned tasks (Belletier et al., 2019; Logie, 2018; Morrison, Rosenbaum, Fair, & Chein, 2016). By embracing these two approaches, and exploring the extent to which theories are complementary rather than adversarial, we argue that there is considerable scope for interrupting the infinite cycle of unresolved debate to make substantial advances in the understanding of WM.

References

Allen, T. W., Marcell, M. M., & Anderson, P. (1978). Modality-specific interference with verbal and nonverbal stimulus information. *Memory & Cognition*, 6, 184–188.

Anderson, J. R. (1996). ACT: A simple theory of complex cognition. *American Psychologist*, 51, 355–365.

Atkinson, R. C., & Shiffrin, R. M. (1968). Human memory: A proposed system and its control processes. In K. W. Spence & J. T. Spence (Eds.), *The psychology of learning and motivation: Advances in research and theory* (Vol. 2, pp. 89–195). New York, UK: Academic Press.

Baddeley, A. D. (1986). *Working memory*. Oxford, UK: Oxford University Press.

Baddeley, A. D. (1996). Exploring the central executive. *Quarterly Journal of Experimental Psychology*, 49A, 5–28.

Baddeley A. D. (2000). The episodic buffer: a new component of working memory? *Trends in Cognitive Sciences*, 4, 417–423.

Baddeley, A. D. (2007). *Working memory: Theory and practice*. Oxford, UK: Oxford University Press.

Baddeley, A. D., Allen, R., & Vargha-Khadem, F. (2009). Is the hippocampus necessary for visual and verbal binding in working memory? *Neuropsychologia*, 48, 1089–1095.

Baddeley, A. D., Bressi, S., Della Sala, S., Logie, R., & Spinnler, H. (1991). The decline of working memory in Alzheimer's disease. A longitudinal study. *Brain*, 114, 2521–2542.

Baddeley, A. D., Cocchini, G., Della Sala, S., Logie, R. H., & Spinnler, H. (1999). Working memory and vigilance: Evidence from normal aging and Alzheimer's disease. *Brain and Cognition* 41, 87–108.

Baddeley, A. D., & Hitch, G. J. (1974). Working memory. In G. A. Bower (Ed.), *The psychology of learning and motivation* (Vol. 8, pp. 47–89). New York, NY: Academic Press.

Baddeley, A. D., Hitch, G. J., & Allen, R. J. (2009). Working memory and binding in sentence recall. *Journal of Memory and Language*, 61, 438–456.

Baddeley, A. D., Hitch, G. J., & Allen, R. (2021). A multicomponent model of working memory. In R. H. Logie, V. Camos, & N. Cowan (Eds.), *Working Memory: State of the Science* (pp. 10–43). Oxford, UK: Oxford University Press.

Baddeley, A. D., & Logie, R. H. (1999). Working memory: The multiple component model. In A. Miyake & P. Shah (Eds.), *Models of working memory* (pp. 28–61). New York, NY: Cambridge University Press.

Baddeley, A., Logie, R., Bressi, S., Della Sala, S., & Spinnler, H. (1986). Dementia and working memory. *Quarterly Journal of Experimental Psychology A: Human Experimental Psychology*, 38, 603–618.

Baltes, P. B., & Baltes, M. M. (1990). Psychological perspectives on successful aging: The model of selective optimization with compensation. In P. B. Baltes & M. M. Baltes (Eds.), *Successful aging: Perspectives from the behavioral sciences* (pp. 1–34). Cambridge, UK: Cambridge University Press.

Barrouillet, P., & Camos, V. (2017). A European perspective on Robert Siegler's contribution. In P. Lemaire (Ed.), *Cognitive development from a strategy perspective* (pp. 19–36). London, UK: Routledge.

Barrouillet, P., & Camos, V. (2021). The time-based resource-sharing model of working memory. In R. H. Logie, V. Camos, & N. Cowan (Eds.), *Working memory: State of the science* (pp. 85–115). Oxford, UK: Oxford University Press.

Basso, A., Spinnler, H., Vallar, G., & Zanobio, M. E. (1982). Left hemisphere damage and selective impairment of auditory verbal short-term memory. A case study. *Neuropsychologia*, 20, 263–274.

Belletier, C., Charkhabi, M., de Andrade Silva, G. P., Ametepe, K., Lutz, M., & Izaute, M. (2019). Wearable cognitive assistants in a factory setting: a critical review of a promising way of enhancing cognitive performance and well-being. *Cognition, Technology & Work*, 1–14. doi:10.1007/s10111-019-00610-2

Boring, E. G. (1923). Intelligence as the tests test it. *New Republic*, 35, 35–37.

Borst, G., Niven, E. H., & Logie, R. H. (2012). Visual mental image generation does not overlap with visual short-term memory: A dual task interference study. *Memory & Cognition*, 40, 360–372.

Brandimonte, M. A., Hitch, G. J., & Bishop, D. (1992). Influence of short-term memory codes on visual image processing: Evidence from image transformation tasks. *Journal of Experimental Psychology: Learning, Memory, and Cognition*, 18, 157–165.

Broadbent, D. E. (1958). *Perception and communication*. London, UK: Pergamon Press.

Broadbent, D. E., & Broadbent, M. H. P. (1981). Recency effects in visual memory. *Quarterly Journal of Experimental Psychology*, 33A, 1–15.

Brooks, L. R. (1967). The suppression of visualisation by reading. *Quarterly Journal of Experimental Psychology*, 19, 289–299.

Brown, L. A., Forbes, D., & McConnell, J. (2006). Limiting the use of verbal coding in the Visual Patterns Test. *Quarterly Journal of Experimental Psychology*, 59, 1169–1176.

Buchsbaum, B. R., & D'Esposito, M. (2019). A sensorimotor view of verbal working memory. *Cortex*, *112*, 134–148.

Charlton, R. A., & Morris, R. G. (2015). Associations between working memory and white matter integrity in normal ageing. In R. H. Logie & R. G. Morris (Eds.), *Working memory and aging* (pp. 97–128). Hove, UK: Psychology Press.

Charness, N. (1976). Memory for chess positions: Resistance to interference. *Journal of Experimental Psychology: Human Learning and Memory*, *2*, 641–653.

Cocchini, G., Logie, R. H., Della Sala, S., & MacPherson, S. E. (2002). Concurrent performance of two memory tasks: evidence for domain specific working memory systems. *Memory & Cognition*, *30*, 1086–1095.

Coltheart, M. (2006). What has functional neuroimaging told us about the mind (so far)? *Cortex*, *42*, 323–331.

Coltheart, M. (2013). How can functional neuroimaging inform cognitive theories? *Perspectives on Psychological Science*, *8*, 98–103.

Connor, J. M., & Hoyer, R. G. (1976). Auditory and visual similarity effects in recognition and recall. *Memory & Cognition*, *4*, 261–264.

Conrad, R. (1964). Acoustic confusions in immediate memory. *British Journal of Psychology*, *55*, 75–84.

Cornoldi, C., Logie, R. H., Brandimonte, M. A., Kaufmann, G., & Reisberg, D. (1996). *Stretching the imagination: Representation and transformation in mental imagery*. New York, NY: Oxford University Press.

Cowan, N. (1988). Evolving conceptions of memory storage, selective attention, and their mutual constraints within the human information processing system. *Psychological Bulletin*, *104*, 163–191.

Cowan, N. (1995). *Attention and memory: An integrated framework*. Oxford Psychology Series (No. 26). New York, NY: Oxford University Press.

Cowan, N. (2005). *Working memory capacity*. Hove, UK: Psychology Press.

Cowan N. (2017). The many faces of working memory and short-term storage. *Psychonomic Bulletin & Review*, *24*, 1158–1170.

Cowan, N. (2019). Short-term memory based on activated long-term memory: a review in response to Norris (2017). *Psychological Bulletin*, *145*, 822–847.

Cowan, N., Morey, C., & Naveh-Benjamin, M. (2021). An embedded-processes approach to working memory: How is it distinct from other approaches, and to what ends? In R. H. Logie, V. Camos, & N. Cowan (Eds.), *Working memory: State of the science* (pp. 44–84). Oxford, UK: Oxford University Press.

Cowan, N., Saults, J. S., & Blume, C. L. (2014). Central and peripheral components of working memory storage. *Journal of Experimental Psychology: General*, *143*, 1806–1836.

Crawford, T. J., Higham, S., Renvoize, T., Patel, J., Dale, M., Suriya, A., & Tetley, S. (2005). Inhibitory control of saccadic eye movements and cognitive impairment in Alzheimer's disease. *Biological Psychiatry*, *57*, 1052–1060.

Daneman, M., & Carpenter, P. A. (1980). Individual differences in working memory and reading. *Journal of verbal learning and verbal behavior*, *19*, 450–466.

Daneman, M., & Hannon, B. (2007). What do working memory span tasks like reading span really measure? In N. Osaka, R. H. Logie, & M. D'Esposito (Eds.), *The cognitive neuroscience of working memory* (pp. 21–58). Oxford, UK: Oxford University Press.

Della Sala, S., Baddeley, A., Papagno, C., & Spinnler, H. (1995). Dual-task paradigm: A means to examine the central executive. *Annals of the New York Academy of Sciences*, *769*, 161–171.

Della Sala, S., Cocchini, G., Logie, R. H., & MacPherson, S. E. (2010). Dual task during encoding, maintenance and retrieval in Alzheimer disease and healthy ageing. *Journal of Alzheimer's Disease*, *19*, 503–515.

Della Sala, S., & Logie, R. (1993). When working memory does not work: The role of working memory in neuropsychology. In F. Boller & H. Spinnler (Eds.), *Handbook of neuropsychology* (Vol. 8, pp. 1–63). Amsterdam, The Netherlands: Elsevier Publishers BV.

Della Sala, S., Gray, C., Baddeley, A., Allamano, N., & Wilson, L. (1999). Pattern span: a tool for unwelding visuo-spatial memory. *Neuropsychologia*, *37*, 1189–1199.

Della Sala, S., Logie, R. H., Beschin, N., & Denis, M. (2004). Preserved visuo-spatial transformations in representational neglect. *Neuropsychologia, 42*, 1358–1364.

De Renzi, E., & Nichelli, P. (1975). Verbal and non-verbal short-term memory impairment following hemispheric damage. *Cortex, 11*, 341–354.

Doherty, J. M. (2016). *What limits dual-tasking in working memory? An investigation of the effect of sub-task demand on maintenance mechanisms employed during dual-tasking* [Unpublished PhD thesis]. University of Edinburgh.

Doherty, J. M., Belletier, C., Rhodes, S., Jaroslawska, A., Barrouillet, P., Camos, V., . . . Logie, R. H. (2019). Dual-task costs in working memory: An adversarial collaboration. *Journal of Experimental Psychology: Learning, Memory, and Cognition, 45*, 1529–1551.

Doherty, J. M., & Logie, R. H. (2016). Resource-sharing in multiple component working memory. *Memory & Cognition, 44*, 1157–1167.

Duncan, J. (2005). Frontal lobe function and general intelligence: Why it matters. *Cortex, 41*, 215–217.

Eisenreich, B. R., Akaishi, R., & Hayden, B. Y. (2017). Control without controllers: Toward a distributed neuroscience of executive control. *Journal of Cognitive Neuroscience, 29*, 1684–1698.

Endress, A. D. (2019). Duplications and domain-generality. *Psychological Bulletin, 12*, 1154–1175.

Engle, R. W., Kane, M. J., & Tuholski, S. W. (1999). Individual differences in working memory capacity and what they tell us about controlled attention, general fluid intelligence, and functions of the prefrontal cortex. In A. Miyake & P. Shah (Eds.), *Models of working memory* (pp. 102–134). New York, NY: Cambridge University Press.

Engle, R. W., & Martin, J. D. (2018). Is a science of the mind even possible? Reply to Logie (2018). *Journal of Applied Research in Memory and Cognition, 7*, 493–498.

Ericsson, K. A. (2014). Expertise. *Current Biology, 24*, 508–510.

Ericsson, K. A., Chase, W. G., & Faloon, S. (1980). Acquisition of a memory skill. *Science, 208*, 1181–1182.

Ericsson, K. A., Cheng, X., Pan, Y., Ku, Y., Ge, Y., & Hu, Y. (2017). Memory skills mediating superior memory in a world-class memorist. *Memory, 25*, 1294–1302.

Ericsson, K. A., & Kintsch, W. (1995). Long-term working memory. *Psychological Review, 102*, 211–245.

Ericsson, K. A., & Polson, P. G. (1988). An experimental analysis of a memory skill for dinner-orders. *Journal of Experimental Psychology: Learning, Memory, and Cognition, 14*, 305–316.

Farmer, E. W., Berman, J. V., & Fletcher, Y. L. (1986). Evidence for a visuo-spatial scratch-pad in working memory. *Quarterly Journal of Experimental Psychology A: Human Experimental Psychology, 38*, 675–688.

Gathercole, S., & Baddeley, A. D. (1989). Evaluation of the role of phonological STM in the development of vocabulary in children: A longitudinal study. *Journal of Memory and Language, 28*, 200–213.

Gathercole, S. E., Dunning, D. L., Holmes, J., & Norris, D. (2019). Working memory training involves learning new skills. *Journal of Memory and Language, 105*, 19–42.

Gathercole, S. E., Woolgar, F., CALM team, Kievet, R. A., Astle, D., Manly, T., & Holmes, J. (2016). How common are WM deficits in children with difficulties in reading and mathematics? *Journal of Applied Research in Memory and Cognition, 5*, 384–394.

Gilhooly, K. J., Logie, R. H., Wetherick, N. E., & Wynn, V. (1993). Working memory and strategies in syllogistic reasoning tasks. *Memory & Cognition, 21*, 115–124.

Hambrick, D. Z., Burgoyne, A. P., & Araujo, D. (2021). Working memory and expertise: An ecological perspective. In R. H. Logie, V. Camos, & N. Cowan (Eds.), *Working memory: State of the science* (pp. 212–234). Oxford, UK: Oxford University Press.

Hanley, J. R., & Young, A. W. (2019). ELD revisited: A second look at a neuropsychological impairment of working memory affecting retention of visuo-spatial material. *Cortex, 112*, 172–179.

Hanley, J. R., Young, A. W., & Pearson, N. A. (1991). Impairment of the visuo-spatial sketch pad. *Quarterly Journal of Experimental Psychology, 43A*, 101–125.

Haslam, C., & Kessels, R. P. C. (2018). *Errorless learning in neuropsychological rehabilitation: Mechanisms, efficacy and application*. London, UK: Taylor & Francis.

Hazy, T. E., Frank, M. J., & O'Reilly, R. C. (2006). Banishing the homunculus: Making working memory work. *Neuroscience, 139*, 105–118.

Hazy, T. E., Frank, M. J., & O'Reilly, R. C. (2007). Towards an executive without a homunculus: Computational models of the prefrontal cortex/basal ganglia system. *Philosophical Transactions of the Royal Society of London B, 362*, 1601–1613.

Helstrup, T., & Logie, R. H. (Eds.) (1999). *Working memory and mental discovery*. Hove, UK: Psychology Press.

Hitch, G. J. (1978). The role of short-term working memory in mental arithmetic. *Cognitive Psychology, 10*, 302–323.

Holtzer, R., Burright, R. G., & Donovick, P. J. (2004). The sensitivity of dual-task performance to cognitive status in aging. *Journal of the International Neuropsychological Society, 10*, 230–238.

Hulme, C., Maughan, S., & Brown, G. D. (1991). Memory for familiar and unfamiliar words: Evidence for a long-term memory contribution to short-term memory span. *Journal of Memory and Language, 30*, 685–701.

Hulme, C., Roodenrys, S., Brown, G., & Mercer, R. (1995). The role of long-term memory mechanisms in memory span. *British Journal of Psychology, 86*, 527–536.

Jacobs, J. (1887). Experiments on "prehension". *Mind, 12*, 75–79.

Jaroslawska, A. J., Gathercole, A. E., Logie, M. R., & Homes, J. (2016). Following instructions in a virtual school: Does working memory play a role? *Memory & Cognition, 44*, 580–589.

James, W. (1890). *Principles of psychology*. New York, NY: Holt, Rinehart and Winston.

Johnson, W., Logie, R. H., & Brockmole, J. R. (2010). Working memory tasks differ in factor structure across age cohorts: Implications for dedifferentiation. *Intelligence, 38*, 513–528.

Jones, D. M., & Macken, W. (2018). In the beginning was the deed: Verbal short-term memory as object-oriented action. *Current Directions in Psychological Science, 27*, 351–356.

Kane, M. J., Conway, A. R. A., Miura, T. K., & Colflesh, G. J. H. (2007). Working memory, attention control, and the N-back task: A question of construct validity. *Journal of Experimental Psychology: Learning, Memory, and Cognition, 33*, 615–622.

Karpicke, J. D., & Roediger, H. L. (2008). The critical importance of retrieval for learning. *Science, 319*, 966–968.

Kaschel, R., Logie, R. H., Kazén, M., & Della Sala, S. (2009). Alzheimer's disease, but not ageing or chronic depression, affects dual-tasking. *Journal of Neurology, 256*, 1860–1868.

Kovacs, K., & Conway, A. R. A. (2016). Process overlap theory: A unified account of the general factor of intelligence. *Psychological Inquiry, 27*, 151–177.

Lautrey, J. (2018). Cognitive development is a reconstruction process that may follow different pathways: The case of number. *Journal of Intelligence, 6*, 15.

Locke, J. (1690). *An essay concerning human understanding*. Book II, Chapter X, 1–2. [First edition consulted in University of Aberdeen, UK, Archive Library.]

Logie, R. H. (1995). *Visuo-spatial working memory*. Hove, UK: Lawrence Erlbaum Associates.

Logie, R. H. (1996). The seven ages of working memory. In J. T. E. Richardson, R. W. Engle, L. Hasher, R. H. Logie, E. R. Stoltzfus, & R. T. Zacks (Eds.), *Working memory and human cognition* (pp. 31–65). New York, NY: Oxford University Press.

Logie, R. H. (2003). Spatial and visual working memory: A mental workspace. In D. Irwin & B. Ross (Eds.), *Cognitive vision: The psychology of learning and motivation* (Vol 42, pp. 37–78). Philadelphia, PA: Elsevier Science.

Logie, R. H. (2011). The functional organisation and the capacity limits of working memory. *Current Directions in Psychological Science, 20*, 240–245.

Logie, R. H. (2012). Cognitive training: Strategies and the multicomponent cognitive system. *Journal of Applied Research in Memory and Cognition, 1*, 206–207.

Logie, R. H. (2016). Retiring the central executive. *Quarterly Journal of Experimental Psychology, 69*, 2093–2109.

Logie, R. H. (2018). Human cognition: Common principles and individual variation. *Journal of Applied Research in Memory and Cognition, 7*, 471–486.

Logie, R. H. (2019). Converging sources of evidence and theory integration in working memory: A commentary on Morey, Rhodes, and Cowan (2019). *Cortex, 112*, 162–171.

Logie, R. H., & Baddeley, A. D. (1987). Cognitive processes in counting. *Journal of Experimental Psychology: Learning, Memory, and Cognition, 13*, 310–326.

Logie, R. H., Baddeley, A. D., Mane, A., Donchin, E., & Sheptak, R. (1989). Working memory and the analysis of a complex skill by secondary task methodology. *Acta Psychologica, 71*, 53–87.

Logie, R. H., Brockmole, J. R., & Vandenbroucke, A. (2009). Bound feature combinations in visual short-term memory are fragile but influence long-term learning. *Visual Cognition, 17*, 160–179.

Logie, R. H., Cocchini, G., Della Sala, S., & Baddeley, A. D. (2004). Is there a specific executive capacity for dual task coordination? Evidence from Alzheimer's disease. *Neuropsychology, 18*(3), 504–513.

Logie, R. H., & Cowan, N. (2015). Perspectives on working memory. *Memory & Cognition, 43*, 315–324.

Logie, R. H., & Della Sala, S. (2005). Disorders of visuo-spatial working memory. In P. Shah & A. Miyake (Eds.), *Handbook of visuospatial thinking* (pp. 81–120). New York, NY: Cambridge University Press.

Logie, R. H., Della Sala, S., Laiacona, M., Chalmers, P., & Wynn, V. (1996). Group aggregates and individual reliability: The case of verbal short-term memory. *Memory & Cognition, 24*, 305–321.

Logie, R. H., Della Sala, S., Wynn, V., & Baddeley, A. D. (2000). Visual similarity effects in immediate verbal serial recall. *Quarterly Journal of Experimental Psychology, 53A*, 626–646.

Logie, R. H., & Duff, S. C. (2007). Separating processing from storage in working memory operation span. In N. Osaka, R. H. Logie, & M. D'Esposito (Eds.), *The cognitive neuroscience of working memory* (pp. 119–135). Oxford, UK: Oxford University Press.

Logie, R. H., Gilhooly, K. J., & Wynn, V. (1994). Counting on working memory in arithmetic problem solving. *Memory & Cognition, 22*, 395–410.

Logie, R. H., Horne, M. J., & Pettit, L. D. (2015). When cognitive performance does not decline across the lifespan. In R. H. Logie & R. Morris (Eds.), *Working memory and ageing* (pp. 21–47). Hove, UK: Psychology Press.

Logie, R. H., & Morris, R. G. (Eds.) (2015). *Working memory and ageing*. Hove, UK: Psychology Press.

Logie, R. H., Parra, M. A., & Della Sala, S. (2015). From cognitive science to dementia assessment. *Policy Insights from the Behavioral and Brain Sciences, 2*, 81–91.

Logie, R. H., & Pearson, D. G. (1997). The inner eye and the inner scribe of visuo-spatial working memory: Evidence from developmental fractionation. *European Journal of Cognitive Psychology, 9*, 241–257.

Logie, R. H., Pernet, C. R., Buonocore, A., & Della Sala, S. (2011). Low and high imagers activate networks differentially in mental rotation. *Neuropsychologia, 49*, 3071–3077.

Logie, R. H., Saito, S., Morita, A., Varma, S., & Norris, D. (2016). Recalling visual serial order for verbal sequences. *Memory & Cognition, 44*, 590–607.

Logie, R. H., Trawley, S., & Law, A. S. (2011). Multitasking: multiple, domain-specific cognitive functions in a virtual environment. *Memory & Cognition, 39*, 1561–1574.

Logie, R. H., Venneri, A., Della Sala, S., Redpath, T., & Marshall, I. (2003). Brain activation and the phonological loop: The impact of rehearsal. *Brain and Cognition, 53*, 293–296.

Logie, R. H., Wolters, M., & Niven, E. H. (2018). Preserving and forgetting in the human brain. In V. Mezaris, C. Niederee, & R. Logie (Eds.), *Personal multimedia preservation: Remembering or forgetting images and video* (pp. 9–45). Cham, Switzerland: Springer.

Logie, R., Wright, R., & Decker, S. (1992). Recognition memory performance and residential burglary. *Applied Cognitive Psychology, 6*, 109–123.

Logie, R. H., Zucco, G., & Baddeley, A. D. (1990). Interference with visual short-term memory. *Acta Psychologica, 75*, 55–74.

MacPherson, S. E., & Della Sala, S. (Eds.) (2019). *Cases of amnesia*. New York, NY: Routledge.

MacPherson, S. E., Della Sala, S., Logie, R. H., & Willcock, G. K. (2007). Specific AD impairment in concurrent performance of two memory tasks. *Cortex, 43*, 858–865.

Marks, D. F. (1973). Visual imagery differences in the recall of pictures. *British Journal of Psychology, 64*, 17–24.

Marks, D. F. (1995). New directions for mental imagery research. *Journal of Mental Imagery, 19*, 153–167.

Martin, R. C., Rapp, B., & Purcell, J. (2021). Domain-specific working memory: Perspectives from cognitive neuropsychology. In R. H. Logie, V. Camos, & N. Cowan (Eds.), *Working memory: State of the science* (pp. 235–281). Oxford, UK: Oxford University Press.

Mashburn, C., Tsukahara, J., & Engle, R. W. (2021). Individual differences in attention control: Implications for the relationship between working memory capacity and fluid intelligence. In R. H. Logie, V. Camos, & N. Cowan (Eds.), *Working memory: State of the science* (pp. 175–211). Oxford, UK: Oxford University Press.

Maylor, E. A., & Logie, R. H. (2010). A large-scale comparison of prospective and retrospective memory development from childhood to middle-age. *Quarterly Journal of Experimental Psychology*, *63*, 442–451.

Meyer, D. E., & Kieras, D. E. (1997). A computational theory of executive cognitive processes and multiple-task performance: Part 1. Basic mechanisms. *Psychological Review*, *104*, 3–65.

Miyake, A., Friedman, N. P., Emerson, M. J., Witzki, A. H., Howerter, A., & Wager, T. D. (2000). The unity and diversity of executive functions and their contributions to complex "front lobe" tasks: A latent variable analysis. *Cognitive Psychology*, *41*, 49–100.

Miyake, A., & Shah, P. (Eds.) (1999). *Models of working memory*. New York, NY: Cambridge University Press.

Morgan, G. (1986). *Images of organization*. London, UK: Sage.

Morris, P. E., Tweedy, M., & Gruneberg, M. M. (1985). Interest, knowledge and the memorizing of soccer scores. *British Journal of Psychology*, *76*, 415–425.

Morris, R. G. (1986). Short-term forgetting in senile dementia of the Alzheimer type. *Cognitive Neuropsychology*, *3*, 77–97.

Morris, R. G., & Baddeley, A. D. (1988). Primary and working memory functioning in Alzheimer type dementia. *Journal of Clinical and Experimental Neuropsychology*, *10*, 279–296.

Morrison, A. B., Rosenbaum, G. M., Fair, D., & Chein, J. M. (2016). Variation in strategy use across measures of verbal working memory. *Memory & Cognition*, *44*, 922–936.

Nair, S., & Szaflarski, J. P. (2020). Neuroimaging of memory in frontal lobe epilepsy. *Epilepsy and Behavior*, *103*, 106857.

Nascimento, N. M., & Lucena, C. J. P. (2017). FIoT: An agent-based framework for self-adaptive and self-organizing applications based on the Internet of Things. *Information Sciences*, *378*, 161–176.

Newell, A. (1990). *Unified theories of cognition*. Cambridge, MA: Harvard University Press.

Niederee, C. Kanhabua, N., Gallo, F., & Logie, R. H. (2015). Forgetful digital memory: Towards brain-inspired long-term data and information management. *ACM Digital Library: SIGMOD Record*, *44*, 41–46.

Nijboer, M., Borst, J., van Rijn, H., & Taatgen, N. (2014). Single-task fMRI overlap predicts concurrent multitasking interference. *Neuroimage*, *100*, 60–74.

Norris, D. (2019). Even an activated long-term memory system still needs a separate short-term store: A reply to Cowan (2019). *Psychological Bulletin*, *145*, 848–853.

Oberauer, K., Lewandowsky, S., Awh, E., Brown, G. D. A., Conway, A., Cowan, N., . . . Ward, G. (2018). Benchmarks for models of short term and working memory. *Psychological Bulletin*, *144*, 885–958.

Osaka, N., Logie, R. H., & D'Esposito, M. (Eds.) (2007). *The cognitive neuroscience of working memory*. Oxford, UK: Oxford University Press.

Paivio, A. (1971). *Imagery and verbal processes*. New York, NY: Holt, Rinehart and Winston.

Paivio, A., & Csapo, K. (1969). Concrete image and verbal memory codes. *Journal of Experimental Psychology*, *80*, 279–285.

Page, M. A. (2006). What can't functional neuroimaging tell the cognitive neuropsychologist? *Cortex*, *42*, 428–443.

Park, D. C., & Reuter-Lorenz, P. A. (2009). The adaptive brain: Ageing and neurocognitive scaffolding. *Annual Review Psychology*, *60*, 173–196.

Parra, M. A., Abrahams, S., Fabi, K., Logie, R., Luzzi, S., & Della Sala, S. (2009). Short term memory binding deficits in Alzheimer's disease. *Brain*, *132*, 1057–1066.

Parra, M. A., Abrahams, S., Logie, R. H., Mendez, L. G., Lopera, F., & Della Sala, S. (2010). Visual short-term memory binding deficits in familial Alzheimer's disease. *Brain*, *133*, 2702–2713.

Parra, M. A., Della Sala, S., Logie, R. H., & Abrahams, S. (2009). Selective impairment in visual short-term memory binding. *Cognitive Neuropsychology, 26*, 583–605.

Perry, R. J., & Hodges, J. R. (1999). Attention and executive deficits in Alzheimer's disease: A critical review. *Brain, 122*, 383–404.

Phillips, W. A., & Christie, D. F. (1977). Interference with visualization. *Quarterly Journal of Experimental Psychology, 29*, 637–650.

Pylyshyn, Z. W. (1973). What the mind's eye tells the mind's brain: a critique of mental imagery. *Psychological Bulletin, 80*, 1–24.

Rabbitt, P. M. A. (2005). *Methodology of frontal and executive function*. Hove, UK: Psychology Press.

Reuchlin, M. (1978). Processus vicariants et différences individuelles [Vicarious processes and individual differences]. *Journal de Psychologie, 2*, 133–145.

Rhodes, S., Jaroslawska, A. J., Doherty, J. M., Belletier, C., Naveh-Benjamin, M., Cowan, N., . . . Logie, R. H. (2019). Storage and processing in working memory: Assessing dual task performance and task prioritization across the adult lifespan. *Journal of Experimental Psychology: General, 148*, 1204–1227.

Saariluoma, P. (1989). Chess players' recall of auditorily presented chess positions. *European Journal of Cognitive Psychology, 1*, 309–320.

Saito, S., Logie, R. H., Morita, A., & Law, A. (2008). Visual and phonological similarity effects in verbal immediate serial recall: A test with kanji materials. *Journal of Memory and Language, 59*, 1–17.

Sanfratello, L., Caprihan, A., Stephen, J. M., Knoefel, J. E., Adair, J. C., Qualls, C., . . . Aine, C. J. (2014). Same task, different strategies: how brain networks can be influenced by memory strategy. *Human Brain Mapping, 35*, 5127–5140.

Schooler, J. W., & Engstler-Schooler, T. Y. (1990). Verbal overshadowing of visual memories: Some things are better left unsaid. *Cognitive Psychology, 22*, 36–71.

Scoville, W. B., & Milner, B. (1957). Loss of recent memory after bilateral hippocampal lesions. *Journal of Neurology, Neurosurgery and Psychiatry, 20*, 11–21.

Sebastian, M. V., Menor, J., & Elosua, M. R. (2006). Attentional dysfunction of the central executive in AD: Evidence from dual task and perseveration errors. *Cortex, 42*, 1015–1020.

Shallice, T., & Papagno, C. (2019). Impairments of auditory-verbal short-term memory: Do selective deficits of the input phonological buffer exist? *Cortex, 112*, 107–121.

Shepard, R. N., & Metzler, J. (1971). Mental rotation of three-dimensional objects. *Science, 171*, 701–703.

Shimi, A., & Logie, R. H. (2019). Feature binding in short-term memory and long-term learning. *Quarterly Journal of Experimental Psychology, 72*, 1387–1400.

Stuss, D. T. (2011). Functions of the frontal lobes: Relation to executive functions. *Journal of the International Neuropsychological Society, 17*, 759–765.

Thomas, R. C., Weywadt, C. R., Anderson, J. L., Martinez-Papponi, B., & McDaniel, M. A. (2018). Testing encourages transfer between factual and application questions in an online learning environment. *Journal of Applied Research in Memory and Cognition, 7*, 252–260.

Tree, J. J., & Playfoot, D. (2019). How to get by with half a loop – an investigation of visual and auditory codes in a case of impaired phonological short-term memory (pSTM). *Cortex, 112*, 23–36.

Tullberg, M., Fletcher, E., DeCarli, C., Mungas, D., Reed, B. R., Harvey, D. J., . . . Jagust, W. J. (2004). White matter lesions impair frontal lobe function regardless of their location. *Neurology, 63*, 246–253.

Tresch, M. C., Sinnamon, H. M., & Seamon, J. G. (1993). Double dissociation of spatial and object visual memory: evidence from selective interference in intact human subjects. *Neuropsychologia, 31*, 211–219.

Van der Meulen, M., Logie, R. H., Freer, Y., Sykes, C., McIntosh, N., & Hunter, J. (2010). When a graph is poorer than 100 words: A comparison of computerised natural language generation, human generated descriptions and graphical displays in neonatal intensive care. *Applied Cognitive Psychology, 24*, 77–89.

Vallar, G. (2019). A "purest" impairment of verbal short-term memory. The case of PV and the phonological short-term store. In S. MacPherson & S. Della Sala (Eds.), *Cases of amnesia: Contributions to understanding memory and the brain* (pp. 261–291). New York, NY: Routledge.

Vallar, G., & Shallice, T. (Eds.) (1990). *Neuropsychological impairments of short-term memory.* Cambridge, UK: Cambridge University Press.

Vandierendonck, A. (2021). Multicomponent working memory system with distributed executive control. In R. H. Logie, V. Camos, & N. Cowan (Eds.), *Working memory: State of the science* (pp. 150–174). Oxford, UK: Oxford University Press.

Wang, X., Logie, R. H., & Jarrold, C. (2016). Interpreting potential markers of storage and rehearsal: Implications for studies of verbal short-term memory and neuropsychological cases. *Memory & Cognition, 44,* 910–921.

Warrington, E. K., & Rabin, P. (1971). Visual span of apprehension in patients with unilateral cerebral lesions. *Quarterly Journal of Experimental Psychology, 23,* 423–431.

Warrington, E. K., & Shallice, T. (1972). Neuropsychological evidence of visual storage in short-term memory tasks. *Quarterly Journal of Experimental Psychology, 24,* 30–40.

Waters, G. S., & Caplan, D. (2003). The reliability and stability of verbal working memory measures. *Behavior Research Methods, Instruments and Computers, 35,* 550–564.

Watkins, M. J. (1984). Models as toothbrushes. *Behavioral and Brain Sciences, 7,* 55–94.

Wickens, C. D., & Liu, Y. (1988). Codes and modalities in multiple resources: A success and a qualification. *Human Factors, 30,* 599–616.

Wijeakumar, S., & Spencer, J. (2021). A dynamic field theory of visual working memory. In R. H. Logie, V. Camos, & N. Cowan (Eds.), *Working memory: State of the science* (pp. 358–388). Oxford, UK: Oxford University Press.

Willshaw, D. (2006). Self-organization in the nervous system. In R. G. M. Morris, L. Tarrassenko, & M. Kenward (Eds.), *Cognitive systems: Information processing meets brain science* (pp. 5–33). London, UK: Academic Press.

Wilson, B. A. (1987). *Rehabilitation of memory.* New York, NY: Guilford Press.

Wright, R., Logie, R. H., & Decker, S. (1995). Criminal expertise and offender decision-making: An experimental study of the target selection process in residential burglary. *Journal of Research in Crime and Delinquency, 32,* 39–53.

Zacks, J. M. (2008). Neuroimaging studies of mental rotation: A meta analysis and review. *Journal of Cognitive Neuroscience, 20,* 1–19.

Zeman, A., Della Sala, Torrens, L., Gountouna, E., McGonigle, D., & Logie, R. H. (2010). Loss of imagery phenomenology with intact visual imagery performance. *Neuropsychologia, 48,* 145–155.

Index